Elizabethan and Jacobean Tragedy:

AN ANTHOLOGY

Elizabethan AND Jacobean TRAGEDY:

AN ANTHOLOGY

Edited by

Robert Ornstein
University of Illinois

and

Hazelton Spencer
late of Johns Hopkins University

D. C. HEATH AND COMPANY
Lexington, Massachusetts • Toronto • London

Printed in the United States of America.

CONTENTS

GENERAL INTRODUCTION

THE plays in this anthology are a sampling of the greatness of Elizabethan and Jacobean tragedy, a greatness which began in the 1580's with Kyd's *The Spanish Tragedy* and which found its conclusion almost a half-century later in Ford's *The Broken Heart*. In addition to *The Spanish Tragedy* and *The Broken Heart*, this volume includes tragedies by Marlowe, Chapman, Webster, and Middleton, which, after Shakespeare's, are the finest expression of a tragic art unparalleled except by the drama of classical Athens.

Because there were no established rules or prescribed materials for tragic drama in Renaissance England, Elizabethan and Jacobean tragedies are remarkably free and diverse in form and substance. Unlike the Greek tragedians, who inherited a traditional body of religious legends which contained the mystery and terror of tragic myth, the English playwrights had, to a large extent, to fashion their own tragic myths or to adapt them from contemporary myths of Italianate evil and Machiavellian satanism. Sometimes they invented their plots, but more often they drew their tragic fables from a wide variety of sources: from the English Chronicles, from ancient and modern European history, and from popular collections of tales of intrigue and passionate revenge. But despite the variety of their source materials and the freedom to innovate and experiment which their stage allowed, the English playwrights created a relatively coherent tradition of tragic drama. Though decades separate the plays of Kyd and Marlowe from those of Webster, Middleton, and Ford, we can trace in them a significant continuity of artistic thought and practice. We see the recurring theme of revenge, and the recurring figures of the revenger and the malcontent. We see that a struggle between good and evil is often at the heart of Elizabethan and Jacobean tragedy, and that again and again sexual passion and ambition intertwine as the motivating forces of tragic action.

To some extent, the continuity of artistic thought and practice in Elizabethan and Jacobean tragedy was simply the result of theatrical conditions. A playwright like Kyd or Marlowe who made an extraordinary success inevitably had a host of imitators; a play like *The Spanish Tragedy* was rifled by dramatists hoping to exploit or rival its success. But quite apart from the borrowings inspired by commercial rivalries and ambitions, the tragedians learned from one another because they were often friends and collaborators as well as competitors, and they shared common artistic ideals and concerns. Although they paid little attention to neo-Aristotelian rules of dramatic practice, they did not happen on great tragedy while merely attempting to provide popular entertainment. Their prefaces reveal that they thought much about tragedy even if they did not theorize about it. They were profoundly aware of the high calling of their tragic art, and they sought to recreate in contemporary terms the grandeur of classical tragedy.

With hindsight we can say that the late Elizabethan age offered fertile soil for the growth of tragedy. It was not only an age of great poetry but also one when poets were attracted by the challenge and potentialities of a newly formed and thriving professional theater. It was a period of intense literary idealism and humanistic absorption in ethical and philosophical issues; it was a time of tremendous economic, social, and political changes, when supreme adventure and heroic fulfillment as well as precipitous disaster were possible and frequent. With hindsight we can see what the greatest tragedians intuitively perceived: that though their civilization was poised at its height, its greatness was threatened by the decay of ancient aristocratic norms and by the growing factionalism of class and religious sect.

Of course we cannot explain the flowering of Elizabethan tragedy near the close of the sixteenth century by reference to cultural conditions, many of which existed some twenty or thirty years before the appearance of *The Spanish Tragedy*. Great tragedy is created only when dramatists of genius attempt it and in turn inspire and fertilize the imaginations of later writers. Indeed, when we compare the plays of Kyd and Marlowe to those which immediately preceded theirs on the popular and academic stages, we find an astonishing leap forward from pedestrian verse to poetic splendor, from shallow characterizations to vivid dramatic personalities, and from rambling or turgid plots to effective dramatic structure. Yet even as Kyd and Marlowe first created the high art of Elizabethan tragedy, they were themselves influenced by earlier concepts of tragedy and by earlier dramatic practice. The interest in tales of calamitous misfortune had been created centuries before by medieval writers who demonstrated the fragility of human greatness by endless examples drawn from the Bible, history, and legend. Simple and repetitious as was the pattern of tragic fall in Boccaccio's *De Casibus Virorum Illustrium* and Lydgate's *The Fall of Princes*, it had an enormous fascination for contemporary readers. And the taste for moralized calamity persisted throughout the Renaissance, as is witnessed by the great popularity of *The Mirror for Magistrates*, which was intended as a supplement to Lydgate.

While there is little evidence that *The Mirror for Magistrates* was an important direct influence on the Elizabethan dramatists, it was one of the main channels by which the medieval idea of tragedy reached Elizabethan readers. Sackville's *Induction* to *The Mirror*, which is reprinted in this volume, is especially fascinating because it seems to bridge two worlds of thought and to suggest some of the ways in which the medieval idea of tragedy was transformed in the Elizabethan era. The archaisms of the *Induction*, its allegorical figures, its references to Troy, and its emphasis on the vanity of human strivings, all are in a medieval vein. But the realistic details of Sackville's portraits of Old Age and Malady give a very human particularity to these abstractions, and his sympathy with wholly irrational clingings to life alters the lesson of human vanity. By allowing Buckingham to relate his own tragic tale, to lament his wretched destiny, and to rail at deceiving fortune, Sackville moves from the medieval tragedy of futile human aspiration towards the Renaissance tragedy of human disillusionment.

The most immediate parallel between *The Mirror for Magistrates* and the tragedies in this volume is one of style, for the heavy atmosphere of gloom and rhetoric of lamentation in the *Induction* are very close to what is customarily called the "Senecan style" of *The Spanish Tragedy*. Less obvious is the relation of the simple undramatic pattern of medieval tragedy to the complicated plots of Elizabethan and Jacobean tragedies, which more often depict the fierce encounter of opposing wills than a simple heroic fall. But then the genius of the dramatists lay in their ability to sophisticate the naive tragic ideas they inherited from earlier literature. In their plays a tragic fall need not be from prosperity or power; it can be, as in *Doctor Faustus* and *The Changeling*, a fall from innocence in a tragedy of moral degradation. Or it may be a descent into melancholy or madness in a tragedy of disillusionment or despair. The tragedy may be more public than personal in that it involves the fall of a society or a state rather than of a single tragic figure.

Medieval tragedy demands only a precipitous fall from prosperity and high degree; Elizabethan and Jacobean tragedies insist upon a deadly catastrophe, if not a final slaughter which strews the stage with bodies. Quite apart from their bloody plots, however, there is in the tragedies of Kyd, Marlowe, Chapman, and Webster an intellectual and emotional fascination with the moment of death and its meaning to the tragic hero. It is often justly said that the Elizabethan artists' preoccupation with death is the obverse of their humanistic sense of man's potentialities. But this preoccupation is an inherited rather than acquired characteristic of Renaissance thought; it derives, at least in part, from the late medieval absorption in "last things," in man's preparation for death.

When Marlowe, in *Doctor Faustus*, uses the allegorical framework of the Morality play, the link between Elizabethan tragedy and late medieval thought becomes clear. For the new value which Renaissance humanism placed on man's aspirations gave new meaning to the challenge of death so powerfully expressed in *Everyman*, the finest of the Moralities. Again and again the Elizabethan and Jacobean tragedians re-stage in contemporary dramatic form the Dance of Death, which was a major artistic and intellectual influence on the author of *Everyman;*

again and again they visualize life as a pilgrimage towards death in which the readiness or ripeness is all. In *Everyman*, as in *Doctor Faustus*, the burden of choice and action falls on the human protagonist. God appears in *Everyman* only to summon Death; He appears to Faustus in his mortal agony, but not to Marlowe's audience. In both plays the hero's crucial need is for knowledge of himself and of his world; in both plays death defines the folly and vanity of the hero's worldly achievements.

The anguishing sense of loss that accompanies human mortality is also present in *The Spanish Tragedy*. But Kyd is less indebted to the medieval *memento mori* than to Senecan tragedy, from which he takes his ghostly chorus, and to medieval traditions of chivalry and courtly love, which figure prominently in his opening scenes. To trace the plot of *The Spanish Tragedy*, however, is to see the Elizabethan imagination casting loose from conventional literary materials and embarking on its own voyage of artistic discovery. For Kyd soon dispenses with Senecan and medieval ideas and finds his true direction in portraying Hieronimo's secret despairing struggle to avenge his son. Though the lines of *The Spanish Tragedy* impressed Kyd's contemporaries and even today have a certain massive effectiveness, Kyd was not an inspired poet. His genius lay in his instinct for effective theater, for the complications of intrigue plotting, and for grim verbal and dramatic ironies. Time could not wither his most effective dramatic ideas, which survived almost fifty years of continuous employment on the stage. Well into the Jacobean period we find revenges accomplished in deadly masques; and we hear malcontented revengers crying out against the false appearances of life. As we would expect, later dramatists sophisticated Kyd's plotting and added greater depth and subtlety to his character types. But his vivid portrayals of Hieronimo, Lorenzo, and Bel-Imperia require no apology, and his plotting suffers from an excess rather than a lack of vitality. Perhaps without realizing its full meaning, Kyd introduced to the Elizabethan stage the tragic question of action in a world where the sacred bonds of trust that bind human beings to one another are violated, and the revenger's victory may be won at the price of his own degradation.

Like *The Spanish Tragedy*, Marlowe's *Doctor Faustus* had an extraordinary appeal for contemporary audiences. Wreathed in the mysteries of Marlowe's life, it continues to fascinate modern readers, perhaps as much by its difficulties as by its exalted theme and poetry. We cannot say for certain how much of the play as we know it is Marlowe's or to what extent it has been mangled by successive revisions and textual corruptions. But with all its question marks, its structural failings, and its somewhat tedious comic scenes, it is nevertheless a powerful and moving drama. For Marlowe is able to capture eternal polarities of human experience in Faustus' early Promethean longings and in his final spiritual isolation and despair. Perhaps no other work of literature captures so memorably the romantic sense that man's greatness is his tragedy because his infinite longings outreach his finite human situation, and he is driven to seek fulfillment in forbidden and illicit ways.

To be sure, *Doctor Faustus* is not simply a romantic hymn to the godlike in man or to heroic rebelliousness. If its comic scenes have any function, it is to suggest the futility of the powers for which Faustus barters his immortal soul. And though Faustus' artistic and intellectual longings are crowned with exquisite poetry, his arrogance and willful blindness are as evident as is the irony of his delusions about his mastery over Mephistophilis. Still Marlowe's play does not cheerfully reconcile us to an orthodox view of Creation, or to the God of power and implacable rage who appears to Faustus in the last scene. Too often opposing interpretations of the play insist that we see Marlowe either as a religious didacticist or as a religious rebel. But perhaps the problem is not to choose one or the other Marlowe but to understand a playwright who could not reconcile his sense of man's heroic potentialities with a religious ethic that assumes that human fulfillment comes only with an act of submission.

Since Chapman admired Marlowe, it seems an easy and natural step from *Doctor Faustus* to *Bussy D'Ambois*, particularly since Chapman creates in Bussy a titanic hero whose passionate soul is expressed in lines of Marlovian sweep, and whose tragic career is also shadowed by apparent ironies of self-delusion. But the melodramatic intrigue plotting of *Bussy D'Ambois* — the duels, love affair, the scenes of spirits, ghosts, torture and revenge — serve to remind us of other, unMarlovian influences at work on Chapman's imagination. Significantly, the pattern of tragic conflict in *Bussy D'Ambois* derives from the line of tragedies originated by Kyd.

Like Hieronimo, Bussy is malcontented in a society dominated by vicious aristocrats. Knowing that sycophancy is the surest way to advancement, Bussy nevertheless pursues a path of moral action. Too bold to adopt Hieronimo's secrecy, however, he launches a public crusade against the corrupt nobility, who are explicitly identified as disciples of the murderous Machiavel.

It is one of the chief ironies of intellectual history that Machiavelli, who sought to eradicate political illusions, was indirectly responsible for the grand political myth of the Renaissance and unwittingly supplied the Elizabethan dramatists with a fascinating archetype of unscrupulous and intellectual villainy. We no longer believe, as did earlier scholars, that Gentillet's *Contre-Machiavel* was the chief source of the myth of Machiavellian evil in Elizabethan England, for we know that first-hand knowledge of Machiavelli's works was fairly extensive among Elizabethan intellectuals. But whether we label the *Contre-Machiavel* as a source or a background material, it is fruitful reading because its analysis of Machiavelli's doctrine illuminates the ideas in Chapman's play. From the portions of the *Contre-Machiavel* reprinted in this volume, we can see that the charges which Bussy hurls against Monsieur are precisely those which Gentillet levels against Machiavelli; we see also that the key snarlword of Chapman's play, *policy*, is the chief heading under which Gentillet dissects Machiavelli's political errors. And of course the French court which Gentillet claims is under Machiavellian influence is the very court which Chapman depicts in his play.

Although Gentillet distorts Machiavelli's ideas, he seeks to document his charges by citing Machiavelli's own words. And like Machiavelli he seeks to deal with political realities — to refute the devilish Florentine on his own grounds of utility by demonstrating that Machiavelli's political principles can breed only disaster. The furious emotionality of Chapman's assault on policy is in striking contrast to Gentillet's controlled though contemptuous outrage; but then Chapman sees Machiavellianism not simply as an immoral doctrine but as a mythic force which is responsible for the decay of aristocratic ideals of "noblesse." His Bussy is a model of ancient, unsullied aristocratic virtue who would wage Gentillet's intellectual battle on the fields of action, who would scourge the politicians and reform his society by self-example. As the play proceeds, however, we see much in Bussy's nature and in his acts — his arrogance, bravado, and his contempt for ordinary morality — which seems to disqualify him as a moral Savior. Indeed, when the affair with Tamyra sidetracks Bussy's reforming energies, we wonder just what view Chapman intends us to have of his once pristine hero.

But if it is true that the moral design of *Bussy D'Ambois* grows somewhat opaque, its poetic splendor never dims. And though we do not easily penetrate to the heart of Bussy's inner law, we can still respond to his fiercely sought integrity and individualism. If we assume, as I think Chapman wished us to, that Bussy's integrity of spirit is untarnished by his acts, then we can agree with those in the play who see Bussy's tragedy as inevitable in a fallen world which wars on virtue and which allows heroic men only destructive means of self-realization. Recent critics have suggested that Chapman's view of Bussy is ironic rather than tragic; but the speeches near the close of the play suggest that Bussy's virtue is insufficient to alter his world rather than specious or corrupted.

Because Elizabethan and Jacobean tragedy deals with the fates of princes or of noblemen like Bussy, its natural setting is the court, the center of power and wealth in the Renaissance. And more often than not, the court is portrayed in Jacobean tragedy as a place of vicious appetites, intrigues, and Machiavellian ambition. Whatever opinions the Jacobean dramatists may have had of the court of James I, they prudently set their tragedies of decadent aristocracy in foreign courts; and they commonly chose for their settings the Italy which popular imagination conceived as a lair of sinister papists, sensualists, and Machiavels. We should keep in mind, however, that the Elizabethans did not wholly imagine the Italianate evil in their tragedies. The plot of *The White Devil*, for example, was drawn from fairly recent Italian history, and the historical facts which Webster transformed were in many respects as terrible as the story which *The White Devil* unfolds.

The White Devil is as passionate a drama as *Bussy D'Ambois*, but its emotional and poetic energy is not focused in a single heroic figure. Able to draw compelling portraits of innocence as well as glorious villains, Webster creates a tragic world of varied and individualized characters: Vittoria, Brachiano, Flamineo, Cornelia, Isabella, Francisco de Medicis, and Lodovico.

Chapman astonishes us by his ability to sustain a single passionate heroic impulse; Webster commands a far greater range of poetic utterance that moves from the lyric pathos of an exquisite elegy to the bitter sarcasm of a contemptuous epithet. His viewpoint is sardonic, his poetic imagination fantastically macabre. What might outrage Chapman — the mockery of justice in Vittoria's trial — is cynically accepted by a Webster who sees wealth and prerogative as ultimate forces in a society which pays only lip service to moral law. Like earlier tragedies, *The White Devil* is a drama of evil; but its tragic theme is not the assault of evil on the integrity of a Hieronimo or a Bussy. In Flamineo the malcontent loses all vestige of moral purpose, though he remains a choric dissector of his society's vices. Now the tragic protagonists are individualists whose passionate wills obliterate all tenets of religion and morality, and all ties of family and blood. We cannot complain that Webster is too fond of his glorious villains or that he admires them uncritically, for Brachiano's sensuality is not attractive, Flamineo's ambition is contemptible, and Lodovico's revenge is animal-like. Yet the quality of life and courage in these figures, their wit and their contempt for painted words is in some way redeeming; for if they delude themselves, they are not completely mistaken about the nature of their canting society. And despite their vices, they possess in no small measure one of the primary tragic virtues — the strength to endure.

After the great flowering of tragic art in the first decade of the seventeenth century, the appearance of a play like *The Changeling* was a rare occurrence on the Jacobean stage. In fact Middleton did not so much continue the great tradition of tragedy as recall it at a time when frivolity and mediocrity prevailed in the theaters. His portrayal of Beatrice is a masterly study of a personality in the throes of self-discovery and self-destruction; his probing of the individual consciousness has a Shakespearean depth and acuteness. But compared to earlier tragedians, Middleton has very limited interests. He is so absorbed in delineating the relationship of Beatrice and De Flores that he scarcely bothers to develop his lesser characters or to create a social milieu to serve as the world of his play, though a social milieu of some kind is implied by the romantic ideals, the codes of honor, and the moral responses of his characters.

The absence of larger philosophical concerns and of social or political commentary distinguishes *The Changeling* from earlier tragedies. New also is the restraint and detachment with which Middleton handles even the most melodramatic details of his plot. The brilliant scenes between Beatrice and De Flores are not visually exciting. What is fascinating and harrowing is the utter clarity of the perception of Beatrice, childishly infatuated with the thought of murder, tempting De Flores while refusing to see his desire for her, but made at last to see herself as he sees her. Characteristically Middleton's poetry is memorable for its preciseness of statement, not for its metaphorical richness. Again and again he places in De Flores' mouth a single unforgettable phrase that penetrates even the obtuseness of Beatrice, the "deed's creature."

The simplicity of his tragic action and the clarity of Middleton's poetry and characterizations avoid the perplexities created by the involved plots and the stormy rhetoric of earlier tragedies. Yet *The Changeling* poses its own singular problems of interpretation. Although Beatrice and De Flores are superbly drawn, lesser figures like Vermandero, Alsemero, and the two Piracquos are somewhat opaque and shadowy. Necessary for the plot, they seem to be curiously neutral figures and therefore not engaged in the tragic action in the way that all of Webster's characters are. Even more difficult to understand than the relation of the minor characters to the central tragic idea is the relation of the tragic plot to the comic or seriocomic scenes in the asylum. Though we can find parallels of theme, character and situation that link both plots, we still wonder at the incongruity of plot and subplot, which come together very loosely only in the last scene.

When we turn to the source of *The Changeling*, which is reprinted in this volume, we realize that Middleton did not require Rowley's aid in fleshing out a skeletal tale. On the contrary, Middleton eliminated many of the incidents in Reynolds' story to allow for a subplot which was immensely popular with contemporary audiences. Were it not for its relation to *The Changeling*, Reynolds' tale would have little interest for modern readers. That relation is important, however, because it leaves no doubt of the freedom and the creativity with which Middleton (like so many other tragedians) transformed his source materials. Much of the popularity of Reynolds' book stemmed from its fervid moralizings and its satisfying recountings of divine retribution. Equally popular was Reynolds' subject matter: his novella-like tales of illicit lust and violence, which are related in tantalizing detail. Reynolds judged his audience shrewdly — he offered sensational and erotic matter but at the same time edified his readers with pietistic sentiments and glosses. Whatever doubts we may have about the subplot of *The Changeling*, it is clear that Middleton's tragic intention is nobler and more elevated than Reynolds' and his vision of character more penetrating and profoundly ethical. We can scarcely exaggerate the difference between Middleton's characterizations and the shallow, conventional figures in Reynolds' story, who are blown to destruction by sudden, incredible gales of passion.

Though Reynolds' talent was thoroughly pedestrian, he aspired to a literary style, especially in the expression of courtly sentiments and declarations of love. This conventional romantic strain is echoed in the speeches of Alsemero and Beatrice even as it is parodied by De Flores' service of love and by the fantastic "love-errantry" in the asylum scenes. The romanticism of *The Broken Heart*, which also has a Petrarchan and courtly flavor, is untouched by the ironies which surround romantic affection in *The Changeling*. Unlike Kyd, who exploits in the opening scenes of *The Spanish Tragedy* the eroticism of courtly love, Ford chastely depicts nuances of refined emotion. His ideal of love, which is inseparable from nobility of character, reaches its paramount expression in the tortured gentility of Penthea and the stoical acceptance of Calantha, whose breaking heart is masked by queenly observance of her role. For Chapman and Webster, the court is a source of vicious desires; in *The Broken Heart* it is a fountainhead of genuinely aristocratic codes of conduct and love.

Ford's deep concern with standards of conduct, explicitly stated in the philosophizing of Tecnicus and embodied in his dramatic portraits, refutes the charges of decadence hurled by those who see *The Broken Heart* as an assault on the sanctity of marriage or a placing of love outside the bounds of moral judgment. But to recognize the perplexing difficulties of Penthea's relationships with Orgilus, Bassanes, and Ithocles, is to be wary of a simple response to Ford's art. He depicts tragic situations which, by their very nature, challenge conventional moral attitudes. Moreover, though immoral acts are committed by Orgilus, even as vile thoughts are expressed by Bassanes, neither character is evil in the way that Chapman's and Webster's villains are. However tormented by their emotions or warped by hopeless circumstances, Ford's characters are all capable of an essential nobility. Like Shakespeare, Ford is noted for his portraits of women; and like Shakespeare, he understands the difference between the aggressive and possessive masculine ego and the more passive, generous feminine capacity for surrender of self. If we wish, we may call Penthea a study in psycho-pathology; but it would be more accurate to say that she embodies an emotional and moral integrity which is not despoiled by the pathological situation in which she is placed by brother, husband, and former lover.

Separating the quiet depths of Ford from the heroic tempests of Kyd, Marlowe, and Chapman was a revolution in literary tastes and a series of radical changes in the nature of the theaters, their audiences, and the drama itself. Yet the high seriousness of Ford's tragic intention testifies to the vitality of a tragic tradition and ideal which were capable of inspiring men of genius long after tragedy itself had ceased to dominate the stage.

ROBERT ORNSTEIN

The Spanish Tragedie

OR,

Hieronimo is mad againe.

Containing the lamentable end of *Don Horatio*, and *Belimperia*; with the pittifull death of *Hieronimo*.

Newly corrected, amended, and enlarged with new Additions of the *Painters* part, and others, as it hath of late been diuers times acted.

LONDON,
Printed by W. White, for I. White and T. Langley, and are to be sold at their Shop ouer against the Sarazens head without New-gate. 1615.

Revenge tragedy

physically + psy to satisfy ē need to be frightened

hero turned villian in order to do
what his initial virtue ē his
victimization demand

tragedy of blood
focus on revenge ē the horror
attendant on it

Ham + S.T.
mumming of play with-in
ghost
madness of hero
activity on stage (stabbing)

INTRODUCTORY NOTE

FEW if any of the Elizabethan plays equalled *The Spanish Tragedy* in popularity or influence. Playgoers and play readers alike devoured it, and many of its features may be traced in subsequent tragedies. To be sure, there are bombast and rawness and clumsiness in *The Spanish Tragedy;* to be sure, it lacks the winged imagination and superb rhetoric that redeem Marlowe's bombast. But a lively melodrama is always preferable to a dead tragedy, and Kyd's play is no ordinary melodrama. Its great merit, as a piece of the 1580's, resides in the author's sincerity and his absorption in the human passions which his story involves. Of all the immediate predecessors of Shakespeare, Kyd is the one with the real flair for the stage. As an example of construction, this play is open to much objection, especially for its labored beginning; and Kyd is stylistically quite inferior to his colleagues. But he surpasses them all in building his scenes around the emotional responses of his characters to the pressure of circumstances, in effective preparation for scenes of rapid action, and in employing a more definitely theatrical technique to move the hearts of his audience. All of which is only saying that Kyd's genius was a more dramatic genius than that of the others.

No source for the plot has been found; yet it is not unlikely that Kyd took it from some romantic tale which has not survived. The political and military background of the play is unhistorical, though there was war between Spain and Portugal in 1580. The influence of Seneca (translated in 1581) is obvious in the frequent stichomythia, the messenger, the ghost, and the revenge theme with its attendant horrors. It is highly significant that the Senecan machinery appears here in, not an academic, but a popular play. Elizabethan tragedy was to continue to be molded more or less of the Senecan clay; it was Kyd who breathed life into it. Besides Seneca, Garnier (translated in 1585) and Vergil are drawn upon for some details.

As the London drama developed, and taste and craft were more refined, *The Spanish Tragedy,* though still a great popular success, became an object of scorn to the sophisticated. From a derisive reference by Jonson in the induction to *Bartholemew Fair*, it seems likely that the play was produced between 1584 and 1589. The absence of any allusion to the Armada suggests an earlier date than 1588; c. 1586 cannot be far out of the way. Apparently the play was often called simply *Jeronimo.* Of its long theatrical career there can be no doubt, but records of actual performances are scanty. It was played sixteen times at the Rose by Lord Strange's Men between March 14, 1592, and January 22, 1593, sometimes in conjunction with *The Spanish Comedy of Don Horatio.* Neither that play, nor *The Comedy of Jeronimo* (their texts have not survived, and they may be alternative titles for the same piece), nor the (probably) later *First Part of Jeronimo* (printed in 1605) had, as far as is known, any connection with Kyd himself. Another substantial run of *The Spanish Tragedy* is recorded, this time by the Admiral's Men, who acted it thirteen times between January 7 and October 11, 1597.

The standard edition of Kyd's works is that of F. S. Boas (1901). *The Spanish Tragedy* has been separately edited by Josef Schick (1898) and by W. W. Greg (1925). No copy of the original edition of the play is known to have survived and but one of the second, an undated octavo in the British Museum, conjecturally assigned by Greg to 1592. The second surviving edition appeared in 1594, and the third in 1599. The next was the Quarto of 1602, "newly corrected, amended, and enlarged." It was reprinted in 1603, 1611, 1615, 1618, 1623, and 1633, the last four quartos carrying on their title pages a woodcut which depicts the discovery of Horatio's body. This second version (1602, *et seq.*) contains the added passages printed in smaller type in the present edition. They have been ascribed to Ben Jonson because Henslowe twice during the season of 1601–1602 records advancing him considerable sums for additions to this play. It is argued, without much cogency, that these cannot be the additions of Quarto

1602, because their romantic fervor is unlike the bulk of Jonson's work. More impressive are Dr. Greg's suggestions that Jonson appears to have received as large a fee as was ordinarily paid for a new play, that the surviving additions are not sufficiently extensive to warrant it, and that it seems unlikely that the company would have permitted the publication of a version so newly made. The additions of Quarto 1602 may, therefore, represent a still earlier revision. There must have been at least one such, for in 1597 Henslowe entered the play in his "Diary" as "new", and in *Cynthia's Revels* (1600) Jonson refers to it "as it was first acted."

As for Kyd's authorship of the original, our chief reliance is on the quotation and ascription to him of V, i, 83–85, by Thomas Heywood in his *Apology for Actors* (1612). The present text is based on Boas's reprint of the first surviving edition and on his and Greg's reprints of the additions of 1602. It has also been collated throughout with Greg's text of Q 1602 and with his list of the variants between that edition and the earliest.

THE SPANISH TRAGEDY

OR

HIERONIMO IS MAD AGAIN

BY

THOMAS KYD

[DRAMATIS PERSONAE

GHOST OF ANDREA, a Spanish courtier, } Chorus.
REVENGE, } Chorus.
KING OF SPAIN.
DON CYPRIAN, DUKE OF CASTILE, his brother.
LORENZO, the Duke's son.
VICEROY OF PORTUGAL.
BALTHAZAR, his son.
DON PEDRO, brother to the Viceroy.
HIERONIMO, Marshal of Spain.
HORATIO, his son.
Spanish General.
Deputy.
DON BAZULTO, an old man.
Three Citizens.
Portuguese Ambassador.
ALEXANDRO, } Portuguese Noblemen.
VILLUPPO,[1] } Portuguese Noblemen.
Two Portuguese.
PEDRINGANO, servant to Bel-imperia.
CHRISTOPHIL, custodian of Bel-imperia.
Page to Lorenzo.
SERBERINE, servant to Balthazar.
Messenger.
Hangman.
BAZARDO, a painter, } in the additions.
PEDRO and JAQUES, Hieronimo's servants, } in the additions.
Army, Royal Suites, Nobles, Halberdiers, Officers, Three Watchmen, Servants, etc.

BEL-IMPERIA, daughter to Don Cyprian.
ISABELLA, wife to Hieronimo.
Maid to Isabella.

SOLIMAN, Sultan of Turkey (Balthazar), } in Hieronimo's play.
ERASTUS, Knight of Rhodes (Lorenzo), } in Hieronimo's play.
BASHAW (Hieronimo), } in Hieronimo's play.
PERSEDA (Bel-imperia), } in Hieronimo's play.

Three Kings and three Knights, in the first dumb show.
HYMEN and two torchbearers, in the second.]

ACT I

[CHORUS]

Enter the GHOST OF ANDREA, *and with him* REVENGE.

GHOST. When this eternal substance of my soul
Did live imprison'd in my wanton flesh,
Each in their function serving other's need,
I was a courtier in the Spanish court.
My name was Don Andrea; my descent,
Though not ignoble, yet inferior far
To gracious fortunes of my tender youth.
For there in prime and pride of all my years,
By duteous service and deserving love,
In secret I possess'd a worthy dame,
Which hight sweet Bel-imperia by name.
But in the harvest of my summer joys
Death's winter nipp'd the blossoms of my bliss,
Forcing divorce betwixt my love and me.
For in the late conflict with Portingale
My valor drew me into danger's mouth
Till life to death made passage through my wounds.
When I was slain, my soul descended straight [2]

[1] An Italian word, = confusion.

[2] The rest of the speech is adapted from Vergil's *Aeneid*, Book VI. The opening lines imitate the appearance of the ghost of Tantalus, with which Seneca's *Thyestes* begins.

To pass the flowing stream of Acheron;
But churlish Charon, only boatman there,
Said that, my rites of burial not perform'd,
I might not sit amongst his passengers.
Ere Sol had slept three nights in Thetis' lap,
And slak'd his smoking chariot in her flood,
By Don Horatio, our knight marshal's son,
My funerals and obsequies were done.
Then was the ferryman of Hell content
To pass me over to the slimy strond
That leads to fell Avernus' ugly waves.
There, pleasing Cerberus with honey'd speech,
I pass'd the perils of the foremost porch.
Not far from hence, amidst ten thousand souls,
Sat Minos, Aeacus, and Rhadamanth;
To whom no sooner 'gan I make approach,
To crave a passport for my wand'ring ghost,
But Minos, in graven leaves of lottery,
Drew forth the manner of my life and death.
"This knight," quoth he, "both liv'd and died in love,
And for his love tried fortune of the wars,
And by war's fortune lost both love and life."
"Why then," said Aeacus, "convey him hence,
To walk with lovers in our fields of love,
And spend the course of everlasting time
Under green myrtle trees and cypress shades."
"No, no," said Rhadamanth, "it were not well
With loving souls to place a martialist.
He died in war and must to martial fields,
Where wounded Hector lives in lasting pain,
And Achilles' Myrmidons do scour the plain."
Then Minos, mildest censor of the three,
Made this device to end the difference:
"Send him," quoth he, "to our infernal King,
To doom him as best seems his Majesty."
To this effect my passport straight was drawn.
In keeping on my way to Pluto's court,
Through dreadful shades of ever-glooming night,
I saw more sights than thousand tongues can tell,
Or pens can write, or mortal hearts can think.
Three ways there were: that on the right-hand side
Was ready way unto the 'foresaid fields,
Where lovers live and bloody martialists,
But either sort contain'd within his bounds.
The left-hand path, declining fearfully,
Was ready downfall to the deepest hell,
Where bloody Furies shakes their whips of steel,
And poor Ixion turns an endless wheel;
Where usurers are chok'd with melting gold,
And wantons are embrac'd with ugly snakes,
And murderers groan with never-killing wounds,
And perjur'd wights scalded in boiling lead,
And all foul sins with torments overwhelm'd.
'Twixt these two ways I trod the middle path,
Which brought me to the fair Elysian green,[3]
In midst whereof there stands a stately tower,
The walls of brass, the gates of adamant.
Here finding Pluto with his Proserpine,
I show'd my passport, humbled on my knee;
Whereat fair Proserpine began to smile,
And begg'd that only she might give my doom.
Pluto was pleas'd, and seal'd it with a kiss.
Forthwith, Revenge, she rounded[4] thee in th' ear,
And bade thee lead me through the gates of hor[n],
Where dreams have passage in the silent night.
No sooner had she spoke but we were here
(I wot not how) in twinkling of an eye.

REVENGE. Then know, Andrea, that thou art arriv'd
Where thou shalt see the author of thy death,
Don Balthazar, the Prince of Portingale,
Depriv'd of life by Bel-imperia.
Here sit we down to see the mystery,
And serve for Chorus in this tragedy.

[SCENE I][5]

Enter SPANISH KING, General, CASTILE, [*and*] HIERONIMO.

KING. Now say, Lord General, how fares our camp?

GEN. All well, my sovereign Liege, except some few
That are deceas'd by fortune of the war.

KING. But what portends thy cheerful countenance,
And posting to our presence thus in haste?
Speak, man, hath fortune given us victory?

GEN. Victory, my Liege, and that with little loss.

KING. Our Portingals will pay us tribute then?

[3] In the prefatory epistle to *Menaphon*, Nash sneers at "those that thrust Elysium into hell."
[4] Whispered.
[5] Before a castle of the Spanish King.

GEN. Tribute and wonted homage therewithal.
KING. Then bless'd be Heaven and Guider of the Heavens,
From whose fair influence such justice flows.
CAST. *O multum dilecte Deo, tibi militat aether,*
Et conjuratae curvato poplit[e] gentes
Succumbunt: recti soror est victoria juris.[6]
KING. Thanks to my loving brother of Castile. —
But, General, unfold in brief discourse
Your form of battle and your war's success,
That, adding all the pleasure of thy news
Unto the height of former happiness,
With deeper wage and greater dignity
We may reward thy blissful chivalry.
GEN. Where Spain and Portingale do jointly knit
Their frontiers, leaning on each other's bound,
There met our armies in their proud array;
Both furnish'd well, both full of hope and fear,
Both menacing alike with daring shows,
Both vaunting sundry colors of device,[7]
Both cheerly sounding trumpets, drums, and fifes,
Both raising dreadful clamors to the sky,
That[8] valleys, hills, and rivers made rebound,
And heaven itself was frighted with the sound.
Our battles[9] both were pitch'd in squadron form,
Each corner strongly fenc'd with wings of shot;
But ere we join'd and came to push of pike,
I brought a squadron of our readiest shot
From out our rearward to begin the fight.
They brought another wing to encounter us.
Meanwhile, our ordnance play'd on either side,
And captains strove to have their valors tried.
Don Pedro, their chief horsemen's colonel,
Did with his cornet[10] bravely make attempt
To break the order of our battle ranks;
But Don Rogero, worthy man of war,
March'd forth against him with our musketeers,
And stopp'd the malice of his fell approach.
While they maintain hot skirmish to and fro,
Both battles join and fall to handy-blows,
Their violent shot resembling th' ocean's rage,
When, roaring loud, and with a swelling tide,
It beats upon the rampires[11] of huge rocks
And gapes to swallow neighbor-bounding lands.
Now, while Bellona rageth here and there,
Thick storms of bullets [rain][12] like winter's hail,
And shivered lances dark[13] the troubled air.
Pede pes et cuspide cuspis;
[Arma] sonant [armis],[14] *vir petiturque viro.*
On every side drop captains to the ground,
And soldiers, some ill-maim'd, some slain outright;
Here falls a body s[u]nd'red from his head,
There legs and arms lie bleeding on the grass,
Mingled with weapons and unbowell'd steeds,
That scattering overspread the purple plain.
In all this turmoil, three long hours and more,
The victory to neither part inclin'd;
Till Don Andrea, with his brave lanciers,
In their main battle made so great a breach,
That, half dismay'd, the multitude retir'd;
But Balthazar, the Portingals' young Prince,
Brought rescue and encourag'd them to stay.
Here-hence the fight was eagerly renew'd,
And in that conflict was Andrea slain,
Brave man at arms, but weak to Balthazar.
Yet while the Prince, insulting[15] over him,
Breath'd out proud vaunts, sounding to our reproach,
Friendship and hardy valor, join'd in one,
Prick'd forth Horatio, our knight marshal's son,
To challenge forth that Prince in single fight.
Not long between these twain the fight endur'd,
But straight the Prince was beaten from his horse,
And forc'd to yield him prisoner to his foe.
When he was taken, all the rest they fled,
And our carbines pursued them to the death,
Till, Phoebus waving[16] to the western deep,
Our trumpeters were charg'd to sound retreat.

[6] O much loved of God, Heaven wars for thee, and on bended knee fall the conspiring nations: victory is the sister of just equity. (Adapted from Claudian's *De Tertio Consulatu Honorii*, ll. 96–98.)

[7] Proudly displaying their heraldic bearings, painted in various colors.

[8] So that.

[9] Armies. "Battle" could also mean a subdivision of an army, as in l. 66. "Squadron" here = square.

[10] Troop.

[11] Ramparts.

[12] Emend. Editor; old eds. *ran.*

[13] Q 1594 *et seq.*, *darkt* or *dark'd.*

[14] Cor. Q 1633; earlier eds. *Anni . . . annis.* "Foot against foot and point against point; arms clash on arms, and man rushes on man." These lines are adapted from Statius's *Thebais*, viii, 399, and Curtius's *De Gestis Alexandri Magni*, iii, 2.

[15] Exulting.

[16] Declining. (*N. E. D.*)

KING. Thanks, good Lord General, for these good news;
And for some argument[17] of more to come,
Take this and wear it for thy sovereign's sake.
Give him his chain.
But tell me now, hast thou confirm'd a peace?
GEN. No peace, my Liege, but peace conditional,
That if with homage tribute be well paid,
The fury of your forces will be stay'd;
And to this peace their viceroy hath subscrib'd,
Give the KING *a paper.*
And made a solemn vow that, during life,
His tribute shall be truly paid to Spain.
KING. These words, these deeds, become thy person well.
But now, Knight Marshal, frolic with thy king,
For 't is thy son that wins this battle's prize.
HIER. Long may he live to serve my sovereign Liege,
And soon decay, unless he serve my Liege.
KING. Nor thou nor he shall die without reward. *A tucket afar off.*
What means this warning of this trumpet's sound?
GEN. This tells me that your Grace's men of war,
Such as war's fortune hath reserv'd from death,
Come marching on towards your royal seat,
To show themselves before your Majesty;
For so I gave in charge at my depart.
Whereby by demonstration shall appear
That all, except three hundred or few more,
Are safe return'd, and by their foes enrich'd.

The Army *enters;* BALTHAZAR, *between* LORENZO *and* HORATIO, *captive.*

KING. A gladsome sight! I long to see them here. *They enter and pass by.*
Was that the warlike Prince of Portingale,
That by our nephew was in triumph led?
GEN. It was, my Liege, the Prince of Portingale.
KING. But what was he that on the other side
Held him by th' arm, as partner of the prize?
HIER. That was my son, my gracious Sovereign;
Of whom though from his tender infancy
My loving thoughts did never hope but well,
He never pleas'd his father's eyes till now,
Nor fill'd my heart with overcloying joys.
KING. Go, let them march once more about these walls.
That, staying them, we may confer and talk
With our brave prisoner and his double guard.
[*Exit a* Messenger.]
Hieronimo, it greatly pleaseth us
That in our victory thou have a share,
By virtue of thy worthy son's exploit.

Enter again.

Bring hither the young Prince of Portingale.
The rest march on; but, ere they be dismiss'd,
We will bestow on every soldier
Two ducats and on every leader ten,
That they may know our largess welcomes them.
Exeunt all [*the* Army] *but* BALTHAZAR, LORENZO, [*and*] HORATIO.
Welcome, Don Balthazar! welcome, Nephew!
And thou, Horatio, thou art welcome too.
Young Prince, although thy father's hard misdeeds,
In keeping back the tribute that he owes,
Deserve but evil measure at our hands,
Yet shalt thou know that Spain is honorable.
BAL. The trespass that my father made in peace
Is now controll'd[18] by fortune of the wars;
And cards once dealt, it boots not ask why so.
His men are slain, a weakening to his realm;
His colors seiz'd, a blot unto his name;
His son distress'd, a corsive[19] to his heart:
These punishments may clear his late offence.
KING. Ay, Balthazar, if he observe this truce,
Our peace will grow the stronger for these wars.
Meanwhile live thou, though not in liberty,
Yet free from bearing any servile yoke;
For in our hearing thy deserts were great,
And in our sight thyself art gracious.
BAL. And I shall study to deserve this grace.
KING. But tell me — for their holding makes me doubt —
To which of these twain art thou prisoner?
LOR. To me, my Liege.
HOR. To me, my Sovereign.
LOR. This hand first took his courser by the reins.
HOR. But first my lance did put him from his horse.

[17] Evidence.

[18] Checked.

[19] Corrosive.

LOR. I seiz'd his weapon, and enjoy'd it first.
HOR. But first I forc'd him lay his weapons down.
KING. Let go his arm, upon our privilege.[20]
Let him go.
Say, worthy Prince, to whether [21] didst thou yield?
BAL. To him in courtesy, to this perforce.
He spake me fair, this other gave me strokes;
He promis'd life, this other threat'ned death;
He won my love, this other conquered me,
And, truth to say, I yield myself to both.
HIER. But that I know your Grace for just and wise,
And might seem partial in this difference,
Enforc'd by nature and by law of arms
My tongue should plead for young Horatio's right.
He hunted well that was a lion's death,
Not he that in a garment wore his skin;
So hares may pull dead lions by the beard.
KING. Content thee, Marshal, thou shalt have no wrong;
And, for thy sake, thy son shall want no right.
Will both abide the censure of my doom?
LOR. I crave no better than your Grace awards.
HOR. Nor I, although I sit beside my right.
KING. Then, by my judgment, thus your strife shall end:
You both deserve, and both shall have reward. —
Nephew, thou took'st his weapon and his horse;
His weapons and his horse are thy reward. —
Horatio, thou didst force him first to yield;
His ransom therefore is thy valor's fee:
Appoint the sum, as you shall both agree. —
But, Nephew, thou shalt have the Prince in guard,
For thine estate best fitteth such a guest;
Horatio's house were small for all his train.
Yet, in regard thy substance passeth his,
And that just guerdon may befall desert,
To him we yield the armor of the Prince. —
How likes Don Balthazar of this device?
BAL. Right well, my Liege, if this proviso were,
That Don Horatio bear us company,
Whom I admire and love for chivalry.

[20] Royal right. A king's presence was supposed to be immune from witnessing a brawl.
[21] Which of the two.

KING. Horatio, leave him not that loves thee so. —
Now let us hence to see our soldiers paid,
And feast our prisoner as our friendly guest.
Exeunt.

[SCENE II] [22]

Enter VICEROY, ALEXANDRO, VILLUPPO, [*and* Attendants.]

VIC. Is our ambassador despatch'd for Spain?
ALEX. Two days, my Liege, are past since his depart.
VIC. And tribute payment gone along with him?
ALEX. Ay, my good Lord.
VIC. Then rest we here awhile in our unrest,
And feed our sorrows with some inward sighs,
For deepest cares break never into tears.
But wherefore sit I in a regal throne?
This better fits a wretch's endless moan. —
Yet this is higher than my fortunes reach,
And therefore better than my state deserves. —
Falls to the ground.
Ay, ay, this earth, image of melancholy,
Seeks him whom fates adjudge to misery.
Here let me lie; now am I at the lowest.
Qui jacet in terra, non habet unde cadat.
In me consumpsit vires fortuna nocendo;
Nil superest ut jam possit obesse magis.[23]
Yes, Fortune may bereave me of my crown:
Here, take it now; let Fortune do her worst,
She will not rob me of this sable weed.
O no, she envies none but pleasant things.
Such is the folly of despiteful chance.
Fortune is blind, and sees not my deserts;
So is she deaf, and hears not my laments;
And could she hear, yet is she wilful-mad,
And therefore will not pity my distress.
Suppose that she could pity me, what then?
What help can be expected at her hands
Whose foot [is] [24] standing on a rolling stone,
And mind more mutable than fickle winds?
Why wail I, then, where 's hope of no redress?
O yes, complaining makes my grief seem less.
My late ambition hath distain'd my faith;

[22] The throne-room in the palace of the Portuguese Viceroy.
[23] Who lies on the ground can fall no further. Fortune has used up all her power to harm me. Nothing is left now that can hurt me any more. (The source of these lines has not been found.)
[24] Add. Dodsley.

My breach of faith occasion'd bloody wars;
Those bloody wars have spent my treasure;[25]
And with my treasure[25] my people's blood;
And with their blood, my joy and best beloved,
My best beloved, my sweet and only son.
O, wherefore went I not to war myself?
The cause was mine; I might have died for both.
My years were mellow, his but young and green;
My death were natural, but his was forced.

ALEX. No doubt, my Liege, but still the Prince survives.

VIC. Survives! Ay, where?

ALEX. In Spain, a prisoner by mischance of war.

VIC. Then they have slain him for his father's fault.

ALEX. That were a breach to common law of arms.

VIC. They reck no laws that meditate revenge.

ALEX. His ransom's worth will stay from foul revenge.

VIC. No; if he lived, the news would soon be here.

ALEX. Nay, evil news fly faster still[26] than good.

VIC. Tell me no more of news, for he is dead.

VIL. My Sovereign, pardon the author of ill news,
And I'll bewray[27] the fortune of thy son.

VIC. Speak on; I'll guerdon thee, whate'er it be.
Mine ear is ready to receive ill news,
My heart grown hard 'gainst mischief's battery.
Stand up, I say, and tell thy tale at large.

VIL. Then hear that truth which these mine eyes have seen.
When both the armies were in battle join'd,
Don Balthazar, amidst the thickest troops,
To win renown did wondrous feats of arms.
Amongst the rest, I saw him, hand to hand,
In single fight with their lord general;
Till Alexandro, that here counterfeits
Under the color of a duteous friend,
Discharged his pistol at the Prince's back
As though he would have slain their general;
But therewithal Don Balthazar fell down;
And when he fell, then we began to fly;
But, had he lived, the day had sure been ours.

ALEX. O wicked forgery! O traitorous miscreant!

VIC. Hold thou thy peace! — But now, Villuppo, say,
Where then became[28] the carcass of my son?

VIL. I saw them drag it to the Spanish tents.

VIC. Ay, ay, my nightly dreams have told me this. —
Thou false, unkind, unthankful, traitorous beast,
Wherein had Balthazar offended thee,
That thou shouldst thus betray him to our foes?
Was 't Spanish gold that bleared so thine eyes
That thou couldst see no part of our deserts?
Perchance, because thou art Terceira's[29] lord,
Thou hadst some hope to wear this diadem,
If first my son and then myself were slain;
But thy ambitious thought shall break thy neck.
Ay, this was it that made thee spill his blood;

Take the crown and put it on again.

But I'll now wear it till thy blood be spilt.

ALEX. Vouchsafe, dread Sovereign, to hear me speak.

VIC. Away with him! His sight is second hell.
Keep him till we determine of his death. —
If Balthazar be dead, he shall not live.
Villuppo, follow us for thy reward.

Exit VICEROY, [*with* ALEXANDRO, *guarded*.]

VIL. Thus have I with an envious,[30] forged tale
Deceived the King, betray'd mine enemy,
And hope for guerdon of my villainy. *Exit.*

[SCENE III][31]

Enter HORATIO *and* BEL-IMPERIA.

BEL. Signior Horatio, this is the place and hour
Wherein I must entreat thee to relate
The circumstance of Don Andrea's death,
Who, living, was my garland's sweetest flower,
And in his death hath buried my delights.

HOR. For love of him and service to yourself,
I nill[32] refuse this heavy doleful charge;
Yet tears and sighs, I fear, will hinder me.

[25] Trisyllabic.
[26] Always.
[27] Reveal.

[28] What then became of.
[29] Terceira is one of the Azores.
[30] Malicious.
[31] A banqueting hall at the Spanish court, though it does not become localized as such till l. 110.
[32] Will not.

When both our armies were enjoin'd in fight,
Your worthy chevalier amidst the thick'st,
For glorious cause still aiming at the fairest,
Was at the last by young Don Balthazar
Encount'red hand to hand. Their fight was long,
Their hearts were great, their clamors menacing,
Their strength alike, their strokes both dangerous.
But wrathful Nemesis, that wicked power,
Envying[33] at Andrea's praise and worth,
Cut short his life, to end his praise and worth.
She, she herself, disguis'd in armor's mask,
As Pallas was before proud Pergamus,[34]
Brought in a fresh supply of halberdiers,
Which paunch'd[35] his horse and ding'd[36] him to the ground.
Then young Don Balthazar with ruthless rage,
Taking advantage of his foe's distress,
Did finish what his halberdiers begun,
And left not till Andrea's life was done.
Then, though too late, incens'd with just remorse,[37]
I with my band[38] set forth against the Prince,
And brought him prisoner from his halberdiers.

BEL. Would thou hadst slain him that so slew my love!
But then was Don Andrea's carcass lost?

HOR. No, that was it for which I chiefly strove;
Nor stepp'd I back till I recover'd him.
I took him up and wound him in mine arms,
And wielding him unto my private tent
There laid him down and dew'd him with my tears,
And sighed and sorrowed as became a friend.
But neither friendly sorrow, sighs, nor tears
Could win pale Death from his usurped right.
Yet this I did, and less I could not do:
I saw him honored with due funeral.
This scarf I pluck'd from off his lifeless arm,
And wear it in remembrance of my friend.

BEL. I know the scarf; would he had kept it still!
For had he lived, he would have kept it still,
And worn it for his Bel-imperia's sake;
For 't was my favor at his last depart.
But now wear thou it both for him and me;
For after him thou hast deserved it best.
But, for thy kindness in his life and death,
Be sure, while Bel-imperia's life endures,
She will be Don Horatio's thankful friend.

HOR. And, madam, Don Horatio will not slack
Humbly to serve fair Bel-imperia.
But now, if your good liking stand thereto,
I'll crave your pardon to go seek the Prince;
For so the Duke, your father, gave me charge.
Exit.

BEL. Ay, go, Horatio; leave me here alone;
For solitude best fits my cheerless mood. —
Yet what avails to wail Andrea's death,
From whence Horatio proves my second love?
Had he not loved Andrea as he did,
He could not sit in Bel-imperia's thoughts.
But how can love find harbor in my breast
Till I revenge the death of my beloved?
Yes, second love shall further my revenge:
I'll love Horatio, my Andrea's friend,
The more to spite the Prince, that wrought his end.
And where[39] Don Balthazar, that slew my love,
Himself now pleads for favor at my hands,
He shall, in rigor of my just disdain,
Reap long repentance for his murderous deed!
For what was 't else but murderous cowardice,
So many to oppress one valiant knight,
Without respect of honor in the fight?
And here he comes that murd'red my delight.

Enter LORENZO *and* BALTHAZAR.

LOR. Sister, what means this melancholy walk?

BEL. That for a while I wish no company.

LOR. But here the Prince is come to visit you.

BEL. That argues that he lives in liberty.

BAL. No, madam, but in pleasing servitude.

BEL. Your prison then, belike, is your conceit.[40]

BAL. Ay, by conceit my freedom is enthrall'd.

BEL. Then with conceit enlarge yourself again.

BAL. What, if conceit have laid my heart to gage?

BEL. Pay that you borrowed, and recover it.

BAL. I die, if it return from whence it lies.

[33] Accented on the second syllable.
[34] Cf. Vergil's *Aeneid*, ii, 615, 616.
[35] Stabbed in the belly.
[36] Knocked.
[37] Pity, regret.
[38] So Greg; Boas *hand*.
[39] Whereas.
[40] Imagination.

BEL. A heartless man, and live? A miracle!
BAL. Ay, lady, love can work such miracles.
LOR. Tush, tush, my Lord! let go these ambages,[41]
And in plain terms acquaint her with your love.
BEL. What boots complaint, when there's no remedy?
BAL. Yes, to your gracious self must I complain,
In whose fair answer lies my remedy,
On whose perfection all my thoughts attend,
On whose aspect mine eyes find beauty's bower,
In whose translucent breast my heart is lodg'd.
BEL. Alas, my Lord, these are but words of course,[42]
And but [devis'd] [43] to drive me from this place.

She, in going in, lets fall her glove, which HORATIO, *coming out, takes up.*

HOR. Madam, your glove.
BEL. Thanks, good Horatio; take it for thy pains.
BAL. Signior Horatio stoop'd in happy time.
HOR. I reap'd more grace than I deserv'd or hop'd.
LOR. My Lord, be not dismay'd for what is past;
You know that women oft are humorous.[44]
These clouds will overblow with little wind;
Let me alone; [45] I'll scatter them myself.
Meanwhile, let us devise to spend the time
In some delightful sports and revelling.
HOR. The King, my Lords, is coming hither straight,
To feast the Portingal ambassador;
Things were in readiness before I came.
BAL. Then here it fits us to attend the King,
To welcome hither our ambassador,
And learn my father and my country's health.

Enter [46] *the banquet*, Trumpets, *the* KING, [DON CYPRIAN, Lords, Ladies,] *and* Ambassador.

KING. See, Lord Ambassador, how Spain entreats
Their prisoner Balthazar, thy viceroy's son.
We pleasure more in kindness than in wars.
AMB. Sad is our king, and Portingale laments,
Supposing that Don Balthazar is slain.
BAL. [*aside to* BEL-IMPERIA]. So am I slain, by beauty's tyranny! —
You see, my Lord, how Balthazar is slain:
I frolic with the Duke of Castile's son,
Wrapp'd every hour in pleasures of the court,
And grac'd with favors of his Majesty.
KING. Put off your greetings, till our feast be done;
Now come and sit with us, and taste our cheer.

Sit to the banquet.

Sit down, young Prince; you are our second guest.
Brother, sit down; and, Nephew, take your place.
Signior Horatio, wait thou upon our cup;
For well thou hast deserved to be honored.
Now, Lordings, fall to; Spain is Portugal,
And Portugal is Spain; we both are friends;
Tribute is paid, and we enjoy our right.
But where is old Hieronimo, our marshal?
He promis'd us, in honor of our guest,
To grace our banquet with some pompous [47] jest. —

Enter HIERONIMO, *with a drum, three* Knights, *each his scutcheon; then he fetches three* Kings; *they take their crowns and them captive.*

Hieronimo, this masque contents mine eye,
Although I sound not well the mystery.
HIER. The first arm'd knight, that hung his scutcheon up,

He takes the scutcheon and gives it to the KING.

Was English Robert, Earl of Gloucester,
Who, when King Stephen bore sway in Albion,
Arrived with five-and-twenty thousand men
In Portingale, and by success of war
Enforc'd the king, then but a Saracen,
To bear the yoke of the English monarchy.[48]
KING. My Lord of Portingale, by this you see
That which may comfort both your king and you,
And make your late discomfort seem the less. —
But say, Hieronimo, what was the next?

[41] Circumlocutions.
[42] Conventional phrases.
[43] Cor. ed. 1599; earlier eds. *deuise.*
[44] Capricious.
[45] Leave it to me.
[46] Mod. eds. begin a new scene here.
[47] Stately.
[48] Moorish Lisbon was taken in 1147 with the help of an English fleet, but Robert of Gloucester was not present.

HIER. The second knight, that hung his scutcheon up, (*He doth as he did before.*)
Was Edmund, Earl of Kent in Albion,
When English Richard wore the diadem.
He came likewise, and razed Lisbon walls,
And took the King of Portingale in fight;
For which and other such like service done,
He after was created Duke of York.[49]

KING. This is another special argument,
That Portingale may deign to bear our yoke,
When it by little England hath been yok'd. —
But now, Hieronimo, what were the last?

HIER. The third and last, not least, in our account, *Doing as before.*
Was, as the rest, a valiant Englishman,
Brave John of Gaunt, the Duke of Lancaster,
As by his scutcheon plainly may appear.
He with a puissant army came to Spain
And took our King of Castile prisoner.[50]

AMB. This is an argument for our viceroy
That Spain may not insult for her success,
Since English warriors likewise conquered Spain,
And made them bow their knees to Albion.

KING. Hieronimo, I drink to thee for this device,
Which hath pleas'd both the ambassador and me.
Pledge me, Hieronimo, if thou love the King. — *Takes the cup of* HORATIO.
My Lord, I fear we sit but overlong,
Unless our dainties were more delicate;
But welcome are you to the best we have.
Now let us in, that you may be despatch'd;
I think our council is already set.

Exeunt omnes.

[CHORUS]

ANDREA. Come we for this from depth of underground,
To see him feast that gave me my death's wound?
These pleasant sights are sorrow to my soul!
Nothing but league, and love, and banqueting?

REVENGE. Be still, Andrea; ere we go from hence,
I'll turn their friendship into fell despite,
Their love to mortal hate, their day to night,
Their hope into despair, their peace to war,
Their joys to pain, their bliss to misery.

ACT II — [SCENE I][1]

Enter LORENZO *and* BALTHAZAR.

LOR. My Lord, though Bel-imperia seem thus coy,
Let reason hold you in your wonted joy.
In time the savage bull sustains the yoke,[2]
In time all haggard[3] hawks will stoop to lure,
In time small wedges cleave the hardest oak,
In time the flint is pierc'd with softest shower,
And she in time will fall from her disdain
And rue the sufferance of your friendly pain.

BAL. No, she is wilder, and more hard withal,
Than beast, or bird, or tree, or stony wall.
But wherefore blot I Bel-imperia's name?
It is my fault, not she, that merits blame.
My feature is not to content her sight;
My words are rude and work her no delight.
The lines I send her are but harsh and ill,
Such as do drop from Pan and Marsyas' quill.
My presents are not of sufficient cost,
And being worthless, all my labor 's lost.
Yet might she love me for my valiancy —
Ay, but that 's sland'red by captivity.
Yet might she love me to content her sire —
Ay, but her reason masters his desire.
Yet might she love me as her brother's friend —
Ay, but her hopes aim at some other end.
Yet might she love me to uprear her state —
Ay, but perhaps she hopes some nobler mate.
Yet might she love me as her [beauty's][4] thrall —
Ay, but I fear she cannot love at all.

LOR. My Lord, for my sake leave [this ecstasy,][5]
And doubt not but we 'll find some remedy.
Some cause there is that lets you not be loved;
First that must needs be known, and then removed.
What if my sister love some other knight?

BAL. My summer's day will turn to winter's night.

[49] Edmund Langley, fifth son of Edward III, made an expedition to Portugal in 1381, but it came to nothing. His dukedom was awarded later, for service against the Scots.

[50] On the contrary he had to retreat from Spain, though he afterwards married one of his daughters to the heir of Castile.

[1] A room in the palace of Don Cyprian.

[2] Ll. 3–6 and 9, 10 are adapted from Thomas Watson's *Hecatompathia*, Sonnet 47, which in turn adapts ll. 1–4 of Sonnet 103 of Serafino d'Acquila.

[3] Wayward, fractious. — "Lure" = bait, a device to entice the hawk to return.

[4] Cor. Q 1615; earlier eds. *beauteous*.

[5] Emend. Schick; old eds. *these extasies*.

LOR. I have already found a stratagem
To sound the bottom of this doubtful theme.
My Lord, for once you shall be rul'd by me;
Hinder me not, whate'er you hear or see.
By force or fair means will I cast about
To find the truth of all this question out. —
Ho, Pedringano!
PED. [*within*] *Signior!*
LOR. *Vien qui presto.*[6]

Enter PEDRINGANO.

PED. Hath your Lordship any service to command me?
LOR. Ay, Pedringano, service of import;
And, not to spend the time in trifling words,
Thus stands the case: it is not long, thou know'st,
Since I did shield thee from my father's wrath,
For thy conveyance [7] in Andrea's love,
For which thou wert adjudg'd to punishment.
I stood betwixt thee and thy punishment;
And since, thou knowest how I have favored thee.
Now to these favors will I add reward,
Not with fair words, but store of golden coin,
And lands and living join'd with dignities,
If thou but satisfy my just demand.
Tell truth, and have me for thy lasting friend.
PED. Whate'er it be your Lordship shall demand,
My bounden duty bids me tell the truth,
If case it lie in me to tell the truth.
LOR. Then, Pedringano, this is my demand:
Whom loves my sister Bel-imperia?
For she reposeth all her trust in thee.
Speak, man, and gain both friendship and reward.
I mean, whom loves she in Andrea's place?
PED. Alas, my Lord, since Don Andrea's death
I have no credit with her as before,
And therefore know not if she love or no.
LOR. Nay, if thou dally, then I am thy foe;
[*Draw his sword.*] [8]
And fear shall force what friendship cannot win.
Thy death shall bury what thy life conceals;
Thou diest for more esteeming her than me.
PED. O, stay, my Lord.
LOR. Yet speak the truth, and I will guerdon thee,
And shield thee from whatever can ensue,
And will conceal whate'er proceeds from thee.
But if thou dally once again, thou diest.
PED. If madam Bel-imperia be in love —
LOR. What, villain, — if's and and's? [9]
[*Offer to kill him.*] [8]
PED. O, stay, my Lord: she loves Horatio.
BALTHAZAR *starts back.*
LOR. What, Don Horatio, our knight marshal's son?
PED. Even him, my Lord.
LOR. Now say but how knowest thou he is her love,
And thou shalt find me kind and liberal.
Stand up, I say, and fearless tell the truth.
PED. She sent him letters, which myself perus'd,
Full-fraught with lines and arguments of love,
Preferring him before Prince Balthazar.
LOR. Swear on this cross [10] that what thou sayest is true,
And that thou wilt conceal what thou hast told.
PED. I swear to both, by Him that made us all.
LOR. In hope thine oath is true, here's thy reward;
But if I prove thee perjur'd and unjust,
This very sword whereon thou took'st thine oath
Shall be the worker of thy tragedy.
PED. What I have said is true, and shall, for me,[11]
Be still conceal'd from Bel-imperia.
Besides, your Honor's liberality
Deserves my duteous service, even till death.
LOR. Let this be all that thou shalt do for me:
Be watchful when and where these lovers meet,
And give me notice in some secret sort.
PED. I will, my Lord.
LOR. Then shalt thou find that I am liberal.
Thou know'st that I can more advance thy state
Than she; be therefore wise, and fail me not.
Go and attend her, as thy custom is,
Lest absence make her think thou dost amiss.
Exit PEDRINGANO.
Why so! *Tam armis quam ingenio:*
Where words prevail not, violence prevails;
But gold doth more than either of them both.
How likes Prince Balthazar this stratagem?

[6] Come here quickly.
[7] Acting as a medium of communication.
[8] Add. Q 1602.

[9] In his jeering allusions to Kyd in the prefatory epistle to *Menaphon*, Nash accuses him of "bodging up a blank verse with 'if's' and 'and's.'"
[10] Probably the hilt of his sword.
[11] As far as I am concerned.

BAL. Both well and ill; it makes me glad and sad:
Glad that I know the hinderer of my love,
Sad that I fear she hates me whom I love;
Glad that I know on whom to be reveng'd,
Sad that she'll fly me if I take revenge.
Yet must I take revenge, or die myself,
For love resisted grows impatient.
I think Horatio be my destin'd plague!
First, in his hand he brandished a sword,
And with that sword he fiercely waged war,
And in that war he gave me dangerous wounds,
And by those wounds he forced me to yield,
And by my yielding I became his slave;
Now in his mouth he carries pleasing words,
Which pleasing words do harbor sweet conceits,
Which sweet conceits are lim'd with sly deceits,
Which sly deceits smooth Bel-imperia's ears,
And through her ears dive down into her heart,
And in her heart set him where I should stand.
Thus hath he ta'en my body by his force,
And now by sleight would captivate my soul;
But in his fall I'll tempt the Destinies,
And either lose my life or win my love.

LOR. Let's go, my Lord; your staying stays revenge.
Do you but follow me, and gain your love;
Her favor must be won by his remove. *Exeunt.*

[SCENE II] [12]

Enter HORATIO *and* BEL-IMPERIA.

HOR. Now, madam, since by favor of your love
Our hidden smoke is turned to open flame,
And that [13] with looks and words we feed our thoughts
(Two chief contents, where more cannot be had);
Thus, in the midst of love's fair blandishments,
Why show you sign of inward languishments?

PEDRINGANO *showeth all to the* PRINCE *and* LORENZO, *placing them in secret.*

BEL. My heart, sweet friend, is like a ship at sea:
She wisheth port, where, riding all at ease,
She [may] [14] repair what stormy times have worn,
And, leaning on the shore, may sing with joy
That pleasure follows pain, and bliss annoy.
Possession of thy love is th' only port
Wherein my heart, with fears and hopes long toss'd,
Each hour doth wish and long to make resort,
There to repair the joys that it hath lost,
And, sitting safe, to sing in Cupid's choir
That sweetest bliss is crown of love's desire.

BALTHAZAR [*and* LORENZO *speak*] *above.*

BAL. O sleep, mine eyes: see not my love profan'd;
Be deaf, my ears: hear not my discontent;
Die, heart: another joys what thou deservest.

LOR. Watch still, mine eyes, to see this love disjoin'd;
Hear still, mine ears, to hear them both lament;
Live, heart, to joy at fond Horatio's fall.

BEL. Why stands Horatio speechless all this while?

HOR. The less I speak, the more I meditate.

BEL. But whereon dost thou chiefly meditate?

HOR. On dangers past, and pleasures to ensue.

BAL. On pleasures past, and dangers to ensue.

BEL. What dangers and what pleasures dost thou mean?

HOR. Dangers of war, and pleasures of our love.

LOR. Dangers of death, but pleasures none at all.

BEL. Let dangers go; thy war shall be with me,
But such a warring as breaks no bond of peace.
Speak thou fair words, I'll cross them with fair words;
Send thou sweet looks, I'll meet them with sweet looks;
Write loving lines, I'll answer loving lines;
Give me a kiss, I'll countercheck thy kiss:
Be this our warring peace, or peaceful war.

HOR. But, gracious madam, then appoint the field
Where trial of this war shall first be made.

BAL. Ambitious villain, how his boldness grows!

BEL. Then be thy father's pleasant bower the field,
Where first we vow'd a mutual amity.
The court were dangerous; that place is safe.
Our hour shall be when Vesper 'gins to rise,

[12] Another room. The eavesdroppers doubtless appear either on the balcony above the inner stage or at a window.
[13] Since.
[14] Cor. Q 1602; earlier eds. *mad, made.*

That summons home distressful travaillers.[15]
There none shall hear us but the harmless birds;
Happily the gentle nightingale
Shall carol us asleep, ere we be 'ware,
And, singing with the prickle [16] at her breast,
Tell our delight and mirthful dalliance.
Till then each hour will seem a year and more.
HOR. But, honey-sweet and honorable love,
Return we now into your father's sight;
Dangerous suspicion waits on our delight.
LOR. Ay, danger mix'd with jealous [17] despite
Shall send thy soul into eternal night.
Exeunt.

[SCENE III] [18]

Enter KING OF SPAIN, Portingale Ambassador, DON CYPRIAN, *etc.*

KING. Brother of Castile, to the Prince's love
What says your daughter, Bel-imperia?
CYP. Although she coy it, as becomes her kind,
And yet dissemble that she loves the Prince,
I doubt not, I, but she will stoop in time.
And were she froward, which she will not be,
Yet herein shall she follow my advice,
Which is to love him, or forgo my love.
KING. Then, Lord Ambassador of Portingale,
Advise thy King to make this marriage up,
For strengthening of our late-confirmed league;
I know no better means to make us friends.
Her dowry shall be large and liberal;
Besides that she is daughter and half heir
Unto our brother here, Don Cyprian,
And shall enjoy the moiety of his land,
I'll grace her marriage with an uncle's gift;
And this it is, in case the match go forward:
The tribute which you pay shall be releas'd;
And if by Balthazar she have a son,
He shall enjoy the kingdom after us.
AMB. I'll make the motion to my sovereign liege,
And work it, if my counsel may prevail.
KING. Do so, my Lord; and, if he give consent,
I hope his presence here will honor us,
In celebration of the nuptial day;
And let himself determine of the time.
AMB. Will't please your Grace command me aught beside?
KING. Commend me to the King, and so farewell.
But where's Prince Balthazar to take his leave?
AMB. That is perform'd already, my good Lord.
KING. Amongst the rest of what you have in charge,
The Prince's ransom must not be forgot.
That's none of mine, but his that took him prisoner;
And well his forwardness deserves reward.
It was Horatio, our knight marshal's son.
AMB. Between us there's a price already pitch'd,
And shall be sent with all convenient speed.
KING. Then once again farewell, my Lord.
AMB. Farewell, my Lord of Castile, and the rest. *Exit.*
KING. Now, Brother, you must take some little pains
To win fair Bel-imperia from her will.
Young virgins must be ruled by their friends.
The Prince is amiable, and loves her well;
If she neglect him and forgo his love,
She both will wrong her own estate and ours.
Therefore, whiles I do entertain the Prince
With greatest pleasure that our court affords,
Endeavor you to win your daughter's [thought]: [19]
If she give back, all this will come to naught.
Exeunt.

[SCENE IV] [20]

Enter HORATIO, BEL-IMPERIA, *and* PEDRINGANO.

HOR. Now that the night begins with sable wings
To overcloud the brightness of the sun,
And that in darkness pleasures may be done,
Come, Bel-imperia, let us to the bower,
And there in safety pass a pleasant hour.
BEL. I follow thee, my love, and will not back,
Although my fainting heart controls my soul.

[15] Toilers. Qq 1623, 1633, *travailers;* earlier eds. *travellers.*
[16] Thorn. Cf. *Friar Bacon and Friar Bungay,* IV, i, 70, and note.
[17] Trisyllabic: jealious. (Kittredge, cited by Manly.)
[18] A room in the royal palace.
[19] Cor. Q 1615; earlier eds. *thoughts.*
[20] Hieronimo's garden, the inner stage representing the arbor.

HOR. Why, make you doubt of Pedringano's faith?
BEL. No, he is as trusty as my second self.
Go, Pedringano, watch without the gate,
And let us know if any make approach.
PED. [*aside*] Instead of watching, I'll deserve more gold
By fetching Don Lorenzo to this match.
Exit PEDRINGANO.
HOR. What means my love?
BEL. I know not what myself;
And yet my heart foretells me some mischance.
HOR. Sweet, say not so; fair fortune is our friend,
And heavens have shut up day to pleasure us.
The stars, thou seest, hold back their twinkling shine,
And Luna hides herself to pleasure us.
BEL. Thou hast prevail'd; I'll conquer my misdoubt,
And in thy love and counsel drown my fear.
I fear no more; love now is all my thoughts.
Why sit we not? for pleasure asketh ease.
HOR. The more thou sitt'st within these leafy bowers,
The more will Flora deck it with her flowers.
BEL. Ay, but if Flora spy Horatio here,
Her jealous eye will think I sit too near.
HOR. Hark, madam, how the birds record [21] by night,
For joy that Bel-imperia sits in sight.
BEL. No, Cupid counterfeits the nightingale,
To frame sweet music to Horatio's tale.
HOR. If Cupid sing, then Venus is not far;
Ay, thou art Venus, or some fairer star.
BEL. If I be Venus, thou must needs be Mars;
And where Mars reigneth, there must needs be [wars].[22]
HOR. Then thus begin our wars: put forth thy hand,
That it may combat with my ruder hand.
BEL. Set forth thy foot to try the push of mine.
HOR. But first my looks shall combat against thine.
BEL. Then ward thyself: I dart this kiss at thee.
HOR. Thus I retort the dart thou threw'st at me.
BEL. Nay, then, to gain the glory of the field,
My twining arms shall yoke and make thee yield.
HOR. Nay, then, my arms are large and strong withal:
Thus elms by vines are compass'd, till they fall.
BEL. O, let me go, for in my troubled eyes
Now mayst thou read that life in passion dies.
HOR. O, stay awhile, and I will die with thee;
So shalt thou yield, and yet have conquer'd me.
BEL. Who's there, Pedringano? We are betray'd!

Enter LORENZO, BALTHAZAR, SERBERINE, [*and*] PEDRINGANO, *disguised.*

LOR. My Lord, away with her; take her aside.—
O, sir, forbear; your valor is already tri'd.
Quickly dispatch, my masters.
They hang him in the arbor.
HOR. What, will you murder me?
LOR. Ay, thus, and thus! these are the fruits of love. *They stab him.*
BEL. O, save his life, and let me die for him!
O, save him, Brother; save him, Balthazar!
I loved Horatio but he loved not me.
BAL. But Balthazar loves Bel-imperia.
LOR. Although his life were still ambitious-proud,
Yet is he at the highest now he is dead.
BEL. Murder! murder! Help, Hieronimo, help!
LOR. Come, stop her mouth; away with her. *Exeunt.*

Enter HIERONIMO *in his shirt, etc.*

HIER. What outcries pluck me from my naked bed,
And chill my throbbing heart with trembling fear,
Which never danger yet could daunt before?
Who calls Hieronimo? Speak, here I am.—
I did not slumber; therefore 't was no dream.
No, no, it was some woman cri'd for help,
And here within this garden did she cry,
And in this garden must I rescue her.—
But stay, what murd'rous spectacle is this?
A man hang'd up and all the murderers gone!
And in my bower, to lay the guilt on me!
This place was made for pleasure, not for death.
He cuts him down.
Those garments that he wears I oft have seen—

[21] Pipe. [22] Cor. Schick; old eds. *warre.*

Alas, it is Horatio, my sweet son!
O no, but he that whilom was my son!
O, was it thou that call'dst me from my bed?
O speak, if any spark of life remain!
I am thy father. Who hath slain my son?
What savage monster, not of human kind,
Hath here been glutted with thy harmless blood,
And left thy bloody corpse dishonored here,
For me, amidst [these][23] dark and deathful shades,
To drown thee with an ocean of my tears?
O Heavens, why made you night to cover sin?
By day this deed of darkness had not been.
O earth, why didst thou not in time devour
The vild profaner of this sacred bower?
O poor Horatio, what hadst thou misdone,
To leese[24] thy life, ere life was new begun?
O wicked butcher, whatsoe'er thou wert,
How could thou strangle virtue and desert?
Ay me most wretched, that have lost my joy,
In leesing my Horatio, my sweet boy!

Enter ISABELL[A].

ISAB. My husband's absence makes my heart to throb! —
Hieronimo!
HIER. Here, Isabella, help me to lament;
For sighs are stopp'd, and all my tears are spent.
ISAB. What world of grief! my son, Horatio!
Oh, where's the author of this endless woe?
HIER. To know the author were some ease of grief,
For in revenge my heart would find relief.
ISAB. Then is he gone? and is my son gone too?
O, gush out, tears, fountains and floods of tears;
Blow, sighs, and raise an everlasting storm;
For outrage fits our cursed wretchedness.

[25] [Ay me, Hieronimo, sweet husband, speak!
HIER. He supp'd with us to-night, frolic and merry,
And said he would go visit Balthazar
At the Duke's palace; there the Prince doth lodge.
He had no custom to stay out so late;
He may be in his chamber; some go see.
Roderigo, ho!

Enter PEDRO *and* JAQUES.

ISAB. Ay me, he raves! — Sweet Hieronimo!
HIER. True, all Spain takes note of it.
Besides, he is so generally beloved;
His Majesty the other day did grace him
With waiting on his cup: these be favors
Which do assure me he cannot be short-lived.
ISAB. Sweet Hieronimo!
HIER. I wonder how this fellow got his clothes! —
Sirrah, sirrah, I'll know the truth of all! —
Jaques, run to the Duke of Castile's presently,
And bid my son Horatio to come home.
I and his mother have had strange dreams to-night.
Do ye hear me, sir?
JAQUES. Ay, sir.
HIER. Well, sir, begone. —
Pedro, come hither; knowest thou who this is?
PED. Too well, sir.
HIER. Too well! Who, who is it? — Peace, Isabella! —
Nay, blush not, man.
PED. It is my Lord Horatio.
HIER. Ha, ha, St. James! but this doth make me laugh,
That there are more deluded than myself.
PED. Deluded?
HIER. Ay! I would have sworn, myself, within this hour,
That this had been my son Horatio —
His garments are so like.
Ha! are they not great persuasions?
ISAB. O, would to God it were not so!
HIER. Were not, Isabella? Doest thou dream it is?
Can thy soft bosom entertain a thought
That such a black deed of mischief should be done
On one so [pure][26] and spotless as our son?
Away, I am ashamed.
ISAB. Dear Hieronimo,
Cast a more serious eye upon thy grief;
Weak apprehension gives but weak belief.
HIER. It was a man, sure, that was hanged up here;
A youth, as I remember. I cut him down.
If it should prove my son now after all!
Say you? say you? — Light! lend me a taper;
Let me look again. — O God!
Confusion, mischief, torment, death, and hell,
Drop all your stings at once in my cold bosom,
That now is stiff with horror; kill me quickly!
Be gracious to me, thou infective[27] night,
And drop this deed of murder down on me;
Gird in my waste of grief with thy large darkness,
And let me not survive to see the light
May put me in the mind I had a son.
ISAB. O sweet Horatio! O my dearest son!
HIER. How strangely had I lost my way to grief!]

Sweet, lovely rose, ill-pluck'd before thy time,
Fair, worthy son, not conquer'd, but betray'd,
I'll kiss thee now, for words with tears are [stay'd].[28]
ISAB. And I'll close up the glasses of his sight,
For once these eyes were only my delight.
HIER. Seest thou this handkercher besmear'd with blood?
It shall not from me till I take revenge.
Seest thou those wounds that yet are bleeding fresh?
I'll not entomb them till I have reveng'd.
Then will I joy amidst my discontent;
Till then my sorrow never shall be spent.

[23] Old eds. *this*.
[24] Qq 1623, 1633, *lose*.
[25] First passage of additions begins here.
[26] Cor. Q 1615; earlier eds. *poore*.
[27] Infectious.
[28] Cor. Q 1603; earlier eds. *stainde*.

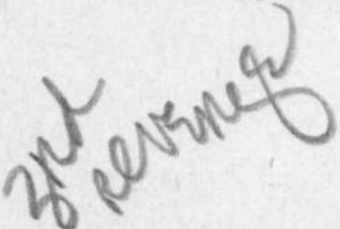

ISAB. The Heavens are just; murder cannot be hid;
Time is the author both of truth and right,
And time will bring this treachery to light.

HIER. Meanwhile, good Isabella, cease thy plaints,
Or, at the least, dissemble them awhile;
So shall we sooner find the practice[29] out,
And learn by whom all this was brought about.
Come, Isabel, now let us take him up,

They take him up.

And bear him in from out this cursed place.
I'll say his dirge; singing fits not this case.

[30] *O aliquis mihi quas pulchrum v[e]r educ[a]t herbas,*

(HIERONIMO *sets his breast unto his sword.*)

Misceat, et nostro detur medicina dolori;
Aut, si qui faciunt ann[or]um obli[v]ia, succos
Pr[ae]beat; ipse met[a]m magn[u]m quaecunque per orbem
Gramina Sol pulchras [*effert*][31] *in luminis oras;*
Ipse bibam quicquid meditatur saga vene[n]i,
Quicquid et [*herbarum vi caeca nenia*][32] *nectit:*
Omnia perpetiar, lethum quoque, dum semel omnis
Noster in extincto moriatur pector[e] sensus.—
Ergo tuos oculos nunquam, mea vita, videbo,
Et tua perpetuus sepelivit lumina somnus?
Emoriar tecum: sic, juvat ire sub umbras.—
At tamen absistam properato cedere letho,
Ne mortem vindicta tuam tam nulla sequatur.

(*Here he throws it from him and bears the body away.*)

[CHORUS]

ANDREA. Brought'st thou me hither to increase my pain?
I look'd that Balthazar should have been slain;
But 'tis my friend Horatio that is slain,
And they abuse fair Bel imperia,
O[n] whom I doted more than all the world,
Because she lov'd me more than all the world.

REVENGE. Thou talkest of harvest, when the corn is green;
The end is crown of every work well done;
The sickle comes not till the corn be ripe.
Be still; and ere I lead thee from this place,
I'll show thee Balthazar in heavy case.

ACT III — [SCENE I][1]

Enter VICEROY OF PORTINGALE, Nobles, [*and*] VILLUPPO.

VIC. Infortunate condition of kings,
Seated amidst so many helpless doubts!
First we are plac'd upon extremest height,
And oft supplanted with exceeding [hate],[2]
But ever subject to the wheel of chance;
And at our highest never joy we so
As we both doubt and dread our overthrow.
So striveth not the waves with sundry winds
As Fortune toileth in the affairs of kings,
That would be fear'd, yet fear to be beloved,
Sith fear or love to kings is flattery.[3]
For instance, Lordings, look upon your king,
By hate deprived of his dearest son,
The only hope of our successive line.

[1] NOB. I had not thought that Alexandro's heart
Had been envenom'd with such extreme hate;
But now I see that words have several works,
And there's no credit in the countenance.

VIL. No; for, my Lord, had you beheld the train[4]
That feigned love had colored in his looks,
When he in camp consorted[5] Balthazar,
Far more inconstant had you thought the sun,
That hourly coasts[6] the centre of the earth,
Than Alexandro's purpose to the Prince.

VIC. No more, Villuppo; thou hast said enough;
And with thy words thou slayest our wounded thoughts.
Nor shall I longer dally with the world,

[29] Plot.

[30] This passage is a hodgepodge of tags from classical poetry and lines of Kyd's own composition. (Boas.) "Oh, may someone blend me the herbs that beauteous Spring doth bear, and let our anguish be medicined; or let him proffer potions, if such there be that cause forgetfulness of the years. May I myself reap throughout the wide world whatever plants the sun's warmth brings forth to earthly realms of light. May I drink any poison the wise woman may prepare, and whatever herbs her incantation unites in occult power. Let me endure all, nay death also, if once for all may die all feeling in a heart that is dead. Nevermore, then, shall I see thy eyes, my life? And has an everlasting slumber buried thy light? With thee may I perish: so would I go into the shadows. But nevertheless I shall hold off from yielding speedily to death, lest then no vengeance follow thy death."

[31] Conj. Traube (quoted by Schick); old eds. *effecit*.

[32] So Schick; old eds. *irraui euecaeca menia*.

[1] The Portuguese court. A place of execution.

[2] Cor. Q 1599; earlier eds. *heat*.

[3] Adapted from Seneca's *Agamemnon*, ll. 57–73.

[4] Guile.

[5] Accompanied.

[6] Moves around.

Procrastinating Alexandro's death. —
Go some of you, and fetch the traitor forth,
[*Exit a* Nobleman.]
That, as he is condemned, he may die.

Enter ALEXANDRO *with a* Nobleman *and* Halberds.

[1] NOB. In such extremes will nought but patience serve.
ALEX. But in extremes what patience shall I use?
Nor discontents it me to leave the world,
With whom there nothing can prevail but wrong.
NOB. Yet hope the best.
ALEX. 'T is Heaven is my hope.
As for the earth, it is too much infect
To yield me hope of any of her mold.
VIC. Why linger ye? Bring forth that daring fiend,
And let him die for his accursed deed.
ALEX. Not that I fear the extremity of death
(For nobles cannot stoop to servile fear)
Do I, O King, thus discontented live.
But this, O this, torments my laboring soul,
That thus I die suspected of a sin
Whereof, as Heavens have known my secret thoughts,
So am I free from this suggestion.[7]
VIC. No more, I say! to the tortures! When![8]
Bind him, and burn his body in those flames
They bind him to the stake.
That shall prefigure those unquenched fires
Of Phlegethon,[9] prepared for his soul.
ALEX. My guiltless death will be aveng'd on thee,
On thee, Villuppo, that hath malic'd[10] thus,
Or for thy meed hast falsely me accus'd.
VIL. Nay, Alexandro, if thou menace me,
I'll lend a hand to send thee to the lake
Where those thy words shall perish with thy works,
Injurious traitor! monstrous homicide!

Enter Ambassador [*and* Attendants].

AMB. Stay, hold a while;
And here, with pardon of his Majesty,
Lay hands upon Villuppo.
VIC. Ambassador,
What news hath urg'd this sudden entrance?

[7] Temptation, incitement to evil.
[8] An exclamation of impatience.
[9] The fiery river of Hades.
[10] Desired to injure.

AMB. Know, Sovereign Lord, that Balthazar doth live.
VIC. What sayest thou? Liveth Balthazar, our son?
AMB. Your Highness' son, Lord Balthazar, doth live;
And, well entreated in the court of Spain,
Humbly commends him to your Majesty.
These eyes beheld, and these my followers;
With these, the letters of the King's commends, *Gives him letters.*
Are happy witnesses of his Highness' health.
The King looks on the letters, and proceeds.
VIC. "Thy son doth live; your tribute is receiv'd;
Thy peace is made, and we are satisfied.
The rest resolve upon as things propos'd
For both our honors and thy benefit."
AMB. These are his Highness' farther articles. *He gives him more letters.*
VIC. Accursed wretch, to intimate these ills
Against the life and reputation
Of noble Alexandro! — Come, my Lord, unbind him. —
Let him unbind thee, that is bound to death,
To make a quital[11] for thy discontent.
They unbind him.
ALEX. Dread Lord, in kindness[12] you could do no less
Upon report of such a damned fact;[13]
But thus we see our innocence hath sav'd
The hopeless life which thou, Villuppo, sought
By thy suggestions to have massacred.
VIC. Say, false Villuppo, wherefore didst thou thus
Falsely betray Lord Alexandro's life?
Him whom thou knowest that no unkindness else
But even the slaughter of our dearest son
Could once have moved us to have misconceived.
ALEX. Say, treacherous Villuppo, tell the King:
Or wherein hath Alexandro used thee ill?
VIL. Rent with remembrance of so foul a deed,
My guilty soul submits me to thy doom;
For not for Alexandro's injuries,
But for reward and hope to be preferr'd,
Thus have I shamelessly hazarded his life.
VIC. Which, villain, shall be ransomed with thy death;

[11] Requital. [12] Nature. [13] Deed.

And not so mean [14] a torment as we here
Devis'd for him who, thou said'st, slew our son,
But with thy bitterest torments and extremes
That may be yet invented for thine end.

ALEXANDRO *seems to entreat.*

Entreat me not. — Go, take the traitor hence. —

Exit VILLUPPO [*guarded*].

And, Alexandro, let us honor thee
With public notice of thy loyalty. —
To end those things articulated here
By our great lord, the mighty King of Spain,
We with our council will deliberate.
Come, Alexandro, keep us company.

Exeunt.

[SCENE II] [15]

Enter HIERONIMO.

HIER. O eyes! no eyes, but fountains fraught with tears; [16]
O life! no life, but lively form of death;
O world! no world, but mass of public wrongs,
Confus'd and fill'd with murder and misdeeds.
O sacred Heav'ns! if this unhallowed deed,
If this inhuman and barbarous attempt,
If this incomparable murder thus
Of mine, but now no more my son,
Shall unreveal'd and unrevenged pass,
How should we term your dealings to be just,
If you unjustly deal with those that in your justice trust? [17]
The night, sad secretary [18] to my moans,
With direful visions wake my vexed soul,
And with the wounds of my distressful son
Solicit me for notice of his death.
The ugly fiends do sally forth of hell,
And frame my steps to unfrequented paths,
And fear my heart with fierce inflamed thoughts.
The cloudy day my discontents records,
Early begins to register my dreams,
And drive me forth to seek the murderer.
Eyes, life, world, Heav'ns, hell, night, and day,
See, search, show, send some man, some mean, that may — *A letter falleth.*
What 's here? a letter? Tush! it is not so! —
A letter written to Hieronimo! — *Red ink.*
"For want of ink, receive this bloody writ.
Me hath my hapless brother hid from thee;
Revenge thyself on Balthazar and him:
For these were they that murd'red thy son.
Hieronimo, revenge Horatio's death,
And better fare than Bel-imperia doth." —
What means this unexpected miracle?
My son slain by Lorenzo and the Prince!
What cause had they Horatio to malign? [19]
Or what might move thee, Bel-imperia,
To accuse thy brother, had he been the mean?
Hieronimo, beware! — thou art betray'd,
And to entrap thy life this train [20] is laid.
Advise thee, therefore; be not credulous:
This is devised to endanger thee,
That thou, by this, Lorenzo shouldst accuse;
And he, for thy dishonor done, should draw
Thy life in question and thy name in hate.
Dear was the life of my beloved son,
And of his death behoves me be reveng'd.
Then hazard not thine own, Hieronimo,
But live t' effect thy resolution.
I therefore will by circumstances [21] try,
What I can gather to confirm this writ;
And, hearkening near the Duke of Castile's house,
Close, if I can, with Bel-imperia,
To listen more, but nothing to bewray.

Enter PEDRINGANO.

Now, Pedringano.

PED. Now, Hieronimo.

HIER. Where 's thy lady?

PED. I know not; here 's my lord.

Enter LORENZO.

LOR. How now, who 's this? Hieronimo?

HIER. My Lord.

PED. He asketh for my Lady Bel-imperia.

LOR. What to do, Hieronimo? The Duke, my father, hath
Upon some disgrace awhile remov'd her hence;
But, if it be aught I may inform her of,
Tell me, Hieronimo, and I'll let her know it.

HIER. Nay, nay, my Lord, I thank you; it shall not need.
I had a suit unto her, but too late;
And her disgrace makes me unfortunate.

LOR. Why so, Hieronimo; use me.

[14] Moderate.
[15] Spain. Before the palace of Don Cyprian.
[16] The opening lines of this speech were much parodied.
[17] A fourteener.
[18] *I.e.*, confidant.
[19] Plot against.
[20] Snare.
[21] Indirect methods.

HIER. O no, my Lord, I dare not; it must not be.
I humbly thank your Lordship.

[22] [HIER. Who? you, my Lord?
I reserve your favor for a greater honor;
This is a very toy,[23] my Lord, a toy.
LOR. All 's one,[24] Hieronimo; acquaint me with it.
HIER. I' faith, my Lord, it is an idle thing;
I must confess I ha' been too slack, too tardy,
Too remiss unto your Honor.
LOR. How now, Hieronimo?
HIER. In troth, my Lord, it is a thing of nothing:
The murder of a son, or so ——
A thing of nothing, my Lord!]

LOR. Why then, farewell.
HIER. [*aside*] My grief no heart, my thoughts no tongue can tell. *Exit.*
LOR. Come hither, Pedringano; seest thou this?
PED. My Lord, I see it, and suspect it too.
LOR. This is that damned villain, Serberine,
That hath, I fear, reveal'd Horatio's death.
PED. My Lord, he could not, 't was so lately done;
And since, he hath not left my company.
LOR. Admit he have not, his condition[25]'s such
As fear or flattering words may make him false.
I know his humor,[25] and therewith repent
That e'er I us'd him in this enterprise.
But, Pedringano, to prevent the worst,
And 'cause I know thee secret as my soul,
Here, for thy further satisfaction, take thou this, *Gives him more gold.*
And hearken to me: thus it is devis'd.
This night thou must (and, prithee, so resolve),
Meet Serberine at Saint Luigi's Park —
Thou knowest 't is here hard by behind the house; —
There take thy stand, and see thou strike him sure,
For die he must, if we do mean to live.
PED. But how shall Serberine be there, my Lord?
LOR. Let me alone; I'll send to him to meet
The Prince and me, where thou must do this deed.
PED. It shall be done, my Lord; it shall be done;
And I'll go arm myself to meet him there.
LOR. When things shall alter, as I hope they will,
Then shalt thou mount for this; thou knowest my mind. *Exit* PEDRINGANO.
Che le Ieron![26]

Enter Page.

PAGE. My Lord?
LOR. Go, sirrah,
To Serberine, and bid him forthwith meet
The Prince and me at Saint Luigi's Park,
Behind the house, this evening, boy.
PAGE. I go, my Lord.
LOR. But, sirrah, let the hour be eight a'clock:
Bid him not fail.
PAGE. I fly, my Lord. *Exit.*
LOR. Now to confirm the complot thou hast cast[27]
Of all these practices,[28] I'll spread the watch,
Upon precise commandment from the King,
Strongly to guard the place where Pedringano
This night shall murder hapless Serberine.
Thus must we work that will avoid distrust;
Thus must we practise to prevent mishap,
And thus one ill another must expulse.
This sly enquiry of Hieronimo
For Bel-imperia breeds suspicion,
And this suspicion bodes a further ill.
As for myself, I know my secret fault,
And so do they; but I have dealt for them.
They that for coin their souls endangered,
To save my life for coin shall venture theirs;
And better it 's that base companions[29] die
Than by their life to hazard our good haps.
Nor shall they live, for me to fear their faith:
I'll trust myself, myself shall be my friend;
For die they shall: slaves are ordain[e]d to no other end.[30] *Exit.*

[SCENE III][31]

Enter PEDRINGANO, *with a pistol.*

PED. Now, Pedringano, bid thy pistol hold;
And hold on, Fortune! once more favor me;
Give but success to mine attempting spirit,
And let me shift[32] for taking of mine aim.
Here is the gold: this is the gold propos'd;
It is no dream that I adventure for,
But Pedringano is possess'd thereof.

[22] Second passage of additions begins here, replacing ll. 65, 66.
[23] Trifle.
[24] It's all the same, just the same, no matter.
[25] Disposition.

[26] Apparently a corruption of the summons, or perhaps of the page's name.
[27] Planned.
[28] Schemes.
[29] Fellows.
[30] A fourteener.
[31] Saint Luigi's Park.
[32] Leave it to me.

And he that would not strain his conscience
For him that thus his liberal purse hath stretch'd,
Unworthy such a favor, may he fail,
And, wishing, want when such as I prevail.
As for the fear of apprehension,
I know, if need should be, my noble lord
Will stand between me and ensuing harms;
Besides, this place is free from all suspect.
Here therefore will I stay and take my stand.

Enter the Watch [*unobserved by* PEDRINGANO].

1 [WATCH]. I wonder much to what intent it is
That we are thus expressly charg'd to watch.
2 [WATCH]. 'T is by commandment in the King's own name.
3 [WATCH]. But we were never wont to watch and ward
So near the Duke his brother's house before.
2 [WATCH]. Content yourself; stand close; there's somewhat in 't.

Enter SERBERINE.

SER. Here, Serberine, attend and stay thy pace;
For here did Don Lorenzo's page appoint
That thou by his command shouldst meet with him.
How fit a place, if one were so dispos'd,
Methinks this corner is to close with one.[33]
PED. [*aside*] Here comes the bird that I must seize upon.
Now, Pedringano, or never, play the man!
SER. I wonder that his Lordship stays so long,
Or wherefore should he send for me so late.
PED. For this, Serberine; and thou shalt ha 't. *Shoots the dag.*[34]
So, there he lies; my promise is perform'd.

The Watch [*advances*].

1 [WATCH]. Hark, gentlemen, this is a pistol shot.
2 [WATCH]. And here's one slain. Stay the murderer.[35]
PED. Now by the sorrows of the souls in hell, *He strives with the* Watch.
Who first lays hand on me, I'll be his priest.[36]
3 [WATCH]. Sirrah, confess, and therein play the priest;
Why hast thou thus unkindly[37] kill'd the man?
PED. Why? Because he walk'd abroad so late.
3 [WATCH]. Come, sir, you had been better kept your bed,
Than have committed this misdeed so late.
2 [WATCH]. Come, to the Marshal's with the murderer.
1 [WATCH]. On to Hieronimo's! Help me here
To bring the murd'red body with us too.
PED. Hieronimo? Carry me before whom you will.
Whate'er he be, I'll answer him and you;
And do your worst, for I defy you all.
Exeunt.

[SCENE IV][38]

Enter LORENZO *and* BALTHAZAR.

BAL. How now, my Lord, what makes you rise so soon?
LOR. Fear of preventing our mishaps too late.
BAL. What mischief is it that we not mistrust?
LOR. Our greatest ills we least mistrust, my Lord,
And inexpected harms do hurt us most.
BAL. Why, tell me, Don Lorenzo, tell me, man,
If aught concerns our honor and your own.
LOR. Nor you, nor me, my Lord, but both in one;
For I suspect, and the presumption's great,
That by those base confederates in our fault
Touching the death of Don Horatio,
We are betray'd to old Hieronimo.
BAL. Betray'd, Lorenzo? Tush, it cannot be.
LOR. A guilty conscience, urged with the thought
Of former evils, easily cannot err.
I am persuaded, and dissuade me not,
That all's revealed to Hieronimo.
And therefore know that I have cast it thus —

[*Enter* Page.][39]

But here's the page. How now? what news with thee?

[33] To meet a person secretly.
[34] Pistol.
[35] Note the metrical value of the pause.
[36] Be in attendance at his death; *i.e.*, kill him.
[37] Unnaturally.
[38] Unlocated; presumably a room in the palace of Don Cyprian.
[39] Add. Q 1615.

PAGE. My Lord, Serberine is slain.
BAL. Who? Serberine, my man?
PAGE. Your Highness' man, my Lord.
LOR. Speak, page, who murdered him?
PAGE. He that is apprehended for the fact.[40]
LOR. Who?
PAGE. Pedringano.
BAL. Is Serberine slain, that lov'd his lord so well?
Injurious villain, murderer of his friend!
LOR. Hath Pedringano murdered Serberine?
My Lord, let me entreat you to take the pains
To exasperate and hasten his revenge
With your complaints unto my Lord the King.
This their dissension breeds a greater doubt.
BAL. Assure thee, Don Lorenzo, he shall die,
Or else his Highness hardly shall deny.[41]
Meanwhile I'll haste the marshal sessions,
For die he shall for this his damned deed.

Exit BALTHAZAR.

LOR. [*aside*] Why, so; this fits our former policy,
And thus experience bids the wise to deal.
I lay the plot; he prosecutes the point.
I set the trap; he breaks the worthless twigs,
And sees not that wherewith the bird was lim'd.[42]
Thus hopeful men, that mean to hold their own,
Must look like fowlers to their dearest friends.
He runs to kill whom I have holp[43] to catch,
And no man knows it was my reaching f[e]tch.[44]
'T is hard to trust unto a multitude,
Or any one, in mine opinion,
When men themselves their secrets will reveal. —

Enter a Messenger *with a letter.*

Boy!
PAGE. My Lord.
LOR. What's he?
MES. I have a letter to your Lordship.
LOR. From whence?
MES. From Pedringano, that's imprisoned.
LOR. So he is in prison, then?
MES. Ay, my good Lord.
LOR. What would he with us? — He writes us here,
To stand good lord, and help him in distress. —
Tell him I have his letters, know his mind;
And what we may, let him assure him of.
Fellow, begone; my boy shall follow thee. —

Exit Messenger.

[*aside*] This works like wax; yet once more try thy wits. —
Boy, go, convey this purse to Pedringano;
Thou knowest the prison; closely[45] give it him,
And be advis'd that none be thereabout.
Bid him be merry still, but secret;
And though the marshal sessions be to-day,
Bid him not doubt of his delivery.
Tell him his pardon is already sign'd,
And thereon bid him boldly be resolved;
For, were he ready to be turned off[46] —
As 't is my will the uttermost be tri'd —
Thou with his pardon shalt attend him still.
Show him this box, tell him his pardon's in 't;
But open 't not, an if thou lovest thy life;
But let him wisely keep his hopes unknown.
He shall not want while Don Lorenzo lives.
Away!
PAGE. I go, my Lord, I run.
LOR. But, sirrah, see that this be cleanly[47] done. — *Exit* Page.
Now stands our fortune on a tickle[48] point,
And now or never ends Lorenzo's doubts.
One only thing is uneffected yet,
And that's to see the executioner.
But to what end? I list not trust the air
With utterance of our pretence[49] therein,
For fear the privy whisp'ring of the wind
Convey our words amongst unfriendly ears,
That lie too open to advantages.
[*E*][50] *quel che voglio i*[*o*], *nessun lo sa;*
Intendo io: quel mi [*basterà*].[51] *Exit.*

[SCENE V][52]

Enter Boy *with the box.*

[BOY.] My master hath forbidden me to look in this box; and, by my troth, 't is likely, if he had not warned me, I should not have had so much idle time; for we men's-kind in our

[40] Deed.
[41] *I.e.*, I will make it hard for him to deny my request.
[42] Caught. Small birds were caught by smearing twigs with sticky lime.
[43] Helped.
[44] Far-reaching stratagem.

[45] Secretly.
[46] Hanged.
[47] Without bungling.
[48] Insecure, critical.
[49] Intention.
[50] Old eds. *Et.*
[51] So Schick; old eds. *bassāra*. "And what I desire none knows; I know: which is enough for me."
[52] Unlocated; presumably a street.

minority are like women in their uncertainty: that they are most forbidden, they will soonest attempt. So I now. — By my bare honesty, here's nothing but the bare empty box! Were it not sin against secrecy, I would say it were a piece of gentlemanlike knavery. I must go to Pedringano, and tell him his pardon is in this box; nay, I would have sworn it, had I not seen the contrary. I cannot choose but smile to think how the villain will flout the gallows, scorn the audience, and descant on the hangman, and all presuming of his pardon from hence. Will 't not be an odd jest for me to stand and grace every jest he makes, pointing my finger at this box, as who would say, "Mock on; here's thy warrant." Is't not a scurvy jest that a man should jest himself to death? Alas! poor Pedringano, I am in a sort sorry for thee; but if I should be hanged with thee, I cannot weep. *Exit.*

[Scene VI] [53]

Enter Hieronimo *and the* Deputy.

Hier. Thus must we toil in other men's extremes,
That know not how to remedy our own,
And do them justice, when unjustly we,
For all our wrongs, can compass no redress.
But shall I never live to see the day
That I may come, by justice of the Heavens,
To know the cause that may my cares allay?
This toils my body, this consumeth age,
That only I to all men just must be,
And neither gods nor men be just to me.

Dep. Worthy Hieronimo, your office asks
A care to punish such as do transgress.

Hier. So is't my duty to regard his death
Who, when he lived, deserved my dearest blood.
But come, for that we came for. Let's begin,
For here lies that [54] which bids me to be gone.

Enter Officers, Boy, *and* Pedringano, *with a letter in his hand, bound.*

Dep. Bring forth the prisoner, for the court is set.

Ped. Gramercy, boy, but it was time to come;
For I had written to my Lord anew
A nearer matter that concerneth him,
For fear his Lordship had forgotten me.
But sith [55] he hath remembr'ed me so well,
Come, come, come on, when shall we to this gear? [56]

Hier. Stand forth, thou monster, murderer of men,
And here, for satisfaction of the world,
Confess thy folly, and repent thy fault;
For there's thy place of execution.

Ped. This is short work. Well, to your Marshalship
First I confess, nor fear I death therefore,
I am the man, 't was I slew Serberine.
But, sir, then you think this shall be the place
Where we shall satisfy you for this gear?

Dep. Ay, Pedringano.

Ped. Now I think not so.

Hier. Peace, impudent; for thou shalt find it so;
For blood with blood shall, while I sit as judge,
Be satisfied, and the law discharg'd.
And though myself cannot receive the like,
Yet will I see that others have their right.
Despatch; the fault's approved [57] and confess'd,
And by our law he is condemn'd to die.

[*Enter* Hangman.] [58]

Hangm. Come on, sir; are you ready?

Ped. To do what, my fine, officious knave?

Hangm. To go to this gear.

Ped. O sir, you are too forward: thou wouldst fain furnish me with a halter, to disfurnish me of my habit.[59] So I should go out of this gear, my raiment, into that gear, the rope. But, hangman, now I spy your knavery, I'll not change without boot,[60] that's flat.

Hangm. Come, sir.

Ped. So, then, I must up?

Hangm. No remedy.

Ped. Yes, but there shall be for my coming down.

Hangm. Indeed, here's a remedy for that.

Ped. How? be turn'd off?

Hangm. Ay, truly. Come, are you ready? I pray, sir, dispatch; the day goes away.

Ped. What, do you hang by the hour? If you do, I may chance to break your old custom.

[53] A place of justice, with a gallows.
[54] The handkerchief besmeared with Horatio's blood.

[55] Since. [56] Affair. [57] Proved.
[58] Add. Q 1615, though the hangman might well enter with the other officers.
[59] The hangman got the clothes of those he executed.
[60] Additional compensation.

HANGM. Faith, you have reason; for I am like to break your young neck.

PED. Dost thou mock me, hangman? Pray God, I be not preserved to break your knave's pate for this.

HANGM. Alas, sir, you are a foot too low to reach it, and I hope you will never grow so high while I am in the office.

PED. Sirrah, dost see yonder boy with the box in his hand?

HANGM. What, he that points to it with his finger?

PED. Ay, that companion.

HANGM. I know him not; but what of him?

PED. Dost thou think to live till his old doublet will make thee a new truss?[61]

HANGM. Ay, and many a fair year after, to truss up many an honester man than either thou or he.

PED. What hath he in his box, as thou think'st?

HANGM. Faith, I cannot tell, nor I care not greatly. Methinks you should rather hearken to your soul's health.

PED. Why, sirrah hangman, I take it that that is good for the body is likewise good for the soul; and it may be in that box is balm for both.

HANGM. Well, thou art even the merriest piece of man's flesh that e'er groan'd at my office door.

PED. Is your roguery become an office with a knave's name?

HANGM. Ay, and that shall all they witness that see you seal it with a thief's name.

PED. I prithee, request this good company to pray with me.

HANGM. Ay, marry, sir, this is a good motion.[62] My masters, you see here's a good fellow.

PED. Nay, nay, now I remember me, let them alone till some other time; for now I have no great need.

HIER. I have not seen a wretch so impudent.
O monstrous times, where murder's set so light,
And where the soul, that should be shrin'd in Heaven,
Solely delights in interdicted things,
Still wand'ring in the thorny passages
That intercepts itself of[63] happiness.
Murder! O bloody monster! God forbid
A fault so foul should scape unpunished.
Dispatch, and see this execution done! —
This makes me to remember thee, my son.

Exit HIERONIMO.

PED. Nay, soft, no haste.

DEP. Why, wherefore stay you? Have you hope of life?

PED. Why, ay.

HANGM. As how?

PED. Why, rascal, by my pardon from the King.

HANGM. Stand you on that? Then you shall off with this.

He turns him off.

DEP. So, executioner; convey him hence;
But let his body be unburied:
Let not the earth be choked or infect
With that which Heavens contemns, and men neglect.

Exeunt.

[61] Jacket.
[62] Proposal.
[63] Bar it from.

[SCENE VII][64]

Enter HIERONIMO.

HIER. Where shall I run to breathe abroad my woes,
My woes, whose weight hath wearied the earth?
Or mine exclaims, that have surcharg'd the air
With ceaseless plaints for my deceased son?
The blust'ring winds, conspiring with my words,
At my lament have moved the leafless trees,
Disrob'd the meadows of their flow'red green,
Made mountains marsh with spring tides of my tears,
And broken through the brazen gates of hell.
Yet still tormented is my tortured soul
With broken sighs and restless passions,
That, winged, mount and, hovering in the air,
Beat at the windows of the brightest Heavens,
Soliciting for justice and revenge.
But they are plac'd in those empyreal[65] heights,
Where, countermur'd[66] with walls of diamond,
I find the place impregnable; and they
Resist my woes, and give my words no way.

Enter Hangman *with a letter.*

HANGM. O Lord, sir! God bless you, sir! the man, sir, Petergade, sir, he that was so full of merry conceits —

[64] Unlocated; presumably a room in Hieronimo's house.
[65] Cor. Schick; old eds. *imperiall.*
[66] Defended by a wall within a wall; *i.e.*, doubly walled.

HIER. Well, what of him?

HANGM. O Lord, sir, he went the wrong way; the fellow had a fair commission to the contrary. Oh, here is his passport; I pray you, sir, we have done him wrong.

HIER. I warrant thee; give it me.

HANGM. You will stand between the gallows and me?

HIER. Ay, ay.

HANGM. I thank your Lord Worship.

Exit Hangman.

HIER. And yet, though somewhat nearer me concerns,
I will, to ease the grief that I sustain,
Take truce with sorrow while I read on this.
"My lord, I [writ][67] as mine extremes requir'd,
That you would labor my delivery;
If you neglect, my life is desperate,
And in my death I shall reveal the troth.
You know, my Lord, I slew him for your sake,
And was confederate with the Prince and you;
Won by rewards and hopeful promises,
I holp to murder Don Horatio too." —
Holp he to murder mine Horatio?
And actors in th' accursed tragedy
Wast thou, Lorenzo, Balthazar and thou,
Of whom my son, my son, deserved so well?
What have I heard, what have mine eyes beheld?
O sacred Heavens, may it come to pass
That such a monstrous and detested deed,
So closely smother'd, and so long conceal'd,
Shall thus by this be venged or reveal'd?
Now see I what I durst not then suspect,
That Bel-imperia's letter was not feign'd.
Nor feigned she, though falsely they have wrong'd
Both her, myself, Horatio, and themselves.
Now may I make compare 'twixt hers and this,
Of every accident I ne'er could find
Till now, and now I feelingly perceive
They did what Heav'n unpunish'd would not leave.
O false Lorenzo, are these thy flattering looks?
Is this the honor that thou didst my son?
And Balthazar — bane to thy soul and me —
Was this the ransom he reserv'd thee for?
Woe to the cause of these constrained wars!
Woe to thy baseness and captivity!
Woe to thy birth, thy body, and thy soul,
Thy cursed father, and thy conquered self!
And bann'd with bitter execrations be
The day and place where he did pity thee!
But wherefore waste I mine unfruitful words,
When naught but blood will satisfy my woes?
I will go plain me to my Lord the King,
And cry aloud for justice through the court,
Wearing the flints with these my withered feet,
And either purchase justice by entreats,
Or tire them all with my revenging threats.

Exit.

[67] Emend. Manly; old eds. *write.* (Cf. IV, ii, 7.)

[ACT IV — SCENE I][1]

Enter ISABELL[A] *and her* Maid.

ISAB. So that you say this herb will purge the eye,
And this, the head?
Ah, but none of them will purge the heart.
No, there's no medicine left for my disease,
Nor any physic to recure[2] the dead.

She runs lunatic.

Horatio! O, where's Horatio?

MAID. Good madam, affright not thus yourself
With outrage[3] for your son Horatio.
He sleeps in quiet in the Elysian fields.

ISAB. Why, did I not give you gowns and goodly things,
Bought you a whistle and a whipstalk too,
To be revenged on their villainies?

MAID. Madam, these humors[4] do torment my soul.

ISAB. "My soul" — poor soul, thou talks of things
Thou know'st not what — my soul hath silver wings,
That mounts me up unto the highest Heavens.
To Heaven! Ay, there sits my Horatio,
Back'd with a troop of fiery cherubins,
Dancing about his newly healed wounds,
Singing sweet hymns and chanting heavenly notes,
Rare harmony to greet his innocence,
That died, ay died, a mirror in our days.
But say, where shall I find the men, the murderers,

[1] Unlocated; presumably the same. According to the old eds. the play is in four acts, separated by the Chorus. If this division is correct, Act III constitutes nearly half the play. There may have been no Chorus to introduce Act IV, or it may have been omitted, as Greg suggests, accidentally. The present edition follows Hawkins in beginning Act IV here.

[2] Recover. [3] Outcry. [4] Whims.

That slew Horatio? Whither shall I run
To find them out that murdered my son?
Exeunt.

[Scene II] [5]

Bel-imperia, *at a window.*

Bel. What means this outrage that is offered me?
Why am I thus sequest'red from the court?
No notice! Shall I not know the cause
Of this [6] my secret and suspicious ills?
Accursed brother, unkind murderer,
Why bends thou thus thy mind to martyr me?
Hieronimo, why writ I of thy wrongs,
Or why art thou so slack in thy revenge?
Andrea, O Andrea! that thou sawest
Me for thy friend Horatio handled thus,
And him for me thus causeless murdered! —
Well, force perforce, I must constrain myself
To patience, and apply me [7] to the time,
Till Heaven, as I have hoped, shall set me free.

Enter Christophil.

Chris. Come, Madam Bel-imperia, this may not be. *Exeunt.*

[Scene III] [8]

Enter Lorenzo, Balthazar, *and the* Page.

Lor. Boy, talk no further; thus far things go well.
Thou art assur'd that thou sawest him dead?
Page. Or else, my Lord, I live not.
Lor. That's enough.
As for his resolution in his end,
Leave that to him with whom he sojourns now.
Here, take my ring and give it Christophil,
And bid him let my sister be enlarg'd,
And bring her hither straight. — *Exit* Page.
This that I did was for a policy,
To smooth and keep the murder secret,
Which, as a nine-days' wonder, being o'erblown,
My gentle sister will I now enlarge.
Bal. And time, Lorenzo; for my Lord the Duke,
You heard, inquired for her yesternight.
Lor. Why, and, my Lord, I hope you heard me say
Sufficient reason why she kept away;
But that's all one.[9] My Lord, you love her?
Bal. Ay.
Lor. Then in your love beware; deal cunningly;
Salve all suspicions; only soothe me up; [10]
And if she hap to stand on terms [11] with us,
As for her sweetheart and concealment so,
Jest with her gently: under feigned jest
Are things conceal'd that else would breed unrest.
But here she comes.

Enter Bel-imperia.

Now, Sister —
Bel. Sister? No!
Thou art no brother, but an enemy;
Else wouldst thou not have used thy sister so:
First, to affright me with thy weapons drawn,
And with extremes abuse my company; [12]
And then to hurry me, like whirlwind's rage,
Amidst a crew of thy confederates,
And clap me up where none might come at me,
Nor I at any to reveal my wrongs.
What madding fury did possess thy wits?
Or wherein is't that I offended thee?
Lor. Advise you better, Bel-imperia,
For I have done you no disparagement;
Unless, by more discretion than deserv'd,
I sought to save your honor and mine own.
Bel. Mine honor? Why, Lorenzo, wherein is't
That I neglect my reputation so,
As you, or any, need to rescue it?
Lor. His Highness and my father were resolv'd
To come confer with old Hieronimo
Concerning certain matters of estate
That by the Viceroy was determined.
Bel. And wherein was mine honor touch'd in that?
Bal. Have patience, Bel-imperia; hear the rest.
Lor. Me, next in sight, as messenger they sent
To give him notice that they were so nigh.
Now, when I came, consorted with the Prince,
And unexpected in an arbor there
Found Bel-imperia with Horatio —
Bel. How then?
Lor. Why, then, rememb'ring that old disgrace,

[5] Before the palace of Don Cyprian.
[6] Q 1633 *these.*
[7] Conform myself to.
[8] Unlocated; presumably a room in the palace of Don Cyprian.
[9] It makes no difference.
[10] Corroborate my story.
[11] Make conditions.
[12] Companion.

Which you for Don Andrea had endur'd,
And now were likely longer to sustain,
By being found so meanly accompanied,
Thought rather, for I knew no readier mean,
To thrust Horatio forth my father's way.

BAL. And carry you obscurely somewhere else,
Lest that his Highness should have found you there.

BEL. Ev'n so, my Lord? And you are witness
That this is true which he entreateth of?
You, gentle Brother, forged this for my sake,
And you, my Lord, were made his instrument!
A work of worth, worthy the noting too!
But what 's the cause that you conceal'd me since?

LOR. Your melancholy, Sister, since the news
Of your first favorite Don Andrea's death,
My father's old wrath hath exasperate.

BAL. And better was 't for you, being in disgrace,
To absent yourself, and give his fury place.

BEL. But why had I no notice of his ire?

LOR. That were to add more fuel to your fire,
Who burnt like Aetna for Andrea's loss.

BEL. Hath not my father then inquir'd for me?

LOR. Sister, he hath; and thus excus'd I thee: *He whispereth in her ear.*
But Bel-imperia, see the gentle Prince;
Look on thy love, behold young Balthazar,
Whose passions by thy presence are increas'd;
And in whose melancholy thou mayest see
Thy hate, his love; thy flight, his following thee.

BEL. Brother, you are become an orator —
I know not, I, by what experience —
Too politic for me, past all compare,
Since last I saw you; but content yourself:
The Prince is meditating higher things.

BAL. 'T is of thy beauty, then, that conquers kings;
Of those thy tresses, Ariadne's twines,
Wherewith my liberty thou hast surpris'd;
Of that thine ivory front,[13] my sorrow's map,
Wherein I see no haven to rest my hope.

BEL. To love and fear, and both at once, my Lord,
In my conceit, are things of more import
Than women's wits are to be busied with.

BAL. 'T is I that love.

BEL. Whom?

BAL. Bel-imperia.

BEL. But I that fear.

BAL. Whom?

BEL. Bel-imperia.

LOR. Fear yourself?

BEL. Ay, Brother.

LOR. How?

BEL. As those
That what they love are loth and fear to lose.

BAL. Then, fair, let Balthazar your keeper be.

BEL. No, Balthazar doth fear as well as we:
Et[14] *tremulo metui pavidum iunxere timorem —*
Est vanum stolidae proditionis opus.[15]

LOR. Nay, and you argue things so cunningly,
We 'll go continue this discourse at court.

BAL. Led by the loadstar of her heavenly looks,
Wends poor oppressed Balthazar,
As o'er the mountains walks the wanderer,
Incertain to effect his pilgrimage. *Exeunt.*

[SCENE IV][16]

Enter two Portingales, *and* HIERONIMO *meets them.*

1 [PORT]. By your leave, sir.

HIER. [17]['T is neither as you think, nor as you think,
Nor as you think;[18] you 're wide all:
These slippers are not mine; they were my son Horatio's.
My son — and what 's a son? A thing begot
Within a pair of minutes, thereabout;
A lump bred up in darkness, and doth serve
To ballace[19] these light creatures we call women;
And, at nine months' end, creeps forth to light.
What is there yet in a son,
To make a father dote, rave, or run mad?
Being born, it pouts, cries, and breeds teeth.
What is there yet in a son? He must be fed,
Be taught to go,[20] and speak. Ay, or yet
Why might not a man love a calf as well?
Or melt in passion o'er a frisking kid,
As for a son? Methinks, a young bacon,[21]
Or a fine little smooth horse colt,
Should move a man as much as doth a son.
For one of these, in very little time,
Will grow to some good use; whereas a son,
The more he grows in stature and in years,
The more unsquar'd, unbevelled,[22] he appears,
Reckons his parents among the rank of fools,

[13] Face.

[14] Transposed with *Est* in old eds.

[15] Another patchwork. "And I feared to add dreadful alarm to a trembling man — vain is the work of senseless treachery."

[16] A street near Don Cyprian's palace.

[17] Third passage of additions begins here.

[18] Perhaps addressed to the audience.

[19] Ballast.

[20] Walk.

[21] Pig.

[22] *I.e.*, uneven [and] unsmoothed.

Strikes care upon their heads with his mad riots,
Makes them look old before they meet with age.
This is a son! And what a loss were this,
Consider'd truly? —— O, but my Horatio
Grew out of reach of these insatiate humors:
He loved his loving parents;
He was my comfort, and his mother's joy,
The very arm that did hold up our house:
Our hopes were stored up in him.
None but a damned murderer could hate him.
He had not seen the back of nineteen year,
When his strong arm unhors'd
The proud Prince Balthazar, and his great mind,
Too full of honor, took him [unto][23] mercy,
That valiant but ignoble Portingale.
Well, Heaven is Heaven still;
And there is Nemesis, and Furies,
And things call'd whips,
And they sometimes do meet with murderers;
They do not always scape; that's some comfort.
Ay, ay, ay; and then time steals on,
And steals, and steals, till violence leaps forth
Like thunder wrapp'd in a ball of fire,
And so doth bring confusion to them all.]

Good leave have you; nay, I pray you go,
For I'll leave you, if you can leave me so.
2 [Port]. Pray you, which is the next way to my Lord the Duke's?
Hier. The next way from me.
1 [Port]. To his house, we mean.
Hier. O, hard by; 't is yon house that you see.
2 [Port]. You could not tell us if his son were there?
Hier. Who, my Lord Lorenzo?
1 [Port]. Ay, sir.
He goeth in at one door and comes out at another.
Hier. O, forbear!
For other talk for us far fitter were.
But if you be importunate to know
The way to him, and where to find him out,
Then list to me, and I'll resolve your doubt.
There is a path upon your left-hand side
That leadeth from a guilty conscience
Unto a forest of distrust and fear,
A darksome place, and dangerous to pass.
There shall you meet with melancholy thoughts,
Whose baleful humors if you but uphold,[24]
It will conduct you to despair and death;
Whose rocky cliffs when you have once beheld,
Within a hugy dale of lasting night,
That, kindled with the world's iniquities,
Doth cast up filthy and detested fumes, —
Not far from thence, where murderers have built
A habitation for their cursed souls,
There, in a brazen caldron, fix'd by Jove,
In his fell wrath, upon a sulphur flame,
Yourselves shall find Lorenzo bathing him
In boiling lead and blood of innocents.
1 [Port]. Ha, ha, ha!
Hier. Ha, ha, ha! Why, ha, ha, ha! Farewell, good ha, ha, ha! *Exit.*
2 [Port]. Doubtless this man is passing lunatic,
Or imperfection of his age doth make him dote.
Come, let's away to seek my Lord the Duke.
Exeunt.

[23] Cor. Boas; old eds. *vs to.*
[24] Preserve, maintain.

[Scene V][25]

Enter Hieronimo, *with a poniard in one hand and a rope in the other.*

Hier. Now, sir, perhaps I come and see the King;
The King sees me, and fain would hear my suit.
Why, is not this a strange and seld-seen thing,
That standers-by with toys should strike me mute?
Go to; I see their shifts, and say no more.
Hieronimo, 't is time for thee to trudge.
Down by the dale that flows with purple gore
Standeth a fiery tower; there sits a judge
Upon a seat of steel and molten brass,
And 'twixt his teeth he holds a firebrand,
That leads unto the lake where hell doth stand.
Away, Hieronimo! to him be gone.
He'll do thee justice for Horatio's death.
Turn down this path; thou shalt be with him straight;
Or this, and then thou need'st not take thy breath.
This way or that way? — Soft and fair, not so!
For if I hang or kill myself, let's know
Who will revenge Horatio's murder then?
No, no! fie, no! pardon me, I'll none of that.
He flings away the dagger and halter.
This way I'll take, and this way comes the King:
He takes them up again.
And here I'll have a fling at him; that's flat.
And, Balthazar, I'll be with thee to bring,[26]
And thee, Lorenzo! Here's the King — nay, stay;
And here, ay here — there goes the hare away.[27]

[25] Unlocated, but presumably a hall in the royal palace.
[26] Bring thee to reason, chastise thee. (Boas.)
[27] That's the upshot.

Enter KING, Ambassador, CASTILE, *and* LORENZO.

KING. Now show, ambassador, what our viceroy saith.
Hath he receiv'd the articles we sent?
HIER. Justice, oh, justice to Hieronimo.
LOR. Back! seest thou not the King is busy?
HIER. Oh, is he so?
KING. Who is he that interrupts our business?
HIER. Not I. — [*aside*] Hieronimo, beware! go by, go by![28]
AMB. Renowned King, he hath received and read
Thy kingly proffers, and thy promis'd league;
And, as a man extremely overjoy'd
To hear his son so princely entertain'd,
Whose death he had so solemnly bewail'd,
This for thy further satisfaction
And kingly love he kindly lets thee know:
First, for the marriage of his princely son
With Bel-imperia, thy beloved niece,
The news are more delightful to his soul
Than myrrh or incense to the offended Heavens.
In person, therefore, will he come himself,
To see the marriage rites solemnized,
And, in the presence of the court of Spain,
To knit a sure [inexplicable][29] band
Of kingly love and everlasting league
Betwixt the crowns of Spain and Portingal.
There will he give his crown to Balthazar,
And make a queen of Bel-imperia.
KING. Brother, how like you this our viceroy's love?
CAST. No doubt, my Lord, it is an argument
Of honorable care to keep his friend,
And wondrous zeal to Balthazar his son;
Nor am I least indebted to his Grace,
That bends his liking to my daughter thus.
AMB. Now last, dread Lord, here hath his Highness sent
(Although he send not that his son return)
His ransom due to Don Horatio.
HIER. Horatio! who calls Horatio?
KING. And well rememb'red; thank his Majesty.
Here, see it given to Horatio.
HIER. Justice, oh, justice, justice, gentle King!
KING. Who is that? Hieronimo?
HIER. Justice, oh, justice! oh, my son, my son,
My son, whom naught can ransom or redeem!
LOR. Hieronimo, you are not well-advis'd.
HIER. Away, Lorenzo, hinder me no more;
For thou hast made me bankrupt of my bliss.
Give me my son! you shall not ransom him!
Away! I'll rip the bowels of the earth,
He diggeth with his dagger.
And ferry over to th' Elysian plains,
And bring my son to show his deadly wounds.
Stand from about me!
I'll make a pickaxe of my poniard,
And here surrender up my marshalship;
For I'll go marshal up the fiends in hell,
To be avenged on you all for this.
KING. What means this outrage?[30]
Will none of you restrain his fury?
HIER. Nay, soft and fair! you shall not need to strive.
Needs must he go that the devils drive.
Exit.
KING. What accident hath happ'd Hieronimo?
I have not seen him to demean him so.
LOR. My gracious Lord, he is with extreme pride,
Conceiv'd of young Horatio, his son,
And covetous of having to himself
The ransom of the young Prince Balthazar,
Distract, and in a manner lunatic.
KING. Believe me, Nephew, we are sorry for't;
This is the love that fathers bear their sons. —
But, gentle Brother, go give to him this gold,
The Prince's ransom; let him have his due.
For what he hath, Horatio shall not want;
Haply Hieronimo hath need thereof.
LOR. But if he be thus helplessly distract,
'T is requisite his office be resign'd,
And given to one of more discretion.
KING. We shall increase his melancholy so.
'T is best that we see further in it first,
Till when, ourself will exempt[31] the place.
And, Brother, now bring in the ambassador,
That he may be a witness of the match
'Twixt Balthazar and Bel-imperia,
And that we may prefix a certain time,
Wherein the marriage shall be solemnized,
That we may have thy lord, the Viceroy, here.

[28] This sentence became a stock expression.

[29] Inextricable. So old eds. except the first, which reads *inexecrable*.

[30] Outburst.

[31] *I.e*, we will hold it immune from the necessity of being filled (by someone else). (But there may be a corruption here.)

AMB. Therein your Highness highly shall content
His Majesty, that longs to hear from hence.
KING. On, then, and hear you, Lord Ambassador — *Exeunt.*

[SCENE VI] [32]

[33] [Enter JAQUES and PEDRO.

JAQ. I wonder, Pedro, why our master thus
At midnight sends us with our torches light,
When man and bird and beast are all at rest,
Save those that watch for rape and bloody murder.
PED. O Jaques, know thou that our master's mind
Is much distraught, since his Horatio died,
And — now his aged years should sleep in rest,
His heart in quiet — like a desperate man,
Grows lunatic and childish for his son.
Sometimes, as he doth at his table sit,
He speaks as if Horatio stood by him;
Then starting in a rage, falls on the earth,
Cries out, "Horatio, where is my Horatio?"
So that with extreme grief and cutting sorrow
There is not left in him one inch of man.
See, where he comes.

Enter HIERONIMO.

HIER. I pry through every crevice of each wall,
Look on each tree, and search through every brake,
Beat at the bushes, stamp our grandam earth,
Dive in the water, and stare up to Heaven,
Yet cannot I behold my son Horatio. —
How now, who's there? sprites, sprites?
PED. We are your servants, that attend you, sir.
HIER. What make you with your torches in the dark?
PED. You bid us light them, and attend you here.
HIER. No, no, you are deceiv'd! — not I; you are deceiv'd!
Was I so mad to bid you light your torches now?
Light me your torches at the mid of noon,
Whenas the sun god rides in all his glory;
Light me your torches then.
PED. Then we burn [34] daylight.
HIER. Let it be burnt; Night is a murderous slut,
That would not have her treasons to be seen;
And yonder pale-fac'd Hecate there, the moon,
Doth give consent to that is done in darkness;
And all those stars that gaze upon her face,
Are ag[le]ts [35] on her sleeve, pins on her train;
And those that should be powerful and divine
Do sleep in darkness when they most should shine.
PED. Provoke them not, fair sir, with tempting words;
The Heavens are gracious, and your miseries
And sorrow makes you speak you know not what.
HIER. Villain, thou liest! and thou doest naught
But tell me I am mad. Thou liest! I am not mad!
I know thee to be Pedro, and he Jaques.
I'll prove it to thee; and were I mad, how could I?
Where was she that same night when my Horatio
Was murd'red? She should have shone; search thou the book.
Had the moon shone, in my boy's face there was a kind of grace,
That I know — nay, I do know — had the murderer seen him,
His weapon would have fall'n and cut the earth,
Had he been framed of naught but blood and death.
Alack, when mischief doth it knows not what,
What shall we say to mischief?

Enter ISABELLA.

ISAB. Dear Hieronimo, come in a'doors;
O, seek not means so to increase thy sorrow.
HIER. Indeed, Isabella, we do nothing here;
I do not cry — ask Pedro, and ask Jaques;
Not I, indeed; we are very merry, very merry.
ISAB. How? be merry here, be merry here?
Is not this the place, and this the very tree,
Where my Horatio [d]ied, where he was murdered?
HIER. Was — do not say what; let her weep it out.
This was the tree; I set it of a kernel;
And when our hot Spain could not let it grow,
But that the infant and the human sap
Began to wither, duly twice a morning
Would I be sprinkling it with fountain water.
At last it grew and grew, and bore and bore,
Till at the length
It grew a gallows and did bear our son;
It bore thy fruit and mine — O wicked, wicked plant!
One knocks within at the door.
See who knocks there.
PED. It is a painter, sir.
HIER. Bid him come in, and paint some comfort;
For surely there's none lives but painted comfort.
Let him come in! — One knows not what may chance:
God's will that I should set this tree! — But even so
Masters ungrateful servants rear from naught,
And then they hate them that did bring them up.

Enter the Painter.

PAINT. God bless you, sir.
HIER. Wherefore? Why, thou scornful villain?
How, where, or by what means should I be bless'd?
ISAB. What wouldst thou have, good fellow?
PAINT. Justice, madam.
HIER. O ambitious beggar,
Wouldest thou have that that lives not in the world?
Why, all the undelved mines cannot buy
An ounce of justice, 't is a jewel so inestimable.
I tell thee, God hath engrossed all justice in his hands,
And there is none but what comes from him.
PAINT. O, then I see
That God must right me for my murd'red son.
HIER. How, was thy son murdered?
PAINT. Ay, sir; no man did hold a son so dear.
HIER. What, not as thine? That's a lie,
As massy as the earth. I had a son
Whose least unvalued hair did weigh
A thousand of thy sons; and he was murdered.
PAINT. Alas, sir, I had no more but he.
HIER. Nor I, nor I; but this same one of mine
Was worth a legion. But all is one.
Pedro, Jaques, go in a'doors; Isabella, go;
And this good fellow here and I
Will range this hideous orchard [36] up and down,
Like to two lions reaved [37] of their young.
Go in a'doors, I say.
Exeunt. The Painter *and he sits down.*
Come, let's talk wisely now.
Was thy son murdered?
PAINT. Ay, sir.
HIER. So was mine.
How dost take it? Art thou not sometimes mad?
Is there no tricks [38] that comes before thine eyes?

[32] Hieronimo's garden.
[33] Fourth passage of additions begins here.
[34] *I.e.*, waste.
[35] Ornamental tags or laces of metal. (Cor. Q 1611; Q 1602 *aggots*.)

[36] Garden. [37] Robbed. [38] Illusions.

PAINT. O Lord, yes, sir.

HIER. Art a painter? Canst paint me a tear, or a wound, a groan, or a sigh? Canst paint me such a tree[39] as this?

PAINT. Sir, I am sure you have heard of my painting; my name's Bazardo.

HIER. Bazardo! Afore God, an excellent fellow. Look you, sir, do you see? I'd have you paint me my gallery, in your oil-colors matted,[40] and draw me five years younger than I am — do ye see, sir, let five years go, let them go — like the marshal of Spain; my wife Isabella standing by me, with a speaking look to my son Horatio, which should intend to this or some such like purpose: "God bless thee, my sweet son"; and my hand leaning upon his head, thus, sir, do you see? May it be done?

PAINT. Very well, sir.

HIER. Nay, I pray mark me, sir. Then, sir, would I have you paint me this tree, this very tree. Canst paint a doleful cry?

PAINT. Seemingly, sir.

HIER. Nay, it should cry; but all is one. Well, sir, paint me a youth run thorough and thorough with villains' swords, hanging upon this tree. Canst thou draw a murderer?

PAINT. I'll warrant you, sir; I have the pattern of the most notorious villains that ever lived in all Spain.

HIER. O, let them be worse, worse; stretch thine art, and let their beards be of Judas his own color;[41] and let their eyebrows jutty over — in any case observe that. Then, sir, after some violent noise, bring me forth in my shirt, and my gown under mine arm, with my torch in my hand, and my sword reared up, thus — and with these words:

"What noise is this? Who calls Hieronimo?"

May it be done?

PAINT. Yea, sir.

HIER. Well, sir; then bring me forth, bring me thorough alley and alley, still with a distracted countenance going along, and let my hair heave up my nightcap. Let the clouds scowl, make the moon dark, the stars extinct, the winds blowing, the bells tolling, the owl shrieking, the toads croaking, the minutes j[a]rring,[42] and the clock striking twelve. And then at last, sir, starting, behold a man hanging, and tottering and tottering, as you know the wind will wave a man, and I with a trice to cut him down. And looking upon him by the advantage of my torch, find it to be my son Horatio. There you may [show][43] a passion, there you may show a passion! Draw me like old Priam of Troy, crying, "The house is afire, the house is afire, as the torch over my head!" Make me curse, make me rave, make me cry, make me mad, make me well again, make me curse hell, invocate Heaven, and in the end leave me in a trance — and so forth.

PAINT. And is this the end?

HIER. O no, there is no end; the end is death and madness. As I am never better than when I am mad; then methinks I am a brave fellow; then I do wonders; but reason abuseth[44] me, and there's the torment, there's the hell. At the last, sir, bring me to one of the murderers; were he as strong as Hector, thus would I tear and drag him up and down.

He beats the Painter *in, then comes out again, with a book in his hand.*]

Enter HIERONIMO, *with a book in his hand.*

Vindicta mihi!

Ay, Heaven will be revenged of every ill;
Nor will they suffer murder unrepaid.
Then stay, Hieronimo, attend their will;
For mortal men may not appoint their time.
Per scelus semper tutum est sceleribus iter:[45]
Strike, and strike home, where wrong is off'red thee;
For evils unto ills conductors be,
And death's the worst of resolution.[46]
For he that thinks with patience to contend
To quiet life, his life shall easily end.[47] —
Fata si miseros juvant, habes salutem;
Fata si vitam negant, habes sepulchrum:[48]
If destiny thy miseries do ease,
Then hast thou health, and happy shalt thou be.
If destiny deny thee life, Hieronimo,
Yet shalt thou be assured of a tomb;
If neither, yet let this thy comfort be:
Heaven covereth him that hath no burial.
And to conclude, I will revenge his death.
But how? Not as the vulgar wits of men,
With open, but inevitable ills,[49]
As by a secret, yet a certain mean,
Which under kindship[50] will be cloaked best.
Wise men will take their opportunity,
Closely and safely fitting things to time.
But in extremes advantage hath no time;
And therefore all times fit not for revenge.
Thus therefore will I rest me in unrest,
Dissembling quiet in unquietness,
Not seeming that I know their villainies,
That my simplicity[51] may make them think
That ignorantly I will let all slip;
For ignorance, I wot, and well they know,
Remedium malorum iners est.[52]
Nor aught avails it me to menace them,
Who, as a wintry storm upon a plain,
Will bear me down with their nobility.
No, no, Hieronimo, thou must enjoin
Thine eyes to observation, and thy tongue
To milder speeches than thy spirit affords,
Thy heart to patience, and thy hands to rest,

[39] Boas notes *teare* as the reading of at least one copy of Q 1602.

[40] Like a mat; *i.e.*, laid on thick.

[41] Red.

[42] Ticking.

[43] Add. Schick.

[44] Deceives.

[45] Crime's safest course leads ever through more crime. (Adapted from Seneca's *Agamemnon*, l. 115.)

[46] *I.e.*, the worst that can happen as a consequence of a bold course is only death. (Or, since "resolution" sometimes = "dissolution", "death", perhaps: the worst thing that can happen is only death.)

[47] *I.e.*, the man who thinks he can win a quiet life by the exercise of patient endurance may lose his life [as] easily [as a bold man may].

[48] Seneca, *Troades*, ll. 511, 512.

[49] Not with open but with inevitable injuries. (Neilson.)

[50] Kindness.

[51] Stupidity, ignorance.

[52] Is an idle remedy for ills. (Adapted from Seneca's *Oedipus*, l. 515.)

Thy cap to courtesy, and thy knee to bow,
Till to revenge thou know when, where, and how. *A noise within.*
How now, what noise? What coil [53] is that you keep?

Enter a Servant.

SERV. Here are a sort [54] of poor petitioners
That are importunate, an it shall please you, sir,
That you should plead their cases to the King.
HIER. That I should plead their several actions?
Why, let them enter, and let me see them.

Enter three Citizens *and an* Old Man.

1 [CIT].[55] So; I tell you this: for learning and for law,
There is not any advocate in Spain
That can prevail, or will take half the pain
That he will, in pursuit of equity.
HIER. Come near, you men, that thus importune me.—
[*aside*] Now must I bear a face of gravity;
For thus I us'd, before my marshalship,
To plead in causes as corregidor.—[56]
Come on, sirs, what's the matter?
2 CIT. Sir, an action.
HIER. Of battery?
1 CIT. Mine of debt.
HIER. Give place.
2 CIT. No, sir, mine is an action of the case.[57]
3 CIT. Mine an *ejectione firma*[e] [58] by a lease.
HIER. Content you, sirs; are you determined
That I should plead your several actions?
1 CIT. Ay, sir, and here's my declaration.
2 CIT. And here is my band.[59]
3 CIT. And here is my lease.
They give him papers.
HIER. But wherefore stands yon silly [60] man so mute,
With mournful eyes and hands to Heaven uprear'd?
Come hither, father, let me know thy cause.

[53] Disturbance. [54] Group, set.
[55] Om. throughout these speech-tags, in old eds.
[56] Properly, "magistrate"; but evidently taken by Kyd as "advocate."
[57] "An universal remedy . . . so called because the plaintiff's whole . . . cause of complaint is set forth at length in the original writ." (Blackstone, cited by *N. E. D.*)
[58] Writ of ejection against a tenant.
[59] Bond.
[60] Humble, simple.

SENEX. O worthy sir, my cause, but slightly known,
May move the hearts of warlike Myrmidons,
And melt the Corsic rocks [61] with ruthful tears.
HIER. Say, father, tell me, what's thy suit?
SENEX. No, sir; could my woes
Give way unto my most distressful words,
Then should I not in paper, as you see,
With ink bewray what blood began in me.
HIER. What's here? "The humble supplication
Of Don Bazulto for his murd'red son."
SENEX. Ay, sir.
HIER. No, sir; it was my murd'red son!
O my son, my son, O my son Horatio!
But mine, or thine, Bazulto, be content.
Here, take my handkercher and wipe thine eyes,
Whiles wretched I in thy mishaps may see
The lively portrait of my dying self.
He draweth out a bloody napkin.
O no, not this; Horatio, this was thine;
And when I dy'd it in thy dearest blood,
This was a token 'twixt thy soul and me
That of thy death revenged I should be.
But here, take this, and this — what, my purse? —
Ay, this, and that, and all of them are thine;
For all as one are our extremities.
1 CIT. O, see the kindness of Hieronimo!
2 CIT. This gentleness shows him a gentleman.
HIER. See, see; oh, see thy shame, Hieronimo!
See here a loving father to his son!
Behold the sorrows and the sad laments,
That he delivereth for his son's decease!
If love's effects so strives in lesser things,
If love enforce such moods in meaner wits,
If love express such power in poor estates,
Hieronimo, [as when] [62] a raging sea,
Toss'd with the wind and tide, [o'erturneth] [63] then
The upper billows, course of waves to keep,
Whilst lesser waters labor in the deep,

[61] Mentioned in Seneca's *Octavia*, l. 382.
[62] Emend. Kittredge (in Manly); old eds. *when as.*
[63] Emend. Hawkins; old eds. *oreturnest, oreturned.* The sense of this clumsy, if not corrupt, passage seems to be: "If the force of love is so mighty in those of low estate, just as when a raging sea is agitated in its upper waters, only to continue its course in its depths; then art not thou, Hieronimo, ashamed to neglect [being a man of high estate] the pursuit of thy vengeance?" The infelicity of the marine simile arises from the lack of harmony between its indirect reference to the high rank of Hieronimo and its direct applicability to the humble station of Bazulto.

Then shamest thou not, Hieronimo, to neglect
The sweet revenge of thy Horatio?
Though on this earth justice will not be found,
I'll down to hell, and in this passion
Knock at the dismal gates of Pluto's court,
Getting by force, as once Alcides did,
A troop of Furies and tormenting hags
To torture Don Lorenzo and the rest.
Yet, lest the triple-headed porter should
Deny my passage to the slimy strond,
The Thracian poet thou shalt counterfeit.
Come on, old father, be my Orpheus,
And if thou canst[64] no notes upon the harp,
Then sound the burden of thy sore heart's grief,
Till we do gain that Proserpine may grant
Revenge on them that murd'red my son.
Then will I rent and tear them, thus, and thus,
Shivering their limbs in pieces with my teeth.
Tear the papers.

1 Cit. O sir, my declaration!
Exit Hieronimo, *and they after.*

2. Cit. Save my bond!

Re-enter Hieronimo.

2 Cit. Save my bond!

3 Cit. Alas, my lease! it cost me ten pound,
And you, my Lord, have torn the same.

Hier. That cannot be; I gave it never a wound.
Show me one drop of blood fall from the same!
How is it possible I should slay it, then?
Tush, no; run after, catch me if you can.
Exeunt all but the Old Man. Bazulto *remains till* Hieronimo *enters again, who, staring him in the face, speaks.*

Hier. And art thou come, Horatio, from the depth,
To ask for justice in this upper earth,
To tell thy father thou art unreveng'd,
To wring more tears from Isabella's eyes,
Whose lights are dimm'd with overlong laments?
Go back, my son; complain to Aeacus,
For here's no justice; gentle boy, begone,
For justice is exiled from the earth;
Hieronimo will bear thee company.
Thy mother cries on righteous Rhadamanth
For just revenge against the murderers.

Senex. Alas, my Lord, whence springs this troubled speech?

Hier. But let me look on my Horatio.
Sweet boy, how art thou chang'd in death's black shade!
Had Proserpine no pity on thy youth,
But suffered thy fair crimson-colored spring
With withered winter to be blasted thus?
Horatio, thou art older than thy father.
Ah, ruthless [fate],[65] that favor[66] thus transforms!

Baz. Ah, my good Lord, I am not your young son.

Hier. What, not my son? Thou then a Fury art,
Sent from the empty kingdom of black night
To summon me to make appearance
Before grim Minos and just Rhadamanth,
To plague Hieronimo that is remiss,
And seeks not vengeance for Horatio's death.

Baz. I am a grieved man, and not a ghost,
That came for justice for my murdered son.

Hier. Ay, now I know thee, now thou namest thy son.
Thou art the lively image of my grief;
Within thy face my sorrows I may see.
Thy eyes are gumm'd with tears, thy cheeks are wan,
Thy forehead troubled, and thy mutt'ring lips
Murmur sad words abruptly broken off
By force of windy sighs thy spirit breathes;
And all this sorrow riseth for thy son,
And selfsame sorrow feel I for my son.
Come in, old man, thou shalt to Isabel.
Lean on my arm; I thee, thou me, shalt stay;
And thou, and I, and she will sing a song,
Three parts in one, but all of discords fram'd.—
Talk not of cords, but let us now be gone;
For with a cord Horatio was slain. *Exeunt.*

[Scene VII][67]

Enter [*on one side*] King of Spain, *the* Duke, Lorenzo, Balthazar, Bel-imperia, [*and* Attendants; *and, on the other,*] Viceroy, Don Pedro, [*and* Attendants].

King. Go, Brother, it is the Duke of Castile's cause;
Salute the Viceroy in our name.

Cast. I go.

Vic. Go forth, Don Pedro, for thy nephew's sake,
And greet the Duke of Castile.

[64] Knowest; *i.e.*, canst play.

[65] Emend. Dodsley; old eds. *Father*.

[66] Face, appearance.

[67] Unlocated; presumably at or near the royal palace.

PED. It shall be so.
KING. And now to meet these Portuguese;
For as we now are, so sometimes were these,
Kings and commanders of the western Indies.
Welcome, brave Viceroy, to the court of Spain,
And welcome all his honorable train!
'T is not unknown to us for why you come,
Or have so kingly cross'd the seas.
Sufficeth it, in this we note the troth
And more than common love you lend to us.
So is it that mine honorable niece
(For it beseems us now that it be known)
Already is betroth'd to Balthazar;
And by appointment and our condescent [68]
To-morrow are they to be married.
To this intent we entertain thyself,
Thy followers, their pleasure, and our peace.
Speak, men of Portingal, shall it be so?
If ay, say so; if not, say flatly no.
VIC. Renowmed King, I come not, as thou think'st,
With doubtful followers, unresolved men,
But such as have upon thine articles
Confirmed thy motion, and contented me.
Know, Sovereign, I come to solemnize
The marriage [69] of thy beloved niece,
Fair Bel-imperia, with my Balthazar,
With thee, my son; whom sith I live to see,
Here take my crown; I give it her and thee;
And let me live a solitary life,
In ceaseless prayers,
To think how strangely Heaven hath thee preserved.
KING. See, Brother, see, how nature strives in him!
Come, worthy Viceroy, and accompany
Thy friend with thine extremities; [70]
A place more private fits this princely mood.
VIC. Or here, or where your Highness thinks it good.
Exeunt all but CASTILE *and* LORENZO.
CAST. Nay, stay, Lorenzo; let me talk with you.
Seest thou this entertainment of these kings?
LOR. I do, my Lord, and joy to see the same.
CAST. And knowest thou why this meeting is?
LOR. For her, my Lord, whom Balthazar doth love,
And to confirm their promised marriage.
CAST. She is thy sister?
LOR. Who, Bel-imperia? Ay,
My gracious Lord, and this is the day
That I have long'd so happily to see.
CAST. Thou wouldst be loth that any fault of thine
Should intercept her in her happiness?
LOR. Heavens will not let Lorenzo err so much.
CAST. Why then, Lorenzo, listen to my words:
It is suspected, and reported too,
That thou, Lorenzo, wrong'st Hieronimo,
And in his suits towards his Majesty
Still keep'st him back, and seeks to cross his suit.
LOR. That I, my Lord?
CAST. I tell thee, Son, myself have heard it said,
When, to my sorrow, I have been ashamed
To answer for thee, though thou art my son.
Lorenzo, knowest thou not the common love
And kindness that Hieronimo hath won
By his deserts within the court of Spain?
Or seest thou not the King my brother's care
In his behalf, and to procure his health?
Lorenzo, shouldst thou thwart his passions,
And he exclaim against thee to the King,
What honor were 't in this assembly,
Or what a scandal were 't among the kings
To hear Hieronimo exclaim on thee?
Tell me — and look thou tell me truly too —
Whence grows the ground of this report in court?
LOR. My Lord, it lies not in Lorenzo's power
To stop the vulgar, liberal of their tongues.
A small advantage makes a water-breach,
And no man lives that long contenteth all.
CAST. Myself have seen thee busy to keep back
Him and his supplications from the King.
LOR. Yourself, my Lord, hath seen his passions,
That ill beseem'd the presence of a king;
And, for I pitied him in his distress,
I held him thence with kind and courteous words
As free from malice to Hieronimo
As to my soul, my Lord.
CAST. Hieronimo, my son, mistakes thee then.
LOR. My gracious father, believe me, so he doth.
But what 's a silly man, distract in mind
To think upon the murder of his son?

[68] Consent. [69] Trisyllabic.
[70] Unrestrained manifestations of emotion. L. 33 is presumably pieced out by them.

Alas, how easy is it for him to err!
But for his satisfaction and the world's,
'T were good, my Lord, that Hieronimo and I
Were reconcil'd, if he misconster me.
CAST. Lorenzo, thou hast said; it shall be so.—
Go one of you, and call Hieronimo.[71]

Re-enter BALTHAZAR *and* BEL-IMPERIA.

BAL. Come, Bel-imperia, Balthazar's content,
My sorrow's ease and sovereign of my bliss,
Sith Heaven hath ordain'd thee to be mine;
Disperse those clouds and melancholy looks,
And clear them up with those thy sun-bright eyes,
Wherein my hope and Heaven's fair beauty lies.
BEL. My looks, my Lord, are fitting for my love,
Which, new-begun, can show [no][72] brighter yet.
BAL. New-kindled flames should burn as morning sun.
BEL. But not too fast, lest heat and all be done.
I see my Lord my father.
BAL. Truce, my love;
I will go salute him.
CAST. Welcome, Balthazar,
Welcome, brave Prince, the pledge of Castile's peace;
And welcome, Bel-imperia. — How now, girl?
Why comest thou sadly to salute us thus?
Content thyself, for I am satisfied.
It is not now as when Andrea liv'd;
We have forgotten and forgiven that,
And thou art graced with a happier love. —
But, Balthazar, here comes Hieronimo;
I'll have a word with him.

Enter HIERONIMO *and a* Servant.

HIER. And where's the Duke?
SERV. Yonder.
HIER. Even so. —
[*aside*] What new device have they devised, trow?[73]
Pocas palabras![74] mild as the lamb!
Is't I will be reveng'd? No, I am not the man.
CAST. Welcome, Hieronimo.
LOR. Welcome, Hieronimo.
BAL. Welcome, Hieronimo.
HIER. My Lords, I thank you for Horatio.
CAST. Hieronimo, the reason that I sent
To speak with you, is this.
HIER. What, so short?
Then I'll be gone; I thank you for 't.
CAST. Nay, stay, Hieronimo! — Go, call him, Son.
LOR. Hieronimo, my father craves a word with you.
HIER. With me, sir? — Why, my Lord, I thought you had done.
LOR. No. — [*aside*] Would he had!
CAST. Hieronimo, I hear
You find yourself aggrieved at my son,
Because you have not access unto the King;
And say 't is he that intercepts your suits.
HIER. Why, is not this a miserable thing, my Lord?
CAST. Hieronimo, I hope you have no cause,
And would be loth that one of your deserts
Should once have reason to suspect my son,
Considering how I think of you myself.
HIER. Your son Lorenzo! Whom, my noble Lord?
The hope of Spain, mine honorable friend?
Grant me the combat of them, if they dare!
Draws out his sword.
I'll meet him face to face, to tell me so!
These be the scandalous reports of such
As love not me, and hate my Lord too much.
Should I suspect Lorenzo would prevent
Or cross my suit, that lov'd my son so well?
My Lord, I am ashamed it should be said.
LOR. Hieronimo, I never gave you cause.
HIER. My good Lord, I know you did not.
CAST. There then pause;
And for the satisfaction of the world,
Hieronimo, frequent my homely house,
The Duke of Castile, Cyprian's ancient seat;
And when thou wilt, use me, my son, and it;
But here, before Prince Balthazar and me,
Embrace each other, and be perfect friends.
HIER. Ay, marry, my Lord, and shall.
Friends, quoth he? See, I'll be friends with you all!
Especially with you, my lovely Lord;
For divers causes it is fit for us
That we be friends: the world is suspicious,
And men may think what we imagine not.
BAL. Why, this is friendly done, Hieronimo.
LOR. And that, I hope, old grudges are forgot.
HIER. What else? It were a shame it should not be so.

[71] Castile evidently calls off stage.
[72] Add. ed. 1594.
[73] I wonder, do you suppose?
[74] Few words.

CAST. Come on, Hieronimo, at my request;
Let us entreat your company to-day.
Exeunt [*all but* HIERONIMO].

HIER. Your Lordship's to command. — Pah! keep your way:
[*Chi mi fa più carezze che non suole,*
Tradito mi ha, o tradir mi vuole.] [75] *Exit.*

[CHORUS] [76]

GHOST. Awake, Ericht[ho]! Cerberus, awake!
Solicit Pluto, gentle Proserpine!
To combat, Ach[er]on and Er[eb]us!
For ne'er, by Styx and Phlegethon in hell, [77]
[O'er] [78] ferried Charon to the fiery lakes
Such fearful sights as poor Andrea see[s]. [79]
Revenge, awake!

REVENGE. Awake? For why?

GHOST. Awake, Revenge! for thou art ill-advis'd
T[o] sleep away what thou art warn'd to watch.

REVENGE. Content thyself, and do not trouble me.

GHOST. Awake, Revenge! if love — as love hath had —
Have yet the power or prevalence in hell!
Hieronimo with Lorenzo is join'd in league,
And intercepts our passage to revenge.
Awake, Revenge, or we are woebegone!

REVENGE. Thus worldlings ground what they have dream'd upon. [80]
Content thyself, Andrea; though I sleep,
Yet is my mood soliciting their souls.
Sufficeth thee that poor Hieronimo
Cannot forget his son Horatio.
Nor dies Revenge, although he sleep awhile;
For in unquiet, quietness is feign'd,
And slumb'ring is a common worldly wile.
Behold, Andrea, for an instance, how
Revenge hath slept, and then imagine thou,
What 't is to be subject to destiny.

Enter a Dumb Show.

GHOST. Awake, Revenge; reveal this mystery.

REVENGE. The two first the nuptial torches bore
As brightly burning as the midday's sun;
But after them doth Hymen hie as fast,
Clothed in sable and a saffron robe,
And blows them out, and quencheth them with blood,
As discontent that things continue so.

GHOST. Sufficeth me; thy meaning's understood;
And thanks to thee and those infernal powers
That will not tolerate a lover's woe.
Rest thee, for I will sit to see the rest.

REVENGE. Then argue not, for thou hast thy request. [81]

ACT [V — SCENE I] [1]

Enter BEL-IMPERIA *and* HIERONIMO.

BEL. Is this the love thou bear'st Horatio?
Is this the kindness that thou counterfeits?
Are these the fruits of thine incessant tears?
Hieronimo, are these thy passions,
Thy protestations and thy deep laments,
That thou wert wont to weary men withal?
O unkind father! O deceitful world!
With what excuses canst thou show thyself [2]
From this dishonor and the hate of men,
Thus to neglect the loss and life of him
Whom both my letters and thine own belief
Assures thee to be causeless slaughtered?
Hieronimo, for shame, Hieronimo,
Be not a history to aftertimes
Of such ingratitude unto thy son!
Unhappy mothers of such children then!
But monstrous fathers to forget so soon
The death of those whom they with care and cost
Have tend'red so, thus careless should be lost!
Myself, a stranger in respect of thee,
So loved his life, as still I wish their deaths.
Nor shall his death be unreveng'd by me,
Although I bear it out for fashion's sake.
For here I swear, in sight of Heaven and earth,
Shouldst thou neglect the love thou shouldst retain,
And give it over and devise no more,
Myself should send their hateful souls to hell
That wrought his downfall with extremest death.

HIER. But may it be that Bel-imperia
Vows such revenge as she hath deign'd to say?

[75] So Schick, correcting the corrupt text of the old eds. "Who me caresses more than was his way Has me betrayed — or wishes to betray."
[76] Old eds. *Enter Ghost and Revenge.*
[77] Old eds. attach *in hell* to l. 3.
[78] Emend. Schick; old eds. *Nor.*
[79] Cor. Q 1602; earlier eds. *see.*
[80] Rely on what they have dreamed.

[81] Old eds. add *Exeunt.*
[1] Unlocated; perhaps a room in the palace of Don Cyprian. Old eds. *Actus Quartus.*
[2] Old eds. perpetuate the compositor's blunder by inserting between ll. 8 and 9 *With what dishonour and the hate of men.*

Why, then I see that Heaven applies our drift,[3]
And all the saints do sit soliciting
For vengeance on those cursed murderers.
Madam, 't is true, and now I find it so,
I found a letter, written in your name,
And in that letter, how Horatio died.
Pardon, O pardon, Bel-imperia,
My fear and care in not believing it;
Nor think I thoughtless think upon a mean
To let his death be unreveng'd at full.
And here I vow — so[4] you but give consent,
And will conceal my resolution —
I will ere long determine of their deaths
That causeless thus have murdered my son.

BEL. Hieronimo, I will consent, conceal,
And aught that may effect for thine avail
Join with thee to revenge Horatio's death.

HIER. On, then; whatsoever I devise,
Let me entreat you, grace my practices;
Forwhy[5] the plot 's already in mine head.
Here they are.

Enter BALTHAZAR *and* LORENZO.

BAL. How now, Hieronimo?
What, courting Bel-imperia?

HIER. Ay, my Lord;
Such courting as, I promise you,
She hath my heart;[6] but you, my Lord, have hers.

LOR. But now, Hieronimo, or never, we
Are to entreat your help.

HIER. My help?
Why, my good Lords, assure yourselves of me;
For you have giv'n me cause — ay, by my faith have you!

BAL. It pleas'd you, at the entertainment of the ambassador,
To grace the King so much as with a show.
Now, were your study so well furnished,
As, for the passing of the first night's sport,
To entertain my father with the like,
Or any such like pleasing motion,[7]
Assure yourself, it would content them well.

HIER. Is this all?

BAL. Ay, this is all.

HIER. Why then, I 'll fit you; say no more.
When I was young, I gave my mind
And pli'd myself to fruitless poetry;
Which though it profit the professor naught,
Yet is it passing pleasing to the world.

LOR. And how for that?

HIER. Marry, my good Lord, thus:
And yet methinks, you are too quick with us —
When in Toledo there I studied,
It was my chance to write a tragedy —
See here, my Lords — *He shows them a book.*
Which, long forgot, I found this other day.
Now would your Lordships favor me so much
As but to grace me with your acting it —
I mean each one of you to play a part —
Assure you it will prove most passing strange,
And wondrous plausible[8] to that assembly.

BAL. What! would you have us play a tragedy?

HIER. Why, Nero thought it no disparagement,
And kings and emperors have ta'en delight
To make experience of their wits in plays.

LOR. Nay, be not angry, good Hieronimo;
The Prince but ask'd a question.

BAL. In faith, Hieronimo,
An you be in earnest, I 'll make one.

LOR. And I another.

HIER. Now, my good Lord, could you entreat
Your sister, Bel-imperia, to make one?
For what 's a play without a woman in it?

BEL. Little entreaty shall serve me, Hieronimo;
For I must needs be employed in your play.

HIER. Why, this is well. I tell you, Lordings,
It was determined to have been acted
By gentlemen and scholars too,
Such as could tell what to speak.

BAL. And now
It shall be play'd by princes and courtiers,
Such as can tell how to speak —
If, as it is our country manner,
You will but let us know the argument.

HIER. That shall I roundly. The chronicles of Spain
Record this written of a knight of Rhodes:
He was betrothed, and wedded at the length,
To one Perseda, an Italian dame,
Whose beauty ravished all that her beheld,
Especially the soul of Soliman,[9]
Who at the marriage was the chiefest guest.

[3] Allies itself to our plan.
[4] Provided that.
[5] Because.
[6] Playing on "heart" = secrets.
[7] Show. (Usually puppet show; but Nash, cited by *N. E. D.*, links "pomps, pageants, motions, masks.")
[8] Pleasing.
[9] The anonymous *Tragedy of Soliman and Perseda* (entered in the Stationers' Register in 1592) has been ascribed by some to Kyd. It is based on Henry Wotton's *Courtly Controversy of Cupid's Cautels* (1578), a translation of Jaques Yver's *Printemps d'Iver* (1572).

By sundry means sought Soliman to win
Perseda's love, and could not gain the same.
Then 'gan he break his passions to a friend,
One of his bashaws,[10] whom he held full dear.
Her had this bashaw long solicited,
And saw she was not otherwise to be won
But by her husband's death, this knight of Rhodes,
Whom presently by treachery he slew.
She, stirr'd with an exceeding hate therefore,
As cause of this slew Soliman,
And, to escape the bashaw's tyranny,
Did stab herself; and this the tragedy.
LOR. Oh, excellent!
BEL. But say, Hieronimo,
What then became of him that was the bashaw?
HIER. Marry, thus: moved with remorse of his misdeeds,
Ran to a mountain top, and hung himself.
BAL. But which of us is to perform that part?
HIER. Oh, that will I, my Lords; make no doubt of it:
I'll play the murderer, I warrant you;
For I already have conceited that.
BAL. And what shall I?
HIER. Great Soliman, the Turkish emperor.
LOR. And I?
HIER. Erast[o], the knight of Rhodes.
BEL. And I?
HIER. Perseda, chaste and resolute.
And here, my Lords, are several abstracts drawn,
For each of you to note your parts,
And act it, as occasion's off'red you.
You must provide a Turkish cap,
A black mustachio, and a falchion;
Gives a paper to BALTHAZAR.
You, with a cross, like to a knight of Rhodes;
Gives another to LORENZO.
And, madam, you must attire yourself
He giveth BEL-IMPERIA *another*.
Like Phoebe, Flora, or the Huntress,[11]
Which to your discretion shall seem best.
And as for me, my Lords, I'll look to one,[12]
And, with the ransom that the Viceroy sent,
So furnish and perform this tragedy
As all the world shall say Hieronimo
Was liberal in gracing of it so.
BAL. Hieronimo, methinks a comedy were better.
HIER. A comedy?
Fie! comedies are fit for common wits;
But to present a kingly troop withal,
Give me a stately-written tragedy;
Tragoedia cothurnata, fitting kings,
Containing matter, and not common things.
My Lords, all this must be performed,
As fitting for the first night's revelling.
The Italian tragedians were so sharp of wit,
That in one hour's meditation
They would perform anything in action.
LOR. And well it may; for I have seen the like
In Paris 'mongst the French tragedians.
HIER. In Paris? mass, and well rememb'red!
There's one thing more that rests for us to do.
BAL. What's that, Hieronimo? Forget not anything.
HIER. Each one of us
Must act his part in unknown languages,
That it may breed the more variety:
As you, my Lord, in Latin, I in Greek,
You in Italian; and, for because I know
That Bel-imperia hath practised the French,
In courtly French shall all her phrases be.
BEL. You mean to try my cunning then, Hieronimo?
BAL. But this will be a mere confusion
And hardly shall we all be understood.
HIER. It must be so; for the conclusion
Shall prove the invention[13] and all was good.
And I myself in an oration,
And with a strange and wondrous show besides,[14]
That I will have there behind a curtain,
Assure yourself, shall make the matter known;
And all shall be concluded in one scene,
For there's no pleasure ta'en in tediousness.
BAL. How like you this?
LOR. [*aside to* BALTHAZAR] Why, thus, my Lord,
We must resolve to soothe his humors up.
BAL. On then, Hieronimo; farewell till soon.
HIER. You'll ply this gear?
LOR. I warrant you.
Exeunt all but HIERONIMO.
HIER. Why so!
Now shall I see the fall of Babylon,
Wrought by the Heavens in this confusion.
And if the world like not this tragedy,
Hard is the hap of old Hieronimo. *Exit*.

[10] Pashas. [11] Diana. *Huntress* is trisyllabic.
[12] Get a costume.

[13] So Greg and Schick; Boas *intention*.
[14] Transposed with preceding line in first three editions.

[SCENE II] [15]

Enter ISABELLA *with a weapon.*

ISAB. Tell me no more! — Oh, monstrous homicides!
Since neither piety or pity moves
The King to justice or compassion,
I will revenge myself upon this place,
Where thus they murdered my beloved son.
She cuts down the arbor.
Down with these branches and these loathsome boughs
Of this unfortunate and fatal pine!
Down with them, Isabella; rent them up,
And burn the roots from whence the rest is sprung!
I will not leave a root, a stalk, a tree,
A bough, a branch, a blossom, nor a leaf,
No, not an herb within this garden plot,
Accursed complot [16] of my misery!
Fruitless for ever may this garden be,
Barren the earth, and blissless whosoever
Imagines not to keep it unmanur'd! [17]
An eastern wind, commix'd with noisome airs,
Shall blast the plants and the young saplings;
The earth with serpents shall be pestered,
And passengers, for fear to be infect,
Shall stand aloof, and, looking at it, tell:
"There, murd'red, died the son of Isabel."
Ay, here he di'd, and here I him embrace!
See, where his ghost solicits with his wounds
Revenge on her that should revenge his death.
Hieronimo, make haste to see thy son;
For sorrow and despair hath cited me
To hear Horatio plead with Rhadamanth.
Make haste, Hieronimo, to hold excus'd
Thy negligence in pursuit [18] of their deaths
Whose hateful wrath bereav'd him of his breath.
Ah, nay, thou doest delay their deaths,
Forgives the murderers of thy noble son,
And none but I bestir me — to no end!
And as I curse this tree from further fruit,
So shall my womb be cursed for his sake;
And with this weapon will I wound the breast,
The hapless breast, that gave Horatio suck.
She stabs herself.

[15] Hieronimo's garden.
[16] Co-plotter, accomplice. Properly, "conspiracy." Note the pun.
[17] Uncultivated.
[18] Accented on first syllable.

[SCENE III] [19]

Enter HIERONIMO; *he knocks up the curtain.*[20] *Enter the* DUKE OF CASTILE.

CAST. How now, Hieronimo, where's your fellows,
That you take all this pain?
HIER. O sir, it is for the author's
Credit, to look that all things may go well.
But, good my Lord, let me entreat your Grace
To give the King the copy of the play:
This is the argument of what we show.
CAST. I will, Hieronimo.
HIER. One thing more, my good Lord.
CAST. What's that?
HIER. Let me entreat your Grace
That, when the train are pass'd into the gallery,
You would vouchsafe to throw me down the key.
CAST. I will, Hieronimo. *Exit* CASTILE.
HIER. What, are you ready, Balthazar?
Bring a chair and a cushion for the King.

Enter BALTHAZAR, *with a chair.*

Well done, Balthazar;
Hang up the title: our scene is Rhodes. What, is your beard on?
BAL. Half on; the other is in my hand.
HIER. Dispatch for shame;
Are you so long? — *Exit* BALTHAZAR.
Bethink thyself, Hieronimo,
Recall thy wits, recount thy former wrongs
Thou hast received by murder of thy son,
And lastly, not least, how Isabel,
Once his mother and thy dearest wife,
All woebegone for him, hath slain herself.
Behoves thee then, Hieronimo, to be reveng'd.
The plot is laid of dire revenge!
On, then, Hieronimo, pursue revenge;
For nothing wants but acting of revenge.

Enter SPANISH KING, VICEROY, DUKE OF CASTILE, [DON PEDRO], *and their train* [*to the gallery*].[21] *Exit Hieronimo.*

KING. Now, Viceroy, shall we see the tragedy

[19] A hall in Don Cyprian's palace. Presumably Isabella's suicide has taken place on the inner stage, the curtains of which are then closed.
[20] See V, i, 177, 178; and V, iii, 111.
[21] Add. Manly. The gallery (see ll. 9, 10) was doubtless the balcony over the inner stage. Castile locks the doors to it and throws the key down to Hieronimo. In the old eds. the latter's exit is given before the entrance of the royal party.

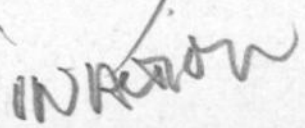

Of Soliman, the Turkish emperor,
Perform'd of pleasure by your son the Prince,
My nephew Don Lorenzo, and my niece.
Vic. Who? Bel-imperia?
King. Ay, and Hieronimo, our marshal,
At whose request they deign to do 't themselves.
These be our pastimes in the court of Spain.
Here, Brother, you shall be the bookkeeper:
This is the argument of that they show.
He giveth him a book.

(*Gentlemen, this play of* Hieronimo, *in sundry languages, was thought good to be set down in English, more largely for the easier understanding to every public reader.*)

Enter *Balthazar, Bel-imperia,* and *Hieronimo.*

Bal. *Bashaw, that Rhodes is ours, yield Heavens the honor,*
And holy Mahomet, our sacred prophet!
And be thou grac'd with every excellence
That Soliman can give, or thou desire.
But thy desert in conquering Rhodes is less
Than in reserving this fair Christian nymph,
Perseda, blissful lamp of excellence,
Whose eyes compel, like pow'rful adamant,
The warlike heart of Soliman to wait.

King. See, Viceroy, that is Balthazar, your son,
That represents the emperor Soliman:
How well he acts his amorous passion!
Vic. Ay, Bel-imperia hath taught him that.
Cast. That 's because his mind runs all on Bel-imperia.

Hier. *Whatever joy earth yields betide your Majesty.*
Bal. *Earth yields no joy without Perseda's love.*
Hier. *Let then Perseda on your Grace attend.*
Bal. *She shall not wait on me, but I on her:*
Drawn by the influence of her lights,[22] *I yield.*
But let my friend, the Rhodian knight, come forth.
Erasto, dearer than my life to me,
That he may see Perseda, my beloved.

Enter *Erasto.*

King. Here comes Lorenzo: look upon the plot,
And tell me, Brother, what part plays he?

[22] Eyes.

Bel. *Ah, my Erasto, welcome to Perseda.*
Lor. *Thrice happy is Erasto that thou livest;*
Rhodes' loss is nothing to Erasto's joy;
Sith his Perseda lives, his life survives.
Bal. *Ah, bashaw, here is love betwixt Erasto*
And fair Perseda, sovereign of my soul.
Hier. *Remove Erasto, mighty Soliman,*
And then Perseda will be quickly won.
Bal. *Erasto is my friend; and while he lives,*
Perseda never will remove her love.
Hier. *Let not Erasto live to grieve great Soliman.*
Bal. *Dear is Erasto in our princely eye.*
Hier. *But if he be your rival, let him die.*
Bal. *Why, let him die — so love commandeth me;*
Yet grieve I that Erasto should so die.
Hier. *Erasto, Soliman saluteth thee,*
And lets thee wit by me his Highness' will,
Which is, thou shouldst be thus employ'd.
Stab him.
Bel. *Ay me,*
Erasto! See, Soliman; Erasto's slain!
Bal. *Yet liveth Soliman to comfort thee.*
Fair queen of beauty, let not favor die,
But with a gracious eye behold his grief,
That with Perseda's beauty is increas'd,
If by Perseda [*his*][23] *grief be not releas'd.*
Bel. *Tyrant, desist soliciting vain suits;*
Relentless are mine ears to thy laments,
As thy butcher is pitiless and base,
Which seiz'd on my Erasto, harmless knight.
Yet by thy power thou thinkest to command,
And to thy power Perseda doth obey;
But, were she able, thus she would revenge
Thy treacheries on thee, ignoble Prince:
Stab him.
And on herself she would be thus reveng'd.
Stab herself.

King. Well said![24] — Old Marshal, this was bravely done!
Hier. But Bel-imperia plays Perseda well!
Vic. Were this in earnest, Bel-imperia,
You would be better to my son than so.
King. But now what follows for Hieronimo?
Hier. Marry, this follows for Hieronimo; —
Here break we off our sundry languages,
And thus conclude I in our vulgar tongue.
Haply you think — but bootless are your thoughts —
That this is fabulously counterfeit,
And that we do as all tragedians do:

[23] So Schick; old eds. s. [24] Good, well done.

To die to-day, for fashioning our scene —
The death of Ajax or some Roman peer —
And in a minute, starting up again,
Revive to please to-morrow's audience.
No, Princes; know I am Hieronimo,
The hopeless father of a hapless son,
Whose tongue is tun'd to tell his latest tale,
Not to excuse gross errors in the play.
I see your looks urge instance of these words;
Behold the reason urging me to this!

Shows his dead son.

See here my show; look on this spectacle!
Here lay my hope, and here my hope hath end!
Here lay my heart, and here my heart was slain!
Here lay my treasure, here my treasure lost!
Here lay my bliss, and here my bliss bereft!
But hope, heart, treasure, joy, and bliss,
All fled, fail'd, died, yea, all decay'd, with this.
From forth these wounds came breath that gave me life;
They murd'red me that made these fatal marks.
The cause was love, whence grew this mortal hate;
The hate, Lorenzo and young Balthazar;
The love, my son to Bel-imperia.
But night, the coverer of accursed crimes,
With pitchy silence hush'd these traitors' harms,
And lent them leave, for they had sorted [25] leisure
To take advantage in my garden plot
Upon my son, my dear Horatio.
There merciless they butcher'd up my boy,
In black, dark night, to pale, dim, cruel death.
He shrieks; I heard — and yet, methinks, I hear —
His dismal outcry echo in the air.
With soonest speed I hasted to the noise,
Where hanging on a tree I found my son,
Through-girt [26] with wounds, and slaught'red as you see.
And grieved I, think you, at this spectacle?
Speak, Portuguese, whose loss resembles mine:
If thou canst weep upon thy Balthazar,
'T is like I wail'd for my Horatio. —
And you, my Lord, whose reconciled son
March'd in a net, and thought himself unseen,
And rated me for brainsick lunacy,
With "God amend that mad Hieronimo!" —
How can you brook our play's catastrophe? —
And here behold this bloody handkerchief,
Which at Horatio's death I weeping dipp'd
Within the river of his bleeding wounds:
It, as propitious, see, I have reserved,
And never hath it left my bloody heart,
Soliciting remembrance of my vow
With these, oh, these accursed murderers!
Which now perform'd, my heart is satisfied.
And to this end the bashaw I became,
That might revenge me on Lorenzo's life,
Who therefore was appointed to the part,
And was to represent the knight of Rhodes,
That I might kill him more conveniently.
So, Viceroy, was this Balthazar, thy son,
That Soliman which Bel-imperia,
In person of Perseda, murdered,
Solely appointed to that tragic part
That she might slay him that offended her.
Poor Bel-imperia miss'd her part in this;
For though the story saith she should have died,
Yet I of kindness, and of care to her,
Did otherwise determine of her end;
But love of him whom they did hate too much
Did urge her resolution [27] to be such.
And, Princes, now behold Hieronimo,
Author and actor in this tragedy,
Bearing his latest fortune in his fist;
And will as resolute conclude his part
As any of the actors gone before.
And, gentles, thus I end my play;
Urge no more words — I have no more to say.

He runs to hang himself.

KING. O hearken, Viceroy! — Hold, Hieronimo!
Brother, my nephew and thy son are slain!

VIC. We are betray'd; my Balthazar is slain!
Break ope the doors; run, save Hieronimo.

[*They break in and hold* HIERONIMO.] [28]

Hieronimo, do but inform the King of these events;
Upon mine honor, thou shalt have no harm.

HIER. Viceroy, I will not trust thee with my life,
Which I this day have offered to my son. —
Accursed wretch,
Why stayest thou him that was resolv'd to die?

KING. Speak, traitor! damned, bloody murderer, speak!
For now I have thee, I will make thee speak.
Why hast thou done this undeserving deed?

[25] Chosen.

[26] Pierced, smitten through.

[27] Either "death" or "determination."

[28] Add. Q 1602.

VIC. Why hast thou murdered my Balthazar?
CAST. Why hast thou butchered both my children thus?
HIER. O, good words![29]
As dear to me was my Horatio
As yours, or yours, or yours, my Lord, to you.
My guiltless son was by Lorenzo slain,
And by Lorenzo and that Balthazar
Am I at last revenged thoroughly,
Upon whose souls may Heavens be yet avenged
With greater far than these afflictions.
CAST. But who were thy confederates in this?
VIC. That was thy daughter, Bel-imperia;
For by her hand my Balthazar was slain:
I saw her stab him.
KING. Why speakest thou not?
HIER. What lesser liberty can kings afford
Than harmless silence? Then afford it me.
Sufficeth, I may not, nor I will not tell thee.
KING. Fetch forth the tortures! Traitor as thou art,
I'll make thee tell.
HIER. Indeed,
Thou mayest torment me as his wretched son
Hath done in murd'ring my Horatio;
But never shalt thou force me to reveal
The thing which I have vow'd inviolate.
And therefore, in despite of all thy threats,
Pleas'd with their deaths, and eas'd with their revenge,
First take my tongue, and afterwards my heart.

[30] [HIER. But are you sure they are dead?
CAST. Ay, slave,[31] too sure.
HIER. What, and yours too?
VIC. Ay, all are dead; not one of them survive.
HIER. Nay, then I care not; come, and we shall be friends;
Let us lay our heads together:
See, here's a goodly noose will hold them all.
VIC. O damned devil, how secure[32] he is!
HIER. Secure? Why, doest thou wonder at it?
I tell thee, Viceroy, this day I have seen [revenge],
And in that sight am grown a prouder monarch
Than ever sat under the crown of Spain.
Had I as many lives as there be stars,
As many Heavens to go to, as those lives,
I'd give them all, ay, and my soul to boot,
But I would see thee ride in this red pool.
CAST. Speak! who were thy confederates in this?
VIC. That was thy daughter Bel-imperia;
For by her hand my Balthazar was slain:
I saw her stab him.
HIER. O, good words!
As dear to me was my Horatio,
As yours, or yours, or yours, my Lord, to you.
My guiltless son was by Lorenzo slain,
And by Lorenzo and that Balthazar
Am I at last revenged thoroughly;
Upon whose souls may Heavens be yet revenged
With greater far than these afflictions.
Methinks, since I grew inward[33] with revenge,
I cannot look with scorn enough on death.
KING. What, doest thou mock us, slave? — Bring tortures forth!
HIER. Do, do, do; and meantime I'll torture you.
You had a son, as I take it; and your son
Should ha' been married to your daughter.
Ha, was 't not so? — You had a son, too;
He was my Liege's nephew. He was proud
And politic; had he lived, he might 'a' come
To wear the crown of Spain. I think 't was so —
'T was I that killed him; look you, this same hand,
'T was it that stabb'd his heart — do you see? this hand —
For one Horatio, if you ever knew him: a youth,
One that they hanged up in his father's garden;
One that did force your valiant son to yield,
While your more valiant son did take him prisoner.
VIC. Be deaf, my senses; I can hear no more.
KING. Fall, Heaven, and cover us with thy sad ruins.
CAST. Roll all the world within thy pitchy cloud.
HIER. Now do I applaud what I have acted.
Nunc [*iners cadat*][34] *manus!*
Now to express the rupture of my part —
First take my tongue, and afterward my heart.
[*He bites out his tongue.*]

KING. O monstrous resolution of a wretch!
See, Viceroy, he hath bitten forth his tongue,
Rather than to reveal what we requir'd.
CAST. Yet can he write.
KING. And if in this he satisfy us not,
We will devise th' extremest kind of death
That ever was invented for a wretch.
Then he makes signs for a knife to mend his pen.
CAST. Oh, he would have a knife to mend his pen.
VIC. Here, and advise thee that thou write the troth.
KING. Look to my brother! save Hieronimo![35]
He with a knife stabs the DUKE *and himself.*
What age hath ever heard such monstrous deeds?
My brother, and the whole succeeding hope
That Spain expected after my decease!
Go, bear his body hence, that we may mourn
The loss of our beloved brother's death,
That he may be entomb'd, whate'er befall.
I am the next, the nearest, last of all.

[29] Ll. 191–215 were replaced by the added passage, ll. 216–265.

[30] Fifth passage of additions begins here. See on l. 191.

[31] Some copies read *slaine*. [32] Sure of himself.

[33] Got on intimate terms.

[34] Emend. Schick; old eds. *mors caede, mers cadae.* "Now let the hand fall idle."

[35] Old eds. give this line to Viceroy; cor. Boas.

VIC. And thou, Don Pedro, do the like for us;
Take up our hapless son, untimely slain;
Set me with him, and he with woeful me,
Upon the mainmast of a ship unmann'd,
And let the wind and tide [hale] [36] me along
To Scylla's barking and untamed [gulf,] [37]
Or to the loathsome pool of Acheron,
To weep my want for my sweet Balthazar;
Spain hath no refuge for a Portingale.

The trumpets sound a dead march; [exeunt omnes,] the KING OF SPAIN *mourning after his brother's body, and the* KING OF PORTINGAL *bearing the body of his son.*

[CHORUS] [38]

GHOST. Ay, now my hopes have end in their effects,
When blood and sorrow finish my desires:
Horatio murdered in his father's bower,
Vild Serberine by Pedringano slain,
False Pedringano hang'd by quaint device,
Fair Isabella by herself misdone,
Prince Balthazar by Bel-imperia stabb'd,
The Duke of Castile and his wicked son
Both done to death by old Hieronimo,
My Bel-imperia fall'n as Dido fell,
And good Hieronimo slain by himself:
Ay, these were spectacles to please my soul.
Now will I beg at lovely Proserpine
That, by the virtue of her princely doom,
I may consort my friends in pleasing sort,
And on my foes work just and sharp revenge.
I'll lead my friend Horatio through those fields
Where never-dying wars are still inur'd; [39]
I'll lead fair Isabella to that train
Where pity weeps, but never feeleth pain;
I'll lead my Bel-imperia to those joys
That vestal virgins and fair queens possess;
I'll lead Hieronimo where Orpheus plays,
Adding sweet pleasure to eternal days. —
But say, Revenge, for thou must help, or none,
Against the rest how shall my hate be shown?

REV. This hand shall hale them down to deepest hell,
Where none but Furies, bugs, [40] and tortures dwell.

GHOST. Then, sweet Revenge, do this at my request:
Let me be judge, and doom them to unrest.
Let loose poor Tityus from the vulture's gripe,
And let Don Cyprian supply his room;
Place Don Lorenzo on Ixion's wheel,
And let the lover's endless pains surcease
(Juno forgets old wrath, and grants him ease);
Hang Balthazar about Chimaera's neck,
And let him there bewail his bloody love,
Repining at our joys that are above;
Let Serberine go roll the fatal stone,
And take from Sisyphus his endless moan;
False Pedringano, for his treachery,
Let him be dragg'd through boiling Acheron,
And there live, dying still in endless flames,
Blaspheming gods and all their holy names.

REV. Then haste we down to meet thy friends and foes:
To place thy friends in ease, the rest in woes;
For here though death hath end their misery
I'll there begin their endless tragedy.

Exeunt.

[36] Cor. ed. 1599; earlier eds. *hall*.
[37] Cor. Q 1623; earlier eds. *greefe*.
[38] Old eds. *Enter Ghost and Revenge*.

[39] Waged.
[40] Bugbears, terrors.

THE TRAGICALL

Hiſtory of D. Fauſtus.

As it hath bene Acted by the Right Honorable the Earle of Nottingham his ſeruants.

Written by Ch. Marl.

LONDON

Printed by V. S. for Thomas Buſhell. 1604.

INTRODUCTORY NOTE

As Tamburlaine aspired to the world's mastery by force of arms, Faustus sought it through knowledge; thus Marlowe exhibits in this play another aspect of the Renaissance will to freedom. In its original form *Doctor Faustus* must have been a sublime poem, and it still retains what *Tamburlaine* lacks, scenes of primarily dramatic power. Unfortunately, though the play was probably produced about 1589 (Boas inclines to 1592 but minimizes the significance of a ballad on Faustus licensed in 1589 and presumably inspired by the play), the first edition appeared only in 1604. By that time, eleven years after the author's death, the piece had been mangled by stage alterations.

In 1602 Henslowe, whose company, the Admiral's (or Nottingham's) Men, acted it, paid £4 to William Bird and Samuel Rowley for additions. And doubtless, both before and after their work, there was fairly constant tampering. The Quarto of 1616 gives us a version widely different from the first edition, and the Quarto of 1663 contains grotesque additions partly adapted from *The Jew of Malta.* The tendency of the early stage was to treat the Devil as a comic character; and as new material was successively introduced for the low comedians, the original was repeatedly pared down to make room for it. *Doctor Faustus,* then, is to be approached like a temple of the antique world; we are the losers if we allow partial collapse, inartistic restoration, and unauthentic and impudent addition to obscure the surviving traces of its beauty. (For a sketch of the probable process of corruption see Percy Simpson's article in *Essays and Studies by Members of the English Association*, VII, 143–155.) Aside from interpolation and excision, the most notable changes are the mangling of metre and the substitution of prose paraphrases for the original verse.

Marlowe's source was evidently not the German *Historia Von D. Johann Fausten* (Frankfurt am Main, 1587), but the not very faithful English translation of it, the *Historie of Doctor Iohn Faustus* (London, 1592), which Marlowe (unless we are to date the play after its appearance) must have read in MS or in an earlier edition. The moral application of the story is a prominent feature of the source, which also shows an anti-Papal bias. The play closely follows selected materials of the English Faust Book; but, as Boas remarks, "it is the questing spirit of the youthful Marlowe that transfigures it." The core of the legend is the compact with the Devil and the consequent retribution. The interval of twenty years is replete in the Faust Book with a great variety of experiences, including the episodes with the Pope, the horse-courser, and the clowns. It is generally believed that Marlowe's soaring pen was incapable of the comic scenes and that a collaborator furnished them. Marlowe was clearly more interested in the aspiration of Faustus, and with that fact in mind the reader must attempt as best he may to hold in his mind's eye the noble outlines of the original structure. "How greatly," said Goethe, "is it all planned."

Whatever the date of the original production, Henslowe records performances of *Doctor Faustus* by the Admiral's Men, with Edward Alleyn in the title rôle, in 1594–97. It continued to be acted, in more and more degraded versions, till well into the eighteenth century. The Case edition of this play is the work of F. S. Boas (1932).[1] Among other editions are Hermann Breymann's parallel texts of Qq 1604 and 1616 (vol. II of the *Historisch-Kritische Ausgabe* of Marlowe's Works, 1889); modernized editions by A. W. Ward (fourth edition, 1901), and I. Gollancz (1897); and a facsimile of Q 1604 by J. S. Farmer (1920). Professor Brooke (*Philological Quarterly*, January, 1933) has supplemented these editions with several valuable bibliographical and exegetical notes.

[1] The present edition has profited, during correction of proofs, by T. M. Parrott's review of Boas (*Modern Language Notes*, June, 1933).

Faustus was first printed, in quarto, in 1604 (reprinted 1609, 1611). In 1616 (reprinted 1619, 1620, 1624, 1628, 1631) a new version added about 550 lines and rewrote much of the play. Since Q 1616 evidently rests in part, not on an earlier quarto, but on independent MS authority, an extremely difficult textual problem is presented. Boas thinks Q 1616 more authentic; but the present edition is based on Breymann's and Brooke's reprints of Q 1604, though with indicated restorations and rearrangements from Q 1616 as given by them; for Q 1604 presents a badly cut and garbled stage version. Q 1616, on the contrary, constantly betrays, in the opinion of the present editor, the hand of an "improver", who smooths out difficult expressions; and it contains a number of new passages that are certainly not Marlovian.

As for the authorship of the version of 1604, Boas's conclusions seem reasonable and may be applied as follows. Marlowe probably wrote the first two acts, through II, ii (the episode of the Seven Deadly Sins is a possible exception); the chorus and the next fifty-three lines of Act III; Act IV, chorus, i, ii, (1–9), iii; and Act V. The prose comic scenes may be a collaborator's subsequently modified, in any case, by the steady pressure of theatrical conditions.

[The most authoritative study of the text of *Doctor Faustus* is by W. W. Greg in *Marlowe's "Doctor Faustus" 1606–1616: Parallel Texts* (Oxford, 1950). Greg also prepared *A Conjectural Reconstruction* of the play (Oxford, 1950). A modernized text based on Greg's textual arguments was edited by John D. Jump (Harvard, 1962) for the Revels Plays series. R. O.]

THE TRAGICAL HISTORY OF DOCTOR FAUSTUS

BY

CHRISTOPHER MARLOWE

[DRAMATIS PERSONAE

THE POPE.
CARDINAL OF LORRAINE.
CHARLES V, EMPEROR OF GERMANY.
DUKE OF VANHOLT.[1]
FAUSTUS.
VALDES, } friends to FAUSTUS.
CORNELIUS, }
WAGNER, servant to FAUSTUS.
Clown.
ROBIN.
RALPH.
Vintner.
Horse-Courser.[2]
Knight.
Old Man.

Scholars, Friars, and Attendants.

DUCHESS OF VANHOLT.

LUCIFER.
BELZEBUB.
MEPHISTOPHILIS.
Good Angel.
Evil Angel.
The Seven Deadly Sins.
Devils.
Spirits in the shapes of ALEXANDER THE GREAT, of his Paramour, and of HELEN of TROY.
Chorus.]

[ACT I]

Enter Chorus.

[CHORUS.] Not marching now in fields of Thrasimene,
Where Mars did mate [3] the Carthaginians;
Nor sporting in the dalliance of love,
In courts of kings where state is overturn'd;
Nor in the pomp of proud, audacious deeds,
Intends our Muse to [vaunt] [4] his [5] heavenly verse: —
Only this, gentlemen: we must perform
The form of Faustus' fortunes, good or bad.
To patient judgments we appeal our plaud,[6]
And speak for Faustus in his infancy.
Now is he born, his parents base of stock,
In Germany, within a town call'd Rhodes; [7]
Of riper years to Wittenberg he went,
Whereas his kinsmen chiefly brought him up.
So soon he profits in divinity,
The fruitful plot of scholarism grac'd,[8]
That shortly he was grac'd [9] with doctor's name,
Excelling all whose sweet delight disputes
In heavenly matters of theology;
Till, swoln with cunning,[10] of a self-conceit,
His waxen [11] wings did mount above his reach,
And melting Heavens conspir'd his overthrow;
For, falling to a devilish exercise,
And glutted more [12] with learning's golden gifts,
He surfeits upon cursed necromancy.
Nothing so sweet as magic is to him,
Which he prefers before his chiefest bliss.
And this [13] the man that in his study sits.
Exit.

[1] Anholt. [2] Horse trader.
[3] Defeat. But Hannibal won this battle. The author may be confused; and the whole speech may be non-Marlovian.
[4] Proudly display; so Q 1616; earlier eds. *daunt*.
[5] Cf. Shakespeare, *Sonnets*, XXI, 1, 2.
[6] For our applause. Q 1616: *And now to patient iudgements we appeale*, typical of that ed.'s efforts to smooth the original version.
[7] Roda, in the Duchy of Saxe-Altenburg.

[8] Full of graces. (Cf. *Macbeth*, III, iv, 41.)
[9] Punning on the official "grace" (at Cambridge) by virtue of which a candidate took his degree.
[10] Puffed up with knowledge.
[11] *I.e.*, insecure, like the wings of Icarus.
[12] Q 1616 *now*.
[13] This is.

[SCENE I] [14]

Enter FAUSTUS *in his study.*

FAUST. Settle thy studies, Faustus, and begin
To sound the depth of that thou wilt profess.
Having commenc'd,[15] be a divine in show;
Yet level [16] at the end of every art,
And live and die in Aristotle's works.
Sweet Analytics,[17] 't is thou hast ravish'd me,
Bene disserere est finis logices.
Is to dispute well logic's chiefest end?
Affords this art no greater miracle?
Then read no more; thou hast attain'd the end —
A greater subject fitteth Faustus' wit.
Bid [ὂν καὶ μὴ ὄν] [18] farewell, Galen come:
Seeing *Ubi desinit philosophus, ibi incipit medicus;* [19]
Be a physician, Faustus, heap up gold,
And be eterniz'd for some wondrous cure.
Summum bonum medicinæ sanitas:
The end of physic is our body's health.
Why, Faustus, hast thou not attain'd that end?
Is not thy common talk sound Aphorisms? [20]
Are not thy bills [21] hung up as monuments,
Whereby whole cities have escap'd the plague,
And thousand desp'rate maladies been eas'd?
Yet art thou still but Faustus and a man.
Wouldst thou make man [22] to live eternally,
Or, being dead, raise them to life again?
Then this profession were to be esteem'd.
Physic, farewell. Where is Justinian?
[*Reads.*]
Si una eademque res legatur duobus,
Alter rem, alter valorem rei, &c.[23]
A pretty [24] case of paltry legacies! [*Reads.*]
Exhæreditare filium non potest pater nisi. . . [25]
Such is the subject of the Institute
And universal body of the [law].[26]
His [27] study fits a mercenary drudge,
Who aims at nothing but external trash; [28]
[Too servile] [29] and illiberal for me.
When all is done, divinity is best;
Jerome's Bible,[30] Faustus, view it well.
[*Reads.*]
Stipendium peccati mors est. Ha! *Stipendium, &c.:*
The reward of sin is death. — That 's hard.
[*Reads.*]
Si peccasse negamus, fallimur, et nulla est in nobis veritas:
If we say that we have no sin we deceive ourselves, and there 's no truth in us. — Why then, belike we must sin and so consequently die.
Ay, we must die an everlasting death.
What doctrine call you this, *Che sera, sera:*
"What will be shall be?" — Divinity, adieu!
These metaphysics of magicians
And necromantic books are heavenly;
Lines, circles, scenes,[31] letters, and characters,
Ay, these are those that Faustus most desires.
O what a world of profit and delight,
Of power, of honor, of omnipotence
Is promis'd to the studious artisan!
All things that move between the quiet [32] poles
Shall be at my command. Emperors and kings
Are but obey'd in their several provinces,
Nor can they raise the wind or rend the clouds;
But his dominion that exceeds [33] in this
Stretcheth as far as doth the mind of man.
A sound magician is a mighty god:
Here, Faustus, try thy [34] brains to gain [35] a deity.

Enter WAGNER.

Wagner! commend me to my dearest friends,
The German Valdes and Cornelius; [36]
Request them earnestly to visit me.
WAG. I will, sir. *Exit.*

[14] Wittenberg. Faustus is "discovered" on the inner stage.
[15] Taken a degree.
[16] Aim.
[17] Aristotelian logic.
[18] Aristotle's "being and not being"; emend. Bullen; Q1 *Oncaymaeon;* later eds. *Oeconomy.*
[19] Where the philosopher leaves off, there the physician begins. (Adapted from Aristotle, as is l. 16.)
[20] Medical memoranda, so called from the Aphorisms of Hippocrates. (Ward.)
[21] Prescriptions. (Wheeler.)
[22] Qq 1, 2; later eds. *men.*
[23] If one and the same thing is bequeathed to two persons, one shall take the thing and the other its value. (An incorrect version of a rule in the *Institutes.*) (Boas.)
[24] Q 1616 *petty.*
[25] A father cannot disinherit his son, except . . . (Adapted from the *Institutes* of Justinian, codifier of the Roman law.)
[26] Q 1616; earlier eds. *Church.*
[27] Its.
[28] *I.e.*, money.
[29] Q 1616; earlier eds. *The deuill.*
[30] The Vulgate.
[31] Logeman conj. *schemes.*
[32] *I.e.*, fixed.
[33] Excels.
[34] Q 1616 *tire my.*
[35] Q 1616 *get.*
[36] Marlowe takes this name from Henry Cornelius Agrippa von Nettesheim, a friend of Faustus and a magician; but this character is not Agrippa (see ll. 116, 117). Brooke suggests that "the German Valdes" is a complimentary title for a mythical character, in allusion to the sixteenth-century Spanish humanist, Juan de Valdes.

FAUST. Their conference [37] will be a greater help to me
Than all my labours, plod I ne'er so fast.

Enter the Good Angel *and the* Evil Angel.

G. ANG. O Faustus, lay that damned book aside,
And gaze not on it lest it tempt thy soul
And heap God's heavy wrath upon thy head.
Read, read the Scriptures; that is blasphemy.

E. ANG. Go forward, Faustus, in that famous art,
Wherein all Nature's treasury is contain'd;
Be thou on earth as Jove is in the sky,
Lord and commander of these elements.

Exeunt [Angels.]

FAUST. How am I glutted with conceit of this! [38]
Shall I make spirits fetch me what I please,
Resolve me of all ambiguities,
Perform what desperate enterprise I will?
I'll have them fly to India [39] for gold,
Ransack the ocean for orient [40] pearl,
And search all corners of the new-found world
For pleasant fruits and princely delicates.
I'll have them read me strange philosophy
And tell the secrets of all foreign kings;
I'll have them wall all Germany with brass,
And make swift Rhine circle fair [Wittenberg]; [41]
I'll have them fill the public schools [42] with [silk], [43]
Wherewith the students shall be bravely clad;
I'll levy soldiers with the coin they bring,
And chase the Prince of Parma [44] from our land,
And reign sole king of all our provinces;
Yea, stranger engines for the brunt of war
Than was the fiery keel [45] at Antwerp's bridge,
I'll make my servile spirits to invent.
Come, German Valdes and Cornelius,
And make me blest with your sage conference.

Enter VALDES *and* CORNELIUS.

Valdes, sweet Valdes, and Cornelius,
Know that your words have won me at the last
To practise magic and concealed arts;
Yet not your words only, but mine own fantasy,
That will receive no object; [46] for my head
But ruminates on necromantic skill.
Philosophy is odious and obscure;
Both law and physic are for petty wits;
Divinity is basest of the three,
Unpleasant, harsh, contemptible, and vild; [47]
'T is magic, magic, that hath ravish'd me.
Then, gentle friends, aid me in this attempt;
And I that have with concise syllogisms
Gravell'd the pastors of the German church,
And made the flow'ring pride of Wittenberg
Swarm to my problems, [48] as the infernal spirits
On sweet Musæus, when he came to hell,
Will be as cunning as Agrippa was,
Whose shadows [49] made all Europe honor him.

VALD. Faustus, these books, thy wit, and our experience
Shall make all nations to canonize us.
As Indian Moors [50] obey their Spanish lords,
So shall the subjects [51] of every element
Be always serviceable to us three;
Like lions shall they guard us when we please;
Like Almain rutters [52] with their horsemen's staves,
Or Lapland giants, trotting by our sides;
Sometimes like women or unwedded maids,
Shadowing [53] more beauty in their airy [54] brows
Than in [the] [55] white breasts of the Queen of Love:
[From] [56] Venice shall they drag huge argosies, [57]
And from America the golden fleece

[37] Conversation.
[38] How am I filled with this notion.
[39] Probably, the West Indies, America.
[40] Lustrous.
[41] For the *Wittenberge* of Q 1616, Q_1 has *Wertenberge.* Brooke suggests that Marlowe thought of the university town as the capital of Würtemberg.
[42] University lecture-halls.
[43] Emend. Dyce; old eds. *skill.* Brooke cites Cambridge regulations which forbade the wearing of silk by the students.
[44] The Spanish governor-general (1579–1592) of the Netherlands, nominally a part of the Empire.
[45] A Dutch "devil-ship" (filled with explosives) which damaged Parma's bridge at the siege of Antwerp.
[46] *I.e.*, my own fancy, which will entertain no regular academic subject — nor anything else but necromancy. Brooke differs from mod. eds., who insert the semicolon and omit the old texts' comma after "head"; but the antithesis is between "words" and "fantasy."
[47] Vile.
[48] Mathematical and logical lectures. (Ward.)
[49] Shades raised from the dead.
[50] American Indians.
[51] Q 1616 *spirits.*
[52] German troopers.
[53] Shadowing forth, portraying.
[54] Because insubstantial.
[55] Q 1616; Q_1 *their.* Q 1616 reads *has* for *in.*
[56] Cor. Q 1609; Q_1 *For.*
[57] Large merchantmen.

That yearly stuffs [58] old Philip's treasury;
If learned Faustus will be resolute.
FAUST. Valdes, as resolute am I in this
As thou to live; therefore object it not.
CORN. The miracles that magic will perform
Will make thee vow to study nothing else.
He that is grounded in astrology,
Enrich'd with tongues, well seen [59] [in] [60] minerals,
Hath all the principles magic doth require.
Then doubt not, Faustus, but to be renowm'd,
And more frequented for this mystery
Than heretofore the Delphian oracle.
The spirits tell me they can dry the sea
And fetch the treasure of all foreign wracks,
Ay, all the wealth that our forefathers hid
Within the massy entrails of the earth;
Then tell me, Faustus, what shall we three want?
FAUST. Nothing, Cornelius. O, this cheers my soul!
Come, show me some demonstrations magical,
That I may conjure in some lusty [61] grove,
And have these joys in full possession.
VALD. Then haste thee to some solitary grove,
And bear wise Bacon's [62] and Albanus' [63] works,
The Hebrew Psalter and New Testament;
And whatsoever else is requisite
We will inform thee ere our conference cease.
CORN. Valdes, first let him know the words of art;
And then, all other ceremonies learn'd,
Faustus may try his cunning by himself.
VALD. First I'll instruct thee in the rudiments,
And then wilt thou be perfecter than I.
FAUST. Then come and dine with me, and after meat
We'll canvass every quiddity [64] thereof;
For ere I sleep I'll try what I can do:
This night I'll conjure though I die therefore.
Exeunt.

[58] Q 1616 *stuff'd*, altered after the death of Philip II. Note inconsistency with the appearance of Charles V in this play.
[59] Versed.
[60] Add. Q 2.
[61] Pleasant. Qq 2, 3, *little*; Q 1616 *bushy*.
[62] Roger Bacon's.
[63] Possibly Pietro d'Albano, a thirteenth-century alchemist; or, misprinted, Albertus Magnus, the German Dominican of the same century, supposed to be a magician.
[64] Essential point.

[SCENE II] [65]

Enter two Scholars.

1 SCHOL. I wonder what's become of Faustus, that was wont to make our schools ring with *sic probo?* [66]

2 SCHOL. That shall we know, for see here comes his boy.

Enter WAGNER.

1 SCHOL. How now, sirrah! Where's thy master?

WAG. God in Heaven knows.

2 SCHOL. Why, dost not thou know?

WAG. Yes, I know; but that follows not.

1 SCHOL. Go to, sirrah; leave your jesting, and tell us where he is.

WAG. That follows not necessary by force of argument, that you, being licentiate, [67] should stand upon 't; therefore acknowledge your error and be attentive.

2 SCHOL. Why, didst thou not say thou knew'st?

WAG. Have you any witness on 't?

1 SCHOL. Yes, sirrah, I heard you.

WAG. Ask my fellow if I be a thief.

2 SCHOL. Well, you will not tell us?

WAG. Yes, sir, I will tell you; yet if you were not dunces, you would never ask me such a question; for is not he *corpus naturale?* [68] and is not that *mobile?* Then wherefore should you ask me such a question? But that I am by nature phlegmatic, slow to wrath, and prone to lechery — to love, I would say, — it were not for you to come within forty foot of the place of execution, [69] although I do not doubt to see you both hang'd the next sessions. Thus having triumph'd over you, I will set my countenance like a precisian, [70] and begin to speak thus: — Truly, my dear brethren, my master is within at dinner, with Valdes and Cornelius, as this wine, if it could speak, it would inform your Worships; and so the Lord bless you, preserve you, and keep you, my dear brethren, my dear brethren. *Exit.*

1 SCHOL. Nay, then, I fear he has fall'n into

[65] Before Faustus's house.
[66] Thus I prove (a scholastic formula).
[67] Licensed to ascend to a Master's or Doctor's degree. (Bòas.)
[68] "'Corpus naturale seu mobile' is the current scholastic expression for the subject-matter of physics." (Ward.)
[69] *I.e.*, the dining-room. (Wagner.)
[70] Puritan.

that damned art, for which they two are infamous through the world.

2 SCHOL. Were he a stranger, and not allied to me, yet should I grieve for him. But come, let us go and inform the Rector,[71] and see if he by his grave counsel can reclaim him.

1 SCHOL. O, but I fear me nothing can reclaim him.

2 SCHOL. Yet let us try what we can do.

Exeunt.

[SCENE III] [72]

Enter FAUSTUS *to conjure.*

FAUST. Now that the gloomy shadow of the earth,[73]
Longing to view Orion's drizzling look,
Leaps from th' antar[c]tic world unto the sky
And dims the welkin with her pitchy breath,
Faustus, begin thine incantations,
And try if devils will obey thy hest,
Seeing thou hast pray'd and sacrific'd to them.
Within this circle is Jehovah's name,
Forward and backward anagrammatiz'd,
The breviated names of holy saints,
Figures of every adjunct to [74] the Heavens,
And characters of signs and erring stars,[75]
By which the spirits are enforc'd to rise.
Then fear not, Faustus, but be resolute,
And try the uttermost magic can perform.

Sint mihi Dei Acherontis propitii! Valeat numen triplex Iehovae! Ignei, aerii, aquatani [76] *spiritus, salvete! Orientis Princeps Belzebub, inferni ardentis monarcha, et Demogorgon, propitiamus vos, ut appareat et surgat Mephistophilis.* [*Quid tu moraris?*] [77] *Per Iehovam, Gehennam, et consecratam aquam quam nunc spargo, signumque crucis quod nunc facio, et per vota nostra, ipse nunc surgat nobis dicatus* [78] *Mephistophilis!* [79]

Enter [MEPHISTOPHILIS,] [80] *a* Devil.

I charge thee to return and change thy shape;
Thou art too ugly to attend on me.
Go, and return an old Franciscan friar;
That holy shape becomes a devil best.

Exit Devil.

I see there's virtue in my heavenly words;
Who would not be proficient in this art?
How pliant is this Mephistophilis,
Full of obedience and humility!
Such is the force of magic and my spells.
[Now,] [81] Faustus, thou art conjuror laureate;
Thou canst command great Mephistophilis:
Quin regis Mephistophilis fratris imagine.[82]

Re-enter MEPHISTOPHILIS [*like a Franciscan Friar*].

MEPH. Now, Faustus, what wouldst thou have me do?

FAUST. I charge thee wait upon me whilst I live,
To do whatever Faustus shall command,
Be it to make the moon drop from her sphere
Or the ocean to overwhelm the world.

MEPH. I am a servant to great Lucifer,
And may not follow thee without his leave;
No more than he commands must we perform.

FAUST. Did he not charge thee to appear to me?

MEPH. No, I came now hither of mine own accord.

FAUST. Did not my conjuring speeches raise thee? Speak!

MEPH. That was the cause, but yet per accident;
For when we hear one rack [83] the name of God,

[71] The head of the university.

[72] A grove.

[73] Q 1616 *night*. But, as Brooke notes, Orion is a winter constellation (hence "drizzling"), and when it is visible the sun is below the equator; thus the earth's shadow "can be said to be projected from the southern hemisphere . . . unto the sky."

[74] Every star joined to.

[75] Planets.

[76] So old eds. Emend. Brooke *aquatici*.

[77] Conj. Schröer; old eds. *quod tumeraris*. For *Mephastophilis* of the earlier eds., Qq 1616 *et seq.* have *Mephostophilis Dragon*. Boas conj. *Enter Dragon above*. This is unlikely, but there may have been a note anticipatory of some feature of the entrance of "a Devil" immediately after this speech. The whole question is discussed by Root, *Englische Studien*, XLIII, 144–149.

[78] Cor. Q 1620; earlier eds. *dicatis*.

[79] Unto me be the gods of Acheron propitious. May the triple name of Jehovah prevail. Spirits of fire, air, and water, hail! Belzebub, Prince of the East, Sovereign of burning Hell, and Demogorgon, we propitiate you, that Mephistophilis may appear and rise. Why delayest thou? By Jehovah, Gehenna, and the holy water which now I sprinkle, and the sign of the cross which now I make, and by our prayer, may Mephistophilis, by us summoned, now arise.

[80] But not the actor who played Mephistophilis. Cf. on l. 21. In the Faust Book "a mighty Dragon" appears at this point.

[81] Emend. Albers; old eds. *No*.

[82] Indeed thou rulest Mephistophilis in his likeness of a friar. (Boas, who adopts, however, Taylor's emendation, *redis* for *regis*.)

[83] Torture into anagrams.

Abjure the Scriptures and his Savior Christ,
We fly, in hope to get his glorious soul;
Nor will we come, unless he use such means
Whereby he is in danger to be damn'd.
Therefore the shortest cut for conjuring
Is stoutly to abjure the Trinity,
And pray devoutly to the Prince of Hell.

FAUST. So Faustus hath
Already done, and holds this principle:
There is no chief but only Belzebub,
To whom Faustus doth dedicate himself.
This word "damnation" terrifies not him,
For he confounds hell in [84] Elysium;
His ghost be with the old philosophers!
But, leaving these vain trifles of men's souls,
Tell me what is that Lucifer, thy lord?

MEPH. Arch-regent and commander of all spirits.

FAUST. Was not that Lucifer an angel once?

MEPH. Yes, Faustus, and most dearly lov'd of God.

FAUST. How comes it then that he is prince of devils?

MEPH. Oh, by aspiring pride and insolence,
For which God threw him from the face of Heaven.

FAUST. And what are you that live with Lucifer?

MEPH. Unhappy spirits that fell with Lucifer,
Conspir'd against our God with Lucifer,
And are for ever damn'd with Lucifer.

FAUST. Where are you damn'd?

MEPH. In hell.

FAUST. How comes it then that thou art out of hell?

MEPH. Why this is hell, nor am I out of it!
Think'st thou that I, who saw the face of God,
And tasted the eternal joys of Heaven,
Am not tormented with ten thousand hells
In being depriv'd of everlasting bliss?
O Faustus, leave these frivolous demands,
Which strike a terror to my fainting soul.

FAUST. What, is great Mephistophilis so passionate [85]
For being depriv'd of the joys of Heaven?
Learn thou of Faustus manly fortitude,
And scorn those joys thou never shalt possess.
Go bear [these] [86] tidings to great Lucifer:
Seeing Faustus hath incurr'd eternal death
By desp'rate thoughts against Jove's [87] deity,
Say he surrenders up to him his soul,
So [88] he will spare him four-and-twenty years,
Letting him live in all voluptuousness,
Having thee ever to attend on me,
To give me whatsoever I shall ask,
To tell me whatsoever I demand,
To slay mine enemies, and aid my friends,
And always be obedient to my will.
Go, and return to mighty Lucifer,
And meet me in my study at midnight,
And then resolve [89] me of thy master's mind.

MEPH. I will, Faustus. *Exit.*

FAUST. Had I as many souls as there be stars,
I'd give them all for Mephistophilis.
By him I'll be great emp'ror of the world,
And make a bridge through [90] the moving air,
To pass the ocean with a band of men;
I'll join the hills that bind the Afric shore,
And make that [country] [91] continent to [92] Spain,
And both contributory to my crown.
The Emperor shall not live but by my leave,
Nor any potentate of Germany.
Now that I have obtain'd what I desire,
I'll live in speculation [93] of this art
Till Mephistophilis return again. *Exit.*

[SCENE IV] [94]

Enter WAGNER *and the* Clown.

WAG. Sirrah boy, come hither.

CLOWN. How, "boy"! Swowns,[95] "boy"! I hope you have seen many boys with such pickadevaunts [96] as I have. "Boy," quotha!

WAG. Tell me, sirrah, hast thou any comings in?

CLOWN. Ay, and goings out too. You may see else.

WAG. Alas, poor slave! See how poverty jesteth in his nakedness! The villain is bare and out of service, and so hungry that I know he would give his soul to the Devil for a shoulder of mutton, though it were blood-raw.

CLOWN. How? My soul to the Devil for a shoulder of mutton, though 't were blood-raw! Not so, good friend. By 'r Lady, I had need

[84] Makes no distinction between hell and.
[85] Emotionally disturbed, grieved.
[86] Cor. Q 1616; earlier eds. *those*.
[87] Common in Elizabethan literature for the Christian God.
[88] Provided that.
[89] Inform.
[90] Dissyllabic.
[91] Q 1616; earlier eds. *land*.
[92] Adjoining.
[93] Contemplative study.
[94] Unlocated; perhaps a field or wood near Wittenberg.
[95] Zounds, God's wounds.
[96] Pointed beards.

have it well roasted and good sauce to it, if I pay so dear.

WAG. Well, wilt thou serve me, and I'll make thee go like *Qui mihi discipulus?*[97]

CLOWN. How, in verse?

WAG. No, sirrah; in beaten silk[98] and stavesacre.[99]

CLOWN. How, how, Knave's acre![100] Ay, I thought that was all the land his father left him. Do ye hear? I would be sorry to rob you of your living.

WAG. Sirrah, I say in stavesacre.

CLOWN. Oho! Oho! Stavesacre! Why, then, belike, if I were your man I should be full of vermin.

WAG. So thou shalt, whether thou beest with me or no. But, sirrah, leave your jesting, and bind yourself presently unto me for seven years, or I'll turn all the lice about thee into familiars, and they shall tear thee in pieces.

CLOWN. Do you hear, sir? You may save that labor; they are too familiar with me already. Swowns! they are as bold with my flesh as if they had paid for my meat and drink.

WAG. Well, do you hear, sirrah? Hold, take these guilders.

CLOWN. Gridirons! what be they?

WAG. Why, French crowns.

CLOWN. Mass, but for the name of French crowns, a man were as good have as many English counters. And what should I do with these?

WAG. Why, now, sirrah, thou art at an hour's warning, whensoever or wheresoever the Devil shall fetch thee.

CLOWN. No, no. Here, take your gridirons again.

WAG. Truly, I'll none of them.

CLOWN. Truly, but you shall.

WAG.[101] Bear witness I gave them him.

CLOWN. Bear witness I give them you again.

WAG. Well, I will cause two devils presently to fetch thee away — Baliol[102] and Belcher.

CLOWN. Let your Baliol and your Belcher come here, and I'll knock them, they were never so knock'd since they were devils. Say I should kill one of them, what would folks say? "Do ye see yonder tall[103] fellow in the round slop?[104] — he has kill'd the Devil." So I should be call'd Kill-devil all the parish over.

WAG. Baliol and Belcher! (*Enter two* Devils *and the* Clown *runs up and down crying.*) Spirits, away! *Exeunt* [Devils].

CLOWN. What, are they gone? A vengeance on them; they have vild long nails! There was a he-devil, and a she-devil; I'll tell you how you shall know them: all he-devils has horns, and all she-devils has clifts and cloven feet.

WAG. Well, sirrah, follow me.

CLOWN. But, do you hear — if I should serve you, would you teach me to raise up Banios and Belcheos?

WAG. I will teach thee to turn thyself to anything; to a dog, or a cat, or a mouse, or a rat, or anything.

CLOWN. How? a Christian fellow to a dog or a cat, a mouse, or a rat? No, no, sir; if you turn me into anything, let it be in the likeness of a little pretty frisking flea, that I may be here and there and everywhere. O, I'll tickle the pretty wenches' plackets[105]; I'll be amongst them, i' faith.

WAG. Well, sirrah, come.

CLOWN. But, do you hear, Wagner?

WAG. How! — Baliol and Belcher!

CLOWN. O Lord! I pray, sir, let Banio and Belcher go sleep.

WAG. Villain, call me Master Wagner, and let thy left eye be diametarily fix'd upon my right heel, with *quasi vestigias nostras insistere.*[106] *Exit.*

CLOWN. God forgive me, he speaks Dutch fustian![107] Well, I'll follow him; I'll serve him; that's flat. *Exit.*

[ACT II — SCENE I]

Enter FAUSTUS *in his study.*

FAUST. Now, Faustus, must
Thou needs be damn'd,[1] and canst thou not be saved!
What boots it then to think of God or Heaven?
Away with such vain fancies, and despair
Despair in God, and trust in Belzebub

[97] The first words of W. Lily's *Ad discipulos carmen de moribus*. (Dyce.)
[98] Silk with metal embroidery hammered into it.
[99] A kind of larkspur, used to kill lice.
[100] Poultney Street, Soho, where junk-dealers were established.
[101] To the audience.
[102] Belial.
[103] Valiant.
[104] Loose breeches.
[105] Slits in skirts and petticoats.
[106] As if to tread my tracks.
[107] Highfalutin.
[1] Dyce's line division; in old eds. l. 1 ends here.

Now go not backward; no, Faustus, be resolute.
Why waverest thou? O, something soundeth in mine ears,
"Abjure this magic; turn to God again."
Ay, and Faustus will turn to God again.
To God? — He loves thee not;
The God thou servest is thine own appetite,
Wherein is fix'd the love of Belzebub;
To him I'll build an altar and a church,
And offer lukewarm blood of newborn babes.

Enter Good Angel *and* Evil [Angel].

G. Ang. Sweet Faustus, leave that execrable art.
[E. Ang. Go forward, Faustus, in that famous art.[2]]
Faust. Contrition, prayer, repentance! What of them?
G. Ang. O, they are means to bring thee unto Heaven.
E. Ang. Rather illusions, fruits of lunacy,
That makes men foolish that do trust them most.
G. Ang. Sweet Faustus, think of Heaven, and heavenly things.
E. Ang. No, Faustus, think of honor and[3] wealth. *Exeunt* [Angels].
Faust. Of wealth!
Why, the signiory of Emden[4] shall be mine.
When Mephistophilis shall stand by me,
What God can hurt thee, Faustus? Thou art safe;
Cast[5] no more doubts. Come, Mephistophilis,
And bring glad tidings from great Lucifer! —
Is 't not midnight? — Come, Mephistophilis:
Veni, veni, Mephistophile!

Enter Mephistophilis.

Now tell [me],[6] what says Lucifer, thy lord?
Meph. That I shall wait on Faustus while [he lives],[7]
So[8] he will buy my service with his soul.
Faust. Already Faustus hath hazarded that for thee.
Meph. But, Faustus, thou must bequeath it solemnly
And write a deed of gift with thine own blood,
For that security craves great Lucifer.
If thou deny it, I will back to hell.
Faust. Stay, Mephistophilis! and tell me what good
Will my soul do thy lord.
Meph. Enlarge his kingdom.
Faust. Is that the reason [why][9] he tempts us thus?
Meph. *Solamen miseris socios habuisse doloris.*[10]
Faust. [Why],[11] have you any pain, that tortures others?
Meph. As great as have the human souls of men.
But tell me, Faustus, shall I have thy soul?
And I will be thy slave, and wait on thee,
And give thee more than thou hast wit to ask.
Faust. Ay, Mephistophilis, I give it thee.
Meph. Then, [Faustus],[12] stab thine arm courageously,
And bind thy soul that at some certain day
Great Lucifer may claim it as his own;
And then be thou as great as Lucifer.
Faust. Lo, Mephistophilis, for love of thee
I cut mine arm, and with my proper blood
Assure my soul to be great Lucifer's,
Chief lord and regent of perpetual night.
View here the blood that trickles from mine arm,
And let it be propitious for my wish.
Meph. But, Faustus, thou must
Write it in manner of a deed of gift.
Faust. Ay, so I will. [*Writes.*] But, Mephistophilis,
My blood congeals, and I can write no more.
Meph. I'll fetch thee fire to dissolve it straight. *Exit.*
Faust. What might the staying of my blood portend?
Is it unwilling I should write this bill?
Why streams it not that I may write afresh?
"Faustus gives to thee his soul." Ah, there it stay'd.
Why shouldst thou not? Is not thy soul thine own?
Then write again, "Faustus gives to thee his soul."

Re-enter Mephistophilis *with a chafer of coals.*

Meph. Here's fire. Come, Faustus, set it[13] on.
Faust. So; now the blood begins to clear again;

[2] Add. Q 1616, before l. 15.
[3] Q_2 adds *of*.
[4] Then a great port.
[5] Reckon up.
[6] Add. Q 1616.
[7] Q 1616; earlier eds. *I liue.*
[8] Provided that.
[9] Add. Q 1616.
[10] *I.e.*, misery loves company.
[11] Add. Q 1616.
[12] Add. Q 1616.
[13] The dish of blood.

Now will I make an end immediately. [*Writes.*]

MEPH. [*aside*] O, what will not I do to obtain his soul?

FAUST. *Consummatum est*: this bill is ended,
And Faustus hath bequeath'd his soul to Lucifer.
But what is this inscription on mine arm?
Homo, fuge! Whither should I fly?
If unto God, he'll throw thee down to hell.
My senses are deceiv'd; here's nothing writ!—
I see it plain; here in this place is writ
Homo, fuge! Yet shall not Faustus fly.

MEPH. [*aside*] I'll fetch him somewhat to delight his mind. *Exit.*

Re-enter [MEPHISTOPHILIS] *with* Devils, *giving crowns and rich apparel to* FAUSTUS, *and dance, and then depart.*

FAUST. Speak, Mephistophilis; what means this show?

MEPH. Nothing, Faustus, but to delight thy mind withal,
And to show thee what magic can perform.

FAUST. But may I raise up spirits when I please?

MEPH. Ay, Faustus, and do greater things than these.

FAUST. Then there's enough for a thousand souls.
Here, Mephistophilis, receive this scroll,
A deed of gift of body and of soul;
But yet conditionally that thou perform
All articles prescrib'd between us both.

MEPH. Faustus, I swear by hell and Lucifer
To effect all promises between us made.

FAUST. Then hear me read them: "On these conditions following. First, that Faustus may be a spirit in form and substance. Secondly, that Mephistophilis shall be his servant, and at his command. Thirdly, that Mephistophilis shall do for him and bring him whatsoever. Fourthly, that he shall be in his chamber or house invisible. Lastly, that he shall appear to the said John Faustus, at all times, in what form or shape soever he please. I, John Faustus, of Wittenberg, Doctor, by these presents do give both body and soul to Lucifer, Prince of the East, and his minister, Mephistophilis; and furthermore grant unto them, that four-and-twenty years being expired, the articles above written inviolate, full power to fetch or carry the said John Faustus, body and soul, flesh, blood, or goods, into their habitation wheresoever. By me, John Faustus."

MEPH. Speak, Faustus; do you deliver this as your deed?

FAUST. Ay, take it, and the Devil give thee good on 't.

MEPH. Now, Faustus, ask what thou wilt.

FAUST. First will I question with thee about hell.
Tell me, where is the place that men call hell?

MEPH. Under the Heavens.

FAUST. Ay, [so are all things else;][14] but whereabout?

MEPH. Within the bowels of these elements,
Where we are tortur'd and remain for ever;
Hell has no limits, nor is circumscrib'd
In one self place; for where we are is hell,
And where hell is [there][14] must we ever be;
And, to conclude, when all the world dissolves,
And every creature shall be purified,
All places shall be hell that is not Heaven.

FAUST. Come, I think hell's a fable.

MEPH. Ay, think so still, till experience change thy mind.

FAUST. Why, think'st thou then that Faustus shall be damn'd?

MEPH. Ay, of necessity; for here's the scroll
Wherein thou hast given thy soul to Lucifer.

FAUST. Ay, and body too; but what of that?
Think'st thou that Faustus is so fond[15] to imagine
That after this life there is any pain?
Tush! these are trifles, and mere old wives' tales!

MEPH. But, Faustus, I am an instance to prove the contrary,
For I am damn'd, and am now in hell.

FAUST. How! now in hell!
Nay, an this be hell, I'll willingly be damn'd here;
What,[16] walking, disputing, etc?
But, leaving off this, let me have a wife,
The fairest maid in Germany;
For I am wanton and lascivious,
And cannot live without a wife.

MEPH. How! a wife?
I prithee, Faustus, talk not of a wife.

FAUST. Nay, sweet Mephistophilis, fetch me one, for I will have one.

MEPH. Well, thou wilt have one. Sit there till I come;
I'll fetch thee a wife in the Devil's name.
[*Exit.*]

[14] Add. Q 1616.
[15] Foolish.
[16] Q 1616 adds *sleeping, eating.*

Re-enter [MEPHISTOPHILIS] *with a* Devil *dress'd like a woman, with fireworks.*

MEPH. Tell, Faustus, how dost thou like thy wife?
FAUST. A plague on her for a hot whore!
MEPH. Tut, Faustus,
Marriage is but a ceremonial toy;
If thou lovest me, think [no] [17] more of it.
I'll cull thee out the fairest courtesans
And bring them ev'ry morning to thy bed;
She whom thine eye shall like, thy heart shall have,
Be she as chaste as was Penelope,
As wise as Saba,[18] or as beautiful
As was bright Lucifer before his fall.
Hold, take this book; peruse it thoroughly:
The iterating of these lines brings gold;
The framing of this circle on the ground
Brings whirlwinds, tempests, thunder and lightning;
Pronounce this thrice devoutly to thyself,
And men in armor shall appear to thee,
Ready to execute what thou desir'st.

FAUST. Thanks, Mephistophilis; yet fain would I have a book wherein I might behold all spells and incantations, that I might raise up spirits when I please.

MEPH. Here they are, in this book. *There turn to them.*

FAUST. Now would I have a book where I might see all characters and planets of the Heavens, that I might know their motions and dispositions.

MEPH. Here they are too. *Turn to them.*

FAUST. Nay, let me have one book more — and then I have done — wherein I might see all plants, herbs, and trees that grow upon the earth.

MEPH. Here they be.

FAUST. O, thou art deceived.

MEPH. Tut, I warrant thee. *Turn to them.* [*Exeunt.*]

[SCENE II] [19]

[*Enter* FAUSTUS *in his study, and* MEPHISTOPHILIS.] [20]

FAUST. When I behold the Heavens, then I repent,
And curse thee, wicked Mephistophilis,
Because thou hast depriv'd me of those joys.
MEPH. Why, Faustus,
Think'st thou Heaven is such a glorious thing?
I tell thee 't is not half so fair as thou,
Or any man that breathes on earth.
FAUST. How provest thou that?
MEPH. It was made for man; therefore is man more excellent.
FAUST. If it were made for man, 't was made for me!
I will renounce this magic and repent.

Enter Good Angel *and* Evil Angel.

G. ANG. Faustus, repent; yet God will pity thee.
E. ANG. Thou art a spirit; God cannot pity thee.
FAUST. Who buzzeth in mine ears I am a spirit?
Be I a devil, yet God may pity me;
Ay, God will pity me if I repent.
E. ANG. Ay, but Faustus never shall repent.
Exeunt [Angels].
FAUST. My heart's so hard'ned I cannot repent.
Scarce can I name salvation, faith, or Heaven,
But fearful echoes thunder in mine ears
"Faustus, thou art damn'd!" Then swords and knives,
Poison, guns, halters, and envenom'd steel
Are laid before me to despatch myself;
And long ere this I should have slain myself,
Had not sweet pleasure conquer'd deep despair.
Have I not made blind Homer sing to me
Of Alexander's [21] love and Œnon's death?
And hath not he that built the walls of Thebes
With ravishing sound of his melodious harp
Made music with my Mephistophilis?
Why should I die then, or basely despair?
I am resolv'd; Faustus shall ne'er repent.
Come, Mephistophilis, let us dispute again,
And argue of divine astrology.
Tell me, are there many heavens above the moon?
Are all celestial bodies but one globe,
As is the substance of this centric earth?
MEPH. As are the elements, such are the spheres
Mutually folded in each other's orb,
And, Faustus,
All jointly move upon one axletree,
Whose terminine is term'd the world's wide pole;

[17] Add. Q2.
[18] The Queen of Sheba.
[19] The same.
[20] Add. Q 1616, which prefaces the entrance with a short version of Wagner's speech at the opening of Act III. Q1 has no break. Evidently the end of Sc. i was tampered with before 1604; it may originally have been followed by a comic scene.
[21] Paris's.

Nor are the names of Saturn, Mars, or Jupiter
Feign'd, but are erring stars.

FAUST. But tell me, have they all one motion, both *situ et tempore?*[22]

MEPH. All jointly move from east to west in four-and-twenty hours upon the poles of the world, but differ in their motion upon the poles of the zodiac.

FAUST. Tush! These slender trifles Wagner can decide.
Hath Mephistophilis no greater skill?
Who knows not the double motion of the planets?
The first is finish'd in a natural day;
The second thus: as Saturn in thirty years; Jupiter in twelve; Mars in four; the Sun, Venus, and Mercury in a year; the moon in twenty-eight days. Tush, these are freshmen's suppositions. But tell me, hath every sphere a dominion or *intelligenti*[a]?

MEPH. Ay.

FAUST. How many heavens, or spheres, are there?

MEPH. Nine: the seven planets, the firmament, and the empyreal heaven.

FAUST. Well, resolve me in this question: Why have we not conjunctions, oppositions, aspects, eclipses, all at one time, but in some years we have more, in some less?

MEPH. *Per inæqualem motum respectu totius.*[23]

FAUST. Well, I am answered. Tell me who made the world.

MEPH. I will not.

FAUST. Sweet Mephistophilis, tell me.

MEPH. Move me not, for I will not tell thee.

FAUST. Villain, have I not bound thee to tell me anything?

MEPH. Ay, that is not against our kingdom; but this is.
Think thou on hell, Faustus, for thou art damn'd.

FAUST. Think, Faustus, upon God that made the world.

MEPH. Remember this. *Exit.*

FAUST. Ay, go, accursed spirit, to ugly hell;
'T is thou hast damn'd distressed Faustus' soul.
Is 't not too late?

Re-enter Good Angel *and* Evil [Angel].

E. ANG. Too late.

G. ANG. Never too late, if Faustus can repent.

E. ANG. If thou repent, devils shall tear thee in pieces.

G. ANG. Repent, and they shall never raze thy skin.

Exeunt [Angels].

FAUST. Ah, Christ, my Savior,
Seek to save distressed Faustus' soul.

Enter LUCIFER, BELZEBUB, *and* MEPHISTOPHILIS.

LUC. Christ cannot save thy soul, for he is just;
There's none but I have int'rest in the same.

FAUST. O, who art thou that look'st so terrible?

LUC. I am Lucifer,
And this is my companion prince in hell.

FAUST. O Faustus, they are come to fetch away thy soul!

LUC. We come to tell thee thou dost injure us;
Thou talk'st of Christ, contrary to thy promise;
Thou shouldst not think of God: think of the Devil,
And of his dam, too.[24]

FAUST. Nor will I henceforth; pardon me in this,
And Faustus vows never to look to Heaven,
Never to name God, or to pray to Him,
To burn his Scriptures, slay his ministers,
And make my spirits pull his churches down.

LUC. Do so, and we will highly gratify thee. Faustus, we are come from hell to show thee some pastime. Sit down, and thou shalt see all the Seven Deadly Sins appear in their proper shapes.

FAUST. That sight will be pleasing unto me
As Paradise was to Adam the first day
Of his creation.

LUC. Talk not of Paradise nor creation, but mark this show; talk of the Devil, and nothing else. — Come away!

Enter the Seven Deadly Sins.

Now, Faustus, examine them of their several names and dispositions.

FAUST. What art thou — the first?

PRIDE. I am Pride. I disdain to have any

[22] In both the direction and the duration of their revolutions.

[23] On account of their unequal motion in relation to the whole. — After l. 65 Q 1616 adds:
Faust. But is there not *Cœlum igneum, & Cristalinum?*
Meph. No Faustus they be but Fables.

[24] Evidently an actor's gag.

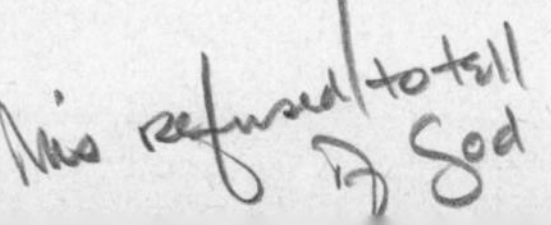

parents. I am like to Ovid's flea[25]: I can creep into every corner of a wench; sometimes, like a periwig, I sit upon her brow;[26] or like a fan of feathers, I kiss her lips;[27] indeed I do — what do I not? But, fie, what a scent is here! I'll not speak another word, except the ground were perfum'd, and covered with cloth of arras.

Faust. What art thou — the second?

Covet. I am Covetousness, begotten of an old churl in an old leathern bag; and might I have my wish, I would desire that this house and all the people in it were turn'd to gold, that I might lock you up in my good chest. O, my sweet gold!

Faust. What art thou — the third?

Wrath. I am Wrath. I had neither father nor mother: I leap'd out of a lion's mouth when I was scarce half an hour old; and ever since I have run up and down the world with this case[28] of rapiers, wounding myself when I had nobody to fight withal. I was born in hell; and look to it, for some of you shall be[29] my father.

Faust. What art thou — the fourth?

Envy. I am Envy, begotten of a chimney sweeper and an oyster-wife. I cannot read, and therefore wish all books were burnt. I am lean with seeing others eat. O, that there would come a famine through all the world, that all might die, and I live alone! Then thou shouldst see how fat I would be. But must thou sit and I stand? Come down with a vengeance!

Faust. Away, envious rascal! — What art thou — the fifth?

Glut. Who, I, sir? I am Gluttony. My parents are all dead, and the devil a penny they have left me, but a bare pension, and that is thirty meals a day and ten bevers[30] — a small trifle to suffice nature. O, I come of a royal parentage! My grandfather was a gammon of bacon, my grandmother a hogshead of claret wine; my godfathers were these: Peter Pickleherring and Martin Martlemas-beef.[31] O, but my godmother, she was a jolly gentlewoman, and well beloved in every good town and city; her name was Mistress Margery March-beer. Now, Faustus, thou hast heard all my progeny,[32] wilt thou bid me to supper?

Faust. No, I'll see thee hanged; thou wilt eat up all my victuals.

Glut. Then the Devil choke thee!

Faust. Choke thyself, glutton! — Who art thou — the sixth?

Sloth. I am Sloth. I was begotten on a sunny bank, where I have lain ever since; and you have done me great injury to bring me from thence. Let me be carried thither again by Gluttony and Lechery. I'll not speak another word for a king's ransom.

Faust. What are you, Mistress Minx, — the seventh and last?

Lech. Who, I, sir? I am one that loves an inch of raw mutton[33] better than an ell of fried stockfish;[34] and the first letter of my name begins with Lechery.

Luc. Away! to hell, to hell!

Exeunt the Sins.

— Now, Faustus, how dost thou like this?

Faust. O, this feeds my soul!

Luc. Tut, Faustus, in hell is all manner of delight.

Faust. O might I see hell, and return again,
How happy were I then!

Luc. Thou shalt; I will send for thee at midnight.
In meantime take this book; peruse it throughly,
And thou shalt turn thyself into what shape thou wilt.

Faust. Great thanks, mighty Lucifer!
This will I keep as chary as my life.

Luc. Farewell, Faustus, and think on the Devil.

Faust. Farewell, great Lucifer! — Come, Mephistophilis.

Exeunt omnes.

[Scene III][35]

Enter Robin *the Ostler with a book in his hand.*

Robin. O, this is admirable! Here I ha' stol'n one of Dr. Faustus' conjuring books,

[25] The *Carmen de Pulice*, probably of medieval origin, was attributed to Ovid. (Boas.)

[26] Q 1616 adds *next, like a Necke-lace I hang about her Necke.*

[27] In place of the next seven words Q 1616 reads *And then turning my selfe to a wrought Smocke do what I list.*

[28] Pair.

[29] One of you devils is doubtless.

[30] Between-meal refreshments.

[31] The feast of St. Martin (Nov. 11) "was the customary time for hanging up [salted] provisions." (Nares.)

[32] Lineage.

[33] Punning on "mutton" = wench, harlot.

[34] Salted or dried fish.

[35] An inn-yard. Q_1 places this scene, erroneously, after the chorus which opens Act IV, and immediately before the comic scene, III, ii. Q 1616

and i' faith I mean to search some circles[36] for my own use! Now will I make all the maidens in our parish dance at my pleasure, stark naked before me; and so by that means I shall see more than e'er I felt or saw yet.

Enter RALPH[37] *calling* ROBIN.

RALPH. Robin, prithee come away; there 's a gentleman tarries to have his horse, and he would have his things rubb'd and made clean. He keeps such a chafing with my mistress about it; and she has sent me to look thee out. Prithee come away.

ROBIN. Keep out, keep out, or else you are blown up, you are dismemb'red, Ralph; keep out, for I am about a roaring piece of work.

RALPH. Come, what doest thou with that same book? Thou canst not read.

ROBIN. Yes, my master and mistress shall find that I can read, he for his forehead,[38] she for her private study; she 's born to bear with me, or else my art fails.

RALPH. Why, Robin, what book is that?

ROBIN. What book! Why, the most intolerable book for conjuring that e'er was invented by any brimstone devil.

RALPH. Canst thou conjure with it?

ROBIN. I can do all these things easily with it: first, I can make thee drunk with ippocras[39] at any ta[v]ern in Europe for nothing; that 's one of my conjuring works.

RALPH. Our Master Parson says that 's nothing.

ROBIN. True, Ralph; and more, Ralph, if thou hast any mind to Nan Spit, our kitchenmaid, then turn her and wind her to thy own use, as often as thou wilt, and at midnight.

RALPH. O brave, Robin, shall I have Nan Spit, and to mine own use? On that condition I 'll feed thy devil with horsebread as long as he lives, of free cost.

ROBIN. No more, sweet Ralph; let 's go and make clean our boots, which lie foul upon our hands, and then to our conjuring in the Devil's name. *Exeunt.*

correctly places II, iii, though in an altered version; Ralph becomes Dick, a hostler, and Robin seems to be the clown of I, iv. Brooke suggests that the appearance of II, iii, and III, iii, consecutively in Q_1 "is presumably due to the fact that they were not in the original MS, but formed a supplement on separate sheets."

[36] Common with a double meaning in these plays.

[37] Old eds. *Rafe*, throughout.

[38] Innumerable jests in these plays allude to the horns which were supposed to grow in the brows of a deceived husband.

[39] A drink made of wine, sugared and spiced.

[ACT III]

Enter WAGNER, *solus* [*as* Chorus].[1]

WAGNER. Learned Faustus, to know the secrets of astronomy
Graven in the book of Jove's high firmament,
Did mount himself to scale Olympus' top,
Being seated in a chariot burning bright,
Drawn by the strength of yoky dragons'[2] necks.
[He views the clouds, the planets, and the stars,
The tropic zones, and quarters of the sky,
From the bright circle of the horned moon
Even to the height of *Primum Mobile*;[3]
And, whirling round with this circumference,
Within the concave compass of the pole,
From east to west his dragons swiftly glide
And in eight days did bring him home again.
Not long he stayed within his quiet house,
To rest his bones after his weary toil;
But new exploits do hale him out again,
And, mounted then upon a dragon's back,
That with his wings did part the subtle air,]
He now is gone to prove cosmography,
[That measures coasts and kingdoms of the earth:]
And, as I guess, will first arrive at Rome,
To see the Pope and manner of his court,
And take some part of holy Peter's feast,
That to this day is highly solemniz'd.
Exit WAGNER.

[SCENE I][4]

Enter FAUSTUS *and* MEPHISTOPHILIS.

FAUST. Having now, my good Mephistophilis,
Pass'd with delight the stately town of Trier,[5]
Environ'd round with airy mountain-tops,
With walls of flint, and deep entrenched lakes,
Not to be won by any conquering prince;
From Paris next, coasting the realm of France,
We saw the river Maine fall into Rhine,

[1] In Q_1 this speech, assigned to Wagner, and cut for the stage, comes between II, ii, and III, i. In Q 1616 it appears, incorrectly, between II, i and ii, and again (assigned to Chorus) to open Act III, with the addition of the bracketed lines.

[2] Among properties for this play Henslowe lists a dragon. Wagner suggests that Faustus may have alighted from it at the opening of III, i. But see, also, on S. D. following I, iii, 25.

[3] "The axle of the heavens, that moveth the whole firmament." (English Faust Book.)

[4] Rome. The Pope's privy-chamber.

[5] Treves.

Whose banks are set with groves of fruitful vines;
Then up to Naples, rich Campania,[6]
Whose buildings fair and gorgeous to the eye,
The streets straight forth, and pav'd with finest brick,
Quarters the town in four equivalents.
There saw we learned Maro's[7] golden tomb,
The way he cut, an English mile in length,
Thorough a rock of stone in one night's space;
From thence to Venice, Padua, and the rest,
In midst of which a sumptuous temple stands;[8]
That threats the stars with her aspiring top,
[Whose frame is paved with sundry-colored stones
And roof'd aloft with curious work in gold.]
Thus hitherto hath Faustus spent his time:
But tell me, now, what resting-place is this?
Hast thou, as erst I did command,
Conducted me within the walls of Rome?

MEPH. [I have, my Faustus; and, for proof thereof,
This is the goodly palace of the Pope;
And 'cause we are no common guests,
I choose his privy-chamber for our use.][9]

FAUST. I hope his Holiness will bid us welcome.

MEPH. [All's one, for we'll be bold with his ven'son.]
And now, my Faustus, that thou mayst perceive
What Rome containeth to delight thee with,
Know that this city stands upon seven hills
That underprops the groundwork of the same.
[Just through the midst runs flowing Tiber's stream,
With winding banks that cut it in two parts,][10]
Over the which four stately bridges lean,
That makes safe passage to each part of Rome.
Upon the bridge call'd Ponto Angelo
Erected is a castle passing strong,
Within whose walls such store of ordnance are,
And double cannons, fram'd of carved brass,
As match the days within one complete year;
Besides the gates and high pyramides,
Which Julius Cæsar brought from Africa.

FAUST. Now by the kingdoms of infernal rule,
Of Styx, Acheron, and the fiery lake
Of ever-burning Phlegethon, I swear
That I do long to see the monuments
And situation of bright-splendent Rome:
Come, therefore; let's away.

MEPH. Nay, Faustus, stay; I know you'd fain see the Pope,
And take some part of holy Peter's feast,
[11] Where thou shalt see a troop of bald-pate friars,
Whose *summum bonum* is in belly-cheer.

FAUST. Well, I am content to compass, then, some sport,
And by their folly make us merriment.
Then charm me, that I may be invisible, to do what I please,
Unseen of any whilst I stay in Rome.

[MEPHISTOPHILIS *charms him.*]

MEPH. So, Faustus; now
Do what thou wilt, thou shalt not be discerned.

Sound a sennet.[12] *Enter the* POPE *and the* CARDINAL *of* LORRAINE *to the banquet, with* Friars *attending.*

POPE. My Lord of Lorraine, wilt please you draw near?

FAUST. Fall to, and the Devil choke you an[13] you spare!

POPE. How now! Who's that which spake? — Friars, look about.

[1] FRIAR. Here's nobody, if it like your Holiness.

POPE. My Lord, here is a dainty dish was sent me from the Bishop of Milan.

FAUST. I thank you, sir. *Snatch it.*

POPE. How now! Who's that which snatch'd the meat from me? Will no man look? — My Lord, this dish was sent me from the Cardinal of Florence.

[6] The English Faust Book reads "to Campania [*i.e.*, the province] in the Kingdom of Naples." Brooke observes that Marlowe evidently took "Campania" as another name for the *city* of Naples.

[7] Virgil's. A tunnel near it was supposed to be the work of his magic.

[8] St. Mark's, at Venice; not, as Brooke suggests, a "composite structure in a nameless city." Though in the Faust Book Padua is visited and St. Anthony's there is admired, "sumptuous" occurs in the E. F. B.'s description of St. Mark's, and any great church may be said to be lofty. For "and the rest", Q 1616 misunderstandingly reads "and the East", and for "in *midst* of which" it despairingly reads "in *one* of which," another indication of its inferiority. Padua is here taken as a Venetian possession; "the rest" are the other territories of Venice. Ll. 19, 20, unquestionably genuine, are added (*i.e.*, preserved) by Q 1616.

[9] This speech, and the next line of Mephistophilis, are from Q 1616; earlier eds. replace them by actors' garbled prose.

[10] Add. Q 1616.

[11] The next seven lines are replaced in Q 1616 by an addition of 205 ll., probably by Rowley, in which Faust and Mephistophilis, disguised as cardinals, play a part in the Pope's disposition of a rival, the "Saxon Bruno."

[12] Fanfare of trumpets.

[13] If.

FAUST. You say true; I'll ha't.

[*Snatches it.*]

POPE. What, again? — My Lord, I'll drink to your Grace.

FAUST. I'll pledge your Grace.

[*Snatches the cup.*]

C. of LOR. My Lord, it may be some ghost newly crept out of purgatory, come to beg a pardon of your Holiness.

POPE. It may be so. — Friars, prepare a dirge to lay the fury of this ghost. — Once again, my Lord, fall to.

The POPE *crosseth himself.*

FAUST. What, are you crossing of yourself? Well, use that trick no more, I would advise you. — (*Cross again.*) Well, there's the second time. Aware the third, I give you fair warning.

Cross again, and FAUSTUS *hits him a box of the ear; and they all run away.*

Come on, Mephistophilis, what shall we do?

MEPH. Nay, I know not. We shall be curs'd with bell, book, and candle.

FAUST. How! bell, book, and candle, — candle, book, and bell,
Forward and backward to curse Faustus to hell!
Anon you shall hear a hog grunt, a calf bleat, and an ass bray,
Because it is Saint Peter's holiday.

Re-enter all the Friars *to sing the dirge.*

[1] FRIAR. Come, brethren, let's about our business with good devotion.

Sing this:

Cursed be he that stole away his Holiness' meat from the table! *Maledicat Dominus!* [14]

Cursed be he that struck his Holiness a blow on the face! *Maledicat Dominus!*

Cursed be he that took Friar Sandelo a blow on the pate! *Maledicat Dominus!*

Cursed be he that disturbeth our holy dirge! *Maledicat Dominus!*

Cursed be he that took away his Holiness' wine! *Maledicat Dominus! Et omnes sancti!* [15] *Amen!*

[MEPHISTOPHILIS *and* FAUSTUS] *beat the* Friars, *and fling fireworks among them, and so exeunt.*

[14] May the Lord curse him.

[15] And all the Saints.

[SCENE II] [16]

Enter ROBIN *and* RALPH [17] *with a silver goblet.*

ROBIN. Come, Ralph, did not I tell thee we were for ever made by this Doctor Faustus book? *Ecce signum*, here's a simple purchase [18] for horsekeepers; our horses shall eat no hay as long as this lasts.

Enter the Vintner.

RALPH. But, Robin, here comes the vintner.

ROBIN. Hush! I'll gull him supernaturally. — Drawer, I hope all is paid; God be with you. — Come, Ralph.

VINT. Soft, sir; a word with you. I must yet have a goblet paid from you, ere you go.

ROBIN. I, a goblet, Ralph; I, a goblet! I scorn you, and you are but a &c.[19] I, a goblet! Search me.

VINT. I mean so, sir, with your favor.

[*Searches him.*]

ROBIN. How say you now?

VINT. I must say somewhat to your fellow. You, sir!

RALPH. Me, sir! me, sir! Search your fill. [Vintner *searches him.*] Now, sir, you may be ashamed to burden honest men with a matter of truth.[20]

VINT. Well, t' one of you hath this goblet about you.

ROBIN. [*aside*] You lie, drawer; 't is afore me. — Sirrah you, I'll teach ye to impeach honest men; stand by; I'll scour you for a goblet! Stand aside you had best, I charge you in the name of Belzebub.—[*aside to* RALPH] Look to the goblet, Ralph.

VINT. What mean you, sirrah?

ROBIN. I'll tell you what I mean. (*He reads* [*from the book.*]) *Sanctobulorum, Periphrasticon* — Nay, I'll tickle you, vintner. — [*aside to* RALPH] Look to the goblet, Ralph. — [*Reads.*] *Polypragmos Belseborams framanto pacostiphos tostu, Mephistophilis, etc.*

Enter MEPHISTOPHILIS, *sets squibs at their backs,* [*and then exit*].[21] *They run about.*

[16] An inn. In Q 1616 this scene, as here, follows III, i. In Q_1 the order is III, i; chorus to IV; II, iii; III, ii. The scene in Q 1616 differs widely.

[17] Old eds. *Rafe* throughout.

[18] Piece of loot.

[19] The low comedian was expected to supply a string of racy invectives.

[20] A question of honesty.

[21] Add. Dyce, in view of Mephistophilis's reentry. The double entrance indicates textual corruption. The squibs were "an afterthought." (Simpson.)

VINT. *O nomine Domine!* [22] what mean'st thou, Robin? Thou hast no goblet.

RALPH. *Peccatum peccatorum!* [23] Here's thy goblet, good vintner.

ROBIN. *Misericordia pro nobis!* [24] What shall I do? Good Devil, forgive me now, and I'll never rob thy library more.

Re-enter to them MEPHISTOPHILIS.

MEPH. Vanish, villains!
Th' one like an ape, another like a bear, the third an ass, for doing this enterprise. — [25]
[*Exit* Vintner.]
Monarch of hell, under whose black survey
Great potentates do kneel with awful fear,
Upon whose altars thousand souls do lie,
How am I vexed with these villains' charms!
From Constantinople am I hither come
Only for pleasure of these damned slaves.

ROBIN. How? from Constantinople? You have had a great journey. Will you take sixpence in your purse to pay for your supper, and be gone?

MEPH. Well, villains, for your presumption, I transform thee into an ape, and thee into a dog; and so, begone! *Exit.*

ROBIN. How, into an ape? That's brave! I'll have fine sport with the boys. I'll get nuts and apples enow.

RALPH. And I must be a dog.

ROBIN. I' faith thy head will never be out of the pottage pot. *Exeunt.*

[ACT IV]

Enter Chorus.[26]

CHORUS. When Faustus had with pleasure ta'en the view
Of rarest things and royal courts of kings,
He stay'd his course and so returned home;
Where such as bear his absence but with grief,
I mean his friends and near'st companions,
Did gratulate his safety with kind words,
And in their conference of what befell,
Touching his journey through the world and air,
They put forth questions of astrology,
Which Faustus answer'd with such learned skill
As they admir'd and wond'red at his wit.
Now is his fame spread forth in every land;
Amongst the rest the Emperor is one;
Carolus the Fifth, at whose palace now
Faustus is feasted 'mongst his noblemen.
What there he did in trial of his art,
I leave untold — your eyes shall see perform'd.
Exit.

[SCENE I] [27]

Enter EMPEROR, FAUSTUS, [MEPHISTOPHILIS,] *and a* Knight, *with attendants.*

EMP. Master Doctor Faustus, I have heard strange report of thy knowledge in the black art, how that none in my empire nor in the whole world can compare with thee for the rare effects of magic; they say thou hast a familiar spirit, by whom thou canst accomplish what thou list. This, therefore, is my request, that thou let me see some proof of thy skill, that mine eyes may be witnesses to confirm what mine ears have heard reported; and here I swear to thee, by the honor of mine imperial crown, that, whatever thou doest, thou shalt be no ways prejudiced or endamaged.

KNIGHT. (*aside*) I' faith he looks much like a conjuror.

FAUST. My gracious Sovereign, though I must confess myself far inferior to the report men have published, and nothing answerable [28] to the honor of your imperial Majesty, yet for that love and duty binds me thereunto, I am content to do whatsoever your Majesty shall command me.

EMP. Then, Doctor Faustus, mark what I shall say.
As I was sometime solitary set
Within my closet, sundry thoughts arose
About the honor of mine ancestors,
How they had won by prowess such exploits,
Got such riches, subdued so many kingdoms,
As we that do succeed, or they that shall
Hereafter possess our throne, shall
(I fear me) ne'er attain to that degree
Of high renown and great authority;
Amongst which kings is Alexander the Great,
Chief spectacle of the world's preëminence,

[22] The Vintner's imperfect Latin for "in the name of the Lord."
[23] Sin of sins.
[24] Mercy on us.
[25] Mod. eds. omit this speech; it may be an alternative ending for the scene. The double transformation indicates corruption.
[26] Q 1616 om. this speech; in Q_1 it appears, misplaced, after III, i.
[27] A room in the imperial palace (at Innsbruck). Q 1616 rewrites and expands this scene, which it prefaces with another at the Emperor's court.
[28] In no respect adequate.

The bright shining of whose glorious acts
Lightens the world with his[29] reflecting beams,
As, when I heard but motion[30] made of him,
It grieves my soul I never saw the man.
If, therefore, thou by cunning of thine art
Canst raise this man from hollow vaults below,
Where lies entomb'd this famous conqueror,
And bring with him his beauteous paramour,
Both in their right shapes, gesture, and attire
They us'd to wear during their time of life,
Thou shalt both satisfy my just desire
And give me cause to praise thee whilst I live.

FAUST. My gracious Lord, I am ready to accomplish your request so far forth as by art, and power of my spirit, I am able to perform.

KNIGHT. (*aside*) I' faith that 's just nothing at all.

FAUST. But, if it like your Grace, it is not in my ability to present before your eyes the true substantial bodies of those two deceased princes, which long since are consumed to dust.

KNIGHT. (*aside*) Ay, marry, Master Doctor, now there 's a sign of grace in you, when you will confess the truth.

FAUST. But such spirits as can lively resemble Alexander and his paramour shall appear before your Grace in that manner that they best liv'd in, in their most flourishing estate; which I doubt not shall sufficiently content your imperial Majesty.

EMP. Go to, Master Doctor; let me see them presently.[31]

KNIGHT. Do you hear, Master Doctor? You bring Alexander and his paramour before the Emperor!

FAUST. How then, sir?

KNIGHT. I' faith that 's as true as Diana turn'd me to a stag!

FAUST. No, sir, but when Actæon died, he left the horns for you. Mephistophilis, begone. *Exit* MEPHISTOPHILIS.

KNIGHT. Nay, an you go to conjuring, I 'll be gone. *Exit* Knight.

FAUST. I 'll meet with you anon for interrupting me so. — Here they are, my gracious Lord.

Re-enter MEPHISTOPHILIS *with* [Spirits *in the shapes of*] ALEXANDER *and his* Paramour.

EMP. Master Doctor, I heard this lady while she liv'd had a wart or mole in her neck. How shall I know whether it be so or no?

FAUST. Your Highness may boldly go and see. [*Exeunt* Spirits.]

EMP. Sure these are no spirits, but the true substantial bodies of those two deceased princes.

FAUST. Will 't please your Highness now to send for the knight that was so pleasant with me here of late?

EMP. One of you call him forth. [*Exit* Attendant.]

Re-enter the Knight *with a pair of horns on his head.*

How now, Sir Knight! Why I had thought thou hadst been a bachelor; but now I see thou hast a wife, that not only gives thee horns, but makes thee wear them. Feel on thy head.

KNIGHT. Thou damned wretch and execrable dog,
Bred in the concave of some monstrous rock,
How dar'st thou thus abuse a gentleman?
Villain, I say, undo what thou hast done!

FAUST. O, not so fast, sir; there 's no haste; but, good, are you rememb'red how you crossed me in my conference with the Emperor? I think I have met with you for it.

EMP. Good Master Doctor, at my entreaty release him; he hath done penance sufficient.

FAUST. My gracious Lord, not so much for the injury he off'red me here in your presence, as to delight you with some mirth, hath Faustus worthily requited this injurious knight; which being all I desire, I am content to release him of his horns; and, Sir Knight, hereafter speak well of scholars. — Mephistophilis, transform him straight. [MEPHISTOPHILIS *removes the horns.*] Now, my good Lord, having done my duty I humbly take my leave.

EMP. Farewell, Master Doctor; yet, ere you go,
Expect from me a bounteous reward. [*Exeunt.*]

[SCENE II][32]

[*Enter* FAUSTUS *and* MEPHISTOPHILIS.]

FAUST. Now, Mephistophilis, the restless course
That Time doth run with calm and silent foot,
Short'ning my days and thread of vital life,
Calls for the payment of my latest years;

[29] Its. [30] Mention. [31] At once.

[32] A green; afterwards Faustus's house. The wreckage of several scenes probably confronts us here; most of this is rubbish, but note the Marlovian column still standing in ll. 45–50. Two additional scenes precede this in Q 1616, which reduces our Sc. ii.

Therefore, sweet Mephistophilis, let us
Make haste to Wittenberg.

MEPH. What, will you go on horseback or on foot?

FAUST. Nay, till I am past this fair and pleasant green,
I'll walk on foot.

Enter a Horse-Courser.

HORSE-C. I have been all this day seeking one Master Fustian; mass, see where he is! — God save you, Master Doctor!

FAUST. What, horse-courser! You are well met.

HORSE-C. Do you hear, sir? I have brought you forty dollars for your horse.

FAUST. I cannot sell him so; if thou lik'st him for fifty, take him.

HORSE-C. Alas, sir, I have no more. — I pray you speak for me.

MEPH. I pray you let him have him; he is an honest fellow, and he has a great charge, neither wife nor child.

FAUST. Well, come, give me your money. [Horse-Courser *gives* FAUSTUS *the money*.] My boy will deliver him to you. But I must tell you one thing before you have him: ride him not into the water at any hand.

HORSE-C. Why, sir, will he not drink of all waters?

FAUST. O yes, he will drink of all waters, but ride him not into the water; ride him over hedge or ditch, or where thou wilt, but not into the water.

HORSE-C. Well, sir. — [*aside*] Now am I made man for ever. I'll not leave my horse for forty.[33] If he had but the quality of hey ding ding, hey ding ding, I'd make a brave living on him; he has a buttock as slick as an eel. — Well, God buy, sir; your boy will deliver him me. But hark ye, sir; if my horse be sick or ill at ease, if I bring his water to you, you'll tell me what it is?

Exit Horse-Courser.

FAUST. Away, you villain; what, dost think I am a horse-doctor? —
What art thou, Faustus, but a man condemn'd to die?
Thy fatal time doth draw to final end;
Despair doth drive distrust unto my thoughts.
Confound these passions with a quiet sleep.
Tush, Christ did call the thief upon the cross;
Then rest thee, Faustus, quiet in conceit.

Sleep in his chair.

[33] *I.e.*, any number of others. (Boas.)

Re-enter Horse-Courser, *all wet, crying*.

HORSE-C. Alas, alas! Doctor Fustian, quotha? Mass, Doctor Lopus[34] was never such a doctor. Has given me a purgation has purg'd me of forty dollars; I shall never see them more. But yet, like an ass as I was, I would not be ruled by him, for he bade me I should ride him into no water. Now I, thinking my horse had had some rare quality that he would not have had me known of, I, like a vent'rous youth, rid him into the deep pond at the town's end. I was no sooner in the middle of the pond, but my horse vanish'd away, and I sat upon a bottle[35] of hay, never so near drowning in my life. But I'll seek out my Doctor, and have my forty dollars again, or I'll make it the dearest horse — O, yonder is his snipper-snapper.[36] — Do you hear? You hey-pass,[37] where's your master?

MEPH. Why, sir, what would you? You cannot speak with him.

HORSE-C. But I will speak with him.

MEPH. Why, he's fast asleep. Come some other time.

HORSE-C. I'll speak with him now, or I'll break his glass windows about his ears.

MEPH. I tell thee he has not slept this eight nights.

HORSE-C. An he have not slept this eight weeks, I'll speak with him.

MEPH. See where he is, fast asleep.

HORSE-C. Ay, this is he. — God save ye, Master Doctor! Master Doctor, Master Doctor Fustian! — Forty dollars, forty dollars for a bottle of hay!

MEPH. Why, thou seest he hears thee not.

HORSE-C. So ho, ho! — so ho, ho! (*Holla in his ear.*) No, will you not wake? I'll make you wake ere I go. (*Pull him by the leg, and pull it away.*) Alas, I am undone! What shall I do?

FAUST. O my leg, my leg! Help, Mephistophilis! Call the officers. My leg, my leg!

MEPH. Come, villain, to the constable.

HORSE-C. O Lord, sir, let me go, and I'll give you forty dollars more.

MEPH. Where be they?

HORSE-C. I have none about me. Come to my ostry[38] and I'll give them you.

[34] Queen Elizabeth's physician, Roderigo Lopez, a Spanish Jew, charged with conspiring to poison her and executed in 1594 — nearly a year after Marlowe's death!

[35] Truss.

[36] Whippersnapper.

[37] Juggler, since this was his cry. (Dyce, Ward.)

[38] Hostelry, inn.

MEPH. Begone quickly.

Horse-Courser runs away.

FAUST. What, is he gone? Farewell he! Faustus has his leg again, and the horse-courser, I take it, a bottle of hay for his labor. Well, this trick shall cost him forty dollars more.

Enter WAGNER.

How now, Wagner, what's the news with thee?

WAG. Sir, the Duke of Vanholt doth earnestly entreat your company.

FAUST. The Duke of Vanholt! an honorable gentleman, to whom I must be no niggard of my cunning. Come, Mephistophilis, let's away to him. *Exeunt.*

[SCENE III] [39]

Enter [40] *the* DUKE [*of* VANHOLT], *the* DUCHESS, [FAUSTUS, *and* MEPHISTOPHILIS.]

DUKE. Believe me, Master Doctor, this merriment hath much pleased me.

FAUST. My gracious Lord, I am glad it contents you so well. — But it may be, madam, you take no delight in this. I have heard that great-bellied women do long for some dainties or other. What is it, madam? Tell me, and you shall have it.

DUCHESS. Thanks, good Master Doctor; and for I see your courteous intent to pleasure me, I will not hide from you the thing my heart desires; and were it now summer, as it is January and the dead time of the winter, I would desire no better meat than a dish of ripe grapes.

FAUST. Alas, madam, that's nothing. Mephistophilis, begone. (*Exit* MEPHISTOPHILIS.) Were it a greater thing than this, so it would content you, you should have it.

Re-enter MEPHISTOPHILIS *with the grapes.*

Here they be, madam; wilt please you taste on them?

DUKE. Believe me, Master Doctor, this makes me wonder above the rest, that being in the dead time of winter and in the month of January, how you should come by these grapes.

FAUST. If it like your Grace, the year is divided into two circles over the whole world, that, when it is here winter with us, in the contrary circle it is summer with them, as in India, Saba,[41] and farther countries in the East; and by means of a swift spirit that I have, I had them brought hither, as ye see. — How do you like them, madam; be they good?

DUCHESS. Believe me, Master Doctor, they be the best grapes that e'er I tasted in my life before.

FAUST. I am glad they content you so, madam.

DUKE. Come, madam, let us in, where you must well reward this learned man for the great kindness he hath show'd to you.

DUCHESS. And so I will, my Lord; and, whilst I live, rest beholding for this courtesy.

FAUST. I humbly thank your Grace.

DUKE. Come, Master Doctor, follow us and receive your reward. *Exeunt.*

[ACT V — SCENE I] [1]

Enter WAGNER, *solus.*

WAG. I think my master means to die shortly,
For he hath given to me all his goods;
And yet, methinks if that death were near,
He would not banquet and carouse and swill
Amongst the students, as even now he doth,
Who are at supper with such belly-cheer
As Wagner ne'er beheld in all his life.
See where they come! Belike the feast is ended. [*Exit.*]

Enter FAUSTUS, *with two or three* Scholars [*and* MEPHISTOPHILIS].

1 SCHOL. Master Doctor Faustus, since our conference about fair ladies, which was the beautiful'st in all the world,[2] we have determined with ourselves that Helen of Greece was the admirablest lady that ever lived. Therefore, Master Doctor, if you will do us that favor, as to let us see that peerless dame of Greece, whom all the world admires for majesty, we should think ourselves much beholding unto you.

FAUST. Gentlemen,
For that I know your friendship is unfeigned,
And Faustus' custom is not to deny

[39] A residence of the Duke of "Vanholt." In Q 1616 another comic scene, with the horse-courser, precedes this. Sc. iii is expanded in Q 1616.

[40] Q₁ adds *to them*, indicating corruption, since Faust and Mephistophilis have just left the stage.

[41] Sheba.

[1] Wittenberg. A room in Faustus's house.

[2] Simpson notes the survival of a Marlovian line, beginning "which", indicating that this prose is an adapter's work.

The just requests of those that wish him well,
You shall behold that peerless dame of Greece,
No otherways for pomp and majesty
Than when Sir Paris cross'd the seas with her
And brought the spoils to rich Dardania.
Be silent, then ; for danger is in words.

Music sounds, and HELEN *passeth over the stage.*

2 SCHOL. Too simple is my wit to tell her praise,
Whom all the world admires for majesty.

3 SCHOL. No marvel though the angry Greeks pursu'd
With ten years' war the rape [3] of such a queen,
Whose heavenly beauty passeth all compare.

1 SCHOL. Since we have seen the pride of Nature's works
And only paragon of excellence,
Let us depart ; and for this glorious deed
Happy and blest be Faustus evermore.

FAUSTUS. Gentlemen, farewell ; the same I wish to you.

Exeunt Scholars.

Enter an Old Man.

OLD MAN. Ah, Doctor Faustus, that I might prevail
To guide thy steps unto the way of life,
By which sweet path thou mayst attain the goal
That shall conduct thee to celestial rest !
Break heart, drop blood, and mingle it with tears,
Tears falling from repentant heaviness
Of thy most vild and loathsome filthiness,
The stench whereof corrupts the inward soul
With such flagitious crimes of heinous sins
As no commiseration may expel,
But mercy, Faustus, of thy Savior sweet,
Whose blood alone must wash away thy guilt.

FAUST. Where art thou, Faustus? Wretch, what hast thou done?
Damn'd art thou, Faustus, damn'd ; despair and die !
Hell calls for right, and with a roaring voice
Says " Faustus, come ; thine hour is [almost] [4] come ! "
And Faustus [now] [4] will come to do thee right.

MEPHISTOPHILIS *gives him a dagger.*

OLD MAN. Ah, stay, good Faustus, stay thy desperate steps !
I see an angel hovers o'er thy head,
And, with a vial full of precious grace,
Offers to pour the same into thy soul ;
Then call for mercy, and avoid despair.

FAUST. Ah, my sweet friend, I feel
Thy words do comfort my distressed soul.
Leave me awhile to ponder on my sins.

OLD MAN. I go, sweet Faustus, but with heavy cheer,
Fearing the ruin of thy hopeless soul. [*Exit.*]

FAUST. Accursed Faustus, where is mercy now?
I do repent, and yet I do despair ;
Hell strives with grace for conquest in my breast.
What shall I do to shun the snares of death?

MEPH. Thou traitor, Faustus, I arrest thy soul
For disobedience to my sovereign lord ;
Revolt, or I 'll in piecemeal tear thy flesh.

FAUST. [I do repent I e'er offended him ;] [5]
Sweet Mephistophilis, entreat thy lord
To pardon my unjust presumption,
And with my blood again I will confirm
My former vow I made to Lucifer.

MEPH. Do it now then quickly, with unfeigned heart,
Lest danger do attend thy drift.

FAUST. Torment, sweet friend, that base and crooked age [6]
That durst dissuade me from my Lucifer,
With greatest torments that our hell affords.

MEPH. His faith is great ; I cannot touch his soul ;
But what I may afflict his body with
I will attempt, which is but little worth.

FAUST. One thing, good servant, let me crave of thee,
To glut the longing of my heart's desire,
That I might have unto my paramour
That heavenly Helen, which I saw of late,
Whose sweet embracings may extinguish clean
These thoughts that do dissuade me from my vow,
And keep mine oath I made to Lucifer.

MEPH. Faustus, this or what else thou shalt desire
Shall be perform'd in twinkling of an eye.

Re-enter HELEN.

FAUST. Was this the face that launch'd a thousand ships,
And burnt the topless [7] towers of Ilium?

[3] Capture.

[4] Add. Q 1616.

[5] Add. Q 1616.

[6] Old man.

[7] Incomparably lofty.

Sweet Helen, make me immortal with a kiss. —
Her lips sucks forth my soul; see where it flies! —
Come, Helen, come, give me my soul again.
Here will I dwell, for Heaven be in these lips,
And all is dross that is not Helena.
I will be Paris, and for love of thee,
Instead of Troy shall Wittenberg be sack'd;
And I will combat with weak Menelaus,
And wear thy colors on my plumed crest;
Yea, I will wound Achilles in the heel,
And then return to Helen for a kiss.
O, thou art fairer than the evening air
Clad in the beauty of a thousand stars;
Brighter art thou than flaming Jupiter
When he appear'd to hapless Semele;
More lovely than the monarch of the sky
In wanton Arethusa's azur'd arms;[8]
And none but thou shalt be my paramour.

Re-enter Old Man.[9] *Exeunt* [*the others*].

Old Man. Accursed Faustus, miserable man,
That from thy soul exclud'st the grace of Heaven,
And fliest the throne of his tribunal seat!

Enter the Devils.

Satan begins to sift[10] me with his pride.[11]
As in this furnace God shall try my faith,
My faith, vile hell, shall triumph over thee.
Ambitious fiends, see how the Heavens smiles
At your repulse, and laughs your state to scorn!
Hence, hell! for hence I fly unto my God.
Exeunt.

[Scene II][12]

Enter Faustus *with the* Scholars.

Faust. Ah, gentlemen!

1 Schol. What ails Faustus?

Faust. Ah, my sweet chamber-fellow, had I lived with thee, then had I lived still! but now I die eternally. Look, comes he not? comes he not?

2 Schol. What means Faustus?

3 Schol. Belike he is grown into some sickness by being oversolitary.

1 Schol. If it be so, we'll have physicians to cure him. — 'T is but a surfeit; never fear, man.

Faust. A surfeit of deadly sin that hath damn'd both body and soul.

2 Schol. Yet, Faustus, look up to Heaven; remember God's mercies are infinite.

Faust. But Faustus' offence can ne'er be pardoned; the serpent that tempted Eve may be sav'd, but not Faustus. Ah, gentlemen, hear me with patience, and tremble not at my speeches. Though my heart pants and quivers to remember that I have been a student here these thirty years, oh, would I had never seen Wittenberg, never read book! And what wonders I have done, all Germany can witness, yea, all the world; for which Faustus hath lost both Germany and the world, yea, Heaven itself, Heaven, the seat of God, the throne of the blessed, the kingdom of joy; and must remain in hell for ever, hell, ah, hell, for ever! Sweet friends, what shall become of Faustus, being in hell for ever?

3 Schol. Yet, Faustus, call on God.

Faust. On God, whom Faustus hath abjur'd! on God, whom Faustus hath blasphemed! Ah, my God, I would weep, but the Devil draws in my tears. Gush forth blood instead of tears! Yea, life and soul — Oh, he stays my tongue! I would lift up my hands, but see, they hold them, they hold them!

All. Who, Faustus?

Faust. Lucifer and Mephistophilis.[13] Ah, gentlemen! I gave them my soul for my cunning.[14]

All. God forbid!

Faust. God forbade it indeed; but Faustus hath done it. For vain pleasure of four-and-twenty years hath Faustus lost eternal joy and felicity. I writ them a bill with mine own blood; the date is expired, the time will come, and he will fetch me.

1 Schol. Why did not Faustus tell us of this before, that divines might have prayed for thee?

Faust. Oft have I thought to have done so; but the Devil threat'ned to tear me in pieces if I nam'd God; to fetch both body and soul if I once gave ear to divinity; and

[8] No such episode is known to classical mythology. (Boas.) Brooke suggests that *Arethusa* may be a slip (or possibly an intentional alteration) for Leucothoe, beloved by Apollo. (See Ovid's *Metamorphoses*, IV, 230, ff.)

[9] Om. Q 1616; in Q_1 placed before l. 101.

[10] Cf. *Luke*, xxii, 31.

[11] Display (of power).

[12] The same.

[13] In Q 1616 Lucifer, Belzebub, and Mephistophilis open the scene, and the last speaks twice in an interpolation of 48 ll., which comes after l. 77.

[14] Knowledge.

now 't is too late. Gentlemen, away! lest you perish with me.

2 SCHOL. Oh, what shall we do to [save] [15] Faustus?

FAUST. Talk not of me, but save yourselves, and depart.

3 SCHOL. God will strengthen me. I will stay with Faustus.

1 SCHOL. Tempt not God, sweet friend; but let us into the next room, and there pray for him.

FAUST. Ay, pray for me, pray for me! and what noise soever ye hear come not unto me, for nothing can rescue me.

2 SCHOL. Pray thou, and we will pray that God may have mercy upon thee.

FAUST. Gentlemen, farewell. If I live till morning I'll visit you; if not, Faustus is gone to hell.

ALL. Faustus, farewell!

Exeunt Scholars. *The clock strikes eleven.*

FAUST. Ah, Faustus,
Now hast thou but one bare hour to live,
And then thou must be damn'd perpetually!
Stand still, you ever-moving spheres of Heaven,
That time may cease, and midnight never come;
Fair Nature's eye, rise, rise again and make
Perpetual day; or let this hour be but
A year, a month, a week, a natural day,
That Faustus may repent and save his soul!
O lente, lente, currite noctis equi! [16]
The stars move still, [17] time runs, the clock will strike,
The Devil will come, and Faustus must be damn'd.
O, I'll leap up to my God! Who pulls me down?
See, see where Christ's blood streams in the firmament!
One drop would save my soul — half a drop! ah, my Christ! —
Ah, rend not my heart for naming of my Christ! —
Yet will I call on him! — O, spare me, Lucifer! —
Where is it now? 'T is gone; and see where God
Stretcheth out his arm, and bends his ireful brows! —
Mountain and hills, come, come and fall on me,
And hide me from the heavy wrath of God!
No! no! —
Then will I headlong run into the earth! —
Earth, gape! — O no, it will not harbor me! —
You stars that reign'd at my nativity,
Whose influence hath allotted death and hell,
Now draw up Faustus like a foggy mist
Into the entrails of yon lab'ring cloud,
That when you vomit forth into the air,
My limbs may issue from their smoky mouths, [18]
So [19] that my soul may but ascend to Heaven.

The watch strikes.

Ah, half the hour is past! 'T will all be past anon!
O God,
If thou wilt not have mercy on my soul,
Yet for Christ's sake, whose blood hath ransom'd me,
Impose some end to my incessant pain;
Let Faustus live in hell a thousand years,
A hundred thousand, and at last be sav'd! —
O, no end is limited to damned souls!
Why wert thou not a creature wanting soul?
Or why is this immortal that thou hast?
Ah, Pythagoras' metempsychosis! were that true,
This soul should fly from me, and I be chang'd
Unto some brutish beast! All beasts are happy,
For, when they die,
Their souls are soon dissolv'd in elements;
But mine must live, still to be plagu'd in hell.
Curs'd be the parents that engend'red me!
No, Faustus, curse thyself, curse Lucifer,
That hath depriv'd thee of the joys of Heaven.

The clock striketh twelve.

O, it strikes, it strikes! Now, body, turn to air,
Or Lucifer will bear thee quick to hell!

Thunder and lightning.

O soul, be chang'd into little water-drops,
And fall into the ocean — ne'er be found! —
My God, my God, look not so fierce on me!

[15] Add. Q 1616.

[16] Run slowly, slowly, steeds of the night. (Ovid, *Amores*, I, xiii, 40.)

[17] Unceasingly.

[18] Brooke, calling attention to the censor's mutilation of this soliloquy in Q 1616, and to the actors' unmetrical insertions in Q 1, suggests that ll. 106, 107, may have stood in place of the "doubtless histrionic" l. 99. "Their dislocation may have been occasioned by the fact that originally each movement of the invocation ended [with l. 108]."

[19] Provided that.

Enter Devils.

Adders and serpents, let me breathe awhile!
Ugly hell, gape not! — Come not, Lucifer! —
I'll burn my books! — Ah, Mephistophilis! [20]
Exeunt [Devils] *with him.*

Enter Chorus.

CHO. Cut is the branch that might have grown full straight,
And burned is Apollo's laurel bough,
That sometime [21] grew within this learned man.
Faustus is gone; regard his hellish fall,
Whose fiendful fortune may exhort the wise
Only to wonder at unlawful things,
Whose deepness doth entice such forward wits
To practise more than heavenly power permits.
[*Exit.*]

Terminat hora diem; terminat author opus.[22]

[20] Q 1616 adds 18 lines, in which the scholars discover Faustus's dismembered body.

[21] Formerly.

[22] The hour ends the day; the author ends his work.

lacking in humility & greedy for the satisfaction

struggle between forces of good & evil for the soul of a representative man

ascribes his downfall in part to his learning

—

to embody the new inquiring & aspiring spirit of the age — recognition of where it could lead

—

conflict between slavery to demonic power and spiritual freedom

"The God thou serv'st is thine own appetite"

exultant individualism & despairing fatalism

middle section — slowly degrading acts —

→ mind upon verge of dissolution is given over to pure fear — absorbed by horror of doom — soul disintegrates

Bussy D'Ambois:

A TRAGEDIE:

As it hath been often Acted with great Applause.

Being much corrected and amended by the Author before his death,

LONDON:
Printed by *A. N.* for Robert Lunne.
1641.

INTRODUCTORY NOTE

Chapman's most famous play was acted, according to the title page of the first edition, by the Boys of St. Paul's. Since that company disappears in 1606, since a leap year is indicated by I, ii, 85, and since allusions to Elizabeth and to the new knights are evidently subsequent to the accession of James, 1604 seems probable for the date of composition. The play is one of a group which Chapman founded on recent French history. Here, as elsewhere, the inspiration of Marlowe is apparent, for some of the same characters appear in *The Massacre at Paris*. Nor is Bussy, with his reckless individualism and romantic extravagance, far removed from Marlowe's aspiring heroes.

Extant accounts of this intrepid chevalier and his spectacular end appeared only after the play had been published; the precise sources of Chapman's information remain unknown. Louis de Clermont d'Amboise, Seigneur de Bussy, was born in 1549 of a noble house. At a tender age he won military distinction, during the massacre of St. Bartholomew murdered a Huguenot cousin with whom he had a lawsuit, in the civil wars was repeatedly wounded, and became withal a brilliant figure at court, the lover of Marguerite de Valois, and a colonel in the service of the Duc d'Anjou, who stood next to Henry III in the succession. This prince, the Machiavellian Monsieur of our play, finally broke with Bussy, whom he had made governor of Anjou, and told the King of his intrigue with Françoise de Maridort. Henry at once betrayed him to her husband, Charles de Chambes, Comte de Montsoreau, who forced her to make an assignation with Bussy on the night of August 15, 1579, when with an overwhelming party the Count attacked and killed him. Though their agreement may be fortuitous, it is possible that Chapman and Dumas Père (in his *La Dame de Montsoreau*) derived from some common source their departure from the historical facts as we know them. Both make Monsieur the direct informant of the Count, and motivate the former's treachery by ascribing to him an unsuccessful passion for the Countess.

Though this is his earliest surviving tragedy, Chapman surpasses in his structural treatment of these materials the epic method of all save the last of Marlowe's important plays. Characterization, except for the hero, is inadequate; but the plot is dramatically conceived, and the play abounds in effective situations. Chapman had not observed in vain the technical advances made by Shakespeare. He was also influenced, like all the Elizabethan tragic writers, by the plays of Seneca, most notably in the employment of the Messenger and the Ghost, and (by his *Hercules Oetaeus*) in the handling of Bussy's death. It is, of course, Bussy as an acting rôle that makes the play. His Titanic energy, though not expressed in poetry equal to Marlowe's, is reminiscent of the heroes of the earlier dramatist, but is more thoroughly worked up in terms of action. And his end is genuinely moving, because he is more than a mere swordsman. The sceptical and stoical temper of Chapman gives Bussy a philosophy of self-reliance: once again we look on while Fate grinds the individual into less than dust.

The play may well have been written, as Professor Parrott thinks, for the Children at the Blackfriars, and been carried to the Paul's Boys when Kirkham went over to them in 1605. From the prologue in the Quarto of 1641 we learn that the famous Nat Field had played the title rôle, very likely for the Queen's Revels at Whitefriars in 1609–1612. It was afterwards revived by the King's Men, evidently in competition with a rival company; it was acted by them at least as late as 1634, when there was a performance at court. The surviving prologue was presumably written for it. The eminent Restoration tragedian, Charles Hart, had much success as Bussy; and in 1691 the play was again revived in an adaptation by Tom Durfey.

The standard edition of Chapman's plays is that of T. M. Parrott (1910). This tragedy has also been edited, along with its inferior sequel, *The Revenge of Bussy d'Ambois*, by F. S. Boas (1905). With a number of additions and corrections from the first edition, the Quarto of 1607 (reissued 1608), the present text is based on that of the Quarto of 1641 (reissued 1646 and 1657), which was "much corrected and amended by the author before his death."

BUSSY D'AMBOIS

BY

GEORGE CHAPMAN

[DRAMATIS PERSONAE

HENRY III, King of France.
MONSIEUR,[1] his brother.
DUKE OF GUISE.[2]
COUNT OF MONTSURRY.
BUSSY D'AMBOIS.
BARRISOR, L'ANOU, PYRHOT, } courtiers; enemies to D'Ambois.
BRISAC, MELYNELL, } courtiers; friends to D'Ambois.
BEAUMOND, an attendant on King Henry.
FRIAR COMOLET.
MAFFÉ, steward to Monsieur.
NUNTIUS.
Murderers.
BEHEMOTH, CARTOPHYLAX, } spirits.
UMBRA OF FRIAR.

ELENOR, Duchess of Guise.
TAMYRA, Countess of Montsurry.
BEAUPRÉ, niece to Elenor.
ANNABELLE, maid to Elenor.
PERO, maid to Tamyra.
CHARLOTTE, maid to Beaupré.
PYRA, a court lady.

Courtiers, Ladies, Pages, Servants, Spirits, etc.

THE SCENE — *Paris*.]

PROLOGUE [3]

NOT out of confidence that none but we [4]
Are able to present this tragedy,
Not out of envy at the grace of late
It did receive, nor yet to derogate
From their deserts who [5] give out boldly that
They move with equal feet on the same flat;
Neither for all nor any of such ends
We offer it, gracious and noble friends,
To your review; we, far from emulation
And (charitably judge) from imitation,
With this work entertain you, a piece known
And still believ'd in Court to be our own.
To quit our claim, doubting our right or merit,
Would argue in us poverty of spirit
Which we must not subscribe to. Field [6] is gone,
Whose action first did give it name, and one [7]
Who came the nearest to him is deni'd
By his gray beard to show the height and pride
Of D'Ambois' youth and bravery; yet to hold
Our title still afoot, and not grow cold
By giving it o'er, a third man [8] with his best
Of care and pains defends our interest;
As Richard [9] he was lik'd, nor do we fear
In personating D'Ambois he 'll appear
To faint, or go less, so [10] your free consent,
As heretofore, give him encouragement.

[1] A title given to the next younger brother of the King of France. This Duke of Anjou is the same prince as the Duke of Alençon who courted Queen Elizabeth.
[2] The great Catholic leader in the civil wars.
[3] Probably not by Chapman. It first appears in Q 1641.
[4] The King's Men.
[5] Some rival company.
[6] Formerly one of the King's Men.
[7] Perhaps Taylor. (Chambers.)
[8] Probably Eliard Swanston.
[9] Probably Shakespeare's Richard III, not Ricardo in Massenger's *The Picture*.
[10] Provided that.

ACT I — Scene I[11]

Enter Bussy D'Ambois, *poor.*

Bus. Fortune, not Reason, rules the state of things ;
Reward goes backwards, Honor on his head ;
Who is not poor, is monstrous ; only need
Gives form and worth to every human seed.
As cedars beaten with continual storms,
So great men flourish ; and do imitate
Unskilful statuaries, who suppose,
In forming a Colossus, if they make him
Straddle enough, strut, and look big, and gape,
Their work is goodly : so men merely great[12]
In their affected gravity of voice,
Sourness of countenance, manners' cruelty,
Authority, wealth, and all the spawn of fortune,
Think they bear all the kingdom's worth before them ;
Yet differ not from those colossic statues,
Which, with heroic forms without o'erspread,
Within are nought but mortar, flint, and lead.
Man is a torch borne in the wind ; a dream
But of a shadow, summ'd with all his substance ;
And as great seamen, using all their wealth[13]
And skills in Neptune's deep invisible paths,
In tall ships richly built and ribb'd with brass,
To put a girdle round about the world,
When they have done it (coming near their haven)
Are glad to give a warning-piece,[14] and call
A poor, staid fisherman, that never pass'd
His country's sight, to waft and guide them in :
So when we wander furthest through the waves
Of glassy glory, and the gulfs of state,
Topp'd with all titles, spreading all our reaches,
As if each private arm would sphere the earth,
We must to Virtue for her guide resort,
Or we shall shipwrack in our safest port.
Procumbit.

[*Enter*] Monsieur, *with two* Pages.

Mons. [*aside*] There is no second place in numerous state[15]
That holds more than a cipher ; in a king
All places are contain'd. His word and looks
Are like the flashes and the bolts of Jove ;
His deeds inimitable, like the sea
That shuts still as it opes, and leaves no tracts[16]
Nor prints of precedent for mean men's facts.[17]
There's but a thread betwixt me and a crown ;
I would not wish it cut, unless by nature.
Yet, to prepare me for that possible fortune,
'T is good to get resolved[18] spirits about me.
I follow'd D'Ambois to this green retreat —
A man of spirit beyond the reach of fear,
Who, discontent with his neglected worth,
Neglects the light and loves obscure abodes ;
But he is young and haughty, apt to take
Fire at advancement, to bear state,[19] and flourish ;
In his rise therefore shall my bounties shine.
None loathes the world so much, nor loves to scoff it,
But gold and grace will make him surfeit of it.
What, D'Ambois?

Bus. He, sir.

Mons. Turn'd to earth, alive?
Up, man ; the sun shines on thee.

Bus. Let it shine ;
I am no mote to play in 't, as great men are.

Mons. Callest thou men great in state, motes in the sun?[20]
They say so that would have thee freeze in shades,
That, like the gross Sicilian gourmandist,
Empty their noses in the cates[21] they love,
That none may eat but they. Do thou but bring
Light to the banquet Fortune sets before thee,
And thou wilt loathe lean darkness like thy death.
Who would believe thy mettle could let sloth
Rust and consume it? If Themistocles
Had liv'd obscur'd thus in th' Athenian state,
Xerxes had made both him and it his slaves.
If brave Camillus had lurk'd so in Rome,
He had not five times been Dictator there,
Nor four times triumph'd. If Epaminondas,
Who liv'd twice twenty years obscur'd in Thebes,
Had liv'd so still, he had been still unnam'd,
And paid his country nor himself their right ;
But, putting forth his strength, he rescu'd both
From imminent ruin, and, like burnish'd steel,
After long use he shin'd ; for, as the light
Not only serves to show, but render us

[11] Unlocated ; but evidently near the court, and out of doors.
[12] Q 1 *our tympanouse statists.*
[13] Q 1 *powers.*
[14] Fire a signal gun.
[15] Punning on (1) the series of numbers, (2) a populous kingdom. (Boas.)
[16] Tracks.
[17] Deeds.
[18] Resolute.
[19] To bear himself proudly.
[20] This speech is a mosaic from Plutarch's *De Latenter Vivendo.* (Parrott.)
[21] Delicacies.

Mutually profitable, so our lives
In acts exemplary, not only win
Ourselves good names, but do to others give
Matter for virtuous deeds, by which we live.
Bus. What would you wish me?
Mons. Leave the troubled streams,
And live, where thrivers do, at the well-head.
Bus. At the well-head? Alas, what should I do
With that enchanted glass? See devils there?
Or, like a strumpet, learn to set my looks
In an eternal brake,[22] or practise juggling,
To keep my face still fast, my heart still loose;
Or bear, like dame's schoolmistresses their riddles,
Two tongues, and be good only for a shift;[23]
Flatter great lords, to put them still in mind
Why they were made lords; or please humorous[24] ladies
With a good carriage, tell them idle tales
To make their physic work; spend a man's life
In sights and visitations, that will make
His eyes as hollow as his mistress' heart;
To do none good, but those that have no need;
To gain being forward, though you break for haste
All the commandments ere you break your fast;
But believe backwards, make your period
And creed's last article, "I believe in God";
And, hearing villainies preach'd, t' unfold their art
Learn to commit them?[25] 'T is a great man's part.
Shall I learn this there?
Mons. No, thou need'st not learn,
Thou hast the theory; now go there and practise.
Bus. Ay, in a threadbare suit; when men come there,
They must have high naps,[26] and go from thence bare.
A man may drown the parts[27] of ten rich men
In one poor suit; brave barks[28] and outward gloss
Attract Court loves, be in parts ne'er so gross.
Mons. Thou shalt have gloss enough, and all things fit
T' enchase in all show thy long-smothered spirit.
Be rul'd by me, then. The old Scythians
Painted blind Fortune's powerful hands with wings,
To show her gifts come swift and suddenly,
Which, if her favorite be not swift to take,
He loses them for ever. Then be wise:
Stay but awhile here, and I'll send to thee.

Exit Monsieur [*with* Pages].

Bus. What will he send? some crowns? It is to sow them
Upon my spirit, and make them spring a crown
Worth millions of the seed-crowns he will send.
Like to disparking[29] noble husbandmen,
He'll put his plow into me, plow me up.
But his unsweating thrift is policy,
And learning-hating policy is ignorant
To fit his seed-land soil[30]; a smooth, plain ground
Will never nourish any politic seed.
I am for honest actions, not for great;
If I may bring up a new fashion,
And rise in court for virtue, speed his plow!
The King hath known me long as well as he,
Yet could my fortune never fit the length
Of both their understandings till this hour.
There is a deep nick in Time's restless wheel
For each man's good, when which nick comes, it strikes;
As rhetoric yet works not persuasion,
But only is a mean to make it work,
So no man riseth by his real merit,
But when it cries "clink" in his raiser's spirit.
Many will say, that cannot rise at all,
Man's first hour's rise is first step to his fall.
I'll venture that; men that fall low must die,
As well as men cast headlong from the sky.

Enter Maffé.

Maf. Humor of princes! Is this wretch endu'd
With any merit worth a thousand crowns?
Will my Lord have me be so ill a steward
Of his revenue,[31] to dispose a sum
So great with so small cause as shows in him?
I must examine this. Is your name D'Ambois?
Bus. Sir?
Maf. Is your name D'Ambois?
Bus. Who have we here?
Serve you the Monsieur?

[22] Vise; *i.e.*, assume a mask.
[23] Piece of trickery.
[24] Capricious. Q 1 *portly*.
[25] Hearing villainies preached against, study to commit them, in order to exemplify their ingenuity.
[26] *I.e.*, good clothes.
[27] Accomplishments, abilities.
[28] Fine coverings.

[29] Putting parks into cultivation.
[30] Q 1 reads (for *To . . . soil*). *But he 's no husband heere*, and omits ll. 122–125.
[31] Accented on second syllable.

MAF. How?
BUS. Serve you the Monsieur?
MAF. Sir, y 'are very hot. I do serve the Monsieur;
But in such place as gives me the command
Of all his other servants. And because
His Grace's pleasure is to give your good
His pass [32] through my command, methinks you might
Use me with more respect.
BUS. Cry you mercy! [33]
Now you have opened my dull eyes, I see you,
And would be glad to see the good you speak of.
What might I call your name?
MAF. Monsieur Maffé.
BUS. Monsieur Maffé? Then, good Monsieur Maffé,
Pray let me know you better.
MAF. Pray do so,
That you may use me better. For yourself,
By your no better outside, I would judge you
To be some poet; have you given my Lord
Some pamphlet?
BUS. Pamphlet?
MAF. Pamphlet, sir, I say.
BUS. Did your great master's goodness leave the good
That is to pass your charge to my poor use,
To your discretion?
MAF. Though he did not, sir,
I hope 't is no rude office to ask reason
How that his Grace gives me in charge, goes from me?
BUS. That 's very perfect, sir.
MAF. Why, very good, sir.
I pray then give me leave; if for no pamphlet,
May I not know what other merit in you
Makes his compunction willing to relieve you?
BUS. No merit in the world, sir.
MAF. That is strange.
Y' are a poor soldier, are you?
BUS. That I am, sir.
MAF. And have commanded?
BUS. Ay, and gone without, sir.
MAF. [*aside*] I see the man; a hundred crowns will make him
Swagger and drink healths to his Grace's bounty,
And swear he could not be more bountiful;
So there 's nine hundred crowns sav'd.— Here, tall [34] soldier.

[32] Its passage.
[33] I beg your pardon.
[34] Bold.

His Grace hath sent you a whole hundred crowns.
BUS. A hundred, sir! Nay, do his Highness right;
I know his hand is larger, and perhaps
I may deserve more than my outside shows.
I am a scholar, as I am a soldier,
And I can poetize [35] and, being well encourag'd,
May sing his fame for giving, yours for delivering,
Like a most faithful steward, what he gives.
MAF. What shall your subject be?
BUS. I care not much
If to his bounteous Grace I sing the praise
Of fair great noses,[36] and to you of long ones.
What qualities have you, sir, beside your chain
And velvet jacket? [37] Can your Worship dance?
MAF. [*aside*] A pleasant fellow, faith; it seems my Lord
Will have him for his jester; and, by 'r lady,
Such men are now no fools; 't is a knight's place.
If I, to save his Grace some crowns, should urge him
T 'abate his bounty, I should not be heard;
I would to Heaven I were an errant ass,
For then I should be sure to have the ears
Of these great men, where now their jesters have them.
'T is good to please him, yet I 'll take no notice
Of his preferment,[38] but in policy
Will still be grave and serious, lest he think
I fear his wooden dagger.[39] Here, Sir Ambo!
BUS. How, Ambo, sir?
MAF. Ay, is not your name Ambo?
BUS. You call'd me lately D'Ambois; has your Worship
So short a head?
MAF. I cry thee mercy, D'Ambois.
A thousand crowns I bring you from my Lord.
[Serve God;] [40] play the good husband, you may make
This a good standing living: 't is a bounty
His Highness might perhaps have bestow'd better.
BUS. Go, y' are a rascal; hence, away, you rogue!

[35] The historical Bussy could, and did.
[36] Monsieur's nose was a mark for the satirists of the time. (Parrott.)
[37] The symbols of his office.
[38] Advancement.
[39] Carried by Fools.
[40] So Q_1; Q 1641 *If you be thriftie, and*, in deference to the statute against profanity.

MAF. What mean you, sir?
BUS. Hence! prate no more!
Or, by thy villain's blood, thou prat'st thy last!
A barbarous groom grudge at his master's bounty!
But since I know he would as much abhor
His hind should argue what he gives his friend,
Take that, sir, for your aptness to dispute.
[*Strikes him.*] *Exit.*
MAF. These crowns are set in blood; blood be their fruit. *Exit.*

[SCENE II] [41]

HENRY [*and*] GUISE [*are discovered at chess; also enter*] MONTSURRY, ELENOR, TAMYRA, BEAUPRÉ, PERO, CHARLOTTE, PYRA,[42] [*and*] ANNABELLE.[43]

HEN. Duchess of Guise, your Grace is much enrich'd
In the attendance of that English virgin,[44]
That will initiate her prime of youth,
Dispos'd to court conditions, under the hand
Of your preferr'd instructions and command,
Rather than any in the English court,
Whose ladies are not match'd in Christendom
For graceful and confirm'd behaviors,
More than the court where they are bred is equall'd.
GUISE. I like not their court fashion; it is too crestfall'n
In all observance, making demigods
Of their great nobles, and of their old queen
An ever-young and most immortal goddess.
MONS. No question she's the rarest queen in Europe.
GUISE. But what's that to [45] her immortality? [46]
HEN. Assure you, cousin Guise, so great a courtier,
So full of majesty and royal parts,
No queen in Christendom may vaunt herself.
Her court approves it, that's a court indeed,
Not mix'd with clowneries us'd in common houses,
But, as courts should be, th' Abstracts of their kingdoms,
In all the beauty, state, and worth they hold;
So is hers, amply, and by her inform'd.
The world is not contracted in a man
With more proportion and expression,
Than in her court, her kingdom. Our French court
Is a mere mirror of confusion to it:
The king and subject, lord and every slave,
Dance a continual hay; [47] our rooms of state
Kept like our stables; no place more observ'd
Than a rude market-place: and though our custom
Keep this assur'd confusion from our eyes,
'T is ne'er the less essentially unsightly,
Which they would soon see, would they change their form
To this of ours, and then compare them both;
Which we must not affect,[48] because in kingdoms
Where the king's change doth breed the subject's terror,
Pure innovation is more gross than error.
MONS. No question we shall see them imitate,
Though afar off, the fashions of our courts,
As they have ever ap'd us in attire.
Never were men so weary of their skins,
And apt to leap out of themselves as they;
Who, when they travail [49] to bring forth rare men,
Come home, delivered of a fine French suit.
Their brains lie with their tailors, and get babies
For their most complete issue; he's sole heir
To all the moral virtues that first greets
The light with a new fashion, which becomes them
Like apes, disfigur'd with the attires of men.
HEN. No question they much wrong their real worth
In affectation of outlandish scum;
But they have faults, and we more; they foolish-proud
To jet [50] in others' plumes so haughtily;
We proud, they that are proud of foolery,
Holding our worths more complete for their vaunts.

[41] A room in the royal palace. That the source of Q 1641 was the prompt-copy (or a transcription of it) is indicated by the following notation, which it prints after I, i, 153: *Table, Chesbord & Tapers behind the Arras.* "Arras" = the curtains of the inner stage.
[42] No speeches are assigned to this character, which suggests that the original version of the play may have been longer.
[43] Old eds. *Annable*, throughout.
[44] Annabelle.
[45] What has that to do with.
[46] Ll. 14, 15, om. Q_1.
[47] A winding rustic dance.
[48] Desire.
[49] Old eds. *travell*, punning on both meanings, which were not distinguished in spelling.
[50] Strut. Q_1 *To be the pictures of our vanitie*, omitting the following line.

Enter MONSIEUR [*and*] D'AMBOIS.

MONS. Come, mine own sweetheart, I will enter thee. —
Sir, I have brought a gentleman to court,
And pray you would vouchsafe to do him grace.

HEN. D'Ambois, I think?

BUS. That's still my name, my Lord,
Though I be something altered in attire.

HEN. We like your alteration, and must tell you
We have expected [51] th' offer of your service;
For we, in fear to make mild virtue proud,
Use not to seek her out in any man.

BUS. Nor doth she use to seek out any man:
He that will win must woo her; [she's not shameless.] [52]

MONS. I urg'd her modesty in him, my Lord,
And gave her those rites that he says she merits.

HEN. If you have woo'd and won, then, Brother, wear him.

MONS. Th' art mine, sweetheart. See, here's the Guise's Duchess,
The Countess of Montsurreau, Beaupré.
Come, I'll enseam [53] thee. Ladies, y' are too many
To be in council; I have here a friend
That I would gladly enter in your graces.

BUS. Save you, ladies.

DUCH. If you enter him in our graces, my Lord, methinks by his blunt behavior he should come out of himself.

TAM. Has he never been courtier, my Lord?

MONS. Never, my Lady.

BEAU. And why did the toy [54] take him in th' head now?

BUS. 'T is leap year, lady, and therefore very good to enter a courtier.

HEN. Mark, Duchess of Guise, there is one is not bashful.

DUCH. No, my Lord, he is much guilty of the bold extremity.

TAM. The man's a courtier at first sight.

BUS. I can sing pricksong,[55] lady, at first sight; and why not be a courtier as suddenly?

BEAU. Here's a courtier rotten before he be ripe.

BUS. Think me not impudent, lady; I am yet no courtier; I desire to be one, and would gladly take entrance, madam, under your princely colors.

Enter BARRISOR, L'ANOU, [*and*] PYRHOT.

DUCH. Soft, sir, you must rise by degrees, first being the servant [56] of some common lady, or knight's wife; then a little higher to a lord's wife; next a little higher to a countess; yet a little higher to a duchess, and then turn the ladder.[57]

BUS. Do you allow a man, then, four mistresses when the greatest mistress is allowed but three servants?

DUCH. Where find you that statute, sir?

BUS. Why, be judged by the groom-porters.[58]

DUCH. The groom-porters?

BUS. Ay, madam; must not they judge of all gamings i' th' court?

DUCH. You talk like a gamester.

GUISE. Sir, know you me?

BUS. My Lord?

GUISE. I know not you. Whom do you serve?

BUS. Serve, my Lord?

GUISE. Go to, companion,[59] your courtship's too saucy.

BUS. [*aside*] Saucy! Companion! 'T is the Guise, but yet those terms might have been spared of the Guisard.[60] Companion! He's jealous, by this light. Are you blind [61] of that side, Duke? I'll to her again for that. — Forth, princely mistress, for the honor of courtship. Another riddle!

GUISE. Cease your courtship, or by Heaven I'll cut your throat.

BUS. Cut my throat? Cut a whetstone, young Accius Naevius.[62] Do as much with your tongue, as he did with a razor. Cut my throat!

BAR. What new-come gallant have we here, that dares mate [63] the Guise thus?

L'AN. 'Sfoot, 't is D'Ambois. The Duke mistakes him, on my life, for some knight of the new edition.[64]

BUS. Cut my throat! I would the King fear'd thy cutting of his throat no more than I fear thy cutting of mine.

[51] Been waiting for.
[52] So Q 1; om. Q 1641.
[53] Introduce.
[54] Whim.
[55] Vocal music written down with points.

[56] Cavalier, professed admirer.
[57] Probably = turn off the ladder, be hanged to you. (Parrott.)
[58] Who at the English court had charge of gaming and the implements for it.
[59] Fellow.
[60] Adherent of the Guise; probably with a pun on "gizzard", *i.e.*, throat.
[61] Unguarded, assailable.
[62] Attus Navius, the Roman augur who performed the feat before Tarquin.
[63] Claim equality with.
[64] Alluding to the cheapening of the order by James's numerous creations.

GUISE. I'll do 't, by this hand.

BUS. That hand dares not do 't. Y' ave cut too many throats already, Guise; and robb'd the realm of many thousand souls, more precious than thine own.[65] — Come madam, talk on. 'Sfoot, can you not talk? Talk on, I say; another riddle.

PYR. Here 's some strange distemper.

BAR. Here 's a sudden transmigration with D'Ambois — out of the knight's ward [66] into the Duchess' bed.

L'AN. See what a metamorphosis a brave suit can work.

PYR. 'Slight, step to the Guise and discover him.

BAR. By no means; let the new suit work; we 'll see the issue.

GUISE. Leave your courting.

BUS. I will not. — I say, mistress, and I will stand unto it, that if a woman may have three servants, a man may have threescore mistresses.

GUISE. Sirrah, I'll have you whipp'd out of the court for this insolence.

BUS. Whipp'd? Such another syllable out a' th' presence, if thou dar'st, for thy dukedom.

GUISE. Remember, poltroon.

MONS. Pray thee, forbear.

BUS. Passion of death! Were not the king here, he should strow [67] the chamber like a rush.

MONS. But leave courting his wife, then.

BUS. I will not. I'll court her in despite of him. Not court her! — Come, madam, talk on; fear me nothing. — [*to* GUISE] Well mayst thou drive thy master from the court, but never D'Ambois.

MONS. His great heart will not down; 't is like the sea,
That partly by his own internal heat,
Partly the stars' daily and nightly motion,
Their heat and light, and partly of the place
The divers frames,[68] but chiefly by the moon,
Bristled with surges, never will be won
(No, not when th' hearts of all those powers are burst)
To make retreat into his settled home,
Till he be crown'd with his own quiet foam.

HEN. You have the mate.[69] Another.

GUISE. No more. *Flourish short.*

Exit GUISE, *after him the* KING, MONSIEUR *whispering.*

BAR. Why, here 's the lion, scar'd with the throat of a dunghill cock, a fellow that has new shak'd off his shackles; now does he crow for that victory.

L'AN. 'T is one of the best jigs [70] that ever was acted.

PYR. Whom does the Guise suppose him to be, trow? [71]

L'AN. Out of doubt, some new denizen'd lord,[72] and thinks that suit newly drawn out a' th' mercer's books.

BAR. I have heard of a fellow, that by a fix'd imagination looking upon a bull-baiting, had a visible pair of horns grew out of his forehead; and I believe this gallant, overjoyed with the conceit of Monsieur's cast [73] suit, imagines himself to be the Monsieur.

L'AN. And why not; as well as the ass, stalking in the lion's case,[74] bare himself like a lion, braying all the huger beasts out of the forest?

PYR. Peace, he looks this way.

BAR. Marry, let him look, sir. What will you say now if the Guise be gone to fetch a blanket [75] for him?

L'AN. Faith, I believe it for his honor sake.

PYR. But, if D'Ambois carry it clean? [76]

Exeunt Ladies.

BAR. True, when he curvets in the blanket.

PYR. Ay, marry, sir.

L'AN. 'Sfoot, see how he stares on 's.

BAR. Lord bless us, let 's away.

BUS. Now, sir, take your full view; how does the object please ye?

BAR. If you ask my opinion, sir, I think your suit sits as well as if 't had been made for you.

BUS. So, sir; and was that the subject of your ridiculous jollity?

L'AN. What 's that to you, sir?

BUS. Sir, I have observ'd all your fleerings; [77] and resolve yourselves ye shall give a strict account for 't.

Enter BRISAC [*and*] MELYNELL.

BAR. Oh, miraculous jealousy! [78] Do you think yourself such a singular subject for

[65] Alluding to the Massacre of St. Bartholomew.
[66] A part of the Counter, a prison for poor debtors.
[67] Strew.
[68] Nature or structure of "the place", the ocean's bed.
[69] Checkmate, in the game of chess.

[70] Farcical entertainments.
[71] Do you suppose?
[72] Alluding to the Scots who swarmed to London upon the accession of James.
[73] Discarded.
[74] Covering, skin.
[75] To toss him in.
[76] Come off superior.
[77] Scoffs.
[78] Suspicion.

laughter that none can fall into the matter of our merriment but you?

L'AN. This jealousy of yours, sir, confesses some close defect in yourself, that we never dream'd of.

PYR. We held discourse of a perfum'd ass that, being disguis'd in a lion's case, imagin'd himself a lion. I hope that touch'd not you.

BUS. So, sir; your descants [79] do marvellous well fit this ground.[80] We shall meet where your buffoonly laughters will cost ye the best blood in your bodies.

BAR. For life's sake let's be gone; he'll kill's outright else.

BUS. Go, at your pleasures; I'll be your ghost to haunt you; an ye sleep on't, hang me.

L'AN. Go, go, sir; court your mistress.

PYR. And be advis'd; we shall have odds against you.

BUS. Tush! valor stands not in number; I'll maintain it, that one man may beat three boys.

BRIS. Nay, you shall have no odds of him in number, sir; he's a gentleman as good as the proudest of you, and ye shall not wrong him.

BAR. Not, sir?

MEL. Not, sir; though he be not so rich, he's a better man than the best of you; and I will not endure it.

L'AN. Not you, sir?

BRIS. No, sir, nor I.

BUS. I should thank you for this kindness, if I thought these perfum'd musk cats, being out of this privilege,[81] durst but once mew at us.

BAR. Does your confident spirit doubt that, sir? Follow us and try.

L'AN. Come, sir, we'll lead you a dance.

Exeunt.

ACT II — SCENE I [1]

[*Enter*] HENRY, GUISE, [BEAUMOND,] [2] *and* Attendants.

HEN. This desperate quarrel sprung out of their envies
To D'Ambois' sudden bravery,[3] and great spirit.

GUISE. Neither is worth their envy.

HEN. Less than either
Will make the gall of envy overflow.
She feeds on outcast entrails like a kite;
In which foul heap, if any ill lies hid,
She sticks her beak into it, shakes it up,
And hurls it all abroad, that all may view it.
Corruption is her nutriment; but touch her
With any precious ointment, and you kill her.
Where she finds any filth in men, she feasts,
And with her black throat bruits it through the world,
(Being [4] sound and healthful). But if she but taste
The slenderest pittance of commended virtue,
She surfeits [5] of it, and is like a fly
That passes all the body's soundest parts,
And dwells upon the sores; or if her squint eye
Have power to find none there, she forges some.
She makes that crooked ever which is straight;
Calls valor giddiness, justice tyranny;
A wise man may shun her, she not herself;
Whithersoever she flies from her harms,
She bears her foe still clasp'd in her own arms:
And therefore, Cousin Guise, let us avoid her.

Enter NUNTIUS.

NUN. What Atlas or Olympus lifts his head
So far past covert, that with air enough
My words may be inform'd, and from their height
I may be seen and heard through all the world?
A tale so worthy, and so fraught with wonder,
Sticks in my jaws and labors with event.

HEN. Com'st thou from D'Ambois?

NUN. From him, and the rest,
His friends and enemies; whose stern fight I saw,
And heard their words before and in the fray.

HEN. Relate at large what thou hast seen and heard.

NUN. I saw fierce D'Ambois and his two brave friends
Enter the field, and at their heels their foes;
Which were the famous soldiers, Barrisor,
L'Anou, and Pyrhot, great in deeds of arms;
All which arriv'd at the evenest piece of earth
The field afforded, the three challengers
Turn'd head, drew all their rapiers, and stood rank'd;

[79] Punning on the two meanings: "comments" and "musical embellishment." Descant was the earliest form of counterpoint.

[80] Punning on the two meanings: "place" (where there can be no fighting) and "musical theme."

[81] *I.e.*, the court, where any fighting was an affront to the sovereign.

[1] The same.

[2] So Q_1; Q 1641 *Montsurry*, economizing in personnel, though in the next scene Montsurry is informed by Guise of the pardon. Ll. 1–50, however, of II, ii, are omitted in Q 1641.

[3] Finery.

[4] She being.

[5] Sickens from over-feeding, is disgusted by.

When face to face the three defendants met them,
Alike prepar'd, and resolute alike.
Like bonfires of contributory wood
Every man's look show'd, fed with either's spirit;
As one had been a mirror to another,
Like forms of life and death, each took from other;
And so were life and death mix'd at their heights,
That you could see no fear of death, for life,
Nor love of life, for death; but in their brows
Pyrrho's [6] opinion in great letters shone:
That life and death in all respects are one.

HEN. Pass'd there no sort of words at their encounter?

NUN. As Hector, 'twixt the hosts of Greece and Troy,
When Paris and the Spartan king should end
The nine years' war, held up his brazen lance
For signal that both hosts should cease from arms,
And hear him speak: so Barrisor, advis'd,[7]
Advanc'd his naked rapier 'twixt both sides,
Ripp'd up [8] the quarrel, and compar'd six lives
Then laid in balance with six idle words;
Offer'd remission and contrition too;
Or else that he and D'Ambois might conclude
The others' dangers. D'Ambois lik'd the last;
But Barrisor's friends, being equally engag'd
In the main quarrel, never would expose
His life alone to that they all deserv'd.
And, for the other offer of remission,
D'Ambois, that like a laurel put in fire
Sparkl'd and spit, did much more than scorn
That his wrong should incense him so like chaff
To go so soon out, and like lighted paper
Approve his spirit at once both fire and ashes.
So drew they lots and in them fates appointed
That Barrisor should fight with fiery D'Ambois;
Pyrhot with Melynell; with Brisac, L'Anou:
And then like flame and powder they commix'd,
So spritely, that I wish'd they had been spirits,
That the ne'er-shutting wounds they needs must open
Might, as they open'd, shut, and never kill.
But D'Ambois' sword, that light'ned as it flew,
Shot like a pointed comet at the face
Of manly Barrisor; and there it stuck.
Thrice pluck'd he [9] at it, and thrice drew on thrusts,
From him [10] that of himself [10] was free as fire,
Who [10] thrust still as he [9] pluck'd, yet (past belief)
He [9] with his subtle eye, hand, body, scap'd.
At last, the deadly bitten point tugg'd off,
On fell his yet undaunted foe so fiercely
That, only made [11] more horrid with his wound,
Great D'Ambois shrunk, and gave a little ground;
But soon return'd, redoubled [12] in his danger,
And at the heart of Barrisor seal'd his anger.
Then, as in Arden [13] I have seen an oak
Long shook with tempests, and his lofty top
Bent to his root, which being at length made loose
Even groaning with his weight, he 'gan to nod
This way and that, as loth his curled brows,
Which he had oft wrapp'd in the sky with storms,
Should stoop; and yet, his radical fibres burst,
Storm-like he fell, and hid the fear-cold earth:
So fell stout Barrisor, that had stood the shocks
Of ten set battles in your Highness' war,
'Gainst the sole soldier of the world, Navarre.

GUISE. Oh, piteous and horrid murder!

BEAUM. Such a life
Methinks had metal [14] in it to survive
An age of men.

HEN. Such often soonest end.
Thy felt report calls on [15]: we long to know
On what events the other have arriv'd.

NUN. Sorrow and fury, like two opposite fumes
Met in the upper region of a cloud,
At the report made by this worthy's fall,
Brake from the earth, and with them rose Revenge,
Ent'ring with fresh powers his two noble friends;
And under that odds fell surcharg'd [16] Brisac,
The friend of D'Ambois, before fierce L'Anou;
Which D'Ambois seeing, as I once did see,
In my young travels through Armenia,
An angry unicorn in his full career

[6] Pyrrhon, the sceptic, of Elis.
[7] *I.e.*, with deliberation.
[8] Analyzed.
[9] Bussy.
[10] Barrisor.
[11] Barrisor only being made.
[12] Thrusting himself into danger for the second time.
[13] The Ardennes.
[14] Undistinguished in spelling from "mettle."
[15] Thy report, heard by us with emotion, incites us.
[16] Overborne, vanquished.

Charge with too swift a foot a jeweller
That watch'd him for the treasure of his brow,[17]
And, ere he could get shelter of a tree,
Nail him with his rich antler to the earth:
So D'Ambois ran upon reveng'd L'Anou,
Who eying th' eager point borne in his face,
And giving back, fell back; and in his fall
His foe's uncurbed sword stopp'd in his heart;
By which time all the life-strings of th' tw' other
Were cut, and both fell as their [spirits][18] flew
Upwards; and still hunt honor at the view:[19]
And now, of all the six, sole D'Ambois stood
Untouch'd save only with the others' blood.

HEN. All slain outright?

NUN. All slain outright but he,
Who kneeling in the warm life of his friends,
All freckled with the blood his rapier rain'd,
He kiss'd their pale lips, and bade both farewell:
And see the bravest man the French earth bears!

Enter MONSIEUR [*and*] D'AMBOIS *bare.*[20]

BUS. Now is the time; y' are princely vow'd my friend;
Perform it princely, and obtain my pardon.

MONS. Else Heaven forgive not me! Come on, brave friend! —
If ever nature[21] held herself her own,
When the great trial of a king and subject
Met in one blood, both from one belly springing;
Now prove her virtue[22] and her greatness one,
Or make the tone the greater with the tother,
As true kings should, and for your brother's love,
Which is a special species of true virtue,
Do that you could not do, not being a king.

HEN. Brother, I know your suit; these wilful murders
Are ever past our pardon.

MONS. Manly slaughter
Should never bear th' account of wilful murder;
It being a spice[23] of justice, where with life
Offending past[24] law, equal life is laid
In equal balance, to scourge that offence
By law of reputation, which to men
Exceeds all positive law, and what that[25] leaves
To true men's valors (not prefixing[26] rights
Of satisfaction, suited to their wrongs)
A free man's eminence may supply and take.

HEN. This would make every man that thinks him wrong'd
Or is offended, or in wrong or right,
Lay on this violence, and all vaunt themselves
Law-menders and suppliers, though mere butchers;
Should this fact[27] (though of justice) be forgiven?

MONS. Oh, no, my Lord; it would make cowards fear
To touch the reputations of true men
When only they are left to imp[28] the law.
Justice will soon distinguish murderous minds
From just revengers. Had my friend been slain,
His enemy surviving, he[29] should die,
Since he had added to a murder'd fame,
Which was in his intent, a murdered man,
And this had worthily been wilful murder;
But my friend only sav'd his fame's dear life,
Which is above life, taking th' under value,
Which in the wrong it did, was forfeit to him;
And in this fact only preserves a man
In his uprightness, worthy to survive
Millions of such as murder men alive.

HEN. Well, Brother, rise, and raise your friend withal
From death to life; and D'Ambois, let your life,
Refin'd, by passing through this merited death,
Be purg'd from more such foul pollution;
Nor on your scape nor valor more presuming
To be again so daring.[30]

BUS. My Lord,
I loathe as much a deed of unjust death
As law itself doth, and to tyrannize,
Because I have a little spirit to dare
And power to do, as to be tyranniz'd.
This is a grace that, on my knees redoubled,[31]
I crave, to double this, my short life's gift;
And shall your royal bounty centuple:
That I may so make good what [God][32] and nature

[17] His horn, supposed to have medicinal properties.
[18] So Q 1; Q 1641 *spirit*.
[19] *I.e.*, like hounds in sight of the quarry.
[20] Bareheaded.
[21] *I.e.*, the natural bond between brothers.
[22] Power.
[23] Kind.
[24] Beyond, outside.
[25] *I.e.*, positive law.
[26] Settling beforehand.
[27] Deed.
[28] Graft onto, piece out.
[29] The enemy.
[30] Q 1 *violent*.
[31] Kneeling a second time.
[32] So Q 1; Q 1641 *Law*.

Have given me for my good; since I am free,
Offending no just law, let no law make
By any wrong it does, my life her slave;
When I am wrong'd, and that law fails to right me,
Let me be king myself (as man was made),
And do a justice that exceeds the law;
If my wrong pass the power of single valor
To right and expiate, then be you my king,
And do a right, exceeding law and nature.
Who to himself is law, no law doth need,
Offends no law, and is a king indeed.

HEN. Enjoy what thou entreat'st; we give but ours.

BUS. What you have given, my Lord, is ever yours.

Exit REX *cum* BEAUMOND.

GUISE. [*Mort dieu!*][33] who would have pardon'd such a murder? *Exit.*

MONS. Now vanish horrors into court attractions,
For which let this balm make thee fresh and fair.
And now forth with thy service to the Duchess,
As my long love will to Montsurry's Countess. *Exit.*

BUS. To whom my love hath long been vow'd in heart,
Although in hand for show I held[34] the Duchess.
And now, through blood and vengeance, deeds of height
And hard to be achiev'd, 't is fit I make
Attempt of her perfection. I need fear
No check in his rivality, since her virtues
Are so renown'd, and he of all dames hated.[35] *Exit.*

[SCENE II][36]

[*Enter* MONTSURRY, TAMYRA, BEAUPRÉ, PERO, CHARLOTTE, [*and*] PYRA.

MONT. He will have pardon, sure.

TAM. 'T were pity, else:
For though his great spirit something overflow,
All faults are still borne that from greatness grow;
But such a sudden courtier saw I never.

BEAU. He was too sudden, which indeed was rudeness.

TAM. True, for it argued his no due conceit[37]
Both of the place and greatness of the persons,
Nor of our sex: all which (we all being strangers
To his encounter) should have made more manners
Deserve more welcome.

MONT. All this fault is found
Because he lov'd the Duchess and left you.

TAM. Alas, love give her joy; I am so far
From envy of her honor, that I swear,
Had he encounter'd me with such proud slight,
I would have put that project[38] face of his
To a more test than did her Duchessship.

BEAU. Why, by your leave, my Lord, I'll speak it here,
Although she be my aunt, she scarce was modest,
When she perceived the Duke, her husband, take
Those late exceptions to her servant's courtship,
To entertain him.

TAM. Ay, and stand him still,
Letting her husband give her servant place.
Though he did manly, she should be a woman.

Enter GUISE.

GUISE. D'Ambois is pardon'd! Where 's a king? where law?
See how it runs, much like a turbulent sea,
Here high and glorious as it did contend
To wash the heavens and make the stars more pure,
And here so low it leaves the mud of hell
To every common view; come, Count Montsurry,
We must consult of this.

TAM. Stay not, sweet lord.

MONT. Be pleased, I'll straight return.

Exit cum GUISE.

TAM. [*aside*] Would that would please me!

BEAU. I'll leave you, madam, to your passions;
I see there 's change of weather in your looks.

Exit cum suis. [TAMYRA *and* PERO *remain.*]

TAM. I cannot cloak it; but, as when a fume,
Hot, dry, and gross, within the womb of earth

[33] So Q_1; om. Q 1641.
[34] *I.e.*, Although for the sake of appearances I deceived.
[35] Ll. 210–218 om. Q_1.
[36] A room in Montsurry's house. The first part of this scene, through l. 50, is omitted in Q 1641.
[37] Understanding.
[38] Base. (*N.E.D.*)

Or in her superficies begot,
When extreme cold hath struck it to her heart,
The more it is compress'd, the more it rageth,
Exceeds his prison's strength that should contain it;
And then it tosseth temples in the air,
All bars made engines to his insolent fury;
So, of a sudden, my licentious fancy
Riots within me: not my name and house
Nor my religion, to this hour observ'd,
Can stand above it. I must utter that
That will in parting break more strings in me
Than death when life parts; and that holy man
That, from my cradle, counsell'd for my soul,
I now must make an agent for my blood.[39]]

Enter MONSIEUR.[40]

[MONS. Yet, is my mistress gracious?
TAM. Yet unanswered?]
MONS. Pray thee regard thine own good, if not mine,
And cheer my love for that; you do not know
What you may be by me, nor what without me;
I may have power t' advance and pull down any.
TAM. That 's not my study. One way I am sure
You shall not pull down me; my husband's height
Is crown to all my hopes; and his retiring
To any mean state, shall be my aspiring;
My honor 's in mine own hands, spite of kings.
MONS. Honor, what 's that? Your second maidenhead!
And what is that? A word. The word is gone,
The thing remains: the rose is pluck'd, the stalk
Abides; an easy loss where no lack 's found.
Believe it, there 's as small lack in the loss
As there is pain i' th' losing; archers ever
Have two strings to a bow; and shall great Cupid
Archer of archers both in men and women,
Be worse provided than a common archer?
A husband and a friend [41] all wise wives have.
TAM. Wise wives they are that on such strings depend,
With a firm husband joining a loose friend!
MONS. Still you stand on your husband; so do all
The common sex of you, when y' are encounter'd
With one ye cannot fancy. All men know
You live in court, here, by your own election,
Frequenting all our common sports and triumphs,
All the most youthful company of men.
And wherefore do you this? To please your husband?
'T is gross and fulsome! if your husband's pleasure
Be all your object, and you aim at honor
In living close to him, get you from court —
You may have him at home; these common put-offs
For common women serve: "My honor! husband!"
Dames maritorious[42] ne'er were meritorious.
Speak plain, and say, "I do not like you, sir;
Y' are an ill-favor'd[43] fellow in my eye;"
And I am answer'd.
TAM. Then, I pray, be answer'd:
For in good faith, my Lord, I do not like you
In that sort [44] you like.
MONS. Then have at you, here!
Take, with a politic hand, this rope of pearl;
And though you be not amorous, yet be wise:
Take me for wisdom; he that you can love
Is ne'er the further from you.
TAM. Now it comes
So ill-prepar'd, that I may take a poison,
Under a medicine as good cheap [45] as it;
I will not have it were it worth the world.
MONS. Horror of death! could I but please your eye,
You would give me the like, ere you would lose me.
"Honor and husband!"
TAM. By this light, my Lord,
Y' are a vile fellow, and I 'll tell the King
Your occupation of dishonoring ladies
And of his court. A lady cannot live
As she was born, and with that sort of pleasure
That fits her state, but she must be defam'd
With an infamous lord's detraction.
Who would endure the court if these attempts
Of open and profess'd lust must be borne? —
Who 's there? Come on, dame; you are at your book

[39] Passion.
[40] Q 1641 adds *Tamyra and Pero with a book.*
[41] Lover.
[42] Overfond of their husbands.
[43] Ugly.
[44] Way.
[45] At as good a bargain; *i.e.*, as readily as.

When men are at your mistress; have I taught you
Any such waiting woman's quality?
MONS. Farewell, good "husband."
Exit MONSIEUR.
TAM. Farewell, wicked lord.

Enter MONTSURRY

MONT. Was not the Monsieur here?
TAM. Yes, to good purpose;
And your cause is as good to seek him, too,
And haunt his company.
MONT. Why, what's the matter?
TAM. Matter of death, were I some husbands' wife.
I cannot live at quiet in my chamber,
For opportunities [46] almost to rapes
Offer'd me by him.
MONT. Pray thee bear with him.
Thou know'st he is a bachelor and a courtier,
Ay, and a prince; and their prerogatives
Are to their laws, as to their pardons are
Their reservations, after parliaments [47] —
One quits another; form gives all their essence.
That prince doth high in virtue's reckoning stand
That will entreat a vice, and not command.
So far bear with him; should another man
Trust to his privilege, he should trust to death.
Take comfort, then, my comfort; nay, triumph
And crown thyself, thou part'st [48] with victory;
My presence is so only dear to thee
That other men's appear worse than they be.
For this night yet, bear with my forced absence;
Thou know'st my business; and with how much weight.
My vow hath charg'd it.
TAM. True, my Lord, and never
My fruitless love shall let [49] your serious honor: [50]
Yet, sweet lord, do no[t] stay; you know my soul
Is so long time without me, and I dead,
As you are absent.
MONT. By this kiss, receive
My soul for hostage, till I see my love.
TAM. The morn shall let me see you?
MONT. With the sun
I'll visit thy more comfortable [51] beauties.
TAM. This is my comfort, that the sun hath left
The whole world's beauty ere my sun leaves me.
MONT. 'T is late night now indeed; farewell, my light. *Exit.*
TAM. Farewell, my light and life — but not in him:
In mine own dark love and light bent to another.
Alas that in the [wane] [52] of our affections
We should supply it with a full dissembling,
In which each youngest maid is grown a mother;
Frailty is fruitful, one sin gets another.
Our loves like sparkles are that brightest shine
When they go out; most vice shows most divine. —
Go, maid, to bed; lend me your book, I pray;
Not like yourself for form; I'll this night trouble
None of your services. Make sure the doors,
And call your other fellows to their rest.
PERO. I will. — [*aside*] Yet I will watch [53] to know why you watch. *Exit.*
TAM. Now all ye peaceful regents of the night,
Silently gliding exhalations,
Languishing winds, and murmuring falls of waters,
Sadness of heart and ominous secureness,
Enchantments, dead sleeps, all the friends of rest,
That ever wrought upon the life of man,
Extend your utmost strengths, and this charm'd hour
Fix like the centre; [54] make the violent wheels
Of Time and Fortune stand; and great Existence,
The Maker's treasury, now not seem to be,
To all but my approaching friends and me.
They come; alas, they come! Fear, fear and hope
Of one thing, at one instant fight in me;
I love what most I loathe, and cannot live
Unless I compass that which holds my death;
For life's mere death, loving one that loathes me,
And he I love will loathe me, when he sees

[46] Importunities.
[47] *I.e.*, the royal prerogative bears the same relation to the laws as a monarch's exceptions (from pardons) made after Parliament is prorogued do to the original pardons.
[48] Leavest (the field).
[49] Hinder.
[50] Q_1 *profit*.
[51] Comforting.
[52] Emend. Dilke; old eds. *wave*.
[53] Stay up.
[54] Of the earth.

I fly my sex, my virtue, my renown,
To run so madly on a man unknown.

The vault opens.

See, see, a vault is opening that was never
Known to my lord and husband, nor to any
But him that brings the man I love, and me.
How shall I look on him? How shall I live,
And not consume in blushes? I will in,
And cast myself off, as I ne'er had been.[55]

Exit.

Ascendit FRIAR *and* D'AMBOIS.

FRIAR. Come, worthiest son, I am past measure glad,
That you, whose worth I have approv'd so long,
Should be the object of her fearful love;
Since both your wit and spirit can adapt
Their full force to supply her utmost weakness.
You know her worths and virtues, for report
Of all that know is to a man a knowledge;
You know besides, that our affections' storm,
Rais'd in our blood, no reason can reform.
Though she seek then their satisfaction
(Which she must needs, or rest unsatisfied),
Your judgment will esteem her peace, thus wrought,
Nothing less dear than if yourself had sought;
And (with another color,[56] which my art
Shall teach you to lay on) yourself must seem
The only agent, and the first orb move [57]
In this our set and cunning world of love.

BUS. Give me the color, my most honor'd father,
And trust my cunning then to lay it on.

FRIAR. 'T is this, good son: Lord Barrisor, whom you slew,
Did love her dearly, and with all fit means
Hath urg'd his acceptation, of all which
She keeps one letter written in his blood.
You must say thus, then, that you heard from me
How much herself was touch'd in conscience
With a report, which is in truth dispers'd
That your main quarrel grew about her love,
Lord Barrisor imagining your courtship
Of the great Guise's Duchess in the presence,
Was by you made to his elected mistress
And so made me your mean now to resolve her,
Choosing, by my direction, this night's depth
For the more clear avoiding of all note
Of your presumed presence; and with this,
To clear her hands of such a lover's blood,
She will so kindly thank and entertain you —
Methinks I see how — ay, and ten to one,
Show you the confirmation in his blood,
Lest you should think report and she did feign,
That you shall so have circumstantial means
To come to the direct, which must be used:
For the direct is crooked; love comes flying;
The height of love is still won with denying.

BUS. Thanks, honor'd father.

FRIAR. She must never know
That you know anything of any love
Sustain'd on her part: for, learn this of me,
In anything a woman does alone,
If she dissemble, she thinks 't is not done;
If not dissemble, nor a little chide,
Give her her wish, she is not satisfi'd;
To have a man think that she never seeks,
Does her more good than to have all she likes:
This frailty sticks in them beyond their sex,
Which to reform, reason is too perplex.
Urge reason to them, it will do no good;
Humor, that is the chariot of our food
In everybody, must in them be fed,
To carry their affections by it bred.
Stand close.

Re-enter TAMYRA *with a book.*

TAM. Alas, I fear my strangeness [58] will retire him.
If he go back, I die; I must prevent it,
And cheer his onset with my sight at least,
And that's the most; though every step he takes
Goes to my heart. I'll rather die than seem
Not to be strange to that I most esteem.

FRIAR. Madam.

TAM. Ah!

FRIAR. You will pardon me, I hope,
That so beyond your expectation,
And at a time for visitants so unfit,
I, with my noble friend here, visit you.
You know that my access at any time
Hath ever been admitted; and that friend
That my care will presume to bring with me
Shall have all circumstance of worth in him
To merit as free welcome as myself.

TAM. Oh, father! but at this suspicious hour
You know how apt best men are to suspect us,
In any cause that makes suspicious shadow

[55] Undress as if I had never been watching here. (Boas.)

[56] Pretence.

[57] *I.e.*, must move initially yourself, thus setting her passion in action; just as, in the Ptolemaic system, the Primum Mobile, the tenth and outer sphere, impelled the motion of all the inner spheres.

[58] Coyness.

No greater than the shadow of a hair;
And y' are to blame. What though my lord and husband
Go forth to-night, and, since I cannot sleep
When he is absent, I sit up to-night?
Though all the doors are sure, and all our servants
As sure bound with their sleeps, yet there is One
That wakes above, whose eye no sleep can bind.
He sees through doors and darkness and our thoughts;
And therefore as we should avoid with fear
To think amiss ourselves before his search,
So should we be as curious to shun
All cause that other think not ill of us.

BUS. Madam, 't is far from that; I only heard,
By this my honor'd father, that your conscience
Made some deep scruple with a false report
That Barrisor's blood should something touch your honor,
Since he imagin'd I was courting you,
When I was bold to change words with the Duchess,
And therefore made his quarrel; his long love
And service, as I hear, being deeply vowed
To your perfections, which my ready presence,
Presum'd on with my father at this season
For the more care of your so curious [59] honor,
Can well resolve [60] your conscience, is most false.

TAM. And is it therefore that you come, good sir?
Then crave I now your pardon and my father's,
And swear your presence does me so much good,
That all I have it binds to your requital.
Indeed, sir, 't is most true that a report
Is spread, alleging that his love to me
Was reason of your quarrel, and because
You shall not think I feign it for my glory
That he importun'd me for his court service, [61]
I 'll show you his own hand, set down in blood
To that vain purpose. Good sir, then come in.
Father, I thank you now a thousand fold.

Exit TAMYRA *and* D'AMBOIS.

FRIAR. May it be worth it to you, honor'd daughter.

Descendit FRIAR.

[59] Scrupulous.
[60] Assure.
[61] *I.e.*, to be my "servant", according to the terminology of courtly love.

ACT III — SCENE I [1]

Enter D'AMBOIS, [*and*] TAMYRA *with a chain of pearl.*

BUS. Sweet mistress, cease! Your conscience is too nice, [2]
And bites too hotly of the Puritan spice.

TAM. Oh, my dear servant, in thy close embraces,
I have set open all the doors of danger
To my encompass'd honor, and my life.
Before I was secure against death and hell,
But now am subject to the heartless fear
Of every shadow and of every breath,
And would change firmness with an aspen leaf;
So confident a spotless conscience is,
So weak a guilty. Oh, the dangerous siege
Sin lays about us, and the tyranny
He exercises when he hath expugn'd! [3]
Like to the horror of a winter's thunder,
Mix'd with a gushing storm, that suffer nothing
To stir abroad on earth but their own rages,
Is sin, when it hath gathered head above us;
No roof, no shelter can secure us so,
But he will drown our cheeks in fear or woe.

BUS. Sin is a coward, madam, and insults
But on our weakness, in his truest valor; [4]
And so our ignorance tames us, that we let
His shadows fright us; and like empty clouds,
In which our faulty apprehensions forge
The forms of dragons, lions, elephants,
When they hold no proportion, the sly charms
Of the witch, Policy, makes him like a monster
Kept only to show men for servile money.
That false hag often paints him in her cloth
Ten times more monstrous than he is in troth.
In three of us, the secret of our meeting
Is only guarded, and three friends as one
Have ever been esteem'd, as our three powers [5]
That in [our] [6] one soul are as one united.
Why should we fear then? For myself I swear

[1] The same.
[2] Scrupulous.
[3] Taken by storm.
[4] Only triumphs over our weakness, if its valor be accurately estimated.
[5] The vegetative, sensitive, and reasoning faculties. (Boas.)
[6] So Q_1; om. Q 1641.

Sooner shall torture be the sire to pleasure,
And health be grievous to one long time sick,
Than the dear jewel of your fame in me
Be made an outcast to your infamy;
Nor shall my value, sacred to your virtues,
Only give free course to it, from myself,
But make it fly out of the mouths of kings
In golden vapors and with awful wings.

TAM. It rests as [7] all kings' seals were set in thee.
Now let us call my father, whom I swear
I could extremely chide, but that I fear
To make him so suspicious of my love
Of which, sweet servant, do not let him know
For all the world.

BUS. Alas! he will not think it.

TAM. Come, then. — Ho! Father, ope, and take your friend. *Ascendit* FRIAR.

FRIAR. Now, honor'd daughter, is your doubt resolv'd.

TAM. Ay, father, but you went away too soon.

FRIAR. Too soon?

TAM. Indeed you did; you should have stayed;
Had not your worthy friend been of your bringing,
And that contains all laws to temper me,
Not all the fearful danger that besieged us,
Had aw'd my throat from exclamation.

FRIAR. I know your serious disposition well. —
Come, son, the morn comes on.

BUS. Now, honor'd mistress,
Till farther service call, all bliss supply you.

TAM. And you this chain of pearl, and my love only.

Descendit FRIAR *and* D'AMBOIS.

It is not I, but urgent destiny,
That, as great statesmen for their general end
In politic justice make poor men offend,
Enforceth my offence to make it just.
What shall weak dames do, when th' whole work of nature
Hath a strong finger in each one of us?
Needs must that sweep away the silly cobweb
Of our still-undone labors; that lays still
Our powers to it,[8] as to the line, the stone,
Not to the stone, the line should be oppos'd;
We cannot keep our constant course in virtue.
What is alike at all parts? Every day
Differs from other: every hour and minute;
Ay, every thought in our false clock of life,
Ofttimes inverts the whole circumference:
We must be sometimes one, sometimes another.
Our bodies are but thick clouds to our souls,
Through which they cannot shine when they desire.
When all the stars, and even the sun himself,
Must stay the vapors' times that he exhales
Before he can make good his beams to us,
Oh, how can we, that are but motes to him,
Wand'ring at random in his ordered rays,
Disperse our passions' fumes with our weak labors,
That are more thick and black than all earth's vapors?

Enter MONTSURRY.

MONT. Good day, my love; what, up and ready [9] too!

TAM. Both, my dear Lord; not all this night made I
Myself unready, or could sleep a wink.

MONT. Alas! what troubled my true love, my peace,
From being at peace within her better self?
Or how could sleep forbear to seize thine eyes
When he might challenge them as his just prize?

TAM. I am in no pow'r earthly, but in yours;
To what end should I go to bed, my Lord,
That wholly miss'd the comfort of my bed?
Or how should sleep possess my faculties,
Wanting the proper closer of mine eyes?

MONT. Then will I nevermore sleep night from thee.
All mine own business, all the King's affairs,
Shall take the day to serve them; every night
I'll ever dedicate to thy delight.

TAM. Nay, good my Lord, esteem not my desires
Such doters on their humors that my judgment
Cannot subdue them to your worthier pleasure;
A wife's pleas'd husband must her object be
In all her acts, not her sooth'd fantasy.[10]

MONT. Then come, my love, now pay those rites to sleep
Thy fair eyes owe him. Shall we now to bed?

TAM. Oh, no, my Lord; your holy friar says

[7] Remains (as inviolable) as if.

[8] Nature ever brings our powers into line with itself, just as the builder brings the stone into line with his plan.

[9] Dressed.

[10] Caprice, whim.

All couplings in the day that touch the bed
Adulterous are, even in the married;
Whose grave and worthy doctrine, well I know,
Your faith in him will liberally allow.
MONT. He's a most learned and religious man.
Come to the presence, then, and see great D'Ambois,
Fortune's proud mushroom shot up in a night,
Stand like an Atlas under our King's arm;
Which greatness [11] with him Monsieur now envies [12]
As bitterly and deadly as the Guise.
TAM. What, he that was but yesterday his maker,
His raiser and preserver?
MONT. Even the same.
Each natural agent works but to this end,
To render that it works on like itself;
Which since the Monsieur in his act on D'Ambois
Cannot to his ambitious end effect,
But that, quite opposite, the King hath power
In his love borne to D'Ambois, to convert
The point of Monsieur's aim on his own breast,
He turns his outward love to inward hate.
A prince's love is like the lightning's fume,
Which no man can embrace, but must consume. *Exeunt.*

[SCENE II] [13]

Enter HENRY, D'AMBOIS, MONSIEUR, GUISE, DUCHESS, ANNABELLE, CHARLOTTE, [*and*] Attendants.

HEN. Speak home, Bussy; [14] thy impartial words
Are like brave falcons that dare truss [15] a fowl
Much greater than themselves; flatterers are kites
That check at [16] sparrows; thou shalt be my eagle,
And bear my thunder underneath thy wings;
Truth's words like jewels hang in th' ears of kings.
BUS. Would I might live to see no Jews hang there
Instead of jewels; sycophants, I mean,
Who use truth like the Devil, his true foe,
Cast by the angel to the pit of fears,
And bound in chains; truth seldom decks kings' ears.
Slave Flattery (like a rippier's [17] legs roll'd up
In boots of hay ropes) with kings' soothed guts
Swaddled and strappl'd, [18] now lives only free.
Oh, 't is a subtle knave; how like the plague
Unfelt he strikes into the brain of man,
And rageth in his entrails, when he can,
Worse than the poison of a red-hair'd man! [19]
HEN. Fly at him and his brood; I cast thee off, [20]
And once more give thee surname of mine eagle.
BUS. I'll make you sport enough, then; let me have
My lucerns [21] too, or dogs inur'd to hunt
Beasts of most rapine, but to put them up, [22]
And if I truss not, let me not be trusted.
Show me a great man (by the people's voice,
Which is the voice of God) that by his greatness
Bombasts [23] his private roofs with public riches;
That affects royalty, rising from a clapdish; [24]
That rules so much more by his suffering king, [25]
That he makes kings of his subordinate slaves:
Himself and them graduate [26] like woodmongers,
Piling a stack of billets from the earth,
Raising each other into steeples' heights;
Let him convey this on the turning props
Of Protean [27] law, and, his own counsel keeping, [28]
Keep all upright; let me but hawk at him,
I'll play the vulture, and so thump his liver,
That, like a huge unlading argosy,
He shall confess all, and you then may hang him.

[11] *I.e.*, favor.
[12] Accented on second syllable.
[13] Unlocated. Presumably within the royal palace; certainly, after Maffé's entrance, the apartments of Monsieur.
[14] Q 1 *my Bussy.*
[15] Seize.
[16] Turn from the game, to pursue.

[17] *Rippier* = "one who carries fish inland to sell." (*N.E.D.*)
[18] Strapped, bound.
[19] *I.e.*, from his body; the common representation of Judas as red-headed seems to have given rise to this superstition.
[20] Loose thee at the game.
[21] Here = "hounds", though properly "lynxes."
[22] Start them up.
[23] Stuffs.
[24] The wooden dish of the beggar, who clapped the cover against it to attract attention.
[25] By his king's sufferance. Q 1 *than.*
[26] Rise by steps.
[27] *I.e.*, assuming various forms to suit various exigencies.
[28] *I.e.*, retaining a lawyer especially for his affairs.

Show me a clergyman, that is in voice
A lark of heaven, in heart a mole of earth ;
That hath good living, and a wicked life ;
A temperate look, and a luxurious gut ;
Turning the rents of his superfluous cures [29]
Into your pheasants and your partridges ;
Venting their quintessence as men read Hebrew ; [30]
Let me but hawk at him, and, like the other,
He shall confess all, and you then may hang him.
Show me a lawyer that turns sacred law
(The equal rend'rer of each man his own,
The scourge of rapine and extortion,
The sanctuary and impregnable defence
Of retir'd learning and besieged virtue)
Into a harpy, that eats all but 's own,
Into the damned sins it punisheth ;
Into the synagogue of thieves and atheists,
Blood into gold, and justice into lust ;
Let me but hawk at him, as at the rest,
He shall confess all, and you then may hang him.

Enter MONTSURRY, TAMYRA, *and* PERO.

GUISE. Where will you find such game as you would hawk at?
BUS. I 'll hawk about your house for one of them.
GUISE. Come, y' are a glorious [31] ruffian, and run proud
Of the King's headlong graces. Hold your breath,
Or, by that poison'd vapor, not the King
Shall back your murderous valor against me.
BUS. I would the King would make his presence free
But for one bout betwixt us : by the reverence
Due to the sacred space 'twixt kings and subjects,
Here would I make thee cast that popular [32] purple,[33]
In which thy proud soul sits and braves thy sovereign.
MONS. Peace, peace, I pray thee peace.
BUS. Let him peace first
That made the first war.
MONS. He 's the better man.
BUS. And therefore may do worst?
MONS. He has more titles.
BUS. So Hydra had more heads.
MONS. He 's greater known.
BUS. His greatness is the people's ; mine 's mine own.
MONS. He 's [nobler] [34] born.
BUS. He is not, I am noble ;
And noblesse in his [35] blood hath no gradation,
But in his merit.
GUISE. Th' art not nobly born,
But bastard to the Cardinal of Ambois.[36]
BUS. Thou liest, proud Guiserd. — Let me fly, my Lord.
HEN. Not in my face, my eagle ; violence flies
The sanctuaries of a prince's eyes.
BUS. Still shall we chide and foam upon this bit?
Is the Guise only great in faction? [37]
Stands he not by himself? Proves he th' opinion
That men's souls are without them? Be a duke,[38]
And lead me to the field.
GUISE. Come, follow me.
HEN. Stay them ! — Stay, D'Ambois. — Cousin Guise, I wonder
Your honor'd disposition brooks so ill
A man so good, that only would uphold
Man in his native noblesse, from whose fall
All our dimensions rise ; that in himself,
Without the outward patches of our frailty,
Riches and honor, knows he comprehends
Worth with the greatest. Kings had never borne
Such boundless empire over other men,
Had all maintain'd the spirit and state of D'Ambois ;
Nor had the full impartial hand of nature
That all things gave in her original [39]
Without these definite terms of mine and thine,
Been turn'd unjustly to the hand of Fortune,
Had all preserv'd her in her prime, like D'Ambois.
No envy, no disjunction had dissolv'd,
Or pluck'd one stick out of the golden faggot
In which the world of Saturn [40] bound our lives,
Had all been held together with the nerves,

[29] As a pluralist.
[30] Backwards.
[31] Vainglorious, bragging.
[32] Alluding to the fact that Guise was more popular than Henry with the Parisians.
[33] *I.e.*, the garment betokening your royal blood.
[34] Emend. Neilson ; old eds. *nobly*.
[35] Its.
[36] He was actually Bussy's great-uncle, and died long before the latter's birth.
[37] As a fomenter of political faction.
[38] Since *dux* = leader.
[39] Beginning.
[40] The Golden Age.

The genius, and th' ingenuous [41] soul of D'Ambois.
Let my hand therefore be the Hermean rod [42]
To part and reconcile, and so conserve you,
As my combin'd embracers and supporters.
BUS. 'T is our King's motion, and we shall not seem
To worst eyes womanish, though we change thus soon
Never so great grudge for his greater pleasure.
GUISE. I seal to that; and, so the manly freedom
That you so much profess, hereafter prove not
A bold and glorious license to deprave,[43]
To me his hand shall hold the Hermean virtue
His Grace affects, in which submissive sign
On this his sacred right hand I lay mine.
BUS. 'T is well, my Lord, and, so your worthy greatness
Decline not to the greater insolence,
Nor make you think it a prerogative
To rack men's freedoms with the ruder wrongs,
My hand, stuck full of laurel, in true sign
'T is wholly dedicate to righteous peace,
In all submission kisseth th' other side.
HEN. Thanks to ye both; and kindly I invite ye
Both to a banquet, where we'll sacrifice
Full cups to confirmation of your loves;
At which, fair ladies, I entreat your presence;
And hope you, madam, will take one carouse
For reconcilement of your lord and servant.
DUCH. If I should fail, my Lord, some other lady
Would be found there to do that for my servant.
MONS. Any of these here?
DUCH. Nay, I know not that.
BUS. Think your thoughts like my mistress', honor'd lady?
TAM. I think not on you, sir; y' are one I know not.
BUS. Cry you mercy, madam.
MONT. Oh, sir, has she met you?

Exeunt HENRY, D'AMBOIS, [*and*] Ladies.

MONS. What had my bounty drunk when it rais'd him?
GUISE. Y' ave stuck us up a very worthy flag,
That takes more wind than we with all our sails.
MONS. Oh, so he spreads and flourishes.
GUISE. He must down;
Upstarts should never perch too near a crown.
MONS. 'T is true, my Lord; and as this doting hand,
Even out of earth, like Juno, struck this giant,[44]
So Jove's great ordnance shall be here impli'd
To strike him under th' Ætna of his pride;
To which work lend your hands, and let us cast [45]
Where we may set snares for his ranging [46] greatness.
I think it best, amongst our greatest women;
For there is no such trap to catch an upstart
As a loose downfall; for you know their falls
Are th' ends of all men's rising. If great men
And wise make scapes to please advantage,[47]
'T is with a woman: women that worst may
Still hold men's candles;[48] they direct and know
All things amiss in all men; and their women [49]
All things amiss in them; through whose charm'd mouths,
We may see all the close scapes of the court.
When the most royal beast of chase, the hart,
Being old and cunning in his lairs and haunts,
Can never be discovered to the bow,
The piece,[50] or hound; yet where, behind some quitch,[51]
He breaks his gall, and rutteth with his hind,
The place is mark'd, and by his venery
He still is taken. Shall we then attempt
The chiefest mean to that discovery here,
And court our greatest ladies' chiefest women
With shows of love and liberal promises?
'T is but our breath. If something given in hand
Sharpen their hopes of more, 't will be well ventur'd.
GUISE. No doubt of that; and 't is the cunning'st point
Of your devis'd investigation.

[41] So Q 1; Q 1641 *ingenious*. The words were not distinguished in spelling.
[42] The caduceus. Its twining serpents had been fighting when Hermes separated them with his rod.
[43] Malign.
[44] An allusion to the myth of Typhon.
[45] Plan.
[46] Q 1 *gadding*.
[47] Indulge in escapades which give (their enemies) opportunity. Parrott emends *advantages*.
[48] Women that can actually do least, nevertheless see all that is going on.
[49] Waiting women.
[50] Gun.
[51] Grass.

MONS. I have broken The ice to it already with the woman Of your chaste lady, and conceive good hope I shall wade thorough to some wished shore At our next meeting.

MONT. Nay, there 's small hope there.

GUISE. Take say [52] of her, my Lord, she comes most fitly.

MONS. Starting back?

Enter CHARLOTTE, ANNABELLE, [*and*] PERO.

GUISE. Y' are engag'd, indeed.

ANNA. Nay, pray, my Lord, forbear.

MONT. [*drawing* ANNABELLE *aside*] What, skittish, servant?

ANNA. No, my Lord, I am not so fit for your service.

CHAR. Pray pardon me now, my Lord; my Lady expects me.

GUISE. [*drawing* CHARLOTTE *aside*] I 'll satisfy her expectation, as far as an uncle may.

MONS. Well said; a spirit of courtship of all hands. — [*drawing* PERO *aside*] Now mine own Pero, hast thou remembr'ed me for the discovery I entreated thee make of thy mistress? Speak boldly, and be sure of all things I have sworn to thee.

PERO. Building on that assurance, my Lord, I may speak; and much the rather, because my Lady hath not trusted me with that I can tell you; for now I cannot be said to betray her.

MONS. That 's all one, so we reach our objects. Forth, I beseech thee.

PERO. To tell you truth, my Lord, I have made a strange discovery.

MONS. Excellent! Pero, thou reviv'st me. May I sink quick to perdition if my tongue discover [53] it.

PERO. 'T is thus, then: this last night, my Lord lay forth; and I, watching my lady's sitting up, stole up at midnight from my pallet; and (having before made a hole both through the wall and arras to her inmost chamber) I saw D'Ambois and herself reading a letter.[54]

MONS. D'Ambois?

PERO. Even he, my Lord.

MONS. Dost thou not dream, wench?

PERO. I swear he is the man.

MONS. The Devil he is, and thy lady his dam! — [*aside*] Why, this was the happiest shot that ever flew! The just plague of hypocrisy levell'd [55] it. Oh, the infinite regions betwixt a woman's tongue and her heart! Is this our goddess of chastity? I thought I could not be so slighted if she had not her fraught besides, and therefore plotted this with her woman, never dreaming of D'Ambois. — Dear Pero, I will advance thee for ever; but tell me now — God's precious, it transforms me with admiration [56] — sweet Pero, whom should she trust with this conveyance? Or, all the doors being made sure, how should his conveyance be made?

PERO. Nay, my Lord, that amazes me; I cannot by any study so much as guess at it.

MONS. Well, let 's favor our apprehensions with forbearing that a little; for if my heart were not hoop'd with adamant, the conceit [57] of this would have burst it. But hark thee. *Whispers.*

[CHAR. I swear to your Grace, all that I can conjecture touching my Lady your niece, is a strong affection she bears to the English Milor'.

GUISE. All, quod you? 'T is enough, I assure you; but tell me —] [58]

MONT. I pray thee, resolve me; the Duke will never imagine that I am busy about 's wife. Hath D'Ambois any privy access to her?

ANNA. No, my Lord; D'Ambois neglects her, as she takes it, and is therefore suspicious that either your lady, or the Lady Beaupré hath closely [59] entertain'd him.

MONT. By 'r lady, a likely suspicion, and very near the life,[60] especially of my wife.

MONS. Come, we 'll disguise all with seeming only to have courted. — Away, dry palm: [61] sh'as a liver [62] as dry as a biscuit; a man may go a whole voyage with her, and get nothing but tempests from her windpipe.

GUISE. Here 's one, I think, has swallowed a porcupine, she casts pricks from her tongue so.

MONT. And here 's a peacock seems to have devour'd one of the Alps, she has so swelling a spirit, and is so cold of her kindness.

CHAR. We are no windfalls, my Lord; ye must gather us with the ladder of matrimony, or we 'll hang till we be rotten.

[52] Make trial. [53] Reveal.
[54] For "herself . . . letter" Q 1 reads *she set close at a banquet.*

[55] Aimed. [56] Wonder.
[57] Thought. [58] So Q 1; om. Q 1641.
[59] Secretly.
[60] Q 1 inserts *if she marks it.*
[61] Supposed to be a sign of chastity.
[62] Supposed to be the seat of love.

MONS. Indeed, that 's the way to make ye right openarses.[63] But, alas! ye have no portions fit for such husbands as we wish you.

PERO. Portions, my Lord? Yes, and such portions as your principality cannot purchase.

MONS. What, woman? what are those portions?

PERO. Riddle my riddle, my Lord.

MONS. Ay, marry, wench, I think thy portion is a right riddle: a man shall never find it out. But let 's hear it.

PERO. You shall, my Lord.

"What 's that, that being most rare 's most cheap?
That when you sow, you never reap?
That when it grows most, most you in[64] it?
And still you lose it when you win it;
That when 't is commonest, 't is dearest,
And when 't is farthest off, 't is nearest?"

MONS. Is this your great portion?

PERO. Even this, my Lord.

MONS. Believe me, I cannot riddle it.

PERO. No, my Lord: 't is my chastity, which you shall neither riddle nor fiddle.

MONS. Your chastity? Let me begin with the end of it; how is a woman's chastity nearest a man when 't is furthest off?

PERO. Why, my Lord, when you cannot get it, it goes to th' heart on you; and that, I think, comes most near you; and I am sure it shall be far enough off. And so we leave you to our mercies.

Exeunt Women.

MONS. Farewell, riddle.

GUISE. Farewell, medlar.

MONT. Farewell, winter plum.

MONS. Now, my Lords, what fruit of our inquisition? Feel you nothing budding yet? Speak, good my Lord Montsurry.

MONT. Nothing but this: D'Ambois is thought negligent in observing the Duchess, and therefore she is suspicious that your niece or my wife closely entertains him.

MONS. Your wife, my Lord? Think you that possible?

MONT. Alas, I know she flies him like her last hour.

MONS. Her last hour? Why, that comes upon her the more she flies it. Does D'Ambois so, think you?

MONT. That 's not worth the answering. 'T is miraculous to think with what monsters women's imaginations engross them when they are once enamor'd, and what wonders they will work for their satisfaction! They will make sheep valiant, a lion fearful.

MONS. [*aside*] And an ass confident. — Well, my Lord, more will come forth shortly; get you to the banquet.

GUISE. Come, my Lord; I have the blind side of one of them.

Exit GUISE *cum* MONTSURRY.

MONS. Oh, the unsounded sea of women's bloods,
That when 't is calmest, is most dangerous;
Not any wrinkle creaming[65] in their faces
When in their hearts are Scylla and Charybdis,
Which still are hid in dark and standing fogs,
Where never day shines, nothing never grows
But weeds and poisons, that no statesman knows;
Not Cerberus ever saw the damned nooks
Hid with the veils of women's virtuous looks.
[66]But what a cloud of sulphur have I drawn
Up to my bosom in this dangerous secret!
Which if my haste with any spark should light,
Ere D'Ambois were engag'd[67] in some sure plot,
I were blown up; he would be, sure, my death.
Would I had never known it, for before
I shall persuade th' importance to Montsurry,
And make him with some studied stratagem
Train D'Ambois to his wreak,[68] his maid may tell it,
Or I, out of my fiery thirst to play
With the fell tiger, up in darkness tied,
And give it some light, make it quite break loose.
I fear it, afore Heaven, and will not see
D'Ambois again, till I have told Montsurry
And set a snare with him to free my fears. —
Who 's there?

Enter MAFFÉ.

MAF. My Lord?

MONS. Go call the Count Montsurry,
And make the doors fast; I will speak with none
Till he come to me.

[63] Medlars, so called with reference to the large open disk between the persistent calyx-lobes. (*N.E.D.*)

[64] Boas emends *thin*.

[65] *I.e.*, wrinkling.

[66] Instead of ll. 338–407, Q_1 reads:

I will conceale all yet, and give more time
To D'Ambois' triall, now upon my hooke;
He awes my throat; else, like Sybillas cave,
It should breathe oracles; I feare him strangely,
And may resemble his advanced valour
Unto a spirit rais'd without a circle,
Endangering him that ignorantly rais'd him,
And for whose furie he hath learn'd no limit.

[67] *I.e.*, caught.

[68] Lure D'Ambois to the vengeance of Montsurry.

MAF. Well, my Lord. *Exiturus.*
MONS. Or else
Send you some other, and see all the doors
Made safe yourself, I pray ; haste, fly about it.
MAF. You 'll speak with none but with the Count Montsurry?
MONS. With none but he, except it be the Guise.
MAF. See even by this, there 's one exception more!
Your Grace must be more firm in the command,
Or else shall I as weakly execute.
The Guise shall speak with you?
MONS. He shall, I say.
MAF. And Count Montsurry?
MONS. Ay, and Count Montsurry.
MAF. Your Grace must pardon me, that I am bold
To urge the clear and full sense of your pleasure ;
Which, whensoever I have known, I hope
Your Grace will say I hit it to a hair.
MONS. You have.
MAF. I hope so, or I would be glad —
MONS. I pray thee get thee gone ; thou art so tedious
In the strict form of all thy services
That I had better have one negligent.
You hit my pleasure well when D'Ambois hit you,
Did you not, think you?
MAF. D'Ambois? Why, my Lord —
MONS. I pray thee talk no more, but shut the doors :
Do what I charge thee.
MAF. I will, my Lord, and yet
I would be glad the wrong I had of D'Ambois —
MONS. Precious! then it is a fate that plagues me
In this man's foolery ; I may be murdered
While he stands on protection of his folly. —
Avaunt ; about thy charge.
MAF. I go, my Lord. —
[*aside*] I had my head broke in his faithful service ;
I had no suit the more, nor any thanks,
And yet my teeth must still be hit with D'Ambois —
D'Ambois, my Lord, shall know —
MONS. The Devil and D'Ambois!
Exit MAFFÉ.
How am I tortur'd with this trusty fool!
Never was any curious in his place
To do things justly, but he was an ass ;
We cannot find one trusty that is witty,[69]
And therefore bear their disproportion.
Grant thou, great star and angel [70] of my life,
A sure lease of it but for some few days,
That I may clear my bosom of the snake
I cherish'd there, and I will then defy
All check to it but Nature's, and her altars
Shall crack with vessels crown'd with every liquor
Drawn from her highest and most bloody humors.
I fear him strangely ; his advanced valor
Is like a spirit rais'd without a circle,[71]
Endangering him that ignorantly rais'd him,
And for whose fury he hath learnt no limit.

Re-enter MAFFÉ *hastily.*

MAF. I cannot help it — what should I do more?
As I was gathering a fit guard to make
My passage to the doors, and the doors sure,
The man of blood is enter'd. [*Exit* MAFFÉ.]
MONS. Rage of death!
If I had told the secret, and he knew it,
Thus had I been endanger'd.

Enter D'AMBOIS.

My sweetheart!
How now, what leap'st thou at?
BUS. O royal object!
MONS. Thou dream'st, awake ; object in th' empty air?
BUS. Worthy the brows of Titan, worth his chair.
MONS. Pray thee, what mean'st thou?
BUS. See you not a crown
Impale [72] the forehead of the great King Monsieur?
MONS. Oh, fie upon thee!
BUS. Prince, that is the subject
Of all these your retir'd and sole discourses.
MONS. Wilt thou not leave that wrongful supposition?
BUS. Why wrongful, to suppose the doubtless right
To the succession worth the thinking on?
MONS. Well, leave these jests. How I am overjoyed

[69] Intelligent.
[70] Tutelary genius.
[71] The magic circle drawn by a conjurer; as long as it intervened he was safe from the spirits he raised.
[72] Surround.

With thy wish'd presence, and how fit thou com'st!
For, of mine honor, I was sending for thee.
Bus. To what end?
Mons. Only for thy company,
Which I have still in thought; but that 's no payment
On thy part made with personal appearance.
Thy absence so long suffered, oftentimes
Put me in some little doubt thou dost not love me.
Wilt thou do one thing therefore now sincerely?
Bus. Ay, anything, but killing of the King.
Mons. Still in that discord, and ill-taken note?
How most unseasonable thou playest the cuckoo,
In this thy fall of friendship!
Bus. Then do not doubt,
That there is any act within my nerves,
But killing of the King, that is not yours.
Mons. I will not, then; to prove which by my love
Shown to thy virtues, and by all fruits else
Already sprung from that still-flourishing tree,
With whatsoever may hereafter spring,
I charge thee utter, even with all the freedom
Both of thy noble nature and thy friendship,
The full and plain state of me in thy thoughts.
Bus. What, utter plainly what I think of you?
Mons. Plain as truth.
Bus. Why, this swims quite against the stream of greatness;
Great men would rather hear their flatteries,
And if they be not made fools, are not wise.[73]
Mons. I am no such great fool, and therefore charge thee,
Even from the root of thy free heart, display me.
Bus. Since you affect[74] it in such serious terms,
If yourself first will tell me what you think
As freely and as heartily of me,
I 'll be as open in my thoughts of you.
Mons. A bargain, of mine honor; and make this,
That prove we in our full dissection
Never so foul, live still the sounder friends.
Bus. What else, sir? Come, pay me home; I 'll bide it bravely.
Mons. I will, I swear. I think thee then a man
That dares as much as a wild horse or tiger,
As headstrong and as bloody; and, to feed
The ravenous wolf of thy most cannibal valor,
Rather than not employ it thou wouldst turn
Hackster[75] to any whore, slave to a Jew
Or English usurer, to force possessions
(And cut men's throats) of mortgaged estates;
Or thou wouldst 'tire thee like a tinker's strumpet,
And murder market-folks, quarrel with sheep,
And run as mad as Ajax;[76] serve a butcher;
Do anything but killing of the King:
That in thy valor th' art like other naturals[77]
That have strange gifts in nature, but no soul
Diffus'd quite through, to make them of a piece,
But stop at humors that are more absurd,
Childish, and villainous than that hackster, whore,
Slave, cutthroat, tinker's bitch, compar'd before;
And in those humors wouldst envy, betray,
Slander, blaspheme, change each hour a religion,
Do anything but killing of the King:
That in thy valor (which is still the dunghill,
To which hath reference[78] all filth in thy house)
Th' art more ridiculous and vainglorious
Than any mountebank, and impudent
Than any painted bawd; which, not to soothe
And glorify thee like a Jupiter Hammon,
Thou eat'st thy heart in vinegar; and thy gall
Turns all thy blood to poison, which is cause
Of that toad-pool that stands in thy complexion,
And makes thee with a cold and earthy moisture,
Which is the dam of putrefaction,
As plague to thy damn'd pride, rot as thou liv'st,
To study calumnies and treacheries,
To thy friends' slaughters like a screech-owl sing,
And do all mischiefs — but to kill the King.
Bus. So! have you said?
Mons. How think'st thou? Do I flatter?
Speak I not like a trusty friend to thee?
Bus. That ever any man was blest withal.
So here 's for me. I think you are, at worst,

[73] Do not consider themselves wise unless they are being made fools of by their flatterers.
[74] Desire.
[75] Bully, hired protector.
[76] See the *Ajax* of Sophocles.
[77] Idiots.
[78] Is carried.

No devil, since y' are like to be no king;
Of which, with any friend of yours, I 'll lay
This poor stillado [79] here, 'gainst all the stars,
Ay, and 'gainst all your treacheries, which are more,
That you did never good, but to do ill;
But ill of all sorts, free and for itself:
That, like a murdering-piece,[80] making lanes in armies,
The first man of a rank,[81] the whole rank falling,
If you have wrong'd one man, you are so far
From making him amends that all his race,
Friends, and associates, fall into your chase:
That y' are for perjuries the very prince
Of all intelligencers; [82] and your voice
Is like an eastern wind, that where it flies
Knits nets of caterpillars, with which you catch
The prime of all the fruits the kingdom yields.
That your political head is the curs'd fount
Of all the violence, rapine, cruelty,
Tyranny, and atheism flowing through the realm:
That y' ave a tongue so scandalous, 't will cut
The purest crystal; [83] and a breath that will
Kill to [84] that wall a spider: you will jest
With God, and your soul to the Devil tender; [85]
For lust kiss horror, and with death engender:
That your foul body is a Lernean fen [86]
Of all the maladies breeding in all men:
That you are utterly without a soul;
And, for your life, the thread of that was spun
When Clotho slept, and let her breathing rock [87]
Fall in the dirt; and Lachesis still draws it,
Dipping her twisting fingers in a bowl
Defil'd, and crown'd [88] with virtue's forced soul:
And lastly (which I must for gratitude
Ever remember) that of all my height
And dearest life, you are the only spring,
Only in royal hope to kill the King.

MONS. Why, now I see thou lov'st me. Come to the banquet. *Exeunt.*

[79] Stiletto.
[80] A small cannon for short ranges.
[81] File.
[82] Spies.
[83] *I.e.*, the diamond. (Parrott.)
[84] At the distance of.
[85] Parrott's punctuation; old eds. have none after *tender*, and a semicolon after *lust*.
[86] The lair of the Hydra.
[87] Her life-giving distaff.
[88] Brimming. The thread of Monsieur's life is stained by Lachesis with evil from a bowl filled with filth and injury to the innocent.

ACT IV — SCENE I [1]

[*Enter*] HENRY, MONSIEUR *with a letter*, GUISE, MONTSURRY, BUSSY, ELENOR, TAMYRA, BEAUPRÉ, PERO, CHARLOTTE, ANNABELLE, [*and*] PYRA, *with four* Pages.

HEN. Ladies, ye have not done our banquet right,
Nor look'd upon it with those cheerful rays
That lately turn'd your breaths to floods of gold;
Your looks, methinks, are not drawn out with thoughts
So clear and free as heretofore, but foul,
As if the thick complexions of men
Govern'd within them.

BUS. 'T is not like, my Lord,
That men in women rule, but contrary;
For as the moon, of all things God created,
Not only is the most appropriate image
Or glass to show them how they wax and wane,
But in her height and motion likewise bears
Imperial influences that command
In all their powers, and make them wax and wane;
So women, that, of all things made of nothing,
Are the most perfect idols [2] of the moon,
Or still-unwean'd sweet moon-calves with white faces,
Not only are patterns of change to men,
But, as the tender moonshine of their beauties
Clears or is cloudy, make men glad or sad;
So then they rule in men, not men in them.

MONS. But here the moons are chang'd, as the King notes,
And either men rule in them, or some power
Beyond their voluntary faculty,[3]
For nothing can recover their lost faces.

MONT.[4] None can be always one; our griefs and joys
Hold several sceptres in us, and have times
For their divided empires; which [5] grief now, in them
Doth prove as proper to his diadem.

BUS. And grief 's a natural sickness of the blood,
That time to part asks, as his coming had;
Only slight fools griev'd suddenly are glad.
A man may say t' a dead man, "Be reviv'd,"
As well as to one sorrowful, "Be not griev'd;"

[1] A room in the palace.
[2] Q 1 *images*.
[3] Q 1 *motions*.
[4] Q 1 gives this speech to Bussy.
[5] *I.e.*, "times."

And therefore, princely mistress,[6] in all wars
Against these base foes that insult on weakness,
And still fight hous'd behind the shield of Nature,
Of privilege, law, treachery, or beastly need,
Your servant cannot help; authority here
Goes with corruption: something like some states,
That back worst men; valor to them must creep
That, to themselves left, would fear him asleep.

DUCH. Ye all take that for granted that doth rest
Yet to be prov'd; we all are as we were,
As merry and as free in thought as ever.

GUISE. And why then can ye not disclose your thoughts?

TAM. Methinks the man hath answer'd for us well.

MONS. The man? Why, madam, d' ye not know his name?

TAM. Man is a name of honor for a king;
Additions[7] take away from each chief thing;
The school of modesty not to learn learns dames:
They sit in high forms[8] there, that know men's names.

MONS. [*to* BUSSY] Hark! sweetheart, here 's a bar set to your valor;
It cannot enter here; no, not to notice
Of what your name is. Your great eagle's beak,
Should you fly at her, had as good encounter
An Albion cliff, as her more craggy liver.[9]

BUS. I'll not attempt her, sir; her sight and name,
By which I only know her, doth deter me.

HEN. So do they all men else.

MONS. You would say so[10]
If you knew all.

TAM. Knew all, my Lord? What mean you?

MONS. All that I know, madam.

TAM. That you know? Speak it.

MONS. No, 't is enough I feel it.

HEN. But, methinks
Her courtship is more pure than heretofore;
True courtiers should be modest, and not nice;[11]
Bold, but not impudent; pleasure love, not vice.

MONS. [*aside to* BUSSY] Sweetheart! come hither, what if one should make
Horns at Montsurry? Would it not strike him jealous
Through all the proofs of his chaste lady's virtues?

BUS. [*aside to* MONSIEUR] If he be wise, not.

MONS. [*aside to* BUSSY] What? Not if I should name the gardener
That I would have him think hath grafted him?

BUS. [*aside to* MONSIEUR] So the large licence that your greatness uses
To jest at all men may be taught indeed
To make a difference of the grounds you play on,
Both in the men you scandal, and the matter.

MONS. [*aside to* BUSSY] As how? as how?

BUS. [*aside to* MONSIEUR] Perhaps led with a train[12]
Where you may have your nose made less and slit,
Your eyes thrust out.

MONS. [*aside to* BUSSY] Peace, peace, I pray thee peace.
Who dares do that? The brother of his king?

BUS. [*aside to* MONSIEUR] Were your king-brother in you; all your powers
(Stretch'd in the arms of great men and their bawds),
Set close down by you; all your stormy laws
Spouted with lawyers' mouths, and gushing blood
Like to so many torrents; all your glories
Making you terrible, like enchanted flames
Fed with bare cockscombs and with crooked hams;
All your prerogatives, your shames, and tortures;
All daring Heaven, and opening hell about you:
Were I the man ye wrong'd so and provok'd,
Though ne'er so much beneath you, like a box tree[13]
I would out of the [toughness][14] of my root
Ram hardness, in my lowness, and like death
Mounted on earthquakes, I would trot through all
Honors and horrors, thorough foul and fair,

[6] The Duchess.
[7] Titles.
[8] On stools of disgrace. (Boas.)
[9] The seat of love. There is also an allusion to the myth of Prometheus.
[10] *I.e.*, all men except Bussy.
[11] Overfastidious.
[12] By a trick.
[13] Symbol of lowliness.
[14] So Q_1; Q 1641 *roughness*.

And from your whole strength toss you into the air.
MONS. [*aside to* BUSSY] Go, th' art a devil; such another spirit
Could not be still'd from all th' Armenian dragons.
O my love's glory! Heir to all I have,
(That 's all I can say, and that all I swear)
If thou outlive me, as I know thou must,
Or else hath nature no proportion'd end
To her great labors; she hath breath'd a mind
Into thy entrails, of desert to swell
Into another great Augustus Cæsar,
Organs and faculties fitted to her greatness;
And should that perish like a common spirit,
Nature 's a courtier and regards no merit.
HEN. Here 's naught but whispering with us; like a calm
Before a tempest, when the silent air
Lays her soft ear close to the earth to hearken
For that she fears steals on to ravish her;
Some fate doth join our ears to hear it coming.
Come, my brave eagle, let 's to covert fly;
I see almighty Aether in the smoke
Of all his clouds descending; and the sky
Hid in the dim ostents [15] of tragedy.

Exit HENRY *with* D'AMBOIS *and* Ladies.

GUISE. Now stir the humor, and begin the brawl.
MONT. The King and D'Ambois now are grown all one.
MONS. Nay, they are two,[16] my Lord.
MONT. How 's that?
MONS. No more.
MONT. I must have more, my Lord.
MONS. What, more than two?
MONT. How monstrous is this!
MONS. Why?
MONT. You make me horns.
MONS. Not I; it is a work without my power;
Married men's ensigns are not made with fingers;
Of divine fabric they are, not men's hands.
Your wife, you know, is a mere [17] Cynthia,[18]
And she must fashion horns out of her nature.
MONT. But doth she — dare you charge her? Speak, false prince.
MONS. I must not speak, my Lord; but if you 'll use
The learning of a nobleman, and read,
Here 's something to those points; soft, you must pawn [19]
Your honor having read it to return it.

Enter TAMYRA [*and*] PERO.

MONT. Not I. I pawn mine honor for a paper!
MONS. You must not buy it under.

Exeunt GUISE *and* MONSIEUR.

MONT. Keep it then,
And keep fire in your bosom.
TAM. What says he?
MONT. You must make good the rest.
TAM. How fares my Lord?
Takes my love anything to heart he says?
MONT. Come y' are a ——
TAM. What, my Lord?
MONT. The plague of Herod [20]
Feast in his rotten entrails.
TAM. Will you wreak
Your anger 's just cause given by him, on me?
MONT. By him?
TAM. By him, my Lord. I have admir'd [21]
You could all this time be at concord with him,
That still hath play'd such discords on your honor.
MONT. Perhaps 't is with some proud [22] string of my wife's.
TAM. How 's that, my Lord?
MONT. Your tongue will still admire,
Till my head be the miracle of the world.
TAM. Oh, woe is me!

She seems to swound.

PERO. What does your Lordship mean? —
Madam, be comforted; my Lord but tries you.
Madam! — Help, good my Lord, are you not mov'd?
Do your set looks print in your words your thoughts?
Sweet Lord, clear up those eyes, [for shame of noblesse,] [23]
Unbend that masking forehead; whence is it
You rush upon her with these Irish wars,[24]

[15] Manifestations.
[16] Here Monsieur makes the sign of the cuckold at Montsurry.
[17] Absolute.
[18] A double allusion to Diana as goddess of chastity and as the horned moon.
[19] Pledge. The historical Bussy was betrayed by a letter to Monsieur in which he boasted of his conquest of the Countess.
[20] See *Acts*, xii, 23.
[21] Wondered.
[22] Lascivious.
[23] So Q_1; om. Q 1641.
[24] They are not mentioned in Q_1. Parrott dates the revision of the play shortly after the Irish troubles of 1607 and 1608, since thereafter Ireland was at peace till after Chapman's death. Q_1 (for ll. 152–154), *Mercilesse creature; but it is enough.*

More full of sound than hurt? But it is enough;
You have shot home; your words are in her heart,
She has not liv'd to bear a trial now.
MONT. Look up, my love, and by this kiss receive
My soul amongst thy spirits for supply
To thine, chas'd with my fury.
TAM. Oh, my Lord,
I have too long liv'd to hear this from you.
MONT. 'T was from my troubled blood, and not from me. —
[*aside*] I know not how I fare; a sudden night
Flows through my entrails, and a headlong chaos
Murmurs within me, which I must digest,
And not drown her in my confusions,
That was my life's joy, being best inform'd.[25]—
Sweet, you must needs forgive me, that my love,
Like to a fire disdaining his suppression,
Rag'd being discourag'd; my whole heart is wounded
When any least thought in you is but touch'd,
And shall be till I know your former merits,
Your name and memory, altogether crave
In just oblivion their eternal grave;
And then, you must hear from me, there 's no mean
In any passion I shall feel for you.
Love is a razor, cleansing being well us'd,
But fetcheth blood still being the least abus'd.
To tell you briefly all: the man that left me
When you appear'd, did turn me worse than woman,
And stabb'd me to the heart thus, with his fingers.
TAM. Oh, happy woman! Comes my stain from him?
It [26] is my beauty, and that innocence proves
That slew Chimaera, rescued Peleus
From all the savage beasts in Pelion,
And rais'd the chaste Athenian prince [27] from hell;
All suffering with me, they for women's lusts,
I for a man's, that the Augean stable
Of his foul sin would empty in my lap.
How his guilt shunn'd me, sacred innocence
That where thou fear'st, art dreadful! [28] and his face
Turn'd in flight from thee, that had thee in chase!
Come, bring me to him; I will tell the serpent
Even to his venom'd teeth, from whose curs'd seed
A pitch'd field starts up 'twixt my lord and me,[29]
That his throat lies, and he shall curse his fingers,
For being so govern'd by his filthy soul.
MONT. I know not if himself, will vaunt t' have been
The princely author of the slavish sin,
Or any other; he would have resolv'd [30] me
Had you not come; not by his word, but writing,
Would I have sworn to give it him again,
And pawn'd mine honor to him for a paper.
TAM. See how he flies me still; 't is a foul heart
That fears his own hand.[31] Good my Lord, make haste
To see the dangerous paper; papers hold
Ofttimes the forms and copies of our souls,
And, though the world despise them, are the prizes
Of all our honors; make your honor then
A hostage for it, and with it confer
My nearest woman here, in all she knows;
Who, if the sun or Cerberus could have seen
Any stain in me, might as well as they;
And, Pero, here I charge thee by my love,
And all proofs of it, which I might call bounties,
By all that thou hast seen seem good in me,
And all the ill which thou shouldst spit from thee,
By pity of the wound this touch hath given me,
Not as thy mistress now, but a poor woman
To death given over, rid me of my pains,
Pour on thy powder, clear thy breast of me.
My Lord is only here; here speak thy worst:
Thy best will do me mischief. If thou spar'st me,
Never shine good thought on thy memory!
Resolve my Lord, and leave me desperate.
PERO. My Lord! My Lord hath play'd a prodigal's part,
To break his stock for nothing; and an insolent,

[25] When I am not reduced to chaos by suspicion. (Parrott.)
[26] My stain.
[27] Bellerophon (who slew the Chimaera), Peleus, and Hippolytus (whom Aesculapius restored to earth) all rejected adulterous advances by women.
[28] Inspirest terror even in those of whom thou art afraid. (Boas.)
[29] Alluding to Cadmus and the dragon's teeth.
[30] Informed.
[31] Implying that Monsieur had forged the paper.

To cut a gordian when he could not loose it.
What violence is this, to put true fire
To a false train? to blow up long-crown'd peace
With sudden outrage, and believe a man
Sworn to the shame of women, 'gainst a woman,
Born to their honors? But I will to him.

TAM. No, I will write (for I shall never more
Meet with the fugitive) where I will defy him,
Were he ten times the brother of my king.
To him, my Lord, and I 'll to cursing him.

Exeunt.

[SCENE II][32]

Enter D'AMBOIS *and* FRIAR.

BUS. I am suspicious, my most honor'd father,
By some of Monsieur's cunning passages,
That his still ranging and contentious nostrils,
To scent the haunts of Mischief, have so us'd
The vicious virtue of his busy sense,
That he trails hotly of him,[33] and will rouse him,
Driving him all enrag'd and foaming on us;
And therefore have entreated your deep skill
In the command of good aërial spirits,
To assume these magic rites, and call up one
To know if any have reveal'd unto him
Anything touching my dear love and me.

FR. Good son, you have amaz'd me but to make
The least doubt of it, it concerns so nearly
The faith and reverence of my name and order.
Yet will I justify, upon my soul,
All I have done. If any spirit i' th' earth or air
Can give you the resolve,[34] do not despair.

[They retire.]

Music: and TAMYRA *enters with* PERO, *her maid, bearing a letter.*

TAM. Away, deliver it. *Exit* PERO.
— Oh, may my lines,
Fill'd with the poison of a woman's hate,
When he shall open them shrink up his curs'd eyes
With torturous darkness, such as stands in hell,
Stuck full of inward horrors, never lighted,
With which are all things to be fear'd, affrighted. —[35]

BUS. [*advancing*][36] How is it with my honor'd mistress?

TAM. Oh, servant, help, and save me from the gripes
Of shame and infamy. Our love is known;
Your Monsieur hath a paper where is writ
Some secret tokens that decipher it.

BUS. What cold, dull northern brain, what fool but he
Durst take into his Epimethean[37] breast
A box of such plagues as the danger yields
Incurr'd in this discovery? He had better
Ventur'd his breast in the consuming reach
Of the hot surfeits cast out of the clouds,
Or stood the bullets that, to wreak the sky,[38]
The Cyclops ram in Jove's artillery.[39]

FRIAR. We soon will take the darkness from his face
That did that deed of darkness; we will know
What now the Monsieur and your husband do,
What is contain'd within the secret paper
Offer'd by Monsieur, and your love's events:
To which ends, honor'd daughter, at your motion,
I have put on these exorcising rites,
And, by my power of learned holiness
Vouchsaf'd me from above, I will command
Our resolution of[40] a raised spirit.

TAM. Good father, raise him in some beauteous form
That with least terror I may brook his sight.

FRIAR. Stand sure together, then, whate'er you see;
And stir not, as ye tender all our lives.

He puts on his robes.

Occidentalium legionum spiritualium imperator (magnus ille Behemoth) veni, veni, comitatus cum Asaroth locotenente invicto. Adjuro te per Stygis inscrutabilia arcana, per ipsos irremeabiles anfractus Averni: adesto o Behemoth, tu cui pervia sunt Magnatum scrinia; veni, per Noctis & tenebrarum abdita profundissima; per labentia sydera; per ipsos motus horarum furtivos, Hecatesq[ue] altum silentium! Appare in

[32] Unlocated; presumably a room in Montsurry's house. Ll. 1–18, and S. D., are added by Q 1641.
[33] Is hot on the trail of Mischief. [34] Information.
[35] By which (even) all fear-inspiring things are themselves frightened.
[36] Q_1 Continues Tamyra's speech: *Father;* a S. D. follows: *Ascendit Bussy with Comolet.* This was cut in the version of Q 1641 because of the new lines at the beginning of the scene.
[37] It was Epimetheus who opened Pandora's box.
[38] To avenge Uranus, deposed by Saturn and the Titans. (Parrott.)
[39] In Jove's war against the Titans.
[40] Information from.

forma spiritali, lucente, splendida, & amabili.[41]

Thunder. Ascendit [BEHEMOTH *with* CARTOPHYLAX [42] *and other spirits*].

BEH. What would the holy Friar?
FRIAR. I would see
What now the Monsieur and Montsurry do,
And see the secret paper that the Monsieur
Offer'd to Count Montsurry, longing much
To know on what events the secret loves
Of these two honor'd persons shall arrive.
BEH. Why call'dst thou me to this accursed light
To these light purposes? I am emperor
Of that inscrutable darkness where are hid
All deepest truths and secrets never seen,
All which I know; and command legions
Of knowing spirits that can do more than these.
Any of this my guard that circle me
In these blue fires, and out of whose dim fumes
Vast murmurs use to break, and from their sounds
Articulate voices, can do ten parts more
Than open such slight truths as you require.
FRIAR. From the last night's black depth I call'd up one
Of the inferior ablest ministers,
And he could not resolve me. Send one then
Out of thine own command, to fetch the paper
That Monsieur hath to show to Count Montsurry.
BEH. I will. — Cartophylax, thou that properly
Hast in thy power all papers so inscrib'd,
Glide through all bars to it and fetch that paper.
CAR. I will. *A* Torch *removes.*
FRIAR. Till he returns, great Prince of darkness,
Tell me if Monsieur and the Count Montsurry
Are yet encounter'd?
BEH. Both them and the Guise
Are now together.
FRIAR. Show us all their persons,
And represent the place, with all their actions.
BEH. The spirit will straight return, and then I'll show thee. [*A* Torch *returns.*]
See, he is come. — Why brought'st thou not the paper?
CAR. He hath prevented me, and got a spirit
Rais'd by another, great in our command,[43]
To take the guard of it before I came.
BEH. This is your slackness, not t' invoke our powers
When first your acts set forth to their effects;
Yet shall you see it and themselves. Behold
They come here, and the Earl now holds the paper.

Enter MONSIEUR, GUISE, [*and*] MONTSURRY *with a paper.*

BUS. May we not hear them?
[FRIAR.] [44] No, be still and see.
BUS. I will go fetch the paper.
FRIAR. Do not stir;
There's too much distance and too many locks
'Twixt you and them, how near soe'er they seem,
For any man to interrupt their secrets.
TAM. O honor'd spirit, fly into the fancy
Of my offended lord, and do not let him
Believe what there the wicked man hath written.
BEH. Persuasion hath already enter'd him
Beyond reflection; peace till their departure!

MONS. There is a glass of ink [45] where you may see
How to make ready black-fac'd tragedy.
You now discern, I hope, through all her paintings,
Her gasping wrinkles and fame's sepulchres.[46]
GUISE. Think you he feigns, my Lord? What hold you now?
Do we malign your wife, or honor you?
MONS. What, stricken dumb! Nay fie, Lord, be not daunted;
Your case is common; were it ne'er so rare,
Bear it as rarely. Now to laugh were manly.
A worthy man should imitate the weather,
That sings in tempests, and being clear is silent.
GUISE. Go home, my Lord, and force your wife to write
Such loving lines to D'Ambois as she us'd
When she desir'd his presence.
MONS. Do, my Lord,

[41] Emperor of the legions of the western spirits, great Behemoth, come, come, attended by [Ashtoreth], thy unconquered lieutenant. I adjure thee by the Styx's inscrutable secrets, by the windings of Avernus, whence there is no return, appear, O Behemoth, thou unto whom are accessible the letter-files of the great. Come! — by the hidden deeps of Night and of the infernal regions, by the wandering stars, by the stealthy motion of the hours, and the deep silence of Hecate! Appear in the form of a spirit, bright, resplendent, and amiable.

[42] Guardian of papers.

[43] Legion.

[44] Cor. Boas; old eds. *Monsieur*.

[45] *I.e.*, this paper is a mirror.

[46] The tomb of her reputation.

And make her name her conceal'd messenger,
That close and most inenarrable [47] pander,
That passeth all our studies to exquire ; [48]
By whom convey the letter to her love.
And so you shall be sure to have him come
Within the thirsty reach of your revenge ;
Before which, lodge an ambush in her chamber,
Behind the arras, of your stoutest men
All close and soundly arm'd ; and let them share
A spirit amongst them that would serve a thousand.

Enter PERO *with a letter.*

GUISE. Yet stay a little ; see, she sends for you.
MONS. Poor, loving lady ; she 'll make all good yet,
Think you not so, my Lord?
Exit MONTSURRY *and stabs* PERO.
GUISE. Alas, poor soul !
MONS. That was cruelly done, i' faith.
PERO. 'T was nobly done.
And I forgive his Lordship from my soul.
MONS. Then much good do 't thee, Pero ! Hast a letter?
PERO. I hope it rather be a bitter volume
Of worthy curses for your perjury.
GUISE. To you, my Lord.
MONS. To me? Now, out upon her.
GUISE. Let me see, my Lord.
MONS. You shall presently. How fares my Pero?

Enter Servant.

Who 's there? Take in this maid — sh'as caught a clap ;
And fetch my surgeon to her. Come, my Lord,
We 'll now peruse our letter.
Exeunt MONSIEUR [*and*] GUISE.
Lead her out.
PERO. Furies rise
Out of the black lines, and torment his soul.

TAM. Hath my Lord slain my woman?
BEH. No, she lives.
FRIAR. What shall become of us?
BEH. All I can say,
Being call'd thus late, is brief, and darkly this :
If D'Ambois' mistress dye not [her] [49] white hand
In her forc'd blood, he shall remain untouch'd ;
So, father, shall yourself, but by yourself.
To make this augury plainer : when the voice
Of D'Ambois shall invoke me, I will rise,
Shining in greater light, and show him all
That will betide ye all. Meantime be wise,
And curb his valor with your policies.
Descendit cum suis.
BUS. Will he appear to me when I invoke him?
FRIAR. He will, be sure.
BUS. It must be shortly then ;
For his dark words have tied my thoughts on knots,
Till he dissolve and free them.
TAM. In meantime,
Dear servant, till your powerful voice revoke him, [50]
Be sure to use the policy he advis'd ;
Lest fury in your too quick knowledge taken
Of our abuse, and your defence of me,
Accuse me more than any enemy.
And, father, you must on my Lord impose
Your holiest charges, and the Church's power,
To temper his hot spirit and disperse
The cruelty and the blood I know his hand
Will shower upon our heads, if you put not
Your finger to the storm, and hold it up,
As my dear servant here must do with Monsieur.
BUS. I 'll soothe his plots, and strow my hate with smiles,
Till all at once the close mines of my heart
Rise at full date, and rush into his blood.
I 'll bind his arm in silk, and rub his flesh,
To make the vein swell, that his soul may gush
Into some kennel, [51] where it longs [52] to lie,
And policy shall be flank'd [53] with policy.
Yet shall the feeling [54] center [55] where we meet
Groan with the weight of my approaching feet ;
I 'll make th' inspired thresholds of his court
Sweat with the weather of my horrid steps,
Before I enter ; yet will I appear
Like calm security before a ruin.
A politician must, like lightning, melt
The very marrow, and not taint the skin ;
His ways must not be seen ; the superficies
Of the green center must not taste his feet,

[47] Indescribable.
[48] That is beyond all our efforts to find out.
[49] Emend. Dilke. Qq *his*.
[50] Call him back.
[51] Gutter.
[52] Belongs, is fitting.
[53] Outflanked.
[54] With a proleptic sense : Bussy's feet will make it feel.
[55] Earth, the centre of the Ptolemaic system.

When hell is plow'd up with his wounding tracts;
And all his harvest reap'd by hellish facts.
Exeunt.

ACT V — Scene I [56]

[*Enter*] Montsurry *bare, unbrac'd, pulling* Tamyra *in by the hair;* Friar; [*and*] One *bearing light, a standish,*[57] *and paper, which sets a table* [*and exit.*]

Tam. Oh, help me, father.
Friar. Impious Earl, forbear.
Take violent hand from her, or by mine order
The King shall force thee.
Mont. 'T is not violent;
Come you not willingly?
Tam. Yes, good my Lord.
Friar. My Lord, remember that your soul must seek
Her peace, as well as your revengeful blood.[58]
You ever to this hour have prov'd yourself
A noble, zealous, and obedient son,
T' our Holy Mother; be not an apostate.
Your wife's offence serves not, were it the worst
You can imagine, without greater proofs,
To sever your eternal bonds and hearts,
Much less to touch her with a bloody hand;
Nor is it manly, much less husbandly,
To expiate any frailty in your wife
With churlish strokes or beastly odds of strength.
The stony birth of clouds [59] will touch no laurel,
Nor any sleeper; your wife is your laurel,
And sweetest sleeper; do not touch her then;
Be not more rude than the wild seed of vapor,
To her that is more gentle than that [60] rude; [21
In whom kind nature suffer'd one offence
But to set off her other excellence.
Mont. Good father, leave us; interrupt no more
The course I must run for mine honor sake.
Rely on my love to her, which her fault
Cannot extinguish. Will she but disclose
Who was the secret minister of her love,
And through what maze he serv'd it, we are friends.
Friar. It is a damn'd work to pursue those secrets
That would ope more sin, and prove springs of slaughter;
Nor is 't a path for Christian feet to tread,
But out of all way to the health of souls;
A sin impossible to be forgiven,
Which he that dares commit ——
Mont. Good father, cease your terrors;
Tempt not a man distracted; I am apt
To outrages that I shall ever rue;
I will not pass the verge that bounds a Christian,
Nor break the limits of a man nor husband.
Friar. Then [God] [61] inspire you both with thoughts and deeds
Worthy his high respect, and your own souls.
Tam. Father!
Friar. I warrant thee, my dearest daughter,
He will not touch thee; think'st thou him a pagan?
His honor and his soul lies for thy safety
Exit.
Mont. Who shall remove the mountain from my breast?
Stand the opening [62] furnace of my thoughts,
And set fit outcries for a soul in hell?
Montsurry *turns a key.*
For now it nothing fits my woes to speak
But thunder, or to take into my throat
The trump of Heaven, with whose determinate [63] blasts
The winds shall burst and the devouring seas
Be drunk up in his sounds; that my hot woes,
Vented enough, I might convert to vapor,
Ascending from my infamy unseen;
Shorten the world, preventing the last breath [64]
That kills the living and regenerates death.[65]
Tam. My Lord, my fault, as you may censure [66] it
With too strong arguments, is past your pardon;
But how the circumstances may excuse me
[God] knows, and your more temperate mind hereafter
May let my penitent miseries make you know.
Mont. Hereafter? 'T is a suppos'd infinite,
That from this point will rise eternally.
Fame grows in going; in the scapes [67] of virtue

[56] A room in Montsurry's house.
[57] Stand for ink and pens.
[58] As well as the indulgence of your passion for revenge.
[59] Thunderstone, thunderbolt.
[60] That is.
[61] So Q_1; Q 1641 *Heaven.* So also in l. 60.
[62] Q_1 *Ope the seven-times heat*[*ed*].
[63] Final.
[64] *I.e.*, anticipating the Last Trump.
[65] The dead. [66] Judge. [67] Escapades.

Excuses damn her: they be fires in cities
Enrag'd with those winds that less lights extinguish.
Come, siren, sing, and dash against my rocks
Thy ruffian galley,[68] rigg'd with quench for[69] lust;
Sing, and put all the nets into thy voice
With which thou drew'st into thy strumpet's lap
The spawn of Venus; and in which ye danc'd[70];
That, in thy lap's stead, I may dig his tomb,
And quit his manhood with a woman's sleight,
Who never is deceiv'd in her deceit.
Sing — that is, write, — and then take from mine eyes
The mists that hide the most inscrutable pander
That ever lapp'd up an adulterous vomit,
That I may see the devil, and survive
To be a devil, and then learn to wive;
That I may hang him, and then cut him down,
Then cut him up, and with my soul's beams search
The cranks and caverns of his brain, and study
The errant wilderness of a woman's face;
Where men cannot get out, for[71] all the comets[72]
That have been lighted at it; though they know
That adders lie a-sunning in their[73] smiles,
That basilisks drink their poison from their eyes,
And no way there to coast out to their hearts;
Yet still they[74] wander there,[75] and are not stay'd
Till they be fetter'd, nor secure before
All cares devour them, nor in human consort,[76]
Till they embrace within their wife's two breasts
All Pelion and Cythaeron with their beasts.
Why write you not?

TAM. O good my Lord, forbear
In wreak of great faults, to engender greater,
And make my love's corruption generate murder.

MONT. It follows needfully as child and parent;
The chain-shot of thy lust is yet aloft,
And it must murder; 't is thine own dear twin:
No man can add height to a woman's sin.
Vice never doth her just hate so provoke
As when she rageth under virtue's cloak.
Write! for it must be — by this ruthless steel,
By this impartial torture, and the death
Thy tyrannies have invented in my entrails,
To quicken life in dying, and hold up
The spirits in fainting, teaching to preserve
Torments in ashes, that will ever last.
Speak! Will you write?

TAM. Sweet Lord, enjoin my sin
Some other penance than what makes it worse;
Hide in some gloomy dungeon my loath'd face,
And let condemned murderers let me down,
Stopping their noses, my abhorred food;
Hang me in chains, and let me eat these arms
That have offended; bind me face to face
To some dead woman, taken from the cart
Of execution, till death and time
In grains of dust dissolve me: I'll endure;
Or any torture that your wrath's invention
Can fright all pity from the world withal.
But to betray a friend with show of friendship,
That is too common for the rare revenge
Your rage affecteth. Here then are my breasts,
Last night your pillows; here my wretched arms,
As late the wished confines of your life;
Now break them as you please, and all the bounds
Of manhood, noblesse, and religion.

MONT. Where all these have been broken, they are kept
In doing their justice there with any show
Of the like[77] cruelty; thine arms have lost
Their privilege in lust, and in their torture
Thus they must pay it. *Stabs her.*

TAM. O Lord!

MONT. Till thou writ'st,
I'll write in wounds, my wrong's fit characters,
Thy right of sufferance. Write.

TAM. Oh, kill me, kill me;
Dear husband, be not crueller than death.
You have beheld some Gorgon; feel, oh, feel
How you are turn'd to stone. With my heart-blood
Dissolve yourself again, or you will grow

[68] *I.e.*, Bussy.
[69] Q$_1$ *laden for thy.*
[70] *I.e.*, acted under the delusion that you were unobserved.
[71] In spite of.
[72] Which were portents of disaster.
[73] Women's.
[74] Men.
[75] In the wilderness of a woman's face.
[76] Lacking human fellowship.
[77] Q 1641 inserts *cruel*, probably through the compositor's blunder, as Parrott observes. Q$_1$ omits *with . . . cruelty*.

Into the image of all tyranny.
MONT. As thou art of adultery! I will ever
Prove thee my parallel, being most a monster,
Thus I express thee[78] yet. *Stabs her again.*
TAM. And yet I live.
MONT. Ay, for thy monstrous idol is not done yet;[79]
This tool hath wrought enough; now, torture, use

Enter Servants [*and put her on the rack*].

This other engine on th' habituate powers
Of her thrice-damn'd and whorish fortitude.
Use the most madding pains in her that ever
Thy venoms soak'd through, making most of death;
That she may weigh her wrongs with them, and then
Stand, Vengeance, on thy steepest rock, a victor.
TAM. Oh, who is turn'd into my lord and husband?
Husband! My lord! None but my lord and husband!
Heaven, I ask thee remission of my sins,
Not of my pains; husband, oh, help me, husband!

Ascendit FRIAR *with a sword drawn.*

FRIAR. What rape of honor and religion —
Oh, wrack of nature! *Falls and dies.*
TAM. Poor man; oh, my father.
Father, look up; oh, let me down, my Lord,
And I will write.
MONT. Author of prodigies!
What new flame breaks out of the firmament,
That turns up counsels never known before?
Now is it true earth moves and Heaven stands still;
Even Heaven itself must see and suffer ill.
The too huge bias[80] of the world hath sway'd
Her back part upwards, and with that she braves
This hemisphere, that long her mouth hath mock'd;[81]
The gravity of her religious face,
Now grown too weighty with her sacrilege
And here discern'd sophisticate enough,
Turns to th' antipodes, and all the forms
That her illusions have impress'd in her,
Have eaten through her back; and now all see
How she is riveted with[82] hypocrisy. —
Was this the way? Was he the mean betwixt you?
TAM. He was, he was; kind, worthy man, he was.
MONT. Write, write a word or two.
TAM. I will, I will —
[*aside*] I'll write, but with my blood, that he[83] may see
These lines come from my wounds, and not from me. *Writes.*
MONT. Well might he[84] die for thought; methinks the frame
And shaken joints of the whole world should crack
To see her parts so disproportionate;
And that his[85] general beauty cannot stand
Without these stains in the particular man.
Why wander I so far?[86] Here, here was she
That was a whole world without spot to me,
Though now a world of spots. Oh, what a lightning
Is man's delight in women! What a bubble
He builds his state, fame, life on, when he marries!
Since all earth's pleasures are so short and small,
The way t' enjoy it is t' abjure it all.
Enough! I must be messenger myself,
Disguis'd like this strange creature. — In,[87] I'll after,
To see what guilty light gives this cave eyes,
And to the world sing new impieties.

He puts the FRIAR *in the vault and follows. She wraps herself in the arras.*[88] *Exeunt* [Servants].

[SCENE II][89]

Enter MONSIEUR *and* GUISE.

MONS. Now shall we see that Nature hath no end

[78] *I.e.*, by being monstrous, and so continuing to be a parallel to you.
[79] *I.e.*, I have not yet completed my image of you.
[80] Tendency (toward wickedness).
[81] The world has reversed itself, so Montsurry concludes upon learning that the pander was the Friar; it has turned upside down; its back part now shows itself arrogantly to our side of the universe, which formerly the world's mouth had mocked (by pretending virtue).
[82] *I.e.*, that her real structure is.
[83] Bussy.
[84] The Friar.
[85] Referring to *man*, in the next line.
[86] For an example.
[87] To the Friar's body.
[88] The curtains of the inner stage.
[89] Another room in Montsurry's house. This scene appears in Q_1 at the beginning of V, iv, with the omission of ll. 54–59 and the S. D. for Montsurry's entrance.

In her great works responsive [90] to their worths;
That she, that makes so many eyes and souls
To see and foresee, is stark blind herself;
And as illiterate men say Latin prayers
By rote of heart and daily iteration,
Not knowing what they say,[91] so Nature lays
A deal of stuff together, and by use,
Or by the mere necessity of matter,
Ends such a work, fills it, or leaves it empty
Of strength or virtue, error or clear truth,
Not knowing what she does; but usually
Gives that which [we call] [92] merit to a man,
And [believe should] [93] arrive him on [94] huge riches,
Honor, and happiness, that effects his ruin;
Even as in ships of war, whose lasts [95] of powder
Are laid, men think,[96] to make them last, and guard [them],[97]
When a disorder'd spark, that powder taking,
Blows up with sudden violence and horror
Ships that kept empty had [98] sail'd long, with terror.[99]

GUISE. He that observes, but like a worldly man,
That which doth oft succeed, and by th' events
Values the worth of things, will think it true
That Nature works at random, just with you;
But with as much proportion she may make
A thing that from the feet up to the throat
Hath all the wondrous fabric man should have,
And leave it headless, for a perfect man,
As give a full man valor, virtue, learning,
Without an end more excellent than those
On whom she no such worthy part bestows.

MONS. Yet shall you see it here [100]; here will be one
Young, learned, valiant, virtuous, and full mann'd;
One on whom Nature spent so rich a hand
That with an ominous eye she wept to see
So much consum'd her virtuous treasury.[1]
Yet, as the winds sing through a hollow tree,
And, since it lets them pass through, lets it stand;
But a tree solid, since it gives no way
To their wild rage, they rend up by the root;
So this whole man,
That will not wind with every crooked way,
Trod by the servile world, shall reel and fall
Before the frantic puffs of blind-born chance,
That pipes through empty men, and makes them dance.
Not so the sea raves on the Lybian sands,[2]
Tumbling her billows in each other's neck;
Not so the surges of the Euxine sea
Near to the frosty pole, where free Boötes
From those dark deep waves turns his radiant team,
Swell, being enrag'd even from their inmost drop,
As Fortune swings about the restless state
Of virtue, now thrown into all men's hate.

Enter MONTSURRY *disguis'd, with the* Murderers.

Away, my Lord, you are perfectly disguis'd;
Leave us to lodge your ambush.

MONT. Speed me, vengeance. *Exit.*

MONS. Resolve, my masters, you shall meet with one
Will try what proofs your privy coats [3] are made on;
When he is ent'red, and you hear us stamp,
Approach, and make all sure.

MURD. We will, my Lord. *Exeunt.*

[SCENE III] [4]

[*Enter*] D'AMBOIS, *with two* Pages *with tapers.*

BUS. Sit up to-night, and watch; I'll speak with none
But the old Friar, who bring to me.

PAGES. We will, sir. *Exeunt.*

BUS. What violent heat is this? Methinks the fire
Of twenty lives doth on a sudden flash
Through all my faculties; the air goes high
In this close chamber, and the frighted earth
Thunder.

---

[90] Answerable, corresponding.

[91] For *Not . . . say* Q_1 reads:

In whose hot zeale a man would thinke they knew
What they ranne so away with, and were sure
To have rewards proportion'd to their labours;
Yet may implore their owne confusions
For anything they know, which oftentimes
It fals out they incurre.

[92] So Q_1; Q 1641 *she calls*. As Parrott notes, Chapman corrected this speech but was misread by the printer; the version of Q 1641 is unintelligible.

[93] So Q_1; Q 1641 *beliefe must*.

[94] Bring him to.

[95] A last of powder = 24 barrels.

[96] Boas and Parrott emend *methinks*.

[97] So Q_1; om. Q 1641.

[98] Would have.

[99] *I.e.*, to their enemies.

[100] In the case of Bussy.

[1] Stock of virtues.

[2] Ll. 46–53 are adapted from Seneca's *Agamemnon*, ll. 64–72. (Boas.)

[3] Hidden shirts of mail.

[4] A room in Bussy's house.

Trembles, and shrinks beneath me; the whole house
Nods with his[5] shaken burthen —

Enter Umbra Friar.

Bless me, Heaven!

Umb. Note what I want, dear son, and be forewarn'd;
Oh, there are bloody deeds past and to come.
I cannot stay; a fate doth ravish me;
I'll meet thee in the chamber of thy love.

Exit.

Bus. What dismal change is here; the good old Friar
Is murder'd, being made known to serve my love;
And now his restless spirit would forewarn me
Of some plot dangerous and imminent.
Note what he wants? He wants his upper weed,[6]
He wants his life and body; which of these
Should be the want he means, and may supply me
With any fit forewarning? This strange vision,
Together with the dark prediction
Us'd by the Prince of Darkness that was rais'd
By this embodied shadow,[7] stir my thoughts
With reminiscion of the spirit's promise,
Who told me that by any invocation
I should have power to raise him, though it wanted
The powerful words and decent rites of art.
Never had my set[8] brain such need of spirit
T' instruct and cheer it; now, then, I will claim
Performance of his free and gentle vow
T' appear in greater light, and make more plain
His rugged oracle. I long to know
How my dear mistress fares, and be inform'd
What hand she now holds on the troubled blood[9]
Of her incensed lord. Methought the spirit,
When he had utter'd his perplex'd presage
Threw his chang'd countenance headlong into clouds;
His forehead bent, as it would hide his face,
He knock'd his chin against his dark'ned breast,
And struck a churlish silence through his powers.
Terror of darkness! O thou King of flames![10]
That with thy music-footed horse dost strike
The clear light out of crystal on dark earth,
And hurl'st instructive fire about the world,
Wake, wake the drowsy and enchanted night,
That sleeps with dead eyes in this heavy riddle!
Or thou great prince of shades, where never sun
Sticks his far-darted beams, whose eyes are made
To shine in darkness, and see ever best
Where men are blindest, open now the heart
Of thy abashed oracle, that, for fear
Of some ill it includes, would fain lie hid,
And rise thou with it in thy greater light.

Thunders. Surgit Spiritus cum suis.

[Beh.][11] Thus to observe my vow of apparition
In greater light, and explicate thy fate,
I come; and tell thee that if thou obey
The summons that thy mistress next will send thee,
Her hand shall be thy death.

Bus. When will she send?

Beh. Soon as I set again, where late I rose.

Bus. Is the old Friar slain?

Beh. No, and yet lives not.

Bus. Died he a natural death?

Beh. He did.

Bus. Who then
Will my dear mistress send?

Beh. I must not tell thee.

Bus. Who lets[12] thee?

Beh. Fate.

Bus. Who are Fate's ministers?

Beh. The Guise and Monsieur.

Bus. A fit pair of shears
To cut the threads of kings and kingly spirits,
And consorts fit to sound forth harmony,
Set to the falls of kingdoms. Shall the hand
Of my kind mistress kill me?

Beh. If thou yield
To her next summons. Y' are fair-warn'd; farewell!

Thunders. Exit [cum suis].

Bus. I must fare well, however, though I die,
My death consenting[13] with his augury.

[5] Its.
[6] His outer garment, his gown (which Montsurry has donned.)
[7] This ghost when it was still alive.
[8] Determined.
[9] Passion (of anger).
[10] The sun-god.
[11] Old eds. *Sp.*, throughout.
[12] Stops.
[13] If my death agrees.

Should not my powers obey when she commands,
My motion must be rebel to my will,
My will to life ; if, when I have obey'd,
Her hand should so reward me, they must arm it,
Bind me or force it ; or, I lay my life,
She rather would convert it many times
On her own bosom, even to many deaths.
But were there danger of such violence,
I know 't is far from her intent to send ;
And who she should send is as far from thought,
Since he is dead, whose only mean she us'd. — *Knocks.*
Who 's there? Look to the door, and let him in,
Though politic Monsieur or the violent Guise.

Enter MONTSURRY, *like the Friar, with a letter written in blood.*

MONT. Hail to my worthy son.
BUS. Oh, lying spirit,
To say the Friar was dead ! I 'll now believe
Nothing of all his forg'd predictions. —
My kind and honor'd father, well reviv'd ;
I have been frighted with your death and mine,
And told my mistress' hand should be my death
If I obey'd this summons.
MONT. I believ'd
Your love had been much clearer than to give
Any such doubt a thought, for she is clear ;
And having freed her husband's jealousy,
Of which her much abus'd hand here is witness,
She prays, for urgent cause, your instant presence.
BUS. Why, then your prince of spirits may be call'd
The prince of liars.
MONT. Holy Writ so calls him.
BUS. What, writ in blood?
MONT. Ay, 't is the ink of lovers.
BUS. Oh 't is a sacred witness of her love.
So much elixir of her blood as this
Dropp'd in the lightest dame, would make her firm
As heat to fire ; and, like to all the signs,[14]
Commands the life confin'd in all my veins.
Oh, how it multiplies my blood with spirit,
And makes me apt t' encounter death and hell. —
But come, kind father, you fetch me to Heaven,
And to that end your holy weed was given. *Exeunt.*

[14] Of the heavenly bodies.

[SCENE IV][15]

Thunder. Intrat UMBRA FRIAR, *and discovers* TAMYRA.[16]

UMB. Up with these stupid thoughts, still loved daughter,
And strike away this heartless trance of anguish.
Be like the sun, and labor in eclipses ;
Look to the end of woes : oh, can you sit
Mustering the horrors of your servant's slaughter
Before your contemplation, and not study
How to prevent it? Watch when he shall rise,
And with a sudden outcry of his murder,
Blow[17] his retreat before he be revenged.
TAM. O father, have my dumb woes wak'd your death?
When will our human griefs be at their height?
Man is a tree that hath no top in cares,
No root in comforts ; all his power to live
Is given to no end, but ['t][18] have power to grieve.
UMB. It is the misery of our creation. Your true friend,[19]
Led by your husband, shadowed in my weed,
Now enters the dark vault.
TAM. But, my dearest father,
Why will not you appear to him yourself,
And see that none of these deceits annoy him?
UMB. My power is limited ; alas ! I cannot.
All that I can do — see, the cave opens.
Exit. D'AMBOIS *at the gulf.*
TAM. Away, my love, away ; thou wilt be murder'd !

Enter MONSIEUR *and* GUISE *above.*

BUS. Murder'd? I know not what that Hebrew means :
That word had ne'er been nam'd had all been D'Ambois.

[15] A room in Montsurry's house.
[16] By opening the curtains of the inner stage, in which she wrapped herself at the close of V, i. Q_1: *Intrat umbra Comolet to the Countesse, wrapt in a canapie.*
[17] Sound a call for.
[18] So Q_1; om. Q 1641.
[19] For ll. 15–21 Q_1 reads:

Tis the just curse of our abus'd creation,
Which wee must suffer heere, and scape heereafter:
He hath the great mind that submits to all
He sees inevitable; he the small
That carps at earth, and her foundation shaker,
And rather than himselfe, will mend his maker.

Murder'd? By Heaven he is my murderer
That shows me not a murderer; what such bug[20]
Abhorreth not the very sleep of D'Ambois?
Murder'd? Who dares give all the room I see
To D'Ambois' reach? or look with any odds
His fight i' th' face, upon whose hand sits death,
Whose sword hath wings, and every feather pierceth?
If I scape Monsieur's 'pothecary shops,
Foutre[21] for Guise's shambles! 'T was ill plotted;
They should have maul'd me here,
When I was rising. I am up and ready.
Let in my politic visitants, let them in,
Though ent'ring like so many moving armors,
Fate is more strong than arms and sly than treason,
And I at all parts buckl'd in my fate.

MONS. }
GUISE. } [*aside*] Why enter not the coward villains?

BUS. Dare they not come?

Enter Murderers, *with* [UMBRA] FRIAR *at the other door.*

TAM. They come.

1 MUR. Come all at once.

UMB. Back, coward murderers, back.

OMN. Defend us, Heaven.

Exeunt all but the First.

1 MUR. Come ye not on?

BUS. No, slave, nor goest thou off. — [*Thrusts at him.*]
Stand you so firm? Will it not enter here?[22]
You have a face yet. — So! [*Kills him.*] — In thy life's flame,
I burn the first rites to my mistress' fame.

UMB. Breathe thee, brave son, against the other charge.

BUS. Oh, is it true then that my sense first told me?
Is my kind father dead?

TAM. He is, my love.
'T was the Earl, my husband, in his weed that brought thee.

BUS. That was a speeding sleight,[23] and well resembled.
Where is that angry Earl? — My Lord, come forth
And show your own face in your own affair;
Take not into your noble veins the blood
Of these base villains, nor the light reports
Of blister'd tongues for clear and weighty truth:
But me against the world, in pure defence
Of your rare lady, to whose spotless name
I stand here as a bulwark, and project
A life to her renown, that ever yet
Hath been untainted, even in envy's eye,
And, where it would protect, a sanctuary.
Brave Earl, come forth, and keep your scandal in;
'T is not our fault if you enforce the spot,[24]
Nor the wreak yours if you perform it not.

Enter MONTSURRY, *with all the* Murderers.[25]

MONT. Cowards, a fiend or spirit beat ye off!
They are your own faint spirits that have forg'd
The fearful shadows that your eyes deluded.
The fiend was in you; cast him out then, thus.

D'AMBOIS *hath* MONTSURRY *down.*

TAM. Favor my Lord, my love, oh, favor him!

BUS. I will not touch him. — Take your life, my Lord,
And be appeas'd. — *Pistols shot within.*
Oh, then the coward Fates
Have maim'd themselves, and ever lost their honor.

UMB. What have ye done, slaves? — Irreligious lord!

BUS. Forbear them, father; 't is enough for me
That Guise and Monsieur, death and destiny,
Come behind D'Ambois. — Is my body, then,
But penetrable flesh? And must my mind
Follow my blood? Can my divine part add
No aid to th' earthly in extremity?
Then these divines are but for form, not fact.[26]
Man is of two sweet courtly friends compact,
A mistress and a servant;[27] let my death
Define life nothing but a courtier's breath.
Nothing is made of nought, of all things made,
Their abstract being a dream but of a shade.
I'll not complain to earth yet, but to Heaven,
And, like a man, look upwards even in death.
And if Vespasian thought in majesty

[20] Bugbear; *i.e.*, threat of murder.
[21] An obscene expression of contempt.
[22] An account of a "privy coat."
[23] Successful trick.

[24] Emphasize the stain on your honor. (Boas.)
[25] Q 1 *with others*.
[26] *I.e.*, theologians are unrealistic.
[27] *I.e.*, body and soul are like mistress and lover, the second of each pair being dependent on the first.

An emperor might die standing, why not I?
She offers to help him.
Nay, without help, in which I will exceed him;
For he died splinted with his chamber grooms.
Prop me, true sword, as thou hast ever done;
The equal thought I bear of life and death
Shall make me faint on no side; I am up.
Here like a Roman statue I will stand
Till death hath made me marble. O my fame,
Live in despite of murder; take thy wings
And haste thee where the grey-ey'd morn perfumes
Her rosy chariot with Sabaean spices;
Fly where the evening from th' Iberian vales
Takes on her swarthy shoulders Hecate,
Crown'd with a grove of oaks; fly where men feel
The burning axletree; and those that suffer
Beneath the chariot of the snowy Bear;
And tell them all that D'Ambois now is hasting
To the eternal dwellers, that a thunder
Of all their sighs together (for their frailties
Beheld in me) may quit my worthless[28] fall
With a fit volley for my funeral.
UMB. Forgive thy murderers.
BUS. I forgive them all;
And you, my Lord, their fautor;[29] for true sign
Of which unfeign'd remission, take my sword;
Take it, and only give it motion,
And it shall find the way to victory
By his own brightness, and th' inherent valor
My fight hath still'd into 't, with charms of spirit.
Now let me pray you that my weighty blood
Laid in one scale of your impartial spleen,
May sway the forfeit of my worthy love
Weigh'd in the other;[30] and be reconcil'd
With all forgiveness to your matchless wife.
TAM. Forgive thou me, dear servant, and this hand
That led thy life to this unworthy end;
Forgive it, for the blood with which 't is stain'd,
In which I writ the summons of thy death —
The forced summons, by this bleeding wound,
By this here is my bosom, and by this
That makes me hold up both my hands imbru'd
For thy dear pardon.
BUS. Oh, my heart is broken!
Fate, nor these murderers, Monsieur nor the Guise,
Have any glory in my death, but this,
This killing spectacle, this prodigy.
My sun is turn'd to blood, in whose red beams
Pindus and Ossa, hid in drifts of snow
Laid on my heart and liver, from their veins
Melt like two hungry torrents, eating rocks
Into the ocean of all human life,
And make it bitter, only with my blood.[31]
O frail condition of strength, valor, virtue,
In me (like warning fire upon the top
Of some steep beacon on a steeper hill)
Made to express it: like a falling star
Silently glanc'd, that like a thunderbolt
Look'd to have stuck[32] and shook the firmament.
Moritur.
UMB. [My terrors are struck inward, and no more
My penance will allow they shall enforce
Earthly afflictions but upon myself.][33] —
Farewell, brave relics of a complete man!
Look up and see thy spirit made a star;
[Join] flames with [Hercules,][34] and when thou sett'st
Thy radiant forehead in the firmament,
Make the vast crystal[35] crack with thy receipt;
Spread to a world of fire; and the aged sky
Cheer with new sparks of old humanity. —
[*To* MONT.] Son of the earth, whom my unrested soul,
Rues t' have begotten in the faith of Heaven,
[Since thy revengeful spirit hath rejected
The charity it commands, and the remission
To serve and worship the blind rage of blood,][36]
Assay to gratulate[37] and pacify
The soul fled from this worthy by performing
The Christian reconcilement he besought

[28] Unworthy.

[29] Protector.

[30] *I.e.*, may my blood, balanced impartially in the scale of your anger, outweigh the claim (to vengeance) you have as a result of my worthy love to the Countess.

[31] *I.e.*, Tamyra, the light of my life, is bleeding; the sight of those bloody rays sweeps away my life into the ocean of eternity and embitters it with my blood (which has itself been embittered by the sight) — sweeps away my life as when on Pindus and Ossa the sun melts the snow and the ensuing torrents sweep even rocks away.

[32] Pierced. Boas emends *struck*.

[33] Q 1641 omits the first three lines of this speech; the first ten, in Q 1, form the closing speech of the play.

[34] So Q 1; Q 1641 garbles: *Jove flames with her rules.*

[35] The highest, or crystalline, sphere, in which Bussy is to be set as a star.

[36] So Q 1; om. Q 1641.

[37] Gratify.

Betwixt thee and thy lady. Let her wounds,
Manlessly [38] digg'd in her, be eas'd and cur'd
With balm of thine own tears; or be accurs'd
Never to rest free from my haunt and horror.

MONT. See how she merits this, still kneeling by,
And mourning his fall more than her own fault.

UMB. Remove, dear daughter, and content thy husband;
So piety wills thee, and thy servant's peace.
[*Exit.*] [39]

TAM. O wretched piety, that are so distract
In thine own constancy, and in thy right
Must be unrighteous. If I right my friend,
I wrong my husband; if his wrong I shun,
The duty of my friend I leave undone.
Ill plays on both sides; here and there it riseth;
No place, no good, so good but ill compriseth.
[My soul more scruple breeds, than my blood, sin.
Virtue imposeth more than any stepdame.] [40]
O had I never married but for form,
Never vow'd faith but purpos'd to deceive,
Never made conscience of any sin,
But cloak'd it privately and made it common,
Nor never honor'd been in blood or mind,
Happy had I been then, as others are
Of the like licence; I had then been honor'd;
Liv'd without envy; custom had benumb'd
All sense of scruple, and all note of frailty;
My fame had been untouch'd, my heart unbroken:
But, shunning all, I strike on all offence.
O husband! Dear friend! O my conscience!

MONS. Come, let's away; my senses are not proof
Against those plaints.
Exeunt GUISE [*and*] MONSIEUR; D'AMBOIS *is borne off.*

MONT. I must not yield to pity, nor to love.
So servile and so traitorous. Cease, my blood,[41]
To wrastle with my honor, fame, and judgment. —
Away! Forsake my house; forbear complaints
Where thou hast bred them: here all things [are] [42] full
Of their own shame and sorrow. Leave my house.

TAM. Sweet lord, forgive me, and I will be gone;
And till these wounds, that never balm shall close
Till death hath enter'd at them, so I love them,
Being opened by your hands, by death be cur'd,
I never more will grieve you with my sight,
Never endure that any roof shall part
Mine eyes and Heaven, but to the open deserts,
Like to a hunted tigress, I will fly,
Eating my heart, shunning the steps of men,
And look on no side till I be arriv'd.

MONT. I do forgive thee, and upon my knees,
With hands held up to Heaven, wish that mine honor
Would suffer reconcilement to my love;
But since it will not, honor never serve
My love with flourishing object till it starve; [43]
And as this taper, though it upwards look,
Downwards must needs consume, so let our love;
As having lost his honey, the sweet taste
Runs into savor, and will needs retain
A spice of his first parents,[44] till, like life,
It sees and dies; so let our love; and lastly,
As when the flame is suffer'd to look up,
It keeps his lustre, but, being thus turn'd down,
His natural course of useful light inverted,
His own stuff [45] puts it out; so let our love.
Now turn from me, as here I turn from thee,
And may both points of Heaven's straight axletree
Conjoin in one, before thyself and me.
Exeunt severally.

EPILOGUE [46]

WITH many hands you have seen D'Ambois slain,
Yet by your grace he may revive again,
And every day grow stronger in his skill
To please, as we presume he is in will.
The best deserving actors of the time
Had their ascents, and by degrees did climb
To their full height, a place to study due.
To make him tread in their path lies in you;
He'll not forget his makers, but still prove
His thankfulness as you increase your love.

[38] Unmanfully.
[39] Add. Parrott.
[40] So Q 1; om. Q 1641.
[41] Emotions (of love and pity).
[42] Add. Dilke.
[43] Perish.
[44] The bees.
[45] The melting wax.
[46] First appears in Q 1641.

THE WHITE DIVEL,

OR,

The Tragedy of *Paulo Giordano Ursini*, Duke of *Brachiano*,

With

The Life and Death of Vittoria Corombona the famous Venetian Curtizan.

Acted by the Queenes Maiesties Seruants..

Written by IOHN WEBSTER.

Non inferiora secutus.

LONDON,
Printed by *N.O.* for *Thomas Archer*, and are to be sold at his Shop in Popes head Pallace, neere the Royall Exchange. 1612.

INTRODUCTORY NOTE

WEBSTER's reputation rests almost wholly on two plays. Both are passionate dramas of amorous and political intrigue; both are set in Renaissance Italy, where to a contemporary Englishman's notion anything could happen; both are marked by Webster's crabbed but searing commentary on the folly of human complacency and the vanity of human wishes; both are replete with double-entendres, and occasionally condescend to a rude employment of physical horror; and both remain, for all these, romantic tragedies of great power, surpassed only by Shakespeare's in their own time, and since unequalled, except perhaps by Otway's pair of masterpieces, till Ibsen gave Europe a new conception of the tragic drama's function.

Yet none of Shakespeare's colleagues has been more bedevilled in our own day. A "Tussaud laureate", jeers Mr. Shaw, a greater dramatist, a twentieth-century dramatist, but an uncertain and still nineteenth-century critic. Before the second great renascence of the British drama was possible, it was necessary to break the strangle-hold of Shakespeare and the Elizabethans. Shaw's iconoclasm was not only healthy, it was indispensable; but it is so no longer, and is in fact definitely outmoded. Realism and naturalism have run their course, and drama is turning back from the analysis of social problems to the reconstruction of life. Here the Elizabethans have much to teach us, Webster not least. Every word, indeed, in the attacks of Shaw and Archer is hardly less applicable to Shakespeare himself. The differences are vast enough, but they reside in degree, not in kind. The better you like Shakespeare the greater Webster will seem to you.

Comparison between Webster's twin peaks of achievement is inevitable. *The White Devil* has come again to its own within the last few years, and there can be little question that in this play we have one of the supreme heights of the Jacobean range. The magnificent *Duchess of Malfy* is almost as effective till the death of the heroine, which comes rather too early; after that the play falls off. *The White Devil*, however, unlike as it is in most respects to Greek tragedy, comes closer to the best of it than any of the great Elizabethan plays except *Othello* in maintaining the highest tension throughout the entire action. Not once does it slacken: from the bitter protest "Banish'd!" which is the opening word, and Brachiano's "Quite lost, Flamineo", through the great trial scene, the lovers' anguished quarrel, and all the strivings and the agonies, to the Duke's terrible cry, "Vittoria! Vittoria!" and her desperate "O me! this place is hell"; through the cynicism of Flamineo's speeches, which are like salt rubbed in open wounds, and Cornelia's misery ("Call for the robin redbreast and the wren"), to the treachery and bloody horror of the final episode, and Lodovico's black benediction:

> I do glory yet
> That I can call this act mine own. For my part,
> The rack, the gallows, and the torturing wheel
> Shall be but sound sleeps to me; here 's my rest:
> I limn'd this night-piece, and it was my best.

The White Devil was published in 1612. It was probably not written before 1609, for the allusion in V, iii, 188, is to Sir Hugh Myddleton's New River, which was begun in that year; and Perseus, in III, ii, 135, comes from Jonson's *Masque of Queens*, which was produced on February 2 of the same year. 1611–1612 is probably correct. The source was the tragic life of Vittoria Accoramboni, which ended with her murder on December 22, 1585. Whether her story reached Webster in written form is unknown. There were several such accounts; but while many details of the play are based on the actual facts, there are so many departures from them, some obviously due to the dramatic adaptation but others apparently unintentional, that Lucas concludes that Webster relied on a circumstantial but oral account. Virginio Orsini, the Giovanni of *The White Devil*, visited England in 1601.

The original reception of the play is described in Webster's address to the reader. It was successfully revived once more under the Restoration. In 1707 Nahum Tate's ridiculous adaptation, *Injured Love*, was published as it was "design'd to be Acted at the Theatre Royal." The standard edition of Webster is that of F. L. Lucas (1928). *The White Devil* and *The Duchess of Malfy* occupy a volume in the Belles Lettres Series, edited by M. W. Sampson (1904). The First Quarto of the former, 1612, was followed by others in 1631, 1665, and 1672. The present text is based on the Harvard copy of Q 1612, which is in agreement with the Garrick copy, cited by Lucas as superior in most signatures to the Dyce copy. It has also been collated with the copy of the Folger Shakespeare Library, which usually, though not invariably, agrees with the Garrick-Harvard State.

[A new modernized text of *The White Devil* was edited by John R. Brown (Harvard, 1960) for the Revels Plays series. R. O.]

THE WHITE DEVIL[1]

OR

VITTORIA COROMBONA

BY

JOHN WEBSTER

To The Reader

In publishing this tragedy I do but challenge to myself that liberty which other men have ta'en before me; not that I affect praise by it, for *nos haec novimus esse nihil:*[2] only, since it was acted in so dull a time of winter, presented in so open and black[3] a theatre, that it wanted that which is the only grace and setting out of a tragedy, a full and understanding auditory; and that since that time I have noted most of the people that come to that playhouse resemble those ignorant asses who, visiting stationers' shops, their use is not to inquire for good books, but new books; I present it to the general view with this confidence:

Nec rhoncos metues maligniorum,
Nec scombris tunicas dabis molestas.[4]

If it be objected this is no true dramatic poem, I shall easily confess it: *non potes in nugas dicere plura meas: Ipse ego quam dixi,*[5] willingly and not ignorantly in this kind have I faulted; for should a man present to such an auditory the most sententious tragedy that ever was written, observing all the critical laws, as heighth of style and gravity of person, enrich it with the sententious Chorus, and as it were lifen death in the passionate and weighty Nuntius;[6] yet, after all this divine rapture, *O dura messorum ilia,*[7] the breath that comes from the uncapable multitude is able to poison it; and ere it be acted let the author resolve to fix to every scene this of Horace:

— Haec hodie Porcis comedenda relinques.[8]

To those who report I was a long time in finishing this tragedy, I confess I do not write with a goose quill, winged with two feathers; and if they will needs make it my fault, I must answer them with that of Euripides to Alcestides,[9] a tragic writer: Alcestides objecting that Euripides had only in three days composed three verses, whereas himself had written three hundred, "Thou tell'st truth," quoth he, "but here's the difference: thine shall only be read for three days, whereas mine shall continue three ages."

Detraction is the sworn friend to ignorance; for mine own part I have ever truly cherish'd my good opinion of other men's worthy labors: especially of that full and height'ned style of Master Chapman; the labor'd and understanding works of Master Jonson; the no less worthy composures of the both worthily excellent Master Beaumont and Master Fletcher; and lastly,

[1] *I.e.*, a devil disguised under a fair appearance.

[2] We are aware that these things are negligible. (Martial, XIII, 2.)

[3] The Red Bull, a large, partly roofless theatre in Clerkenwell, saw the first performance of *The White Devil.* Toward the end of a winter afternoon it would be getting dark. Malone emends *bleak.* The company was the Queen's Men, formerly the Earl of Worcester's. It seems probable that Webster had severed his connection with them before the publication of this play. His next, *The Duchess of Malfy*, was produced by the King's Men.

[4] You, [my book,] shall not fear the turned-up noses of the malicious, nor shall you provide wrapping-paper for mackerel. (Martial, IV, 86.)

[5] You can not say more against these trifles of mine than I have said myself. (Martial, XIII, 2.)

[6] Give a lively account of the deaths of the characters by means of the . . . classical Messenger.

[7] Oh, the strong stomachs of harvesters. (Horace, *Epodes*, III.)

[8] These you will leave for the swine to eat today. (*Epistles*, I, 7.)

[9] The anecdote is told by Valerius Maximus (III, 7). *Alcestides* is Webster's blunder for *Alcestis*, itself (Lucas suggests) a blunder for the tragic poet *Acestor*. The Latin account specifies one, not three, hundred lines.

without wrong last to be named, the right happy and copious industry of M. Shakespeare, M. Dekker, and M. Heywood; wishing what I write may be read by their light: protesting that, in the strength of mine own judgment, I know them so worthy that, though I rest silent in my own work, yet to most of theirs I dare, without flattery, fix that of Martial:

— non norunt, Haec monumenta mori.[10]

[THE PERSONS[11]

MONTICELSO, a cardinal, afterwards Pope Paul the Fourth.[12]

FRANCISCO DE MEDICIS,[13] Duke of Florence; in the fifth act disguis'd for a Moor, under the name of Mulinassar.

BRACHIANO, otherwise PAULO GIORDANO ORSINI,[14] Duke of Brachiano; husband to Isabella, and in love with Vittoria.

GIOVANNI,[15] his son, by Isabella.

LODOVICO,[16] an Italian count, but decay'd.

ANTONELLI, } his friends, and dependents of
GASPARO, } the Duke of Florence.

CAMILLO,[17] husband to Vittoria.

HORTENSIO, one of Brachiano's officers.

MARCELLO,[18] an attendant of the Duke of Florence, and brother to Vittoria.

FLAMINEO,[19] secretary to Brachiano, brother to Vittoria.

JAQUES, a Moor, servant to Giovanni.

CARDINAL OF ARRAGON.

DOCTOR JULIO.

CHRISTOPHERO, his assistant.

Ambassadors, courtiers, lawyers, officers, physicians, conjuror, armorer, and attendants.

ISABELLA,[20] sister to Francisco de Medicis, and wife to Brachiano.

VITTORIA COROMBONA, a Venetian[21] lady; first marri'd to Camillo, afterwards to Brachiano.

CORNELIA,[22] mother to Vittoria, Flamineo, and Marcello.

ZANCHE, a Moor, servant to Vittoria.

Matron of a house of convertites.

THE SCENE — *Rome and Padua.*]

[ACT I — SCENE I][1]

Enter COUNT LODOVICO, ANTONELLI, *and* GASPARO.

LOD. Banish'd!
ANT. It griev'd me much to hear the sentence.
LOD. Ha, ha! O Democritus, thy gods
That govern the whole world! courtly reward
And punishment![2] Fortune's a right whore:
If she give aught, she deals it in small parcels,
That she may take away all at one swoop.
This 't is to have great enemies: God quit[3] them!
Your wolf no longer seems to be a wolf
Than when she's hungry.[4]
GAS. You term those enemies
[5]Are men of princely rank.
LOD. Oh, I pray for them.
The violent thunder is adored by those
Are pash'd in pieces by it.
ANT. Come, my Lord,
You are justly doom'd: look but a little back
Into your former life; you have in three years
Ruin'd the noblest earldom.
GAS. Your followers

[10] These monuments know not how to die. (Martial, X, 2.)

[11] Based on the list first given in Q_3, but with several additions and minor changes.

[12] Historically, Cardinal Montalto, afterwards Sextus V.

[13] Francesco de' Medici.

[14] Bracciano . . . Paolo . . . Orsini; old eds. *Ursini* here, but elsewhere, *Orsini*. Webster's spelling *Brachiano* is intended to indicate the Italian pronunciation, *Bracciano*.

[15] Historically, Virginio.

[16] Historically, Lodovico degli Orsini di Monterotondo, a younger kinsman of Bracciano.

[17] Nephew to the Cardinal; historically, Francesco Peretti.

[18] Younger than the Flamineo of the play; historically, Flamineo.

[19] Historically, Marcello.

[20] The historical Isabella was murdered in revenge for her intrigue with Troilo Orsini.

[21] The historical Vittoria Accoramboni was an Umbrian.

[22] Historically, Tarquinia. She probably planned her son-in-law's assassination.

[1] Rome, but not precisely located.

[2] Opposed to all the known sayings of Democritus. (Sampson.)

[3] Repay, requite.

[4] *I.e.*, prosperous wolves are not regarded as wolves.

[5] The relative is often omitted in this play.

Have swallowed you like mummia,[6] and, being sick
With such unnatural and horrid physic,
Vomit you up i' th' kennel.[7]
ANT. All the damnable degrees
Of drinkings have you stagger'd through: one citizen
Is lord of two fair manors call'd you master,
Only for caviare.[8]
GAS. Those noblemen
Which were invited to your prodigal feasts,
Wherein the phoenix scarce could scape your throats,
Laugh at your misery, as fore-deeming you
An idle meteor, which, drawn forth the earth,[9]
Would be soon lost i' th' air.
ANT. Jest upon you,
And say you were begotten in an earthquake,
You have ruin'd such fair lordships.
LOD. Very good;
This well goes with two buckets: I must tend[10]
The pouring out of either.
GAS. Worse than these:
You have acted certain murders[11] here in Rome,
Bloody and full of horror.
LOD. 'Las! they were flea-bitings.
Why took they not my head then?
GAS. Oh, my Lord,
The law doth sometimes mediate, thinks it good
Not ever to steep violent sins in blood;
This gentle penance may both end your crimes,
And in the example better these bad times.
LOD. So; but I wonder then some great men scape
This banishment: there's Paulo Giordano Orsini,
The Duke of Brachiano, now lives in Rome,
And by close panderism seeks to prostitute
The honor of Vittoria Corombona —
Vittoria, she that might have got my pardon
For one kiss to the Duke.
ANT. Have a full man within you.
We see that trees bear no such pleasant fruit
There where they grew first as where they are new set;
Perfumes, the more they are chaf'd, the more they render
Their pleasing scents; and so affliction
Expresseth virtue fully, whether true
Or else adulterate.
LOD. Leave your painted comforts;[12]
I'll make Italian cut-works[13] in their guts,
If ever I return.
GAS. Oh, sir!
LOD. I am patient.
I have seen some ready to be executed
Give pleasant looks and money, and grown familiar
With the knave hangman; so do I, I thank them,
And would account them nobly merciful,
Would they dispatch me quickly.
ANT. Fare you well;
We shall find time, I doubt not, to repeal
Your banishment.
LOD. I am ever bound to you.
This is the world's alms; pray, make use of it.[14]
Great men sell sheep thus, to be cut in pieces
When first they have shorn them bare and sold their fleeces. *Exeunt.*

SCENE II[1]

Sennet.[2] *Enter* BRACHIANO, CAMILLO, FLAMINEO, VITTORIA COROMBONA, [*and* Servants *with torches*].

BRACH. Your best of rest!
VIT. Unto my Lord the Duke
The best of welcome! — More lights! attend the Duke.
[*Exeunt* CAMILLO *and* VITTORIA.]
BRACH. Flamineo!
FLAM. My Lord?
BRACH. Quite lost, Flamineo!
FLAM. Pursue your noble wishes; I am prompt
As lightning to your service. Oh, my Lord —
(*whisper*) The fair Vittoria, my happy sister,
Shall give you present audience. — Gentlemen,
Let the caroche[3] go on; and 't is his pleasure

[6] Mummy was formerly used medicinally.
[7] Gutter.
[8] *I.e.*, you have spent for caviare alone the proceeds of the sale of two of your manors.
[9] Meteors were supposed to be "exhalations" from the earth, drawn up by the sun.
[10] Await.
[11] The historical Lodovico had murdered Vincenzo Vitelli.

[12] Specious consolations.
[13] Open-work patterns.
[14] *I.e.*, profit by my experience.
[1] "Vaguely Camillo's house, here perhaps the entrance-hall, later the banqueting-house." (Lucas.)
[2] Flourish of trumpets. Qq om., but after i, 59 give the prompter's note: *Enter Senate.*
[3] Coach.

You put out all your torches, and depart.
[*Exeunt* Attendants.]

BRACH. Are we so happy?

FLAM. Can 't be otherwise?
Observ'd you not to-night, my honor'd Lord,
Which way soe'er you went she threw her eyes?
I have dealt already with her chambermaid,
Zanche, the Moor; and she is wondrous proud
To be the agent for so high a spirit.

BRACH. We are happy above thought, because 'bove merit.

FLAM. 'Bove merit! — we may now talk freely — 'bove merit! What is 't you doubt?[4] her coyness? that 's but the superficies of lust most women have; yet why should ladies blush to hear that nam'd which they do not fear to handle? Oh, they are politic! They know our desire is increas'd by the difficulty of enjoying, where[5] a satiety is a blunt, weary, and drowsy passion. If the buttery-hatch at court stood continually open, there would be nothing so passionate crowding, nor hot suit after the beverage.

BRACH. Oh, but her jealous husband!

FLAM. Hang him! a gilder that hath his brains perish'd with quicksilver[6] is not more cold in the liver;[7] the great barriers[8] moulted not more feathers[9] than he hath shed hairs, by the confession of his doctor;[10] an Irish gamester that will play himself naked, and then wage all downward[11] at hazard, is not more venturous; so unable to please a woman, that, like a Dutch doublet,[12] all his back is shrunk into his breeches.
Shroud you within this closet, good my Lord:
Some trick now must be thought on to divide
My brother-in-law from his fair bedfellow.

BRACH. Oh, should she fail to come —

FLAM. I must not have your Lordship thus unwisely amorous. I myself have loved a lady, and pursued her with a great deal of under-age protestation,[13] whom some three or four gallants that have enjoyed would with all their hearts have been glad to have been rid of. 'T is just like a summer bird-cage in a garden: the birds that are without despair to get in, and the birds that are within despair and are in a consumption for fear they shall never get out.[14] Away, away, my Lord!
[*Exit* BRACHIANO.]
See, here he comes. This fellow by his apparel
Some men would judge a politician;
But, call his wit in question, you shall find it
Merely an ass in 's footcloth.[15]

Re-enter CAMILLO.

How now, Brother?
What, travelling to bed to your kind wife?

CAM. I assure you, Brother, no; my voyage lies
More northerly, in a far colder clime;
I do not well remember, I protest,
When I last lay with her.

FLAM. Strange you should lose your count.

CAM. We never lay together, but ere morning
There grew a flaw[16] between us.

FLAM. 'T had been your part
To have made up that flaw.

CAM. True, but she loathes
I should be seen in 't.

FLAM. Why, sir, what 's the matter?

CAM. The Duke, your master, visits me, I thank him;
And I perceive how, like an earnest bowler,
He very passionately leans that way
He should have his bowl run.

FLAM. I hope you do not think —

CAM. That noblemen bowl booty?[17] Faith, his cheek[18]
Hath a most excellent bias;[19] it would fain

[4] Fear.

[5] Whereas. Dyce may be right in emending *where a* to *whereas.*

[6] *I.e.*, from mercurial poisoning. Mercury was used in the process of gold-plating.

[7] The seat of love.

[8] A form of jousting; the participants fought across waist-high barriers.

[9] The shorn helmet plumes.

[10] The mercurial treatment of syphilis had this effect.

[11] Sykes quotes from Stanyhurst's *Description of Ireland* an account of certain Irish gamesters who after playing away their clothes would wager their testes. The imputation is that Camillo's are valueless, and that his impotence would make him bold to stake them.

[12] Which, unlike their breeches, was tight-fitting.

[13] Inexperienced love-making.

[14] From Florio's translation of Montaigne's Essays, "Of Marriage."

[15] A rich cloth laid over a horse's back; it nearly touched the ground.

[16] Quarrel, with an obvious double entente.

[17] Join with confederates to victimize another player.

[18] Brachiano's cheek, which, like the round cheek of a bowl, is trying to touch that of the "mistress."

[19] Bowls were shaped or weighted so as to roll in a curve (bias) around an object that might bar the way to the "mistress."

Jump with [20] my mistress.[21]
FLAM. Will you be an ass,
Despite you[r] Aristotle? or a cuckold,
Contrary to your Ephemerides,[22]
Which shows you under what a smiling planet
You were first swaddled?
CAM. Pew-wew, sir, tell not me
Of planets nor of Ephemerides;
A man may be made cuckold in the daytime,
When the stars' eyes are out.
FLAM. Sir, God boy you; [23]
I do commit you to your pitiful pillow
Stuff'd with horn-shavings.[24]
CAM. Brother —
FLAM. God refuse me!
Might I advise you now, your only course
Were to lock up your wife.
CAM. 'T were very good.
FLAM. Bar her the sight of revels.
CAM. Excellent.
FLAM. Let her not go to church, but, like a hound,
In leon [25] at your heels.
CAM. 'T were for her honor.
FLAM. And so you should be certain in one fortnight,
Despite her chastity or innocence,
To be cuckolded, which yet is in suspense:
This is my counsel, and I ask no fee for 't.
CAM. Come, you know not where my night-cap wrings me.

FLAM. Wear it a' th' old fashion; let your large ears come through, it will be more easy. Nay, I will be bitter. Bar your wife of her entertainment? Women are more willingly and more gloriously chaste when they are least restrained of their liberty. It seems you would be a fine, capricious, mathematically jealous coxcomb; take the height of your own horns with a Jacob's staff [26] afore they are up. These politic inclosures [27] for paltry mutton [28] makes more rebellion in the flesh than all the provocative electuaries doctors have uttered [29] since last jubilee.[30]

CAM. This doth not physic me.

FLAM. It seems you are jealous; I'll show you the error of it by a familiar example. I have seen a pair of spectacles fashion'd with such perspective art, that, lay down but one twelvepence a' th' board, 't will appear as if there were twenty; now, should you wear a pair of these spectacles, and see your wife tying her shoe, you would imagine twenty hands were taking up of your wife's clothes, and this would put you into a horrible causeless fury.

CAM. The fault there, sir, is not in the eyesight.

FLAM. True; but they that have the yellow jaundice think all objects they look on to be yellow. Jealousy is worser: her fits present to a man, like so many bubbles in a basin of water, twenty several crabbed faces; many times makes his own shadow his cuckold-maker.

Re-enter [VITTORIA] COROMBONA.

See, she comes. What reason have you to be jealous of this creature? What an ignorant ass or flattering knave might he be counted that should write sonnets to her eyes, or call her brow the snow of Ida or ivory of Corinth, or compare her hair to the blackbird's bill,[31] when 't is liker the blackbird's feather! This is all; be wise, I will make you friends; and you shall go to bed together. Marry, look you, it shall not be your seeking; do you stand upon that by any means; [32] walk you aloof; I would not have you seen in 't. [CAMILLO *retires.*] — Sister, — [*aside*] my Lord attends you in the banqueting-house. Your husband is wondrous discontented.

VIT. I did nothing to displease him; I carved [33] to him at supper-time.

FLAM. [*aside*] You need not have carved [34] him, in faith: they say he is a capon already. I must now seemingly fall out with you. — Shall a gentleman so well descended as Camillo, — [*aside*] a lousy slave, that within this twenty years rode with the black guard [35] in the Duke's carriage, 'mongst spits and dripping-pans. —

CAM. [*aside*] Now he begins to tickle [36] her!

[20] Coincide with, touch.
[21] Or jack, the object-ball at which the bowls were aimed.
[22] Astrological tables. [23] God be with you, goodbye.
[24] Alluding to the horns of the cuckold.
[25] A variant of *leam* or *lyam* = leash.
[26] An instrument for measuring heights and distances.
[27] An allusion to a grievance of the time, the inclosure of common lands by rich landowners for sheep pasturage.
[28] Slang for "loose women."
[29] Issued, sold.
[30] 1600. The first year of jubilee was proclaimed by Pope Boniface VIII in 1300.
[31] Which is yellow. Gentlemen still preferred blondes to brunettes, at any rate theoretically.
[32] Stick to that on any account.
[33] Was courteous. [34] *I.e.*, gelded.
[35] The lowest menials. "Carriage" = baggage train.
[36] Excite.

FLAM. An excellent scholar, — [*aside*] one that hath a head fill'd with calves' brains without any sage [37] in them, — come crouching in the hams to you for a night's lodging, — [*aside*] that hath an itch in 's hams, which like the fire at the glass-house [38] hath not gone out this seven years? — Is he not a courtly gentleman? — [*aside*] When he wears white satin, one would take him by his black muzzle to be no other creature than a maggot. — You are a goodly foil, I confess, well set out, — [*aside*] but cover'd with a false stone, yon counterfeit diamond.

CAM. [*aside*] He will make her know what is in me.

FLAM. Come, my Lord attends you; thou shalt go to bed to my Lord —

CAM. [*aside*] Now he comes to 't.

FLAM. [*aside*] With a relish as curious as a vintner going to taste new wine. — [*to* CAMILLO] I am opening your case hard.

CAM. [*aside*] A virtuous brother, a' my credit!

FLAM. He will give thee a ring with a philosopher's stone in it.

CAM. [*aside*] Indeed, I am studying alchemy.

FLAM. [*aside*] Thou shalt lie in a bed stuff'd with turtles' feathers; swoon in perfumed linen, like the fellow was smothered in roses. So perfect shall be thy happiness that, as men at sea think land and trees and ships go that way they go, so both heaven and earth shall seem to go your voyage. Shalt meet him; 't is fix'd with nails of diamonds to inevitable necessity.

VIT. [*aside*] How shall 's rid him hence?

FLAM. [*aside*] I will put brees [39] in 's tail — set him gadding presently.[40] — [*to* CAMILLO] I have almost wrought her to it: I find her coming; [41] but, might I advise you now, for this night I would not lie with her; I would cross her humor,[42] to make her more humble.

CAM. Shall I, shall I?

FLAM. It will show in you a supremacy of judgment.

CAM. True, and a mind differing from the tumultuary [43] opinion; for, *quae negata, grata.*[44]

FLAM. Right; you are the adamant [45] shall draw her to you, though you keep distance off.

CAM. A philosophical reason.

FLAM. Walk by her a' the nobleman's fashion, and tell her you will lie with her at the end of the progress.[46]

CAM. [*coming forward*] Vittoria, I cannot be induc'd, or, as a man would say, incited —

VIT. To do what, sir?

CAM. To lie with you to-night. Your [47] silkworm useth to fast every third day, and the next following spins the better. To-morrow at night I am for you.

VIT. You 'll spin a fair thread, trust to 't.

FLAM. [*aside to* CAMILLO] But, do you hear, I shall have you [48] steal to her chamber about midnight.

CAM. [*aside*] Do you think so? why, look you, Brother, because you shall not think I'll gull [49] you, take the key, lock me into the chamber, and say [50] you shall be sure of me.

FLAM. [*aside*] In troth, I will; I'll be your jailer once. But have you ne'er a false door?

CAM. [*aside*] A pox on 't, as I am a Christian! Tell me to-morrow how scurvily she takes my unkind parting.

FLAM. [*aside*] I will.

CAM. [*aside*] Didst thou not [mark] [51] the jest of the silkworm? Good-night. In faith, I will use this trick often.

FLAM. [*aside*] Do, do, do. — *Exit* CAMILLO. So; [52] now you are safe. Ha, ha, ha! thou entanglest thyself in thine own work like a silkworm. — Come, Sister; darkness hides your blush. Women are like curst [53] dogs: civility [54] keeps them tied all daytime, but they are let loose at midnight; then they do most good, or most mischief. — My Lord, my Lord!

[37] An obvious pun.
[38] It stood near the Blackfriars Theatre. There are numerous allusions to London in this play, despite its setting.
[39] Gadflies.
[40] At once.
[41] *I.e.*, favorably disposed.
[42] Whim, inclination.
[43] Hurriedly formed, unsystematic.
[44] What is refused is pleasing.
[45] Magnet.
[46] Royal journey to visit various parts of the realm.
[47] The.
[48] I shall find you, I fear you will.
[49] Deceive.
[50] Tate's *Injured Love* reads *so*, perhaps rightly. Daniel proposed the emendation.
[51] So Q_4; earlier Qq *make*.
[52] Locking the door.
[53] Ugly, fierce.
[54] Decency. Q_2, *et seq.*, *cruelty*.

Re-enter BRACHIANO. ZANCHE *brings out a carpet, spreads it, and lays on it two fair cushions.*

BRACH. Give credit I could wish time would stand still,
And never end this interview, this hour;
But all delight doth itself soon'st devour.

Enter CORNELIA [*behind*].

Let me into your bosom, happy lady,
Pour out, instead of eloquence, my vows.
Loose me not, madam; for, if you forgo me,
I am lost eternally.
VIT. Sir, in the way of pity,
I wish you heart-whole.
BRACH. You are a sweet physician.
VIT. Sure, sir, a loathed cruelty in ladies
Is as to doctors many funerals:
It takes away their credit.
BRACH. Excellent creature!
We call the cruel fair; what name for you
That are so merciful?
ZAN. See, now they close.
FLAM. Most happy union!
CORN. [*aside*] My fears are fall'n upon me. Oh, my heart!
My son the pander! now I find our house
Sinking to ruin. Earthquakes leave behind,
Where they have tyrannized, iron or lead or stone;
But, woe to ruin, violent lust leaves none!
BRACH. What value is this jewel?
VIT. 'T is the ornament
Of a weak fortune.
BRACH. In sooth, I'll have it; nay, I will but change
My jewel for your jewel.
FLAM. [*aside*] Excellent!
His jewel for her jewel: well put in, Duke.
BRACH. Nay, let me see you wear it.
VIT. Here, sir?
BRACH. Nay, lower, you shall wear my jewel lower.
FLAM. [*aside*] That's better: she must wear his jewel lower.
VIT. To pass away the time, I'll tell your Grace
A dream I had last night.
BRACH. Most wishedly.
VIT. A foolish, idle dream.
Methought I walk'd, about the mid of night,
Into a churchyard, where a goodly yew tree
Spread her large root in ground. Under that yew,[55]
As I sat sadly leaning on a grave
Chequered with cross sticks,[56] there came stealing in
Your duchess and my husband; one of them
A pickaxe bore, th' other a rusty spade;
And in rough terms they 'gan to challenge me
About this yew.
BRACH. That tree?
VIT. This harmless yew.
They told me my intent was to root up
That well-grown yew, and plant i' th' stead of it
A withered blackthorn; and for that they vow'd
To bury me alive. My husband straight
With pickaxe 'gan to dig, and your fell duchess
With shovel, like a Fury, voided out
The earth, and scattered bones. Lord, how methought
I trembled; and yet, for all this terror,
I could not pray.
FLAM. [*aside*] No; the Devil was in your dream.
VIT. When to my rescue there arose, methought,
A whirlwind, which let fall a massy arm
From that strong plant;
And both were struck dead by that sacred yew,
In that base shallow grave that was their due.
FLAM. [*aside*] Excellent devil! she hath taught him in a dream
To make away his duchess and her husband.
BRACH. Sweetly shall I interpret this your dream.
You are lodged within his arms who shall protect you
From all the fevers of a jealous husband,
From the poor envy[57] of our phlegmatic duchess.
I'll seat you above law and above scandal;
Give to your thoughts the invention of delight,
And the fruition; nor shall government
Divide me from you longer than a care
To keep you great: you shall to me at once
Be dukedom, health, wife, children, friends, and all.

[55] With a play on "you." Old eds. spell *Eu* or *Ewe*.

[56] Probably, as Sampson suggests, "crosses stuck in the grave."

[57] Malice.

CORN. [*coming forward*] Woe to light hearts! they still forerun our fall.
FLAM. What Fury rais'd thee up? — Away, away! *Exit* ZANCHE.
CORN. What make [58] you here, my Lord, this dead of night?
Never dropp'd mildew on a flower here
Till now.
FLAM. I pray, will you go to bed, then,
Lest you be blasted?
CORN. Oh, that this fair garden
Had [with] [59] all poisoned herbs of Thessaly [60]
At first been planted; made a nursery
For witchcraft, rather [than] [59] a burial plot
For both your honors!
VIT. Dearest Mother, hear me.
CORN. Oh, thou dost make my brow bend to the earth,
Sooner than nature! See, the curse of children!
In life they keep us frequently [61] in tears;
And in the cold grave leaves us in pale fears.
BRACH. Come, come, I will not hear you.
VIT. Dear my Lord —
CORN. Where is thy duchess now, adulterous Duke?
Thou little dream'dst this night she is come to Rome.
FLAM. How! come to Rome?
VIT. The Duchess!
BRACH. She had been better —
CORN. The lives of princes should like dials move,
Whose regular example is so strong
They make the times by them go right or wrong.
FLAM. So; have you done?
CORN. Unfortunate Camillo!
VIT. I do protest, if any chaste denial,
If anything but blood could have allayed
His long suit to me —
CORN. I will join with thee, [62]
To the most woeful end e'er mother kneel'd:
If thou dishonor thus thy husband's bed,
Be thy life short as are the funeral tears
In great men's — [63]
BRACH. Fie, fie, the woman's mad.
CORN. Be thy act Judas-like — betray in kissing!
Mayst thou be envied [64] during his short breath,
And pitied like a wretch after [his] [65] death!
VIT. O me accurs'd! *Exit* VITTORIA.
FLAM. Are you out of your wits, my Lord?
I'll fetch her back again!
BRACH. No, I'll to bed;
Send Doctor Julio to me presently. —
Uncharitable woman, thy rash tongue
Hath rais'd a fearful and prodigious [66] storm:
Be thou the cause of all ensuing harm.
Exit BRACHIANO.
FLAM. Now, you that stand so much upon your honor,
Is this a fitting time a' night, think you,
To send a duke home without e'er a man? [67]
I would fain know where lies the mass of wealth
Which you have hoarded for my maintenance,
That I may bear my beard out of the level
Of my Lord's stirrup. [68]
CORN. What! because we are poor,
Shall we be vicious?
FLAM. Pray, what means have you
To keep me from the galleys — or the gallows?
My father prov'd himself a gentleman —
Sold all's land, and, like a fortunate fellow,
Died ere the money was spent. You brought me up
At Padua, I confess, where, I protest,
For want of means (the university judge me),
I have been fain to heel my tutor's stockings, [69]
At least seven years; conspiring with a beard
Made me a graduate; then to this duke's service.
I visited the court, whence I return'd
More courteous, more lecherous by far,
But not a suit the richer; and shall I,
Having a path so open and so free
To my preferment, still retain your milk
In my pale forehead? [70] No, this face of mine
I'll arm and fortify with lusty wine,
'Gainst shame and blushing.
CORN. Oh, that I ne'er had borne thee!
FLAM. So would I;
I would the common'st courtezan in Rome

[58] Do.
[59] Add. Q_2.
[60] In classical literature a great haunt of witches.
[61] Repeatedly.
[62] In kneeling.
[63] Old eds. have a full stop instead of a dash.
[64] Hated.
[65] Q_1 *this*.
[66] Portentous.
[67] An attendant.
[68] *I.e.*, leave off having to run at his stirrup like a footman.
[69] *I.e.*, act as his servant.
[70] *I.e.*, be womanish.

Had been my mother, rather than thyself.
Nature is very pitiful to whores,
To give them but few children, yet those children
Plurality of fathers: they are sure
They shall not want. Go, go,
Complain unto my great Lord Cardinal;
Yet maybe he will justify the act.
Lycurgus [71] wond'red much men would provide
Good stallions for their mares, and yet would suffer
Their fair wives to be barren.

CORN. Misery of miseries!

Exit CORNELIA.

FLAM. The Duchess come to court! I like not that.
We are engag'd to mischief, and must on;
As rivers, to find out the ocean,
Flow with crook bendings beneath forced banks;
Or as we see, to aspire some mountain's top,
The way ascends not straight, but imitates
The subtle foldings of a winter's snake;
So who knows policy and her true aspect
Shall find her ways winding and indirect.

[ACT II — SCENE I] [1]

Enter FRANCESCO DE MEDICIS, CARDINAL MONTICELSO, ISABELLA, *young* GIOVANNI, *with little* JAQUES *the Moor*.

FRAN. Have you not seen your husband since you arrived?

ISA. Not yet, sir.

FRAN. Surely he is wondrous kind.
If I had such a dovehouse as Camillo's,
I would set fire on 't, were 't but to destroy
The polecats [2] that haunt to 't. —

[*Enter* MARCELLO.]

My sweet Cousin! [3]

GIOV. Lord Uncle, you did promise me a horse
And armor.

FRAN. That I did, my pretty Cousin. —
Marcello, see it fitted.

MAR. My Lord, the Duke is here.

FRAN. Sister, away! you must not yet be seen.

ISA. I do beseech you,
Entreat him mildly; let not your rough tongue
Set us at louder variance: all my wrongs
Are freely pardoned; and I do not doubt,
As men, to try the precious unicorn's horn, [4]
Make of the powder a preservative circle
And in it put a spider, [5] so these arms
Shall charm his poison, force it to obeying,
And keep him chaste from an infected straying.

FRAN. I wish it may. Begone.

[*Exeunt* ISABELLA, GIOVANNI, *and* JAQUES.]

Enter BRACHIANO *and* FLAMINEO.

Void the chamber. —

[*Exeunt* MARCELLO *and* FLAMINEO.]

You are welcome; will you sit? — I pray, my Lord,
Be you my orator: my heart 's too full;
I 'll second you anon.

MONT. Ere I begin,
Let me entreat your Grace forgo all passion
Which may be raised by my free discourse.

BRACH. As silent as i' th' church — [6] you may proceed.

MONT. It is a wonder to your noble friends,
That you, have, [7] as 'twere, ent'red the world
With a free sceptre in your able hand,
And have to th' use of nature well applied
High gifts of learning, should in your prime age
Neglect your awful throne for the soft down
Of an insatiate bed. O, my Lord,
The drunkard after all his lavish cups
Is dry, and then is sober; so at length,
When you awake from this lascivious dream,
Repentance then will follow, like the sting
Plac'd in the adder's tail. Wretched are princes
When fortune blasteth but a petty flower
Of their unwieldly crowns or ravisheth
But one pearl from their scepter; [8] but, alas,
When they to wilful shipwrack lose good fame,
All princely titles perish with their name!

BRACH. You have said, my Lord.

MONT. Enough to give you taste
How far I am from flattering your greatness!

[71] In Plutarch's Life of him.
[1] A room in Francisco's palace.
[2] Prostitutes.
[3] Here = nephew.

[4] Supposed to be an antidote.
[5] Whose inability to cross the ring of powder would prove its efficacy. [6] Qq_{1-3} have no stop.
[7] So Q_1; Qq_{2-4} *you having*. Lucas needlessly inserts *that*, but see on I, i, 10. [8] Qq_{2-4} *scepters*.

BRACH. Now you that are his second, what say you?
Do not, like young hawks, fetch a course about:[9]
Your game flies fair and for you.
FRAN. Do not fear it.
I 'll answer you in your own hawking phrase:
Some eagles that should gaze upon the sun
Seldom soar high, but take their lustful ease,
Since they from dunghill birds their prey can seize.
You know Vittoria?
BRACH. Yes.
FRAN. You shift your shirt there,
When you retire from tennis?
BRACH. Happily.[10]
FRAN. Her husband is lord of a poor fortune,
Yet she wears cloth of tissue.[11]
BRACH. What of this? —
Will you urge that, my good Lord Cardinal,
As part of her confession at next shrift,
And know from whence it sails?
FRAN. She is your strumpet.
BRACH. Uncivil sir, there 's hemlock in thy breath
And that black slander — were she[12] a whore of mine,
All thy loud cannons, and thy borrowed[13] Switzers,
Thy galleys, nor thy sworn confederates,
Durst not supplant her.
FRAN. Let 's not talk on thunder.
Thou hast a wife, our sister; would I had given
Both her white hands to death, bound and lock'd fast
In her last winding sheet, when I gave thee
But one!
BRACH. Thou hadst given a soul to God, then.
FRAN. True;
Thy ghostly father, with all 's absolution,
Shall ne'er do so by thee.
BRACH. Spit thy poison!
FRAN. I shall not need; lust carries her sharp whip
At her own girdle. Look to 't, for our anger
Is making thunderbolts.
BRACH. Thunder? in faith,
They are but crackers.
FRAN. We 'll end this with the cannon.
BRACH. Thou 'lt get naught by it but iron in thy wounds
And gunpowder in thy nostrils.
FRAN. Better that
Than change perfumes for plasters.[14]
BRACH. Pity on thee!
'T were good you 'd show your slaves or men condemn'd
Your new-plow'd[15] forehead.[16] Defiance! and I 'll meet thee,
Even in a thicket of thy ablest men.
MONT. My Lords, you shall not word it any further
Without a milder limit.
FRAN. Willingly.
BRACH. Have you proclaimed a triumph, that you bait
A lion thus?
MONT. My Lord!
BRACH. I am tame, I am tame, sir.
FRAN. We send unto the Duke for conference
'Bout levies 'gainst the pirates; my Lord Duke
Is not at home; we come ourself in person;
Still my Lord Duke is busied. But, we fear,
When Tiber to each prowling passenger
Discovers flocks of wild ducks, then, my Lord
('Bout moulting time I mean), we shall be certain
To find you sure enough and speak with you.
BRACH. Ha!
FRAN. A mere tale of a tub: my words are idle;
But to express the sonnet[17] by natural reason:
When stags grow melancholic, you 'll find the season.[18]
MONT. No more, my Lord; here comes a champion[19]

[9] *I.e.*, turn tail.
[10] Perhaps, haply.
[11] A rich cloth, often interwoven with gold or silver.
[12] Even if she were.
[13] *I.e.*, mercenary.
[14] *I.e.*, than endure venereal disease after your amour.
[15] *I.e.*, furrowed in anger.
[16] Old eds. have no stop.
[17] Used of any short poem.
[18] Ll. 86–93 have baffled all the commentators. The sense seems to be that Brachiano's irregularities, to which are now due his absences from home, will eventually infect him with venereal disease, which will lay him up at home. "A tale of a tub" = an empty yarn, a cock and bull story, with a play on "tub" = the tub used in treating syphilis. Perhaps, as Lucas suggests, "wild ducks" = prostitutes, "birds of the game." On "moulting," cf. on I, ii, 34. The melancholy stag may be compared with ll. 329–331, and Monticelso's gloss. In both passages the point seems to be that excessive sexual indulgence will lead to impotence. "Season" may be intended as a play on the meaning "salt", "pickle", and thus be another allusion to "the powdering tub of infamy."
[19] For, as Lucas notes, the boy returns in the armor mentioned in l. 7.

Shall end the difference between you both:

Re-enter GIOVANNI.

Your son, the Prince Giovanni. See, my Lords,
What hopes you store in him; this is a casket
For both your crowns, and should be held like dear.
Now is he apt for knowledge; therefore know
It is a more direct and even way
To train to virtue those of princely blood
By examples than by precepts. If by examples,
Whom should he rather strive to imitate
Than his own father? Be his pattern, then;
Leave him a stock of virtue that may last,
Should fortune rend his sails and split his mast.

BRACH. Your hand, boy; growing to [a] [20] soldier?

GIO. Give me a pike.

FRAN. What, practising your pike so young, fair Coz?

GIO. Suppose me one of Homer's frogs,[21] my Lord,
Tossing my bullrush thus. Pray, sir, tell me,
Might not a child of good discretion [22]
Be leader to an army?

FRAN. Yes, Cousin, a young prince
Of good discretion [22] might.

GIO. Say you so?
Indeed, I have heard 't is fit a general
Should not endanger his own person oft;
So [23] that he make a noise when he 's a' horseback,
Like a Dansk [24] drummer. Oh, 't is excellent!
He need not fight; methinks his horse as well
Might lead an army for him. If I live,
I 'll charge the French foe in the very front
Of all my troops, the foremost man.

FRAN. What, what!

GIO. And will not bid my soldiers up and follow,
But bid them follow me.

BRACH. Forward [25] lapwing!
He flies with the shell on 's head.

FRAN. Pretty Cousin!

GIO. The first year, Uncle, that I go to war,
All prisoners that I take I will set free
Without their ransom.

FRAN. Ha, without their ransom?
How, then, will you reward your soldiers [26]
That took those prisoners for you?

GIO. Thus, my Lord:
I 'll marry them to all the wealthy widows
That falls that year.

FRAN. Why, then, the next year following,
You 'll have no men to go with you to war.

GIO. Why, then, I 'll press the women to the war,
And then the men will follow.

MONT. Witty prince!

FRAN. See, a good habit makes a child a man;
Whereas a bad one makes a man a beast.
Come, you and I are friends.

BRACH. Most wishedly,
Like bones which, broke in sunder and well set,
Knit the more strongly.

FRAN. Call Camillo hither.[27]
You have received the rumor how Count Lodowick
Is turn'd a pirate?

BRACH. Yes.

FRAN. We are now preparing
Some ships, to fetch him in.

[*Re-enter* ISABELLA.]

Behold your duchess.
We now will leave you, and expect from you
Nothing but kind entreaty.

BRACH. You have charm'd me. —

Exeunt FRANCISCO, MONTICELSO, [*and*] GIOVANNI.

You are in health, we see.

ISA. And above health,
To see my Lord well.

BRACH. So! [28] I wonder much
What amorous whirlwind hurried you to Rome.

ISA. Devotion,[29] my Lord.

BRACH. Devotion? [30]
Is your soul charg'd with any grievous sin?

[20] Add Q_2.
[21] In the *Batrachomyomachia* or *Battle of the Frogs and Mice*, a mock-heroic poem formerly ascribed to Homer.
[22] Quadrisyllabic.
[23] Provided.
[24] Danish.
[25] Precocious. The lapwing often served as a type of precocity.
[26] Trisyllabic.
[27] Dyce adds *Exit Marcello*, who might indeed enter with Giovanni. Lucas notes that Francisco may simply call off stage.
[28] Qq_{1-3} have no stop.
[29] To Brachiano.
[30] To religion.

ISA. 'T is burdened with too many; and I think
The oft'ner that we cast our reckonings up,
Our sleeps will be the sounder.
BRACH. Take your chamber!
ISA. Nay, my dear Lord, I will not have you angry;
Doth not my absence from you,[31] two months,
Merit one kiss?
BRACH. I do not use to kiss.
If that will dispossess your jealousy,
I'll swear it to you.
ISA. O my loved Lord,
I do not come to chide. My jealousy?
I am to learn what that Italian [32] means.
You are as welcome to these longing arms
As I to you a virgin. [*Kisses him.*]
BRACH. Oh, your breath!
Out upon sweetmeats and continued physic!
The plague is in them!
ISA. You have oft for these two lips
Neglected cassia or the natural sweets
Of the spring violet: they are not yet much withered.
My Lord, I should be merry: these your frowns
Show in a helmet lovely; but on me,
In such a peaceful interview, methinks
They are too, too roughly knit.
BRACH. Oh, dissemblance!
Do you bandy factions 'gainst me? have you learnt
The trick of impudent baseness, to complain
Unto your kindred?
ISA. Never, my dear Lord.
BRACH. Must I be haunted out? or was't your trick
To meet some amorous gallant here in Rome,
That must supply our discontinuance?
ISA. I pray, sir, burst my heart; and in my death
Turn to your ancient pity, though not love.
BRACH. Because your brother is the corpulent [33] Duke,

[31] Qq$_{3,4}$, followed by Dyce, add *now*, spoiling the emphasis on "two months."

[32] *I.e.*, what that word in our Italian tongue. Cf. *Bussy d'Ambois*, V, iv, 23: "Murder'd? I know not what that Hebrew means."

[33] Historically it was Bracciano who was fat — monstrously so. Webster may have been adapting his characters to his actors, or may have thought Brachiano's corpulence unromantic, or may have transferred it to Francisco for the sake of this sneer. In any case, he forgot it when he brought the latter in as Mulinassar.

That is, the great Duke,[34] 'sdeath, I shall not shortly
Racket away five hundred crowns at tennis,
But it shall rest upon record![35] I scorn him
Like a shav'd Polack; all his reverend wit
Lies in his wardrobe; he's a discreet fellow,
When he is made up in his robes of state.
Your brother, the great Duke (because h'as galleys
And now and then ransacks a Turkish flyboat [36] —
Now all the hellish Furies take his soul!)
First made this match; accursed be the priest
That sang the wedding mass, and even my issue![37]
ISA. O, too, too far you have curs'd!
BRACH. Your hand I'll kiss;
This is the latest [38] ceremony of my love.
Henceforth I'll never lie with thee; by this,
This wedding ring, I'll ne'er more lie with thee;
And this divorce shall be as truly kept
As if the judge had doom'd it. Fare you well:
Our sleeps are sever'd.
ISA. Forbid it, the sweet union
Of all things blessed! why, the saints in Heaven
Will knit their brows at that.
BRACH. Let not thy love
Make me an unbeliever; this my vow
Shall never, on my soul, be satisfied [39]
With my repentance; let thy brother rage
Beyond a horrid tempest or sea fight,
My vow is fixed.
ISA. O my winding sheet!
Now shall I need thee shortly. — Dear my Lord,
Let me hear once more what I would not hear:
Never?
BRACH. Never!
ISA. O my unkind Lord! may your sins find mercy,
As I upon a woeful widowed bed
Shall pray for you, if not to turn your eyes
Upon your wretched wife and hopeful son,
Yet that in time you'll fix them upon Heaven!
BRACH. No more; go, go complain to the great Duke.
ISA. No, my dear Lord; you shall have present witness

[34] This is a sneer at one of Francisco's titles, that of Grand Duke of Tuscany.

[35] Accented on the second syllable.

[36] A light, fast vessel.

[37] Offspring.

[38] Final.

[39] Discharged.

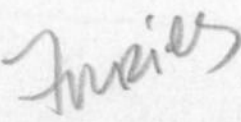

How I'll work peace between you. I will make
Myself the author of your cursed vow;
I have some cause to do it. — You have none.
Conceal it, I beseech you, for the weal
Of both your dukedoms, that you wrought the means
Of such a separation; let the fault
Remain with my supposed jealousy,
And think with what a piteous and rent heart
I shall perform this sad ensuing part.

Re-enter FRANCISCO, FLAMINEO, MONTICELSO, [*and*] MARCELLO.

BRACH. Well, take your course.[40] — My honorable Brother!
FRAN. Sister! — This is not well, my Lord. — Why, Sister! —
She merits not this welcome.
BRACH. Welcome, say?
She hath given a sharp welcome.
FRAN. Are you foolish?
Come, dry your tears; is this a modest course
To better what is naught, to rail and weep?
Grow to a reconcilement, or, by Heaven,
I'll ne'er more deal between you.
ISA. Sir, you shall not;
No, though Vittoria, upon that condition,
Would become honest.[41]
FRAN. Was your husband loud,
Since we departed?
ISA. By my life, sir, no;
I swear by that I do not care to lose.
Are all these ruins of my former beauty
Laid out for a whore's triumph?
FRAN. Do you hear?
Look upon other women, with what patience
They suffer these slight wrongs; with what justice
They study to requite them: take that course.
ISA. Oh, that I were a man, or that I had power
To execute my apprehended wishes!
I would whip some with scorpions.
FRAN. What! turn'd Fury?
ISA. To dig the strumpet's eyes out; let her lie
Some twenty months a-dying; to cut off
Her nose and lips, pull out her rotten teeth,
Preserve her flesh like mummia, for trophies
Of my just anger! Hell, to my affliction,
Is mere snow-water. By your favor, sir —
Brother, draw near, and my Lord Cardinal —
Sir, let me borrow of you but one kiss;
Henceforth I'll never lie with you, by this,
This wedding ring.
FRAN. How? ne'er more lie with him?
ISA. And this divorce shall be as truly kept
As if in thronged court a thousand ears
Had heard it and a thousand lawyers' hands
Seal'd to the separation.
BRACH. Ne'er lie with me?
ISA. Let not my former dotage
Make thee an unbeliever; this my vow
Shall never, on my soul, be satisfied
With my repentance; *manet alta mente* [*repostum*].[42]
FRAN. Now, by my birth, you are a foolish, mad,
And jealous woman.
BRACH. You see 't is not my seeking.
FRAN. Was this your circle of pure unicorn's horn
You said should charm your lord? Now, horns upon thee,
For jealousy deserves them! Keep your vow,
And take your chamber.
ISA. No, sir; I'll presently to Padua;
I will not stay a minute.
MONT. O good madam!
BRACH. 'T were best to let her have her humor:
Some half-day's journey will bring down her stomach,[43]
And then she'll turn in post.[44]
FRAN. To see her come
To my Lord Cardinal for a dispensation
Of her rash vow will beget excellent laughter.
ISA. [*aside*] Unkindness, do thy office; poor heart, break;
Those are the killing griefs which dare not speak. *Exit.*

Enter CAMILLO.

MAR. Camillo's come, my Lord.
FRAN. Where 's the commission?
MAR. 'T is here.
FRAN. Give me the signet.
[FRANCISCO, MONTICELSO, CAMILLO, *and* MARCELLO *retire.*]

FLAM. [*to* BRACHIANO] My Lord, do you mark their whispering? I will compound a medicine, out of their two heads, stronger

[40] Qq_{1-3} have no stop.
[41] Chaste.
[42] It shall remain buried deep in my mind. (Virgil, *Aeneid*, I, 26.) Q_1 *repositum*.
[43] Anger.
[44] Return in haste.

than garlic, deadlier than stibium;[45] the cantharides, which are scarce seen to stick upon the flesh when they work to the heart, shall not do it with more silence or invisible cunning.

BRACH. About the murder.

FLAM. They are sending him to Naples; but I'll send him to Candy.[46]

Enter DOCTOR [JULIO].

Her[e]'s another property too.

BRACH. Oh, the doctor!

FLAM. A poor quacksalving knave, my Lord; one that should have been lash'd for's lechery, but that he confess'd a judgment, had an execution laid upon him, and so put the whip to a *non plus*.

DOCT. And was cozen'd, my Lord, by an arranter knave than myself, and made pay all the colorable[47] execution.

FLAM. He will shoot pills into a man's guts shall make them have more ventages than a cornet[48] or a lamprey;[49] he will poison a kiss; and was once minded, for his masterpiece, because Ireland breeds no poison, to have prepared a deadly vapor in a Spaniard's fart, that should have poison'd all Dublin.[50]

BRACH. Oh, Saint Anthony's fire![51]

DOCT. Your secretary is merry, my Lord.

FLAM. O thou cursed antipathy to nature! — Look, his eye's bloodshed,[52] like a needle a chirurgeon stitcheth a wound with. — Let me embrace thee, toad, and love thee, O thou abominable loathsome gargarism,[53] that will fetch up lungs, lights, heart, and liver, by scruples![54]

BRACH. No more! — I must employ thee, honest doctor;
You must to Padua, and, by the way,
Use some of your skill for us.

DOCT. Sir, I shall.

BRACH. But, for Camillo?

FLAM. He dies this night, by such a politic strain,
Men shall suppose him by's own engine slain.
But, for your Duchess' death —

DOCT. I'll make her sure.

BRACH. Small mischiefs are by greater made secure.

FLAM. Remember this, you slave; when knaves come to preferment, they rise as gallowses[55] are raised i' th' Low Countries, one upon another['s] shoulders.

Exeunt [BRACHIANO, FLAMINEO, *and* DOCTOR JULIO].

MONT. Here is an emblem, Nephew; pray peruse it:
'T was thrown in at your window.

CAM. At my window?
Here is a stag, my Lord, hath shed his horns;
And for the loss of them the poor beast weeps:
The word, "*Inopem me copia fecit.*"[56]

MONT. That is,
"Plenty of horns hath made him poor of horns."[57]

CAM. What should this mean?

MONT. I'll tell you: 't is given out
You are a cuckold.

CAM. Is it given out so?
I had rather such report as that, my Lord,
Should keep within doors.

FRAN. Have you any children?

CAM. None, my Lord.

FRAN. You are the happier.
I'll tell you a tale.

CAM. Pray, my Lord.

FRAN. An old tale.
Upon a time, Phoebus, the god of light,
Or him we call the sun, would need be married.
The gods gave their consent; and Mercury
Was sent to voice it to the general world.
But what a piteous cry there straight arose
Amongst smiths and felt-makers, brewers and cooks,

[45] Antimony.

[46] Crete. Lucas cites, from Nash's *Unfortunate Traveller*: "He is not fit to travel that cannot with the Candians live on serpents, make nourishing food even of poison."

[47] Fictitious. The doctor escaped the lash for his lechery by conspiring with another rascal who agreed to charge him with a defaulted debt, to which the doctor pleaded guilty, thus avoiding penalty on the other charge. But the supposititious creditor played him false and made him pay up as if the debt had been genuine. *Should have* (l. 292) = would have undoubtedly.

[48] An old wind instrument of the oboe family.

[49] Which has seven branchial openings on each side behind its head; they were once supposed to be eyes.

[50] Alluding to "the Don Diego who made himself offensive in St. Paul's (some time before 1598)" (Lucas), and also to the notorious aversion of the Irish to this practice.

[51] Erysipelas.

[52] Bloodshot. [53] Gargle. [54] By minute particles.

[55] Gallows-birds. One was placed on the shoulders of another, who then stepped aside and left his predecessor hanging.

[56] Abundance has left me destitute. (Ovid, *Metamorphoses*, III, 466.)

[57] This is obscure. See on ll. 86–93. Probably both cuckoldry and impotence are glanced at here.

Reapers and butterwomen, amongst fishmongers,
And thousand other trades, which are annoyed
By his excessive heat; 't was lamentable.
They came to Jupiter all in a sweat,
And do forbid the banns. A great fat cook
Was made their speaker, who entreats of Jove
That Phoebus might be gelded; for, if now,
When there was but one sun, so many men
Were like to perish by his violent heat,
What should they do if he were married,
And should beget more, and those children
Make fireworks like their father? So say I;
Only I will apply it to your wife:
Her issue, should not Providence prevent it,
Would make both nature, time, and man repent it.

MONT. Look you, Cousin,
Go, change the air,[58] for shame; see if your absence
Will blast your cornucopia.[59] Marcello
Is chosen with you joint commissioner
For the relieving our Italian coast
From pirates.

MAR. I am much honor'd in 't.

CAM. But, sir,
Ere I return, the stag's horns may be sprouted
Greater than these are shed.

MONT. Do not fear it:
I'll be your ranger.

CAM. You must watch i' th' nights;
Then 's the most danger.

FRAN. Farewell, good Marcello;
All the best fortunes of a soldier's wish
Bring you a-shipboard!

CAM. Were I not best, now I am turn'd soldier,
Ere that I leave my wife, sell all she hath,
And then take leave of her?

MONT. I expect good from you,
Your parting is so merry.

CAM. Merry, my Lord, a' the captain's humor right:[60]
I am resolved to be drunk this night.

[*Exeunt* CAMILLO *and* MARCELLO.]

FRAN. So! 't was well fitted; now shall we discern
How his wish'd absence will give violent way
To Duke Brachiano's lust.

MONT. Why, that was it;
To what scorn'd purpose else should we make choice
Of him for a sea captain? and, besides,
Count Lodowick, which was rumor'd for a pirate,
Is now in Padua.

FRAN. Is 't true?

MONT. Most certain;
I have letters from him, which are suppliant
To work his quick repeal from banishment.
He means to address himself for pension[61]
Unto our sister[62] Duchess.

FRAN. Oh, 't was well;
We shall not want his absence past six days.
I fain would have the Duke Brachiano run
Into notorious scandal; for there 's naught
In such curs'd dotage to repair his name,
Only the deep sense of some deathless shame.

MONT. It may be objected I am dishonorable
To play thus with my kinsman; but I answer,
For my revenge I 'd stake a brother's life,
That, being wrong'd, durst not avenge himself.

FRAN. Come, to observe this strumpet.

MONT. Curse of greatness!
Sure, he 'll not leave her.

FRAN. There 's small pity in 't;
Like mistletoe on sear elms spent by weather,
Let him cleave to her, and both rot together.

Exeunt.

[SCENE II] [63]

Enter BRACHIANO, *with one in the habit of a* Conjuror.

BRACH. Now, sir, I claim your promise; 't is dead midnight,
The time prefix'd to show me, by your art,
How the intended murder of Camillo
And our loathed Duchess grow to action.

CON. You have won me by your bounty to a deed
I do not often practise. Some there are
Which by sophistic tricks aspire that name,
Which I would gladly lose, of nigromancer;[64]
As some that use to juggle upon cards,
Seeming to conjure, when indeed they cheat;

[58] Seek a change of air.
[59] Horn of plenty, another allusion to his cuckoldry. [60] Precisely.

[61] Trisyllabic.
[62] Greg plausibly suggests that Webster has momentarily confused with Cardinal Montalto the Cardinal de' Medici, Isabella's brother.
[63] A room in Camillo's house. [64] Necromancer.

Others that raise up their confederate spirits
'Bout windmills, and endanger their own necks,
For making of a squib; and some there are
Will keep a curtal [65] to show juggling tricks,
And give out 't is a spirit; besides these,
Such a whole realm of almanac-makers, figure-flingers,[66]
Fellows, indeed, that only live by stealth,
Since they do merely lie about stol'n goods —
They'd make men think the Devil were fast and loose,[67]
With speaking fustian [68] Latin. Pray, sit down;
Put on this nightcap, sir: 't is charm'd; and now
I'll show you, by my strong-commanding art,
The circumstance that breaks your Duchess' heart.

A Dumb Show [69]

Enter suspiciously JULIO *and* CHRISTOPHERO: *they draw a curtain* [70] *where Brachiano's picture is; they put on spectacles of glass, which cover their eyes and noses, and then burn perfumes afore the picture, and wash the lips of the picture; that done, quenching the fire and putting off their spectacles, they depart laughing.*

Enter ISABELLA *in her nightgown, as to bedward, with lights after her,* COUNT LODOVICO, GIOVANNI, GUID-ANTONIO,[71] *and others, waiting on her: she kneels down as to prayers, then draws the curtain of the picture, does three reverences to it, and kisses it thrice; she faints, and will not suffer them to come near it; dies: sorrow express'd in* GIOVANNI *and in* COUNT LODOVICO; *she 's convey'd out solemnly.*

BRACH. Excellent! then she 's dead?
CON. She 's poisoned
By the fum'd [72] picture. 'T was her custom nightly,
Before she went to bed, to go and visit
Your picture, and to feed her eyes and lips
On the dead shadow. Doctor Julio,
Observing this, infects it with an oil
And other poison'd stuff, which presently
Did suffocate her spirits.
BRACH. Methought I saw
Count Lodowick there.
CON. He was; and by my art
I find he did most passionately dote
Upon your Duchess. Now turn another way,
And view Camillo's far more politic [fate].[73]
Strike louder, music, from this charmed ground,
To yield, as fits the act, a tragic sound.

The Second Dumb Show

Enter FLAMINEO, MARCELLO, CAMILLO, *with four more as* Captains; *they drink healths and dance: a vaulting-horse is brought into the room:* MARCELLO *and two more whisper'd out of the room, while* FLAMINEO *and* CAMILLO *strip themselves into their shirts, as to vault; compliment* [74] *who shall begin: as* CAMILLO *is about to vault,* FLAMINEO *pitcheth him upon his neck, and, with the help of the rest, writhes his neck about; seems to see if it be broke, and lays him folded double, as 't were under the horse; makes shows to call for help;* MARCELLO *comes in, laments; sends for the* CARDINAL *and* DUKE, *who comes forth with armed men; wonder*[s] *at the act, commands the body to be carried home; apprehends* FLAMINEO, MARCELLO, *and the rest, and go, as 't were to apprehend* VITTORIA.

BRACH. 'T was quaintly [75] done; but yet each circumstance
I taste not fully.
CON. Oh, 't was most apparent:
You saw them enter, charged with their deep healths
To their boon voyage;[76] and, to second that,
Flamineo calls to have a vaulting-horse
Maintain their sport; the virtuous Marcello
Is innocently plotted forth the room;
Whilst your eye saw the rest, and can inform you
The engine of all.
[BRACH.] It seems Marcello and Flamineo
Are both committed.[77]
CON. Yes, you saw them guarded;
And now they are come with purpose to apprehend

[65] Docked horse. An allusion to Morocco, the trained horse of one Banks; there are many references to them.
[66] Horoscope casters.
[67] See on *The Wild-Goose Chase*, III, i, 72.
[68] Claptrap.
[69] Probably on the inner stage.
[70] Dust-curtains were regularly provided for portraits.
[71] Sampson suggests *Gasp*[*aro*] *Anton*[*elli*].
[72] Perfumed.
[73] So Q_4; earlier Qq *face*. "More politic" because it appeared to be an accident. Historically, Vittoria's husband was ambushed and shot.
[74] *I.e.*, polite gestures.
[75] Cleverly.
[76] Bon voyage.
[77] Arrested.

Your mistress, fair Vittoria. We are now
Beneath her roof; 't were fit we instantly
Make out by some back-postern.

BRACH. Noble friend,
You bind me ever to you; this shall stand
As the firm seal annexed to my hand:
It shall enforce a payment.

CON. Sir, I thank you. —

Exit BRACHIANO.

Both flowers and weeds spring when the sun is warm,
And great men do great good or else great harm.

Exit Conjuror.

[ACT III — SCENE I] [1]

Enter FRANCISCO *and* MONTICELSO [*with*] *their* Chancellor *and* Register.

FRAN. You have dealt discreetly, to obtain the presence
Of all the grave lieger [2] ambassadors,
To hear Vittoria's trial.

MONT. 'T was not ill;
For, sir, you know we have naught but circumstances
To charge her with, about her husband's death;
Their approbation, therefore, to the proofs
Of her black lust shall make her infamous
To all our neighboring kingdoms. I wonder
If Brachiano will be here.

FRAN. Oh, fie!
'T were impudence too palpable.

[*Exeunt.*]

Enter FLAMINEO *and* MARCELLO, *guarded, and a* Lawyer.

LAW. What, are you in by the week? [3] so; I will try now whether thy wit be close prisoner. Methinks none should sit upon thy sister but old whoremasters.

FLAM. Or cuckolds; for your cuckold is your most terrible tickler [4] of lechery. Whoremasters would serve; for none are judges at tilting but those that have been old tilters.

LAW. My Lord Duke and she have been very private.[5]

FLAM. You are a dull ass; 't is threat'ned they have been very public.[6]

LAW. If it can be proved they have but kiss'd one another —

FLAM. What then?

LAW. My Lord Cardinal will ferret [7] them.

FLAM. A Cardinal, I hope, will not catch conies.[8]

LAW. For to sow kisses (mark what I say), to sow kisses is to reap lechery; and I am sure, a woman that will endure kissing is half won.

FLAM. True, her upper part, by that rule; if you will win her nether part too, you know what follows.

LAW. Hark; the ambassadors are lighted.[9]

FLAM. [*aside*] I do put on this feigned garb of mirth
To gull suspicion.

MAR. Oh, my unfortunate sister!
I would my dagger's point had cleft her heart
When she first saw Brachiano; you, 't is said,
Were made his engine and his stalking-horse,
To undo [10] my sister.

FLAM. I made a kind of path
To her and mine own preferment.

MAR. Your ruin.

FLAM. Hum! thou art a soldier,
Followest the great Duke, feedest his victories,
As witches do their serviceable spirits,
Even with thy prodigal blood: what hast got,
But, like the wealth of captains, a poor handful,
Which in thy palm thou bear'st as men hold water?
Seeking to grip it fast, the frail reward
Steals through thy fingers.

MAR. Sir!

FLAM. Thou hast scarce maintenance
To keep thee in fresh chamois.[11]

MAR. Brother!

FLAM. Hear me!
And thus, when we have even poured ourselves
Into great fights, for their ambition
Or idle spleen, how shall we find reward?
But, as we seldom find the mistletoe,
Sacred to physic, [on] [12] the builder oak,[13]

[1] Unlocated; perhaps an antechamber or courtyard adjacent to the scene of the examination.

[2] Resident, as distinguished from those sent on special missions.

[3] Deeply involved.

[4] As Lucas notes, = "castigator", but also perhaps with a play on the meaning, "instigator."

[5] Intimate.

[6] Lewd.

[7] Hunt them out.

[8] Rabbits, with various plays on other meanings, *e.g.*, "sweethearts." "To catch conies" = to cheat.

[9] Have alighted.

[10] Ruin.

[11] The chamois jerkin worn under armor. (Lucas.)

[12] Emend. Lucas; old eds. *or*.

[13] Chaucer and Spenser, as Lucas notes, both have *builder oak*.

Without a mandrake [14] by it; so in our quest of gain:
Alas, the poorest of their forc'd dislikes
At a limb proffers, but at heart it strikes!
This is lamented [15] doctrine.

MAR. Come, come.

FLAM. When age shall turn thee
White as a blooming hawthorn —

MAR. I'll interrupt you:
For love of virtue bear an honest heart,
And stride o'er every politic respect,[16]
Which, where they most advance, they most infect.
Were I your father, as I am your brother,
I should not be ambitious to leave you
A better patrimony.

FLAM. I'll think on't. —

Enter SAVOY [Ambassador].

The Lord Ambassadors.

Here there is a passage of the lieger Ambassadors *over the stage severally. Enter* French Ambassador.

LAW. Oh, my sprightly Frenchman! — Do you know him? he's an admirable tilter.

FLAM. I saw him at last tilting: he showed like a pewter candlestick, fashioned like a man in armor, holding a tilting-staff in his hand, little bigger than a candle of twelve i' th' pound.

LAW. Oh, but he's an excellent horseman.

FLAM. A lame one in his lofty tricks; he sleeps a-horseback, like a poulter.[17]

Enter English *and* Spanish [Ambassadors].

LAW. Lo you, my Spaniard!

FLAM. He carries his face in's ruff,[18] as I have seen a serving man carry glasses in a cypress [19] hatband, monstrous steady, for fear of breaking; he looks like the claw of a blackbird, first salted, and then broiled in a candle. *Exeunt.*

[SCENE II] [20] THE ARRAIGNMENT OF VITTORIA

Enter FRANCISCO, MONTICELSO, *the six lieger* Ambassadors, BRACHIANO, [FLAMINEO, MARCELLO,] VITTORIA, [ZANCHE], Lawyer, *and a* Guard.

MONT. Forbear, my Lord; here is no place assign'd you:
This business by his Holiness is left
To our examination.

BRACH. May it thrive with you!
Lays a rich gown under him.

FRAN. A chair there for his Lordship!

BRACH. Forbear your kindness: an unbidden guest
Should travel as Dutchwomen go to church —
Bear their stools with them.

MONT. At your pleasure, sir. —
[*to* VITTORIA] Stand to the table, [gentlewoman].[21] — Now, signior,
Fall to your plea.

[LAW.] *Domine judex, converte oculos in hanc pestem, mulierum corruptissimam.*[22]

VIT. What's he?

FRAN. A lawyer that pleads against you.

VIT. Pray, my Lord, let him speak his usual tongue;
I'll make no answer else.

FRAN. Why? you understand Latin.

VIT. I do, sir; but amongst this auditory
Which come to hear my cause, the half or more
May be ignorant in't.

MONT. Go on, sir.

VIT. By your favor,
I will not have my accusation clouded
In a strange tongue; all this assembly
Shall hear what you can charge me with.

FRAN. Signior,
You need not stand [23] on't much; pray, change your language.

MONT. Oh, for God's sake! — Gentlewoman, your credit [24]
Shall be more famous by it.

LAW. Well, then, have at you!

VIT. I am at the mark, sir: I'll give aim to you,
And tell you how near you shoot.[25]

LAW. Most literated judges, please your Lordships
So to connive your judgments [26] to the view
Of this debauch'd and diversivolent [27] woman;
Who such a black concatenation
Of mischief hath effected, that to extirp

[14] Supposed to be a sinister plant. The point is that there is always a fly in the ointment.
[15] Lamentable; *i.e.*, this is too bad, but it's so.
[16] Consideration of expediency.
[17] On his way to early market.
[18] Spanish ruffs were notoriously large. [19] Crape.
[20] Unlocated. Probably the curtains of the inner stage were now opened.
[21] So Q_4; earlier eds. *gentlewomen*, perhaps rightly.
[22] My Lord Judge, turn your eyes upon this plague, this most corrupt of women.
[23] Insist. [24] Reputation.
[25] The reference is to archery; the marker had the same function as in rifle-practice now.
[26] Presumably he means "bring your judgments into a common understanding."
[27] Desiring or inciting to strife.

The memory of't, must be the consummation
Of her and her projections —[28]
VIT. What's all this?
LAW. Hold your peace!
Exorbitant[29] sins must have exulceration.[30]
VIT. Surely, my Lords, this lawyer here hath swallowed
Some pothecaries' bills or proclamations;
And now the hard and undigestible words
Come up, like stones we use give hawks for physic;
Why, this is Welsh to[31] Latin.
LAW. My Lords, the woman
Knows not her tropes nor figures, nor is perfect
In the academic derivation
Of grammatical elocution.
FRAN. Sir, your pains
Shall be well spared, and your deep eloquence
Be worthily applauded amongst those
Which understand you.
LAW. My good Lord —
FRAN. (*speaks this as in scorn.*) Sir,
Put up your papers in your fustian[32] bag —
Cry mercy, sir; 't is buckram[33] — and accept
My notion of your learn'd verbosity.
LAW. I most graduatically[34] thank your Lordship;
I shall have use for them elsewhere. [*Exit.*]
MONT. I shall be plainer with you, and paint out
Your follies in more natural red and white
Than that upon your cheek.
VIT. Oh, you mistake;
You raise a blood as noble in this cheek
As ever was your mother's.
MONT. I must spare you, till proof cry "whore" to that. —
Observe this creature here, my honored Lords,
A woman of a most prodigious spirit,
In her effected.[35]
VIT. Honorable my Lord,
It doth not suit a reverend cardinal
To play the lawyer thus.
MONT. Oh, your trade
Instructs your language. —
You see, my Lords, what goodly fruit she seems;
Yet, like those apples travellers report
To grow where Sodom and Gomorrah stood,
I will but touch her, and you straight shall see
She'll fall to soot and ashes.
VIT. Your envenom'd
Pothecary should do 't.
MONT. I am resolved,[36]
Were there a second Paradise to lose,
This devil would betray it.
VIT. O poor charity!
Thou art seldom found in scarlet.[37]
MONT. Who knows not how, when several night by night
Her gates were chok'd with coaches, and her rooms
Outbrav'd the stars with several kind of lights,
When she did counterfeit a prince's court
In music, banquets, and most riotous surfeits,
This whore, forsooth, was holy?
VIT. Ha, "whore?" what 's that?
MONT. Shall I expound "whore" to you? sure, I shall;
I'll give their perfect character. They are, first,
Sweetmeats which rot the eater; in man's nostril,
Poison'd perfumes; they are coz'ning alchemy;
Shipwracks in calmest weather! What are whores?
Cold Russian winters, that appear so barren
As if that nature had forgot the spring;
They are the true material fire of hell;
Worse than those tributes i' th' Low Countries payed,
Exactions upon meat, drink, garments, sleep,
Ay, even on man's perdition,[38] his sin;
They are those brittle evidences of law
Which forfeit all a wretched man's estate
For leaving out one syllable. What are whores?
They are those flattering bells have all one tune
At weddings and at funerals. Your rich whores
Are only treasuries by extortion fill'd,
And empt[i]ed by curs'd riot. They are worse,
Worse than dead bodies which are begg'd at gallows,
And wrought upon by surgeons, to teach man
Wherein he is imperfect. What 's a whore?

[28] Projects.
[29] Monstrous.
[30] Sores; but apparently the lawyer means "must be treated like ulcers."
[31] Compared with.
[32] Playing on the meanings: (1) coarse cloth; (2) claptrap.
[33] Stout linen cloth.
[34] As a graduate should.
[35] Brought to pass.
[36] Convinced.
[37] Alluding to the Cardinal's robe, but also, perhaps, as Sampson suggests, to the color of the legal faculty.
[38] Apparently there was a tax on prostitution.

She 's like the guilty counterfeited coin
Which, whosoe'er first stamps it, bring[s] in trouble
All that receive it.

VIT. This character scapes me.

MONT. You, gentlewoman!
Take from all beasts and from all minerals
Their deadly poison —

VIT. Well, what then?

MONT. I 'll tell thee;
I 'll find in thee a pothecary's shop,
To sample them all.

FR. AMB. [*aside*] She hath lived ill.

ENG. AMB. [*aside*] True; but the Cardinal's too bitter.

MONT. You know what "whore" is. Next the devil, adult'ry,
Enters the devil, murder.

FRAN. Your unhappy
Husband is dead.

VIT. Oh, he 's a happy husband:
Now he owes nature nothing.[39]

FRAN. And by a vaulting-engine.

MONT. An active plot;
He jump'd into his grave.

FRAN. What a prodigy was 't
That from some two yards' height a slender man
Should break his neck!

MONT. I' th' rushes! [40]

FRAN. And, what 's more,
Upon the instant lose all use of speech,
All vital motion, like a man had lain
Wound up [41] three days. Now mark each circumstance.

MONT. And look upon this creature was his wife.
She comes not like a widow; she comes arm'd
With scorn and impudence. Is this a mourning habit?

VIT. Had I foreknown his death, as you suggest,
I would have bespoke my mourning.

MONT. Oh, you are cunning.

VIT. You shame your wit and judgment,
To call it so. What, is my just defence
By him that is my judge call'd impudence?
Let me appeal, then, from this Christian court
To the uncivil [42] Tartar.

MONT. See, my Lords,
She scandals [43] our proceedings.

VIT. Humbly thus,
Thus low, to the most worthy and respected
Lieger ambassadors, my modesty
And womanhood I tender; but withal,
So entangled in a cursed accusation,
That my defence, of force,[44] like Perseus',[45]
Must personate masculine virtue.[46] — To the point:
Find me but guilty, sever head from body,
We 'll part good friends; I scorn to hold my life
At yours or any man's entreaty, sir.

ENG. AMB. She hath a brave spirit.

MONT. Well, well, such counterfeit jewels
Make true on[e]s oft suspected.

VIT. You are deceived;
For know that all your strict [47]-combined heads,
Which strike against this mine of diamonds,
Shall prove but glassen hammers: they shall break.
These are but feigned shadows of my evils:
Terrify babes, my Lord, with painted devils;
I am past such needless palsy. For your names
Of "whore" and "murd'ress," they proceed from you
As if a man should spit against the wind;
The filth returns in 's face.

MONT. Pray you, mistress, satisfy me one question:
Who lodg'd beneath your roof that fatal night
Your husband brake his neck?

BRACH. That question
Enforceth me break silence: I was there.

MONT. Your business?

BRACH. Why, I came to comfort her,
And take some course for settling her estate,
Because I heard her husband was in debt
To you, my Lord.

MONT. He was.

BRACH. And 't was strangely fear'd
That you would cozen her.

MONT. Who made you overseer?

BRACH. Why, my charity, my charity, which should flow

[39] For he has paid the debt every man owes — his life, which is but lent him.
[40] With which floors were strewn.
[41] In his winding sheet.
[42] Barbarous.
[43] Defames.
[44] Necessarily.
[45] Perseus appeared for "heroic and masculine virtue" in Jonson's *Masque of Queens* (1609). (Simpson.)
[46] Old eds., perhaps rightly, have no stop.
[47] *I.e.*, closely.

From every generous and noble spirit
To orphans and to widows.
MONT. Your lust.
BRACH. Cowardly dogs bark loudest; Sirrah Priest,
I'll talk with you hereafter. Do you hear?
The sword you frame of such an excellent temper
I'll sheathe in your own bowels.
There are a number of thy coat resemble
Your common postboys.
MONT. Ha?
BRACH. Your mercenary postboys:
Your letters carry truth, but 't is your guise
To fill your mouths with gross and impudent lies. [*He makes for the door.*]
SER. My Lord, your gown.
BRACH. Thou liest: 't was my stool;
Bestow't upon thy master, that will challenge[48]
The rest a' th' household stuff; for Brachiano
Was ne'er so beggarly to take a stool
Out of another's lodging: let him make
Valance[49] for his bed on 't, or a demi-footcloth
For his most reverend moil.[50] Monticelso,
Nemo me impune lacessit.[51] *Exit* BRACHIANO.
MONT. Your champion's gone.
VIT. The wolf may prey the better.
FRAN. My Lord, there's great suspicion of the murder,
But no sound proof who did it. For my part,
I do not think she hath a soul so black
To act a deed so bloody; if she have,
As in cold countries husbandmen plant vines,
And with warm blood manure them, even so
One summer she will bear unsavory fruit,
And ere next spring wither both branch and root.
The act of blood let pass; only descend
To matter of incontinence.
VIT. I discern poison under your gilded pills.
MONT. Now the Duke's gone, I will produce a letter,
Wherein 't was plotted [he][52] and you should meet
At an apothecary's summerhouse,[53]
Down by the river Tiber — view't, my Lords —
Where, after wanton bathing and the heat
Of a lascivious banquet — I pray read it;
I shame to speak the rest.
VIT. Grant I was tempted;
Temptation to lust proves not the act:
Casta est quam nemo rogavit.[54]
You read his hot love to me; but you want
My frosty answer.
MONT. Frost i' th' dog days! strange!
VIT. Condemn you me for that the Duke did love me?
So may you blame some fair and crystal river
For that some melancholic distracted man
Hath drown'd himself in 't.
MONT. Truly drown'd, indeed.
VIT. Sum up my faults, I pray, and you shall find
That beauty and gay clothes, a merry heart,
And a good stomach to [a][55] feast, are all,
All the poor crimes that you can charge me with.
In faith, my Lord, you might go pistol flies;
The sport would be more noble.
MONT. Very good.
VIT. But take you your course; it seems you have beggar'd me first,
And now would fain undo me. I have houses,
Jewels, and a poor remnant of crusadoes.[56]
Would those would make you charitable!
MONT. If the Devil
Did ever take good shape, behold his picture.
VIT. You have one virtue left: you will not flatter me.
FRAN. Who brought this letter?
VIT. I am not compell'd to tell you.
MONT. My Lord Duke sent to you a thousand ducats
The twelfth of August.
VIT. 'T was to keep your cousin[57]
From prison: I paid use[58] for 't.
MONT. I rather think
'T was interest for his lust.
VIT. Who says so
But yourself? If you be my accuser,
Pray cease to be my judge: come from the bench,
Give in your evidence 'gainst me, and let these
Be moderators.[59] My Lord Cardinal,
Were your intelligencing ears as [long][60]
As to my thoughts, had you an honest tongue,
I would not care though you proclaim'd them all.

[48] Claim. [49] Drapery. [50] Mule.
[51] No one hurts me with impunity.
[52] Cor. Q_3; earlier Qq *her*.
[53] Such places, in suburban gardens, were notorious as places of assignation in Elizabethan London.
[54] Chaste is she whom none has tempted. (Ovid, *Amores*, I, viii, 43.) [55] Add. Dyce.
[56] Portuguese coins worth upwards of half a dollar.
[57] Nephew.
[58] Interest. [59] Judges.
[60] Emend. Lucas; old eds. *loving*.

MONT. Go to, go to!
After your goodly and vainglorious banquet,
I'll give you a choke-pear.[61]
VIT. A' your own grafting?
MONT. You were born in Venice, honorably descended
From the Vittelli; [62] 't was my cousin's fate —
Ill may I name the hour — to marry you:
He bought you of your father.
VIT. Ha?
MONT. He spent there in six months
Twelve thousand ducats, and, to my acquaintance,[63]
Received in dowry with you not one julio: [64]
'T was a hard pennyworth,[65] the ware being so light.
I yet but draw the curtain; [66] now to your picture:
You came from thence a most notorious strumpet;
And so you have continued.
VIT. My Lord —
MONT. Nay, hear me;
You shall have time to prate. My Lord Brachiano —
Alas, I make but repetition
Of what is ordinary and Rialto talk,[67]
And ballated,[68] and would be played a' th' stage,
But that vice many times finds such loud friends
That preachers are charm'd silent. —
You gentlemen, Flamineo and Marcello,
The court hath nothing now to charge you with;
Only, you must remain upon your sureties
For your appearance.
FRAN. I stand for Marcello.
FLAM. And my Lord Duke for me.
MONT. For you, Vittoria, your public fault,
Join'd to th' condition of the present time,
Takes from you all the fruits of noble pity.
Such a corrupted trial have you made
Both of your life and beauty, and been styl'd
No less in ominous fate than blazing stars
To princes, here's your sentence: you are confin'd
Unto a house of convertites; and your bawd—
FLAM. [*aside*] Who, I?
MONT. The Moor —
FLAM. [*aside*] Oh, I am a sound man again.
VIT. A house of convertites! what's that?
MONT. A house
Of penitent whores.
VIT. Do the noblemen in Rome
Erect it for their wives, that I am sent to lodge there?
FRAN. You must have patience.
VIT. I must first have vengeance.
I fain would know if you have your salvation
By patent,[69] that you proceed thus.
MONT. Away with her!
Take her hence.
VIT. A rape! a rape!
MONT. How?
VIT. Yes, you have ravish'd justice;
Forc'd her to do your pleasure.
MONT. Fie, she's mad!
VIT. Die with these pills in your most cursed maws
Should bring you health! or while you sit a' th' bench
Let your own spittle choke you! —
MONT. She's turn'd Fury.
VIT. That the last day of judgment may so find you,
And leave you the same devil you were before!
Instruct me, some good horse-leech,[70] to speak treason;
For, since you cannot take my life for deeds,
Take it for words! O woman's poor revenge,
Which dwells but in the tongue! I will not weep;
No, I do scorn to call up one poor tear
To fawn on your injustice. Bear me hence
Unto this house of — what's your mitigating title?
MONT. Of convertites.
VIT. It shall not be a house of convertites;
My mind shall make it honester to me
Than the Pope's palace, and more peaceable
Than thy soul, though thou art a cardinal.
Know this, and let it somewhat raise your spite:
Through darkness diamonds spread their richest light. *Exit* VITTORIA. [

Re-enter BRACHIANO.

BRACH. Now you and I are friends, sir, we'll shake hands

[61] *I.e.*, I'll give you something to silence you.
[62] This great Roman family had no connection with Vittoria. But see on I, i, 31.
[63] According to my information.
[64] A papal coin worth about twelve cents.
[65] Bargain.
[66] See on II, ii, 23, Dumb Show.
[67] *I.e.*, town talk; the Rialto was the exchange of Venice.
[68] Made into ballads.
[69] In the form of a written warrant or license.
[70] Bloodsucker.

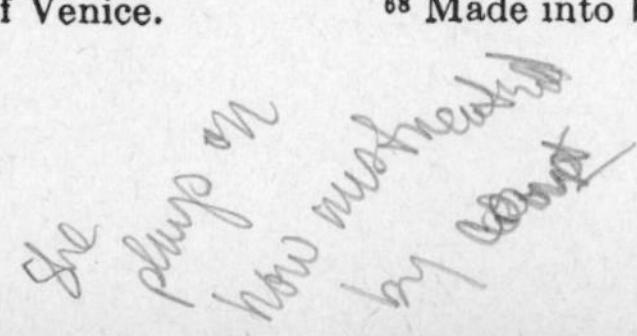

In a friend's grave together: a fit place,
Being the emblem of soft peace, t' atone [71] our hatred.

FRAN. Sir, what's the matter?

BRACH. I will not chase more blood from that lov'd cheek:
You have lost too much already; fare you well. [*Exit.*]

FRAN. How strange these words sound! what's the interpretation?

FLAM. [*aside*] Good; this is a preface to the discovery of the Duchess' death; he carries it well. Because now I cannot counterfeit a whining passion for the death of my Lady, I will feign a mad humor for the disgrace of my sister; and that will keep off idle questions. Treason's tongue hath a villainous palsy in 't; I will talk to any man, hear no man, and for a time appear a politic madman. [*Exit.*]

Enter GIOVANNI [*and*] COUNT LODOVICO.

FRAN. How now, my noble Cousin? what, in black?

GIO. Yes, Uncle, I was taught to imitate you
In virtue, and you must imitate me
In colors for your garments. My sweet mother
Is —

FRAN. How! where?

GIO. Is there; no, yonder; indeed, sir, I'll not tell you,
For I shall make you weep.

FRAN. Is dead?

GIO. Do not blame me now;
I did not tell you so.

LOD. She's dead, my Lord.

FRAN. Dead!

MONT. Blessed lady, thou art now above thy woes! —
Will 't please your Lordships to withdraw a little? [*Exeunt* Ambassadors.]

GIO. What do the dead do, Uncle? do they eat,
Hear music, go a-hunting, and be merry,
As we that live?

FRAN. No, Coz; they sleep.

GIO. Lord, Lord, that I were dead!
I have not slept these six nights. — When do they wake?

FRAN. When God shall please.

GIO. Good God, let her sleep ever.
For I have known her wake an hundred nights,
When all the pillow where she laid her head
Was brine-wet with her tears. I am to complain to you, sir;
I'll tell you how they have used her now she's dead:
They wrapp'd her in a cruel fold of lead,
And would not let me kiss her.

FRAN. Thou didst love her.

GIO. I have often heard her say she gave me suck,
And it should seem by that she dearly lov'd me,
Since princes seldom do it.

FRAN. O all of my poor sister that remains! —
Take him away, for God's sake!

MONT. How now, my Lord?

FRAN. Believe me, I am nothing but her grave;
And I shall keep her blessed memory
Longer than thousand epitaphs. [*Exeunt.*]

[SCENE III] [72]

Enter FLAMINEO, *as distracted*, [MARCELLO, *and* LODOVICO.]

FLAM. We endure the strokes like anvils or hard steel,
Till pain itself make us no pain to feel.
Who shall do me right now? Is this the end of service? I'd rather go weed garlic; travel through France, and be mine own ostler; wear sheepskin linings, or shoes that stink of blacking; be ent'red into the list of the forty thousand peddlers in Poland.[73]

Enter [*the* Ambassador of] Savoy.

Would I had rotted in some surgeon's house at Venice, built upon the pox as well as on piles,[74] ere I had serv'd Brachiano!

SAV. [AMB.]. You must have comfort.

FLAM. Your comfortable words are like honey: they relish well in your mouth that's whole, but in mine that's wounded they go

[71] Reconcile.

[72] Doubtless the same as III, i. As Lucas observes, the curtains of the inner stage would probably be closed here, and Sc. iii would proceed with no other break.

[73] Sampson notes the prevalence of Scotch and Irish peddlers there in the seventeenth century, and that the Lithuanian word for peddler is *szatas* = Scot.

[74] An obvious pun.

down as if the sting of the bee were in them. Oh, they have wrought their purpose cunningly, as if they would not seem to do it of malice! In this a politician imitates the Devil, as the Devil imitates a cannon: wheresoever he comes to do mischief, he comes with his backside towards you.

Enter the French [Ambassador].

FRENCH [AMB.] The proofs are evident.

FLAM. Proof! 't was corruption. O gold, what a god art thou! and O man, what a devil art thou to be tempted by that cursed mineral! [Yon] [75] diversivolent [76] lawyer, mark him; knaves turn informers, as maggots turn to flies; you may catch gudgeons [77] with either. A cardinal! I would he would hear me: there's nothing so holy but money will corrupt and putrefy it, like victual under the line.[78]

[*Enter the*] English Ambassador.

You are happy in England, my Lord: here they sell justice with those weights they press men to death with.[79] O horrible salary!

ENG. [AMB.]. Fie, fie, Flamineo!

[*Exeunt* Ambassadors.] [80]

FLAM. Bells ne'er ring well till they are at their full pitch; [81] and I hope yon cardinal shall never have the grace to pray well till he come to the scaffold. If they were rack'd now to know the confederacy! But your noblemen are privileged from the rack; and well may, for a little thing would pull some of them a-pieces [82] afore they came to their arraignment. Religion, oh, how it is commeddled [83] with policy! The first bloodshed in the world happened about religion.[84] Would I were a Jew!

MAR. Oh, there are too many.

FLAM. You are deceiv'd: there are not Jews enough, priests enough, nor gentlemen enough.

MAR. How?

FLAM. I'll prove it: for, if there were Jews enough, so many Christians would not turn usurers; if priests enough, one should not have six benefices; and, if gentlemen enough, so many early mushrooms, whose best growth sprang from a dunghill, should not aspire to gentility. Farewell; let others live by begging; be thou one of them [85] practice the art of Wolner [86] in England, to swallow all 's given thee; and yet let one purgation make thee as hungry again as fellows that work in [a] [87] saw-pit. I'll go hear the screech owl. *Exit.*[88]

LOD. [*aside*] This was Brachiano's pander; and 't is strange
That, in such open and apparent guilt
Of his adulterous sister, he dare utter
So scandalous a passion. I must wind him.[89]

Re-enter FLAMINEO.

FLAM. [*aside*] How dares this banish'd count return to Rome,
His pardon not yet purchas'd? [90] I have heard
The deceas'd Duchess gave him pension,
And that he came along from Padua
I' th' train of the young Prince. There's somewhat in 't;
Physicians that cure poisons still do work
With counter-poisons.

MAR. [*aside*] Mark this strange encounter.

FLAM. [*to* LODOVICO] The god of melancholy turn thy gall to poison,
And let the stigmatic wrinkles in thy face,
Like to the boisterous waves in a rough tide,
One still overtake another.

LOD. I do thank thee,
And I do wish ingeniously [91] for thy sake
The dog days [92] all year long.

FLAM. How croaks the raven?
Is our good Duchess dead?

LOD. Dead.

FLAM. O fate!
Misfortune comes, like the crowner's [93] business,
Huddle [94] upon huddle.

[75] Emend. Lucas; Qq_{1-3} *you;* Q_4, and other mod. eds., *your*.

[76] See on III, ii, 29.

[77] *I.e.*, fools.

[78] Below the equator.

[79] The fate of those who refused to plead guilty or not guilty.

[80] So Dyce, but as Lucas notes they may remain in the background to enhance the pictorial effect.

[81] Height.

[82] Because of their diseased condition. (Sampson.)

[83] Mixed up.

[84] Cain's quarrel with Abel about sacrifice. (Lucas.)

[85] Understand "that."

[86] An early Elizabethan famous for his talent for devouring "iron, glass, oyster shells", etc. In the end, a raw eel was too much for him.

[87] Add. Q_2.

[88] Very likely he merely retires up-stage.

[89] Scent him, hunt him down.

[90] Got.

[91] Ingenuously.

[92] *I.e.*, evil days.

[93] Coroner's.

[94] Heap.

LOD. Shalt thou and I join house-keeping?
FLAM. Yes, content; let's be unsociably sociable.
LOD. Sit some three days together, and discourse —
FLAM. Only with making faces; lie in our clothes.
LOD. With faggots for our pillows —
FLAM. And be lousy.
LOD. In taffeta linings; that's genteel melancholy;
Sleep all day —
FLAM. Yes; and, like your melancholic hare,[95]
Feed after midnight.

Enter ANTONELLI [*and* GASPARO, *behind, laughing.*]

We are observed: see how yon couple grieve!
LOD. What a strange creature is a laughing fool!
As if man were created to no use
But only to show his teeth.
FLAM. I'll tell thee what:
It would do well, instead of looking-glasses,
To set one's face each morning by a saucer
Of a witch's congealed blood.
LOD. Precious [rogue!] [96]
We'll never part.
FLAM. Never, till the beggary of courtiers,
The discontent of churchmen, want of soldiers
And all the creatures that hang manacled,
Worse than strappado'd,[97] on the lowest felly
Of Fortune's wheel, be taught, in our two lives,
To scorn that world which life of means deprives.
ANT. My Lord, I bring good news. The Pope, on's deathbed,
At th' earnest suit of the Great Duke of Florence,
Hath sign'd your pardon, and restor'd unto you —
LOD. I thank you for your news. — Look up again,
Flamineo; see my pardon.
FLAM. Why do you laugh?
There was no such condition in our covenant.
LOD. Why?
FLAM. You shall not seem a happier man than I;
You know our vow, sir; if you will be merry,
Do it i' th' like posture as if some great man
Sat while his enemy were executed;
Though it be very lechery unto thee,
Do't with a crabbed politician's face.
LOD. Your sister is a damnable whore.
FLAM. Ha?
LOD. Look you, I spake that laughing.
FLAM. Dost ever think to speak again?
LOD. Do you hear?
Wilt sell me forty ounces of her blood
To water a mandrake?[98]
FLAM. Poor Lord, you did vow
To live a lousy creature.
LOD. Yes.
FLAM. Like one
That had for ever forfeited the daylight
By being in debt.
LOD. Ha, ha!
FLAM. I do not greatly wonder you do break;[99]
Your Lordship learn't[100] long since; but I'll tell you —
LOD. What?
FLAM. And't shall stick by you —
LOD. I long for it.
FLAM. This laughter scurvily becomes your face;
If you will not be melancholy, be angry.
Strikes him.
See, now I laugh too.
MAR. You are to blame: I'll force you hence.
LOD. [*to* ANTONELLI *and* GASPARO] Unhand me.
[*Exeunt*] MARCELLO *and* FLAMINEO.
That e'er I should be forc'd to right myself
Upon a pander!
ANT. My Lord!
LOD. H' had been as good
Met with his fist a thunderbolt.
GAS. How this shows!
LOD. Ud's death, how did my sword miss him? These rogues
That are most weary of their lives still scape
The greatest dangers.
A pox upon him! all his reputation,

[95] Which was proverbially melancholy.
[96] So Qq 3, 4, Lucas; Q_1 (Garrick) *grine rouge;* Q_1 (Dyce), Q_2, Dyce, Sampson, *gue*.
[97] In torturing by the strappado, the victim's arms were bound behind his back and by them he was hauled up on a pulley and dropped, to be brought up with a dislocating jerk.
[98] Which was supposed to flourish under a gibbet, from the droppings from the decomposing bodies.
[99] Go bankrupt; *i.e.*, break your agreement with me.
[100] For *learn'd't*, which is unpronounceable.

Nay, all the goodness of his family,
Is not worth half this earthquake.
I learnt it of no fencer to shake thus;
Come, I'll forget him, and go drink some wine.
Exeunt.

[ACT IV — SCENE I][1]

Enter FRANCISCO *and* MONTICELSO.

MONT. Come, come, my Lord, untie your folded thoughts,
And let them dangle loose as a bride's hair:[2]
Your sister's poisoned.
FRAN. Far be it from my thoughts
To seek revenge.
MONT. What, are you turn'd all marble?
FRAN. Shall I defy him, and impose a war
Most burdensome on my poor subjects' necks,
Which at my will I have not power to end?
You know, for all the murders, rapes, and thefts,
Committed in the horrid lust of war,
He that unjustly caus'd it first proceed
Shall find it in his grave and in his seed.
MONT. That's not the course I'd wish you; pray, observe me:
We see that undermining more prevails
Than doth the cannon; bear your wrongs conceal'd,
And, patient as the tortoise, let this camel
Stalk o'er your back unbruis'd; sleep with the lion,
And let this brood of secure foolish mice
Play with your nostrils, till the time be ripe
For th' bloody audit and the fatal gripe;
Aim like a cunning fowler, close one eye,
That you the better may your game espy.
FRAN. Free me, my innocence, from treacherous acts!
I know there's thunder yonder,[3] and I'll stand
Like a safe valley, which low bends the knee
To some aspiring mountain, since I know
Treason, like spiders weaving nets for flies,
By her foul work is found, and in it dies.
To pass away these thoughts, my honor'd Lord,
It is reported you possess a book
Wherein you have quoted, by intelligence,[4]
The names of all notorious offenders
Lurking about the city.
MONT. Sir, I do;
And some there are which call it my black book.
Well may the title hold; for, though it teach not
The art of conjuring, yet in it lurk
The names of many devils.
FRAN. Pray, let's see it.
MONT. I'll fetch it to your Lordship.
Exit MONTICELSO.
FRAN. Monticelso,
I'll not trust thee; but in all my plots
I'll rest as jealous as a town besieg'd.
Thou canst not reach[5] what I intend to act.
Your flax soon kindles, soon is out again;
But gold slow heats, and long will hot remain.

Re-enter MONTICELSO. [*Presents* FRANCISCO *with a book.*][6]

MONT. 'T is here, my Lord.
FRAN. First, your[7] intelligencers,[8] pray, let's see.
MONT. Their number rises strangely; and some of them
You'd take for honest men. Next are panders;
These are your pirates; and these following leaves
For base rogues that undo young gentlemen
By taking up commodities;[9] for politic bankrupts;
For fellows that are bawds to their own wives,
Only to put off[10] horses and slight jewels,
Clocks, defac'd plate, and such commodities,
At birth of their first children.
FRAN. Are there such?
MONT. These are for impudent bawds
That go in men's apparel; for usurers
That share with scriveners for their good reportage;[11]

[1] A room in Francisco's palace.
[2] An old custom of virgin brides.
[3] Above.
[4] By information from your spies.
[5] Comprehend.
[6] Om. Garrick-Harvard copies of Q 1, in signature G, in which the Dyce copy is superior, as Lucas notes.
[7] The.
[8] Informers.
[9] A reference to the notorious commodity swindle. A borrower would be required to take the bulk of the loan in the form of some odd sort of goods for which there was little or no demand. Then the lender, through an agent, would buy them back at an outrageous discount.
[10] On the lover; *i.e.*, force him to buy "commodities" at absurd prices.
[11] A form of fee-splitting. "Good reportage" = recommendation.

For lawyers that will antedate their writs;[12]
And some divines you might find folded there,
But that I slip them o'er for conscience' sake.
Here is a general catalogue of knaves;
A man might study all the prisons o'er,
Yet never attain this knowledge.

FRAN. "Murderers"!—
Fold down the leaf, I pray.
Good my Lord, let me borrow this strange doctrine.

MONT. Pray, use 't, my Lord.

FRAN. I do assure your Lordship,
You are a worthy member of the state,
And have done infinite good in your discovery
Of these offenders.

MONT. Somewhat, sir.

FRAN. O God!
Better than tribute of wolves paid in England;[13]
'T will hang their skins o' th' hedge.

MONT. I must make bold
To leave your Lordship.

FRAN. Dearly, sir, I thank you;
If any ask for me at court, report
You have left me in the company of knaves.

Exit MONTICELSO.

I gather now by this, some cunning fellow
That 's my Lord's officer, [one][14] that lately skipp'd
From a clerk's desk up to a justice' chair,
Hath made this knavish summons, and intends,
As th' Irish rebels wont were to sell heads,
So to make prize of these. And thus it happens
Your poor rogues pay for 't which have not the means
To present bribe in fist; the rest o' th' band
Are raz'd out of the knaves' record; or else
My Lord he winks at them with easy will;
His man grows rich; the knaves are the knaves still.
But to the use I 'll make of it: it shall serve
To point me out a [list][15] of murderers,
Agents for any villainy. Did I want
Ten leash[16] of courtezans, it would furnish me;
Nay, laundress[17] three armies. That [in][18] so little paper
Should [lie][19] th' undoing of so many men!
'T is not so big as twenty declarations.[20]
See the corrupted use some make of books;
Divinity,[21] wrested by some factious blood,
Draws swords, swells battles, and o'erthrows all good.
To fashion my revenge more seriously,
Let me remember my dead sister's face;
[Call][22] for her picture? no, I 'll close mine eyes,
And in a melancholic thought I 'll frame
Her figure 'fore me.

Enter ISABELLA'S Ghost.

Now I—d'foot![23] how strong
Imagination works! how she can frame
Things which are not! Methinks she stands afore me,
And by the quick idea of my mind,
Were my skill pregnant, I could draw her picture.
Thought, as a subtle juggler, makes us deem
Things supernatural, which have cause
Common as sickness. 'T is my melancholy.—
How cam'st thou by thy death?—How idle am I
To question mine own idleness!—Did ever
Man dream awake till now?—Remove this object;
Out of my brain with 't! What have I to do
With tombs or deathbeds, funerals or tears,
That have to meditate upon revenge?

[*Exit* Ghost.]

So, now 't is ended, like an old wife's story.
Statesmen think often they see stranger sights
Than madmen. Come, to this weighty business;
My tragedy must have some idle mirth in 't,
Else it will never pass. I am in love,
In love with Corombona; and my suit
Thus halts[24] to her in verse.— *He writes.*
I have done it rarely—oh, the fate of princes!

[12] Lucas suggests an allusion to Dr. Julio's method of escaping conviction on one charge by trumping up and pleading guilty to another, perhaps by falsely dating the second prior to the first.

[13] By the Welsh to King Edgar.

[14] Garrick-Harvard copies of Q 1, *and*.

[15] Garrick-Harvard copies of Q 1, *life*.

[16] Sets of three.

[17] For the women who followed the army and performed this function were not conspicuous for their virtue.

[18] Cor. Q 2; om. Garrick-Harvard copies of Q 1; Dyce copy bungles the correction: *so in*.

[19] Garrick-Harvard copies of Q 1, *be*.

[20] Statements by plaintiffs of their claims.

[21] Theology.

[22] Garrick-Harvard copies of Q 1, *Looke*.

[23] So Garrick-Harvard copies of Q 1; Dyce copy avoids the oath: *ha't*.

[24] Limps.

I am so us'd to frequent flattery,
That, being alone, I now flatter myself;
But it will serve; 't is seal'd. —

Enter Servant.

Bear this
To th' house of convertites, and watch your leisure
To give it to the hands of Corombona,
Or to the matron, when some followers
Of Brachiano may be by. Away!

Exit Servant.

He that deals all by strength, his wit is shallow;
When a man's head goes through, each limb will follow.
The engine for my business, bold Count Lodowick;
'T is gold must such an instrument procure;
With empty fist no man doth falcons lure.[25]
Brachiano, I am now fit for thy encounter;
Like the wild Irish, I'll ne'er think thee dead
Till I can play at football with thy head.
Flectere si nequeo superos, Acheronta movebo.[26]

Exit.[27]

[Scene II] [28]

Enter the Matron *and* Flamineo.

Mat. Should it be known the Duke hath such recourse
To your imprison'd sister, I were like
T' incur much damage by it.

Flam. Not a scruple.
The Pope [29] lies on his deathbed, and their heads
Are troubled now with other business
Than guarding of a lady.

Enter [*Francisco's*] Servant.

Ser. [*aside*] Yonder's Flamineo in conference
With the matrona. — Let me speak with you;
I would entreat you to deliver for me
This letter to the fair Vittoria.

Mat. I shall, sir.

Enter Brachiano.

Ser. With all care and secrecy.
Hereafter you shall know me, and receive
Thanks for this courtesy. [*Exit.*]

Flam. How now? what's that

Mat. A letter.

Flam. To my sister? I'll see 't delivered. [*Exit* Matron.]

Brach. What's that you read, Flamineo?

Flam. Look.

Brach. Ha!
"To the most unfortunate, his best respected Vittoria." —
Who was the messenger?

Flam. I know not.

Brach. No?
Who sent it?

Flam. Ud's foot, you speak as if a man
Should know what fowl is coffin'd in a bak'd meat
Afore you cut it up.

Brach. I'll open't, were't her heart. What's here subscribed?
"Florence!" this juggling [30] is gross and palpable!
I have found out the conveyance.[31] — Read it, read it!

Flam. (*reads the letter.*) "Your tears I'll turn to triumphs, be but mine.
Your prop is fall'n; I pity that a vine
Which princes heretofore have long'd to gather,
Wanting supporters, now should fade and wither." —
Wine, i' faith, my Lord, with lees would serve his turn. —
"Your sad imprisonment I'll soon uncharm,
And with a princely uncontrolled arm
Lead you to Florence, where my love and care
Shall hang your wishes in my silver hair." —
A halter on his strange equivocation! —
"Nor for my years return me the sad willow: [32]
Who prefer blossoms before fruit that's mellow?" —
Rotten, on my knowledge, with lying too long i' th' bed-straw. —
"And all the lines of age this line convinces: [33]
The gods never wax old; no more do princes." —
A pox on't, tear it; let's have no more atheists,[34] for God's sake.

Brach. Ud's death, I'll cut her into atomies,[35]
And let th' irregular [36] north wind sweep her up,

[25] The lure was a decoy of feathers to which the hawk was trained to return.
[26] If the high gods I cannot move, I'll move the powers of hell. (Vergil, *Aeneid*, VII, 312.)
[27] Qq 1-3 *Exit Mon.* [28] The house of convertites.
[29] Gregory XIII (d. 1585).

[30] Trisyllabic.
[31] Trickery.
[32] Symbol of rejected love. [33] Overcomes.
[34] *I.e.*, blasphemers; for he has compared princes to gods. [35] Atoms. [36] Wild.

And blow her int' his nostrils! Where's this whore?
FLAM. What? what do you call her?
BRACH. Oh, I could be mad,
Prevent [37] the curs'd disease she'll bring me to,
And tear my hair off! [38] Where's this changeable stuff? [39]
FLAM. O'er head and ears in water, I assure you:
She is not for your wearing.
BRACH. [In,] [40] you pander!
FLAM. What, me, my Lord? am I your dog?
BRACH. A bloodhound!
Do you brave, do you stand [41] me?
FLAM. Stand you! let those that have diseases run; [42]
I need no plasters.[43]
BRACH. Would you be kick'd?
FLAM. Would you have your neck broke?
I tell you, Duke, I am not in Russia;
My shins must be kept whole.[44]
BRACH. Do you know me?
FLAM. O, my Lord, methodically:
As in this world there are degrees of evils,
So in this world there are degrees of devils;
You're a great duke, I your poor secretary.
I do look now for a Spanish fig or an Italian sallet [45] daily.[46]
BRACH. Pander, ply your convoy,[47] and leave your prating.
FLAM. All your kindness to me is like that miserable courtesy of Polyphemus to Ulysses: you reserve me to be devour'd last; you would dig turves out of my grave to feed your larks; that would be music to you. Come, I'll lead you to her. [*Walks backwards.*]
BRACH. Do you face me?
FLAM. [Oh,] [48] sir, I would not go before a politic enemy with my back towards him, though there were behind me a whirlpool.

Enter VITTORIA *to* BRACHIANO *and* FLAMINEO.

BRACH. Can you read, mistress? Look upon that letter:
There are no characters [49] nor hieroglyphics;
You need no comment; I am grown your receiver.[50]
God's precious! you shall be a brave great lady,
A stately and advanced whore.
VIT. Say, sir?
BRACH. Come, come, let's see your cabinet; discover
Your treasury of love letters. Death and Furies!
I'll see them all.
VIT. Sir, upon my soul,
I have not any. Whence was this directed?
BRACH. Confusion on your politic ignorance!
You are reclaimed,[51] are you? I'll give you the bells,
And let you fly to the Devil.
FLAM. Ware hawk,[52] my Lord!
VIT. "Florence"! this is some treacherous plot, my Lord;
To me he ne'er was [lovely,] [53] I protest,
So much as in my sleep.
BRACH. Right! they are plots.
Your beauty! oh, ten thousand curses on't!
How long have I beheld the Devil in crystal! [54]
Thou hast led me, like an heathen sacrifice,
With music and with fatal yokes of flowers,
To my eternal ruin. Woman to man
Is either a god or a wolf.
VIT. My Lord —
BRACH. Away!
We'll be as differing as two adamants: [55]
The one shall shun the other. What? dost weep?
Procure but ten of thy dissembling trade,
[Ye'd] [56] furnish all the Irish funerals
With howling past wild Irish.
FLAM. Fie, my Lord!
BRACH. That hand, that cursed hand, which I have wearied
With doting kisses! — O my sweetest Duchess,
How lovely art thou now! — Thy loose thoughts

[37] Anticipate.
[38] See on I, ii, 34.
[39] With reference to "watered" taffeta or changeable silk.
[40] So Dyce copy of Q_1; Garrick-Harvard copies, *No;* Q_2, *E'en;* $Qq_{3,4}$, omit.
[41] Stand up to, withstand.
[42] Have running sores.
[43] I'm not diseased, and don't intend to run.
[44] Sykes cites Dekker's allusion, in *Seven Deadly Sins*, to this old Russian method of persuading debtors to pay up.
[45] Salad; *i.e.*, poison.
[46] Possibly, as Lucas asserts, a "fourteener."
[47] Perform your function.
[48] Om. Garrick-Harvard copies of Q_1.
[49] Cipher. (Lucas.)
[50] Pimp.
[51] *I.e.*, a tame hawk.
[52] Look out for a trap.
[53] Garrick-Harvard copies of Q_1, *thought on.*
[54] Cf. "white devil." Crystal was used to enclose spirits.
[55] Magnets.
[56] So Dyce; Q_1 *ee'ld;* other old eds. *Wee'l*, etc.

Scatter like quicksilver! I was bewitch'd;
For all the world speaks ill of thee.
VIT. No matter;
I'll live so now, I'll make that world recant
And change her speeches. You did name your Duchess.
BRACH. Whose death God pardon!
VIT. Whose death God revenge
On thee, most godless Duke!
FLAM. [*aside*] Now for two [57] whirlwinds!
VIT. What have I gain'd by thee but infamy?
Thou hast stain'd the spotless honor of my house,
And frighted thence noble society;
Like those which sick [58] o' th' palsy and retain
Ill-scenting foxes 'bout them, are still shunn'd
By those of choicer nostrils. What do you call this house?
Is this your palace? Did not the judge style it
A house of penitent whores? Who sent me to it?
Who hath the honor to advance Vittoria
To this incontinent college? is't not you?
Is't not your high preferment? Go, go brag
How many ladies you have undone like me.
Fare you well, sir; let me hear no more of you.
I had a limb corrupted to an ulcer;
But I have cut it off, and now I'll go
Weeping to Heaven on crutches. For your gifts,
I will return them all; and I do wish
That I could make you full executor
To all my sins. Oh, that I could toss myself
Into a grave as quickly! for all thou art worth
I'll not shed one tear more. — I'll burst first.
She throws herself upon a bed.
BRACH. I have drunk Lethe. — Vittoria!
My dearest happiness! Vittoria!
What do you ail, my love? why do you weep?
VIT. Yes, I now weep poniards, do you see?
BRACH. Are not those matchless eyes mine?
VIT. I had rather
They were not matches.
BRACH. Is not this lip mine?
VIT. Yes; thus to bite it off, rather than give it thee.
FLAM. Turn to my Lord, good sister.
VIT. Hence, you pander!
FLAM. Pander! am I the author of your sin?
VIT. Yes; he's a base thief that a thief lets in.
FLAM. We're blown up, my Lord.
BRACH. Wilt thou hear me?
Once to be jealous of thee, is t' express
That I will love thee everlastingly,
And never more be jealous.
VIT. O thou fool,
Whose greatness hath by much o'ergrown thy wit!
What dar'st thou do that I not dare to suffer,
Excepting to be still thy whore? for that,
In the sea's bottom sooner thou shalt make
A bonfire.
FLAM. Oh, no oaths, for God's sake!
BRACH. Will you hear me?
VIT. Never.
FLAM. What a damned imposthume [59] is a woman's will!
Can nothing break it? — [*aside*] Fie, fie, my Lord,
Women are caught as you take tortoises;
She must be turn'd on her back. — Sister, by this hand,
I am on your side. — Come, come, you have wrong'd her.
What a strange credulous man were you, my Lord,
To think the Duke of Florence would love her!
Will any mercer take another's ware
When once 't is tous'd and sullied? — And yet, Sister,
How scurvily this frowardness becomes you!
Young leverets stand [60] not long; and women's anger
Should, like their flight, procure a little sport,
A full cry for a quarter of an hour,
And then be put to the dead quat.[61]
BRACH. Shall these eyes,
Which have so long time dwelt upon your face,
Be now put out?
FLAM. No cruel landlady i' th' world, which lends forth groats
To broom-men and takes use [62] for them, would do't. —
Hand her, my Lord, and kiss her; be not like

[57] So Dyce; Dyce copy of Q 1, *tow;* Garrick-Harvard copies, *ten;* other old eds. *the.*
[58] Probably, as Lucas asserts, = sicken.

[59] Abscess.
[60] Hold out.
[61] Squat.
[62] Interest.

A ferret, to let go your hold with blowing.[63]
BRACH. Let us renew right hands.
VIT. Hence!
BRACH. Never shall rage
Or the forgetful wine make me commit
Like fault.
FLAM. [*aside*] Now you are i' th' way on 't, follow 't hard.
BRACH. Be thou[64] at peace with me, let all the world
Threaten the cannon.
FLAM. Mark his penitence;
Best natures do commit the grossest faults
When they 're giv'n o'er to jealousy, as best wine,
Dying, makes strongest vinegar. I 'll tell you:
The sea 's more rough and raging than calm rivers,
But not so sweet nor wholesome. A quiet woman
Is a still water under a great bridge;[65]
A man may shoot her safely.
VIT. Oh, ye dissembling men!
FLAM. We suck'd that, Sister,
From women's breasts, in our first infancy.
VIT. To add misery to misery.
BRACH. Sweetest!
VIT. Am I not low enough?
Ay, ay, your good heart gathers like a snowball,
Now your affection 's cold.
FLAM. Ud'foot, it shall melt
To a heart again, or all the wine in Rome
Shall run o' th' lees for 't.
VIT. Your dog or hawk should be rewarded better
Than I have been. I 'll speak not one word more.
FLAM. Stop her mouth with a sweet kiss my Lord. — [*aside*] So,
Now the tide 's turn'd, the vessel 's come about.
He 's a sweet armful. Oh, we curl'd-hair'd men
Are still most kind to women! This is well.
BRACH. That you should chide thus!
FLAM. [*aside*] Oh, sir, your little chimneys
Do ever cast most smoke! I sweat for you.
Couple together with as deep a silence
As did the Grecians in their wooden horse. —
My Lord, supply your promises with deeds;
You know that painted meat no hunger feeds.
BRACH. Stay — ingrateful Rome —
FLAM. Rome! it deserves
To be call'd Barbary for our villainous usage.
BRACH. Soft! the same project which the Duke of Florence
(Whether in love or gullery I know not)
Laid down for her escape will I pursue.
FLAM. And no time fitter than this night, my Lord,
The Pope being dead, and all the cardinals ent'red
The conclave for th' electing a new pope,
The city in a great confusion.
We may attire her in a page's suit,
Lay her post-horse,[66] take shipping, and amain
For Padua.
BRACH. I 'll instantly steal forth the Prince Giovanni,
And make for Padua. You two, with your old mother,
And young Marcello that attends on Florence,
If you can work him to it, follow me;
I will advance you all. — For you, Vittoria,
Think of a duchess' title.
FLAM. Lo you,[67] Sister! —
Stay, my Lord; I 'll tell you a tale.[68] The crocodile, which lives in the river Nilus, hath a worm breeds i' th' teeth of 't, which puts it to extreme anguish. A little bird, no bigger than a wren, is barber-surgeon to this crocodile; flies into the jaws of 't, picks out the worm, and brings present remedy. The fish, glad of ease, but ingrateful to her that did it, that the bird may not talk largely of her abroad for non-payment, closeth her chaps, intending to swallow her, and so put her to perpetual silence; but nature, loathing such ingratitude, hath arm'd this bird with a quill or prick on the head, top o' th' which wounds the crocodile i' th' mouth, forceth her open her bloody prison, and away flies the pretty toothpicker from her cruel patient.

[63] This, it appears from an anonymous communication cited by Lucas, is only a popular superstition.
[64] If thou art.
[65] Qq 3, 4, *Is like a . . . under London-Bridge.*
[66] Establish relays of post-horses for her.
[67] There you are!, what did I tell you?
[68] Herodotus, Pliny, and others told it, or parts of it.

BRACH. Your application is, I have not rewarded
The service you have done me.[69]

FLAM. No, my Lord. —
You, Sister, are the crocodile: you are blemish'd in your fame; my Lord cures it; and though the comparison hold not in every particle, yet observe, remember what good the bird with the prick i' th' head hath done you, and scorn ingratitude. —
[*aside*] It may appear to some ridiculous
Thus to talk knave and madman, and sometimes
Come in with a dried sentence, stuff'd with sage;
But this allows my varying of shapes;
Knaves do grow great by being great men's apes. *Exeunt.*

[SCENE III][70]

Enter LODOVICO, GASPARO, *and six* Ambassadors; [*and*,] *at another door*, FRANCISCO THE DUKE OF FLORENCE.

FRAN. So, my Lord; I commend your diligence.
Guard well the conclave; and, as the order is,
Let none have conference with the cardinals.

LOD. I shall, my Lord. — Room for the ambassadors!

GAS. They're wondrous brave[71] to-day. Why do they wear
These several habits?

LOD. Oh, sir, they're knights
Of several orders: that lord i' th' black cloak
With the silver cross is Knight of Rhodes;[72] the next,
Knight of St. Michael; that, of the Golden Fleece;
The Frenchman there, Knight of the Holy Ghost;
My Lord of Savoy, Knight of th' Annunciation;
The Englishman is Knight of th' honored Garter,
Dedicated unto their saint, St. George. I could
Describe to you their several institutions,
With the laws annexed to their orders, but that time
Permits not such discovery.

FRAN. Where's Count Lodowick?

LOD. Here, my Lord.

FRAN. 'T is o' th' point of dinner time;
Marshal the cardinals' service.

LOD. Sir, I shall.

Enter Servants, *with several dishes covered.*

Stand! Let me search your dish; who's this for?

SER. For my Lord Cardinal Monticelso.

LOD. Whose this?

SER. For my Lord Cardinal of Bourbon.

FRE. [AMB.] Why doth he search the dishes? to observe
What meat is dress'd?

ENG. [AMB.] No, sir; but to prevent
Lest any letters should be convey'd in
To bribe or to solicit the advancement
Of any cardinal. When first they enter,
'T is lawful for the ambassadors of princes
To enter with them, and to make their suit
For any man their prince affecteth[73] best;
But after, till a general election,
No man may speak with them.

LOD. You that attend on the lord cardinals,
Open the window, and receive their viands!

[SERVANT (*appearing at a window.*)][74] You must return the service: the lord cardinals
Are busied 'bout electing of the pope;
They have given o'er scrutiny,[75] and are fallen
To admiration.[76]

LOD. Away, away! [*Exeunt* Servants.]

FRAN. I'll lay a thousand ducats you hear news
Of a pope presently.

A Cardinal *on the terrace.*[77]

— Hark! sure, he's elected;
Behold, my Lord of Arragon appears
On the church battlements.

ARR. *Denuntio vobis gaudium magnum. Reverendissimus Cardinalis Lorenso de Monticelso electus est in sedem apostolicam, et elegit sibi nomen Paulum Quartum.*

[69] And so of course it is, even though Flamineo proceeds to offer another, dictated possibly by fear that he has gone too far with the Duke, and certainly by the dramatist's inability to resist the double-entendre that had occurred to him.

[70] Before the Vatican.

[71] Splendidly attired.

[72] *I.e.*, of the order of St. John of Jerusalem; their headquarters in 1585 was no longer Rhodes, but Malta. The cross is the Maltese.

[73] Favors, likes.

[74] Old eds. *A Car.*

[75] Balloting.

[76] The proper term is "adoration", *i.e.*, the homage which followed the new pope's investiture.

[77] Arragon appears on the balcony above the inner stage.

OMNES. *Vivat sanctus Pater Paulus Quartus!*

[*Enter a* Servant.]

SER. Vittoria, my Lord,
FRAN. Well, what of her?
SER. Is fled the city, —
FRAN. Ha?
SER. With Duke Brachiano.
FRAN. Fled! Where's the Prince Giovanni?
SER. Gone with his father.
FRAN. Let the matrona of the convertites
Be apprehended. — Fled! oh, damnable! — [*Exit* Servant.]
[*aside*] How fortunate are my wishes! why! 't was this
I only labored. I did send the letter
T' instruct him what to do. Thy fame, fond[78] Duke,
I first have poison'd, directed thee the way
To marry a whore; what can be worse? This follows:
The hand must act to drown the passionate tongue;
I scorn to wear a sword and prate of wrong.

Enter MONTICELSO *in state.*

MONT. *Concedimus vobis apostolicam benedictionem et remissionem peccator*[*u*]*m.*

[FRANCISCO *whispers to him.*][79]

My Lord reports Vittoria Corombona
Is stol'n from forth the house of convertites
By Brachiano, and they're fled the city.
Now, though this be the first day of our seat,[80]
We cannot better please the divine Power
Than to sequester from the Holy Church
These cursed persons. Make it therefore known
We do denounce excommunication
Against them both; all that are theirs in Rome
We likewise banish. — Set on.

Exeunt [*all but* FRANCISCO *and* LODOVICO].

FRAN. Come, dear Lodovico.
You have ta'en the sacrament to prosecute
Th' intended murder.
LOD. With all constancy.
But, sir, I wonder you'll engage yourself
In person, being a great prince.
FRAN. Divert me not.
Most of his court are of my faction,
And some are of my council. Noble friend,
Our danger shall be 'like in this design;
Give leave part of the glory may be mine.

Exit FRANCISCO.

Re-enter MONTICELSO.

MONT. Why did the Duke of Florence with such care
Labor your pardon? say.
LOD. Italian beggars will resolve you that,
Who, begging of an alms, bid those they beg of
Do good for their own sakes; or, 't may be,
He spreads his bounty with a sowing hand,
Like kings, who many times give out of measure,
Not for desert so much as for their pleasure.
MONT. I know you're cunning. Come, what devil was that
That you were raising?
LOD. Devil, my Lord?
MONT. I ask you[81]
How doth the Duke employ you, that his bonnet
Fell with such compliment[82] unto his knee
When he departed from you?
LOD. Why, my Lord,
He told me of a resty[83] Barbary horse
Which he would fain have brought to the career,[84]
The 'sault,[85] and the ring-galliard;[86] now, my Lord,
I have a rare French rider.[87]
MONT. Take you heed
Lest the jade break your neck. Do you put me off
With your wild horse-tricks? Sirrah, you do lie.
Oh, thou 'rt a foul, black cloud, and thou dost threat
A violent storm!
LOD. Storms are i' th' air, my Lord;
I am too low to storm.
MONT. Wretched creature!
I know that thou art fashion'd for all ill;
Like dogs that once get blood, they'll ever kill.
About some murder? was 't not?
LOD. I'll not tell you
And yet I care not greatly if I do;

[78] Foolish. [79] Add. Lucas.
[80] So all old eds. except Dyce (and Folger) copy of Q 1, which reads *state*.

[81] Qq 1, 2, give to Lodovico. [82] Politeness.
[83] *I.e.*, untrained; the word could mean either "restive" or "sluggish."
[84] A rapid run, starting and stopping suddenly.
[85] Bound; horses were trained to leap, curvet, lash out with the heels, etc. These were all "'saults."
[86] A mixture of bounding forward, curvetting, and lashing out with the heels.
[87] They had the name of being the best.

Marry, with this preparation: Holy Father,
I come not to you as an intelligencer,[88]
But as a penitent sinner: what I utter
Is in confession merely; which you know
Must never be reveal'd.

MONT. You have o'erta'en [89] me.

LOD. Sir, I did love Brachiano's Duchess dearly,
Or rather I pursued her with hot lust,
Though she ne'er knew on 't. She was poison'd;
Upon my soul, she was; for which I have sworn
T' avenge her murder.

MONT. To the Duke of Florence?

LOD. To him I have.

MONT. Miserable creature!
If thou persist in this, 't is damnable.
Dost thou imagine thou canst slide on blood,
And not be tainted with a shameful fall?
Or, like the black and melancholic yew tree,
Dost think to root thyself in dead men's graves,
And yet to prosper? Instruction to thee
Comes like sweet showers to overhard'ned ground:
They wet, but pierce not deep. And so I leave thee,
With all the Furies hanging 'bout thy neck,
Till by thy penitence thou remove this evil,
In conjuring from thy breast that cruel devil.
Exit MONTICELSO.

LOD. I'll give it o'er; he says 't is damnable;
Besides I did expect his suffrage,[90]
By reason of Camillo's death.

Re-enter Servant *and* FRANCISCO.

FRAN. Do you know that Count?

SER. Yes, my Lord.

FRAN. Bear him these thousand ducats to his lodging;
Tell him the Pope hath sent them. — [*aside*] Happily
That will confirm [him] [91] more than all the rest.
[*Exit.*]

SER. Sir.

LOD. To me, sir?

SER. His Holiness hath sent you
A thousand crowns, and will[s] you, if you travel,
To make him your patron for intelligence.

LOD. His creature ever to be commanded.
[*Exit* Servant.]
Why, now 't is come about. He rail'd upon me,
And yet these crowns were told [92] out and laid ready
Before he knew my voyage. Oh, the art,
The modest form of greatness! [93] that do sit,
Like brides at wedding dinners, with their looks turn'd
From the least wanton jests, their puling stomach
Sick of the modesty, when their thoughts are loose,
Even acting of those hot and lustful sports
Are to ensue about midnight; such his cunning!
He sounds my depth thus with a golden plummet.
I am doubly arm'd now. Now to th' act of blood.
There's but three Furies found in spacious hell;
But in a great man's breast three thousand dwell.
[*Exit.*]

[88] Informer. [89] Overreached. [90] Trisyllabic. [91] Add. Dyce.

[ACT V — SCENE I] [1]

A passage over the stage of BRACHIANO, FLAMINEO, MARCELLO, HORTENSIO, [VITTORIA] COROMBONA, CORNELIA, ZANCHE, *and others.* [FLAMINEO, MARCELLO, *and* HORTENSIO *remain.*]

FLAM. In all the weary minutes of my life,
Day ne'er broke up [2] till now. This marriage
Confirms me happy.

HORT. 'T is a good assurance.
Saw you not yet the Moor that's come to court?

FLAM. Yes, and conferr'd with him i' th' Duke's closet;
I have not seen a goodlier personage,
Nor ever talk'd with man better experienc'd
In state affairs or rudiments [3] of war.
He hath, by report, serv'd the Venetian [4]
In Candy [5] these twice seven years, and been chief
In many a bold design.

[92] Counted. [93] Great men.
[1] Padua. A room in Brachiano's palace.
[2] Dawned.
[3] Fundamental principles.
[4] Quadrisyllabic. "He" should be slurred.
[5] Crete.

HORT. What are those two
That bear him company?

FLAM. Two noblemen of Hungary, that, living in the Emperor's service as commanders, eight years since, contrary to the expectation of all the court, entered into religion, into the strict [6] order of Capuchins; but, being not well settled in their undertaking, they left their order, and returned to court; for which, being after troubled in conscience, they vowed their service against the enemies of Christ, went to Malta,[7] were there knighted, and in their return back, at this great solemnity, they are resolved for ever to forsake the world, and settle themselves here in a house of Capuchins in Padua.

HORT. 'T is strange.

FLAM. One thing makes it so: they have vowed for ever to wear next their bare bodies those coats of mail they served in.

HORT. Hard penance! Is the Moor a Christian?

FLAM. He is.

HORT. Why proffers he his service to our Duke?

FLAM. Because he understands there's like to grow
Some wars between us and the Duke of Florence,
In which he hopes employment.[8]
I never saw one in a stern bold look
Wear more command, nor in a lofty phrase
Express more knowing or more deep contempt
Of our slight airy courtiers. He talks
As if he had travell'd all the princes' courts
Of Christendom; in all things strives t' express,
That all that should dispute with him may know
Glories, like glowworms, afar off shine bright,
But, look'd to near, have neither heat nor light. —
The Duke!

Enter BRACHIANO, [FRANCISCO DUKE OF] FLORENCE (*disguised like* Mulinassar); LODOVICO [*disguised as* Carlo], ANTONELLI, GASPARO [*disguised as* Pedro]; [*an* Officer,] FARNESE, *bearing their swords and helmets.*

BRACH. You are nobly welcome. We have heard at full
Your honorable service 'gainst the Turk.
To you, brave Mulinassar, we assign
A competent pension, and are inly [9] [sorry][10]
The vows of those two worthy gentlemen
Make them incapable of our proffer'd bounty.
Your wish is you may leave your warlike swords
For monuments in our chapel; I accept it
As a great honor done me, and must crave
Your leave [11] to furnish out our Duchess' revels.
Only one thing, as the last vanity
You e'er shall view, deny me not to stay
To see a barriers [12] prepar'd to-night;
You shall have private standings. It hath pleas'd
The great ambassadors of several princes,
In their return from Rome to their own countries,
To grace our marriage, and to honor me
With such a kind of sport.

FRAN. I shall persuade them
To stay, my Lord.

[BRACH].[13] Set on there to the presence![14]

Exeunt BRACHIANO, FLAMINEO, [HORTENSIO, FARNESE,] *and* MARCELLO.

[LOD.][15] Noble my Lord, most fortunately welcome.

The Conspirators *here embrace.*

You have our vows seal'd with the sacrament,
To second your attempts.

[GAS.][16] And all things ready.
He could not have invented his own ruin,
Had he despair'd, with more propriety.

LOD. You would not take my way.

FRAN. 'T is better ordered.

LOD. T' have poison'd his prayer book, or a pair [17] of beads,
The pommel of his saddle, his looking-glass,
Or th' handle of his racket — Oh, that, that!
That while he had been bandying at tennis,
He might have sworn himself to hell, and struck
His soul into the hazard![18] Oh, my Lord,
I would have our plot be ingenious,
And have it hereafter recorded for example
Rather than borrow example.

FRAN. There's no way
More speeding than this thought on.

[6] At the time when this play was written the Capuchins were still an austere branch of the Franciscans. [7] See on IV, iii, 8.

[8] Qq 1, 2, add *Enter Duke Brachiano*, merely the prompter's warning notation.

[9] Deeply. [10] So Qq 2-4; Q 1 *sorrow.*

[11] For my absence. [12] See on I, ii, 32.

[13] Cor. Dyce; old eds. *Fran.* [14] Presence-chamber.

[15] So Qq 3, 4; Qq 1, 2, *Car[lo].*

[16] So Qq 3, 4; Qq 1, 2, *Ped[ro].* [17] Set.

[18] An inappropriate metaphor, as Lucas notes, since to hit the ball into a hazard scored a point for you.

LOD. On, then.

FRAN. And yet methinks that this revenge is poor,
Because it steals upon him like a thief.
To have ta'en him by the casque in a pitch'd field —
Led him to Florence!

LOD. It had been rare. — And there
Have crown'd him with a wreath of stinking garlic,
T' have shown the sharpness of his government
And rankness of his lust. — Flamineo comes.

Exeunt LODOVICO, ANTONELLI,[19] [*and* GASPARO].

Re-enter FLAMINEO, MARCELLO, *and* ZANCHE.

MAR. [*aside to* FLAMINEO] Why doth this devil [20] haunt you? say!

FLAM. [*aside to* MARCELLO] I know not;
For, by this light, I do not conjure for her.
'T is not so great a cunning as men think
To raise the devil; for here 's one up already;
The greatest cunning were to lay him down.

MAR. [*aside*] She is your shame.

FLAM. [*aside*] I prithee, pardon her.
In faith, you see, women are like to burrs:
Where their affection throws them, there they 'll stick.

ZAN. That is my countryman, a goodly person;
When he 's at leisure, I 'll discourse with him
In our own language.

FLAM. I beseech you do. —

Exit ZANCHE.

How is 't, brave soldier? Oh, that I had seen
Some of your iron days! I pray, relate
Some of your service to us.

FRAN. 'T is a ridiculous thing for a man to be his own chronicle; I did never wash my mouth with mine own praise, for fear of getting a stinking breath.

MAR. You 're too stoical. The Duke will expect other discourse from you.

FRAN. I shall never flatter him; I have studied man too much to do that. What difference is between the Duke and I? No more than between two bricks, all made of one clay; only 't may be one is plac'd on the top of a turret, the other in the bottom of a well, by mere chance. If I were plac'd as high as the Duke, I should stick as fast, make as fair a show, and bear out weather equally.

FLAM. If this soldier had a patent to beg in churches, then he would tell them stories.

MAR. I have been a soldier too.

FRAN. How have you thriv'd?

MAR. Faith, poorly.

FRAN. That 's the misery of peace: only outsides are then respected. As ships seem very great upon the river, which show very little upon the seas; so some men i' th' court seem colossuses in a chamber, who, if they came into the field, would appear pitiful pigmies.

FLAM. Give me a fair room yet hung with arras, and some great cardinal to lug me by th' ears as his endeared minion.

FRAN. And thou mayst do the devil knows what villainy.

FLAM. And safely.

FRAN. Right; you shall see in the country, in harvest time, pigeons, though they destroy never so much corn,[21] the farmer dare not present the fowling-piece to them! Why? because they belong to the lord of the manor; whilst your poor sparrows, that belong to the Lord of Heaven, they go to the pot for 't.

FLAM. I will now give you some politic instruction. The Duke says he will give you pension; that 's but bare promise; get it under his hand;[22] for I have known men that have come from serving against the Turk, for three or four months they have had pension to buy them new wooden legs and fresh plasters; but, after, 't was not to be had; and this miserable courtesy shows as if a tormentor [23] should give hot cordial drinks to one three-quarters dead o' th' rack, only to fetch the miserable soul again to endure more dog days.[24] — [*Exit* FRANCISCO.]

Re-enter HORTENSIO, [*with*] *a* Young Lord, ZANCHE, *and* Two *more*.

How now, gallants. What, are they ready for the barriers?

Y. LORD. Yes; the lords are putting on their armor.

HORT. [*aside to* FLAMINEO] What 's he?

FLAM. [*aside to* HORTENSIO] A new upstart; one that swears like a falc'ner, and will lie in the Duke's ear day by day, like a maker of almanacs; and yet I knew him, since he came to the court, smell worse of sweat than an under tennis-court keeper.

HORT. Look, you, yonder 's your sweet mistress.

[19] Perhaps erroneously listed for this scene.
[20] Referring to her complexion.

[21] Grain. This was a common grievance of the farmers at the time.
[22] In writing.
[23] Torturer, executioner.
[24] See on III, iii, 84.

FLAM. Thou art my sworn brother; I'll tell thee, I do love that Moor, that witch, very constrainedly. She knows some of my villainy. I do love her just as a man holds a wolf by the ears, but for fear of turning upon me and pulling out my throat, I would let her go to the devil.

HORT. I hear she claims marriage of thee.

FLAM. Faith, I made to her some such dark promise; and, in seeking to fly from 't, I run on, like a frighted dog with a bottle at 's tail, that fain would bite it off, and yet dares not look behind him. — Now, my precious gipsy![25]

ZAN. Ay, your love to me rather cools than heats.

FLAM. Marry, I am the sounder lover; we have many wenches about the town heat too fast.

HORT. What do you think of these perfum'd gallants, then?

FLAM. Their satin cannot save them; I am confident
They have a certain spice of the disease;
For they that sleep with dogs shall rise with fleas.[26]

ZAN. Believe it! A little painting and gay clothes
Make you loathe me.

FLAM. How? love a lady for painting or gay apparel? I'll unkennel one example more for thee: Aesop had a foolish dog that let go the flesh to catch the shadow. I would have courtiers be better diners.[27]

ZAN. You remember your oaths?

FLAM. Lovers' oaths are like mariners' prayers, uttered in extremity; but when the tempest is o'er and that[28] the vessel leaves tumbling, they fall from protesting to drinking. And yet, amongst gentlemen, protesting and drinking go together, and agree as well as shoemakers and Westphalia bacon.[29] They are both drawers on; for drink draws on protestation and protestation draws on more drink. Is not this discourse better now than the [morality][30] of your sunburnt gentleman?

Re-enter CORNELIA.

CORN. Is this your perch, you haggard?[31] fly to th' stews.[32] [*Strikes* ZANCHE].

FLAM. You should be clapp'd by the heels now: strike i' th' court!
[Exit CORNELIA.]

ZAN. She's good for nothing but to make her maids
Catch cold a-nights: they dare not use a bedstaff[33]
For fear of her light fingers.

MAR. [*kicking* ZANCHE] You're a strumpet,
An impudent one.

FLAM. Why do you kick her? say,
Do you think that she's like a walnut tree?[34]
Must she be cudgell'd ere she bear good fruit?

MAR. She brags that you shall marry her.

FLAM. What then?

MAR. I had rather she were pitch'd upon a stake
In some new-seeded garden, to affright
Her fellow crows thence.

FLAM. You're a boy, a fool;
Be guardian to your hound; I am of age.

MAR. If I take her near you, I'll cut her throat.

FLAM. With a fan of feathers?

MAR. And, for you, I'll whip
This folly from you.

FLAM. Are you choleric?
I'll purge 't with rhubarb.

HORT. Oh! your brother!

FLAM. Hang him!
He wrongs me most that ought t' offend me least. —
I do suspect my mother play'd foul play
When she conceiv'd thee.

MAR. Now, by all my hopes,
Like the two slaught'red sons[35] of Œdipus,
The very flames of our affection
Shall turn [two][36] ways. Those words I'll make thee answer
With thy heart-blood.

[25] Wench, baggage.
[26] Proverbial.
[27] Old eds. *Diuers*.
[28] When.
[29] For shoemakers draw shoes onto one's feet, and bacon incites thirst.
[30] So Q_4; earlier eds. *mortality*.
[31] Wild female hawk.
[32] Brothels.

[33] Defined by Dr. Johnson as "a wooden pin stuck anciently on the sides of the bedstead, to hold the clothes from slipping on either side." The maids dare not use such a pin lest Cornelia snatch it up and beat them with it. And so the clothes slide off, and the maids catch cold.

[34] Alluding to a very old proverb, thus given by Ray (1670):
"A spaniel, a woman, and a walnut tree,
The more they're beaten the better still they be."

[35] Eteocles and Polynices, who killed each other fighting for the Theban throne. When their bodies were burned, their hatred was still so violent that the flames turned two ways.

[36] Q_1 *10*.

FLAM. Do like the geese in the progress;[37]
You know where you shall find me. [*Exit.*]
MAR. Very good.
An thou beest a noble,[38] friend, bear him my sword,
And bid him fit the length on 't.
YOUNG LORD. Sir, I shall.
[*Exeunt all but* ZANCHE.]
ZAN. He comes. Hence, petty thought of my disgrace! —

Re-enter FRANCISCO, *the* DUKE OF FLORENCE.

I ne'er loved my complexion till now,
'Cause I may boldly say, without a blush,
I love you.

[FRAN]. [39] Your love is untimely sown; there 's a spring at Michaelmas,[40] but 't is but a faint one; I am sunk in years, and I have vowed never to marry.

ZAN. Alas! poor maids get more lovers than husbands. Yet you may mistake my wealth; for, as when ambassadors are sent to congratulate princes, there 's commonly sent along with them a rich present, so that, though the prince like not the ambassador's person nor words, yet he likes well of the presentment; so I may come to you in the same manner, and be better loved for my dowry than my virtue.

[FRAN.] I 'll think on the motion.[41]

ZAN. Do; I 'll now detain you no longer.
At your better leisure I 'll tell you things shall startle your blood.
Nor blame me that this passion I reveal:
Lovers die inward that their flames conceal.
[FRAN.] [*aside*] Of all intelligence this may prove the best;
Sure, I shall draw strange fowl from this foul nest.
Exeunt.

[SCENE II] [42]

Enter MARCELLO *and* CORNELIA [*with a* Page].[43]

CORN. I hear a whispering all about the court
You are to fight. Who is your opposite?
What is the quarrel?
MAR. 'T is an idle rumor.
CORN. Will you dissemble? sure, you do not well
To fright me thus; you never look thus pale,
But when you are most angry. I do charge you
Upon my blessing — nay, I 'll call the Duke,
And he shall school you.
MAR. Publish not a fear
Which would convert to laughter; 't is not so.
Was not this crucifix my father's?
CORN. Yes.
MAR. I have heard you say, giving my brother suck,
He took the crucifix between his hands,
And broke a limb off.
CORN. Yes; but 'tis mended.

Enter FLAMINEO.

FLAM. I have brought your weapon back.
FLAMINEO *runs* MARCELLO *through.*
CORN. Ha! Oh, my horror!
MAR. You have brought it home, indeed.
CORN. Help! Oh, he 's murdered!
FLAM. Do you turn your gall up? I 'll to sanctuary,
And send a surgeon to you. [*Exit.*]

Enter [LODOVICO *as*] Carlo, HORTENSIO, [*and* GASPARO *as*] Pedro.

HORT. How? o' th' ground?
MAR. O Mother, now remember what I told
Of breaking off the crucifix! Farewell.
There are some sins which Heaven doth duly punish
In a whole family. This it is to rise
By all dishonest means! Let all men know
That tree shall long time keep a steady foot
Whose branches spread no [wider] [44] than the root. [*Dies.*]
CORN. Oh, my perpetual sorrow!
HORT. Virtuous Marcello!
He 's dead. — Pray, leave him, lady. — Come, you shall.

CORN. Alas! he is not dead; he 's in a trance. Why, here 's nobody shall get anything by his death. Let me call him again, for God's sake!

[LOD.] I would you were deceiv'd.

CORN. Oh, you abuse me, you abuse me, you abuse me! How many have gone away

[37] Flamineo rushes off abruptly, flinging back the jibe, "Do as the geese do in a goose-procession — follow me, you goose, you!" Cf. Hamlet's exit (IV, ii, 33) with "Hide, fox, and all after." (Kittredge.) Cf. also *The Spanish Tragedy*, IV, vi, 301.

[38] Qq $_{2-4}$ omit comma.

[39] Old eds. *Fla.* here and in ll. 255, 261.

[40] September 29; the allusion is to Indian summer.

[41] Proposal.

[42] The same.

[43] Add. Editor. As Lucas suggests, the Page, for whom no entrance is provided in S. D. of old eds., must witness the murder; see l. 70.

[44] So Q $_4$; earlier Qq *wilder*.

thus, for lack of tendance! Rear up 's head, rear up 's head: his bleeding inward will kill him.

HORT. You see he is departed.

CORN. Let me come to him; give me him as he is, if he be turn'd to earth; let me but give him one hearty kiss, and you shall put us both into one coffin. Fetch a looking-glass: see if his breath will not stain it; or pull out some feathers from my pillow, and lay them to his lips. Will you lose him for a little painstaking?

HORT. Your kindest office is to pray for him.

CORN. Alas! I would not pray for him yet. He may live to lay me i' th' ground, and pray for me, if you 'll let me come to him.

Enter BRACHIANO, *all armed save the beaver, with* FLAMINEO, [*and* FRANCISCO].

BRACH. Was this your handiwork?
FLAM. It was my misfortune.

CORN. He lies, he lies; he did not kill him; these have kill'd him that would not let him be better look'd to.

BRACH. Have comfort, my griev'd Mother.
CORN. Oh, you screech owl!
HORT. Forbear, good madam.
CORN. Let me go, let me go.

She runs to FLAMINEO *with her knife drawn and coming to him lets it fall.*

The God of Heaven forgive thee! Dost not wonder
I pray for thee? I'll tell thee what's the reason:
I have scarce breath to number twenty minutes;
I'd not spend that in cursing. Fare thee well:
Half of thyself lies there; and mayst thou live
To fill an hourglass with his mould'red ashes,
To tell how thou shouldst spend the time to come
In blest repentance!

BRACH. Mother, pray tell me
How came he by his death? What was the quarrel?

CORN. Indeed, my younger boy presum'd too much
Upon his manhood, gave him bitter words,
Drew his sword first; and so, I know not how,
For I was out of my wits, he fell with 's head
Just in my bosom.

PAGE. This is not true, madam.
CORN. I pray thee, peace.
One arrow's [grass'd][45] already; it were vain
T' lose this;[46] for that will ne'er be found again.

BRACH. Go, bear the body to Cornelia's lodging;
And we command that none acquaint our Duchess
With this sad accident. For you, Flamineo,
Hark you, I will not grant your pardon.
FLAM. No?
BRACH. Only a lease of your life; and that shall last
But for one day; thou shalt be forc'd each evening
To renew it, or be hang'd.
FLAM. At your pleasure.

LODOVICO *sprinkles* BRACHIANO'S *beaver with a poison.*

Your will is law now; I'll not meddle with it.

BRACH. You once did brave me in your sister's lodging;
I'll now keep you in awe for't. — Where's our beaver?

FRAN. [*aside*] He calls for his destruction. — Noble youth,
I pity thy sad fate! — [*aside*] Now to the barriers.
This shall his passage to the black lake further;
The last good deed he did, he pardon'd murther. *Exeunt.*

[SCENE III][47]

Charges and shouts. They fight at barriers; first single pairs, then three to three.

Enter BRACHIANO, [FRANCISCO,] *and* FLAMINEO, *with others.*

BRACH. An armorer! ud's death, an armorer!
FLAM. Armorer! where's the armorer?
BRACH. Tear off my beaver.
FLAM. Are you hurt,[48] my Lord?

[45] Lost in the grass; spelled *graz'd* in old eds.
[46] Dyce, perhaps rightly, omits the stop.
[47] A courtyard of the palace, changing at l. 86 to Brachiano's cabinet. Lucas thinks the barriers would be fought on the inner stage, and takes *bar* (l. 8) for a part of the helmet. A better arrangement would be to take *bar* as the barrier across which the contestants fought, and to suppose it was set on the outer stage, which Flamineo's order clears, leaving the inner stage for the bed.
[48] Wounded.

Enter Armorer.

BRACH. Oh, my brain's on fire! the helmet is poison'd.
ARM. My Lord,
Upon my soul —
BRACH. Away with him to torture!
[*Exit* Armorer, *guarded.*]
There are some great ones that have hand in this,
And near about me.

[*Enter* VITTORIA.]

VIT. Oh, my loved Lord! poisoned?
FLAM. Remove the bar. — Here's unfortunate revels! —
Call the physicians.

Enter two Physicians.

A plague upon you!
We have too much of your cunning here already;
I fear the ambassadors are likewise poison'd.
BRACH. Oh, I am gone already! the infection
Flies to the brain and heart. O thou strong heart!
There's such a covenant 'tween the world and it,
They're loth to break.

[*Enter* GIOVANNI.]

GIO. Oh, my most loved father!
BRACH. Remove the boy away. —
Where's this good woman? — Had I infinite worlds,
They were too little for thee. Must I leave thee? —
What say yon screech owls? is the venom mortal?
PHY. Most deadly.
BRACH. Most corrupted politic hangman,
You kill without book;[49] but your art to save
Fails you as oft as great men's needy friends.
I that have given life to offending slaves
And wretched murderers, have I not power
To lengthen mine own a twelvemonth? —
[*to* VITTORIA] Do not kiss me,
For I shall poison thee. This unction is sent
From the great Duke of Florence.
FRAN. Sir, be of comfort.
BRACH. O thou soft natural death, that art joint-twin
To sweetest slumber! no rough-bearded comet
Stares on thy mild departure; the dull owl
Beats not against thy casement; the hoarse wolf
Scents not thy carrion. Pity winds thy corse,
Whilst horror waits on princes.
VIT. I am lost for ever.
BRACH. How miserable a thing it is to die
'Mongst women howling!

[*Enter* LODOVICO *and* GASPARO.]

What are those?
FLAM. Franciscans;[50]
They have brought the extreme[51] unction.
BRACH. On pain of death,
Let no man name death to me; it is a word
Infinitely terrible. Withdraw into our cabinet.

Exeunt [*all*] *but* FRANCISCO *and* FLAMINEO.

FLAM. To see what solitariness is about dying princes! As heretofore they have unpeopled towns, divorc'd friends, and made great houses unhospitable; so now, O justice! where are their flatterers now? Flatterers are but the shadows of princes' bodies: the least thick cloud makes them invisible.

FRAN. There's great moan made for him.

FLAM. Faith, for some few hours salt water will run most plentifully in every office o' th' court; but, believe it, most of them do but weep over their stepmothers' graves.

FRAN. How mean you?

FLAM. Why, they dissemble; as some men do that live within compass o' th' verge.[52]

FRAN. Come, you have thriv'd well under him.

FLAM. Faith, like a wolf[53] in a woman's breast; I have been fed with poultry;[54] but, for money, understand me, I had as good a will to cozen him as e'er an officer of them all; but I had not cunning enough to do it.

FRAN. What didst thou think of him? faith, speak freely.

[49] By heart; *i.e.*, you are virtuosi.

[50] See on V, i, 17.

[51] Accented on first syllable.

[52] The Lord High Steward had jurisdiction over a radius of twelve miles from the court; this area was the verge. The meaning is: as do some men whom I could name, men who live not a thousand miles from court.

[53] Cancer.

[54] The old treatment of cancer was to feed it meat. Bracciano was treated in this fashion for an ulcerous infection of his thigh.

FLAM. He was a kind of statesman that would sooner have reckon'd how many cannon bullets he had discharged against a town, to count his expense that way, than how many of his valiant and deserving subjects he lost before it.

FRAN. Oh, speak well of the Duke.

FLAM. I have done. Wilt hear some of my court wisdom? To reprehend princes is dangerous; and to overcommend some of them is palpable lying.

Re-enter LODOVICO.

FRAN. How is it with the Duke?
LOD. Most deadly ill.
He's fall'n into a strange distraction:
He talks of battles and monopolies,
Levying of taxes; and from that descends
To the most brainsick language. His mind fastens
On twenty several objects, which confound
Deep sense with folly. Such a fearful end
May teach some men that bear too lofty crest,
Though they live happiest, yet they die not best.
He hath conferr'd the whole state of the dukedom
Upon your sister, till the Prince arrive
At mature age.
FLAM. There's some good luck in that yet.
FRAN. See, here he comes.

Enter BRACHIANO, *presented in a bed*, VITTORIA, [GASPARO,] *and others.*[55]

There's death in's face already.
VIT. Oh, my good Lord!
BRACH.[56] Away! you have abus'd me:
You have convey'd coin forth our territories,[57]
Bought and sold offices, oppress'd the poor,
And I ne'er dreamt on't. Make up your accounts;
I'll now be mine own steward.
FLAM. Sir, have patience.
BRACH. Indeed, I am to blame;
For did you ever hear the dusky raven
Chide blackness? or was't ever known the Devil
Rail'd against cloven creatures?
VIT. Oh, my Lord!
BRACH. Let me have some quails to supper.
FLAM. Sir, you shall.
BRACH. No, some fried dogfish; your quails feed on poison.
That old dog-fox, that politician, Florence —
I'll forswear hunting, and turn dog-killer:
Rare! I'll be friends with him; for, mark you, sir,
One dog still sets another a-barking. Peace, peace!
Yonder's a fine slave come in now.
FLAM. Where?
BRACH. Why, there, in a blue bonnet, and a pair
Of breeches with a great codpiece.[58] Ha, ha, ha!
Look you, his codpiece is stuck full of pins,[59]
With pearls o' th' head of them. Do not you know him?
FLAM. No, my Lord.
BRACH. Why, 't is the Devil:
I know him by a great rose[60] he wears on's shoe,
To hide his cloven foot. I'll dispute with him;
He's a rare linguist.[61]
VIT. My Lord, here's nothing.
BRACH. Nothing? rare! nothing! When I want money,
Our treasury is empty: there is nothing;
I'll not be us'd thus.
VIT. Oh, lie still, my Lord!
BRACH. See, see; Flamineo, that kill'd his brother,
Is dancing on the ropes[62] there, and he carries
A moneybag in each hand, to keep him even,
For fear of breaking's neck. And there's a lawyer
In a gown whipp'd[63] with velvet, stares and gapes
When the money will fall. How the rogue cuts capers!

[55] Probably the curtains of the inner stage were opened, these characters were "discovered", and the audience at once accepted the whole stage as the Duke's cabinet.

[56] Old eds. note marginally: *These speeches are several kinds of distractions and in the action should appear.*

[57] To do so was often prohibited by statute.

[58] A baggy appendage at the front of the breeches.

[59] "According to the fashion of the time." (Lucas.)

[60] Rosette.

[61] Talker.

[62] Tight-ropes.

[63] Trimmed.

It should have been in a halter.[64] 'T is there; what's she?
FLAM. Vittoria, my Lord.
BRACH. Ha, ha, ha! Her hair
Is sprinkled with arras-powder,[65] that makes her look
As if she had sinn'd in the pastry.[66] — What's he?
FLAM. A divine, my Lord.

BRACHIANO seems here near his end; LODOVICO and GASPARO, in the habit of Capuchins, present him in his bed with a crucifix and hallowed candle.

BRACH. He will be drunk; avoid him;
Th' argument is fearful, when churchmen stagger in 't.
Look you, six grey rats that have lost their tails
Crawl up the pillow; send for a ratcatcher.
I'll do a miracle. I'll free the court
From all foul vermin. Where's Flamineo?
FLAM. [*aside*] I do not like that he names me so often,
Especially on's deathbed; 't is a sign
I shall not live long. — See, he's near his end.
LOD. Pray, give us leave. — *Attende, Domine Brachiane* —
FLAM. See, see how firmly he doth fix his eye
Upon the crucifix.
VIT. Oh, hold it constant!
It settles his wild spirits; and so his eyes
Melt into tears.
LOD.[67] *Domine Brachiane, solebas in bello tutus esse tuo clypeo; nunc hunc clypeum hosti tuo opponas infernali.*
GAS.[68] *Olim hasta valuisti in bello; nunc hanc sacram hastam vibrabis contra hostem animarum.*
LOD. *Attende, Domine Brachiane; si nunc quoque probas ea quae acta sunt inter nos, flecte caput in dextrum.*
GAS. *Esto securus, Domine Brachiane; cogita quantum habeas meritorum; denique memineris meam animam pro tua oppignoratam si quid esset periculi.*
LOD. *Si nunc quoque probas ea quae acta sunt inter nos, flecte caput in l[ae]vum.* — [69]
He is departing; pray, stand all apart,
And let us only whisper in his ears
Some private meditations, which our order
Permits you not to hear.

Here, the rest being departed, LODOVICO and GASPARO discover themselves.

GAS. Brachiano!
LOD. Devil
Brachiano, thou art damn'd!
GAS. Perpetually!
LOD. A slave condemn'd and given up to the gallows
Is thy great lord and master!
GAS. True; for thou
Art given up to the Devil!
LOD. O you slave!
You that were held the famous politician,
Whose art was poison —
GAS. And whose conscience, murder!
LOD. That would have broke your wife's neck down the stairs,
Ere she was poison'd!
GAS. That had your villainous sallets — [70]
LOD. And fine embroidered bottles and perfumes,
Equally mortal with a winter plague!
GAS. Now there's mercury — [71]
LOD. And copperas — [72]
GAS. And quicksilver —
LOD. With other devilish pothecary stuff,
A-melting in your politic brains — dost hear?
GAS. This is Count Lodovico.
LOD. This, Gasparo;
And thou shalt die like a poor rogue.
GAS. And stink
Like a dead fly-blown dog.
LOD. And be forgotten

[64] He should have danced at the end of the hangman's rope.

[65] Powdered orris (iris) root, with which Vittoria had scented her hair.

[66] *I.e.*, the "office" of the pastry · there would be much flour about.

[67] Old eds. note marginally: By the crucifix.

[68] Old eds. note marginally: By the h[a]llowed taper.

[69] Lord Brachiano, safe wert thou wont to be in battle by virtue of thy shield; this shield shalt thou now oppose to thine infernal enemy. . . . Once by the spear wert thou mighty in battle; now shalt thou shake this spear against the enemy of souls. . . . Hearken, Lord Brachiano; if now thou dost approve of these things done between us, incline thine head to the right. . . . Be thou confident, Lord Brachiano; think upon how much of merit thou hast; and finally remember that my soul is a pledge for thine, should there be aught of peril. . . . If now, likewise, thou dost approve of these things done between us, incline thine head to the left.

[70] Salads.

[71] *I.e.*, corrosive sublimate.

[72] Sulphate of copper, iron, or zinc.

Before thy funeral sermon.
BRACH. Vittoria! Vittoria!
LOD. Oh, the cursed devil!
Come [73] to himself again! We are undone.
FRAN. Strangle him in private.

Re-enter VITTORIA *and the* Attendants.

What, will you call him again
To live in treble torments? For charity,
For Christian charity, avoid the chamber.
[*Exeunt* VITTORIA *and* Attendants.]
LOD. You would prate, sir? This is a true-love knot
Sent from the Duke of Florence
BRACHIANO *is strangled.*
GAS. What, is it done?
LOD. The snuff [74] is out. No woman keeper [75] i' th' world,
Though she had practis'd seven year at the pest-house,
Could have done 't quaintlier.[76] — My Lords, he 's dead.

[*They return.*]

OMNES. Rest to his soul!
VIT. O me! this place is hell.
Exit VITTORIA.
[FRAN.] [77] How heavily she takes it!
FLAM. Oh, yes, yes;
Had women navigable rivers in their eyes,
They would dispend them all. Surely, I wonder
Why we should wish more rivers to the city,[78]
When they sell water so good cheap.[79] I'll tell thee,
These are but moonish [80] shades of griefs or fears;
There 's nothing sooner dry than women's tears.
Why, here 's an end of all my harvest; he [h]as given me nothing.
Court promises! let wise men count them curs'd,
For while you live,[81] he that scores best [82] pays worst.
FRAN. Sure, this was Florence' doing.
FLAM. Very likely.
Those are found weighty strokes which come from th' hand,
But those are killing strokes which come from th' head.
Oh, the rare tricks of a Machiavellian!
He doth not come like a gross, plodding slave,
And buffet you to death; no, my quaint knave!
He tickles you to death, makes you die laughing,
As if you had swallow'd down a pound of saffron.
You see the feat, 't is practis'd in a trice —
To teach court honesty [83] it jumps on ice.
FRAN. Now have the people liberty to talk,
And descant [84] on his vices.
FLAM. Misery of princes,
That must of force [85] be censur'd by their slaves!
Not only blam'd for doing things are ill,
But for not doing all that all men will:
One were better be a thresher. — Ud's death,
I would fain speak with this duke yet.
FRAN. Now he 's dead?
FLAM. I cannot conjure; but, if prayers or oaths
Will get to th' speech of him, though forty devils
Wait on him in his livery of flames,
I'll speak to him, and shake him by the hand,
Though I be blasted. *Exit* FLAMINEO.
FRAN. Excellent Lodovico!
What, did you terrify him at the last gasp?
LOD. Yes, and so idly, that the Duke had like
T' have terrified us.
FRAN. How?
LOD. You shall hear that hereafter.

Enter the Moor [ZANCHE].

See, yon 's the infernal that would make up [86] sport.
Now to the revelation of that secret
She promis'd when she fell in love with you.
FRAN. You 're passionately [87] met in this sad world.
ZAN. I would have you look up, sir; these court tears
Claim not your tribute to them; let those weep

[73] Qq_{2-4}, *Comes.*
[74] Of the candle; *i.e.*, of Brachiano's life.
[75] Nurse.
[76] More neatly.
[77] Early eds. confuse *Flo[rence]* and *Fra.* throughout the rest of this scene.
[78] Sir Hugh Myddleton's New River was completed in 1613.
[79] At such a bargain.
[80] Changeable.
[81] Ever.
[82] Runs up the largest account.
[83] Understand "that."
[84] Expatiate.
[85] Necessarily.
[86] Q_4 *us.*
[87] Sorrowfully.

That guiltily partake in the sad cause.
I knew last night, by a sad dream I had,
Some mischief would ensue; yet, to say truth,
My dream most concern'd you.

LOD. Shall 's fall a-dreaming?

FRAN. Yes; and for fashion sake I 'll dream with her.

ZAN. Methought, sir, you came stealing to my bed.

FRAN. Wilt thou believe me, sweeting? by this light,
I was a-dreamt on thee too; for methought
I saw thee naked.

ZAN. Fie, sir! As I told you,
Methought you lay down by me.

FRAN. So dreamt I;
And, lest thou shouldst take cold, I cover'd thee
With this Irish mantle.

ZAN. Verily, I did dream
You were somewhat bold with me; but, to come to 't —

LOD. How, how! I hope you will not go to it here.

FRAN. Nay, you must hear my dream out.

ZAN. Well, sir, forth!

FRAN. When I threw the mantle o'er thee, thou didst laugh
Exceedingly, methought.

ZAN. Laugh?

FRAN. And cri'dst out,
The hair did tickle thee.

ZAN. There was a dream indeed!

LOD. [*aside*] Mark her, I prithee; she simpers like the suds
A collier hath been wash'd in.

ZAN. Come, sir, good fortune tends you. I did tell you
I would reveal a secret: Isabella,
The Duke of Florence' sister, was empoison'd
By a fum'd [88] picture; and Camillo's neck
Was broke by damn'd Flamineo, the mischance
Laid on a vaulting-horse.

FRAN. Most strange!

ZAN. Most true.

LOD. [*aside*] The bed [89] of snakes is broke.

ZAN. I sadly do confess I had a hand
In the black deed.

FRAN. Thou kept's [90] their counsel?

ZAN. Right;
For which, urg'd with contrition, I intend
This night to rob Vittoria.

LOD. [*aside*] Excellent penitence!
Usurers dream on 't while they sleep out sermons.

ZAN. To further our escape, I have entreated
Leave to retire me, till the funeral,
Unto a friend i' th' country; that excuse
Will further our escape. In coin and jewels
I shall at least make good unto your use
An hundred thousand crowns.

FRAN. O noble wench!

LOD. Those crowns we 'll share.

ZAN. It is a dowry,
Methinks, should make that sunburnt proverb false,
" And wash the Ethiop white."

FRAN. It shall. Away!

ZAN. Be ready for our flight.

FRAN. An hour 'fore day.

Exit the Moor.

O strange discovery! why, till now we knew not
The circumstance of either of their deaths.

Re-enter the Moor.

ZAN. You'll wait about midnight in the chapel?

FRAN. There. [*Exit* ZANCHE.]

LOD. Why, now our action 's justified.

FRAN. Tush for justice!
What harms it justice? We now, like the partridge,
Purge the disease with laurel: [91] for the fame
Shall crown the enterprise and quit the shame.

Exeunt.

[SCENE IV] [92]

Enter FLAMINEO *and* GASPARO, *at one door; another way*, GIOVANNI, *attended.*

GAS. The young Duke: did you e'er see a sweeter prince?

FLAM. I have known a poor woman's bastard better favor'd.[93] This is behind him. Now to his face: all comparisons were hateful. Wise was the courtly peacock that, being a great minion, and, being compar'd for beauty, by some dottrels [94] that stood by, to the kingly eagle, said the eagle was a far fairer bird than herself, not in respect of her feathers,

[88] See on II, ii, 25.
[89] Knotted mass.
[90] For the unpronounceable *keptst*.

[91] According to Pliny.
[92] A room in the palace.
[93] Better looking.
[94] A kind of plover, supposed to be especially foolish.

but in respect of her long talons. His will grow out in time. — My gracious Lord!

GIO. I pray, leave me, sir.

FLAM. Your Grace must be merry; 'tis I have cause to mourn; for, wot you, what said the little boy that rode behind his father on horseback?

GIO. Why, what said he?

FLAM. "When you are dead, Father," said he, "I hope then I shall ride in the saddle." Oh, 't is a brave thing for a man to sit by himself! He may stretch himself in the stirrups, look about, and see the whole compass of the hemisphere. You 're now, my Lord, i' th' saddle.

GIO. Study your prayers, sir, and be penitent;
'T were fit you 'd think on what hath former been;[95]
I have heard grief nam'd the eldest child of sin. *Exit* GIOVANNI.

FLAM. Study my prayers! he threatens me divinely;
I am falling to pieces already. I care not, though, like [Anaxarchus],[96] I were pounded to death in a mortar; and yet that death were fitter for usurers — gold and themselves to be beaten together, to make a most cordial cullis[97] for the Devil.
He hath his uncle's villainous look already,
In decimo sexto.[98]

Enter Courtier.

Now, sir, what are you?

COURT. It is the pleasure, sir, of the young Duke,
That you forbear the presence and all rooms
That owe him reverence.

FLAM. So; the wolf and the raven
Are very pretty fools when they are young.
Is it your office, sir, to keep me out?

COURT. So the Duke wills.

FLAM. Verily, Master Courtier, extremity is not to be used in all offices. Say that a gentlewoman were taken out of her bed about midnight, and committed to Castle Angelo,[99] to the Tower[100] yonder, with nothing about her but her smock, would it not show a cruel part in the gentleman-porter to lay claim to her upper garment, pull it o'er her head and ears, and put her in naked?

COURT. Very good; you are merry. [*Exit.*]

FLAM. Doth he make a court ejectment of me? A flaming firebrand casts more smoke without a chimney than within 't. I'll smoor[101] some of them.

Enter FLORENCE.

How now! thou art sad.

FRAN. I met even now with the most piteous sight.

FLAM. Thou mett'st[102] another here: a pitiful
Degraded courtier.

FRAN. Your reverend mother
Is grown a very old woman in two hours.
I found them winding of Marcello's corse;
And there is such a solemn melody,
'Tween doleful songs, tears, and sad elegies,
Such as old grandams watching by the dead
Were wont t' outwear the nights with, that, believe me,
I had no eyes to guide me forth the room,
They were so o'ercharg'd with water.

FLAM. I will see them.

FRAN. 'T were much uncharity in you; for your sight
Will add unto their tears.

FLAM. I will see them;
They are behind the traverse — I'll discover
Their superstitious howling.
[*Draws the curtains.*[103]]

CORNELIA, *the* Moor [ZANCHE], *and three other* Ladies *discovered winding* MARCELLO'S *corse.* *A Song.*

CORN. This rosemary is wither'd; pray get fresh.
I would have these herbs grow up in his grave,
When I am dead and rotten. Reach the bays;
I'll tie a garland here about his head;
'T will keep my boy from lightning.[104] This sheet
I have kept this twenty year, and every day
Hallow'd it with my prayers; I did not think
He should have wore it.

ZAN. Look you who are yonder.

CORN. Oh, reach me the flowers.

ZAN. [*aside*] Her Ladyship's foolish.

[95] Old eds. spell *bin*.
[96] The Thracian philosopher; his death was at the hands of Nicocreon, tyrant of Cyprus. Emend. Sykes; old eds. *Anacharsis*.
[97] Broth.
[98] *I.e.*, in little, on a small scale.
[99] The Castle of St. Angelo, in Rome.
[100] Referring to the Tower of London, but evidently an explanatory note on "Castle Angelo."

[101] Smother.
[102] Q_4 *meet'st*.
[103] Of the inner stage.
[104] An ancient superstition.

LADY. [*aside*] Alas! her grief
Hath turn'd her child again!
CORN. You're very welcome:
There's rosemary for you; (*to* FLAMINEO) and rue for you; —
Heartsease[105] for you; I pray make much of it;
I have left more for myself.
FRAN. Lady, who's this?
CORN. You are, I take it, the gravemaker.
FLAM. So.
ZAN. 'T is Flamineo.
CORN. Will you make me such a fool? here's a white hand:
Can blood so soon be wash'd out? Let me see;
When screech owls croak upon the chimney tops,
And the strange cricket i' th' oven sings and hops,
When yellow spots do on your hands appear,
Be certain then you of a corse shall hear.
Out upon't, how 't is speckled! h'as handled a toad, sure. Cowslip-water is good for the memory; pray buy me three ounces of 't.

FLAM. [*aside*] I would I were from hence.

CORN. Do you hear, sir? I'll give you a saying which my grandmother was wont, when she heard the bell toll, to sing o'er unto her lute.

FLAM. Do, an you will; do.

CORNELIA *doth this in several forms of distraction.*

CORN.

Call for the robin redbreast and the wren,
  Since o'er shady groves they hover,
  And with leaves and flow'rs do cover
The friendless bodies of unburied men.
  Call unto his funeral dole
  The ant, the fieldmouse, and the mole,
To rear him hillocks that shall keep him warm,
And (when gay tombs are robb'd) sustain no harm;
But keep the wolf far thence, that's foe to men;
For with his nails he 'll dig them up again.

They would not bury him 'cause he died in a quarrel;
But I have an answer for them:
"Let holy Church receive him duly,
Since he paid the church-tithes truly."
His wealth is summ'd; and this is all his store:
This poor men get; and great men get no more.
Now the wares are gone, we may shut up shop.
Bless you all, good people.

Exeunt CORNELIA, [ZANCHE,] *and* Ladies.

FLAM. I have a strange thing in me, to th' which
I cannot give a name, without it be
Compassion. I pray, leave me.

Exit FRANCISCO.

This night I'll know the utmost of my fate;
I'll be resolv'd what my rich sister means
T' assign me for my service. I have liv'd
Riotously ill, like some that live in court;
And sometimes, when my face was full of smiles,
Have felt the maze[106] of conscience in my breast.
Oft gay and honor'd robes those tortures try;[107]
We think cag'd birds sing, when indeed they cry.

Enter BRACHIANO's Ghost, *in his leather cassock and breeches, boots* [*and*] *a cowl;* [*in his hand*] *a pot of lily flowers, with a skull in 't.*

Ha! I can stand[108] thee; nearer, nearer yet!
What a mockery hath death made of thee! thou look'st sad.
In what place art thou? in yon starry gallery?
Or in the cursed dungeon? — No? not speak?
Pray, sir, resolve me what religion 's best
For a man to die in? Or is it in your knowledge
To answer me how long I have to live?
That's the most necessary question.
Not answer? are you still like some great men
That only walk like shadows up and down,
And to no purpose? say: —

The Ghost *throws earth upon him, and shows him the skull.*

What's that? Oh, fatal! he throws earth upon me!
A dead man's skull beneath the roots of flowers! —
I pray, speak, sir; our Italian churchmen
Make us believe dead men hold conference
With their familiars, and many times
Will come to bed to them, and eat with them.

Exit Ghost.

[105] Pansies.

[106] Stupefying effect.

[107] *I.e.*, people whose outward appearance indicates happiness often experience the torments of conscience.

[108] Stand up to.

He's gone; and see, the skull and earth are vanish'd.
This is beyond melancholy.[109] I do dare my fate
To do its worst. Now to my sister's lodging,
And sum up all these horrors: the disgrace
The Prince threw on me; next, the piteous sight
Of my dead brother; and my mother's dotage;
And last, this terrible vision — all these
Shall with Vittoria's bounty turn to good,
Or I will drown this weapon in her blood.
Exit.

[SCENE V] [110]

Enter FRANCISCO, LODOVICO, *and* HORTENSIO [*following them*].

LOD. My Lord, upon my soul, you shall no further;
You have most ridiculously engag'd yourself
Too far already. For my part, I have paid
All my debts; so, if I should chance to fall,
My creditors fall not with me; and I vow
To quit [111] all in this bold assembly
To the meanest follower. My Lord, leave the city;
Or I'll forswear the murder.
FRAN. Farewell, Lodovico!
If thou dost perish in this glorious act,
I'll rear unto thy memory that fame
Shall in the ashes keep alive thy name.
[*Exeunt* FRANCISCO *and* LODOVICO.]
HORT. There's some black deed on foot. I'll presently [112]
Down to the citadel, and raise some force.
These strong court factions, that do brook no checks,
In the career [113] oft break the riders' necks.
[*Exit.*]

[SCENE VI] [114]

Enter VITTORIA *with a book in her hand,* [*and*] ZANCHE; FLAMINEO *following them.*

FLAM. What, are you at your prayers? give o'er.
VIT. How, ruffian?
FLAM. I come to you 'bout worldly business;
Sit down, sit down; — nay, stay, blowze,[115] you may hear it;
The doors are fast enough.
VIT. Ha! are you drunk?
FLAM. Yes, yes, with wormwood-water; you shall taste
Some of it presently.
VIT. What intends the [116] fury?
FLAM. You are my Lord's executrix, and I claim
Reward for my long service.
VIT. For your service?
FLAM. Come, therefore; here is pen and ink; set down
What you will give me. *She writes.*
VIT. There!
FLAM. Ha! have you done already?
'T is a most short conveyance.
VIT. I will read it:
"I give that portion to thee, and no other,
Which Cain groan'd under, having slain his brother."
FLAM. A most courtly patent to beg by! [117]
VIT. You are a villain.
FLAM. Is't come to this? The[y] say affrights cure agues.
Thou hast a devil in thee; I will try
If I can scare him from thee. Nay, sit still.
My Lord hath left me yet two case [118] of jewels
Shall make me scorn your bounty; you shall see them. [*Exit.*]
VIT. Sure, he's distracted.
ZAN. Oh, he's desperate;
For your own safety give him gentle language.

He enters with two case [118] *of pistols.*

FLAM. Look, these are better far at a dead lift [119]
Than all your jewel-house.
VIT. And yet, methinks,
These stones have no fair lustre, they are ill set.
FLAM. I'll turn the right side towards you: you shall see
How the[y] will sparkle.
VIT. Turn this horror from me!
What do you want? What would you have me do?
Is not all mine yours? Have I any children?
FLAM. Pray thee, good woman, do not trouble me

[109] *I.e.*, this is not an illusion resulting from a disproportionate amount of black bile.
[110] Unlocated. [111] Requite. [112] Immediately.
[113] See on IV, iii, 94. [114] Vittoria's apartment.

[115] Wench. [116] Lucas queries *thy*.
[117] Such licenses were often issued.
[118] Pairs. [119] At a pinch.

With this vain worldly business; say your prayers:
I made a vow to my deceased lord,
Neither yourself nor I should outlive him
The numbering of four hours.
VIT. Did he enjoin it?
FLAM. He did; and 't was a deadly jealousy
Lest any should enjoy thee after him,
That urg'd him vow me to it. For[120] my death,
I did propound it voluntarily, knowing,
If he could not be safe in his own court,
Being a great duke, what hope, then, for us?
VIT. This is your melancholy and despair.
FLAM. Away! Fool thou art to think that politicians
Do use to kill the effects of injuries,
And let the cause live. Shall we groan in irons,
Or be a shameful and a weighty burden
To a public scaffold? This is my resolve —
I would not live at any man's entreaty,
Nor die at any's bidding.
VIT. Will you hear me?
FLAM. My life hath done service to other men;
My death shall serve mine own turn. Make you ready.
VIT. Do you mean to die indeed?
FLAM. With as much pleasure
As e'er my father gat me.
VIT. [*aside to* ZANCHE] Are the doors lock'd?
ZAN. [*aside*] Yes, madam.
VIT. Are you grown an atheist? will you turn your body,
Which is the goodly palace of the soul,
To the soul's slaughterhouse? Oh, the cursed Devil,
Which doth present us with all other sins
Thrice-candied o'er — despair with gall and stibium,[121]
Yet we carouse it off[122] — [*aside to* ZANCHE] Cry out for help! —
Makes us forsake that which was made for man,
The world, to sink to that was made for devils,
Eternal darkness!
ZAN. Help, help!
FLAM. I'll stop your throat
With winter plums.
VIT. I prithee, yet remember,
Millions are now in graves, which at last day,
Like mandrakes, shall rise shrieking.[123]
FLAM. Leave your prating,
For these are but grammatical[124] laments,
Feminine arguments; and they move me,
As some in pulpits move their auditory,
More with their exclamation than sense
Of reason or sound doctrine.
ZAN. [*aside to* VITTORIA] Gentle madam,
Seem to consent, only persuade him teach
The way to death; let him die first.
VIT. [*aside to* ZANCHE] 'T is good.
I apprehend it. —
To kill one's self is meat that we must take
Like pills, not chew 't, but quickly swallow it;
The smart a' th' wound, or weakness of the hand,
May else bring treble torments.
FLAM. I have held it
A wretched and most miserable life
Which is not able to die.
VIT. Oh, but frailty!
Yet I am now resolv'd. Farewell, affliction!
Behold, Brachiano, I, that while you liv'd
Did make a flaming altar of my heart
To sacrifice unto you, now am ready
To sacrifice heart and all. — Farewell, Zanche!
ZAN. How, madam! do you think that I'll outlive you;
Especially when my best self, Flamineo,
Goes the same voyage?
FLAM. Oh, most loved Moor!
ZAN. Only by all my love let me entreat you,
Since it is most necessary none[125] of us
Do violence on ourselves, let you or I
Be her sad taster;[126] teach her how to die.
FLAM. Thou dost instruct me nobly; take these pistols.
Because my hand is stain'd with blood already,
Two of these you shall level at my breast,

[120] As for.

[121] Antimony.

[122] But presents despair (which leads to suicide), not sugared over, but bitterly; and yet we drink that potion.

[123] A widespread superstition; the mandrake, which like several other vegetables sometimes grows with a forked root somewhat resembling the human form, was supposed to shriek upon being eradicated.

[124] Rhetorical.

[125] Q_{2-4}, *one*, which mod. eds. adopt, misunderstanding ll. 93, 94. Vittoria and Zanche are to take, each, a pair of the pistols. One of each pair is to be aimed at Flamineo; the "other" (*i.e.*, others) are to be aimed by the women at each other, Zanche's against Vittoria, Vittoria's against Zanche. Thus *none* of them does violence to himself.

[126] Continuing the figure of ll. 73, 74.

Th' other 'gainst your own, and so we'll die
Most equally contented; but first swear
Not to outlive me.

VIT. AND ZAN. Most religiously.

FLAM. Then here's an end of me, farewell, daylight!
And, O contemptible physic, that dost take
So long a study only to preserve
So short a life, I take my leave of thee! —
(*showing the pistols*) These are two cupping-glasses[127] that shall draw
All my infected blood out. Are you ready?

BOTH. Ready.

FLAM. Whither shall I go now? O Lucian, thy ridiculous purgatory![128] to find Alexander the Great cobbling shoes, Pompey tagging points,[129] and Julius Cæsar making hair-buttons! Hannibal selling blacking, and Augustus crying garlic! Charlemagne selling lists[130] by the dozen, and King Pepin crying apples in a cart drawn with one horse!
Whether I resolve[131] to fire, earth, water, air,
Or all the elements by scruples, I know not,
Nor greatly care. — Shoot, shoot;
Of all deaths the violent death is best;
For from ourselves it steals ourselves so fast,
The pain, once apprehended, is quite past.

They shoot.

VIT. What, are you dropp'd?

FLAM. I am mix'd with earth already; as you are noble,
Perform your vows, and bravely follow me.

VIT. Whither? to hell?

[*They*] *run to him and tread upon him.*

ZAN. To most assured damnation?

VIT. O thou most cursed devil!

ZAN. Thou art caught —

VIT. In thine own engine. I tread the fire out
That would have been my ruin.

FLAM. Will you be perjur'd? what a religious oath was Styx, that the gods never durst swear by, and violate! Oh, that we had such an oath to minister, and to be so well kept in our courts of justice!

VIT. Think whither thou art going.

ZAN. And remember
What villainies thou hast acted.

VIT. This thy death
Shall make me,[132] like a blazing, ominous star,
Look up and tremble.

FLAM. Oh, I am caught with a springe![133]

VIT. You see the fox comes many times short home;
'T is here prov'd true.

FLAM. Kill'd with a couple of braches![134]

VIT. No fitter off'ring for the infernal Furies
Than one in whom they reign'd while he was living!

FLAM. Oh, the way's dark and horrid! I cannot see;
Shall I have no company?

VIT. Oh, yes, thy sins
Do run before thee to fetch fire from hell,
To light thee thither.

FLAM. Oh, I smell soot,
Most s[t]inking soot! the chimney is[135] afire:
My liver's p[a]rboil'd, like Scotch holly-bread;[136]
There's a plumber laying pipes in my guts; it scalds. —
Wilt thou outlive me?

ZAN. Yes, and drive a stake
Through[137] thy body;[138] for we'll give it out
Thou didst this violence upon thyself.

FLAM. O cunning devils! now I have tri'd your love,
And doubled all your reaches.[139] — I am not wounded;

FLAMINEO *riseth.*

The pistols held no bullets: 't was a plot
To prove[140] your kindness to me; and I live,
To punish your ingratitude. I knew,
One time or other, you would find a way
To give me a strong potion. — O men
That lie upon your deathbeds, and are haunted
With howling wives, ne'er trust them! they'll remarry
Ere the worm pierce your winding sheet, ere the spider
Make a thin curtain for your epitaphs. — How cunning you were to discharge! do you practise at the Artillery Yard?[141] — Trust a woman? never, never! Brachiano be my precedent. We lay our souls to pawn to the Devil for a little pleasure, and a woman makes

[127] Vacuum cups for bleeding.
[128] In his dialogue, "Menippos."
[129] Putting the metal points on the laces that served the Elizabethans for buttons.
[130] Strips of cloth.
[131] Dissolve.

[132] Lucas suggests *men*.
[133] Snare. [134] By . . . bitches. [135] Q *chimneis*.
[136] Sampson cites Cotgrave's Dictionary: "*Pain benist d'Escosse*, a sodden sheep's liver." Holy Bread, notes Lucas, ordinarily meant the bread blessed and distributed after the Eucharist.
[137] Dissyllabic. [138] As a suicide's.
[139] Eluded all your devices. [140] Test.
[141] Near Bishopsgate Street Without.

the bill of sale. That ever man should marry! For one Hypermnestra that saved her lord and husband, forty-nine of her sisters cut their husbands' throats all in one night;[142] there was a shoal of virtuous horse-leeches![143] — [*showing pistols*] Here are two other instruments.

VIT. Help, help!

Enter LODOVICO [*and*] GASPARO [*disguised as*] Carlo [*and*] Pedro.

FLAM. What noise is that? Ha! false keys i' th' court!
LOD. We have brought you a masque.[144]
FLAM. A matachin,[145] it seems
By your drawn swords. Churchmen turn'd revellers!
[GAS.][146] Isabella! Isabella!
LOD. Do you know us now?
FLAM. Lodovico and Gasparo!
LOD. Yes; and that Moor the Duke gave pension to
Was the great Duke of Florence.
VIT. Oh, we are lost!
FLAM. You shall not take justice from forth my hands.
Oh, let me kill her! — I'll cut my safety
Through your coats of steel. Fate's a spaniel;
We cannot beat it from us. What remains now?
Let all that do ill, take this precedent:
Man may his fate foresee, but not prevent;
And, of all axioms, this shall win the prize:
'T is better to be fortunate than wise.
GAS. Bind him to the pillar.[147]
VIT. Oh, your gentle pity!
I have seen a blackbird that would sooner fly
To a man's bosom than to stay the gripe
Of the fierce sparrowhawk.
GAS. Your hope deceives you.
VIT. If Florence be i' th' court, would he would kill me!
GAS. Fool! Princes give rewards with their own hands,
But death or punishment by the hands of others.
LOD. Sirrah, you once did strike me; I'll strike you
Into the centre.
FLAM. Thou 'lt do it like a hangman,[148]
A base hangman, not like a noble fellow;
For thou seest I cannot strike again.
LOD. Dost laugh?
FLAM. Wouldst have me die, as I was born, in whining?
GAS. Recommend yourself to Heaven.
FLAM. No, I will carry
Mine own commendations thither.
LOD. Oh, could I kill you forty times a day,
And use 't four year together, 't were too little!
Naught grieves but that you are too few to feed
The famine of our vengeance. What dost think on?
FLAM. Nothing; of nothing; leave thy idle questions.
I am i' th' way to study a long silence;
To prate were idle. I remember nothing.
There 's nothing of so infinite vexation
As man's own thoughts.
LOD. O thou glorious strumpet!
Could I divide thy breath from this pure air,
When 't leaves thy body, I would suck it up,
And breathe 't upon some dunghill.
VIT. You my deathsman!
Methinks thou doest not look horrid enough;
Thou hast too good a face to be a hangman.
If thou be, do thy office in right form;
Fall down upon thy knees, and ask forgiveness.
LOD. Oh, thou hast been a most prodigious comet;
But I'll cut off your train.[149] — Kill the Moor first.
VIT. You shall not kill her first; behold my breast:
I will be waited on in death; my servant
Shall never go before me.
GAS. Are you so brave?
VIT. Yes, I shall welcome death
As princes do some great ambassadors;
I'll meet thy weapon half way.
LOD. Thou dost tremble.
Methinks fear should dissolve thee into air.
VIT. Oh, thou art deceiv'd, I am too true a woman:
Conceit[150] can never kill me. I'll tell thee what:

[142] In the Greek myth of the Danaides.
[143] *I.e.*, lovers of blood.
[144] Which was marked by the appearance of masked strangers.
[145] A sword-dance performed in fantastic costume.
[146] So $Qq_{3,4}$; $Qq_{1,2}$, *Con;* perhaps for *Car.*, perhaps for *Conspirators*.
[147] Doubtless one of the columns that supported the "Heavens."
[148] Professional executioner.
[149] Punning on "train" = (1) tail of a comet; (2) retinue.
[150] Punning on "conceit" = (1) vanity; (2) imagination.

I will not in my death shed one base tear;
Or, if look pale, for want of blood, not fear.
[GAS.][151] Thou art my task, black Fury.
ZAN. I have blood
As red as either of theirs, wilt drink some!
'Tis good for the falling sickness.[152] I am proud
Death cannot alter my complexion,
For I shall ne'er look pale.
LOD. Strike, strike,
With a joint motion!
[*They strike.* ZANCHE *dies.*]
VIT. 'T was a manly blow!
The next thou giv'st, murder some sucking infant;
And then thou wilt be famous.
FLAM. Oh, what blade is 't?
A Toledo, or an English fox?[153]
I ever thought a cutler should distinguish
The cause of my death, rather than a doctor.
Search my wound deeper; tent[154] it with the steel
That made it.
VIT. Oh, my greatest sin lay in my blood;[155]
Now my blood pays for 't.
FLAM. Th'art a noble sister!
I love thee now; if woman do breed man,
She ought to teach him manhood. Fare thee well.
Know many glorious women that are fam'd
For masculine virtue have been vicious;
Only a happier silence did betide them:[156]
She hath no faults who hath the art to hide them.
VIT. My soul, like to a ship in a black storm,
Is driven I know not whither.
FLAM. Then cast anchor.
Prosperity doth bewitch men, seeming clear;
But seas do laugh, show white, when rocks are near.
We cease to grieve, cease to be fortune's slaves,
Nay, cease to die, by dying. — Art thou[157] gone?
And thou[158] so near the bottom? — False report,
Which says that women vie with the nine Muses
For nine tough durable lives! I do not look
Who went before, nor who shall follow me;
No, at myself I will begin and end.
While we look up to Heaven, we confound
Knowledge with knowledge. Oh, I am in a mist!
VIT. Oh, happy they that never saw the court,
Nor ever knew great men but by report.
VITTORIA *dies.*
FLAM. I recover like a spent taper, for a flash,
And instantly go out.
Let all that belong to great men remember
th' old wives' tradition, to be like the lions
i' th' Tower on Candlemas Day[159]: to mourn
if the sun shine, for fear of the pitiful remainder
of winter to come.
'T is well yet there's some goodness in my death;
My life was a black charnel. I have caught
An everlasting cold; I have lost my voice
Most irrecoverably. — Farewell, glorious villains!
This busy trade of life appears most vain,
Since rest breeds rest, where[160] all seek pain by pain.
Let no harsh flattering bells resound my knell;
Strike, thunder, and strike loud, to my farewell! *Dies.*
ENG. AM. [*within*] This way, this way! break ope the doors! this way!
LOD. Ha! are we betray'd?
Why, then let's constantly die all together,
And, having finish'd this most noble deed,
Defy the worst of fate, not fear to bleed.

Enter AMBASSAD[ORS], GIOVANNI, [*and* Officers].

ENG. [AM.] Keep back the Prince: shoot, shoot.
LOD. Oh, I am wounded!
I fear I shall be ta'en.
GIO. You bloody villains,
By what authority have you committed
This massacre?
LOD. By thine.
GIO. Mine?
LOD. Yes; thy uncle,
Which is a part of thee, enjoin'd us to 't.

[151] Old eds. *Car*.
[152] Epilepsy. According to Pliny the blood was not to be drunk, but smeared on the patient's face.
[153] Sword.
[154] Probe.
[155] Sensual nature.
[156] Let the reader remember it, too. This is Webster's summing up.
[157] Zanche.
[158] Vittoria.
[159] February 2. Cf. St. Swithin's Day and the ground hog.
[160] Whereas.

Thou know'st me, I am sure: I am Count Lodowick;
And thy most noble uncle, in disguise,
Was last night in thy court.

Gio. Ha!

[Gasp.][161] Yes, that Moor
Thy father chose his pensioner.

Gio. He turn'd murderer! —
Away with them to prison and to torture;
All that have hands in this shall taste our justice,
As I hope Heaven.

Lod. I do glory yet
That I can call this act mine own. For my part,
The rack, the gallows, and the torturing wheel
Shall be but sound sleeps to me; here's my rest:
I limn'd this night-piece, and it was my best.

Gio. Remove the bodies. — See, my honored Lord,
What use you ought make of their punishment.
Let guilty men remember their black deeds
Do lean on crutches made of slender reeds.

[*Exeunt.*]

Instead of an epilogue only this of Martial supplies me:

Haec fuerint nobis praemia, si placui.[162]

For the action of the play, 't was generally well,[163] and I dare affirm, with the joint testimony of some of their own quality,[164] for the true imitation of life (without striving to make Nature a monster) the best that ever became them; whereof, as I make a general acknowledgment, so in particular I must remember the well-approved industry of my friend Master Perkins,[165] and confess the worth of his action did crown both the beginning and end.

161 So Qq 3, 4; Qq 1, 2, *Car.*

162 These things will be our reward, if I have pleased you. (Martial, II, 91.)

163 Good.

164 Profession.

165 Richard Perkins, a leading actor, at this time with the Queen's Men.

THE
CHANGELING:

As it was Acted (with great Applause) at the Privat house in DRURY-LANE, and *Salisbury Court.*

Written by {*THOMAS MIDLETON,* and *WILLIAM ROWLEY.*} Gent'.

Never Printed before.

LONDON,
Printed for HUMPHREY MOSELEY, and are to be sold at his shop at the sign of the *Princes-Arms* in St *Pauls* Church-yard, 1653.

INTRODUCTORY NOTE

The Changeling is sadly marred, to a modern taste, by the lunatic divertissements which were always acceptable to the Elizabethans; yet it is none the less among the most powerful tragedies of the seventeenth century. Beatrice-Joanna and De Flores provide acting rôles of tremendous force. In a series of lurid flashes the lightning-like scenes of the tragic plot reveal their Titanic passions and their indomitable wills, while under a sky lowering with almost Websterian darkness and horror the proud heroine is hunted to her doom.

To Middleton's collaborator the comic portion of the play is due; but Rowley is also credited with the opening and the closing of the main plot. Middleton is doubtless the author of the great tragic episodes. They mark the height of his powers, which he seems only to have reached during the period of his association with Rowley.

The source is the fourth story in Book I of John Reynolds's *Triumphs of God's Revenge against Murder* (1621); but the material is freely handled, the deaths of the principal characters being radically altered. The play was probably written c. 1622; it was acted at court on January 4, 1624, and had a long career on the public stage. It was revived after the Restoration, when the great Betterton was much applauded as De Flores.

No edition, however, is known prior to that of 1653, on which the present text is based. A later issue, in 1668, consists merely of the remaindered sheets of 1653, with a new title page. As Oliphant observes, we can have no confidence that the play has reached us in its original state; the thirty years that elapsed between its production and publication afforded ample scope for stage tampering, which is reflected in the broken metre of many of the lines, and in such inconsistencies as the omission of scenes carefully prepared for — *e.g.*, the quarrel between Antonio and Franciscus (see IV, iii, 168, ff.). It is a grievous commentary on public taste that the title alludes to the leading figure of the foolish underplot.

[A new modernized text of *The Changeling* was edited by N. W. Bawcutt (Harvard, 1958) for the Revels Plays series. R. O.]

THE CHANGELING

BY

THOMAS MIDDLETON AND WILLIAM ROWLEY

DRAMATIS PERSONAE

VERMANDERO, [governor of the castle of Alicant,] father to Beatrice.
TOMAZO DE PIRACQUO, a noble lord.
ALONZO DE PIRACQUO, his brother, suitor to Beatrice.
ALSEMERO, a nobleman, afterwards married to Beatrice.
JASPERINO, his friend.
ALIBIUS, a jealous doctor.
LOLLIO, his man.
PEDRO, friend to Antonio.
ANTONIO, the changeling.[1]
FRANCISCUS, the counterfeit madman
DE FLORES, servant to Vermandero.
Madmen.
Servants.

BEATRICE [-JOANNA], daughter to Vermandero.
DIAPHANTA, her waiting woman.
ISABELLA, wife to Alibius.

THE SCENE — *Alicante.*

ACT I — [SCENE I][2]

Enter ALSEMERO.

ALS. 'T was in the temple where I first beheld her,
And now again the same. What omen yet
Follows of that? None but imaginary.
Why should my hopes or fate be timorous?
The place is holy, so is my intent:
I love her beauties to the holy purpose;
And that, methinks, admits comparison
With man's first creation, the place blest,
And is his right home back, if he achieve it.
The church hath first begun our interview,
And that's the place must join us into one;
So there's beginning and perfection too.

Enter JASPERINO.

JAS. Oh, sir, are you here? Come, the wind's fair with you;
Y' are like to have a swift and pleasant passage.
ALS. Sure, y' are deceived, friend, 't is contrary,
In my best judgment.
JAS. What, for Malta?[3]
If you could buy a gale amongst the witches,[4]
They could not serve you such a lucky pennyworth[5]
As comes a' God's name.[6]
ALS. Even now I observ'd
The temple's vane to turn full in my face;
I know 't is against me.
JAS. Against you?
Then you know not where you are.
ALS. Not well, indeed.
JAS. Are you not well, sir?
ALS. Yes, Jasperino,
Unless there be some hidden malady
Within me, that I understand not.
JAS. And that
I begin to doubt,[7] sir. I never knew
Your inclinations to travels at a pause
With any cause to hinder it, till now.
Ashore you were wont to call your servants up,
And help to trap your horses for the speed;[8]
At sea I have seen you weigh the anchor with 'em,
Hoist sails for fear to lose the foremost breath,
Be in continual prayers for fair winds;
And have you chang'd your orisons?

[1] Idiot; with a glance, however, at the meanings: (1) turncoat; (2) child (especially an idiot child), substituted by the fairies for a normal human child which they have stolen from its cradle.
[2] Before a church. — Q *Allegant*, above.
[3] In the source Alsemero was on his way there, hoping to obtain a command against the Turks.
[4] Who had them to sell.
[5] Bargain.
[6] *I.e.*, freely.
[7] Fear, suspect.
[8] In order to hasten the process.

ALS. No, friend;
I keep the same church, same devotion.
JAS. Lover I'm sure y' are none; the stoic was
Found in you long ago; your mother nor
Best friends, who have set snares of beauty, ay,
And choice ones too, could never trap you that way.
What might be the cause?
ALS. Lord, how violent
Thou art! I was but meditating of
Somewhat I heard within the temple.
JAS. Is this
Violence? 'T is but idleness compar'd
With your haste yesterday.
ALS. I'm all this while
A-going, man.

Enter Servants.

JAS. Backwards, I think, sir. Look,
Your servants.
1 SER. The seamen call; shall we board your trunks?
ALS. No, not to-day.
JAS. 'T is the critical day, it seems, and the sign [9] in Aquarius.
2 SER. We must not to sea to-day; this smoke will bring forth fire.
ALS. Keep all on shore; I do not know the end,
Which needs I must do, of an affair in hand
Ere I can go to sea.
1 SER. Well, your pleasure.
2 SER. Let him e'en take his leisure too; we are safer on land. *Exeunt* Servants.

Enter BEATRICE-JOANNA, DIAPHANTA, *and* Servants; [ALSEMERO *accosts the lady and then kisses her.*[10]]

JAS. [*aside*] How now! The laws of the Medes are chang'd sure; salute a woman! He kisses too; wonderful! Where learnt he this? and does it perfectly too. In my conscience,[11] he ne'er rehears'd it before. Nay, go on; this will be stranger and better news at Valencia than if he had ransom'd half Greece from the Turk.
BEAT. You are a scholar, sir?
ALS. A weak one, lady.
BEAT. Which of the sciences is this love you speak of?
ALS. From your tongue I take it to be music.
BEAT. You are skilful in 't, can sing at first sight.
ALS. And I have show'd you all my skill at once;
I want more words to express me further,
And must be forc'd to repetition:
I love you dearly.
BEAT. Be better advis'd, sir;
Our eyes are sentinels unto our judgments,
And should give certain judgment what they see;
But they are rash sometimes, and tell us wonders
Of common things, which when our judgments find,
They can then check the eyes, and call them blind.
ALS. But I am further, lady; yesterday
Was mine eyes' employment, and hither now
They brought my judgment, where are both agreed.
Both houses [12] then consenting, 't is agreed;
Only there wants the confirmation
By the hand royal: that 's your part, lady.
BEAT. Oh, there 's one above me,[13] sir. — [*aside*] For five days past
To be recall'd! Sure mine eyes were mistaken;
This was the man was meant me. That he should come
So near his time, and miss it!
JAS. [*aside*] We might have come by the carriers from Valencia, I see, and sav'd all our sea-provision; we are at farthest, sure. Methinks I should do something too;
I meant to be a venturer [14] in this voyage.
Yonder 's another vessel, I'll board [15] her;
If she be lawful prize, down goes her topsail.[16]
[*Accosts* DIAPHANTA.]

Enter DE FLORES.

DE F. Lady, your father ——
BEAT. Is in health, I hope.
DE F. Your eye shall instantly instruct you, lady;
He 's coming hitherward.
BEAT. What needed then
Your duteous preface? I had rather
He had come unexpected; you must stall [17]
A good presence with unnecessary blabbing;

[9] In the almanac.
[10] A common salutation then, not necessarily indicative of love.
[11] As far as I know.
[12] Of Parliament.
[13] Her father.
[14] Investor.
[15] Accost.
[16] In token of surrender. — Q *Deflores*, throughout.
[17] Forestall.

And how welcome for your part you are,
I'm sure you know.

DE F. [*aside*] Will 't never mend, this scorn,
One side nor other? Must I be enjoin'd
To follow still[18] whilst she flies from me? Well,
Fates, do your worst, I'll please myself with sight
Of her at all opportunities,
If but to spite her anger. I know she had
Rather see me dead than living; and yet
She knows no cause for 't but a peevish will.

ALS. You seem'd displeas'd, lady, on the sudden.

BEAT. Your pardon, sir; 't is my infirmity;
Nor can I other reason render you
Than his or hers, [of][19] some particular thing
They must abandon as a deadly poison,
Which to a thousand other tastes were wholesome;
Such to mine eyes is that same fellow there,
The same that report speaks of the basilisk.[20]

ALS. This is a frequent frailty in our nature;
There 's scarce a man amongst a thousand found
But hath his imperfection: one distastes
The scent of roses, which to infinites
Most pleasing is and odoriferous;
One, oil, the enemy of poison;
Another, wine, the cheerer of the heart
And lively refresher of the countenance.
Indeed this fault, if so it be, is general;
There 's scarce a thing but is both lov'd and loath'd;
Myself, I must confess, have the same frailty.

BEAT. And what may be your poison, sir? I am bold with you.

ALS. What[21] might be your desire, perhaps: a cherry.

BEAT. I am no enemy to any creature
My memory has, but yon gentleman.

ALS. He does ill to tempt your sight, if he knew it.

BEAT. He cannot be ignorant of that, sir,
I have not spar'd to tell him so; and I want[22]
To help myself, since he 's a gentleman
In good respect with my father, and follows him.

ALS. He 's out of his place then now.

[*They talk apart.*]

JAS. I am a mad wag, wench.

DIA. So methinks; but for your comfort, I can tell you, we have a doctor in the city that undertakes the cure of such.

JAS. Tush, I know what physic is best for the state of mine own body.

DIA. 'T is scarce a well-govern'd state, I believe.

JAS. I could show thee such a thing with an ingredian[23] that we two would compound together, and if it did not tame the maddest blood i' th' town for two hours after, I 'll ne'er profess physic again.

DIA. A little poppy, sir, were good to cause you sleep.

JAS. Poppy? I'll give thee a pop i' th' lips for that first, and begin there. Poppy is one simple[24] indeed, and cuckoo (what-you-call 't) another. I'll discover no more now; another time I 'll show thee all. [*Exit.*][25]

Enter VERMANDERO *and* Servants.

BEAT. My father, sir.

VER. Oh, Joanna, I came to meet thee.
Your devotion 's ended?

BEAT. For this time, sir. —
[*aside*] I shall change my saint,[26] I fear me; I find
A giddy turning in me. — Sir, this while
I am beholding[27] to this gentleman,
Who left his own way to keep me company,
And in discourse I find him much desirous
To see your castle. He hath deserv'd it, sir,
If ye please to grant it.

VER. With all my heart, sir.
Yet there 's an article between;[28] I must know
Your country; we use not to give survey
Of our chief strengths[29] to strangers; our citadels
Are plac'd conspicuous to outward view,
On promonts'[30] tops, but within are secrets.

ALS. A Valencian, sir.

VER. A Valencian?
That 's native, sir. Of what name, I beseech you?

ALS. Alsemero, sir.

[18] Always.
[19] Q *or*.
[20] A fabulous serpent, hatched from a cock's egg; it killed with its glance.
[21] Q *And what;* erroneously repeating from the preceding line.
[22] Am unable, lack means.
[23] Ingredient, element.
[24] Remedy.
[25] So Dyce, probably rightly, since Jasperino is not introduced to Vermandero.
[26] *I.e.*, the object of my devotion.
[27] Beholden.
[28] One consideration interposes.
[29] Strongholds.
[30] Promontories'.

VER. Alsemero? Not the son
Of John de Alsemero?
ALS. The same, sir.
VER. My best love bids you welcome.
BEAT. He was wont
To call me so, and then[31] he speaks a most
Unfeigned truth.
VER. Oh, sir, I knew your father;
We two were in acquaintance long ago,
Before our chins were worth iulan[32] down,
And so continued till the stamp of time
Had coin'd us into silver. Well, he's gone;
A good soldier went with him.
ALS. You went together[33] in that, sir.
VER. No, by Saint Jacques, I came behind him;
Yet I've done somewhat too. An unhappy day
Swallowed him at last at Gibraltar,
In fight with those rebellious Hollanders.
Was it not so?
ALS. Whose death I had reveng'd,
Or followed him in fate, had not the late league[34]
Prevented me.
VER. Ay, ay, 't was time to breathe.—
Oh, Joanna, I should ha' told thee news;
I saw Piracquo lately.
BEAT. [*aside*] That's ill news.
VER. He's hot preparing for this day of triumph;[35]
Thou must be a bride within this sevennight.
ALS. [*aside*] Ha!
BEAT. Nay, good sir, be not so violent; with speed
I cannot render satisfaction
Unto the dear companion of my soul,
Virginity, whom I thus long have liv'd with,
And part with it so rude and suddenly.
Can such friends divide, never to meet again,
Without a solemn farewell?
VER. Tush, tush! there's a toy.[36]
ALS. [*aside*] I must now part, and never meet again
With any joy on earth.— Sir, your pardon;
My affairs call on me.
VER. How, sir? By no means;
Not chang'd so soon, I hope! You must see my castle,
And her best entertainment, e'er we part;

[31] In speaking so.
[32] The first tender down (Gk. ἴουλος). (Dyce.)
[33] Were equal.
[34] A truce existed between the Dutch and the Spaniards from 1609 till 1621.
[35] Joy, festivity. [36] Trifle.

I shall think myself unkindly us'd else.
Come, come, let's on; I had good hope your stay
Had been awhile with us in Alicant;
I might have bid you to my daughter's wedding.
ALS. [*aside*] He means to feast me, and poisons me beforehand.—
I should be dearly glad to be there, sir,
Did my occasions suit as I could wish.
BEAT. I shall be sorry if you be not there
When it is done, sir; but not so suddenly.
VER. I tell you, sir, the gentleman's complete,
A courtier and a gallant, enrich'd
With many fair and noble ornaments;
I would not change him for a son-in-law
For any he in Spain, the proudest he,
And we have great ones, that you know.
ALS. He's much
Bound to you, sir.
VER. He shall be bound to me
As fast as this tie can hold him; I'll want
My will else.
BEAT. [*aside*] I shall want mine, if you do it.
VER. But come; by the way I'll tell you more of him.
ALS. [*aside*] How shall I dare to venture in his castle,
When he discharges murderers[37] at the gate?
But I must on, for back I cannot go.
BEAT. [*aside*] Not this serpent gone yet?
[*Drops a glove.*]
VER. Look, girl, thy glove's fallen.
Stay, stay; De Flores, help a little.
DE. F. Here, lady. [*Offers her the glove.*]
BEAT. Mischief on your officious forwardness!
Who bade you stoop? They touch my hand no more—
There! For tother's sake I part with this;
[*Takes off and throws down the other glove.*]
Take 'em, and draw thine own skin off with 'em!
Exeunt [*all but* DE FLORES].
DE F. Here's a favor come with a mischief now! I know
She had rather wear my pelt tann'd in a pair
Of dancing pumps, than I should thrust my fingers
Into her sockets here. I know she hates me,
Yet cannot choose but love her. No matter;

[37] Cannon used to scatter shot at short ranges.

If but to vex her, I'll haunt her still;
Though I get nothing else, I'll have my will.
Exit.

[Scene II] [38]

Enter Alibius *and* Lollio.

Alib. Lollio, I must trust thee with a secret,
But thou must keep it.

Lol. I was ever close [39] to a secret, sir.

Alib. The diligence that I have found in thee,
The care and industry already past,
Assures me of thy good continuance.
Lollio, I have a wife.

Lol. Fie, sir, 't is too late to keep her secret; she's known to be married all the town and country over.

Alib. Thou goest too fast, my Lollio. That knowledge
I allow no man can be barr'd it;
But there is a knowledge which is nearer,
Deeper, and sweeter, Lollio.

Lol. Well, sir, let us handle that between you and I.

Alib. 'T is that I go about, man. Lollio,
My wife is young.

Lol. So much the worse to be kept secret, sir.

Alib. Why, now thou meet'st the substance of the point;
I am old, Lollio.

Lol. No, sir; 't is I am old Lollio.

Alib. Yet why may not this concord and sympathize?
Old trees and young plants often grow together,
Well enough agreeing.

Lol. Ay, sir, but the old trees raise themselves higher and broader than the young plants.

Alib. Shrewd [40] application! There's the fear, man;
I would wear my ring on my own finger;
Whilst it is borrowed, it is none of mine,
But his that useth it.

Lol. You must keep it on still [41] then; if it but lie by, one or other will be thrusting into 't.

Alib. Thou conceiv'st [42] me, Lollio; here thy watchful eye
Must have employment; I cannot always be
At home.

Lol. I dare swear you cannot.

Alib. I must look out.

Lol. I know't, you must look out; 't is every man's case.

Alib. Here, I do say, must thy employment be;
To watch her treadings, and in my absence
Supply my place.

Lol. I'll do my best, sir; yet surely I cannot see who you should have cause to be jealous of.

Alib. Thy reason for that, Lollio? 'T is
A comfortable [43] question.

Lol. We have but two sorts of people in the house, and both under the whip: that's fools [44] and madmen; the one has not wit enough to be knaves, and the other not knavery enough to be fools.

Alib. Ay, those are all my patients, Lollio;
I do profess the cure of either sort;
My trade, my living 't is; I thrive by it;
But here's the care that mixes with my thrift:
The daily visitants, that come to see
My brainsick patients, I would not have
To see my wife. Gallants I do observe
Of quick, enticing eyes, rich in habits,
Of stature and proportion very comely;
These are most shrewd temptations, Lollio.

Lol. They may be easily answered, sir; if they come to see the fools and madmen, you and I may serve the turn, and let my mistress alone; she's of neither sort.

Alib. 'T is a good ward; [45] indeed, come they to see
Our madmen or our fools, let 'em see no more
Than what they come for; by that consequent
They must not see her; I'm sure she's no fool.

Lol. And I'm sure she's no madman.

Alib. Hold that buckler fast; Lollio, my trust
Is on thee, and I account it firm and strong.
What hour is 't, Lollio?

Lol. Towards belly-hour, sir.

Alib. Dinner time? Thou mean'st twelve a'clock?

Lol. Yes, sir, for every part has his hour: we wake at six and look about us, that's eye-hour; at seven we should pray, that's knee-hour; at eight walk, that's leg-hour; at nine gather flowers and pluck a rose, [46] that's nose-hour; at ten we drink, that's mouth-hour; at eleven lay about us for victuals, that's hand-hour; at twelve go to dinner, that's belly-hour.

[38] A room in Alibius's house.
[39] Secret.
[40] Devilish, cursed. Alibius takes the greater height of the old trees as an allusion to the horns of the cuckold.
[41] Continuously.
[42] Understandest.
[43] Comforting.
[44] Imbeciles.
[45] Defensive stroke.
[46] Defecate.

ALIB. Profoundly, Lollio! It will be long
Ere all thy scholars learn this lesson, and
I did look to have a new one ent'red; — stay,
I think my expectation is come home.

Enter PEDRO, *and* ANTONIO [*disguised*] *like an idiot.*

PED. Save you, sir; my business speaks itself:
This sight takes off the labor of my tongue.

ALIB. Ay, ay, sir, 't is plain enough, you mean
Him for my patient.

PED. And if your pains prove but commodious,[47] to give but some little strength to his sick and weak part of nature in him, these are [*giving him money*] but patterns to show you of the whole pieces that will follow to you, beside the charge of diet, washing, and other necessaries, fully defrayed.

ALIB. Believe it, sir, there shall no care be wanting.

LOL. Sir, an officer in this place may deserve something. The trouble will pass through my hands.

PED. 'T is fit something should come to your hands then, sir. [*Gives him money.*]

LOL. Yes, sir, 't is I must keep him sweet,[48] and read to[49] him. What is his name?

PED. His name is Antonio; marry, we use but half to him, only Tony.

LOL. Tony, Tony; 't is enough, and a very good name for a fool. — What's your name, Tony?

ANT. He, he, he! well, I thank you, cousin; he, he, he!

LOL. Good boy! hold up your head. — He can laugh; I perceive by that he is no beast.

PED. Well, sir,
If you can raise him but to any height,
Any degree of wit; might he attain,
As I might say, to creep on but all four
Towards the chair of wit, or walk on crutches,
'T would add an honor to your worthy pains,
And a great family might pray for you,
To which he should be heir, had he discretion
To claim and guide his own. Assure you, sir,
He is a gentleman.

LOL. Nay, there's nobody doubted that: at first sight I knew him for a gentleman; he looks no other yet.

PED. Let him have good attendance and sweet lodging.

LOL. As good as my mistress lies in, sir; and as you allow us time and means, we can raise him to the higher degree of discretion.

PED. Nay, there shall no cost want, sir.

LOL. He will hardly be stretch'd up to the wit of a magnifico.[50]

PED. Oh, no, that's not to be expected; far shorter will be enough.

LOL. I'll warrant you [I'll] make him fit to bear office in five weeks; I'll undertake to wind him up to the wit of constable.

PED. If it be lower than that, it might serve turn.

LOL. No, fie; to level him with a headborough,[51] beadle, or watchman, were but little better than he is. Constable I'll able[52] him; if he do come to be a justice afterwards, let him thank the keeper. Or I'll go further with you; say I do bring him up to my own pitch, say I make him as wise as myself.

PED. Why, there I would have it.

LOL. Well, go to; either I'll be as errant a fool as he, or he shall be as wise as I, and then I think 't will serve his turn.

PED. Nay, I do like thy wit passing well.

LOL. Yes, you may; yet if I had not been a fool, I had had more wit than I have too. Remember what state[53] you find me in.

PED. I will, and so leave you. Your best cares, I beseech you. *Exit* PEDRO.

ALIB. Take you none with you; leave 'em all with us.

ANT. Oh, my cousin's gone! cousin, cousin, oh!

LOL. Peace, peace, Tony; you must not cry, child; you must be whipp'd if you do; your cousin is here still; I am your cousin, Tony.

ANT. He, he! then I'll not cry, if thou be'st my cousin; he, he, he!

LOL. I were best try his wit a little, that I may know what form[54] to place him in.

ALIB. Ay, do, Lollio, do.

LOL. I must ask him easy questions at first. — Tony, how many true[55] fingers has a tailor on his right hand?

ANT. As many as on his left, cousin.

LOL. Good; and how many on both?

ANT. Two less than a deuce, cousin.

LOL. Very well answered. I come to you again, cousin Tony; how many fools goes to[56] a wise man?

[47] *I.e.*, serviceable enough.
[48] Clean.
[49] Teach.
[50] Grandee.
[51] A petty parish official.
[52] Vouch for.
[53] Responsible position.
[54] Grade, class.
[55] Honest.
[56] Make.

Ant. Forty in a day sometimes, cousin.

Lol. Forty in a day? How prove you that?

Ant. All that fall out amongst themselves, and go to a lawyer to be made friends.

Lol. A parlous [57] fool! he must sit in the fourth form at least. I perceive that. — I come again, Tony; how many knaves make an honest man?

Ant. I know not that, cousin.

Lol. No, the question is too hard for you. I'll tell you, cousin; there's three knaves may make an honest man: a sergeant, a jailor, and a beadle; the sergeant catches him, the jailor holds him, and the beadle lashes him; and if he be not honest then, the hangman must cure him.

Ant. Ha, ha, ha! that's fine sport, cousin.

Alib. This was too deep a question for the fool, Lollio.

Lol. Yes, this might have serv'd yourself, though I say 't. — Once more and you shall go play, Tony.

Ant. Ay, play at push-pin,[58] cousin; ha, he!

Lol. So thou shalt; say how many fools are here. —

Ant. Two, cousin; thou and I.

Lol. Nay, y'are too forward there, Tony. Mark my question; how many fools and knaves are here; a fool before a knave, a fool behind a knave, between every two fools a knave; how many fools, how many knaves?

Ant. I never learnt so far, cousin.

Alib. Thou putt'st too hard questions to him, Lollio.

Lol. I'll make him understand it easily. — Cousin, stand there.

Ant. Ay, cousin.

Lol. Master, stand you next the fool.

Alib. Well, Lollio.

Lol. Here's my place. Mark now, Tony, there's a fool before a knave.

Ant. That's I, cousin.

Lol. Here's a fool behind a knave — that's I; and between us two fools there is a knave — that's my master; 't is but "We Three" [59] — that's all.

Ant. We three, we three, cousin.

1 Madman. (*within*) Put's head i' th' pillory; the bread's too little.

2 Mad. (*within*) Fly, fly, and he catches the swallow.

3 Mad. (*within*) Give her more onion, or the Devil put the rope about her crag.[60]

Lol. You may hear what time of day it is; the chimes of Bedlam goes.

Alib. Peace, peace, or the wire [61] comes!

3 Mad. (*within*) Cat whore, cat whore! her permasant, her permasant! [62]

Alib. Peace, I say! — Their hour's come; they must be fed, Lollio.

Lol. There's no hope of recovery of that Welsh madman: was undone by a mouse that spoil'd him a permasant; lost his wits for 't.

Alib. Go to your charge, Lollio; I'll to mine.

Lol. Go you to your madmen's ward; let me alone with your fools.[63]

Alib. And remember my last charge, Lollio. *Exit.*

Lol. Of which your patients do you think I am? — Come, Tony, you must amongst your schoolfellows now; there's pretty scholars amongst 'em, I can tell you; there's some of 'em at *stultus, stulta, stultum*.[64]

Ant. I would see the madmen, cousin, if they would not bite me.

Lol. No, they shall not bite thee, Tony.

Ant. They bite when they are at dinner, do they not, coz?

Lol. They bite at dinner, indeed, Tony. Well, I hope to get credit by thee; I like thee the best of all the scholars that ever I brought up, and thou shalt prove a wise man, or I'll prove a fool myself. *Exeunt.*

ACT II — [Scene I] [1]

Enter Beatrice *and* Jasperino *severally.*

Beat. Oh, sir, I'm ready now for that fair service
Which makes the name of friend sit glorious on you!
Good angels and this conduct be your guide!
[*Gives a paper.*]
Fitness of time and place is there set down, sir.

[57] Shrewd.

[58] Or put-pin, a child's game, in which each player pushes or fillips his pin with the object of crossing that of another player. (*N.E.D.*)

[59] A stock joke was a picture of two fools, entitled "We Three", the third of course being the spectator.

[60] Neck. [61] Whip.

[62] Parmesan cheese.

[63] Leave the fools to me.

[64] *I.e.*, so far advanced as to be able to decline *stultus*, = foolish.

[1] Unlocated; presumably a room in the castle.

JAS. The joy I shall return[2] rewards my service. *Exit.*

BEAT. How wise is Alsemero in his friend!
It is a sign he makes his choice with judgment;
Then I appear in nothing more approv'd
Than making choice of him; for 't is a principle,
He that can choose
That bosom well who of his thoughts partakes,
Proves most discreet in every choice he makes.
Methinks I love now with the eyes of judgment,
And see the way to merit, clearly see it.
A true deserver like a diamond sparkles:
In darkness you may see him — that's in absence,
Which is the greatest darkness falls on love;
Yet is he best discern'd then
With intellectual eyesight. What's Piracquo,
My father spends his breath for? And his blessing
Is only mine as I regard his name,
Else it goes from me, and turns head against me,
Transform'd into a curse. Some speedy way
Must be rememb'red. He's so forward too,
So urgent that way, scarce allows me breath
To speak to my new comforts.

Enter DE FLORES.

DE F. [*aside*] Yonder's she;
Whatever ails me, now a' late especially,
I can as well be hang'd as refrain seeing her;
Some twenty times a day, nay, not so little,
Do I force errands, frame ways and excuses,
To come into her sight; and I've small reason for 't,
And less encouragement; for she baits me still
Every time worse than other, does profess herself
The cruellest enemy to my face in town,
At no hand can abide the sight of me,
As if danger or ill luck hung in my looks.
I must confess my face is bad enough,
But I know far worse has better fortune,
And not endur'd alone, but doted on;
And yet such pick-hair'd faces, chins like witches',
Here and there five hairs whispering in a corner,
As if they grew in fear one of another,
Wrinkles like troughs, where swine-deformity swills
The tears of perjury, that lie there like wash
Fallen from the slimy and dishonest eye, —
Yet such a one [plucks][3] sweets without restraint,
And has the grace of beauty to his sweet.[4]
Though my hard fate has thrust me out to servitude,
I tumbled into th' world a gentleman.
She turns her blessed eye upon me now,
And I'll endure all storms before I part with 't.

BEAT. [*aside*] Again?
This ominous ill-fac'd fellow more disturbs me
Than all my other passions.

DE F. [*aside*] Now 't begins again;
I'll stand this storm of hail, though the stones pelt me.

BEAT. Thy business? What's thy business?

DE F. [*aside*] Soft and fair!
I cannot part so soon now.

BEAT. [*aside*] The villain's fix'd. —
Thou standing toad-pool[5] ——

DE F. [*aside*] The show'r falls amain now.

BEAT. Who sent thee? What's thy errand? Leave my sight!

DE F. My Lord your father charg'd me to deliver
A message to you.

BEAT. What, another since?
Do 't, and be hang'd then; let me be rid of thee.

DE F. True service merits mercy.

BEAT. What's thy message?

DE F. Let beauty settle but in patience,
You shall hear all.

BEAT. A dallying, trifling torment!

DE F. Signior Alonzo de Piracquo, lady,
Sole brother to Tomazo de Piracquo ——

BEAT. Slave, when wilt make an end?

DE F. Too soon I shall.

BEAT. What all this while of him?

DE F. The said Alonzo,
With the foresaid Tomazo ——

BEAT. Yet again? [70

DE F. Is new alighted.

BEAT. Vengeance strike the news!
Thou thing most loath'd, what cause was there in this
To bring thee to my sight?

DE F. My Lord your father
Charg'd me to seek you out.

BEAT. Is there no other
To send his errand by?

[2] To Alsemero.

[3] Q *pluckt*.

[4] In his sweetheart's eyes.

[5] *I.e.*, frogpond.

DE F. It seems 't is my luck
To be i' th' way still.
BEAT. Get thee from me!
DE F. So,
[*aside*] Why, am not I an ass to devise ways
Thus to be rail'd at? I must see her still!
I shall have a mad qualm within this hour again,
I know 't; and, like a common Garden[6] bull,
I do but take breath to be lugg'd[7] again.
What this may bode I know not; I'll despair the less,
Because there's daily precedents of bad faces
Belov'd beyond all reason. These foul chops[8]
May come into favor one day 'mongst his[9] fellows.
Wrangling has prov'd the mistress of good pastime;
As children cry themselves asleep, I ha' seen
Women have chid themselves abed to men.
Exit DE FLORES.
BEAT. I never see this fellow but I think
Of some harm towards me; danger's in my mind still;
I scarce leave trembling of an hour after.
The next good mood I find my father in,
I'll get him quite discarded. — Oh, I was
Lost in this small disturbance, and forgot
Affliction's fiercer torrent that now comes
To bear down all my comforts!

Enter VERMANDERO, ALONZO, [*and*] TOMAZO.

VER. Y' are both welcome,
But an especial one belongs to you, sir,
To whose most noble name our love presents
The addition[10] of a son, our son Alonzo.
ALON. The treasury of honor cannot bring forth
A title I should more rejoice in, sir.
VER. You have improv'd it well. — Daughter, prepare;
The day will steal upon thee suddenly.
BEAT. [*aside*] Howe'er, I will be sure to keep[11] the night,
If it should come so near me.
[BEATRICE *and* VERMANDERO *talk apart.*]
TOM. Alonzo.
ALON. Brother?
TOM. In troth I see small welcome in her eye.
ALON. Fie, you are too severe a censurer[12]
Of love in all points, there's no bringing on you.
If lovers should mark everything a fault,
Affection would be like an ill-set[13] book,
Whose faults[14] might prove as big as half the volume.
BEAT. That's all I do entreat.
VER. It is but reasonable;
I'll see what my son says to 't. — Son Alonzo,
Here is a motion made but to reprieve
A maidenhead three days longer: the request
Is not far out of reason, for indeed
The former time is pinching.
ALON. Though my joys
Be set back so much time as I could wish
They had been forward, yet since she desires it,
The time is set as pleasing as before;
I find no gladness wanting.
VER. May I ever
Meet it in that point still! Y' are nobly welcome, sirs.
Exeunt VERMANDERO *and* BEATRICE.
TOM. So; did you mark the dulness of her parting now?
ALON. What dulness? Thou art so exceptious[15] still!
TOM. Why, let it go then; I am but a fool
To mark your harms so heedfully.
ALON. Where's the oversight?
TOM. Come, your faith's cozened[16] in her, strongly cozened.
Unsettle your affection with all speed
Wisdom can bring it to; your peace is ruin'd else.
Think what a torment 't is to marry one
Whose heart is leap'd into another's bosom:
If ever pleasure she receive from thee,
It comes not in thy name, or of thy gift;
She lies but with another in thine arms,
He the half-father unto all thy children
In the conception; if he get 'em not,
She helps to get 'em for him;[17] and how dangerous
And shameful her restraint may [grow][18] in time to,
It is not to be thought on without sufferings.

[6] Bulls and bears were baited at Paris Garden, near the theatres on the Bankside, in Southwark.
[7] Worried by the ear, baited.
[8] *I.e.*, my face.
[9] Its; referring to his face; expressed by "foul chops."
[10] Title.
[11] Heed.
[12] Judge.
[13] Referring to the setting of the types.
[14] *I.e.*, the list of *errata*.
[15] Captious.
[16] Cheated, deceived.
[17] Q adds *in his passions*. Dyce suggests that the author wrote the phrase and failed to strike it out upon revision.
[18] Conj. Bullen; Q *go*.

ALON. You speak as if she lov'd some other, then.
TOM. Do you apprehend so slowly?
ALON. Nay, an that
Be your fear only, I am safe enough.
Preserve your friendship and your counsel, Brother,
For times of more distress; I should depart
An enemy, a dangerous, deadly one,
To any but thyself, that should but think
She knew the meaning of inconstancy,
Much less the use and practice; yet w' are friends.
Pray, let no more be urg'd; I can endure
Much, till I meet an injury to her;
Then I am not myself. Farewell, sweet Brother;
How much w' are bound to Heaven to depart lovingly. *Exit.*
TOM. Why, here is love's tame madness; thus a man
Quickly steals into his vexation. *Exit.*

[SCENE II] [19]

Enter DIAPHANTA *and* ALSEMERO.

DIA. The place is my charge; you have kept your hour,
And the reward of a just meeting bless you!
I hear my lady coming. Complete gentleman,
I dare not be too busy with my praises;
The' are dangerous things to deal with. *Exit.*
ALS. This goes well;
These women are the ladies' cabinets:
Things of most precious trust are lock['d] into 'em.

Enter BEATRICE.

BEAT. I have within mine eye all my desires.
Requests that holy prayers ascend Heaven for,
And brings 'em down to furnish our defects,
Come not more sweet to our necessities
Than thou unto my wishes.
ALS. W' are so like
In our expressions, lady, that unless I borrow
The same words, I shall never find their equals.
BEAT. How happy were this meeting, this embrace,
If it were free from envy! [20] This poor kiss
It has an enemy, a hateful one,
That wishes poison to 't. How well were I now,
If there were none such name known as Piracquo!
Nor no such tie as the command of parents —
I should be but too much blessed.
ALS. One good service
Would strike off both your fears, and I'll go near it too,
Since you are so distress'd. Remove the cause,
The command ceases; so there's two fears blown out
With one and the same blast.
BEAT. Pray, let me find [21] you, sir.
What might that service be, so strangely happy?
ALS. The honorablest piece 'bout man, valor;
I'll send a challenge to Piracquo instantly.
BEAT. How? Call you that extinguishing of fear,
When 't is the only way to keep it flaming?
Are not you ventured [22] in the action,
That's all my joys and comforts? Pray, no more, sir.
Say you prevail'd, you're danger's and not mine then;
The law would claim you from me, or obscurity
Be made the grave to bury you alive.
I'm glad these thoughts come forth; oh, keep not one
Of this condition, sir! Here was a course
Found to bring sorrow on her way to death;
The tears would ne'er 'a' dried, till dust had chok'd 'em.
Blood-guiltiness becomes a fouler visage; —
And now I think on one. — [*aside*] I was to blame,
I ha' marr'd so good a market with my scorn;
'T had been done questionless; the ugliest creature
Creation fram'd for some use; yet to see
I could not mark so much where it should be!
ALS. Lady!
BEAT. [*aside*] Why, men of art make much of poison,
Keep one to expel another. Where was my art?
ALS. Lady, you hear not me.
BEAT. I do especially, sir.
The present times are not so sure of our side

[19] Another room. [20] Malice.

[21] Understand. [22] Risked.

As those hereafter may be; we must use 'em then
As thrifty folks their wealth, sparingly now,
Till the time opens.

ALS. You teach wisdom, lady.

BEAT. Within there! Diaphanta!

Re-enter DIAPHANTA.

DIA. Do you call, madam?

BEAT. Perfect your service, and conduct this gentleman
The private way you brought him.

DIA. I shall, madam.

ALS. My love's as firm as love e'er built upon.

Exeunt DIAPHANTA *and* ALSEMERO.

Enter DE FLORES.

DE F. [*aside*] I have watch'd this meeting, and do wonder much
What shall become of tother; I'm sure both
Cannot be serv'd unless she transgress; happily[23]
Then I'll put in for one; for if a woman
Fly from one point, from him she makes a husband,
She spreads and mounts then like arithmetic:
One, ten, a hundred, a thousand, ten thousand —
Proves in time sutler to an army royal.
Now do I look to be most richly rail'd at,
Yet I must see her.

BEAT. [*aside*] Why, put case[24] I loath'd him
As much as youth and beauty hates a sepulchre,
Must I needs show it? Cannot I keep that secret,
And serve my turn upon him? See, he's here. —
De Flores.

DE F. [*aside*] Ha, I shall run mad with joy!
She call'd me fairly by my name, De Flores,
And neither rogue nor rascal.

BEAT. What ha' you done
To your face a' late? Y' ave met with some good physician;
Y' ave prun'd[25] yourself, methinks; you were not wont
To look so amorously.[26]

DE F. Not I. —
[*aside*] 'T is the same physnomy,[27] to a hair and pimple,
Which she call'd scurvy scarce an hour ago.
How is this?

BEAT. Come hither, nearer, man.

DE F. [*aside*] I'm up to the chin in Heaven!

BEAT. Turn, let me see;
Vauh,[28] 't is but the heat of the liver, I perceive 't;
I thought it had been worse.

DE F. [*aside*] Her fingers touch'd me!
She smells all amber.[29]

BEAT. I'll make a water for you shall cleanse this
Within a fortnight.

DE F. With your own hands, lady?

BEAT. Yes, mine own, sir; in a work of cure
I'll trust no other.

DE F. [*aside*] 'T is half an act of pleasure
To hear her talk thus to me.

BEAT. When w' are us'd
To a hard face, 't is not so unpleasing;
It mends still in opinion, hourly mends;
I see it by experience.

DE F. [*aside*] I was blest
To light upon this minute; I'll make use on 't.

BEAT. Hardness becomes the visage of a man well;
It argues service, resolution, manhood —
If cause were of employment.

DE F. 'T would be soon seen
If e'er your Ladyship had cause to use it;
I would but wish the honor of a service
So happy as that mounts to.

BEAT. [*aside*] We shall try you. —
O my De Flores!

DE F. [*aside*] How's that? She calls me hers
Already! *My* De Flores! — You were about
To sigh out somewhat, madam?

BEAT. No, was I?
I forgot, — oh! ——

DE F. There 't is again, the very
Fellow on 't.

BEAT. You are too quick, sir.

DE F. There's no excuse for 't now: I heard it twice, madam;
That sigh would fain have utterance: take pity on 't,
And lend it a free word. 'Las, how it labors
For liberty! I hear the murmur yet
Beat at your bosom.

BEAT. Would creation ——

DE F. Ay, well said, that 's it.

[23] Perhaps. [24] Suppose. [25] Preened. [26] So like a lover. [27] Physiognomy.

[28] Faugh. [29] Ambergris.

BEAT. Had form'd me man!
DE F. Nay, that's not it.
BEAT. Oh, 't is the soul of freedom!
I should not then be forc'd to marry one
I hate beyond all depths; I should have power
Then to oppose my loathings, nay, remove 'em
For ever from my sight.
DE F. [*aside*] O blest occasion! ——
Without change to your sex you have your wishes;
Claim so much man in me.
BEAT. In thee, De Flores?
There's small cause for that.
DE F. Put it not from me;
It's a service that I kneel for to you. [*Kneels.*]
BEAT. You are too violent to mean faithfully.
There's horror in my service, blood, and danger.
Can those be things to sue for?
DE F. If you knew
How sweet it were to me to be employed
In any act of yours, you would say then
I fail'd, and us'd not reverence enough
When I receive[d] the charge on't.
BEAT. [*aside*] This is much,
Methinks; belike his wants are greedy; and,
To such, gold tastes like angel's food. — Rise.
DE F. I'll have the work first.
BEAT. [*aside*] Possible his need
Is strong upon him. — There's to encourage thee; [*Gives money.*]
As thou art forward, and thy service dangerous,
Thy reward shall be precious.
DE F. That I have thought on;
I have assur'd myself of that beforehand,
And know it will be precious; the thought ravishes!
BEAT. Then take him to thy fury!
DE F. I thirst for him.
BEAT. Alonzo de Piracquo.
DE F. [*rising*] His end's upon him;
He shall be seen no more.
BEAT. How lovely now
Dost thou appear to me! Never was man
Dearlier rewarded.
DE F. I do think of that.
BEAT. Be wondrous careful in the execution.
DE F. Why, are not both our lives upon the cast? [30]
BEAT. Then I throw all my fears upon thy service.

[30] Throw of the dice.

DE F. They ne'er shall rise to hurt you.
BEAT. When the deed's done,
I'll furnish thee with all things for thy flight;
Thou mayst live bravely [31] in another country.
DE F. Ay, ay;
We'll talk of that hereafter.
BEAT. [*aside*] I shall rid myself
Of two inveterate loathings at one time:
Piracquo, and his dog-face. *Exit.*
DE F. O my blood!
Methinks I feel her in mine arms already;
Her wanton fingers combing out this beard,
And, being pleased, praising this bad face.
Hunger and pleasure,[32] they'll commend sometimes
Slovenly dishes, and feed heartily on 'em.
Nay, which is stranger, refuse daintier for 'em.
Some women are odd feeders. — I'm too loud.
Here comes the man goes supperless to bed,
Yet shall not rise to-morrow to his dinner.

Enter ALONZO.

ALON. De Flores.
DE F. My kind, honorable Lord.
ALON. I am glad I ha' met with thee.
DE F. Sir.
ALON. Thou canst show me
The full strength of the castle.
DE F. That I can, sir.
ALON. I much desire it.
DE F. And if the ways and straits
Of some of the passages be not too tedious for you,
I will assure you, worth your time and sight, my Lord.
ALON. Pooh, that shall be no hindrance.
DE F. I'm your servant, then.
'T is now near dinner time; 'gainst [33] your Lordship's rising [34]
I'll have the keys about me.
ALON. Thanks, kind De Flores.
DE F. [*aside*] He's safely thrust upon me, beyond hopes. *Exeunt.*

ACT III — [SCENE I] [1]

Enter ALONZO *and* DE FLORES. (*In the act-time* [2] DE FLORES *hides a naked rapier.*[3])

DE F. Yes, here are all the keys; I was afraid, my Lord,

[31] Splendidly. [32] Lust. [33] Before.
[34] From table. [1] Another room.
[2] *I.e.*, in the interval between the acts.
[3] In the source, behind a door.

I 'd wanted[4] for the postern — this is it.
I 've all, I 've all, my Lord: this for the sconce.[5]

ALON. 'T is a most spacious and impregnable fort.

DE F. You 'll tell me more, my Lord. This descent
Is somewhat narrow, we shall never pass
Well with our weapons, they 'll but trouble us.

ALON. Thou say'st true.

DE F. Pray, let me help your Lordship.

ALON. 'T is done; thanks, kind De Flores.

DE F. Here are hooks, my Lord,
To hang such things on purpose.

[*Hanging up his own sword and that of* ALONZO.]

ALON. Lead, I 'll follow thee.

Exeunt at one door, and enter at the other.

[SCENE II][6]

DE F. All this is nothing; you shall see anon
A place you little dream on.

ALON. I am glad
I have this leisure; all your master's house
Imagine I ha' taken a gondola.

DE F. All but myself, sir, — [*aside*] which makes up my safety. —
My Lord, I 'll place you at a casement here
Will show you the full strength of all the castle.
Look, spend your eye awhile upon that object.

ALON. Here 's rich variety, De Flores.

DE F. Yes, sir.

ALON. Goodly munition.

DE F. Ay, there 's ordnance, sir,
No bastard metal, will ring you a peal like bells
At great men's funerals. Keep your eye straight, my Lord;
Take special notice of that sconce before you;
There you may dwell awhile.

[*Takes the rapier which he has hidden.*]

ALON. I am upon 't.

DE F. And so am I. [*Stabs him.*]

ALON. De Flores! O De Flores!
Whose malice hast thou put on?

DE F. Do you question
A work of secrecy? I must silence you.
[*Stabs him.*]

ALON. O, O, O!

DE F. I must silence you. [*Stabs him.*]
So; here 's an undertaking well accomplish'd.
This vault serves to good use now. Ha, what 's that
Threw sparkles in my eye? — Oh, 't is a diamond
He wears upon his finger; it was well found;
This will approve the work.[7] What, so fast on?
Not part in death? I 'll take a speedy course then.
Finger and all shall off. [*Cuts off the finger.*]
So; now I 'll clear
The passages from all suspect or fear.

Exit with body.

[SCENE III][8]

Enter ISABELLA *and* LOLLIO.

ISA. Why, sirrah, whence have you commission
To fetter the doors against me? If you
Keep me in a cage, pray whistle to me,
Let me be doing something.

LOL. You shall be doing, if it please you;
I 'll whistle to you, if you 'll pipe after.

ISA. Is it your master's pleasure, or your own,
To keep me in this pinfold?[9]

LOL. 'T is for my master's pleasure, lest being taken in another man's corn, you might be pounded[10] in another place.

ISA. 'T is very well, and he 'll prove very wise.

LOL. He says you have company enough in the house, if you please to be sociable, of all sorts of people.

ISA. Of all sorts? Why, here 's none but fools and madmen.

LOL. Very well; and where will you find any other, if you should go abroad? There 's my master and I to boot too.

ISA. Of either sort one, a madman and a fool.

LOL. I would ev'n participate of both, then, if I were as you; I know y' are half mad already; be half foolish too.

ISA. Y' are a brave,[11] saucy rascal! Come on, sir,
Afford me then the pleasure of your bedlam.[12]
You were commending once to-day to me

[4] I lacked the one.
[5] An isolated redoubt.
[6] In the source, the "vault of the casemate."
[7] Prove the work was done.
[8] A room in Alibius's house.
[9] Pound.
[10] Put in a pound, with an obvious double-entendre.
[11] Fine.
[12] Madhouse.

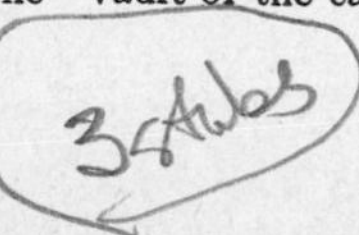

Your last-come lunatic; what a proper[13]
Body there was without brains to guide it,
And what a pitiful delight appear'd
In that defect, as if your wisdom had found
A mirth in madness; pray, sir, let me partake,
If there be such a pleasure.

Lol. If I do not show you the handsomest, discreetest madman, one that I may call the understanding madman, then say I am a fool.

Isa. Well, a match;[14] I will say so.

Lol. When you have a taste of the madman, you shall, if you please, see Fool's College, o' th'[15] side. I seldom lock there; 't is but shooting a bolt or two, and you are amongst 'em. *Exit. Re-enter presently.*[16] — Come on, sir; let me see how handsomely you 'll behave yourself now.

Enter Franciscus.

Fran. How sweetly she looks! Oh, but there 's a wrinkle in her brow as deep as philosophy. Anacreon, drink to my mistress' health; I 'll pledge it. Stay, stay, there 's a spider in the cup! No, 't is but a grapestone; swallow it; fear nothing, poet; so, so, lift higher.

Isa. Alack, alack, 't is too full of pity
To be laugh'd at! How fell he mad? Canst thou tell?

Lol. For love, mistress. He was a pretty poet, too, and that set him forwards first;[17] the Muses then forsook him; he ran mad for a chambermaid, yet she was but a dwarf neither.

Fran. Hail, bright Titania!
Why stand'st thou idle on these flow'ry banks?
Oberon is dancing with his Dryades;
I 'll gather daisies, primrose, violets,
And bind them in a verse of poesy.

Lol. [*holding up a whip*] Not too near!
You see your danger.

Fran. Oh, hold thy hand, great Diomede!
Thou feed 'st thy horses well; they shall obey thee.
Get up, Bucephalus kneels. [*Kneels.*]

Lol. You see how I awe my flock; a shepherd has not his dog at more obedience.

Isa. His conscience is unquiet; sure that was
The cause of this; a proper gentleman!

Fran. Come hither, Æsculapius; hide the poison.

Lol. Well, 't is hid. [*Hides the whip.*]

Fran. Didst thou never hear of one Tiresias,[18]
A famous poet?

Lol. Yes, that kept tame wild-geese.

Fran. That 's he; I am the man.

Lol. No!

Fran. Yes; but make no words on 't. I was a man
Seven years ago.

Lol. A stripling, I think, you might.

Fran. Now I 'm a woman, all feminine.

Lol. I would I might see that!

Fran. Juno struck me blind.

Lol. I 'll ne'er believe that; for a woman, they say, has an eye more than a man.

Fran. I say she struck me blind.

Lol. And Luna made you mad; you have two trades to beg with.

Fran. Luna is now big-bellied, and there 's room
For both of us to ride with Hecate;
I 'll drag thee up into her silver sphere,
And there we 'll kick the dog — and beat the bush —
That barks against the witches of the night;
The swift lycanthropi[19] that walks the round,
We 'll tear their wolvish skins, and save the sheep. [*Attempts to seize* Lollio.]

Lol. Is 't come to this? Nay, then, my poison comes forth again. [*showing the whip*] Mad slave, indeed; abuse your keeper!

Isa. I prithee, hence with him, now he grows dangerous.

Fran. (*sing.*)

Sweet love, pity me;
Give me leave to lie with thee.

Lol. No, I 'll see you wiser first. To your own kennel!

Fran. No noise, she sleeps; draw all the curtains round;
Let no soft sound molest the pretty soul
But love, and love creeps in at a mouse-hole.

Lol. I would you would get into your hole! (*Exit* Franciscus.) — Now, mistress, I will bring you another sort; you shall be fool'd another while. [*Exit, and re-enter.*] — Tony, come hither, Tony: look who 's yonder, Tony.

[13] Handsome.
[14] Agreed.
[15] Mod. eds. add *other*.
[16] At once.
[17] Got him started.
[18] The Theban prophet of classical mythology. According to one version of his story Juno struck him blind. His sexual metamorphoses are also part of his myth. The allusion to the geese is presumably mere nonsensical talk to the supposed lunatic.
[19] Here = werewolves.

Enter ANTONIO.

ANT. Cousin, is it not my aunt?[20]

LOL. Yes, 't is one of 'um, Tony.

ANT. He, he! how do you, Uncle?

LOL. Fear him not, mistress; 't is a gentle nidget;[21] you may play with him, as safely with him as with his bauble.[22]

ISA. How long hast thou been a fool?

ANT. Ever since I came hither, cousin.

ISA. Cousin? I'm none of thy cousins, fool.

LOL. Oh, mistress, fools have always so much wit as to claim their kindred.

MADMAN. [*above*] (*within*) Bounce,[23] bounce! he falls, he falls!

ISA. Hark you, your scholars in the upper room
Are out of order.

LOL. Must I come amongst you there? — Keep you the fool, mistress; I'll go up and play left-handed Orlando[24] amongst the madmen. *Exit.*

ISA. Well, sir.

ANT. 'T is opportuneful now, sweet lady! — nay,
Cast no amazing eye upon this change.

ISA. Ha!

ANT. This shape of folly shrouds your dearest love,
The truest servant to your powerful beauties,
Whose magic had this force thus to transform me.

ISA. You are a fine fool indeed!

ANT. Oh, 't is not strange!
Love has an intellect that runs through all
The scrutinous consciences; and, like a cunning poet,
Catches a quantity of every knowledge,
Yet brings all home into one mystery,
Into one secret that he proceeds in.

ISA. Y' are a parlous fool.

ANT. No danger in me; I bring naught but love
And his soft-wounding shafts to strike you with.
Try but one arrow; if it hurt you, I'll
Stand you twenty back in recompense.
[*Kisses her.*][25]

ISA. A forward fool too!

ANT. This was love's teaching:
A thousand ways [he][26] fashion'd out my way,
And this I found the safest and [the] nearest,
To tread the Galaxia[27] to my star.

ISA. Profound withal! Certain, you dream'd of this;
Love never taught it waking.

ANT. Take no acquaintance
Of these outward follies; there is within
A gentleman that loves you.

ISA. When I see him,
I'll speak with him; so, in the meantime, keep
Your habit; it becomes you well enough.
As you are a gentleman, I'll not discover you;
That's all the favor that you must expect.
When you are weary, you may leave the school,
For all this while you have but play'd the fool.

Re-enter LOLLIO.

ANT. And must again. — He, he! I thank you, cousin;
I'll be your valentine to-morrow morning.

LOL. How do you like the fool, mistress?

ISA. Passing well, sir.

LOL. Is he not witty, pretty well, for a fool?

ISA. If he holds on as he begins, he is like to come to something.

LOL. Ay, thank a good tutor. You may put him to 't; he begins to answer pretty hard questions. — Tony, how many is five times six?

ANT. Five times six is six times five.

LOL. What arithmetician could have answer'd better? How many is one hundred and seven?

ANT. One hundred and seven is seven hundred and one, cousin.

LOL. This is no wit to speak on! — Will you be rid of the fool now?

ISA. By no means: let him stay a little.

MADMAN (*within*) Catch there; catch the last couple in hell![28]

LOL. Again! Must I come amongst you? — Would my master were come home! I am not able to govern both these wards together. *Exit.*

ANT. Why should a minute of love's hour be lost?

[20] The word also meant bawd, mistress, or prostitute. Q *Ant.*
[21] Idiot. Q *nigget.*
[22] The fool's sceptre.
[23] Bang.
[24] Apparently = "strike terror."
[25] Add. Neilson. — *I'll* stands in Q at beginning of l. 151. Q frequently mislines verse.
[26] Q *she.* — Q om. *the,* l. 154.
[27] Milky Way.
[28] Alluding to the game of barley-break; the last couple was left in "hell", the middle of three compartments.

ISA. Fie, out again! I had rather you kept
Your other posture; you become not your tongue
When you speak from [29] your clothes.

ANT. How can he freeze
Lives near so sweet a warmth? Shall I alone
Walk through the orchard of th' Hesperides,
And, cowardly, not dare to pull an apple?

Re-enter LOLLIO, *above.*

This with the red cheeks I must venture for.
[*Attempts to kiss her.*]

ISA. Take heed, there's giants keep 'em.

LOL. [*aside*] How now, fool, are you good at that? Have you read Lipsius? [30] He's past *Ars Amandi* [31]; I believe I must put harder questions to him, I perceive that.

ISA. You are bold without fear too.

ANT. What should I fear,
Having all joys about me? Do you smile,
And love shall play the wanton on your lip,
Meet and retire, retire and meet again;
Look you but cheerfully, and in your eyes
I shall behold mine own deformity,
And dress myself up fairer. I know this shape
Becomes me not, but in those bright mirrors
I shall array me handsomely.

LOL. Cuckoo, cuckoo! [32] *Exit.*

Madmen [*cry*] *above, some as birds, others as beasts.*

ANT. What are these?

ISA. Of fear enough to part us;
Yet are they but our schools of lunatics,
That act their fantasies in any shapes,
Suiting their present thoughts; if sad, they cry;
If mirth be their conceit, they laugh again.
Sometimes they imitate the beasts and birds,
Singing or howling, braying, barking, all
As their wild fancies prompt 'em.

Re-enter LOLLIO.

ANT. These are no fears.

ISA. But here's a large one, my man.

ANT. Ha, he! that's fine sport, indeed, cousin.

LOL. I would my master were come home! 'T is too much for one shepherd to govern two of these flocks; nor can I believe that one churchman can instruct two benefices at once; there will be some incurable mad of the one side, and very fools on the other. — Come, Tony.

ANT. Prithee, cousin, let me stay here still.

LOL. No, you must to your book now; you have play'd sufficiently.

ISA. Your fool is grown wondrous witty.

LOL. Well, I'll say nothing: but I do not think but he will put you down [33] one of these days.

Exeunt LOLLIO *and* ANTONIO.

ISA. Here the restrained current might make breach,
Spite of the watchful bankers.[34] Would a woman stray,
She need not gad abroad to seek her sin:
It would be brought home one ways or other.
The needle's point will to the fixed north;
Such drawing arctics [35] women's beauties are.

Re-enter LOLLIO.

LOL. How dost thou, sweet rogue?

ISA. How now?

LOL. Come, there are degrees; one fool may be better than another.

ISA. What's the matter?

LOL. Nay, if thou giv'st thy mind to fool's flesh, have at thee!

ISA. You bold slave, you!

LOL. I could follow now as tother fool did:
" What should I fear,
Having all joys about me? Do you but smile,
And love shall play the wanton on your lip,
Meet and retire, retire and meet again;
Look you but cheerfully, and in your eyes
I shall behold my own deformity,
And dress myself up fairer. I know this shape
Becomes me not — "
And so as it follows: but is not this the more foolish way? Come, sweet rogue; kiss me, my little Lacedaemonian; let me feel how thy pulses beat. Thou hast a thing about thee would do a man pleasure, I'll lay [36] my hand on 't.

ISA. Sirrah, no more! I see you have discovered

[29] Apart from, out of keeping with.

[30] "Is it necessary to notice that the name of this great scholar is introduced merely for the sake of its first syllable?" (Dyce.) Lipsius was a sixteenth-century Belgian.

[31] *I.e.*, he is evidently able to tackle harder reading than Ovid's *Art of Love*.

[32] Alluding to Alibius's apparently imminent cuckoldom.

[33] Beat you in an argument; with an obvious double-entendre.

[34] Dike-tenders.

[35] Poles. Q *Articks*.

[36] Bet; with an obvious double-entendre.

This love's knight [e]rrant, who hath made adventure
For purchase of [37] my love. Be silent, mute,
Mute as a statue, or his injunction,
For me enjoying, shall be to cut thy throat;
I'll do it, though for no other purpose; and
Be sure he'll not refuse it.

LOL. My share, that's all;
I'll have my fool's part with you.

ISA. No more! Your master.

Enter ALIBIUS.

ALIB. Sweet, how dost thou?

ISA. Your bounden servant, sir.

ALIB. Fie, fie, sweetheart, no more of that.

ISA. You were best lock me up.

ALIB. In my arms and bosom, my sweet Isabella,
I'll lock thee up most nearly. — Lollio,
We have employment, we have task in hand.
At noble Vermandero's, our castle captain,
There is a nuptial to be solemniz'd —
Beatrice-Joanna, his fair daughter, bride, —
For which the gentleman hath bespoke our pains,
A mixture of our madmen and our fools,
To finish, as it were, and make the fag [38]
Of all the revels, the third night from the first;
Only an unexpected passage over,[39]
To make a frightful pleasure, that is all,
But not the all I aim at. Could we so act it,
To teach it in a wild distracted measure,[40]
Though out of form and figure, breaking time's head,
It were no matter, 't would be heal'd again
In one age or other, if not in this;
This, this, Lollio; there's a good reward begun,
And will beget a bounty, be it known.

LOL. This is easy, sir, I'll warrant you; you have about you fools and madmen that can dance very well; and 't is no wonder, your best dancers are not in the wisest men; the reason is, with often jumping they jolt their brains down into their feet, that their wits lie more in their heels than in their heads.

ALIB. Honest Lollio, thou giv'st me a good reason,
And a comfort in it.

ISA. Y'ave a fine trade on 't.
Madmen and fools are a staple commodity.

ALIB. Oh, wife, we must eat, wear clothes, and live.
Just at the lawyer's haven we arrive:
By madmen and by fools we both do thrive.

Exeunt.

[SCENE IV] [41]

Enter VERMANDERO, ALSEMERO, JASPERINO, *and* BEATRICE.

VER. Valencia speaks so nobly of you, sir,
I wish I had a daughter now for you.

ALS. The fellow of this creature were a partner
For a king's love.

VER. I had her fellow once, sir;
But Heaven has married her to joys eternal;
'T were sin to wish her in this vale again.
Come, sir, your friend and you shall see the pleasures
Which my health chiefly joys in.

ALS. I hear
The beauty of this seat largely [commended].[42]

VER. It falls much short of that.

Exeunt [*all but*] BEATRICE.

BEAT. So, here's one step
Into my father's favor; time will fix him.
I've got him now the liberty of the house.
So wisdom, by degrees, works out her freedom;
And if that eye be dark'ned that offends me, —
I wait but that eclipse, — this gentleman
Shall soon shine glorious in my father's liking,
Through the refulgent virtue of my love.

Enter DE FLORES.

DE F. [*aside*] My thoughts are at a banquet; for [43] the deed,
I feel no weight in 't; 't is but light and cheap
For the sweet recompense that I set down for 't.

BEAT. De Flores.

DE F. Lady.

BEAT. Thy looks promise cheerfully.

DE F. All things are answerable: time, circumstance,
Your wishes, and my service.

BEAT. Is it done, then?

DE F. Piracquo is no more.

BEAT. My joys start at mine eyes; our sweet'st delights
Are evermore born weeping.

DE F. I've a token for you.

BEAT. For me?

DE F. But it was sent somewhat unwillingly;

[37] To acquire, to make booty of.
[38] End.
[39] The stage.
[40] Dance.

[41] A room in the castle.
[42] So Dyce and other mod. eds. Om. Q.
[43] As for.

I could not get the ring without the finger.
[*Producing the finger and ring.*]

BEAT. Bless me, what hast thou done?

DE F. Why, is that more
Than killing the whole man? I cut his heart-strings;
A greedy hand thrust in a dish at court,
In a mistake, hath had as much as this.

BEAT. 'T is the first token my father made me send him.

DE F. And I made him send it back again
For his last token. I was loth to leave it,
And I 'm sure dead men have no use of jewels;
He was as loth to part with 't, for it stuck
As if the flesh and it were both one substance.

BEAT. At the stag's fall, the keeper has his fees;
'T is[44] soon appli'd: all dead men's fees are yours, sir.
I pray, bury the finger; but the stone
You may make use on shortly; the true value,
Take 't of my truth, is near three hundred ducats.

DE F. 'T will hardly buy a capcase[45] for one's conscience though,
To keep it from the worm, as fine as 't is.
Well, being my fees, I'll take it;
Great men have taught me that, or else my merit
Would scorn the way on 't.

BEAT. It might justly, sir.
Why, thou mistak'st, De Flores; 't is not given
In state of[46] recompense.

DE F. No, I hope so, lady;
You should soon witness my contempt to 't then.

BEAT. Prithee — thou look'st as if thou wert offended.

DE F. That were strange, lady; 't is not possible
My service should draw such a cause from you.
Offended! Could you think so? That were much
For one of my performance, and so warm
Yet in my service.

BEAT. 'T were misery in me to give you cause, sir.

DE F. I know so much: it were so; misery
In her most sharp condition.

BEAT. 'T is resolv'd[47] then;
Look you, sir, here 's three thousand golden florins;[48]
I have not meanly thought upon thy merit.

DE F. What! salary? Now you move me.

BEAT. How, De Flores?

DE F. Do you place me in the rank of verminous fellows,
To destroy things for wages? Offer gold
For the lifeblood of man? Is anything
Valued too precious for my recompense?

BEAT. I understand thee not.

DE F. I could ha' hir'd
A journeyman in murder at this rate,
And mine own conscience might have [slept at ease],[49]
And have had the work brought home.

BEAT. [*aside*] I 'm in a labyrinth;
What will content him? I'd fain be rid of him. —
I'll double the sum, sir.

DE F. You take a course
To double my vexation, that 's the good you do.

BEAT. [*aside*] Bless me, I am now in worse plight than I was;
I know not what will please him. — For my fear's sake,
I prithee, make away with all speed possible;
And if thou be'st so modest not to name
The sum that will content thee, paper blushes not:
Send thy demand in writing, it shall follow thee;
But, prithee, take thy flight.

DE F. You must fly too, then.

BEAT. I?

DE F. I'll not stir a foot else.

BEAT. What 's your meaning?

DE F. Why, are not you as guilty? In, I'm sure,
As deep as I; and we should stick together.
Come, your fears counsel you but ill; my absence
Would draw suspect upon you instantly;
There were no rescue for you.

BEAT. [*aside*] He speaks home!

DE F. Nor is it fit we two, engag'd so jointly,
Should part and live asunder.

[44] *I.e.*, my remark about the keeper's fees is. Apparently De Flores makes a gesture of inquiry or dissent.

[45] Bandbox.

[46] By way of.

[47] Settled.

[48] The English name for various continental coins. In view of the weight of such a sum in gold Dyce suggests that Beatrice may hand De Flores a paper.

[49] Add. ed. 1816.

BEAT. How now, sir!
This shows not well.
DE F. What makes your lip so strange?[50]
This must not be betwixt us.
BEAT. Thy man talks wildly!
DE F. Come, kiss me with a zeal now.
BEAT. [*aside*] Heaven, I doubt[51] him!
DE F. I will not stand so long to beg 'em shortly.
BEAT. Take heed, De Flores, of forgetfulness;
'T will soon betray us.
DE F. Take you heed first;
Faith, y' are grown much forgetful; y' are to blame in 't.
BEAT. [*aside*] He 's bold, and I am blam'd for 't.
DE F. I have eas'd you
Of your trouble; think on 't: I'm in pain,
And must be eas'd of[52] you; 't is a charity:
Justice invites your blood to understand me.
BEAT. I dare not.
DE F. Quickly!
BEAT. Oh, I never shall!
Speak it yet further off, that I may lose
What has been spoken, and no sound remain on 't;
I would not hear so much offence again
For such another deed.
DE F. Soft, lady, soft!
The last is not yet paid for. Oh, this act
Has put me into spirit; I was as greedy on 't
As the parch'd earth of moisture, when the clouds weep.
Did you not mark I wrought myself into 't,
Nay, sued and kneel'd for 't? Why was all that pains took?
You see I have thrown contempt upon your gold;
Not that I want it [not],[53] for I do piteously;
In order I 'll come unto 't, and make use on 't;
But 't was not held so precious to begin with,
For I place wealth after the heels of pleasure;
And were not I resolv'd in my belief
That thy virginity were perfect in thee,
I should but take my recompense with grudging,[54]
As if I had but half my hopes I agreed for.
BEAT. Why, 't is impossible thou canst be so wicked,
Or shelter such a cunning cruelty,
To make his death the murderer of my honor!
Thy language is so bold and vicious,
I cannot see which way I can forgive it
With any modesty.
DE F. Push! you forget yourself;
A woman dipp'd in blood, and talk of modesty!
BEAT. O misery of sin! would I had been bound
Perpetually unto my living hate
In that Piracquo, than to hear these words!
Think but upon the distance that creation
Set 'twixt thy blood and mine, and keep thee there.
DE F. Look but into your conscience; read me there:—
'T is a true book; you 'll find me there your equal.
Push! fly not to your birth, but settle you
In what the act has made you; y' are no more now.
You must forget your parentage;[55] to me
Y' are the deed 's creature; by that name
You lost your first condition, and I challenge you,
As peace and innocency has turn'd you out,
And made you one with me.
BEAT. With thee, foul villain!
DE F. Yes, my fair murd'ress. Do you urge me,
Though thou writ'st maid, thou whore in thy affection?
'T was chang'd from thy first love, and that 's a kind
Of whoredom in thy heart; and he 's chang'd now
To bring thy second on, thy Alsemero,
Whom, by all sweets that ever darkness tasted,
If I enjoy thee not, thou ne'er enjoy'st!
I 'll blast the hopes and joys of marriage;[56]
I 'll confess all; my life I rate at nothing.
BEAT. De Flores!
DE F. I shall rest from all lovers' plagues then;
I live in pain now: that shooting eye
Will burn my heart to cinders.
BEAT. Oh, sir, hear me!
DE F. She that in life and love refuses me,
In death and shame my partner she shall be.
BEAT. [*kneeling*] Stay, hear me once for all; I make thee master
Of all the wealth I have in gold and jewels;
Let me go poor unto my bed with honor,
And I am rich in all things!

[50] Why do you hold off? [51] Fear. [52] By.
[53] Add. mod. eds.; om. Q. [54] Complaining.
[55] Professor Kittredge places the stop here instead of after "me." [56] Trisyllabic.

De F. Let this silence thee:
The wealth of all Valencia shall not buy
My pleasure from me;
Can you weep Fate from its determin'd purpose?
So soon may [you] weep me.

Beat. Vengeance begins;
Murder, I see, is followed by more sins.
Was my creation in the womb so curs'd,
It must engender with a viper first?

De F. Come, rise and shroud your blushes in my bosom;
Silence is one of pleasure's best receipts;[57]
Thy peace is wrought for ever in this yielding.
'Las! how the turtle[58] pants! Thou 'lt love anon
What thou so fear'st and faint'st to venture on.
Exeunt.

ACT IV

[Dumb Show]

Enter Gentlemen, Vermandero *meeting them with action of wonderment at the flight of Piracquo. Enter* Alsemero *with* Jasperino *and* Gallants: Vermandero *points to him, the* Gentlemen *seeming to applaud the choice.* Alsemero, Jasperino, *and* Gentlemen; Beatrice *the bride following in great state, accompanied with* Diaphanta, Isabella, *and other* Gentlewomen; De Flores *after all, smiling at the accident:* Alonzo's Ghost *appears to* De Flores *in the midst of his smile, startles him, showing him the hand whose finger he had cut off. They pass over in great solemnity.*[1]

[Scene I][2]

Enter Beatrice.

Beat. This fellow has undone me endlessly;
Never was bride so fearfully distress'd.
The more I think upon th' ensuing night,
And whom I am to cope with in embraces:
One both ennobled[3] in blood and mind,
So clear in understanding — that 's my plague now, —
Before whose judgment will my fault appear
Like malefactors' crimes before tribunals.
There is no hiding on 't, the more I dive
Into my own distress. How a wise man
Stands for[4] a great calamity! There 's no venturing
Into his bed, what course soe'er I light upon,
Without my shame, which may grow up to danger.
He cannot but in justice strangle me
As I lie by him — as a cheater use me;
'T is a precious craft to play with a false die
Before a cunning gamester. Here 's his closet;
The key left in 't, and he abroad i' th' park!
Sure 't was forgot; I 'll be so bold as look in 't.
[*Opens closet.*]
Bless me! a right[5] physician's closet 't is,
Set round with vials; every one her mark too.
Sure he does practise physic for his own use,
Which may be safely call'd your great man's wisdom.[6]
What manuscript lies here? "The Book of Experiment,
Call'd Secrets in Nature." So 't is; 't is so.
[*Reads.*] "How to know whether a woman be with child or no."
I hope I am not yet, — if he should try though!
Let me see [*reads*] "folio forty-five," here 't is,
The leaf tuck'd dow[n] upon 't, the place suspicious.
[*Reads.*] "If you would know whether a woman be with child or not, give her two spoonfuls of the white water in glass C ——"
Where 's that glass C? Oh, yonder, I see 't now —
[*Reads.*] "and if she be with child, she sleeps full twelve hours after; if not, not:"
None of that water comes into my belly;
I 'll know you from a hundred; I could break you now,
Or turn you into milk, and so beguile
The master of the mystery; but I 'll look to you.
Ha! that which is next is ten times worse:
[*Reads.*] "How to know whether a woman be a maid or not;"
If that should be appli'd, what would become of me?
Belike he has a strong faith of my purity,
That never yet made proof;[7] but this he calls
[*Reads.*] "A merry sleight,[8] but true experi-

[57] One of the best recipes for sexual gratification.
[58] Dove.
[1] With pomp and circumstance.
[2] Alsemero's apartment in the castle.
[3] Q *both ennobled both.* "Ennobled" is quadrisyllabic.
[4] Stands open to.
[5] True, actual.
[6] Since it safeguards him against poison.
[7] Trial, test.
[8] Artifice.

ment; the author Antonius Mizaldus.[9] Give the party you suspect the quantity of a spoonful of the water in the glass M, which, upon her that is a maid, makes three several effects: 't will make her incontinently[10] gape, then fall into a sudden sneezing, last into a violent laughing; else, dull, heavy, and lumpish."
Where had I been?
I fear it; yet 't is seven hours to bedtime.

Enter DIAPHANTA.

DIA. Cuds,[11] madam, are you here?
BEAT. [*aside*] Seeing that wench now,
A trick comes in my mind; 't is a nice piece[12]
Gold cannot purchase. — I come hither, wench,
To look my lord.
DIA. Would I had such a cause
To look him too! Why, he's i' th' park, madam.
BEAT. There let him be.
DIA. Ay, madam, let him compass
Whole parks and forests, as great rangers do,
At roosting time a little lodge can hold 'em.
Earth-conquering Alexander, that thought the world
Too narrow for him, in th' end had but his pit-hole.
BEAT. I fear thou art not modest, Diaphanta.
DIA. Your thoughts are so unwilling to be known, madam.
'T is ever the bride's fashion, towards bed-time,
To set light by her joys, as if she ow'd[13] 'em not.
BEAT. Her joys? Her fears thou wouldst say.
DIA. Fear of what?
BEAT. Art thou a maid, and talk'st so to a maid?
You leave a blushing business behind;
Beshrew your heart for 't!
DIA. Do you mean good sooth, madam?
BEAT. Well, if I'd thought upon the fear at first,
Man should have been unknown.
DIA. Is 't possible?

[9] A sixteenth-century French astrologer. According to Sampson, the *De Arcanis Naturae* contains no such experiments; but similar ones are found elsewhere in his works.
[10] Immediately.
[11] Probably a corruption of "God save me." Cf. *codes*.
[12] Scrupulous wench.
[13] Possessed.

BEAT. I will give a thousand ducats to that woman
Would try what my fear were, and tell me true
To-morrow, when she gets from 't; as she likes,
I might perhaps be drawn to 't.
DIA. Are you in earnest?
BEAT. Do you get the woman, then challenge me,
And see if I'll fly from 't; but I must tell you
This by the way, she must be a true maid.
Else there's no trial; my fears are not her's else.
DIA. Nay, she that I would put into your hands, madam,
Shall be a maid.
BEAT. You know I should be sham'd else,
Because she lies for me.
DIA. 'T is a strange humor![14]
But are you serious still? Would you resign
Your first night's pleasure, and give money too?
BEAT. As willingly as live. — [*aside*] Alas, the gold
Is but a by[15]-bet to wedge in the honor!
DIA. I do not know how the world goes abroad
For faith or honesty; there's both requir'd in this.
Madam, what say you to me, and stray no further?
I've a good mind, in troth, to earn your money.
BEAT. Y' are too quick,[16] I fear, to be a maid.
DIA. How? not a maid? Nay, then you urge me, madam:
Your honorable self is not a truer,
With all your fears upon you ——
BEAT. [*aside*] Bad enough then.
DIA. Than I with all my lightsome joys about me.
BEAT. I'm glad to hear 't. Then you dare put your honesty[17]
Upon an easy trial.
DIA. Easy? — Anything.
BEAT. I'll come to you straight. [*Goes to the closet.*]
DIA. She will not search me, will she,
Like the forewoman of a female jury?
BEAT. Glass M: ay, this is it. [*Brings vial.*] Look, Diaphanta,
You take no worse than I do. [*Drinks.*]

[14] Whim, notion.
[15] Side. (*N.E.D.*)
[16] Lively, impulsive.
[17] Chastity.

DIA. And in so doing,
I will not question what 't is, but take it. [*Drinks.*]
BEAT. [*aside*] Now if th' experiment be true, 't will praise itself,
And give me noble ease: begins already; [DIAPHANTA *gapes.*]
There 's the first symptom; and what haste it makes
To fall into the second, there by this time! [DIAPHANTA *sneezes.*]
Most admirable secret! on the contrary,
It stirs not me a whit, which most concerns it.
DIA. Ha, ha, ha!
BEAT. [*aside*] Just in all things, and in order
As if 't were circumscrib'd; one accident [18]
Gives way unto another.
DIA. Ha, ha, ha!
BEAT. How now, wench?
DIA. Ha, ha, ha! I am so, so light
At heart — ha, ha, ha! — so pleasurable!
But one swig more, sweet madam.
BEAT. Ay, to-morrow,
We shall have time to sit by 't.
DIA. Now I 'm sad again.
BEAT. [*aside*] It lays itself so gently too! — Come, wench.
Most honest [19] Diaphanta I dare call thee now.
DIA. Pray, tell me, madam, what trick call you this?
BEAT. I 'll tell thee all hereafter; we must study
The carriage of this business.
DIA. I shall carry 't well,
Because I love the burthen.
BEAT. About midnight
You must not fail to steal forth gently,
That I may use the place.
DIA. Oh, fear not, madam;
I shall be cool by that time. The bride's place,
And with a thousand ducats! I'm for a justice now:
I bring a portion with me; I scorn small fools.[20] *Exeunt.*

[SCENE II] [21]

Enter VERMANDERO *and* Servant.

VER. I tell thee, knave, mine honor is in question,
A thing till now free from suspicion,
Nor ever was there cause. Who of my gentlemen
Are absent? Tell me, and truly, how many, and who?
SER. Antonio, sir, and Franciscus.
VER. When did they leave the castle?
SER. Some ten days since, sir; the one intending to
Briamata,[22] th' other for Valencia.
VER. The time accuses 'em; a charge of murder
Is brought within my castle-gate, Piracquo's murder;
I dare not answer faithfully their absence.
A strict command of apprehension
Shall pursue 'em suddenly, and either wipe
The stain off clear, or openly discover it.
Provide me winged warrants for the purpose. *Exit* Servant.
See, I am set on again.

Enter TOMAZO.

TOM. I claim a brother of you.
VER. Y' are too hot;
Seek him not here.
TOM. Yes, 'mongst your dearest bloods,
If my peace find no fairer satisfaction.
This is the place must yield account for him,
For here I left him; and the hasty tie
Of this snatch'd marriage gives strong testimony
Of his most certain ruin.
VER. Certain falsehood!
This is the place indeed; his breach of faith
Has too much marr'd both my abused love,
The honorable love I reserv'd for him,
And mock'd my daughter's joy; the prepar'd morning
Blush'd at his infidelity; he left
Contempt and scorn to throw upon those friends
Whose belief hurt 'em. Oh, 't was most ignoble
To take his flight so unexpectedly,
And throw such public wrongs on those that lov'd him!
TOM. Then this is all your answer.
VER. 'T is too fair
For one of his alliance; [23] and I warn you
That this place no more see you. *Exit.*

[18] Symptom. [19] Chaste.
[20] *I.e.*, I'm for a big fool, a justice.
[21] Another room in the castle.
[22] The source mentions this "fair house" of Vermandero's, ten leagues from Alicante.
[23] Related to him.

Enter De Flores.

Tom. The best is,
There is more ground to meet a man's revenge on. —
Honest De Flores.

De F. That's my name indeed.
Saw you the bride? Good sweet sir, which way took she?

Tom. I have bless'd mine eyes from seeing such a false one.

De F. [*aside*] I'd fain get off; this man's not for my company:
I smell his brother's blood when I come near him.

Tom. Come hither, kind and true one; I remember
My brother lov'd thee well.

De F. Oh, purely,[24] dear sir! —
[*aside*] Methinks I am now again a-killing on him,
He brings it so fresh to me.

Tom. Thou canst guess, sirrah —
[An] [25] honest friend has an instinct of jealousy —
At some foul guilty person.

De F. 'Las! sir,
I am so charitable, I think none
Worse than myself! — You did not see the bride then?

Tom. I prithee, name her not: is she not wicked?

De F. No, no; a pretty, easy, round-pack'd [26] sinner,
As your most ladies are, else you might think
I flatter'd her; but, sir, at no hand wicked,
Till th' are so old their [chins and noses] [27] meet,
And they salute witches. I am call'd, I think, sir. —
[*aside*] His company ev'n o'erlays my conscience. *Exit.*

Tom. That De Flores has a wondrous honest heart!
He'll bring it out in time, I'm assur'd on 't.
Oh, here's the glorious [28] master of the day's joy!
I [29] will not be long till he and I do reckon. —

Enter Alsemero.

Sir.

Als. You are most welcome.

Tom. You may call that word back;
I do not think I am, nor wish to be.

Als. 'T is strange you found the way to this house, then.

Tom. Would I'd ne'er known the cause! I'm none of those, sir,
That come to give you joy, and swill your wine;
'T is a more precious liquor that must lay
The fiery thirst I bring.

Als. Your words and you
Appear to me great strangers.

Tom. Time and our swords
May make us more acquainted. This the business:
I should have had a brother in your place;
How treachery and malice have dispos'd of him
I'm bound to inquire of him which holds his right,
Which never could come fairly.

Als. You must look
To answer for that word, sir.

Tom. Fear you not,
I'll have it ready drawn at our next meeting.
Keep your day solemn: [30] farewell; I disturb it not;
I'll bear the smart with patience for a time. *Exit.*

Als. 'T is somewhat ominous this; a quarrel ent'red
Upon this day; my innocence relieves me —

Enter Jasperino.

I should be wondrous sad else. — Jasperino,
I have news to tell thee, strange news.

Jasp. I ha' some too,
I think as strange as yours. Would I might keep
Mine, so my faith and friendship might be kept in 't!
Faith, sir, dispense a little with my zeal,
And let it cool in this.

Als. This puts me on,[31]
And blames thee for thy slowness.

Jas. All may prove nothing,
Only a friendly fear that leap'd from me, sir.

Als. No question, it may prove nothing; let's partake it though.

Jas. 'T was Diaphanta's chance — for to that wench
I pretend [32] honest love, and she deserves it —

[24] Utterly. [25] Emend. Dyce; Q *One*.
[26] Presumably = "plump."
[27] Conj. Dyce; Q *sins and vices*. [28] Vainglorious.
[29] Dyce emends '*T*.

[30] Go on celebrating your wedding day.
[31] Incites me, arouses me. [32] Offer.

To leave me in a back part of the house,
A place we chose for private conference.
She was no sooner gone, but instantly
I heard your bride's voice in the next room to me ;
And lending more attention, found De Flores
Louder than she.

ALS. De Flores! Thou art out now.

JAS. You'll tell me more anon.

ALS. Still I'll prevent [33] thee :
The very sight of him is poison to her.

JAS. That made me stagger too ; but Diaphanta
At her return confirm'd it.

ALS. Diaphanta!

JAS. Then fell we both to listen, and words pass'd
Like those that challenge interest in a woman.

ALS. Peace! quench thy zeal ; 't is dangerous to thy bosom.

JAS. Then truth is full of peril.

ALS. Such truths are.
Oh, were she the sole glory of the earth,
Had eyes that could shoot fire into kings' breasts,
And touch'd,[34] she sleeps not here! Yet I have time,
Though night be near, to be resolv'd [35] hereof ;
And, prithee, do not weigh me by my passions.[36]

JAS. I never weigh'd friend so.

ALS. Done charitably!
That key will lead thee to a pretty secret,
[*Gives key.*]
By a Chaldean taught me, and I've
My study upon some. Bring from my closet
A glass inscrib'd there with the letter M,
And question not my purpose.

JAS. It shall be done, sir. *Exit.*

ALS. How can this hang together? Not an hour since
Her woman came, pleading her lady's fears,
Deliver'd [37] her for the most timorous virgin
That ever shrunk at man's name, and so modest
She charg'd her weep out her request to me
That she might come obscurely to my bosom.

Enter BEATRICE.

BEAT. [*aside*] All things go well ; my woman's preparing yonder
For her sweet voyage, which grieves me to lose ;
Necessity compels it ; I lose all, else.

ALS. [*aside*] Push! modesty's shrine is set in yonder forehead ;
I cannot be too sure, though. — My Joanna!

BEAT. Sir, I was bold to weep a message to you ;
Pardon my modest fears.

ALS. [*aside*] The dove's not meeker ;
She's abus'd, questionless.

Re-enter JASPERINO [*with vial*].

Oh, are you come, sir?

BEAT. [*aside*] The glass, upon my life! I see the letter.

JAS. Sir, this is M. [*Giving vial.*]

ALS. 'T [i]s it.

BEAT. [*aside*] I am suspected.

ALS. How fitly our bride comes to partake with us!

BEAT. What is't, my Lord?

ALS. No hurt.

BEAT. Sir, pardon me,
I seldom taste of any composition.[38]

ALS. But this, upon my warrant, you shall venture on.

BEAT. I fear't will make me ill.

ALS. Heaven forbid that.

BEAT. [*aside*] I'm put now to my cunning ; th' effects I know,
If I can now but feign 'em handsomely.
[*Drinks.*]

ALS. [*aside to* JASPERINO] It has that secret virtue, it ne'er miss'd, sir,
Upon a virgin.

JAS. Treble-qualitied? [39]
[BEATRICE *gapes and sneezes.*]

ALS. By all that's virtuous, it takes there! proceeds!

JAS. This is the strangest trick to know a maid by.

BEAT. Ha, ha, ha!
You have given me joy of heart to drink, my Lord.

ALS. No, thou hast given me such joy of heart
That never can be blasted.

BEAT. What's the matter, sir?

ALS. [*aside*] See, now 't is settled in a melancholy ;
Keep[s] both the time and method. — My Joanna,

[33] Anticipate.
[34] Tainted.
[35] Satisfied, clear.
[36] Show of emotions.
[37] Reported, described.
[38] *I.e.*, mixed drink.
[39] Cf. IV, i, 51.

Chaste as the breath of Heaven, or morning's womb,
That brings the day forth! thus my love encloses thee. *Exeunt.*

[SCENE III] [40]

Enter ISABELLA *and* LOLLIO.

ISA. O Heaven! is this the [waning] [41] moon? Does love turn fool, run mad, and all at once? Sirrah, here's a madman, akin to the fool too, a lunatic lover.

LOL. No, no, not he I brought the letter from?

ISA. Compare his inside with his out, and tell me.

LOL. The out's mad, I'm sure of that; I had a taste on't. [*Reads letter.*] "To the bright Andromeda, chief chambermaid to the Knight of the Sun,[42] at the sign of Scorpio, in the middle region, sent by the bellows-mender of Aeolus. Pay the post." This is stark madness!

ISA. Now mark the inside. [*Takes the letter and reads.*] "Sweet lady, having now cast off this counterfeit cover of a madman, I appear to your best judgment a true and faithful lover of your beauty."

LOL. He is mad still.

ISA. [*reads.*] "If any fault you find, chide those perfections in you which have made me imperfect; 't is the same sun that causeth to grow and enforceth to wither, ——"

LOL. O rogue!

ISA. [*reads.*] "Shapes and transhapes, destroys and builds again. I come in winter to you, dismantled of my proper ornaments; by the sweet splendor of your cheerful smiles, I spring and live a lover."

LOL. Mad rascal still!

ISA. [*reads.*] "Tread him not under foot that shall appear an honor to your bounties. I remain — mad till I speak with you, from whom I expect my cure, yours all, or one beside himself, FRANCISCUS."

LOL. You are like to have a fine time on't. My master and I may give over our professions; I do not think but you can cure fools and madmen faster than we, with little pains too.

ISA. Very likely.

LOL. One thing I must tell you, mistress: you perceive that I am privy to your skill; if I find you minister once, and set up the trade, I put in for my thirds;[43] I shall be mad or fool else.

ISA. The first place is thine, believe it, Lollio,
If I do fall.

LOL. I fall upon you.

ISA. So.

LOL. Well, I stand to my venture.

ISA. But thy counsel now;
How shall I deal with 'em?

LOL. [Why,] [44] do you mean to deal with 'em?

ISA. Nay, the fair understanding [45] — how to use 'em.

LOL. Abuse [46] 'em! That's the way to mad the fool, and make a fool of the madman, and then you use 'em kindly.[47]

ISA. 'T is easy, I'll practise;[48] do thou observe it.
The key of thy wardrobe.

LOL. There [*giving key*]; fit yourself for 'em, and I'll fit 'em both for you.

ISA. Take thou no further notice than the outside. *Exit.*

LOL. Not an inch; I'll put you to the inside.

Enter ALIBIUS.

ALIB. Lollio, art there? Will all be perfect, think'st thou?
To-morrow night, as if to close up the
Solemnity, Vermandero expects us.

LOL. I mistrust the madmen most; the fools will do well enough; I have taken pains with them.

ALIB. Tush! they cannot miss; the more absurdity,
The more commends it, so no rough behaviors
Affright the ladies; they're nice [49] things, thou know'st.

LOL. You need not fear, sir; so long as we are there with our commanding pizzles,[50] they'll be as tame as the ladies themselves.

ALIB. I will see them once more rehearse before they go.

LOL. I was about it, sir; look you to the madmen's morris,[51] and let me alone with

[40] A room in Alibius's house.
[41] Conj. ed. 1816; Q *waiting*.
[42] Another allusion to the hero of *The Mirror of Knighthood.*
[43] The other sharers to be her husband and her lover.
[44] Q *We.*
[45] *I.e.*, don't take my words in an obscene sense.
[46] Deceive.
[47] According to their natures.
[48] Plot.
[49] Finical.
[50] *I.e.*, whips. Q *pees'es.*
[51] Morris dance.

the other. There is one or two that I mistrust their fooling;[52] I'll instruct them, and then they shall rehearse the whole measure.[53]

ALIB. Do so; I'll see the music prepar'd; but, Lollio,
By the way, how does my wife brook her restraint?
Does she not grudge[54] at it?

LOL. So, so; she takes some pleasure in the house; she would abroad else. You must allow her a little more length; she's kept too short.

ALIB. She shall along to Vermandero's with us;
That will serve her for a month's liberty.

LOL. What's that on your face, sir?

ALIB. Where, Lollio? I see nothing.

LOL. Cry you mercy,[55] sir, 't is your nose; it show'd like the trunk of a young elephant.[56]

ALIB. Away, rascal! I'll prepare the music, Lollio. *Exit* ALIBIUS.

LOL. Do, sir, and I'll dance the whilst. — Tony, where art thou, Tony?

Enter ANTONIO.

ANT. Here, cousin; where art thou?

LOL. Come, Tony, the footmanship I taught you.

ANT. I had rather ride, cousin.

LOL. Ay, a whip take you! but I'll keep you out; vault in: look you, Tony: fa, la, la, la, la. [*Dances.*]

ANT. Fa, la, la, la, la. [*Dances.*]

LOL. There, an honor.[57]

ANT. Is this an honor, coz?

LOL. Yes, an it please your Worship.

ANT. Does honor bend in the hams, coz?

LOL. Marry does it, as low as worship, squireship, nay, yeomanry itself sometimes, from whence it first stiffened: there, rise, a caper.[58]

ANT. Caper after an honor, coz?

LOL. Very proper, for honor is but a caper, rise[s] as fast and high, has a knee or two, and falls to th' ground again. You can remember your figure,[59] Tony? *Exit.*

ANT. Yes, cousin; when I see thy figure, I can remember mine.

[52] Bullen conj. *footing;* cf. l. 97.
[53] Dance.
[54] Complain.
[55] Beg pardon.
[56] It looks as though someone had been pulling your nose. Professor Kittredge adds, "Perhaps with an allusion to being led by the nose."
[57] Bow.
[58] A leap or frisky hop in dancing.
[59] In the dance.

Re-enter ISABELLA, [*dressed as a madwoman.*]

ISA. Hey, how [he][60] treads the air! Shough, shough, tother way! he burns his wings else. Here's wax enough below, Icarus, more than will be cancelled[61] these eighteen moons. He's down, he's down! what a terrible fall he had!
Stand up, thou son of Cretan Daedalus,
And let us tread the lower labyrinth;
I'll bring thee to the clue.

ANT. Prithee, coz, let me alone.

ISA. Art thou not drown'd?
About thy head I saw a heap of clouds
Wrapp'd like a Turkish turban; on thy back
A crook'd chameleon-color'd rainbow hung
Like a tiara down unto thy hams.
Let me suck out those billows in thy belly;
Hark, how they roar and rumble in the [straits]![62]
Bless thee from the pirates!

ANT. Pox upon you, let me alone!

ISA. Why shouldst thou mount so high as Mercury,
Unless thou hadst reversion of[63] his place?
Stay in the moon with me, Endymion,
And we will rule these wild rebellious waves,
That would have drown'd my love.

ANT. I'll kick thee if
Again thou touch me, thou wild unshapen antic;
I am no fool, you bedlam!

ISA. But you are, as sure as I am, mad.
Have I put on this habit of a frantic,
With love as full of fury, to beguile
The nimble eye of watchful jealousy,
And am I thus rewarded?

ANT. Ha! dearest beauty!

ISA. No, I have no beauty now,
Nor never had but what was in my garments.
You a quick-sighted lover! Come not near me:
Keep your caparisons, y' are aptly clad;
I came a feigner, to return stark mad. *Exit.*

ANT. Stay, or I shall change condition,
And become as you are.

Re-enter LOLLIO.

LOL. W[h]y, Tony, whither now? Why, fool!

[60] Emend. Dyce; Q *she.*
[61] In the form of sealing-wax.
[62] Emend. Dyce; Q *streets.*
[63] Promise of succeeding to.

ANT. Whose fool, usher of idiots? You coxcomb!
I have fool'd too much.

LOL. You were best be mad another while then.

ANT. So I am, stark mad; I have cause enough;
And I could throw the full effects on thee,
And beat thee like a fury.

LOL. Do not, do not; I shall not forbear the gentleman under the fool, if you do. Alas! I saw through your fox-skin [64] before now! Come, I can give you comfort; my mistress loves you; and there is as arrant a madman i' th' house as you are a fool, your rival, whom she loves not. If after the masque we can rid her of him, you earn her love, she says, and the fool shall ride her.

ANT. May I believe thee?

LOL. Yes, or you may choose whether you will or no.

ANT. She's eas'd of him; I have a good quarrel on 't.

LOL. Well, keep your old station yet, and be quiet.

ANT. Tell her I will deserve her love.

[*Exit.*]

LOL. And you are like to have your desire.[65]

Enter FRANCISCUS.

FRAN. [*sings.*] "Down, down, down, a-down a-down," — and then with a horse-trick [66]
To kick Latona's [67] forehead, and break her bowstring.

LOL. [*aside*] This is tother counterfeit; I'll put him out of his humor — [*Takes out a letter and reads.*] "Sweet lady, having now cast [68] this counterfeit cover of a madman, I appear to your best judgment a true and faithful lover of your beauty." This is pretty well for a madman.

FRAN. Ha! what's that?

LOL. [*reads.*] "Chide those perfections in you which have made me imperfect."

FRAN. [*aside*] I am discover'd to the fool.

LOL. [*aside*] I hope to discover the fool in you, ere I have done with you. — [*Reads.*] "Yours all, or one beside himself, FRANCISCUS." This madman will mend sure.

FRAN. What do you read, sirrah?

LOL. Your destiny, sir; you'll be hang'd for this trick, and another that I know.

[64] Disguise. [65] Dyce conj. *desert.*
[66] Cf. "horseplay." [67] Diana's. [68] Cast off.

FRAN. Art thou of counsel with thy mistress?

LOL. Next her apron-strings.

FRAN. Give me thy hand.

LOL. Stay, let me put yours in my pocket first. [*Putting letter into his pocket.*] Your hand is true,[69] is it not? It will not pick? I partly fear it, because I think it does lie.

FRAN. Not in a syllable.

LOL. So if you love my mistress so well as you have handled the matter here, you are like to be cur'd of your madness.

FRAN. And none but she can cure it.

LOL. Well, I'll give you over then, and she shall cast your water [70] next.

FRAN. Take for thy pains past.

[*Gives money.*]

LOL. I shall deserve more, sir, I hope. My mistress loves you, but must have some proof of your love to her.

FRAN. There I meet my wishes.

LOL. That will not serve; you must meet her enemy and yours.

FRAN. He's dead already.

LOL. Will you tell me that, and I parted but now with him?

FRAN. Show me the man.

LOL. Ay, that's a right course now; see him before you kill him, in any case; and yet it needs not go so far neither. 'T is but a fool that haunts the house and my mistress in the shape of an idiot; bang but his fool's coat well-favoredly, and 't is well.

FRAN. Soundly, soundly!

LOL. Only reserve him till the masque be past; and if you find him not now in the dance yourself, I'll show you. In, in! my master!

[*Dancing.*]

FRAN. He handles him like a feather. Hey!

Enter ALIBIUS.

ALIB. Well said;[71] in a readiness, Lollio?

LOL. Yes, sir.

ALIB. Away then, and guide them in, Lollio;
Entreat your mistress to see this sight.
Hark, is there not one incurable fool
That might be begg'd?[72] I have friends.

LOL. I have him for you,
One that shall deserve it too.

[69] Honest.
[70] *I.e.*, be your physician.
[71] Well done.
[72] Alluding to the practice of begging the king to grant the guardianship of a wealthy fool for the sake of enjoying the income from his property.

ALIB. Good boy, Lollio!
[*Exit* LOLLIO. *He returns at once with*] *the madmen and fools,* [*who*] *dance.*
'T is perfect; well, fit but once these strains,
We shall have coin and credit for our pains.
Exeunt.

ACT V — [SCENE I][1]

Enter BEATRICE: *a clock strikes one.*

BEAT. One struck, and yet she lies by 't! O my fears!
This strumpet serves her own ends, 't is apparent now,
Devours the pleasure with a greedy appetite
And never minds my honor or my peace,
Makes havoc of my right. But she pays dearly for 't;
No trusting of her life with such a secret,
That cannot rule her blood[2] to keep her promise;
Beside, I have some suspicion of her faith to me,
Because I was suspected of my lord,
And it must come from her. [*Strike two.*] Hark! by my horrors,
Another clock strikes two!

Enter DE FLORES.

DE F. Pist! where are you?
BEAT. De Flores?
DE F. Ay. Is she not come from him yet?
BEAT. As I am a living soul, not!
DE F. Sure the Devil
Hath sow'd his itch[3] within her. Who would trust
A waiting woman?
BEAT. I must trust somebody.
DE F. Push! they are t[e]rmagants;
Especially when they fall upon their masters
And have their ladies' first fruits; th' are mad whelps:
You cannot stave 'em off from game royal; then
You are so [rash][4] and hardy, ask no counsel;
And I could have help'd you to a pothecary's daughter
Would have fall'n off before eleven, and thank you too.
BEAT. O me, not yet! this whore forgets herself.
DE F. The rascal fares so well. Look, y' are undone;
The day-star, by this hand! see [Phosphorus][5] plain yonder.
BEAT. Advise me now to fall upon some ruin;
There is no counsel safe else.
DE F. Peace! I ha 't now,
For we must force a rising; there 's no remedy.
BEAT. How? take heed of that.
DE F. Tush! be you quiet, or else give over all.
BEAT. Prithee, I ha' done then.
DE F. This is my reach:[6] I'll set
Some part afire of Diaphanta's chamber.
BEAT. How? fire, sir? That may endanger the whole house.
DE F. You talk of danger when your fame 's on fire.
BEAT. That 's true; do what thou wilt now.
DE F. Push! I aim
At a most rich success[7] strikes all dead sure.
The chimney being afire, and some light parcels
Of the least danger in her chamber only,
If Diaphanta should be met by chance then
Far from her lodging, which is now suspicious,
It would be thought her fears and affrights then
Drove her to seek for succor; if not seen
Or met at all, as that 's the likeliest,
For her own shame she 'll hasten towards her lodging;
I will be ready with a piece[8] high-charg'd,
As 't were to cleanse the chimney; there 't is proper now,
But she shall be the mark.
BEAT. I'm forc'd to love thee now,
'Cause thou provid'st so carefully for my honor.
DE F. 'Slid, it concerns the safety of us both,
Our pleasure and continuance.
BEAT. One word now,
Prithee; how for the servants?
DE F. I'll dispatch them,
Some one way, some another in the hurry,
For buckets, hooks, ladders; fear not you,
The deed shall find its time; and I've thought since

[1] A gallery in the castle. [2] Sensual nature.
[3] Inclination to evil. [4] Conj. Dyce; Q *harsh*.
[5] Q *Bosphorus*. [6] Scheme.
[7] Understand "which." [8] Gun.

Upon a safe conveyance [9] for the body too!
How this fire purifies wit! Watch you your minute.

BEAT. Fear keeps my soul upon 't, I cannot stray from 't.

Enter ALONZO's Ghost.

DE F. Ha! what art thou that tak'st away the light
Betwixt that star and me? I dread thee not. —
'T was but a mist of conscience; all 's clear again. *Exit.*

BEAT. Who 's that, De Flores? Bless me, it slides by! [*Exit* Ghost.]
Some ill thing haunts the house; 't has left behind it
A shivering sweat upon me; I'm afraid now.
This night hath been so tedious! Oh, this strumpet!
Had she a thousand lives, he should not leave her
Till he had destroy'd the last. List! O my terrors! *Struck three a'clock.*
Three struck by St. Sebastian's!

Within. Fire, fire, fire!

BEAT. Already? How rare is that man 's speed!
How heartily he serves me! his face loathes one;
But look upon his care, who would not love him?
The east is not more beauteous than his service.

Within. Fire, fire, fire!

Re-enter DE FLORES [*and*] Servants: *pass over: ring a bell.*

DE F. Away, dispatch! hooks, buckets, ladders! that 's well said.
The fire bell rings; the chimney works, my charge;
The piece is ready. *Exit.*

BEAT. Here 's a man worth loving!

Enter DIAPHANTA.

O y' are a jewel!

DIA. Pardon frailty, madam;
In troth I was so well, I ev'n forgot myself.

BEAT. Y' have made trim work!

DIA. What?

BEAT. Hie quickly to your chamber;
Your reward follows you.

DIA. I never made
So sweet a bargain. *Exit.*

Enter ALSEMERO.

ALS. O my dear Joanna,
Alas! art thou risen too? I was coming,
My absolute treasure!

BEAT. When I miss'd you,
I could not choose but follow.

ALS. Th 'art all sweetness;
The fire is not so dangerous.

BEAT. Think you so, sir?

ALS. I prithee, tremble not; believe me, 't is not.

Enter VERMANDERO [*and*] JASPERINO.

VER. Oh, bless my house and me!

ALS. My Lord your father.

Re-enter DE FLORES *with a piece.*

VER. Knave, whither goes that piece?

DE F. To scour the chimney. *Exit.*

VER. Oh, well said, well said!
That fellow 's good on all occasions.

BEAT. A wondrous necessary man, my Lord.

VER. He hath a ready wit; he 's worth 'em all, sir;
Dog [10] at a house of [11] fire; I ha' seen him sing'd ere now. — *The piece goes off.*
Ha, there he goes!

BEAT. 'T is done!

ALS. Come, sweet, to bed now;
Alas! thou wilt get cold.

BEAT. Alas! the fear keeps that out!
My heart will find no quiet till I hear
How Diaphanta, my poor woman, fares;
It is her chamber, sir, her lodging chamber.

VER. How should the fire come there?

BEAT. As good a soul as ever lady countenanc'd,
But in her chamber negligent and heavy [12];
She scap'd a mine twice.

VER. Twice?

BEAT. Strangely twice, sir.

VER. Those sleepy sluts are dangerous in a house,
An they be ne'er so good.

Re-enter DE FLORES.

DE F. O poor virginity,
Thou hast paid dearly for 't!

VER. Bless us! What 's that?

[9] Artifice.

[10] Adept. [11] On. [12] Sleepy.

DE F. A thing you all knew once, Diaphanta's burnt.
BEAT. My woman! O my woman!
DE F. Now the flames
Are greedy of her; burnt, burnt, burnt to death, sir!
BEAT. O my presaging soul!
ALS. Not a tear more!
I charge you by the last embrace I gave you
In bed, before this rais'd us.
BEAT. Now you tie me;
Were it my sister, now she gets no more.

Enter Servant.

VER. How now?
SER. All danger's past; you may now take
Your rests, my Lords; the fire is throughly quench'd.
Ah, poor gentlewoman, how soon was she stifled!
BEAT. De Flores, what is left of her inter,
And we as mourners all will follow her.
I will entreat that honor to my servant
Ev'n of my Lord himself.
ALS. Command it, sweetness.
BEAT. Which of you spied the fire first?
DE F. 'T was I, madam.
BEAT. And took such pains in't too? A double goodness!
'T were well he were rewarded.
VER. He shall be. —
De Flores, call upon me.
ALS. And upon me, sir.
Exeunt [*all but* DE FLORES].
DE F. Rewarded? Precious! here's a trick beyond me.
I see in all bouts, both of sport and wit,
Always a woman strives for the last hit.
Exit.

[SCENE II] [13]

Enter TOMAZO.

TOM. I cannot taste the benefits of life
With the same relish I was wont to do.
Man I grow weary of, and hold his fellowship
A treacherous bloody friendship; and because
I'm ignorant in whom my wrath should settle,
I must think all men villains, and the next
I meet, whoe'er he be, the murderer
Of my most worthy brother. Ha! what's he?
Enter DE FLORES [*and*] *passes over the stage.*
Oh, the fellow that some call honest De Flores;
But methinks honesty was hard bestead [14]
To come there for a lodging; as if a queen
Should make her palace of a pesthouse.
I find a contrariety in nature
Betwixt that face and me; the least occasion
Would give me game upon [15] him; yet he's so foul
One would scarce touch [16] with a sword he lov'd
And made account of; so most deadly venomous,
He would go near to poison any weapon
That should draw blood on him; one must resolve
Never to use that sword again in fight,
In way of honest manhood, that strikes him;
Some river must devour it; 't were not fit
That any man should find it. What, again?

Re-enter DE FLORES.

He walks a' purpose by, sure, to choke me up,
T' infect my blood.
DE F. My worthy noble Lord!
TOM. Dost offer to come near and breathe upon me? [*Strikes him.*]
DE F. A blow! [*Draws.*]
TOM. Yea, are you so prepar'd?
I'll rather like a soldier die by th' sword,
Than like a politician by thy poison. [*Draws.*]
DE F. Hold, my Lord, as you are honorable!
TOM. All slaves that kill by poison are still [17] cowards.
DE F. [*aside*] I cannot strike; I see his brother's wounds
Fresh bleeding in his eye, as in a crystal. —
I will not question this: I know y' are noble;
I take my injury with thanks given, sir,
Like a wise lawyer, and as a favor
Will wear it for the worthy hand that gave it. —
[*aside*] Why this from him that yesterday appear'd
So strangely loving to me?
Oh, but instinct [18] is of a subtler strain!
Guilt must not walk so near his lodge again;
He came near me now.[19] *Exit.*
TOM. All league with mankind I renounce for ever,
Till I find this murderer; not so much
As common courtesy but I'll lock up;

[13] Another room in the castle.

[14] Hard up, hard put to it.
[15] Would afford me an occasion to fight.
[16] Mod. eds. insert *him*.
[17] Always.
[18] Accented on second syllable.
[19] He nearly found me out.

For in the state of ignorance I live in,
A brother may salute his brother's murderer,
And wish good speed to th' villain in a greeting.

Enter VERMANDERO, ALIBIUS, *and* ISABELLA.

VER. Noble Piracquo!
TOM. Pray, keep on your way, sir;
I 've nothing to say to you.
VER. Comforts bless you, sir;
TOM. I 've forsworn compliment,[20] in troth I have, sir;
As you are merely man, I have not left
A good wish for you, nor[21] any here.
VER. Unless you be so far in love with grief
You will not part from 't upon any terms,
We bring that news will make a welcome for us.
TOM. What news can that be?
VER. Throw no scornful smile
Upon the zeal I bring you; 't is worth more, sir.
Two of the chiefest men I kept about me
I hide not from the law or your just vengeance.
TOM. Ha!
VER. To give your peace more ample satisfaction,
Thank these discoverers.
TOM. If you bring that calm,
Name but the manner I shall ask forgiveness in
For that contemptuous smile[22] upon you;
I'll perfect it with reverence that belongs
Unto a sacred altar. [*Kneels.*]
VER. Good sir, rise;
Why, now you overdo as much a' this hand
As you fell short a' tother. — Speak, Alibius.
ALIB. 'T was my wife's fortune, as she is most lucky
At a discovery, to find out lately,
Within our hospital of fools and madmen,
Two counterfeits slipp'd into these disguises;
Their names, Franciscus and Antonio.
VER. Both mine, sir, and I ask no favor for 'em.
ALIB. Now that which draws suspicion to their habits,
The time of their disguisings agrees justly[23]
With the day of the murder.
TOM. O blest revelation!
VER. Nay, more, nay, more, sir — I'll not spare mine own
In way of justice — they both feign'd a journey
To Br[i]amata, and so wrought out their leaves[24];
My love was so abus'd[25] in 't.
TOM. Time 's too precious
To run in waste now; you have brought a peace
The riches of five kingdoms could not purchase.
Be my most happy conduct; I thirst for 'em;
Like subtle lightning will I wind about 'em,
And melt their marrow in 'em. *Exeunt.*

[SCENE III][26]

Enter ALSEMERO *and* JASPERINO.

JAS. Your confidence, I 'm sure, is now of proof;
The prospect from the garden[27] has show'd
Enough for deep suspicion.
ALS. The black mask
That so continually was worn upon 't
Condemns the face for ugly ere 't be seen:
Her despite to him, and so seeming bottomless.
JAS. Touch it home then; 't is not a shallow probe
Can search this ulcer soundly; I fear you'll find it
Full of corruption. 'T is fit I leave you;
She meets you opportunely from that walk;
She took the back door at his parting with her. *Exit* JASPERINO.
ALS. Did my fate wait for this unhappy stroke
At my first sight of woman? — She 's here.

Enter BEATRICE.

BEAT. Alsemero!
ALS. How do you?
BEAT. How do I?
Alas! how do you? You look not well.
ALS. You read me well enough; I am not well.
BEAT. Not well, sir? Is 't in my power to better you?
ALS. Yes.
BEAT. Nay, then y' are cur'd again.
ALS. Pray, resolve me[28] one question, lady.
BEAT. If I can.
ALS. None can so sure. Are you honest?[29]
BEAT. Ha, ha, ha! that 's a broad question, my Lord.

[20] Politeness.
[21] Mod. eds. add *for*.
[22] Dyce adds *I threw*, perhaps rightly; cf. l. 57.
[23] Precisely.
[24] Obtained their leaves of absence. [25] Deceived.
[26] Alsemero's apartment. Dyce suggests the location of the earlier part elsewhere, on account of *walk* in l. 10. But note *door* in l. 11.
[27] Trisyllabic. (Dyce.)
[28] Satisfy me concerning. [29] Chaste.

ALS. But that's not a modest answer, my Lady.
Do you laugh? My doubts are strong upon me.

BEAT. 'T is innocence that smiles, and no rough brow
Can take away the dimple in her cheek.
Say I should strain a tear to fill the vault,
Which would you give the better faith to?

ALS. 'T were but hypocrisy of a sadder color,
But the same stuff; neither your smiles nor tears
Shall move or flatter me from my belief:
You are a whore!

BEAT. What a horrid sound it hath!
It blasts a beauty to deformity;
Upon what face soever that breath falls,
It strikes it ugly. Oh, you have ruin'd
What you can ne'er repair again.

ALS. I'll all
Demolish, and seek out truth within you,
If there be any left; let your sweet tongue
Prevent[30] your heart's rifling; there I'll ransack
And tear out my suspicion.

BEAT. You may, sir;
'T is an easy passage; yet, if you please,
Show me the ground whereon you lost your love;
My spotless virtue may but tread on that
Before I perish.

ALS. Unanswerable;
A ground you cannot stand on; you fall down
Beneath all grace and goodness when you set
Your ticklish heel on 't. There was a visor
O'er that cunning face, and that became you;
Now impudence in triumph rides upon 't.
How comes this tender reconcilement else
'Twixt you and your despite, your rancorous loathing,
De Flores? He that your eye was sore at sight of,
He's now become your arm's supporter, your
Lip's saint!

BEAT. Is there the cause?

ALS. Worse, your lust's devil,
Your adultery!

BEAT. Would any but yourself say that,
'T would turn him to a villain!

ALS. 'T was witness'd
By the counsel of your bosom,[31] Diaphanta.

BEAT. Is your witness dead then?

ALS. 'T is to be fear'd
It was the wages of her knowledge; poor soul,
She liv'd not long after the discovery.

BEAT. Then hear a story of not much less horror
Than this your false suspicion is beguil'd with;
To your bed's scandal I stand up innocence,[32]
Which even the guilt of one black other deed
Will stand for proof of: your love has made me
A cruel murd'ress.

ALS. Ha!

BEAT. A bloody one;
I have kiss'd poison for it, strok'd a serpent:
That thing of hate, worthy in my esteem
Of no better employment, and him most worthy
To be so employ'd, I caus'd to murder
That innocent Piracquo, having no
Better means than that worst to assure
Yourself to me.

ALS. Oh, the place itself e'er since
Has crying been for vengeance! the temple,
Where blood and beauty first unlawfully
Fir'd their devotion and quench'd the right one;
'T was in my fears at first, 't will have it now;
Oh, thou art all deform'd!

BEAT. Forget not, sir,
It for your sake was done. Shall greater dangers
Make the less welcome?

ALS. Oh, thou shouldst have gone
A thousand leagues about to have avoided
This dangerous bridge of blood! Here we are lost.

BEAT. Remember, I am true unto your bed.

ALS. The bed itself's a charnel, the sheets shrouds
For murdered carcasses. It must ask pause
What I must do in this; meantime you shall
Be my prisoner only; enter my closet;[33]

Exit BEATRICE [*into closet*].

I'll be your keeper yet. Oh, in what part
Of this sad story shall I first begin? — Ha!
This same fellow has put me in.[34] — De Flores!

Enter DE FLORES.

DE F. Noble Alsemero!

ALS. I can tell you
News, sir; my wife has her commended to you.

DE F. That's news indeed, my Lord; I think she would

[30] Forestall.
[31] By your confidante.
[32] I am innocent.
[33] A small private room.
[34] In the way of beginning.

Commend me to the gallows if she could,
She ever lov'd me so well; I thank her.

ALS. What's this blood upon your band,[35] De Flores?

DE F. Blood! no, sure 't was wash'd since.

ALS. Since when, man?

DE F. Since tother day I got a knock
In a sword-and-dagger school; I think 't is out.

ALS. Yes, 't is almost out, but 't is perceiv'd though.
I had forgot my message; this it is:
What price goes murder?

DE F. How, sir?

ALS. I ask you, sir;
My wife 's behindhand with[36] you, she tells me,
For a brave bloody blow you gave for her sake
Upon Piracquo.

DE F. Upon? 'T was quite through him, sure;
Has she confess'd it?

ALS. As sure as death to both of you;
And much more than that.

DE F. It could not be much more;
'T was but one thing, and that — she 's a whore.

ALS. I[t] could not choose but follow. O cunning devils!
How should blind men know you from fair-fac'd saints?

BEAT. (*within*) He lies! the villain does belie me!

DE F. Let me go to her, sir.

ALS. Nay, you shall to her. —
Peace, crying crocodile, your sounds are heard;
Take your prey to you. — Get you in to her, sir. *Exit* DE FLORES [*into closet*].
I 'll be your pander now; rehearse again
Your scene of lust, that you may be perfect
When you shall come to act it to the black audience,
Where howls and gnashings shall be music to you.
Clip your adult'ress freely; 't is the pilot
Will guide you to the *mare mortuum*,
Where you shall sink to fa[th]oms bottomless.

Enter VERMANDERO, ALIBIUS, ISABELLA, TOMAZO, FRANCISCUS, *and* ANTONIO.

VER. O Alsemero! I have a wonder for you.

ALS. No, sir, 't is I, I have a wonder for you.

VER. I have suspicion near as proof itself
For Piracquo's murder.

ALS. Sir, I have proof.
Beyond suspicion, for Piracquo's murder.

VER. Beseech you, hear me; these two have been disguis'd
E'er since the deed was done.

ALS. I have two other
That were more close disguis'd than your two could be
E'er since the deed was done.

VER. You 'll hear me — these mine own servants ——

ALS. Hear me — those nearer than your servants,
That shall acquit them and prove them guiltless.

FRAN. That may be done with easy truth, sir.

TOM. How is my cause bandied through your delays!
'T is urgent in[37] blood and calls for haste.
Give me a brother[38] alive or dead;
Alive, a wife with him; if dead, for both
A recompense for murder and adultery.

BEAT. (*within*) Oh, oh, oh!

ALS. Hark! 't is coming to you.

DE F. (*within*) Nay, I 'll along for company.

BEAT. (*within*) Oh, oh!

VER. What horrid sounds are these?

ALS. Come forth, you twins
Of mischief!

Re-enter DE FLORES, *bringing in* BEATRICE [*wounded*].

DE F. Here we are; if you have any more
To say to us, speak quickly: I shall not
Give you the hearing else; I am so stout yet,
And so, I think, that broken rib of mankind.

VER. A host of enemies ent'red my citadel
Could not amaze like this. Joanna! Beatrice-Joanna!

BEAT. O, come not near me, sir; I shall defile you!
I am that of your blood[39] was taken from you,
For your better health; look no more upon 't,
But cast it to the ground regardlessly;
Let the common sewer take it from distinction
Beneath the stars; upon yon meteor [*Points to* DE FLORES.]
Ever hang[40] my fate 'mongst things corruptible;
I ne'er could pluck it from him; my loathing

[35] Collar.

[36] Indebted to.

[37] Mod. eds. add *my*.

[38] Mod. eds. add *or*.

[39] Understand "which."

[40] Dyce emends *hung*.

Was prophet to the rest, but ne'er believ'd.
Mine honor fell with him, and now my life. —
Alsemero, I am a stranger to your bed;
Your bed was coz'ned on the nuptial night, —
For which your false bride died.

ALS. Diaphanta!

DE F. Yes, and the while I coupled with your mate
At barley-break; now we are left in hell.[41]

VER. We are all there; it circumscribes[42] here.

DE F. I lov'd this woman in spite of her heart;
Her love I earn'd out of Piracquo's murder.

TOM. Ha! my brother's murderer?

DE F. Yes, and her honor's prize
Was my reward; I thank life for nothing
But that pleasure; it was so sweet to me,
That I have drunk up all, left none behind
For any man to pledge me.

VER. Horrid villain!
Keep life in him for future tortures.

DE F. No!
I can prevent you; here's my penknife still;
It is but one thread more [*stabbing himself*], and now 't is cut. —
Make haste, Joanna, by that token to thee,
Canst[43] not forget, so lately put in mind;
I would not go to leave thee far behind. (*Dies.*)

BEAT. Forgive me, Alsemero, all forgive!
'T is time to die when 't is a shame to live.
Dies.

VER. Oh, my name is ent'red now in that record[44]
Where till this fatal hour 't was never read.

ALS. Let it be blotted out; let your heart lose it,
And it can never look you in the face,
Nor tell a tale behind the back of life
To your dishonor. Justice hath so right[45]
The guilty hit, that innocence is quit
By proclamation, and may joy again. —
Sir, you are sensible of what truth hath done;
'T is the best comfort that your grief can find.

TOM. Sir, I am satisfied; my injuries
Lie dead before me; I can exact no more,
Unless my soul were loose, and could o'ertake
Those black fugitives that are fled from thence,[46]
To take[47] a second vengeance; but there are wraths
Deeper than mine, 't is to be fear'd, about 'em.

ALS. What an opacous[48] body had that moon
That last chang'd on us! Here's beauty chang'd
To ugly whoredom; here servant-obedience
To a master-sin, imperious murder;
I, a suppos'd husband, chang'd embraces
With wantonness — but that was paid before.[49] —
[*to* TOMAZO] Your change is come too, from an ignorant wrath
To knowing friendship. — Are there any more on's?

ANT. Yes, sir, I was chang'd, too, from a little ass as I was to a great fool as I am; and had like to ha' been chang'd to the gallows, but that you know my innocence[50] always excuses me.

FRAN. I was chang'd from a little wit to be stark mad,
Almost for the same purpose.

ISA. Your change is still behind,[51]
But deserve best your transformation;
You are a jealous coxcomb,[52] keep schools of folly,
And teach your scholars how to break your own head.

ALIB. I see all apparent, Wife, and will change now
Into a better husband, and never keep
Scholars that shall be wiser than myself.

ALS. Sir, you have yet a son's duty living;
Please you, accept it; let that your sorrow,
As it goes from your eye, go from your heart:
Man and his sorrow at the grave must part.

EPILOGUE

ALS. All we can do to comfort one another,
To stay a brother's sorrow for a brother,
To dry a child from the kind father's eyes,
Is to no purpose; it rather multiplies:
Your only smiles have power to cause relive
The dead again, or in their rooms to give
Brother a new brother, father a child;
If these appear, all griefs are reconcil'd.

Exeunt omnes.

[41] See on III, iii, 188. [42] Mod. eds. add *us*. [43] Which thou canst. [44] Of dishonor. [45] Precisely. [46] Dyce needlessly emends *hence*.

[47] Receive. [48] Opaque. [49] *I.e.*, Diaphanta paid for that with her life. [50] With a pun on "innocence" = imbecility. [51] To come. [52] Fool.

THE BROKEN HEART.

A Tragedy.

ACTED
By the KINGS Majesties Seruants
at the priuate House in the
BLACK-FRIERS.

Fide Honor.

LONDON:
Printed by I. B. for HUGH BEESTON, and are to
be sold at his Shop, neere the *Castle* in
Corne-hill. 1633.

INTRODUCTORY NOTE

FORD's first publication, *Fame's Memorial*, is a long elegiac poem on Charles Blount, Lord Mountjoy and Earl of Devonshire, whose death in 1606 followed by a few months his marriage to Penelope Rich, *née* Devereux, Sidney's Stella. Her wedded life with Robert, Lord Rich, had been a miserable one, and she had long been Devonshire's mistress, without their incurring serious reprobation. Their marriage, however, after her divorce, was regarded as scandalous, and the Earl died heartbroken at the King's displeasure. The youthful Ford, generous and romantic, was deeply moved by the lovers' trials, and throughout his literary career remained a somewhat quixotic idealist and amorist. For him the spiritual union of lovers is an inviolable thing, and wedlock adulterous without a marriage of true minds. To what extent *The Broken Heart* is influenced by the still earlier relations (whatever they may have been) between Penelope and Sir Philip Sidney is very uncertain, despite Sherman's argument (Introduction, Belles Lettres Series) that their predicament was similar to that of Orgilus and Penthea. In any case, the poet's doctrinaire sympathy with lovers as such, his worship of beauty, and his contempt for conventional morality, are constantly reflected in his works.

Ford, then, is not an echo of Shakespeare, Webster, or Fletcher, but the most original of their immediate successors. He is dominated by an idea or mood, which in his best plays he is able to project with remarkable success. To apply to *The Broken Heart* the test of probability, save in the Aristotelian sense, would be as foolish as to reproach Whistler for not delineating in one of his nocturnes every window and chimney pot on the far side of the river. If in this play we are not sensible of the surge of great power, there is a place for sentiment and pathos, especially when they are rendered with such literary distinction. Ford is perhaps a poet first; yet the dramatic effectiveness of *The Broken Heart* is very considerable. Whether there is any justice in the charge that his works are decadent is an interesting question which the Editor hopes soon to discuss elsewhere.

Despite the assertion in lines fifteen and sixteen of the prologue, no source for the plot has been found. The date of composition, and of production by the King's Men at the Blackfriars, has not been precisely determined. Weber (1811) called attention to the citation (IV, ii, 15) of Thomas Deloney's *Garland of Good Will*, of which there was an edition, though it was not the first, in 1631 (Percy Society Reprints, vol. 30, p. viii). The sole quarto of *The Broken Heart* appeared two years later; c. 1632 seems a likely, though quite unsupported, date for its writing. The Quarto of 1633, on which the present text is based, does not carry the author's name on the title page, save in the anagram, *Fide Honor;* but it is signed to the dedication.

The standard edition of Ford's works is still that of W. Gifford, in the revision of A. Dyce (1869). Excellent reprints of the quartos are provided in W. Bang's *Materialen zur Kunde des Älteren Englischen Dramas*, in vol. XXIII, and in vol. I of the " New Series " by H. De Vocht. *The Broken Heart* and *'T is Pity She's a Whore* were also edited by S. P. Sherman (1915).

THE BROKEN HEART

BY

JOHN FORD

THE SPEAKERS' NAMES FITTED TO THEIR QUALITIES

AMYCLAS, *Common to the Kings of Laconia.*
ITHOCLES, *Honor of loveliness,* a favorite.
ORGILUS, *Angry,* son to Crotolon.
BASSANES, *Vexation,* a jealous nobleman.
ARMOSTES, *An Appeaser,* a councillor of state.
CROTOLON, *Noise,* another councillor.
PROPHILUS, *Dear,* friend to Ithocles.
NEARCHUS, *Young Prince,* Prince of Argos.
TECNICUS, *Artist,* a philosopher.
[HEMOPHIL],[1] *Glutton,* } two courtiers.
GRONEAS, *Tavern-haunter,* } two courtiers.
AMELUS, *Trusty,* friend to Nearchus.
PHULAS, *Watchful,* servant to Bassanes.
Courtiers, Officers, Attendants, etc.]

CALANTHA, *Flower of beauty,* the King's daughter.
PENTHEA, *Complaint,* sister to Ithocles [and wife to Bassanes].
EUPHRANEA, *Joy,* a maid of honor, [daughter to Crotolon].
CHRISTALLA, *Crystal,* } maids of honor.
PHILEMA, *A Kiss,* } maids of honor.
GRAUSIS,[2] *Old Beldam,* overseer of Penthea.

PERSONS INCLUDED

THRASUS, *Fierceness,* father of Ithocles.
APLOTES, *Simplicity,* Orgilus so disguis'd.

[THE SCENE — *Sparta.*]

THE PROLOGUE

OUR scene is Sparta. He whose best of art
Hath drawn this piece calls it *The Broken Heart.*
The title lends no expectation here
Of apish laughter, or of some lame jeer
At place or persons; no pretended [3] clause
Of jests fit for a brothel courts applause
From vulgar admiration: such low songs,
Tun'd to unchaste ears, suit not modest tongues.
The Virgin Sisters [4] then deserv'd fresh bays
When innocence and sweetness crown'd their lays;
Then vices gasp'd for breath, whose whole commerce
Was whipp'd to exile by unblushing verse.
This law we keep in our presentment now,
Not to take freedom more than we allow;
What may be here thought a fiction, when Time's youth
Wanted some riper years was known *A Truth:* [5]
In which, if words have cloth'd the subject right,
You may partake a pity with delight.

[1] Q *Lemophil.*
[2] Q *Gransis,* throughout.
[3] Set forth, offered for consideration.
[4] The Muses.
[5] See introductory note.

ACT I — Scene I [6]

Enter Crotolon *and* Orgilus.

Crot. Dally not further; I will know the reason
That speeds thee to this journey.
Org. Reason? good sir,
I can yield many.
Crot. Give me one, a good one;
Such I expect, and ere we part must have.
Athens! Pray, why to Athens? You intend not
To kick against the world, turn cynic, stoic,
Or read the logic lecture, or become
An Areopagite,[7] and judge in cases
Touching the commonwealth; for, as I take it,
The budding of your chin cannot prognosticate
So grave an honor.
Org. All this I acknowledge.
Crot. You do! Then, son, if books and love of knowledge
Inflame you to this travel, here in Sparta
You may as freely study.
Org. 'T is not that, sir.
Crot. Not that, sir! As a father, I command thee
To acquaint me with the truth.
Org. Thus I obey 'ee.
After so many quarrels as dissension,
Fury, and rage had br[oa]ch'd in blood, and sometimes
With death to such confederates as sided
With now-dead Thrasus and yourself, my Lord;
Our present king, Amyclas, reconcil'd
Your eager swords and seal'd a gentle peace:
Friends you profess'd yourselves; which to confirm,
A resolution for a lasting league
Betwixt your families was entertain'd,
By joining in a Hymenean bond
Me and the fair Penthea, only daughter
To Thrasus.
Crot. What of this?
Org. Much, much, dear sir.
A freedom of converse, an interchange
Of holy and chaste love, so fix'd our souls
In a firm growth of union [8] that no time
Can eat into the pledge; we had enjoy'd
The sweets our vows expected, had not cruelty
Prevented all those triumphs we prepar'd for,
By Thrasus his untimely death.
Crot. Most certain.
Org. From this time sprouted up that poisonous stalk
Of aconite, whose ripened fruit hath ravish'd
All health, all comfort of a happy life;
For Ithocles, her brother, proud of youth,
And prouder in his power, nourish'd closely [9]
The memory of former discontents,
To glory in revenge. By cunning partly,
Partly by threats, 'a [10] woos at once and forces
His virtuous sister to admit [11] a marriage
With Bassanes, a nobleman, in honor
And riches, I confess, beyond my fortunes.
Crot. All this is no sound reason to importune
My leave for thy departure.
Org. Now it follows.
Beauteous Penthea, wedded to this torture
By an insulting [12] brother, being secretly
Compell'd to yield her virgin freedom up
To him who never can usurp her heart,
Before contracted mine, is now so yok'd
To a most barbarous thraldom, misery,
Affliction, that he savors not humanity
Whose sorrow melts not into more than pity
In hearing but her name.
Crot. As how, pray?
Org. Bassanes,
The man that calls her wife, considers truly
What heaven of perfections he is lord of
By thinking fair Penthea his; this thought
Begets a kind of monster-love, which love
Is nurse unto a fear so strong and servile
As brands all dotage with a jealousy:
All eyes who gaze upon that shrine of beauty
He doth resolve [13] do homage to the miracle;
Some one, he is assur'd, may now or then,
If opportunity but sort,[14] prevail.
So much, out of a self-unworthiness,
His fears transport him; not that he finds cause
In her obedience, but his own distrust.
Crot. You spin out your discourse.
Org. My griefs are violent.
For, knowing how the maid was heretofore
Courted by me, his jealousies grow wild
That I should steal again into her favors,

[6] Unlocated; presumably a room in Crotolon's house.

[7] A member of the Areopagus, the famous Athenian court.

[8] Some copies of Q *of holy union.* (Dyce. See also De Vocht.)

[9] Secretly.

[10] He.

[11] Consent to.

[12] Arrogant, insolently triumphant.

[13] Is convinced.

[14] Suit.

And undermine her virtues; which the gods
Know I nor dare nor dream of. Hence, from hence
I undertake a voluntary exile;
First, by my absence to take off the cares
Of jealous Bassanes; but chiefly, sir,
To free Penthea from a hell on earth;
Lastly, to lose the memory of something
Her presence makes to live in me afresh.
CROT. Enough, my Orgilus, enough. To Athens
I give a full consent. — Alas, good lady! —
We shall hear from thee often?
ORG. Often.
CROT. See,
Thy sister comes to give a farewell.

Enter EUPHRANEA.

EUPH. Brother!
ORG. Euphranea, thus upon thy cheeks I print
A brother's kiss; more careful of thine honor,
Thy health, and thy well-doing than my life.
Before we part, in presence of our father,
I must prefer a suit to 'ee.[15]
EUPH. You may style it,
My Brother, a command.
ORG. That you will promise
To pass never to any man, however
Worthy, your faith, till, with our father's leave,
I give a free consent.
CROT. An easy motion![16]
I'll promise for her, Orgilus.
ORG. Your pardon;
Euphranea's oath must yield me satisfaction.
EUPH. By Vesta's sacred fires I swear.
CROT. And I,
By Great Apollo's beams, join in the vow,
Not without thy allowance[17] to bestow her
On any living.
ORG. Dear Euphranea,
Mistake me not; far, far 't is from my thought,
As far from any wish of mine, to hinder
Preferment to an honorable bed
Or fitting fortune; thou art young and handsome,
And 't were injustice, more, a tyranny,
Not to advance thy merit. Trust me, Sister,
It shall be my first care to see thee match'd
As may become thy choice and our contents.
I have your oath.
EUPH. You have. But mean you, Brother,
To leave us, as you say?
CROT. Ay, ay, Euphranea;
He has just grounds[18] direct him. I will prove
A father and a brother to thee.
EUPH. Heaven
Does look into the secrets of all hearts. —
Gods, you have mercy with 'ee, else —
CROT. Doubt nothing;
Thy brother will return in safety to us.
ORG. Souls sunk in sorrows never are without 'em;
They change fresh airs, but bear their griefs about 'em. *Exeunt omnes.*

SCENE II[19]

Flourish. *Enter* AMYCLAS the King, ARMOSTES, PROPHILUS, *and* Attendants.

AMY. The Spartan gods are gracious; our humility
Shall bend before their altars, and perfume
Their temples with abundant sacrifice.
See, Lords, Amyclas, your old king, is ent'ring
Into his youth again! I shall shake off
This silver badge of age, and change this snow
For hairs as gay as are Apollo's locks;
Our heart leaps in new vigor.
ARM. May old time
Run back to double your long life, great sir!
AMY. It will, it must, Armostes: thy bold nephew,
Death-braving Ithocles, brings to our gates
Triumphs and peace upon his conquering sword.
Laconia is a monarchy at length;
Hath in this latter war trod under foot
Messene's pride; Messene[20] bows her neck
To Lacedaemon's royalty. Oh, 't was
A glorious victory, and doth deserve
More than a chronicle — a temple, Lords,
A temple to the name of Ithocles. —
Where didst thou leave him, Prophilus?
PRO. At Pephon,[21]
Most gracious sovereign; twenty of the noblest
Of the Messenians there attend your pleasure,

[15] Common for "ye", though here perhaps = "thee."
[16] Proposal.
[17] Approval.

[18] Understand "that."
[19] Presumably a room in the palace.
[20] The town of this name was not founded till after the overthrow of the Spartan supremacy, but the name was anciently given to Messenia.
[21] Pephnus, a Laconian town on the eastern shore of the Messenian Gulf. It was regarded by the Messenians as the limit of their territories.

For such conditions as you shall propose
In settling peace, and liberty of life.
AMY. When comes your friend, the general?
PRO. He promis'd
To follow with all speed convenient.

Enter CROTOLON, CALANTHA, CHRISTALLA [*and*] PHILEMA [*with a garland*], *and* EUPHRANEA.

AMY. Our daughter! — Dear Calantha, the happy news,
The conquest of Messene, hath already
Enrich'd thy knowledge.
CAL. With the circumstance
And manner of the fight, related faithfully
By Prophilus himself. — But, pray, sir, tell me
How doth the youthful general demean
His actions in these fortunes?
PRO. Excellent Princess,
Your own fair eyes may soon report a truth
Unto your judgment, with what moderation,
Calmness of nature, measure, bounds, and limits
Of thankfulness and joy, 'a doth digest
Such amplitude of his success as would
In others, moulded of a spirit less clear,
Advance 'em to comparison with Heaven;
But Ithocles —
CAL. Your friend —
PRO. He is so, madam,
In which the period of my fate consists:
He, in this firmament of honor, stands
Like a star fix'd, not mov'd with [22] any thunder
Of popular applause or sudden lightning
Of self-opinion; he hath serv'd his country,
And thinks 't was but his duty.
CROT. You describe
A miracle of man.
AMY. Such, Crotolon,
On forfeit of a king's word, thou wilt find him. — *Flourish.*
Hark, warning of his coming! All attend him.

Enter ITHOCLES, HEMOPHIL, *and* GRONEAS; *the rest of the* Lords *ushering him in.*

Return into these arms, thy home, thy sanctuary,
Delight of Sparta, treasure of my bosom,
Mine own, own Ithocles.
ITH. Your humblest subject.
ARM. Proud of the blood I claim an interest in,
As brother to thy mother, I embrace thee,
Right noble Nephew.
ITH. Sir, your love 's too partial.
CROT. Our country speaks by me, who by thy valor,
Wisdom, and service shares in this great action,
Returning thee, in part of thy due merits,
A general welcome.
ITH. You exceed in bounty.
CAL. Christalla, Philema, the chaplet. [*Takes it.*] — Ithocles,
Upon the wings of Fame the singular
And chosen fortune of an high attempt
Is borne so past the view of common sight,
That I myself with mine own hands have wrought,
To crown thy temples, this provincial garland: [23]
Accept, wear, and enjoy it as our gift,
Deserv'd, not purchas'd.
ITH. Y' are a royal maid.
AMY. She is in all our daughter.
ITH. Let me blush,
Acknowledging how poorly I have serv'd,
What nothings I have done, compar'd with th' honors
Heap'd on the issue of a willing mind;
In that lay mine ability, that only.
For who is he so sluggish from his birth,
So little worthy of a name or country,
That owes not out of gratitude for life
A debt of service, in what kind soever
Safety or counsel of the commonwealth
Requires, for payment?
CAL. 'A speaks truth.
ITH. Whom Heaven
Is pleas'd to style victorious, there, to such,
Applause runs madding, like the drunken priests
In Bacchus' sacrifices, without reason,
Voicing the leader-on a demigod;
Whenas, indeed, each common soldier's blood
Drops down as current coin in that hard purchase
As his whose much more delicate condition
Hath suck'd the milk of ease: judgment commands,
But resolution executes. I use not,
Before this royal presence, these fit slights [24]
As in contempt of such as can direct;

[22] By.

[23] "The wreath (of laurel) . . . which the ancients conferred on those who . . . had added a province to the empire." (Gifford.)

[24] *I.e.*, these appropriate depreciatory expressions.

My speech hath other end: not to attribute
All praise to one man's fortune, which is strengthed
By many hands. For instance, here in Prophilus,
A gentleman — I cannot flatter truth —
Of much desert; and, though in other rank,
Both Hemophil and Groneas were not missing
To wish their country's peace; for, in a word,
All there did strive their best, and 't was our duty.

AMY. Courtiers turn soldiers! — We vouchsafe our hand. [*They kiss his hand.*]
Observe your great example.

HEM. With all diligence.

GRO. Obsequiously and hourly.

AMY. Some repose
After these toils are[25] needful. We must think on
Conditions for the conquered; they expect[26] 'em.
On! — Come, my Ithocles.

EUPH. [*to* PROPHILUS] Sir, with your favor,
I need not a supporter.[27]

PRO. Fate instructs me.

Exeunt [*all but*] HEMOPHIL, [*who*] *stays* CHRISTALLA; [*and*] GRONEAS, [*who stays*] PHILEMA.

CHRIS. With me?

PHIL. Indeed, I dare not stay.

HEM. Sweet lady,
Soldiers are blunt — your lip.

CHRIS. Fie, this is rudeness;
You went not hence such creatures.

GRO. Spirit of valor
Is of a mounting nature.

PHIL. It appears so. —
Pray, in earnest, how many men apiece
Have you two been the death of?

GRO. 'Faith, not many;
We were compos'd of mercy.

HEM. For our daring,
You heard the general's approbation
Before the King.

CHRIS. You "wish'd your country's peace;"
That show'd your charity. Where are your spoils,
Such as the soldier fights for?

PHIL. They are coming.

CHRIS. By the next carrier, are they not?

GRO. Sweet Philema,
When I was in the thickest of mine enemies,
Slashing off one man's head, another's nose,
Another's arms and legs —

PHIL. And all together.

GRO. Then would I with a sigh remember thee,
And cry "Dear Philema, 't is for thy sake
I do these deeds of wonder!" — Dost not love me
With all thy heart now?

PHIL. Now as heretofore.
I have not put my love to use;[28] the principal
Will hardly yield an interest.

GRO. By Mars,
I'll marry thee!

PHIL. By Vulcan,[29] y' are forsworn,
Except my mind do alter strangely.

GRO. One word.

CHRIS. You lie beyond all modesty — forbear me.

HEM. I'll make thee mistress of a city; 't is
Mine own by conquest.

CHRIS. By petition; sue for 't
In forma pauperis.[30] — City? kennel! — Gallants,
Off with your f[e]athers; put on aprons, gallants;
Learn to reel,[31] thrum,[32] or trim a lady's dog,
And be good, quiet souls of peace, hobgoblins!

HEM. Christalla!

CHRIS. Practise to drill hogs, in hope
To share in the acorns. — Soldiers? corn-cutters!
But not so valiant: they ofttimes draw blood,
Which you durst never do. When you have practis'd
More wit or more civility, we'll rank 'ee
I' th' list of men: till then, brave things-at-arms,
Dare not to speak to us — most potent Groneas!

PHIL. And Hemophil the hardy! — at your services.

Exeunt CHRISTALLA *and* PHILEMA.

GRO. They scorn us as they did before we went.

[25] Mod. eds. *is*.
[26] Are waiting for.
[27] Evidently Prophilus has offered his arm or hand.

[28] Out at interest; *i.e.*, I have not lent my love to anyone, and therefore am not expecting to receive anything in return.
[29] Who got the better of Mars.
[30] A pauper being entitled to exemption from court costs and to service of counsel gratis.
[31] Wind yarn or thread.
[32] Make tufts in cloth.

HEM. Hang 'em! let us scorn them, and be reveng'd.
GRO. Shall we?
HEM. We will: and when we slight them thus,
Instead of following them, they'll follow us;
It is a woman's nature.
GRO. 'T is a scurvy one. *Exeunt.*

SCENE III[33]

Enter TECNICUS, *a philosopher, and* ORGILUS *disguised like a scholar of his.*

TEC. Tempt not the stars, young man; thou canst not play
With the severity of Fate; this change
Of habit[34] and disguise in outward view
Hides not the secrets of thy soul within thee
From their quick-piercing eyes, which dive at all times
Down to thy thoughts. In thy aspect I note
A consequence of danger.[35]
ORG. Give me leave,
Grave Tecnicus, without foredooming destiny,
Under thy roof to ease my silent griefs
By applying to my hidden wounds the balm
Of thy oraculous lectures. If my fortune
Run such a crooked byway as to wrest
My steps to ruin, yet thy learned precepts
Shall call me back and set my footings straight.
I will not court the world.
TEC. Ah, Orgilus,
Neglects in young men of delights and life
Run often to extremities; they care not
For harms to others who contemn their own.
ORG. But I, most learned artist, am not so much
At odds with nature that I grudge the thrift
Of any true deserver; nor doth malice
Of present hopes[36] so check them with despair
As that I yield to thought of more affliction
Than what is incident to frailty.[37] Wherefore,
Impute not this retired course of living
Some little time to any other cause
Than what I justly render: the information
Of an unsettled mind, as the effect
Must clearly witness.
TEC. Spirit of truth inspire thee!
On these conditions I conceal thy change,
And willingly admit thee for an auditor.—
I'll to my study.
ORG. I to contemplations
In these delightful walks.— [*Exit* TECNICUS.]
Thus metamorph[o]s'd,
I may without suspicion hearken after
Penthea's usage and Euphranea's faith.
Love, thou art full of mystery! The deities
Themselves are not secure[38] in searching out
The secrets of those flames, which, hidden, waste
A breast made tributary to the laws
Of beauty; physic yet hath never found
A remedy to cure a lover's wound.—
Ha! who are those that cross yon private walk
Into the shadowing grove in amorous foldings?

PROPHILUS *passeth over, supporting* EUPHRANEA, *and whispering.*

My sister! Oh, my sister! 't is Euphranea
With Prophilus; supported, too! I would
It were an apparition! Prophilus
Is Ithocles his[39] friend; it strangely puzzles me.
Again? Help me, my book; this scholar's habit
Must stand[40] my privilege. My mind is busy;
Mine eyes and ears are open.
Walk by, reading.

Enter again PROPHILUS *and* EUPHRANEA.

PRO. Do not waste
The span of this stol'n time, lent by the gods
For precious use, in niceness![41] Bright Euphranea,
Should I repeat old vows, or study new,
For purchase of belief to my desires,—
ORG. [*aside*] Desires!
PRO. My service, my integrity,—
ORG. [*aside*] That's better.
PRO. I should but repeat a lesson
Oft conn'd without a prompter but thine eyes.
My love is honorable.
ORG. [*aside*] So was mine
To my Penthea, chastely honorable.
PRO. Nor wants there more addition to my wish
Of happiness than having thee a wife;
Already sure of Ithocles, a friend
Firm and unalterable.
ORG. [*aside*] But a brother
More cruel than the grave.
EUPH. What can you look for,
In answer to your noble protestations,
From an unskilful[42] maid, but language suited
To a divided mind?

[33] A grove in the palace grounds.
[34] Clothing.
[35] Dangerous outcome.
[36] Injury to my present hopes.
[37] *I.e.*, the general frailty of men.
[38] Free from uncertainty.
[39] Ithocles's.
[40] Be.
[41] Coyness.
[42] Inexperienced.

ORG. [*aside*] Hold out, Euphranea!
EUPH. Know, Prophilus, I never undervalued,
From the first time you mentioned worthy love,
Your merit, means, or person; it had been
A fault of judgment in me, and a dullness
In my affections, not to weigh and thank
My better stars that offered me the grace
Of so much blissfulness. For, to speak truth,
The law of my desires kept equal pace
With yours, nor have I left that resolution;
But only, in a word, whatever choice
Lives nearest in my heart must first procure
Consent both from my father and my brother,
Ere he can own me his.
ORG. [*aside*] She is forsworn else.
PRO. Leave me that task.
EUPH. My brother, ere he parted
To Athens, had my oath.
ORG. [*aside*] Yes, yes, 'a had, sure.
PRO. I doubt not, with the means the court supplies,
But to prevail at pleasure.
ORG. [*aside*] Very likely!
PRO. Meantime, best, dearest, I may build my hopes
On the foundation of thy constant suff'rance [43]
In [44] any opposition.
EUPH. Death shall sooner
Divorce life and the joys I have in living
Than my chaste vows from truth.
PRO. On thy fair hand
I seal the like.
ORG. [*aside*] There is no faith in woman.
Passion, oh, be contain'd! My very heart-strings
Are on the tenters.[45]
EUPH. Sir, we are overheard.
Cupid protect us! 'T was a stirring, sir,
Of some one near.
PRO. Your fears are needless, lady;
None have access into these private pleasures [46]
Except some near in court, or bosom-student
From Tecnicus his oratory, granted
By special favor lately from the King
Unto the grave philosopher.
EUPH. Methinks
I hear one talking to himself — I see him.
PRO. 'T is a poor scholar, as I told you, lady.

[43] Endurance; *i.e.*, fidelity. [44] In the event of.
[45] Hooks for stretching cloth.
[46] Pleasure grounds.

ORG. [*aside*] I am discovered. — [*as if studying*] Say it: is it possible,
With a smooth tongue, a leering countenance,
Flattery, or force of reason — I come t' ee sir —
To turn or to appease the raging sea?
Answer to that. — Your art! what art to catch
And hold fast in a net the sun's small atoms?
No, no; they'll out, they'll out: ye may as easily
Outrun a cloud driven by a northern blast
As fiddle-faddle so! Peace, or speak sense.
EUPH. Call you this thing a scholar? 'Las, he's lunatic.
PRO. Observe him, sweet; 't is but his recreation.
ORG. But will you hear a little? You are so tetchy,
You keep no rule in argument. Philosophy
Works not upon impossibilities,
But natural conclusions. — Mew! — absurd! [47]
The metaphysics are but speculations
Of the celestial bodies, or such accidents
As not mix'd perfectly, in the air engend'red
Appear to us unnatural; that's all. —
Prove it; — yet, with a reverence to your gravity,
I'll balk illiterate sauciness, submitting
My sole opinion to the touch of writers.
PRO. Now let us fall in with him.
[*They come forward.*]
ORG. Ha, ha, ha!
These apish boys, when they but taste the grammates [48]
And principles of theory, imagine
They can oppose their teachers. Confidence
Leads many into errors.
PRO. By your leave, sir.
EUPH. Are you a scholar, friend?
ORG. I am, gay creature,
With pardon of your deities, a mushroom
On whom the dew of heaven drops now and then;
The sun shines on me too, I thank his beams!
Sometime I feel their warmth, and eat and sleep.
PRO. Does Tecnicus read to [49] thee?
ORG. Yes, forsooth;
He is my master surely; yonder door
Opens upon his study.

[47] "A term of the schools . . . used when false conclusions are illogically deduced from the opponent's premises." (Gifford.)
[48] Rudiments.
[49] Teach.

PRO. Happy creatures!
Such people toil not, sweet, in heats of state,
Nor sink in thaws of greatness; their affections
Keep order with the limits of their modesty;
Their love is love of virtue. — What's thy name?
ORG. Aplotes, sumptuous master, a poor wretch.
EUPH. Dost thou want anything?
ORG. Books, Venus, books.
PRO. Lady, a new conceit [50] comes in my thought,
And most available for both our comforts.
EUPH. My Lord —
PRO. Whiles I endeavor to deserve
Your father's blessing to our loves, this scholar
May daily at some certain hours attend [51]
What notice I can write of my success,
Here in this grove, and give it to your hands;
The like from you to me: so can we never,
Barr'd of our mutual speech, want sure intelligence,
And thus our hearts may talk when our tongues cannot.
EUPH. Occasion is most favorable; use it.
PRO. Aplotes, wilt thou wait us twice a day,
At nine i' th' morning and at four at night,
Here in this bower, to convey such letters
As each shall send to other? Do it willingly,
Safely, and secretly, and I will furnish
Thy study, or what else thou canst desire.
ORG. Jove, make me thankful, thankful, I beseech thee,
Propitious Jove! I will prove sure and trusty.
You will not fail me books?
PRO. Nor aught besides
Thy heart can wish. This lady's name 's Euphranea,
Mine Prophilus.
ORG. I have a pretty memory;
It must prove my best friend. I will not miss
One minute of the hours appointed.
PRO. Write
The books thou wouldst have bought thee in a note,
Or take thyself some money.
ORG. No, no money;
Money to scholars is a spirit invisible —
We dare not finger it: or books or nothing.
PRO. Books of what sort thou wilt; do not forget
Our names.
ORG. I warrant 'ee, I warrant 'ee.

[50] Idea. [51] Wait for.

PRO. Smile, Hymen, on the growth of our desires;
We'll feed thy torches with eternal fires!
Exeunt [PROPHILUS *and* EUPHRANEA].
ORG. Put out thy torches, Hymen, or their light
Shall meet a darkness of eternal night!
Inspire me, Mercury, with swift deceits.
Ingenious Fate has leap'd into mine arms,
Beyond the compass of my brain.[52] Mortality
Creeps on the dung of earth, and cannot reach [53]
The riddles which are purpos'd by the gods.
Great arts best write themselves in their own stories;
They die too basely who outlive their glories.
Exit.

ACT II — SCENE I [1]

Enter BASSANES *and* PHULAS.

BASS. I'll have that window next the street damm'd up;
It gives too full a prospect to temptation,
And courts a gazer's glances. There's a lust
Committed by the eye, that sweats and travails,
Plots, wakes, contrives, till the deformed bearwhelp,[2]
Adultery, be lick'd into the act,
The very act. That light shall be damm'd up;
D'ee hear, sir?
PHU. I do hear, my Lord; a mason
Shall be provided suddenly.[3]
BASS. Some rogue,
Some rogue of your confederacy — factor [4]
For slaves and strumpets! — to convey close [5] packets
From this spruce springal [6] and the tother youngster,
That gaudy earwig,[7] or my Lord your patron,
Whose pensioner you are. — I'll tear thy throat out,
Son of a cat, ill-looking hound's-head — rip up
Thy ulcerous maw, if I but scent a paper,
A scroll, but half as big as what can cover

[52] Beyond my capacity to plan.
[53] Succeed in understanding.
[1] A room in Bassanes's house.
[2] Which was supposed to be born a "confused lump" (*e.g.*, Burton's *Anatomy of Melancholy*, cited by Sherman), afterwards licked "into form" by the mother.
[3] Immediately.
[4] Agent.
[5] Secret.
[6] Youth.
[7] *I.e.*, insinuating person. Q *Eare-wrig*.

A wart upon thy nose, a spot, a pimple,
Directed to my lady: it may prove
A mystical preparative to lewdness.
PHU. Care shall be had, I will turn every thread
About me to an eye. — [*aside*] Here's a sweet life!
BASS. The city housewives, cunning in the traffic
Of chamber merchandise, set all at price
By wholesale; yet they wipe their mouths and simper,
Cull,[8] kiss, and cry "sweetheart," and stroke the head
Which they have branch'd;[9] and all is well again!
Dull clods of dirt, who dare not feel the rubs
Stuck on [their][10] foreheads!
PHU. 'T is a villainous world;
One cannot hold his own in 't.
BASS. Dames at court,
Who flaunt in riots, run another bias;[11]
Their pleasure heaves the patient ass that suffers
Up on the stilts of office, titles, incomes;
Promotion justifies the shame, and sues for 't.
Poor Honor, thou art stabb'd, and bleed'st to death
By such unlawful hire! The country mistress
Is yet more wary, and in blushes hides
Whatever trespass draws her troth to guilt.
But all are false; on this truth I am bold:
No woman but can fall, and doth or would. —
Now for the newest news about the city;
What blab the voices, sirrah?
PHU. O, my Lord,
The rarest, quaintest, strangest, tickling news
That ever —
BASS. Hey-day! up and ride me, rascal!
What is 't?
PHU. Forsooth, they say the King has mew'd[12]
All his gray beard, instead of which is budded
Another of a pure carnation color,
Speckled with green and russet.
BASS. Ignorant block![13]
PHU. Yes, truly; and 't is talk'd about the streets
That, since Lord Ithocles came home, the lions
Never left roaring, at which noise the bears
Have danc'd their very hearts out.
BASS. Dance out thine too.
PHU. Besides, Lord Orgilus is fled to Athens
Upon a fiery dragon, and 't is thought
'A never can return.
BASS. Grant it, Apollo!
PHU. Moreover, please your Lordship, 't is reported
For certain, that whoever is found jealous
Without apparent proof that 's wife is wanton
Shall be divorc'd; but this is but she-news —
I had it from a midwife. I have more yet.
BASS. Antic,[14] no more! Idiots and stupid fools
Grate my calamities. Why to be fair
Should yield presumption of a faulty soul —
Look to the doors.
PHU. [*aside*] The horn of plenty[15] crest him! *Exit* PHULAS.
BASS. Swarms of confusion huddle in my thoughts
In rare distemper. — Beauty! Oh, it is
An unmatch'd blessing or a horrid curse.

Enter PENTHEA *and* GRAUSIS, *an old Lady.*

She comes, she comes! so shoots the morning forth,
Spangled with pearls of transparent dew.
The way to poverty is to be rich,
As I in her am wealthy; but for her,
In all contents a bankrupt. — Lov'd Penthea!
How fares my heart's best joy?
GRAU. In sooth, not well;
She is so oversad.
BASS. Leave chattering, magpie. —
Thy brother is return'd, sweet — safe, and honor'd
With a triumphant victory; thou shalt visit him.
We will to court, where, if it be thy pleasure,
Thou shalt appear in such a ravishing lustre
Of jewels above value, that the dames
Who brave[16] it there, in rage to be outshin'd,
Shall hide them in their closets, and unseen
Fret in their tears; whiles every wond'ring eye
Shall crave none other brightness but thy presence.
Choose thine own recreations; be a queen
Of what delights thou fanciest best, what company,

[8] Embrace. [9] Horned, cuckolded.
[10] Conj. Dyce; Q *the*.
[11] Course, direction. [12] Moulted. [13] Blockhead.

[14] Fool.
[15] Cornucopia; but allusive to the horns of the cuckold.
[16] Display their finery.

What place, what times; do anything, do all things
Youth can command, so[17] thou wilt chase these clouds
From the pure firmament of thy fair looks.
GRAU. Now 't is well said, my Lord. — What, lady! laugh,
Be merry; time is precious.
BASS. [*aside*] Furies whip thee!
PEN. Alas, my Lord, this language to your handmaid
Sounds as would music to the deaf; I need
No braveries nor cost of art to draw
The whiteness of my name into offence.
Let such, if any such there are, who covet
A curiosity of admiration,
By laying out their plenty to full view,
Appear in gaudy outsides; my attires
Shall suit the inward fashion of my mind;
From which, if your opinion, nobly plac'd,
Change not the livery your words bestow,
My fortunes with my hopes are at the highest.
BASS. This house, methinks, stands somewhat too much inward;
It is too melancholy; we 'll remove
Nearer the court. Or what thinks my Penthea
Of the delightful island we command?
Rule me as thou canst wish.
PEN. I am no mistress.
Whither you please, I must attend; all ways
Are alike pleasant to me.
GRAU. Island? prison!
A prison is as gaysome; we 'll no islands;
Marry, out upon 'em! Whom shall we see there?
Sea gulls, and porpoises, and water rats,
And crabs, and mews,[18] and dogfish; goodly gear
For a young lady's dealing, or an old one's.
On no terms islands; I 'll be stew'd first.
BASS. [*aside to* GRAUSIS] Grausis,
You are a juggling bawd. — This sadness, sweetest,
Becomes not youthful blood. — [*aside to* GRAUSIS] I 'll have you pounded. —
For my sake put on a more cheerful mirth;
Thou 'lt mar thy cheeks, and make me old in griefs.—
[*aside to* GRAUSIS] Damnable bitch-fox!
GRAU. I am thick of hearing,
Still, when the wind blows southerly. — What think 'ee
If your fresh lady breed young bones, my Lord?
Would not a chopping boy d'ee good at heart?
But, as you said —
BASS. [*aside to* GRAUSIS] I 'll spit thee on a stake,
Or chop thee into collops![19]
GRAU. Pray, speak louder.
Sure, sure the wind blows south still.
PEN. Thou prat'st madly.
BASS. 'T is very hot; I sweat extremely.

Re-enter PHULAS.

Now?
PHU. A herd of lords, sir.
BASS. Ha?
PHU. A flock of ladies.
BASS. Where?
PHU. Shoals of horses.
BASS. Peasant, how?
PHU. Caroches[20]
In drifts; th' one enter, th' other stand without, sir;
And now I vanish. *Exit* PHULAS.

Enter PROPHILUS, HEMOPHIL, GRONEAS, CHRISTALLA, *and* PHILEMA.

PRO. Noble Bassanes!
BASS. Most welcome, Prophilus; ladies, gentlemen,
To all my heart is open; you all honor me, —
[*aside*] A tympany[21] swells in my head already —
Honor me bountifully. — [*aside*] How they flutter,
Wagtails[22] and jays together!
PRO. From your brother,
By virtue of your love to him, I require
Your instant presence, fairest.
PEN. He is well, sir?
PRO. The gods preserve him ever! Yet, dear beauty,
I find some alteration in him lately,
Since his return to Sparta. — My good Lord,
I pray, use no delay.
BASS. We had not needed
An invitation, if his sister's health
Had not fallen into question. — Haste, Penthea,

[17] Provided.
[18] Sea gulls.
[19] Small bits, mincemeat.
[20] Coaches.
[21] Swelling; an allusion to the horns of the cuckold.
[22] The name of these birds was often applied to wanton women.

Slack not a minute. — Lead the way, good Prophilus;
I'll follow step by step.
PRO. Your arm, fair madam.
Exeunt [*all but*] [23] BASSANES *and* GRAUSIS.
BASS. One word with your old Bawdship: th' hadst been better
Rail'd at the sins [24] thou worshipp'st than have thwarted
My will. I'll use thee cursedly.
GRAU. You dote;
You are beside yourself. A politician
In jealousy? No, y' are too gross, too vulgar.
Pish, teach not me my trade; I know my cue.
My crossing you sinks me into her trust,
By which I shall know all; my trade 's a sure one.
BASS. Forgive me, Grausis; 't was consideration
I relish'd not; [25] but have a care now.
GRAU. Fear not;
I am no new-come-to-'t.
BASS. Thy life 's upon it,
And so is mine. My agonies are infinite.
Exeunt omnes.

SCENE II [26]

Enter ITHOCLES, *alone.*

ITH. Ambition! 't is of vipers' breed: it gnaws
A passage through the womb that gave it motion.
Ambition, like a seeled [27] dove, mounts upward,
Higher and higher still, to perch on clouds,
But tumbles headlong down with heavier ruin.
So squibs and crackers fly into the air,
Then, only breaking with a noise, they vanish
In stench and smoke. Morality, appli'd
To timely practice, keeps the soul in tune,
At whose sweet music all our actions dance;
But this is form of books and school [28] tradition;
It physics not the sickness of a mind
Broken with griefs. Strong fevers are not eas'd
With counsel, but with best receipts and means;
Means, speedy means and certain; that's the cure.

Enter ARMOSTES *and* CROTOLON.

ARM. You stick, Lord Crotolon, upon a point
Too nice [29] and too unnecessary; Prophilus
Is every way desertful. I am confident
Your wisdom is too ripe to need instruction
From your son's tutelage.
CROT. Yet not so ripe,
My Lord Armostes, that it dares to dote
Upon the painted meat [30] of smooth persuasion,
Which tempts me to a breach of faith.
ITH. Not yet
Resolv'd, my Lord? Why, if your son's consent
Be so available, we'll write to Athens
For his repair to Sparta. The King's hand
Will join with our desires; he has been mov'd to 't.
ARM. Yes, and the King himself importun'd [31] Crotolon
For a dispatch.
CROT. Kings may command; their wills
Are laws not to be questioned.
ITH. By this marriage
You knit an union so devout, so hearty,
Between your loves to me and mine to yours,
As if mine own blood had an interest in it;
For Prophilus is mine, and I am his.
CROT. My Lord, my Lord! —
ITH. What, good sir? Speak your thought.
CROT. Had this sincerity been real once,
My Orgilus had not been now unwiv'd,
Nor your lost sister buried in a bride-bed.
Your uncle here, Armostes, knows this truth;
For had your father Thrasus liv'd, — but peace
Dwell in his grave! I have done.
ARM. Y' are bold and bitter.
ITH. [*aside*] 'A presses home the injury; it smarts. —
No reprehensions, Uncle; I deserve 'em. —
Yet, gentle sir, consider what the heat
Of an unsteady youth, a giddy brain,
Green indiscretion, flattery of greatness,
Rawness of judgment, wilfulness in folly,

[23] Q *omnes sed.*
[24] Gifford emends *saints.*
[25] A point I failed to appreciate.
[26] Unlocated; perhaps a room in the palace.
[27] Temporarily blinded by having had its eyelids sewed up. The dove would then soar straight up till its strength was exhausted, when it would fall at the feet of the "sportsmen."
[28] Scholastic.
[29] Fine, scrupulous.
[30] Gifford conj. *bait.*
[31] Accented on second syllable.

Thoughts vagrant as the wind and as uncertain,
Might lead a boy in years to. 'T was a fault,
A capital fault; for then I could not dive
Into the secrets of commanding love;
Since when, experience, by the extremities (in others),
Hath forc'd me collect.[32] And, trust me, Crotolon,
I will redeem those wrongs with any service
Your satisfaction can require for current.[33]

ARM. Thy acknowledgment is satisfaction. —
What would you more?

CROT. I'm conquer'd; if Euphranea
Herself admit the motion, let it be so;
I doubt not my son's liking.

ITH. Use my fortunes,
Life, power, sword, and heart — all are your own.

Enter BASSANES, PROPHILUS, CALANTHA, PENTHEA, EUPHRANEA, CHRISTALLA, PHILEMA, *and* GRAUSIS.

ARM. The Princess, with your sister.

CAL. I present 'ee
A stranger here in court, my Lord; for did not
Desire of seeing you draw her abroad,
We had not been made happy in her company.

ITH. You are a gracious princess. — Sister, wedlock
Holds too severe a passion in your nature,
Which can engross all duty to your husband,
Without attendance on so dear a mistress. —
[*To* BASSANES] 'T is not my brother's pleasure, I presume,
T' immure her in a chamber.

BASS. 'T is her will;
She governs her own hours. Noble Ithocles,
We thank the gods for your success and welfare.
Our lady has of late been indispos'd,
Else we had waited on you with the first.

ITH. How does Penthea now?

PEN. You best know, Brother,
From whom my health and comforts are deriv'd.

BASS. [*aside*] I like the answer well; 't is sad[34] and modest.
There may be tricks yet, tricks. — Have an eye, Grausis!

CAL. Now, Crotolon, the suit we join'd in must not
Fall by too long demur.

CROT. 'T is granted, Princess,
For my part.

ARM. With condition, that his son
Favor the contract.

CAL. Such delay is easy. —
The joys of marriage make thee, Prophilus,
A proud deserver of Euphranea's love,
And her of thy desert!

PRO. Most sweetly gracious!

BASS. The joys of marriage are the Heaven on earth,
Life's paradise, great Princess, the soul's quiet,
Sinews of concord, earthly immortality,
Eternity of pleasures; no restoratives
Like to a constant woman! — [*aside*] but where is she?
'T would puzzle all the gods but to create
Such a new monster. — I can speak by proof,
For I rest in Elysium; 't is my happiness.

CROT. Euphranea, how are you resolv'd,[35] speak freely,
In your affections to this gentleman?

EUPH. Nor more nor less than as his love assures me;
Which — if your liking with my brother's warrants —
I cannot but approve in all points worthy.

CROT. So, so. — [*to* PROPHILUS] I know your answer.

ITH. 'T had been pity
To sunder hearts so equally consented.

Enter HEMOPHIL.

HEM. The King, Lord Ithocles, commands your presence; —
And, fairest Princess, yours.

CAL. We will attend him.

Enter GRONEAS.

GRO. Where are the lords? All must unto the King
Without delay: the Prince of Argos —

CAL. Well, sir?

GRO. Is coming to the court, sweet lady.

CAL. How!
The Prince of Argos?

GRO. 'T was my fortune, madam,
T' enjoy the honor of these happy tidings.

ITH. Penthea! —

PEN. Brother?

ITH. Let me an hour hence
Meet you alone within the palace grove;
I have some secret with you. — Prithee, friend,

[32] Infer, "gather."
[33] As acceptable, to pass current.
[34] Sober.
[35] Decided.

Conduct her thither, and have special care
The walks be clear'd of any to disturb us.

PRO. I shall.

BASS. [*aside*] How's that?

ITH. Alone, pray be alone. —
I am your creature, Princess. — On, my Lords! *Exeunt* [*all but*] BASSANES.

BASS. Alone! alone! What means that word "alone"?
Why might not I be there? — hum! — he's her brother.
Brothers and sisters are but flesh and blood,
And this same whoreson court-ease is temptation
To a rebellion in the veins.[36] — Besides,
His fine friend Prophilus must be her guardian.
Why may not he dispatch a business nimbly
Before the other come? — or — pand'ring, pand'ring
For one another, — be't to sister, mother,
Wife, cousin, anything, — 'mongst youths of mettle
Is in request; it is so — stubborn fate!
But if I be a cuckold, and can know it,
I will be fell, and fell.

Re-enter GRONEAS.

GRO. My Lord, y' are call'd for.

BAS. Most heartily I thank ye. Where's my wife, pray?

GRO. Retir'd amongst the ladies.

BASS. Still I thank 'ee.
There's an old waiter[37] with her; saw you her too?

GRO. She sits i' th' presence-lobby fast asleep, sir.

BASS. Asleep! [a]sleep, sir!

GRO. Is your Lordship troubled?
You will not to the King?

BASS. Your humblest vassal.

GRO. Your servant, my good Lord.

BASS. I wait your footsteps.
Exeunt.

SCENE III[38]

[*Enter*] PROPHILUS [*and*] PENTHEA.

PRO. In this walk, lady, will your brother find you;
And, with your favor, give me leave a little
To work a preparation. In his fashion
I have observ'd of late some kind of slackness
To such alacrity as nature[39]
And custom took delight in; sadness grows
Upon his recreations, which he hoards
In such a willing silence, that to question
The grounds will argue [little][40] skill in friendship,
And less good manners.

PEN. Sir, I'm not inquisitive
Of secrecies without an invitation.

PRO. With pardon, lady, not a syllable
Of mine implies so rude a sense; the drift —

Enter ORGILUS, [*disguised as before*].

[*to* ORGILUS] Do thy best
To make this lady merry for an hour. *Exit.*

ORG. Your will shall be a law, sir.

PEN. Prithee, leave me;
I have some private thoughts I would account with;
Use thou thine own.

ORG. Speak on, fair nymph; our souls
Can dance as well to music of the spheres
As any's who have feasted with the gods.

PEN. Your school terms are too troublesome.

ORG. What Heaven
Refines mortality from dross of earth
But such as uncompounded beauty hallows
With glorified perfection?

PEN. Set thy wits
In a less wild proportion.

ORG. Time can never
On the white table of unguilty faith
Write counterfeit dishonor; turn those eyes,
The arrows of pure love, upon that fire
Which once rose to a flame, perfum'd with vows
As sweetly scented as the incense smoking
On Vesta's[41] [altars];[42] virgin tears,[43] like
The holiest odors, sprinkled dews to feed 'em
And to increase their fervor.

PEN. Be not frantic.

ORG. All pleasures are but mere imagination,
Feeding the hungry appetite with steam
And sight of banquet, whilst the body pines,
Not relishing the real[43] taste of food:
Such is the leanness of a heart divided
From intercourse of troth-contracted loves;
No horror should deface that precious figure
Seal'd with the lively stamp of equal souls.

[36] In the blood; *i.e.*, in the sensual nature.
[37] Servant.
[38] The grove.
[39] Gifford adds *once;* Weber supplies "as *once his* nature."
[40] Add. Weber.
[41] Q transposes *On Vesta's* and *The holiest.* Cor. Oliphant.
[42] Q *Artars.*
[43] Dissyllabic.

PEN. Away! some Fury hath bewitch'd thy tongue.
The breath of ignorance, that flies from thence,
Ripens a knowledge in me of afflictions
Above all suff'rance. — Thing of talk, begone!
Begone, without reply!

ORG. Be just, Penthea,
In thy commands; when thou send'st forth a doom
Of banishment, know first on whom it lights.
Thus I take off the shroud in which my cares
Are folded up from view of common eyes.
[*Throws off his scholar's dress.*]
What is thy sentence next?

PEN. Rash man! thou layest
A blemish on mine honor, with the hazard
Of thy too desperate life; yet I profess,
By all the laws of ceremonious wedlock,
I have not given admittance to one thought
Of female change since cruelty enforc'd
Divorce betwixt my body and my heart.
Why would you fall from goodness thus?

ORG. Oh, rather
Examine me, how I could live to say
I have been much, much wrong'd. 'T is for thy sake
I put on this imposture. Dear Penthea,
If thy soft bosom be not turn'd to marble,
Thou 't pity our calamities; my interest
Confirms me thou art mine still.

PEN. Lend your hand;
With both of mine I clasp it thus, thus kiss it,
Thus kneel before ye.

ORG. You instruct my duty.
[*They remain for some moments kneeling, with clasped hands.*]

PEN. We may stand up. — Have you aught else to urge
Of new demand? As for the old, forget it;
'T is buried in an everlasting silence,
And shall be, shall be ever. What more would ye?

ORG. I would possess my wife; the equity
Of very reason bids me.

PEN. Is that all?

ORG. Why, 't is the all of me, myself.

PEN. Remove
Your steps some distance from me. — At this space
A few words I dare change; but first put on
Your borrowed shape.

ORG. You are obey'd; 't is done.
[*He resumes his disguise.*]

PEN. How, Orgilus, by promise I was thine
The Heavens do witness; they can witness too
A rape done on my truth; how I do love thee
Yet, Orgilus, and yet, must best appear
In tendering thy freedom; for I find
The constant preservation of thy merit,
By thy not daring to attempt my fame
With injury of any loose conceit,
Which might give deeper wounds to discontents.
Continue this fair race:[44] then, though I cannot
Add to thy comfort, yet I shall more often
Remember from what fortune I am fallen,
And pity mine own ruin. — Live, live happy,
Happy in thy next choice, that thou mayst people
This barren age with virtues in thy issue!
And oh, when thou art married, think on me
With mercy, not contempt! I hope thy wife,
Hearing my story, will not scorn my fall. —
Now let us part.

ORG. Part! yet advise thee better;
Penthea is the wife to Orgilus,
And ever shall be.

PEN. Never shall nor will.

ORG. How!

PEN. Hear me; in a word I'll tell thee why.
The virgin dowry which my birth bestow'd
Is ravish'd by another; my true love
Abhors to think that Orgilus deserv'd
No better favors than a second bed.

ORG. I must not take this reason.

PEN. To confirm it
Should I outlive my bondage, let me meet
Another worse than this and less desir'd,
If, of all the men alive, thou shouldst but touch
My lip or hand again!

ORG. Penthea, now
I tell 'ee, you grow wanton in my sufferance;[45]
Come, sweet, th' art mine.

PEN. Uncivil sir, forbear!
Or I can turn affection into vengeance;
Your reputation, if you value any,
Lies bleeding at my feet. Unworthy man,
If ever henceforth thou appear in language,
Message, or letter, to betray my frailty,
I'll call thy former protestations lust,
And curse my stars for forfeit of my judgment.

[44] Course.
[45] Reckless in regard to my suffering.

Go thou, fit only for disguise, and [walk],[46]
To hide thy shame; this once I spare thy life.
I laugh at mine own confidence; my sorrows
By thee are made inferior to my fortunes.
If ever thou didst harbor worthy love,
Dare not to answer. My good genius guide me,
That I may never see thee more! — Go from me!

ORG. [I'll][47] tear my veil of politic French off,
And stand up like a man resolv'd to do:
Action, not words, shall show me. — O Penthea! *Exit* ORGILUS.

PEN. 'A sigh'd my name, sure, as he parted from me.
I fear I was too rough. Alas, poor gentleman,
'A look'd not like the ruins of his youth,
But like the ruins of those ruins. Honor,
How much we fight with weakness to preserve thee! [*Walks aside.*]

Enter BASSANES *and* GRAUSIS.

BASS. Fie on thee! damn thee, rotten maggot, damn thee!
Sleep? sleep at court? and now? Aches,[48] convulsions,
Imposthumes,[49] rheums, gouts, palsies, clog thy bones
A dozen years more yet!

GRAU. Now y' are in humors.

BASS. She's by herself: there's hope of that; she's sad too;
She's in strong contemplation; yes, and fix'd:
The signs are wholesome.

GRAU. Very wholesome, truly.

BASS. Hold your chops,[50] nightmare! — Lady, come; your brother
Is carried to his closet; you must thither.

PEN. Not well, my Lord?

BASS. A sudden fit; 't will off!
Some surfeit or disorder. How doest, dearest?

PEN. Your news is none o' th' best.

Re-enter PROPHILUS.

PRO. The chief of men,
The excellentest Ithocles, desires
Your presence, madam.

BASS. We are hasting to him.

PEN. In vain we labor in this course of life
To piece our journey out at length, or crave
Respite of breath; our home is in the grave.

BASS. Perfect philosophy![51] Then let us care
To live so, that our reckonings may fall even
When w' are to make account.

PRO. He cannot fear
Who builds on noble grounds: sickness or pain
Is the deserver's exercise;[52] and such
Your virtuous brother to the world is known.
Speak comfort to him, lady; be all gentle.
Stars fall but in the grossness of our sight;
A good man dying, th' earth doth lose a light.
Exeunt omnes.

[46] Emend. Kittredge; Q *walks*. *I.e.*, walk ever in that disguise, to hide thy shameful self.
[47] Q *I'e*.
[48] Dissyllabic.
[49] Abscesses.
[50] Jaws.
[51] Gifford and Dyce assign the rest of this speech to Penthea.
[52] Discipline.

ACT III — SCENE I[1]

Enter TECNICUS, *and* ORGILUS *in his own shape.*

TEC. Be well advis'd;[2] let not a resolution
Of giddy rashness choke the breath of reason.

ORG. It shall not, most sage master.

TEC. I am jealous;[3]
For if the borrowed shape[4] so late put on
Inferr'd a consequence, we must conclude
Some violent design of sudden nature
Hath shook that shadow[5] off, to fly upon
A new-hatch'd execution. Orgilus,
Take heed thou hast not, under our integrity,
Shrouded unlawful plots; our mortal eyes
Pierce not the secrets of your [heart]:[6] the gods
Are only privy to them.

ORG. Learned Tecnicus,
Such doubts are causeless; and, to clear the truth
From misconceit,[7] the present state commands me.
The Prince of Argos comes himself in person
In quest of great Calantha for his bride,
Our kingdom's heir; besides, mine only sister,
Euphranea, is dispos'd[8] to Prophilus;
Lastly, the King is sending letters for me
To Athens, for my quick repair to court.
Please to accept these reasons.

[1] Unlocated; probably the study of Tecnicus.
[2] Cautious.
[3] Suspicious.
[4] Costume, disguise.
[5] Disguise.
[6] Q *hearts*.
[7] Misconception.
[8] Disposed of; *i.e.*, betrothed.

TEC. Just ones, Orgilus,
Not to be contradicted; yet beware
Of an unsure foundation; no fair colors
Can fortify a building faintly jointed.
I have observ'd a growth in thy aspect [9]
Of dangerous extent, sudden, and — look to 't —
I might add, certain —
ORG. My aspect! [9] Could art
Run through mine inmost thoughts, it should not sift
An inclination there more than what suited
With justice of mine honor.
TEC. I believe it.
But know then, Orgilus, what honor is.
Honor consists not in a bare opinion
By doing any act that feeds content,
Brave in appearance, 'cause we think it brave;
Such honor comes by accident, not nature,
Proceeding from the vices of our passion,
Which makes our reason drunk; but real honor
Is the reward of virtue, and acquir'd
By justice, or by valor which for basis
Hath justice to uphold it. He then fails
In honor, who for lucre [or] [10] revenge
Commits thefts, murders, treasons, and adulteries,
With such like, by intrenching on just laws,
Whose sov'reignty is best preserv'd by justice.
Thus, as you see how honor must be grounded
On knowledge, not opinion, — for opinion
Relies on probability and accident,
But knowledge on necessity and truth, —
I leave thee to the fit consideration
Of what becomes the grace of real honor,
Wishing success to all thy virtuous meanings.
ORG. The gods increase thy wisdom, reverend oracle,
And in thy precepts make me ever thrifty! [11]
TEC. I thank thy wish. — *Exit* ORGILUS.
Much mystery of fate
Lies hid in that man's fortunes; curiosity
May lead his actions into rare attempts.
But let the gods be moderators still;
No human power can prevent their will.

Enter ARMOSTES [*with a casket*].

From whence come 'ee?
ARM. From King Amyclas — pardon
My interruption of your studies. — Here,
In this seal'd box, he sends a treasure dear
To him as his crown. 'A prays your Gravity
You would examine, ponder, sift, and bolt
The pith and circumstance of every tittle
The scroll within contains.
TEC. What is 't, Armostes?
ARM. It is the health of Sparta, the King's life,
Sinews and safety of the commonwealth:
The sum of what the oracle deliver'd
When last he visited the prophetic temple
At Delphos.[12] What his reasons are, for which,
After so long a silence, he requires
Your counsel now, grave man, his Majesty
Will soon himself acquaint you with.
TEC. [*taking the casket*] Apollo
Inspire my intellect! — The Prince of Argos
Is entertain'd?
ARM. He is; and has demanded
Our princess for his wife; which I conceive
One special cause the King importunes you
For resolution of the oracle.
TEC. My duty to the King, good peace to Sparta,
And fair day to Armostes!
ARM. Like to Tecnicus! *Exeunt.*

[SCENE II] [13]

Soft music.

A SONG

Can you paint a thought? or number
Every fancy in a slumber?
Can you count soft minutes roving
From a dial's point by moving?
Can you grasp a sigh? or, lastly,
Rob a virgin's honor chastely?
No, oh, no! yet you may
Sooner do both that and this,
This and that, and never miss,
Than by any praise display
Beauty's beauty; such a glory,
As beyond all fate, all story,
All arms, all arts,
All loves, all hearts,
Greater than those or they,
Do, shall, and must obey.

During which time enters PROPHILUS, BASSANES, PENTHEA, GRAUSIS, *passing over the stage.* BASSANES *and* GRAUSIS *enter again softly, stealing to several stands, and listen.*

BASS. All silent, calm, secure. — Grausis, no creaking?
No noise? Dost hear nothing?

[9] Accented on second syllable.
[10] Emend. Gifford; Q *of*.
[11] To avail myself of them.

[12] Delphi, in Phocis.
[13] Ithocles's apartment. The outer stage, till S. D. following l. 32.

GRAU. Not a mouse,
Or whisper of the wind.
BASS. The floor is matted;
The bedposts sure are steel or marble. — Soldiers
Should not affect, methinks, strains so effeminate:
Sounds of such delicacy are but fawnings
Upon the sloth of luxury,[14] they heighten
Cinders of covert lust up to a flame.
GRAU. What do you mean, my Lord? — speak low; that gabbling
Of yours will but undo us.
BASS. Chamber combats
Are felt, not h[e]ard.
PRO. [*within*] 'A wakes.
BASS. What's that?
ITH. [*within*] Who's there?
Sister? — All quit the room else.
BASS. 'T is consented!

Re-enter PROPHILUS.

PRO. Lord Bassanes, your brother would be private;
We must forbear; his sleep hath newly left him.
Please 'ee withdraw.
BASS. By any means;[15] 't is fit.
PRO. Pray, gentlewoman, walk too.
GRAU. Yes, I will, sir. *Exeunt omnes.*

ITHOCLES *discovered in a chair, and* PENTHEA.

ITH. Sit nearer, Sister, to me; nearer yet.
We had one father, in one womb took life,
Were brought up twins together, yet have liv'd
At distance, like two strangers. I could wish
That the first pillow whereon I was cradl'd
Had prov'd to me a grave.
PEN. You had been happy:
Then had you never known that sin of life
Which blots all following glories with a vengeance,
For forfeiting the last will of the dead,
From whom you had your being.
ITH. Sad Penthea,
Thou canst not be too cruel; my rash spleen
Hath with a violent hand pluck'd from thy bosom
A lover-blest[16] heart, to grind it into dust;
For which mine's now a-breaking.
PEN. Not yet, Heaven,
I do beseech thee! First let some wild fires
Scorch, not consume it! may the heat be cherish'd
With desires infinite, but hopes impossible!
ITH. Wrong'd soul, thy prayers are heard.
PEN. Here, lo, I breathe,
A miserable creature, led to ruin
By an unnatural brother!
ITH. I consume
In languishing affections[17] for that trespass;
Yet cannot die.
PEN. The handmaid to the wages
Of country toil drinks the untroubled streams[18]
With leaping kids and with the bleating lambs,
And so allays her thirst secure, whiles I
Quench my hot sighs with fleetings[19] of my tears.
ITH. The laborer doth eat his coarsest bread,
Earn'd with his sweat, and lies him down to sleep;
Which[20] every bit I touch turns in disgestion[21]
To gall as bitter as Penthea's curse.
Put me to any penance for my tyranny,
And I will call thee merciful.
PEN. Pray kill me;
Rid me from living with a jealous husband;
Then we will join in friendship, be again
Brother and sister. — Kill me, pray; nay, will 'ee?
ITH. How does thy lord esteem thee?
PEN. Such an one
As only you have made me: a faith-breaker,
A spotted whore — forgive me: I am one
In [act,][22] not in desires, the gods must witness.
ITH. Thou dost belie thy friend.[23]
PEN. I do not, Ithocles;
For she that's wife to Orgilus, and lives
In known adultery with Bassanes,
Is at the best a whore. Wilt kill me now?
The ashes of our parents will assume
Some dreadful figure, and appear to charge
Thy bloody guilt, that hast betray'd their name
To infamy in this reproachful match.
ITH. After my victories abroad, at home
I meet despair; ingratitude of nature
Hath made my actions monstrous. Thou shalt stand
A deity, my sister, and be worshipp'd

[14] Lust. [15] By all means.
[16] Gifford and Dyce, perhaps rightly, *love-blest*.

[17] Desires.
[18] So Gifford; Q: *The vntroubled of Country toyle, drinkes streames*.
[19] Flowings; *i.e.*, streams.
[20] Gifford and Dyce *While*.
[21] Digestion. [22] Q *art*. [23] Lover.

For thy resolved martyrdom; wrong'd maids
And married wives shall to thy hallowed shrine
Offer their orisons, and sacrifice
Pure turtles,[24] crown'd with myrtle; if thy pity
Unto a yielding brother's pressure lend
One finger but to ease it.

PEN. Oh, no more!

ITH. Death waits to waft me to the Stygian banks
And free me from this chaos of my bondage;
And till thou wilt forgive, I must endure.

PEN. Who is the saint you serve?

ITH. Friendship, or [nearness] [25]
Of birth to any but my sister, durst not
Have mov'd that question, as [26] a secret, Sister,
I dare not murmur to myself.

PEN. Let me,
By your new protestations I conjure 'ee,
Partake her name.

ITH. Her name? — 't is — 't is — I dare not.

PEN. All your respects are forg'd.[27]

ITH. They are not. — Peace!
Calantha is — the Princess — the King's daughter —
Sole heir of Sparta. — Me, most miserable,
Do I now love thee? For my injuries
Revenge thyself with bravery, and gossip
My treasons to the King's ears, do. Calantha
Knows it not yet, nor Prophilus, my nearest.

PEN. Suppose you were contracted to her, would it not
Split even your very soul to see her father
Snatch her out of your arms against her will,
And force her on the Prince of Argos?

ITH. Trouble not
The fountains of mine eyes with thine own story;
I sweat in blood for 't.

PEN. We are reconcil'd.
Alas, sir, being children, but two branches
Of one stock, 't is not fit we should divide.
Have comfort; you may find it.

ITH. Yes, in thee;
Only in thee, Penthea mine.

PEN. If sorrows
Have not too much dull'd my infected brain,
I 'll cheer invention for an active strain.[28]

ITH. Mad man! why have I wrong'd a maid so excellent?

Enter BASSANES *with a poniard;* PROPHILUS, GRONEAS, HEMOPHIL, *and* GRAUSIS.

BASS. I can forbear no longer; more, I will not.
Keep off your hands, or fall upon my point. —
Patience is tir'd; for, like a slow-pac'd ass,
Ye ride my easy nature, and proclaim
My sloth to vengeance a reproach and property.[29]

ITH. The meaning of this rudeness?

PRO. He 's distracted.

PEN. Oh, my griev'd Lord! —

GRAU. Sweet lady, come not near him;
He holds his perilous weapon in his hand
To prick 'a cares not whom nor where — see, see, see!

BASS. My birth is noble; though the popular blast
Of vanity, as giddy as thy youth,
Hath rear'd thy name up to bestride a cloud,
Or progress in the chariot of the sun,
I am no clod of trade, to lackey pride,
Nor, like your slave of expectation,[30] wait
The bawdy hinges of your doors, or whistle
For mystical conveyance to your bed-sports.

GRO. Fine humors! they become him.

HEM. How 'a stares,
Struts, puffs, and sweats! Most admirable [31] lunacy!

ITH. But that I may conceive the spirit of wine
Has took possession of your soberer custom,
I 'd say you were unmannerly.

PEN. Dear Brother! — [

BASS. Unmannerly! — mew, kitling! [32] — smooth formality
Is usher to the rankness of the blood,
But impudence bears up the train. Indeed, sir,
Your fiery mettle, or your springal [33] blaze
Of huge renown, is no sufficient royalty
To print upon my forehead the scorn, "Cuckold."

ITH. His jealousy has robb'd him of his wits;

[24] Doves.
[25] Add. Weber.
[26] Gifford emends *'tis*.
[27] All the considerations you have mentioned are feigned; *i.e.*, your new attitude toward me is not genuine.

[28] *I.e.*, I'll try to think of something that can be done.
[29] Personal characteristic.
[30] *I.e.*, attendant slave.
[31] Remarkable.
[32] Kitten.
[33] Youthful.

'A talks 'a knows not what.

BASS. Yes, and 'a knows
To whom 'a talks; to one that franks[34] his lust
In swine-security of bestial incest.

ITH. Ha, devil!

BASS. I will halloo 't; though I blush more
To name the filthiness than thou to act it.

ITH. Monster!

PRO. Sir, by our friendship —

PEN. By our bloods —
Will you quite both undo us, Brother?

GRAU. Out on him!
These are his megrims,[35] firks,[36] and melancholies.

HEM. Well said, old touchhole.

GRO. Kick him out at doors.

PEN. With favor, let me speak. — My Lord, what slackness
In my obedience hath deserv'd this rage?
Except humility and silent duty
Have drawn on your unquiet, my simplicity
Ne'er studied your vexation.

BASS. Light of beauty,
Deal not ungently with a desperate wound!
No breach of reason dares make war with her
Whose looks are sovereignty, whose breath is balm.
Oh, that I could preserve thee in fruition
As in devotion!

PEN. Sir, may every evil
Lock'd in Pandora's box show'r, in your presence,
On my unhappy head, if, since you made me
A partner in your bed, I have been faulty
In one unseemly thought against your honor!

ITH. Purge not his griefs, Penthea.

BASS. Yes, say on,
Excellent creature! — [*to* ITHOCLES] Good,[37] be not a hindrance
To peace and praise of virtue. — Oh, my senses
Are charm'd with sounds celestial! — On, dear, on:
I never gave you one ill word; say, did I?
Indeed I did not.

PEN. Nor, by Juno's forehead,
Was I e'er guilty of a wanton error.

BASS. A goddess! let me kneel.

GRAU. Alas, kind animal!

ITH. No; but for penance.

BASS. Noble sir, what is it?
With gladness I embrace it; yet, pray let not
My rashness teach you to be too unmerciful.

ITH. When you shall show good proof that manly wisdom,
Not oversway'd by passion or opinion,
Knows how to lead[38] judgment, then this lady,
Your wife, my sister, shall return in safety
Home, to be guided by you; but, till first
I can out of clear evidence approve[39] it,
She shall be my care.

BASS. Rip my bosom up,
I'll stand the execution with a constancy;
This torture is unsufferable.

ITH. Well, sir,
I dare not trust her to your fury.

BASS. But
Penthea says not so.

PEN. She needs no tongue
To plead excuse who never purpos'd wrong.

HEM. Virgin of reverence and antiquity,
Stay you behind.

GRO. [*to* GRAUSIS] The court wants not your diligence.

Exeunt [*all but*] BASSANES *and* GRAUSIS.

GRAU. What will you do, my Lord? My Lady's gone;
I am deni'd to follow.

BASS. I may see her,
Or speak to her once more?

GRAU. And feel her too, man;
Be of good cheer: she's your own flesh and bone.

BASS. Diseases desperate must find cures alike.
She swore she has been true.

GRAU. True, on my modesty.

BASS. Let him want truth who credits not her vows!
Much wrong I did her, but her brother infinite;
Rumor will voice me the contempt of manhood,
Should I run on thus. Some way I must try
To outdo art, and cry a'[40] jealousy.

Exeunt omne[*s*].

[34] Crams, feeds.
[35] Fancies.
[36] Caprices.
[37] *I.e.*, good sir.
[38] Weber conj. the addition of *your*, which Gifford silently adopts.
[39] Prove, make certain of.
[40] Cry on, exclaim against. Gifford emends *jealousy decry*.

[SCENE III] [41]

Flourish. Enter AMYCLAS, NEARCHUS *leading* CALANTHA, ARMOSTES, CROTOLON, EUPHRANEA, CHRISTALLA, PHILEMA, *and* AMELUS.

AMY. Cousin of Argos, what the Heavens have pleas'd
In their unchanging counsels to conclude
For both our kingdoms' weal, we must submit to;
Nor can we be unthankful to their bounties,
Who, when we were even creeping to our [grave],[42]
Sent us a daughter, in whose birth our hope
Continues of succession. As you are
In title next, being grandchild to our aunt,
So we in heart desire you may sit nearest
Calantha's love; since we have ever vow'd
Not to enforce affection by our will,
But by her own choice to confirm it gladly.
NEAR. You speak the nature of a right just father.
I come not hither roughly to demand
My cousin's thralldom, but to free mine own.
Report of great Calantha's beauty, virtue,
Sweetness, and singular perfections, courted
All ears to credit what I find was publish'd
By constant truth; from which, if any service
Of my desert can purchase fair construction,
This lady must command it.
CAL. Princely sir,
So well you know how to profess observance,[43]
That you instruct your hearers to become
Practitioners in duty; of which number
I'll study to be chief.
NEAR. Chief, glorious virgin,
In my devotions, as in all men's wonder.
AMY. Excellent Cousin, we deny no liberty;
Use thine own opportunities. — Armostes,
We must consult with the philosophers;
The business is of weight.
ARM. Sir, at your pleasure.
AMY. You told me, Crotolon, your son's return'd
From Athens. Wherefore comes 'a not to court
As we commanded?
CROT. He shall soon attend
Your royal will, great sir.
AMY. The marriage
Between young Prophilus and Euphranea
Tastes of too much delay.
CROT. My Lord, —
AMY. Some pleasures
At celebration of it would give life
To th' entertainment of the Prince our kinsman;
Our court wears gravity more than we relish.
ARM. Yet the Heavens smile on all your high attempts,
Without a cloud.
CROT. So may the gods protect us.
CAL. A prince a subject?
NEAR. Yes, to beauty's sceptre;
As all hearts kneel, so mine.
CAL. You are too courtly.

[*Enter*] *to them* ITHOCLES, ORGILUS, [*and*] PROPHILUS.

ITH. Your safe return to Sparta is most welcome.
I joy to meet you here, and, as occasion
Shall grant us privacy, will yield you reasons
Why I should covet to deserve the title
Of your respected friend; for, without compliment,
Believe it, Orgilus, 't is my ambition.
ORG. Your Lordship may command me, your poor servant.
ITH. [*aside*] So amorously close! — so soon! — my heart!
PRO. What sudden change is next?
ITH. Life to the King!
To whom I here present this noble gentleman,
New come from Athens. Royal sir, vouchsafe
Your gracious hand in favor of his merit.
CROT. [*aside*] My son preferr'd [44] by Ithocles!
AMY. Our bounties
Shall open to thee, Orgilus; for instance, —
Hark in thine ear, — if, out of those inventions
Which flow in Athens, thou hast there engross'd [45]
Some rarity of wit, to grace the nuptials
Of thy fair sister, and renown our court
In th' eyes of this young prince, we shall be debtor
To thy conceit: think on 't.
ORG. Your Highness honors me.
NEAR. My tongue and heart are twins.

[41] A room in the palace.
[42] Emend. Dyce; Q *graues*.
[43] Courtship.
[44] Put forward.
[45] Acquired.

CAL. A noble birth,
Becoming such a father. — Worthy Orgilus,
You are a guest most wish'd for.
ORG. May my duty
Still rise in your opinion, sacred Princess!
ITH. Euphranea's brother, sir; a gentleman
Well worthy of your knowledge.
NEAR. We embrace him,
Proud of so dear acquaintance.
AMY. All prepare
For revels and disport; the joys of Hymen,
Like Phoebus in his lustre, puts to flight
All mists of dullness. Crown the hours with gladness;
No sounds but music, no discourse but mirth!
CAL. Thine arm, I prithee, Ithocles. — Nay, good
My Lord, keep on your way; I am provided.
NEAR. I dare not disobey.
ITH. Most heavenly lady! *Exeunt.*

[SCENE IV] [46]

Enter CROTOLON [*and*] ORGILUS.

CROT. The King has spoke his mind.
ORG. His will he hath;
But were it lawful to hold plea against
The power of greatness, not the reason, haply
Such undershrubs as subjects sometimes might
Borrow of nature justice, to inform
That license sovereignty holds without check
Over a meek obedience.
CROT. How resolve you
Touching your sister's marriage? Prophilus
Is a deserving and a hopeful youth.
ORG. I envy not his merit, but applaud it;
Could wi[s]h him thrift [47] in all his best desires,
And with a willingness inleague our blood
With his, for purchase of full growth in friendship.
He never touch'd on any wrong that malic'd
The honor of our house nor stirr'd our peace.
Yet, with your favor, let me not forget
Under whose wing he gathers warmth and comfort,
Whose creature he is bound, made, and must live so.
CROT. Son, son, I find in thee a harsh condition; [48]
No courtesy can win it; 't is too rancorous.

[46] Unlocated. [47] Prosperity.
[48] State of mind.

ORG. Good sir, be not severe in your construction;
I am no stranger to such easy calms
As sit in tender bosoms. Lordly Ithocles
Hath grac'd my entertainment [49] in abundance,
Too humbly hath descended from that height
Of arrogance and spleen which wrought the rape
On griev'd Penthea's purity; his scorn
Of my untoward fortunes is reclaim'd
Unto a cou[r]tship, almost to a fawning:
I'll kiss his foot, since you will have it so.
CROT. Since I will have it so! Friend, I will have it so,
Without our ruin by your politic plots,
Or wolf of hatred snarling in your breast.
You have a spirit, sir, have ye? A familiar [50]
That posts i' th' air for your intelligence?
Some such hobgoblin hurried you from Athens,
For yet you come unsent for.
ORG. If unwelcome,
I might have found a grave there.
CROT. Sure, your business
Was soon dispatch'd, or your mind alter'd quickly.
ORG. 'T was care, sir, of my health cut short my journey;
For there a general infection
Threatens a desolation.
CROT. And I fear
Thou hast brought back a worse infection with thee —
Infection of thy mind, which, as thou say'st,
Threatens the desolation of our family.
ORG. Forbid it, our dear genius! [51] I will rather
Be made a sacrifice on Thrasus' monument,
Or kneel to Ithocles, his son, in dust,
Than woo a father's curse. My sister's marriage
With Prophilus is from my heart confirm'd;
May I live hated, may I die despis'd,
If I omit to further it in all
That can concern me!
CROT. I have been too rough.
My duty to my King made me so earnest;
Excuse it, Orgilus.
ORG. Dear sir! —

Enter to them PROPHILUS, EUPHRANEA, ITHOCLES, GRONEAS, [*and*] HEMOPHIL.

CROT. Here comes
Euphranea with Prophilus and Ithocles.

[49] Reception. [50] Spirit. [51] Tutelar deity.

ORG. Most honored! — ever famous!
ITH. Your true friend
On earth not any truer. — With smooth eyes
Look on this worthy couple; your consent
Can only make them one.
ORG. They have it. — Sister,
Thou pawn'dst to me an oath, of which engagement
I never will release thee, if thou aim'st
At any other choice than this.
EUPH. Dear Brother,
At him, or none.
CROT. To which my blessing 's added.
ORG. Which, till a greater ceremony perfect, —
Euphranea, lend thy hand, — here, take her, Prophilus. —
Live long a happy man and wife; and further,
That these in presence may conclude an omen,
Thus for a bridal song I close my wishes:

[*Sings*]

Comforts lasting, loves increasing,
Like soft hours never ceasing;
Plenty's pleasure, peace complying,
Without jars, or tongues' envying;[52]
Hearts by holy union wedded,
More than theirs by custom bedded;
Fruitful issues; life so graced,
Not by age to be defaced,
Budding, as the year ensu'th,
Every spring another youth:
All what thought can add beside
Crown this bridegroom and this bride.

PRO. You have seal'd joy close to my soul. — Euphranea,
Now I may call thee mine.
ITH. I but exchange
One good friend for another.
ORG. If these gallants
Will please to grace a poor invention
By joining with me in some slight device,
I'll venture on a strain my younger days
Have studied for delight.
HEM. With thankful willingness
I offer my attendance.
GRO. No endeavor
Of mine shall fail to show itself.
ITH. We will
All join to wait on thy directions, Orgilus.
ORG. Oh, my good Lord, your favors flow towards
A too unworthy worm; but, as you please;
I am what you will shape me.
ITH. A fast friend.
CROT. I thank thee, son, for this acknowledgment;
It is a sight of gladness.
ORG. But my duty.
Exeunt omnes.

[SCENE V][53]

Enter CALANTHA, PENTHEA, CHRISTALLA, [*and*] PHILEMA.

CAL. Whoe'er would speak with us, deny his entrance;
Be careful of our charge.
CHRIS. We shall, madam.
CAL. Except the King himself, give none admittance;
Not any.
PHIL. Madam, it shall be our care.
Exeunt [CHRISTALLA *and* PHILEMA].
CAL. Being alone, Penthea, you have granted
The opportunity you sought, and might
At all times have commanded.
PEN. 'T is a benefit
Which I shall owe your goodness even in death for.
My glass of life, sweet Princess, hath few minutes
Remaining to run down; the sands are spent;
For by an inward messenger I feel
The summons of departure short and certain.
CAL. You feel too much your melancholy.
PEN. Glories
Of human greatness are but pleasing dreams
And shadows soon decaying: on the stage
Of my mortality my youth hath acted
Some scenes of vanity, drawn out at length
By varied pleasures, sweet'ned in the mixture,
But tragical in issue. Beauty, pomp,
With every sensuality our giddiness
Doth frame an idol, are unconstant friends,
When any troubled passion makes assault
On the unguarded castle of the mind.
CAL. Contemn not your condition for the proof
Of bare opinion only. To what end
Reach all these moral texts?
PEN. To place before 'ee
A perfect mirror, wherein you may see
How weary I am of a ling'ring life,
Who count the best a misery.

[52] Malice.

[53] Calantha's apartment in the palace.

CAL. Indeed
You have no little cause; yet none so great
As to distrust a remedy.
PEN. That remedy
Must be a winding sheet, a fold of lead,
And some untrod-on corner in the earth. —
Not to detain your expectation, Princess,
I have an humble suit.
CAL. Speak; I enjoy[54] it.
PEN. Vouchsafe, then, to be my executrix,
And take that trouble on 'ee to dispose
Such legacies as I bequeath, impartially.
I have not much to give: the pains are easy;
Heaven will reward your piety, and thank it
When I am dead; for sure I must not live —
I hope I cannot.
CAL. Now, beshrew thy sadness,
Thou turn'st me too much woman. [*Weeps.*]
PEN. [*aside*] Her fair eyes
Melt into passion.[55] — Then I have assurance
Encouraging my boldness. In this paper
My will was character'd; which you, with pardon,
Shall now know from mine own mouth.
CAL. Talk on, prithee;
It is a pretty earnest.
PEN. I have left me
But three poor jewels to bequeath. The first is
My youth; for though I am much old in griefs,
In years I am a child.
CAL. To whom that [jewel][56]?
PEN. To virgin wives, such as abuse not wedlock
By freedom of desires, but covet chiefly
The pledges of chaste beds for ties of love,
Rather than ranging of their blood; and next
To married maids, such as prefer the number
Of honorable issue in their virtues
Before the flattery of delights by marriage:
May those be ever young!
CAL. A second jewel
You mean to part with?
PEN. 'T is my fame, I trust
By scandal yet untouch'd; this I bequeath
To Memory, and Time's old daughter, Truth.
If ever my unhappy name find mention
When I am fall'n to dust, may it deserve
Beseeming charity without dishonor!
CAL. How handsomely thou play'st with harmless sport
Of mere imagination! Speak the last.
I strangely like thy will.
PEN. This jewel, madam,
Is dearly precious to me; you must use
The best of your discretion to employ
This gift as I intend it.
CAL. Do not doubt me.
PEN. 'T is long agone since first I lost my heart;
Long I have liv'd without it, else for certain
I should have given that too; but instead
Of it, to great Calantha, Sparta's heir,
By service bound and by affection vow'd,
I do bequeath, in holiest rites of love,
Mine only brother, Ithocles.
CAL. What said'st thou?
PEN. Impute not, heaven-blest lady, to ambition
A faith as humbly perfect as the prayers
Of a devoted suppliant can endow it.
Look on him, Princess, with an eye of pity;
How like the ghost of what he late appear'd
'A moves before you.
CAL. [*aside*] Shall I answer here,
Or lend my ear too grossly?
PEN. First his heart
Shall fall in cinders, scorch'd by your disdain,
Ere he will dare, poor man, to ope an eye
On these divine looks, but with low-bent thoughts
Accusing such presumption; as for words,
'A dares not utter any but of service.
Yet this lost creature loves 'ee. — Be a princess
In sweetness as in blood; give him his doom,
Or raise him up to comfort.
CAL. What new change
Appears in my behavior, that thou dar'st
Tempt my displeasure?
PEN. I must leave the world
To revel [in][57] Elysium, and 't is just
To wish my brother some advantage here;
Yet, by my best hopes, Ithocles is ignorant
Of this pursuit. But if you please to kill him,
Lend him one angry look or one harsh word,
And you shall soon conclude how strong a power
Your absolute authority holds over
His life and end.
CAL. You have forgot, Penthea,
How still I have a father.
PEN. But remember
I am a sister, though to me this brother

[54] Dyce conj. *enjoin*.
[55] Sorrow.
[56] Add. Gifford.
[57] Add. Weber.

Hath been, you know, unkind, oh, most unkind!
CAL. Christalla, Philema, where are 'ee? — Lady,
Your check lies in my silence.

Re-enter CHRISTALLA *and* PHILEMA.

BOTH. Madam, here.
CAL. I think 'ee sleep, 'ee drones; wait on Penthea
Unto her lodging. — [*aside*] Ithocles? Wrong'd lady!
PEN. My reckonings are made even; death or fate
Can now nor strike too soon, nor force too late.
Exeunt.

ACT IV — SCENE I[1]

Enter ITHOCLES *and* ARMOSTES.

ITH. Forbear your inquisition; curiosity
Is of too subtle and too searching nature,
In fears of love too quick, too slow of credit.
I am not what you doubt me.[2]
ARM. Nephew, be, then,
As I would wish; — all is not right. — Good Heaven
Confirm your resolutions for dependence
On worthy ends, which may advance your quiet!
ITH. I did the noble Orgilus much injury,
But griev'd Penthea more: I now repent it —
Now, Uncle, now; this "now" is now too late.
So provident is folly in sad issue,
That after-wit, like bankrupts' debts, stand[s] tallied,
Without all possibilities of payment.
Sure, he 's an honest, very honest gentleman;
A man of single[3] meaning.
ARM. I believe it.
Yet, Nephew, 't is the tongue informs our ears;
Our eyes can never pierce into the thoughts,
For they are lodg'd too inward: — but I question
No truth in Orgilus. — The Princess, sir.
ITH. The Princess? ha!
ARM. With her the Prince of Argos.

[1] Unlocated; presumably a room in the palace.
[2] Suspect me to be.
[3] Simple, sincere.

Enter NEARCHUS *leading* CALANTHA, AMELUS, CHRISTALLA, [*and*] PHILEMA.

NEAR. Great fair one, grace my hopes with any instance
Of livery[4] from the allowance of your favor;
This little spark —
[*Attempts to take a ring from her finger.*]
CAL. A toy!
NEAR. Love feasts on toys,
For Cupid is a child; vouchsafe this bounty —
It cannot be [de]ni'd.
CAL. You shall not value,
Sweet Cousin, at a price, what I count cheap;
So cheap, that let him take it who dares stoop for 't,
And give it at next meeting to a mistress;
She 'll thank him for 't, perhaps.
Casts it to ITHOCLES.
AME. The ring, sir, is
The Princess's; I could have took it up.
ITH. Learn manners, prithee. — To the blessed owner,
Upon my knees —
[*Kneels and offers it to* CALANTHA.]
NEAR. Y' are saucy.
CAL. This is pretty!
I am, belike, "a mistress" — wondrous pretty!
Let the man keep his fortune, since he found it;
He 's worthy on 't. — On, Cousin!
ITH. [*to* AMELUS] Follow, spaniel;
I 'll force 'ee to a fawning else.
AME. You dare not.
Exeunt [*all but*] ITHOCLES *and* ARMOSTES.
ARM. My Lord, you were too forward.
ITH. Look 'ee, Uncle,
Some such there are whose liberal contents
Swarm without care in every sort of plenty;
Who after full repasts can lay them down
To sleep; and they sleep, Uncle: in which silence
Their very dreams present 'em choice of pleasures,
Pleasures — observe me, Uncle — of rare object;
Here heaps of gold, there increments of honors,
Now change of garments, then the votes of people;
Anon varieties of beauties, courting,
In flatteries of the night, exchange of dalliance —

[4] *I.e.*, by giving me something I can wear as a sign that I am in your service.

Yet these are still but dreams. Give me felicity
Of which my senses waking are partakers,
A real, visible, material happiness;
And then, too, when I stagger in expectance
Of the least comfort that can cherish life. —
I saw it, sir, I saw it; for it came
From her own hand.

ARM. The Princess threw it t'ee.

ITH. True; and she said — well I remember what —
Her cousin prince would beg it.

ARM. Yes, and parted
In anger at your taking on't.

ITH. Penthea,
Oh, thou hast pleaded with a powerful language!
I want a fee to gratify [5] thy merit;
But I will do —

ARM. What is't you say?

ITH. In anger!
In anger let him part; for could his breath,
Like whirlwinds, toss such servile slaves as lick
The dust his footsteps print into a vapor,
It durst not stir a hair of mine: it should not;
I'd rend it up by th' roots first. To be anything
Calantha smiles on, is to be a blessing
More sacred than a petty prince of Argos
Can wish to equal, or in worth or title.

ARM. Contain yourself, my Lord: Ixion, aiming
To embrace Juno, bosom'd but a cloud,
And begat centaurs; 't is an useful moral.
Ambition hatch'd in clouds of mere opinion
Proves but in birth a prodigy.[6]

ITH. I thank 'ee;
Yet, with your licence,[7] I should seem uncharitable
To gentler fate, if, relishing the dainties
Of a soul's settled peace, I were so feeble
Not to digest it.

ARM. He deserves small trust
Who is not privy-counsellor to himself.

Re-enter NEARCHUS, ORGILUS, *and* AMELUS.

NEAR. Brave me!

ORG. Your Excellence mistakes his temper;
For Ithocles in fashion of his mind
Is beautiful, soft, gentle, the clear mirror
Of absolute perfection.

AME. Was't your modesty
Term'd any of the Prince his servants "spaniel"?
Your nurse, sure, taught you other language.

ITH. Language!

NEAR. A gallant man at arms is here, a doctor
In feats of chivalry, blunt and rough-spoken,
Vouchsafing not the fustian of civility,
Which [less] [8] rash spirits style good manners!

ITH. Manners!

ORG. No more, illustrious sir; 't is matchless Ithocles.

NEAR. You might have understood who I am.

ITH. Yes.
I did; else — but the presence [9] calm'd th' affront —
Y' are cousin to the Princess.

NEAR. To the King, too;
A certain instrument that lent supportance
To your colossic greatness — to that King, too,
You might have added.

ITH. There is more divinity
In beauty than in majesty.

ARM. O fie, fie!

NEAR. This odd youth's pride turns heretic in loyalty.
Sirrah! low mushrooms never rival cedars.

Exeunt NEARCHUS *and* AMELUS.

ITH. Come back! — What pitiful dull thing am I
So to be tamely scolded at! come back! —
Let him come back, and echo once again
That scornful sound of "mushroom"! painted colts —
Like heralds' coats gilt o'er with crowns and sceptres — [10]
May bait a muzzled lion.

ARM. Cousin, Cousin,
Thy tongue is not thy friend.

ORG. In point of honor
Discretion knows no bounds. Amelus told me
'T was all about a little ring.

ITH. A ring
The Princess threw away, and I took up.
Admit she threw't to me, what arm of brass
Can snatch it hence? No; could 'a grind the hoop
To powder, 'a might sooner reach my heart

[5] Reward.
[6] Monstrosity.
[7] If you will allow me to say so.

[8] Add. Gifford. [9] Of royalty.
[10] "Our old writers used *colt* . . . for a compound of rudeness and folly." (Gifford.) Lions were supposed to fear royalty (and, here, its symbols), as that true lion, Falstaff, makes plain in Shakespeare's *i Henry IV*, II, iv, 299 ff.

Than steal and wear one dust on 't. — Orgilus,
I am extremely wrong'd.
ORG. A lady's favor
Is not to be so slighted.
ITH. Slighted!
ARM. Quiet
These vain unruly passions, which will render ye
Into a madness.
ORG. Griefs will have their vent.

Enter TECNICUS [*with a scroll*].

ARM. Welcome; thou com'st in season, reverend man,
To pour the balsam of a [suppling] [11] patience
Into the festering wound of ill-spent fury.
ORG. [*aside*] What makes he here?
TEC. The hurts are yet but [12] mortal,
Which shortly will prove deadly. To the King,
Armostes, see in safety thou deliver
This seal'd-up counsel; bid him with a constancy
Peruse the secrets of the gods. — O Sparta,
O Lacedaemon! double-nam'd, but one
In fate: when kingdoms reel, — mark well my saw, —
Their heads must needs be giddy. Tell the King
That henceforth he no more must inquire after
My aged head; Apollo wills it so.
I am for Delphos.
ARM. Not without some conference
With our great master?
TEC. Nevermore to see him;
A greater prince commands me. — Ithocles,
When youth is ripe, and age from time doth part,
The lifeless trunk shall wed the broken heart.
ITH. What 's this, if understood?
TEC. List, Orgilus;
Remember what I told thee long before;
These tears shall be my witness.
ARM. 'Las, good man!
TEC. *Let craft with courtesy awhile confer;*
Revenge proves its own executioner.
ORG. Dark sentences are for Apollo's priests;
I am not Oedipus.[13]
TEC. My hour is come;
Cheer up the King; farewell to all. — O Sparta,
O Lacedaemon! *Exit* TECNICUS.
ARM. If prophetic fire
Have warm'd this old man's bosom, we might construe
His words to fatal sense.
ITH. Leave to the powers
Above us the effects of their decrees;
My burthen lies within me: servile fears
Prevent no great effects. — Divine Calantha!
ARM. The gods be still propitious!
Exeunt [ITHOCLES *and* ARMOSTES].
ORG. Something oddly
The book-man prated, yet 'a talk'd it weeping:
Let craft with courtesy a while confer;
Revenge proves its own executioner.
Con it again; for what? It shall not puzzle me;
'T is dotage of a withered brain. — Penthea
Forbade me not her presence; I may see her,
And gaze my fill. Why see her, then, I may,
When, if I faint to speak, I must be silent.
Exit ORGILUS.

[SCENE II] [14]

Enter BASSANES, GRAUSIS, *and* PHULAS.

BASS. Pray, use your recreations, all the service
I will expect is quietness amongst 'ee;
Take liberty at home, abroad, at all times,
And in your charities appease the gods,
Whom I, with my distractions, have offended.
GRAU. Fair blessings on thy heart!
PHU. [*aside*] Here 's a rare change!
My Lord, to cure the itch, is surely gelded;
The cuckold in conceit [15] hath cast [16] his horns.
BASS. Betake 'ee to your several occasions;
And wherein I have heretofore been faulty,
Let your constructions mildly pass it over.
Henceforth I 'll study reformation, — more
I have not for employment.
GRAU. Oh, sweet man!
Thou art the very Honeycomb of Honesty.[17]
PHU. The Garland of Good-will. — Old lady, hold up
Thy reverend snout, and trot behind me softly,

[11] Emend. Gifford; Weber emends *supple;* Q *supplying*.
[12] Gifford conj. *not*. If "but" is right, "mortal" must = threatening death, and "deadly" = actually causing death. (Kittredge.)
[13] Who solved the riddle of the Sphinx.
[14] A room in the house of Bassanes.
[15] Imagination.
[16] Shed.
[17] "Like the 'Garland of Good Will' . . . probably one of the popular miscellanies of the day." (Gifford.) On the former work see introductory note.

As it becomes a moil [18] of ancient carriage.

Exeunt [GRAUSIS *and* PHULAS].

BASS. Beasts, only capable of sense, enjoy
The benefit of food and ease with thankfulness,
Such silly creatures, with a grudging, kick not
Against the portion nature hath bestow'd :
But men, endow'd with reason and the use
Of reason, to distinguish from the chaff
Of abject scarcity the quintessence,
Soul, and elixir of the earth's abundance,
The treasures of the sea, the air, nay, heaven,
Repining at these glories of creation,
Are verier beasts than beasts ; and of those beasts
The worst am I : I, who was made a monarch
Of what a heart could wish for, a chaste wife,
Endeavor'd what in me lay to pull down
That temple built for adoration only,
And level 't in the dust of causeless scandal.
But, to redeem a sacrilege so impious,
Humility shall pour before the deities
I have incens'd a [largess] [19] of more patience
Than their displeased altars can require.
No tempests of commotion shall disquiet
The calms of my composure.

Enter ORGILUS.

ORG. I have found thee,
Thou patron of more horrors than the bulk
Of manhood, hoop'd about with ribs of iron,
Can cram within thy breast. Penthea, Bassanes,
Curs'd by thy jealousies, — more, by thy dotage, —
Is left a prey to words.
BASS. Exercise
Your trials for addition to my penance ;
I am resolv'd.
ORG. Play not with misery
Past cure : some angry minister of fate
Hath depos'd the empress of her soul, her reason,
From its most proper throne ; but, what's the miracle
More new, I, I have seen it, and yet live !
BASS. You may delude my senses, not my judgment ;
'T is anchor'd into a firm resolution ;
Dalliance of mirth or wit can ne'er unfix it :
Practice [20] yet further.
ORG. May thy death of love to her
Damn all thy comforts to a lasting fast
From every joy of life ! Thou barren rock,
By thee we have bee[n] split in ken [21] of harbor.

Enter ITHOCLES, PENTHEA *her hair about her ears,* [ARMOSTES,] PHILEMA, [*and*] CHRISTALLA.

ITH. Sister, look up ; your Ithocles, your brother,
Speaks t' ee ; why do you weep ? Dear, turn not from me. —
Here is a killing sight ; lo, Bassanes,
A lamentable object !
ORG. Man, dost see 't ?
Sports are more gamesome ; am I yet in merriment ?
Why dost not laugh ?
BASS. Divine and best of ladies,
Please to forget my outrage ! Mercy ever
Cannot but lodge under a roo[f] so excellent.
I have cast off that cruelty of frenzy
Which once appear'd, [impostor],[22] and then juggled
To cheat my sleeps of rest.
ORG. Was I in earnest ?
PEN. Sure, if we were all Sirens, we should sing pitifully.
And 't were a comely music, when in parts
One sung another's knell. The turtle [23] sighs
When he hath lost his mate ; and yet some say
'A must be dead first. 'T is a fine deceit
To pass away in a dream ; indeed, I 've slept
With mine eyes open a great while. No falsehood
Equals a broken faith ; there 's not a hair
Sticks on my head but, like a leaden plummet,
It sinks me to the grave. I must creep thither ;
The journey is not long.
ITH. But, thou, Penthea,
Hast many years, I hope, to number yet,
Ere thou canst travel that way.
BASS. Let the [sun] [24] first
Be wrapp'd up in an everlasting darkness,
Before the light of nature, chiefly form'd
For the whole world's delight, feel an eclipse
So universal !
ORG. Wisdom, look 'ee, begins
To rave ! — Art thou mad too, antiquity ?
PEN. Since I was first a wife, I might have been

[18] Mule. [19] Emend. Weber ; Q *largenesse.*
[20] *I.e.*, try me.

[21] Within sight.
[22] Emend. Weber ; Q *Impostors ;* Gifford omits comma and reads *imposture.*
[23] Dove.
[24] Emend. Weber ; Q *Swan.*

Mother to many pretty prattling babes;
They would have smil'd when I smil'd, and for certain
I should have cri'd when they cri'd: — truly, Brother,
My father would have pick'd me out a husband,
And then my little ones had been no bastards;
But 't is too late for me to marry now —
I am past childbearing; 't is not my fault.

BASS. Fall on me, if there be a burning Aetna,
And bury me in flames! Sweats hot as sulphur
Boil through my pores! Affliction hath in store
No torture like to this.

ORG. Behold a patience!
Lay by thy whining gray dissimulation:
Do something worth a chronicle; show justice
Upon the author of this mischief; dig out
The jealousies that hatch'd this thraldom first
With thine own poniard. Every antic rapture
Can roar as thine does.

ITH. Orgilus, forbear.

BASS. Disturb him not; it is a talking motion[25]
Provided for my torment. What a fool am I
To bawdy[26] passion! Ere I'll speak a word,
I will look on and burst.

PEN. [*to* ORGILUS] I lov'd you once.

ORG. Thou didst, wrong'd creature, in despite of malice;
For it I love thee ever.

PEN. Spare your hand;
Believe me, I'll not hurt it.

ORG. Pain my heart too.

[PEN.][27] Complain not though I wring it hard. I'll kiss it;
Oh, 't is a fine soft palm! — Hark, in thine ear;
Like whom do I look, prithee? — Nay, no whispering.
Goodness! we had been happy; too much happiness
Will make folk proud, they say — but that is he — *Points at* ITHOCLES.
And yet he paid for 't home; alas, his heart
Is crept into the cabinet of the Princess;
We shall have points[28] and bride-laces.[29] Remember,
When we last gather'd roses in the garden,
I found my wits; but truly you lost yours.
That 's he, and still 't is he.

ITH. Poor soul, how idly
Her fancies guide her tongue!

BASS. [*aside*] Keep in, vexation,
And break not into clamor.

ORG. [*aside*] She has tutor'd me:
Some powerful inspiration checks my laziness. —
Now let me kiss your hand, griev'd beauty.

PEN. Kiss it. —
Alack, alack, his lips be wondrous cold.
Dear soul, h' as lost his color: have 'ee seen
A straying heart? All crannies! every drop
Of blood is turn'd to an amethyst,
Which married bachelors hang in their ears.

ORG. Peace usher her into Elysium! —
If this be madness, madness is an oracle.
Exit ORGILUS.

ITH. Christalla, Philema, when slept my sister? —
Her ravings are so wild.

CHRIS. Sir, not these ten days.

PHIL. We watch by her continually; besides,
We can not any way pray her to eat.

BASS. Oh, misery of miseries!

PEN. Take comfort;
You may live well, and die a good old man.
By yea and nay, an oath not to be broken,
If you had join'd our hands once in the temple, —
'T was since my father di'd, for had he liv'd
He would have done 't, — I must have call'd you father. —
Oh, my wrack'd honor! ruin'd by those tyrants,
A cruel brother and a desperate dotage!
There is no peace left for a ravish'd wife
Widow'd by lawless marriage; to all memory
Penthea's, poor Penthea's name is strumpeted.
But since her blood was season'd by the forfeit
Of noble shame with mixtures of pollution,
Her blood — 't is just — be henceforth never height'ned
With taste of sustenance! Starve; let that fullness
Whose pleurisy[30] hath fever'd faith and modesty —
Forgive me; oh, I faint!

ARM. Be not so wilful,
Sweet Niece, to work thine own destruction.

[25] Puppet. [26] Dyce emends *bandy*.
[27] Supplied by Weber.
[28] Tagged laces.
[29] Pieces of silk or lace used to tie the sprigs of rosemary in use at weddings.
[30] Excess.

ITH. Nature
Will call her daughter monster! — What! not can?
Refuse the only ordinary means
Which are ordain'd for life? Be not, my sister,
A murd'ress to thyself. — Hear'st thou this, Bassanes?
BASS. Fo! I am busy; for I have not thoughts
Enow to think; all shall be well anon.
'T is tumbling in my head; there is a mastery
In art to fatten and keep smooth the outside,
Yes, and to comfort up the vital spirits
Without the help of food; fumes or perfumes,
Perfumes or fumes. Let her alone; I'll search out
The trick on 't.
PEN. Lead me gently; Heavens reward ye.
Griefs are sure friends: they leave without control
Nor cure nor comforts for a leprous soul.
Exeunt the Maids *supporting* PENTHEA.
BASS. I grant t 'ee; and will put in practice instantly
What you shall still admire: 't is wonderful,
'T is super-singular, not to be match'd;
Yet, when I've done 't, I've done 't: — ye shall all thank me. *Exit* BASSANES.
ARM. The sight is full of terror.
ITH. On my soul
Lies such an infinite clog of massy dullness,
As that I have not sense enough to feel it. —
See, Uncle, th' [angry] [31] thing returns again;
Shall 's welcome him with thunder? We are haunted,
And must use exorcism to conjure down
This spirit of malevolence.
ARM. Mildly, Nephew.

Enter NEARCHUS *and* AMELUS.

NEAR. I come not, sir, to chide your late disorder,
Admitting that th' inurement to a roughness
In soldiers of your years and fortunes, chiefly,
So lately prosperous, hath not yet shook off
The custom of the war in hours of leisure;
Nor shall you need excuse, since y' are to render
Account to that fair excellence, the Princess,
Who in her private gallery expects it
From your own mouth alone; I am a messenger
But to her pleasure.

[31] Weber; Q *augury*.

ITH. Excellent Nearchus,
Be prince still of my services, and conquer
Without the combat of dispute; I honor 'ee.
NEAR. The King is on a sudden indispos'd;
Physicians are call'd for; 't were fit, Armostes,
You should be near him.
ARM. Sir, I kiss your hands.
Exeunt [ITHOCLES *and* ARMOSTES].
NEAR. Amelus, I perceive Calantha's bosom
Is warm'd with other fires than such as can
Take strength from any fuel of the love
I might address to her. Young Ithocles,
Or ever I mistake, is lord ascendant
Of her devotions; one, to speak him truly,
In every disposition nobly fashioned.
AME. But can your Highness brook to be so rivall'd,
Considering th' inequality of the persons?
NEAR. I can, Amelus; for affections injur'd
By tyranny or rigor of compulsion,
Like tempest-threat'ned trees unfirmly rooted,
Ne'er spring to timely growth. Observe, for instance,
Life-spent Penthea and unhappy Orgilus.
AME. How does your Grace determine?
NEAR. To be jealous
In public of what privately I'll further;
And though they shall not know, yet they shall find it. *Exeunt omnes.*

[SCENE III] [32]

Enter HEMOPHIL *and* GRONEAS *leading* AMYCLAS, *and placing him in a chair; followed by* ARMOSTES [*with a box*], CROTOLON, *and* PROPHILUS.

AMY. Our daughter is not near?
ARM. She is retired, sir,
Into her gallery.
AMY. Where 's the Prince our cousin?
PRO. New walk'd into the grove, my Lord.
AMY. All leave us
Except Armostes, and you, Crotolon;
We would be private.
PRO. Health unto your Majesty!
Exeunt PROPHILUS, HEMOPHIL, *and* GRONEAS.
AMY. What! Tecnicus is gone?
ARM. He is, to Delphos;
And to your royal hands presents this box.
AMY. Unseal it, good Armostes; therein lies
The secrets of the oracle; out with it.
[ARMOSTES *takes out the scroll.*]
Apollo live our patron! Read, Armostes.

[32] A room in the palace.

Arm. [*reads.*] "The plot in which the vine takes root
Begins to dry from head to foot;
The stock soon withering, want of sap
Doth cause to quail [33] the budding grape;
But from the neighboring elm a dew
Shall drop, and feed the plot anew."
Amy. That is the oracle. What exposition
Makes the philosopher?
Arm. This brief one only:
[*Reads.*] "The plot is Sparta, the dri'd vine the King;
The quailing grape his daughter; but the thing
Of most importance, not to be reveal'd,
Is a near prince, the elm; the rest conceal'd.
Tecnicus."
Amy. Enough; although the opening [34] of this riddle
Be but itself a riddle, yet we construe
How near our lab'ring age draws to a rest.
But must Calantha quail too, that young grape
Untimely budded? I could mourn for her;
Her tenderness hath yet deserv'd no rigor
So to be cross'd by fate.
Arm. You misapply, sir, —
With favor let me speak it, — what Apollo
Hath clouded in hid sense. I here conjecture
Her marriage with some neighb'ring prince, the dew
Of which befriending elm shall ever strengthen
Your subjects with a sovereignty of power.
Crot. Besides, most gracious Lord, the pith of oracles
Is to be then digested when th' events
Expound their truth, not brought as soon to light
As utter'd. Truth is child of Time; and herein
I find no scruple, rather cause of comfort,
With unity of kingdoms.
Amy. May it prove so,
For weal of this dear nation! — Where is Ithocles? —
Armostes, Crotolon, when this wither'd vine
Of my frail carcass on the funeral pile
Is fir'd into its ashes, let that young man
Be hedg'd about still with your cares and loves.
Much owe I to his worth, much to his service. —
Let such as wait come in now.
Arm. All attend here!

Enter Ithocles, Calantha, Prophilus, Orgilus, Euphranea, Hemophil, *and* Groneas.

Cal. Dear sir! King! Father!
Ith. O my royal master!
Amy. Cleave not my heart, sweet twins of my life's solace,
With your forejudging fears; there is no physic
So cunningly restorative to cherish
The fall of age, or call back youth and vigor,
As your consents in duty. I will shake off
This languishing disease of time, to quicken
Fresh pleasures in these drooping hours of sadness.
Is fair Euphranea married yet to Prophilus?
Crot. This morning, gracious Lord.
Org. This very morning;
Which, with your Highness' leave, you may observe, too.
Our sister looks, methinks, mirthful and sprightly,
As if her chaster fancy could already
Expound the riddle of her gain in losing
A trifle maids know only that they know not. —
Pish! prithee, blush not; 't is but honest change
Of fashion in the garment, loose for strait,
And so the modest maid is made a wife.
Shrewd business — is't not, Sister?
Euph. You are pleasant.
Amy. We thank thee, Orgilus; this mirth becomes thee.
But wherefore sits the court in such a silence?
A wedding without revels is not seemly.
Cal. Your late indisposition, sir, forbade it.
Amy. Be it thy charge, Calantha, to set forward
The bridal sports, to which I will be present;
If not, at least consenting. — Mine own Ithocles,
I have done little for thee yet.
Ith. Y' have built me
To the full height I stand in.
Cal. [*aside*] Now or never! — [35]
May I propose a suit?
Amy. Demand, and have it.
Cal. Pray, sir, give me this young man, and no further
Account him yours than he deserves in all things

[33] Wither.

[34] Exposition.

[35] So Weber, *et al.* Q has no punctuation here.

To be thought worthy mine. I will esteem him
According to his merit.
Amy. Still th' art my daughter,
Still grow'st upon my heart. — [*to* Ithocles]
Give me thine hand. —
Calantha, take thine own; in noble actions
Thou 'lt find him firm and absolute. — I would not
Have parted with thee, Ithocles, to any
But to a mistress who is all what I am.
Ith. A change, great King, most wish'd for, 'cause the same.
Cal. [*aside to* Ithocles] Th' art mine. Have I now kept my word?
Ith. [*aside to* Calantha] Divinely.
Org. Rich fortunes, guard to favor of a princess,[36]
Rock thee, brave man, in ever-crowned plenty!
Y' are minion[37] of the time; be thankful for it. —
[*aside*] Ho! here 's a swing in destiny — apparent!
The youth is up on tiptoe, yet may stumble.
Amy. On to your recreations. — Now convey me
Unto my bedchamber; none on his forehead
Wear a distempered look.
Omnes. The gods preserve 'ee!
Cal. [*aside to* Ithocles] Sweet, be not from my sight.
Ith. [*aside to* Calantha] My whole felicity!
Exeunt, carrying out of the King. Orgilus *stays* Ithocles.
Org. Shall I be bold, my Lord?
Ith. Thou canst not, Orgilus:
Call me thine own; for Prophilus must henceforth
Be all thy sister's. Friendship, though it cease not
In marriage, yet is oft at less command
Than when a single freedom can dispose it.
Org. Most right, my most good Lord, my most great Lord,
My gracious princely Lord, I might add, royal.
Ith. Royal! A subject royal?
Org. Why not, pray, sir?
The sovereignty of kingdoms in their nonage
Stoop'd to desert, not birth; there 's as much merit
In clearness of affection as in puddle
Of generation: you have conquer'd love
Even in the loveliest; if I greatly err not,
The son of Venus hath bequeath'd his quiver
To Ithocles his manage,[38] by whose arrows
Calantha's breast is open'd.
Ith. Can 't be possible?
Org. I was myself a piece of suitor once,
And forward in preferment too; so forward
That, speaking truth, I may without offence, sir,
Presume to whisper that my hopes, and — hark 'ee —
My certainty of marriage, stood assured
With as firm footing — by your leave — as any's
Now at this very instant — but —
Ith. 'T is granted;
And for a league of privacy between us,
Read o'er my bosom and partake a secret:
The Princess is contracted mine.
Org. Still, why not?
I now applaud her wisdom. When your kingdom
Stands seated in your will, secure and settled,
I dare pronounce you will be a just monarch;
Greece must admire and tremble.
Ith. Then the sweetness
Of so imparadis'd a comfort, Orgilus!
It is to banquet with the gods.
Org. The glory
Of numerous children, potency of nobles,
Bent knees, hearts pav'd to tread on!
Ith. With a friendship
So dear, so fast as thine.
Org. I am unfitting
For office; but for service —
Ith. We 'll distinguish
Our fortunes merely in the title, partners
In all respects else but the bed.
Org. The bed!
Forfend it Jove's own jealousy! — till lastly
We slip down in the common earth together,
And there our beds are equal; save some monument
To show this was the king, and this the subject. — *Soft, sad music.*
List, what sad sounds are these? — extremely sad ones.
Ith. Sure, from Penthea's lodgings.

[36] So Sherman; Q omits the comma after *fortunes*; Gifford-Dyce: "Rich fortunes guard, *the* favour of a princess Rock thee . . ."
[37] Darling, favorite.
[38] Ithocles's management.

ORG. Hark! a voice too.

A SONG [*within*]

Oh, no more, no more, too late
Sighs are spent; the burning tapers
Of a life as chaste as fate,
Pure as are unwritten papers,
Are burnt out: no heat, no light
Now remains; 't is ever night.

Love is dead; let lovers' eyes,
Lock'd in endless dreams,
Th' extremes of all extremes,
Ope no more, for now Love dies,
Now Love dies, — implying
Love's martyrs must be ever, ever dying.

ITH. Oh, my misgiving heart!
ORG. A horrid stillness
Succeeds this deathful air; let's know the reason.
Tread softly; there is mystery in mourning.
Exeunt.

SCENE [IV] [39]

Enter CHRISTALLA *and* PHILEMA, *bringing in* PENTHEA *in a chair, veil'd; two other* Servants *placing two chairs, one on the one side, and the other with an engine* [40] *on the other. The* Maids *sit down at her feet, mourning. The* Servants *go out: meet them* ITHOCLES *and* ORGILUS.

SER. [*aside to* ORGILUS] 'T is done; that on her right hand.
ORG. Good; begone.
[*Exeunt* Servants.]
ITH. Soft peace enrich this room!
ORG. How fares the lady?
PHIL. Dead!
CHRIS. Dead!
PHIL. Starv'd!
CHRIS. Starv'd!
ITH. Me miserable!
ORG. Tell us
How parted she from life.
PHIL. She call'd for music,
And begg'd some gentle voice to tune a farewell
To life and griefs. Christalla touch'd the lute;
I wept the funeral song.
CHRIS. Which scarce was ended
But her last breath seal'd up these hollow sounds:
"Oh, cruel Ithocles and injur'd Orgilus!"
So down she drew her veil, so di'd.
ITH. So di'd!
ORG. Up! you are messengers of death; go from us;
Here's woe enough to court without a prompter.
Away; and — hark ye — till you see us next,
No syllable that she is dead. — Away,
Keep a smooth brow.
Exeunt PHILEMA *and* CHRISTALLA.
My Lord, —
ITH. Mine only sister!
Another is not left me.
ORG. Take that chair;
I'll seat me here in this: between us sits
The object of our sorrows; some few tears
We'll part among us. I perhaps can mix
One lamentable story to prepare 'em. —
There, there; sit there, my Lord.
ITH. Yes, as you please.
ITHOCLES *sits down, and is catch'd in the engine.*
What means this treachery?
ORG. Caught! you are caught,
Young master; 't is thy throne of coronation,
Thou fool of greatness! See, I take this veil off;
Survey a beauty wither'd by the flames
Of an insulting [41] Phaëthon, her brother.
ITH. Thou mean'st to kill me basely.
ORG. I foreknew
The last act of her life, and train'd thee hither
To sacrifice a tyrant to a turtle.
You dreamt of kingdoms, did 'ee? How to bosom
The delicacies of a youngling princess;
How with this nod to grace that subtle courtier,
How with that frown to make this noble tremble,
And so forth; whiles Penthea's groans and tortures,
Her agonies, her miseries, afflictions,
Ne'er touch'd upon your thought. As for my injuries,
Alas, they were beneath your royal pity;
But yet they liv'd, thou proud man, to confound thee.
Behold thy fate; this steel!
ITH. Strike home! A courage
As keen as thy revenge shall give it welcome;
But prithee faint not; if the wound close up,
Tent [42] it with double force, and search it deeply.

[39] Penthea's apartment. [40] Mechanism.

[41] See on I, i, 50. [42] Probe.

Thou look'st that I should whine and beg compassion,
As loth to leave the vainness of my glories.
A statelier resolution arms my confidence,
To cozen thee of honor; neither could I
With equal trial of unequal fortune
By hazard of a duel; 't were a bravery
Too mighty for a slave intending murder.
On to the execution, and inherit
A conflict with thy horrors.

ORG. By Apollo,
Thou talk'st a goodly language! for requital
I will report thee to thy mistress richly.
And take this peace along: some few short minutes
Determin'd, my resolves shall quickly follow
Thy wrathful ghost; then, if we tug for mastery,
Penthea's sacred eyes shall lend new courage.
Give me thy hand: be healthful in thy parting
From lost mortality! thus, thus I free it.
Kills him.

ITH. Yet, yet, I scorn to shrink.

ORG. Keep up thy spirit:
I will be gentle even in blood; to linger
Pain, which I strive to cure, were to be cruel.
[*Stabs him again.*]

ITH. Nimble in vengeance, I forgive thee. Follow
Safety, with best success: Oh, may it prosper! —
Penthea, by thy side thy brother bleeds;
The earnest of his wrongs to thy forc'd faith.
Thoughts of ambition, or delicious banquet
With beauty, youth, and love, together perish
In my last breath, which on the sacred altar
Of a long-look'd-for peace — now — moves — to Heaven.
[*Dies.*] [43]

ORG. Farewell, fair spring of manhood! Henceforth welcome
Best expectation of a noble suff'rance.
I'll lock the bodies safe, till what must follow
Shall be approv'd. — Sweet twins, shine stars for ever! —
In vain they build their hopes whose life is shame;
No monument lasts but a happy name. —
Exit ORGILUS.

[43] Q *moritur.*

ACT V — SCENE I [1]

Enter BASSANES, *alone.*

BASS. Athens, to Athens I have sent, the nursery
Of Greece for learning and the fount of knowledge;
For here in Sparta there's not left amongst us
One wise man to direct; we're all turn'd madcaps.
'T is said Apollo is the god of herbs;
Then certainly he knows the virtue of 'em.
To Delphos I have sent, too. If there can be
A help for nature, we are sure yet.

Enter ORGILUS.

ORG. Honor
Attend thy counsels ever!

BASS. I beseech thee
With all my heart, let me go from thee quietly;
I will not aught to do with thee, of all men.
The [doubles] [2] of a hare, or in a morning
Salutes from a splay-footed witch, to drop
Three drops of blood at th' nose just and no more,
Croaking of ravens, or the screech of owls,
Are not so boding mischief as thy crossing
My private meditations. Shun me, prithee;
And if I cannot love thee heartily,
I'll love thee as well as I can.

ORG. Noble Bassanes,
Mistake me not.

BASS. Phew! then we shall be troubled.
Thou wert ordain'd my plague — Heaven make me thankful,
And give me patience too, Heaven, I beseech thee.

ORG. Accept a league of amity; for henceforth,
I vow, by my best genius, [3] in a syllable,
Never to speak vexation. I will study
Service and friendship, with a zealous sorrow
For my past incivility towards 'ee.

BASS. Heyday! good words, good words! I must believe 'em,
And be a coxcomb [4] for my labor.

ORG. Use not
So hard a language; your misdoubt is causeless.

[1] Unlocated; presumably a room in the house of Bassanes.
[2] *I.e.*, the crossing of one's path. Emend. Gifford (silently). Q *doublers*.
[3] See on III, iv, 46.
[4] Fool.

For instance, if you promise to put on
A constancy of patience, such a patience
As chronicle or history ne'er mentioned,
As follows not example, but shall stand
A wonder and theme for imitation,
The first, the index [5] pointing to a second,
I will acquaint 'ee with an unmatch'd secret,
Whose knowledge to your griefs shall set a period.

BASS. Thou canst not, Orgilus; 't is in the power
Of the gods only; yet, for satisfaction,
Because I note an earnest in thine utterance,
Unforc'd and naturally free, be resolute [6]
The virgin bays shall not withstand the lightning
With a more careless danger than my constancy
The full of thy relation. Could it move
Distraction in a senseless marble statue,
It should find me a rock. I do expect now
Some truth of unheard moment.

ORG. To your patience
You must add privacy, as strong in silence
As mysteries lock'd up in Jove's own bosom.

BASS. A skull hid in the earth a treble age
Shall sooner prate.

ORG. Lastly, to such direction
As the severity of a glorious action
Deserves to lead your wisdom and your judgment,
You ought to yield obedience.

BASS. With assurance
Of will and thankfulness.

ORG. With manly courage
Please, then, to follow me.

BASS. Where'er, I fear not.

Exeunt omnes.

SCENE II [7]

Loud music. Enter GRONEAS *and* HEMOPHIL, *leading* EUPHRANEA; CHRISTALLA *and* PHILEMA, *leading* PROPHILUS; NEARCHUS *supporting* CALANTHA; CROTOLON *and* AMELUS. *Cease loud music; all make a stand.*[8]

CAL. We miss our servant Ithocles and Orgilus;
On whom attend they?

CROT. My son, gracious Princess,
Whisper'd some new device, to which these revels
Should be but usher, wherein I conceive
Lord Ithocles and he himself are actors.

CAL. A fair excuse for absence; as for Bassanes,
Delights to him are troublesome. Armostes
Is with the King?

CROT. He is.

CAL. On to the dance! —
Dear Cousin, hand you the bride; the bridegroom must be
Intrusted to my courtship. Be not jealous,
Euphranea; I shall scarcely prove a temptress. —
Fall to our dance.

Music

NEARCHUS *dance with* EUPHRANEA, PROPHILUS *with* CALANTHA, CHRISTALLA *with* HEMOPHIL, PHILEMA *with* GRONEAS.

Dance the first change, during which enter ARMOSTES.

ARM. (*in* CALANTHA'S *ear*) The King your father 's dead.

CAL. To the other change.

ARM. Is 't possible?

Dance again.

Enter BASSANES.

BASS. [*whispering to* CALANTHA] Oh, madam!
Penthea, poor Penthea's starv'd.

CAL. Beshrew thee! —
Lead to the next.

BASS. Amazement dulls my senses.

Dance again.

Enter ORGILUS.

ORG. [*whispering to* CALANTHA] Brave Ithocles is murder'd, murder'd cruelly.

CAL. How dull this music sounds! Strike up more sprightly;
Our footings are not active like our heart,
Which treads the nimbler measure.

ORG. I am thunderstruck.

Last change. Cease music.

CAL. So; let us breathe awhile. — Hath not this motion
Rais'd fresher color on your [9] cheeks?

NEAR. Sweet Princess,
A perfect purity of blood enamels
The beauty of your white.

CAL. We all look cheerfully;
And, Cousin, 't is, methinks, a rare presumption

---

[5] The printer's "fist" or index-hand.
[6] Assured.
[7] A hall in the palace.
[8] Halt.
[9] Weber, perhaps rightly, emends *our*.

In any who prefer our lawful pleasures
Before their own sour censure, to interrupt
The custom of this ceremony bluntly.

NEAR. None dares, lady.

CAL. Yes, yes; some hollow voice deliver'd to me
How that the King was dead.

ARM. The King is dead:
That fatal news was mine; for in mine arms
He breath'd his last, and with his crown bequeath'd 'ee
Your mother's wedding ring, which here I tender.

CROT. Most strange!

CAL. Peace crown his ashes! We are queen, then.

NEAR. Long live Calantha! Sparta's sovereign queen!

OMNES. Long live the Queen!

CAL. What whispered Bassanes?

BASS. That my Penthea, miserable soul,
Was starv'd to death.

CAL. She 's happy; she hath finish'd
A long and painful progress. — A third murmur
Pierc'd mine unwilling ears.

ORG. That Ithocles
Was murder'd; — rather butcher'd, had not bravery
Of an undaunted spirit, conquering terror,
Proclaim'd his last act triumph over ruin.

ARM. How! murder'd!

CAL. By whose hand?

ORG. By mine: this weapon
Was instrument to my revenge; the reasons
Are just, and known; quit him of these, and then
Never liv'd gentleman of greater merit,
Hope or abiliment [10] to steer a kingdom.

CROT. Fie,[11] Orgilus!

EUPH. Fie, Brother!

CAL. You have done it.

BASS. How it was done let him report, the forfeit
Of whose allegiance to our laws doth covet
Rigor of justice; but that done it is,
Mine eyes have been an evidence of credit
Too sure to be convinc'd.[12] Armostes, rent [13] not
Thine arteries with hearing the bare circumstances
Of these calamities; thou'st lost a nephew,
A niece, and I a wife: continue man still;
Make me the pattern of digesting evils,
Who can outlive my mighty ones, not shrinking
At such a pressure as would sink a soul
Into what 's most of death, the worst of horrors.
But I have seal'd a covenant with sadness,
And enter'd into bonds without condition,
To stand these tempests calmly; mark me, nobles,
I do not shed a tear, not for Penthea!
Excellent misery!

CAL. We begin our reign
With a first act of justice: thy confession,
Unhappy Orgilus, dooms thee a sentence;
But yet thy father's or thy sister's presence
Shall be excus'd. — Give, Crotolon, a blessing
To thy lost son; — Euphranea, take a farewell; —
And both be gone.

CROT. [*to* ORGILUS] Confirm thee, noble sorrow,
In worthy resolution!

EUPH. Could my tears speak,
My griefs were slight.

ORG. All good[n]ess dwell amongst ye!
Enjoy my sister, Prophilus; my vengeance
Aim'd never at thy prejudice.[14]

CAL. Now withdraw. —

Exeunt CROTOLON, PROPHILUS, *and* EUPHRANEA.

Bloody relater of thy stains in blood,
For that [15] thou hast reported him, whose fortunes
And life by thee are both at once snatch'd from him,
With honorable mention, make thy choice
Of what death likes [16] thee best; there 's all our bounty. —
But to excuse delays, let me, dear Cousin,
Entreat you and these lords see execution
Instant before 'ee part.

NEAR. Your will commands us.

ORG. One suit, just Queen, my last: vouchsafe your clemency,
That by no common hand I be divided
From this my humble frailty.

CAL. To their wisdoms
Who are to be spectators of thine end
I make the reference. Those that are dead

[10] Capacity, qualification.
[11] Formerly a stronger term of reproach.
[12] Overcome, confuted.
[13] Rend.

[14] At harming thee.
[15] In that.
[16] Is pleasing to.

Are dead; had they not now di'd, of necessity
They must have paid the debt they ow'd to nature
One time or other. — Use dispatch,[17] my Lords;
We'll suddenly prepare our coronation.
Exeunt CALANTHA, PHILEMA, [*and*] CHRISTALLA.

ARM. 'T is strange these tragedies should never touch on
Her female pity.

BASS. She has a masculine spirit;
And wherefore should I pule, and like a girl
Put finger in the eye? Let's be all toughness,
Without distinction betwixt sex and sex.

NEAR. Now, Orgilus, thy choice?

ORG. To bleed to death.

ARM. The executioner?

ORG. Myself, no surgeon;
I am well skill'd in letting blood. Bind fast
This arm, that so the pipes may from their conduits
Convey a full stream; here's a skilful instrument. [*Shows his dagger.*]
Only I am a beggar to some charity
To speed me in this execution
By lending th' other prick to th' tother arm,
When this is bubbling life out.

BASS. I am for 'ee;
It most concerns my art, my care, my credit. —
Quick, fillet[18] both [his][19] arms.

ORG. Gramercy, friendship!
Such courtesies are real which flow cheerfully
Without an expect[a]tion of requital.
Reach me a staff in this hand. — If a proneness
Or custom in my nature from my cradle
Had been inclin'd to fierce and eager bloodshed,
A coward guilt, hid in a coward quaking,
Would have betray'd fame[20] to ignoble flight
And vagabond pursuit of dreadful[21] safety;
But look upon my steadiness, and scorn not
The sickness of my fortune, which, since Bassanes
Was husband to Penthea, had lain bedrid.
We trifle time in words; thus I show cunning
In opening of a vein too full, too lively.
[*Pierces a vein.*]

ARM. Desperate courage!

[NEAR.][22] Honorable infamy!

HEM. I tremble at the sight.

GRO. Would I were loose!

BASS. It sparkles like a lusty wine new broach'd;
The vessel must be sound from which it issues. —
Grasp hard this other stick — I'll be as nimble —
But prithee, look not pale — have at 'ee! stretch out
Thine arm with vigor and[23] unshook virtue.
[*Opens a vein.*]
Good! Oh, I envy not a rival, fitted
To conquer in extremities. This pastime
Appears majestical; some high-tun'd poem
Hereafter shall deliver to posterity
The writer's glory and his subject's triumph.
How is't, man? Droop not yet.

ORG. I feel no palsies.
On a pair royal do I wait in death:
My sovereign, as his liegeman; on my mistress,
As a devoted servant;[24] and on Ithocles,
As if no brave, yet no unworthy enemy.
Nor did I use an engine to entrap
His life out of a slavish fear to combat
Youth, strength, or cunning;[25] but for that I durst not
Engage the goodness of a cause on fortune,
By which his name might have outfac'd my vengeance.
O Tecnicus, inspir'd with Phoebus' fire,
I call to mind thy augury; 't was perfect:
Revenge proves its own executioner.
When feeble man is bending to his mother,
The dust 'a was first fram'd on, thus he totters.

BASS. Life's fountain is dri'd up.

ORG. So falls the standards
Of my prerogative in being a creature!
A mist hangs o'er mine eyes, the sun's bright splendor
Is clouded in an everlasting shadow;
Welcome, thou ice, that sitt'st about my heart:
No heat can ever thaw thee. *Dies.*

NEAR. Speech hath left him.

BASS. 'A has shook hands[26] with Time; his funeral urn
Shall be my charge. Remove the bloodless body.

[17] Hasten.
[18] *I.e.*, bind with a narrow strip, to facilitate the blood-letting.
[19] Q *this*.
[20] *I.e.*, my reputation.
[21] Timorous.
[22] Emend. Gifford; Q *Org.*
[23] Dyce suggests the addition of *with.*
[24] Lover.
[25] Skill.
[26] Said goodbye.

The coronation must require attendance;
That past, my few days can be but one mourning. [*Exeunt*.

[Scene III][27]

An altar covered with white; two lights of virgin wax, during which music of recorders;[28] *enter* Four *bearing* Ithocles *on a hearse, or in a chair, in a rich robe, and a crown on his head; place him on one side of the altar. After him enter* Calantha *in a white robe and crown'd;* Euphranea, Philema, [*and*] Christalla, *in white;* Nearchus, Armostes, Crotolon, Prophilus, Amelus, Bassanes, Hemophil, *and* Groneas.

Calantha *goes and kneels before the altar; the rest stand off, the* Women *kneeling behind. Cease recorders during her devotions. Soft music.* Calantha *and the rest rise, doing obeisance to the altar.*

Cal. Our orisons are heard; the gods are merciful. —
Now tell me, you whose loyalties pays tribute
To us your lawful sovereign, how unskilful
Your duties or obedience is to render
Subjection to the sceptre of a virgin,
Who have been ever fortunate in princes
Of masculine and stirring composition!
A woman has enough to govern wisely
Her own demeanors, passions, and divisions.[29]
A nation warlike and inur'd to practice
Of policy and labor cannot brook
A feminate authority. We therefore
Command your counsel, how you may advise us
In choosing of a husband whose abilities
Can better guide this kingdom.
Near. Royal lady,
Your law is in your will.
Arm. We have seen tokens
Of constancy too lately to mistrust it.
Crot. Yet, if your Highness settle on a choice
By your own judgment both allow'd and lik'd of,
Sparta may grow in power, and proceed
To an increasing height.
Cal. Hold you the same mind?
Bass. Alas, great mistress, reason is so clouded
With the thick darkness of my [infinite][30] woes,
That I forecast nor dangers, hopes, or safety.
Give me some corner of the world to wear out
The remnant of the minutes I must number,
Where I may hear no sounds but sad complaints
Of virgins who have lost contracted partners;
Of husbands howling that their wives were ravish'd
By some untimely fate; of friends divided
By churlish opposition; or of fathers
Weeping upon their children's slaughtered carcasses;
Or daughters groaning o'er their fathers' hearses;
And I can dwell there, and with these keep consort
As musical as theirs. What can you look for
From an old, foolish, peevish, doting man
But craziness of age?
Cal. Cousin of Argos, —
Near. Madam?
Cal. Were I presently
To choose you for my lord, I'll open[31] freely
What articles I would propose to treat on
Before our marriage.
Near. Name them, virtuous lady.
Cal. I would presume you would retain the royalty
Of Sparta in her own bounds; then in Argos
Armostes might be viceroy; in Messene
Might Crotolon bear sway; and Bassanes —
Bass. I, Queen! alas, what I?
Cal. Be Sparta's marshal:
The multitudes of high employments could not
But set a peace to private griefs. These gentlemen,
Groneas and Hemophil, with worthy pensions,
Should wait upon your person in your chamber. —
I would bestow Christalla on Amelus.
She'll prove a constant wife; and Philema
Should into Vesta's Temple.
Bass. [*aside*] This is a testament!
It sounds not like conditions on a marriage.
Near. All this should be perform'd.
Cal. Lastly, for Prophilus,
He should be, Cousin, solemnly invested
In all those honors, titles, and preferments
Which his dear friend and my neglected husband
Too short a time enjoy'd.
Pro. I am unworthy
To live in your remembrance.

[27] A temple.
[28] Flageolets or small flutes.
[29] Discords.
[30] Q *infinites*.
[31] Reveal, explain.

EUPH. Excellent lady!
NEAR. Madam, what means that word, "neglected husband"?
CAL. Forgive me. — [*to the body of* ITHOCLES] Now I turn to thee, thou shadow
Of my contracted lord! — Bear witness all,
I put my mother's wedding ring upon
His finger; 't was my father's last bequest.
Thus I new marry him whose wife I am:
Death shall not separate us. Oh, my Lords,
I but deceiv'd your eyes with antic gesture,
When one news straight came huddling on another
Of death! and death! and death! still I danced forward;
But it struck home, and here, and in an instant.
Be such mere women, who with shrieks and outcries
Can vow a present end to all their sorrows,
Yet live to vow [32] new pleasures, and outlive them.
They are the silent griefs which cut the heart-strings;
Let me die smiling.
NEAR. 'T is a truth too ominous.
CAL. One kiss on these cold lips, my last! — Crack, crack! —
Argos now's Sparta's king. — Command the voices
Which wait at th' altar now to sing the song
I fitted for my end.
NEAR. Sirs, the song!

A SONG

ALL. Glories, pleasures, pomps, delights, and ease
Can but please
[The] [33] outward senses when the mind
Is not [34] untroubled or by peace refin'd.
1 [VOICE.] Crowns may flourish and decay;
Beauties shine, but fade away.
2 [VOICE.] Youth may revel; yet it must
Lie down in a bed of dust.
3 [VOICE.] Earthly honors flow and waste;
Time alone doth change and last.
ALL. Sorrows mingled with contents prepare
Rest for care;
Love only reigns in death; though art
Can find no comfort for a broken heart.

[CALANTHA *dies.*]

ARM. Look to the Queen!
BASS. Her heart is broke, indeed.
O royal maid, would thou hadst miss'd this part!
Yet 't was a brave one. I must weep to see
Her smile in death.
ARM. Wise Tecnicus! thus said he:
"When youth is ripe, and age from time doth part,
The Lifeless Trunk shall wed the Broken Heart."
'T is here fulfill'd.
NEAR. I am your King.
ALL. Long live
Nearchus, King of Sparta!
NEAR. Her last will
Shall never be digress'd from: wait in order
Upon these faithful lovers, as becomes us. —
The counsels of the gods are never known
Till men can call th' effects of them their own.
[*Exeunt.*]

[32] Gifford emends *court*.
[33] A space in Q makes it clear that a word has dropped out here.
[34] Gifford emends *or*. But, as Sherman notes, if "outward" is emphasized the sense is clear enough: "glories, etc., can please only the *outward* senses when the mind is troubled or not refined by peace."

THE EPILOGUE

WHERE noble judgments and clear eyes are fix'd
To grace endeavor, there sits truth, not mix'd
With ignorance; those censures may command
Belief which talk not till they understand.
Let some say, "This was flat;" some, "Here the scene
Fell from its height;" another, that the mean
Was "ill observ'd" in such a growing passion
As it transcended either state or fashion.
Some few may cry, 't was "pretty well, or so,
But — " and there shrug in silence; yet we know
Our writer's aim was in the whole address'd
Well to deserve of *all*, but please the *best*;
Which granted, by th' allowance of this strain
The *Broken Heart* may be piec'd up again.

BACKGROUND AND SOURCE MATERIALS

¶ Here begynneth a treatyse how þ hye fader of heuen sendeth dethe to somon euery creature to come and gyue a counte of theyr lyues in this worlde/and is in maner of a morall playe.

EVERYMAN AND DEATH

INTRODUCTORY NOTE

The Medieval Morality Play: *Everyman*

The Morality play *Everyman* survived in single copies (two only fragmentary) of four separate editions which date from the early decades of the sixteenth century. For years debate continued about the relation of *Everyman* to the Dutch play *Elckerlijk*, which it very nearly resembles. Recent scholarship supports the conclusion that the *Elckerlijk*, which was probably written in the fifteenth century, was the original work from which *Everyman* was translated. But the fact of continental origin does not make *Everyman* in any way less native to the English dramatic tradition. The Morality play was an indigenous dramatic form; the concern with death and "the last things" was a universal concern of late medieval Catholicism; and the style of *Everyman* is admirably clear and natural.

The original editions of *Everyman* were reprinted by W. W. Greg in Bang's *Materialien* (1904, 1909, 1910). Scholarly old-spelling texts can be found in J. Q. Adams' *Chief Pre-Shakespearean Dramas* (Cambridge, Mass., 1924) and A. C. Cawley's *Everyman* (Manchester Univ. Press, 1961). I am indebted to these editions for valuable suggestions about stage directions and textual difficulties.

R. O.

EVERYMAN

[DRAMATIS PERSONAE

Messenger.
God.
Death.
Everyman.
Fellowship.
Cousin.
Kindred.
Goods.
Good Deeds.
Knowledge.
Confession.
Beauty.
Strength.
Discretion.
Five Wits.
Angel.

Doctor.]

Here beginneth a treatise how the High Father of Heaven sendeth Death to summon every creature to come and give account of their lives in this world, and is in manner of a moral play.

[*Enter* Messenger *as Prologue.*]

Messenger. I pray you all give your audience,
And hear this matter with reverence,
By figure a moral play.
The *Summoning of Everyman* called it is,
That of our lives and ending shows
How transitory we be all day.
This matter is wondrous precious,
But the intent of it is more gracious,
And sweet to bear away.
The story saith: Man, in the beginning
Look well, and take good heed to the ending,
Be you never so gay!
Ye think sin in the beginning full sweet,
Which in the end causeth the soul to weep,
When the body lieth in clay.
Here shall you see how Fellowship and Jollity,
Both Strength, Pleasure, and Beauty,
Will fade from thee as flower in May.
For ye shall hear how our Heaven King
Calleth Everyman to a general reckoning.
Give audience, and hear what he doth say.
[*Exit.*]

[God *speaketh from above.*]

God. I perceive, here in my majesty,
How that all creatures be to me unkind,
Living without dread in worldly prosperity;
Of ghostly sight the people be so blind,
Drowned in sin, they know me not for their God.
In worldly riches is all their mind;
They fear not my righteousness, the sharp rod;
My law that I showed when I for them died,
They forget clean, and shedding of my blood red.
I hanged between two thieves, it cannot be denied;
To get them life I suffered to be dead;
I healed their feet, with thorns hurt was my head.
I could do no more than I did, truly;
And now I see the people do clean forsake me.
They use the seven deadly sins damnable,
As pride, covetise, wrath, and lechery,
Now in the world be made commendable;
And thus they leave of angels, the heavenly company.
Every man liveth so after his own pleasure,
And yet of their life they be nothing sure.
I see the more that I them forbear
The worse they be from year to year.
All that liveth appaireth [1] fast.
Therefore I will, in all the haste,
Have a reckoning of every man's person;
For, and I leave the people thus alone
In their life and wicked tempests,
Verily they will become much worse than beasts;
For now one would by envy another up eat;
Charity they all do clean forget.
I hoped well that every man
In my glory should make his mansion,

[1] Becomes worse.

And thereto I had them all elect;
But now I see, like traitors deject,
They thank me not for the pleasure that I to them meant,
Nor yet for their being that I them have lent.
I proffered the people great multitude of mercy,
And few there be that asketh it heartily;
They be so cumbered with worldly riches
That needs on them I must do justice,
On every man living without fear.
Where art thou, Death, thou mighty messenger?

[*Enter* DEATH.]

DEATH. Almighty God, I am here at your will,
Your commandment to fulfil.
GOD. Go thou to Everyman,
And show him, in my name,
A pilgrimage he must on him take,
Which he in no wise may escape;
And that he bring with him a sure reckoning
Without delay or any tarrying.
[God *withdraws*.]
DEATH. Lord, I will in the world go run overall,
And cruelly out search both great and small.
Every man will I beset that liveth beastly
Out of God's laws, and dreadeth not folly.
He that loveth riches I will strike with my dart,
His sight to blind, and from heaven to depart,
Except that alms be his good friend,
In hell for to dwell, world without end.

[*Enter* EVERYMAN.]

Lo, yonder I see Everyman walking.
Full little he thinketh on my coming;
His mind is on fleshly lusts and his treasure;
And great pain it shall cause him to endure
Before the Lord, Heaven King.
Everyman, stand still! whither art thou going
Thus gaily? Hast thou thy Maker forgot?
EVERYMAN. Why askest thou?
Wouldest thou wot? [2]
DEATH. Yea, sir, I will show you:
In great haste I am sent to thee
From god out of his majesty.
EVERYMAN. What, sent to me?
DEATH. Yea, certainly.
Though thou have forgot him here,
He thinketh on thee in the heavenly sphere,
As, or we depart, thou shalt know.
EVERYMAN. What desireth God of me?
DEATH. That shall I show thee:
A reckoning he will needs have
Without any longer respite.
EVERYMAN. To give a reckoning longer leisure I crave;
This blind matter troubleth my wit.
DEATH. On thee thou must take a long journey,
Therefore thy book of count with thee thou bring;
For turn again thou can not by no way.
And look thou be sure of thy reckoning;
For before God thou shalt answer, and show
Thy many bad deeds, and good but a few,
How thou hast spent thy life, and in what wise,
Before the Chief Lord of paradise.
Have ado that we were in that way,
For, wot thou well, thou shalt make none attournay.
EVERYMAN. Full unready I am such reckoning to give.
I know thee not. What messenger art thou?
DEATH. I am Death, that no man dreadeth.[3]
For every man I rest, and no man spareth;
For it is God's commandment
That all to me should be obedient.
EVERYMAN. O Death, thou comest when I had thee least in mind!
In thy power it lieth me to save;
Yet of my good[s] will I give thee, if thou will be kind;
Yea, a thousand pound shalt thou have,
And defer this matter till another day.
DEATH. Everyman, it may not be by no way;
I set not by gold, silver, nor riches,
Nor by pope, emperor, king, duke, nor princes.
For, and I would receive gifts great,
All the world I might get;
But my custom is clean contrary.
I give thee no respite. Come hence, and not tarry.
EVERYMAN. Alas! shall I have no longer respite?
I may say Death giveth no warning.
To think on thee, it maketh my heart sick,
For all unready is my book of reckoning.
But twelve year and I might have abiding.
My counting-book I would make so clear
That my reckoning I should not need to fear.

[2] Know.

[3] That respects no man.

Wherefore, Death, I pray thee, for God's mercy,
Spare me till I be provided of remedy.
DEATH. Thee availeth not to cry, weep, and pray;
But haste thee lightly that thou were gone that journey,
And prove thy friends if thou can.
For wot thou well the tide abideth no man,
And in the world each living creature
For Adam's sin must die of nature.
EVERYMAN. Death, if I should this pilgrimage take,
And my reckoning surely make,
Show me, for saint charity,
Should I not come again shortly?
DEATH. No, Everyman; and thou be once there,
Thou mayst never more come here,
Trust me verily.
EVERYMAN. O gracious God, in the high seat celestial,
Have mercy on me in this most need!
Shall I have no company from this vale terrestrial
Of mine acquaintance that way me to lead?
DEATH. Yea, if any be so hardy
That would go with thee and bear thee company.
Hie thee that thou were gone to God's magnificence,
Thy reckoning to give before his presence.
What! weenest thou life is given thee,
And thy worldly goods also?
EVERYMAN. I had weened so, verily.
DEATH. Nay, nay; it was but lent thee;
For, as soon as thou art gone,
Another a while shall have it, and then go therefrom
Even as thou hast done.
Everyman, thou art mad! thou hast thy wits five,
And here on earth will not amend thy life;
For suddenly I do come.
EVERYMAN. O wretched caitiff! whither shall I flee,
That I might scape this endless sorrow?
Now, gentle Death, spare me till tomorrow,
That I may amend me
With good advisement.
DEATH. Nay, thereto I will not consent,
Nor no man will I respite,
But to the heart suddenly I shall smite
Without any advisement.
And now out of thy sight I will me hie;
See thou make thee ready shortly,
For thou mayst say this is the day
That no man living may scape away.
[*Exit* DEATH.]
EVERYMAN. Alas, I may well weep with sighs deep!
Now have I no manner of company
To help me in my journey, and me to keep;
And also my writing is full unready.
How shall I do now for to excuse me?
I would to God I had never been gete![4]
To my soul a full great profit it had be;
For now I fear pains huge and great.
The time passeth — Lord, help, that all wrought!
For though I mourn it availeth naught.
The day passeth and is almost ago;
I wot not well what for to do.
To whom were I best my complaint to make?
What and I to Fellowship thereof spake,
And showed him of this sudden chance?
For in him is all mine affiance;[5]
We have in the world so many a day
Been good friends in sport and play.
I see him yonder, certainly;
I trust that he will bear me company;
Therefore to him will I speak to ease my sorrow.
Well met, good Fellowship, and good morrow!

FELLOWSHIP *speaketh.*

FELLOWSHIP. Everyman, good morrow; by this day!
Sir, why lookest thou so piteously?
If any thing be amiss, I pray thee me say,
That I may help to remedy.
EVERYMAN. Yea, good Fellowship, yea,
I am in great jeopardy.
FELLOWSHIP. My true friend, show to me your mind;
I will not forsake thee, unto my life's end,
In the way of good company.
EVERYMAN. That was well spoken, and lovingly.
FELLOWSHIP. Sir, I must needs know your heaviness;
I have pity to see you in any distress.
If any have you wronged, ye shall revenged be,
Though I on the ground be slain for thee,
Though that I know before that I should die.
EVERYMAN. Verily, Fellowship, gramercy.
FELLOWSHIP. Tush! by thy thanks I set not a straw!
Show me your grief, and say no more.

[4] Born. [5] Trust.

EVERYMAN. If I my heart should to you break,
And then you to turn your mind from me,
And would not me comfort when you hear me speak,
Then should I ten times sorrier be.
FELLOWSHIP. Sir, I say as I will do in deed.
EVERYMAN. Then be you a good friend at need;
I have found you true herebefore.
FELLOWSHIP. And so ye shall evermore;
For, in faith, and thou go to hell
I will not forsake thee by the way!
EVERYMAN. Ye speak like a good friend; I believe you well;
I shall deserve it, and I may.
FELLOWSHIP. I speak of no deserving, by this day!
For he that will say, and nothing do,
Is not worthy with good company to go;
Therefore show me the grief of your mind,
As to your friend most loving and kind.
EVERYMAN. I shall show you how it is:
Commanded I am to go a journey,
A long way, hard and dangerous,
And give a strait count without delay
Before the high judge, Adonay.[6]
Wherefore, I pray you, bear me company,
As ye have promised, in this journey.
FELLOWSHIP. That is matter indeed! Promise is duty;
But, and I should take such a voyage on me,
I know it well, it should be to my pain;
Also it maketh me afeared, certain.
But let us take counsel here as well as we can,
For your words would fear a strong man.
EVERYMAN. Why, ye said if I had need,
Ye would me never forsake, quick nor dead,
Though it were to hell, truly.
FELLOWSHIP. So I said, certainly,
But such pleasures be set aside, the sooth to say.
And also, if we took such a journey,
When should we again come?
EVERYMAN. Nay, never again till the day of doom.
FELLOWSHIP. In faith, then will not I come there!
Who hath you these tidings brought?
EVERYMAN. Indeed, Death was with me here.
FELLOWSHIP. Now, by God that all hath bought,
If Death were the messenger,
For no man that is living today
I will not go that loath journey —
Not for the father that begat me!
EVERYMAN. Ye promised otherwise, pardie.
FELLOWSHIP. I wot well I said so, truly;
And yet if thou wilt eat, and drink, and make good cheer,
Or haunt to women the lusty company,
I would not forsake you while the day is clear,
Trust me verily!
EVERYMAN. Yea, thereto ye would be ready;
To go to mirth, solace, and play,
Your mind will sooner apply
Than to bear me company in my long journey.
FELLOWSHIP. Now, in good faith, I will not that way;
But and thou will murder, or any man kill,
In that I will help thee with a good will.
EVERYMAN. O, that is a simple advice indeed;
Gentle Fellow, help me in my necessity!
We have loved long, and now I need,
And now, gentle Fellowship, remember me.
FELLOWSHIP. Whether ye have loved me or no,
By Saint John, I will not with thee go.
EVERYMAN. Yet, I pray thee, take the labor, and do so much for me
To bring me forward, for saint charity,
And comfort me till I come without the town.
FELLOWSHIP. Nay, and thou would give me a new gown,
I will not a foot with thee go;
But, and thou had tarried, I would not have left thee so.
And as now God speed thee in thy journey,
For from thee I will depart as fast as I may.
EVERYMAN. Whither away, Fellowship? Will thou forsake me?
FELLOWSHIP. Yea, by my fay, to God I betake thee.
EVERYMAN. Farewell, good Fellowship; for thee my heart is sore;
Adieu for ever! I shall see thee no more.
FELLOWSHIP. In faith, Everyman, farewell now at the end[ing].
For you I will remember that parting is mourning.
[*Exit* FELLOWSHIP.]
EVERYMAN. Alack! shall we thus depart indeed?
Ah, Lady, help! Without any more comfort,
Lo, Fellowship forsaketh me in my most need.
For help in this world whither shall I resort?

[6] Hebrew for God.

Fellowship herebefore with me would merry make,
And now little sorrow for me doth he take.
It is said, "In prosperity men friends may find,
Which in adversity be full unkind."
Now whither for succor shall I flee,
Sith that Fellowship hath forsaken me?
To my kinsmen I will, truly,
Praying them to help me in my neccessity.
I believe that they will do so,
For kind will creep where it may not go.
I will go say, for yonder I see them go.
Where be ye now, my friends and kinsmen?

[*Enter* KINDRED *and* COUSIN.]

KINDRED. Here be we now at your commandment.
Cousin, I pray you show us your intent
In any wise, and [do] not spare.

COUSIN. Yea, Everyman, and to us declare
If ye be disposed to go any whither,
For, wot you well, we will live and die together.

KINDRED. In wealth and woe we will with you hold,
For over his kin a man may be bold.

EVERYMAN. Gramercy, my friends and kinsmen kind.
Now shall I show you the grief of my mind.
I was commanded by a messenger,
That is a high king's chief officer;
He bade me go a pilgrimage, to my pain,
And I know well I shall never come again.
Also I must give a reckoning straight,
For I have a great enemy that hath me in wait,
Which intendeth me for to hinder.

KINDRED. What account is that which ye must render?
That would I know.

EVERYMAN. Of all my works I must show
How I have lived and my days spent;
Also of ill deeds that I have used
In my time, sith life was me lent;
And of all virtues that I have refused.
Therefore I pray you go thither with me,
To help to make mine account, for saint charity.

COUSIN. What, to go thither? Is that the matter?
Nay, Everyman, I had liefer fast bread and water
All this five year and more.

EVERYMAN. Alas, that ever I was bore!
For now shall I never be merry
If that you forsake me.

KINDRED. Ah, sir, what, ye be a merry man!
Take good heart to you, and make no moan.
But one thing I warn you, by Saint Anne,
As for me, ye shall go alone.

EVERYMAN. My cousin, will you not with me go?

COUSIN. No, by our Lady! I have the cramp in my toe.
Trust not to me; for, so God me speed,
I will deceive you in your most need.

KINDRED. It availeth not us to tice.
Ye shall have my maid with all my heart;
She loveth to go to feasts, there to be nice,
And to dance, and abroad to start;
I will give her leave to help you in that journey,
If that you and she may agree.

EVERYMAN. Now show me the very effect of your mind.
Will you go with me, or abide behind?

KINDRED. Abide behind? Yea, that will I, and I may!
Therefore farewell till another day.

[*Exit* KINDRED.]

EVERYMAN. How should I be merry or glad?
For fair promises men to me make,
But when I have most need, they me forsake.
I am deceived; that maketh me sad.

COUSIN. Cousin Everyman, farewell now,
For verily I will not go with you.
Also of mine own life an unready reckoning
I have to account; therefore I make tarrying.
Now, God keep thee, for now I go.

[*Exit* COUSIN]

EVERYMAN. Ah, Jesus! is all come hereto?
Lo, fair words maketh fools fain;
They promise and nothing will do, certain.
My kinsmen promised me faithfully
For to abide with me steadfastly,
And now fast away do they flee;
Even so Fellowship promised me.
What friend were best me of to provide?
I lose my time here longer to abide.
Yet in my mind a thing there is;
All my life I have loved riches;
If that my Good now help me might,
He would make my heart full light.
I will speak to him in this distress.
Where art thou, my Goods and riches?

Goods [*From within*]. Who calleth me? Everyman? What! hast thou haste?
I lie here in corners, trussed and piled so high,
And in chests I am locked so fast,
Also sacked in bags. Thou mayst see with thine eye.
I cannot stir; in packs low I lie.
What would ye have? Lightly me say.

EVERYMAN. Come hither, Good, in all the haste thou may.
For of counsel I must desire thee.

[*Enter* GOODS.]

GOODS. Sir, and ye in the world have sorrow or adversity,
That can I help you to remedy shortly.

EVERYMAN. It is another disease that grieveth me;
In this world it is not, I tell thee so.
I am sent for another way to go,
To give a strait count general
Before the highest Jupiter of all;
And all my life I have had joy and pleasure in thee,
Therefore I pray thee go with me;
For, peradventure, thou mayst before God Almighty
My reckoning help to clean and purify;
For it is said ever among,
That money maketh all right that is wrong.

GOODS. Nay, Everyman; I sing another song,
I follow no man in such voyages;
For, and I went with thee,
Thou shouldst fare much the worse for me;
For because on me thou did set thy mind,
Thy reckoning I have made blotted and blind,
That thine account thou cannot make truly;
And that hast thou for the love of me.

EVERYMAN. That would grieve me full sore,
When I should come to that fearful answer.
Up, let us go thither together.

GOODS. Nay, not so! I am too brittle, I may not endure;
I will follow no man one foot, be ye sure.

EVERYMAN. Alas, I have thee loved, and had great pleasure
All my life-days on good[s] and treasure.

GOODS. That is to thy damnation, without lesing![7]
For my love is contrary to the love everlasting.
But if thou had me loved moderately during,
As to the poor to give part of me,
Then shouldst thou not in this dolor be,
Nor in this great sorrow and care.

EVERYMAN. Lo, now was I deceived ere I was ware,
And all I may wyte my spending of time.[8]

GOODS. What, weenest thou that I am thine?

EVERYMAN. I had weened so.

GOODS. Nay, Everyman, I say no;
As for a while I was lent thee,
A season thou hast had me in prosperity.
My condition is man's soul to kill;
If I save one, a thousand I do spill;
Weenest thou that I will follow thee?
Nay, from this world not, verily.

EVERYMAN. I had weened otherwise.

GOODS. Therefore to thy soul Good is a thief;
For when thou art dead, this is my guise —
Another to deceive in the same wise
As I have done thee, and all to his soul's reprief.

EVERYMAN. O false Good, cursed thou be!
Thou traitor to God, that hast deceived me
And caught me in thy snare.

GOODS. Mary, thou brought thyself in care;
Whereof I am [right] glad.
I must needs laugh, I cannot be sad.

EVERYMAN. Ah, Good, thou hast had long my hearty love;
I gave thee that which should be the Lord's above.
But wilt thou not go with me indeed?
I pray thee truth to say.

GOODS. No, so God me speed!
Therefore farewell, and have good day.

[*Exit* GOODS.]

EVERYMAN. O, to whom shall I make my moan
For to go with me in that heavy journey?
First Fellowship said he would with me gone;
His words were very pleasant and gay,
But afterward he left me alone.
Then spake I to my kinsmen, all in despair,
And also they gave me words fair;
They lacked no fair speaking,
But all forsook me in the ending.
Then went I to my Goods, that I loved best,
In hope to have comfort, but there had I least,
For my Goods sharply did me tell
That he bringeth many into hell.
Then of myself I was ashamed,
And so I am worthy to be blamed;

[7] Lying.

[8] And I may blame all on my wasting of time.

Thus may I well myself hate.
Of whom shall I now counsel take?
I think that I shall never speed
Till that I go to my Good Deed.
But alas! she is so weak
That she can neither go nor speak;
Yet will I venture on her now.
My Good Deeds, where be you?

[Good Deeds *speaks from the ground.*]

Good Deeds. Here I lie, cold in the ground.
Thy sins hath me sore bound,
That I cannot stir.
Everyman. O Good Deeds, I stand in fear!
I must you pray of counsel,
For help now should come right well.
Good Deeds. Everyman, I have understanding
That ye be summoned account to make
Before Messias, of Jerusalem King;
And you do by me,[9] that journey with you will I take.
Everyman. Therefore I come to you my moan to make;
I pray you that ye will go with me.
Good Deeds. I would full fain, but I cannot stand, verily.
Everyman. Why, is there anything on you fall?
Good Deeds. Yea, sir, I may thank you of all.
If ye had perfectly cheered me,
Your book of count full ready had be.
Look, the books of your works and deeds eke;
[Ah, see] how they lie under the feet,
To your soul's heaviness.
Everyman. Our Lord Jesus, help me!
For one letter here I can not see.
Good Deeds. There is a blind reckoning in time of distress.
Everyman. Good Deeds, I pray you help me in this need,
Or else I am for ever damned indeed;
Therefore help me to make my reckoning
Before the Redeemer of all thing,
That King is, and was, and ever shall.
Good Deeds. Everyman, I am sorry of your fall,
And fain would I help you, and I were able.
Everyman. Good Deeds, your counsel I pray you give me.
Good Deeds. That shall I do verily;
Though that on my feet I may not go,
I have a sister that shall with you also,
Called Knowledge, which shall with you abide,
To help you to make that dreadful reckoning.

[*Enter* Knowledge.]

Knowledge. Everyman, I will go with thee, and be thy guide,
In thy most need to go by thy side.
Everyman. In good condition I am now in every thing,
And am wholly content with this good thing;
Thanked be God my [Creator].
Good Deeds. And when she hath brought thee there,
Where thou shalt heal thee of thy smart,
Then go you with your reckoning and your Good Deeds together,
For to make you joyful at heart
Before the blessed Trinity.
Everyman. My Good Deeds, gramercy!
I am well content, certainly,
With your words sweet.
Knowledge. Now go we together lovingly
To Confession, that cleansing river.
Everyman. For joy I weep; I would we were there!
But, I pray you, give me cognition
Where dwelleth that holy man, Confession.
Knowledge. In the house of salvation;
We shall find him in that place,
That shall us comfort, by God's grace.

[Knowledge *leads* Everyman *to* Confession.]

Lo, this is Confession. Kneel down and ask mercy,
For he is in good conceit with God almighty.
Everyman [*Kneeling*]. O glorious fountain, that all uncleanness doth clarify,
Wash from me the spots of vice unclean,
That on me no sin may be seen.
I come with Knowledge, for my redemption,
Redempt with heart and full contrition;
For I am commanded a pilgrimage to take,
And great accounts before God to make.
Now, I pray you, Shrift, mother of salvation,
Help my Good Deeds for my piteous exclamation.
Confession. I know your sorrow well, Everyman.
Because with Knowledge ye come to me,
I will you comfort as well as I can,
And a precious jewel I will give thee,
Called penance, voider of adversity;
Therewith shall your body chastised be,
With abstinence, and perseverance in God's [serviture].

[9] As I advise.

Here shall you receive that scourge of me,

[*Gives* Everyman *a scourge.*]

Which is penance strong that ye must endure,
To remember thy Savior was scourged for thee
With sharp scourges, and suffered it patiently;
So must thou, eve thou scape that painful pilgrimage.
Knowledge, keep him in this voyage,
And by that time Good Deeds will be with thee.
But in any wise be seeker of mercy,
For your time draweth fast, and ye will saved be;
Ask God mercy, and He will grant truly.
When with the scourge of penance man doth him bind,
The oil of forgiveness then shall he find.

[*Exit* Confession.]

Everyman. Thanked be God for his gracious work!
For now I will my penance begin;
This hath rejoiced and lighted my heart,
Though the knots be painful and hard within.

Knowledge. Everyman, look your penance that ye fulfil,
What pain that ever it to you be,
And Knowledge shall give you counsel at will
How your account ye shall make clearly.

Everyman [*kneeling*]. O eternal God! O heavenly figure!
O way of righteousness! O goodly vision!
Which descended down in a virgin pure
Because he would every man redeem,
Which Adam forfeited by his disobedience.
O blessed Godhead, elect and high divine,
Forgive me my grievous offence!
Here I cry thee mercy in this presence.
O ghostly treasure! O ransomer and redeemer!
Of all the world hope and conductor,
Mirror of joy, and founder of mercy,
Which illumineth heaven and earth thereby,
Hear my clamorous complaint, though it late be.
Receive my prayers; unworthy in this heavy life.
Though I be a sinner most abominable,
Yet let my name be written in Moses' table.
O Mary! pray to the Maker of all thing,
Me for to help at my ending,
And save me from the power of my enemy,
For Death assaileth me strongly.
And, Lady, that I may by means of thy prayer
If your Son's glory to be partner,
By the means of his passion, I it crave;
I beseech you, help my soul to save.

[*He rises.*]

Knowledge, give me the scourge of penance.
My flesh therewith shall give acquaintance.
I will now begin, if God give me grace.

Knowledge. Everyman, God give you time and space!
Thus I bequeath you in the hands of our Savior,
Now may you make your reckoning sure.

Everyman. In the name of the Holy Trinity,
My body sore punished shall be.

[*Scourges himself.*]

Take this, body, for the sin of the flesh;
Also thou delightest to go gay and fresh,
And in the way of damnation thou did me bring;
Therefore suffer now strokes of punishing.
Now of penance I will wade the water clear,
To save me from Purgatory, that sharp fire.

[Good Deeds *rises from floor.*]

Good Deeds. I thank God, now I can walk and go,
And am delivered of my sickness and woe.
Therefore with Everyman I will go, and not spare;
His good works I will help him to declare.

Knowledge. Now, Everyman, be merry and glad.
Your Good Deeds cometh now; ye may not be sad;
Now is your Good Deeds whole and sound,
Going upright upon the ground.

Everyman. My heart is light, and shall be evermore;
Now will I smite faster than I did before.

Good Deeds. Everyman, pilgrim, my special friend,
Blessed be thou without end;
For thee is prepared the eternal glory.
Ye have me made whole and sound,
Therefore I will bide by thee in every stound.[10]

Everyman. Welcome, my Good Deeds! now I hear thy voice,
I weep for very sweetness of love.

Knowledge. Be no more sad, but ever rejoice;
God seeth thy living in his throne above.

10 Assault.

Put on this garment to thy behove,
Which is wet with your tears,
Or else before God you may it miss,
When you to your journey's end come shall.

EVERYMAN. Gentle Knowledge, what do ye it call?

KNOWLEDGE. It is the garment of sorrow;
From pain it will you borrow;
Contrition it is
That getteth forgiveness;
It pleaseth God passing well.

GOOD DEEDS. Everyman, will you wear it for your heal?

[EVERYMAN *puts on garment of contrition.*]

EVERYMAN. Now blessed be Jesu, Mary's Son!
For now have I on true contrition.
And let us go now without tarrying;
Good Deeds, have we clear our reckoning?

GOOD DEEDS. Yea, indeed I have [it] here.

EVERYMAN. Then I trust we need not fear.
Now, friends, let us not part in twain.

KNOWLEDGE. Nay, Everyman, that will we not, certain.

GOOD DEEDS. Yet must thou lead with thee
Three persons of great might.

EVERYMAN. Who should they be?

GOOD DEEDS. Discretion and Strength they hight,
And thy Beauty may not abide behind.

KNOWLEDGE. Also ye must call to mind
Your Five Wits as for your counselors.

GOOD DEEDS. You must have them ready at all hours.

EVERYMAN. How shall I get them hither?

KNOWLEDGE. You must call them all together,
And they will hear you incontinent.

EVERYMAN. My friends, come hither and be present;
Discretion, Strength, my Five Wits, and Beauty.

[*Enter* DISCRETION, STRENGTH, FIVE WITS, *and* BEAUTY.]

BEAUTY. Here at your will we be all ready.
What would ye that we should do?

GOOD DEEDS. That ye would with Everyman go,
And help him in his pilgrimage.
Advise you, will ye with him or not in that voyage?

STRENGTH. We will bring him all thither,
To his help and comfort, ye may believe me.

DISCRETION. So will we go with him all together.

EVERYMAN. Almighty God, loved may thou be!
I give thee laud that I have hither brought
Strength, Discretion, Beauty, and Five Wits. Lack I naught;
And my Good Deeds, with Knowledge clear,
All be in company at my will here.
I desire no more to my business.

STRENGTH. And I, Strength, will by you stand in distress,
Though thou would in battle fight on the ground.

FIVE WITS. And though it were through the world round,
We will not depart for sweet nor sour.

BEAUTY. No more will I unto death's hour,
Whatsoever thereof befall.

DISCRETION. Everyman, advise you first of all;
Go with a good advisement and deliberation.
We all give you virtuous monition
That all shall be well.

EVERYMAN. My friends, hearken what I will tell:
I pray God reward you in his heavenly sphere.
Now hearken, all that be here,
For I will make my testament
Here before you all present;
In alms half my good I will give with my hands twain
In the way of charity, with good intent,
And the other half still shall remain,
In [bequest] to be returned there it ought to be.
This I do in despite of the fiend of hell,
To go quite out of his peril
Even after and this day.

KNOWLEDGE. Everyman, hearken what I say;
Go to Priesthood, I you advise,
And receive of him in any wise
The holy sacrament and ointment together.
Then shortly see ye turn again hither;
We will all abide you here.

FIVE WITS. Yea, Everyman, hie you that ye ready were.
There is no emperor, king, duke, nor baron,
That of God hath commission
As hath the least priest in the world being;
For of the blessed sacraments pure and benign
He beareth the keys, and thereof hath the cure
For man's redemption — it is ever sure —
Which God for our soul's medicine
Gave us out of his heart with great pain,

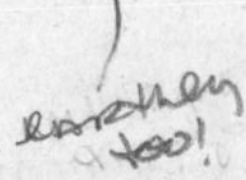

Here in this transitory life, for thee and me.
The blessed sacraments seven there be:
Baptism, confirmation, with priesthood good,
And the sacrament of God's precious flesh and blood,
Marriage, the holy extreme unction, and penance.
These seven be good to have in remembrance,
Gracious sacraments of high divinity.

EVERYMAN. Fain would I receive that holy body
And meekly to my ghostly father I will go.

FIVE WITS. Everyman, that is the best that ye can do.
God will you to salvation bring,
For priesthood exceedeth all other thing;
To us Holy Scripture they do teach,
And converteth man from sin, heaven to reach;
God hath to them more power given
Than to any angel that is in heaven.
With five words he may consecrate
God's body in flesh and blood to make,
And handleth his Maker between his hands.
The priest bindeth and unbindeth all bands,
Both in earth and in heaven
Thou ministers all the sacraments seven;
Though we kissed thy feet, thou wert worthy;
Thou art the surgeon that cureth sin deadly.
No remedy we find under God
But all only priesthood.
Everyman, God gave priest[s] that dignity,
And setteth them in his stead among us to be;
Thus be they above angels in degree.

[*Exit* EVERYMAN *to receive the last rites of the church.*]

KNOWLEDGE. If priests be good, it is so, surely;
But when Jesu hanged on the cross with great smart,
There he gave out of his blessed heart
The same sacrament[s] in great torment.
He sold them not to us, that Lord omnipotent.
Therefore Saint Peter the Apostle doth say
That Jesu's curse hath all they
Which God their Savior do buy or sell,
Or they for any money do take or tell.
Sinful priests giveth the sinners example bad;
Their children sitteth by other men's fires, I have heard;
And some haunteth women's company
With unclean life, as lusts of lechery.
These be with sin made blind.

FIVE WITS. I trust to God no such may we find.
Therefore let us priesthood honor,
And follow their doctrine for our souls' succor.
We be their sheep, and they shepherds be
By whom we all be kept in surety.
Peace! for yonder I see Everyman come,
Which hath made true satisfaction.

GOOD DEEDS. Methinketh it is he indeed.

[*Enter* EVERYMAN.]

EVERYMAN. Now Jesu be your alder speed.[11]
I have received the sacrament for my redemption,
And then mine extreme unction.
Blessed be all they that counseled me to take it!
And now, friends, let us go without longer respite.
I thank God that ye have tarried so long.
Now set each of you on this rod your hand,
And shortly follow me.
I go before, there I would be. God be our guide!

STRENGTH. Everyman, we will not from you go
Till ye have gone this voyage long.

DISCRETION. I, Discretion, will bide by you also.

KNOWLEDGE. And though this pilgrimage be never so strong,
I will never part you fro.
Everyman, I will be as sure by thee
As ever I did by Judas Maccabee.

[*They proceed together to the grave.*]

EVERYMAN. Alas! I am so faint I may not stand,
My limbs under me do fold.
Friends, let us not turn again to this land,
Not for all the world's gold;
For into this cave must I creep
And turn to earth, and there to sleep.

BEAUTY. What, into this grave? Alas!

EVERYMAN. Yea, there shall you consume, more and less.[12]

BEAUTY. And what! should I smother here?

EVERYMAN. Yea, by my faith, and never more appear.
In this world live no more we shall,
But in heaven before the highest Lord of all.

BEAUTY. I cross out all this. Adieu, by Saint John;
I take my "tap in my lap" [13] and am gone.

[11] Give success to all.
[12] The mighty and the lowly.
[13] Proverbial for "I am going" (Cawley).

EVERYMAN. What, Beauty, whither will ye?
BEAUTY. Peace! I am deaf. I look not behind me,
Not and thou would give me all the gold in thy chest.
[*Exit* BEAUTY.]
EVERYMAN. Alas, whereto may I trust?
Beauty goeth fast away from me;
She promised with me to live and die.
STRENGTH. Everyman, I will thee also forsake and deny;
Thy game liketh me not at all.
EVERYMAN. Why, then, ye will forsake me all!
Sweet Strength, tarry a little space.
STRENGTH. Nay, sir, by the rood of grace,
I will hie me from thee fast,
Though thou weep till thy heart to-brast.[14]
EVERYMAN. Ye would ever bide by me, ye said.
STRENGTH. Yea, I have you far enough conveyed;
Ye be old enough, I understand,
Your pilgrimage to take on hand.
I repent me that I hither came.
EVERYMAN. Strength, you to displease I am to blame;
Will you break promise that is debt?
STRENGTH. In faith, I care not;
Thou art but a fool to complain;
You spend your speech and waste your brain;
Go, thrust thee into the ground.
[*Exit* STRENGTH.]
EVERYMAN. I had weened surer I should you have found.
He that trusteth in his Strength,
She him deceiveth at the length.
Both Strength and Beauty forsaketh me,
Yet they promised me fair and lovingly.
DISCRETION. Everyman, I will after Strength be gone;
As for me, I will leave you alone.
EVERYMAN. Why, Discretion, will ye forsake me?
DISCRETION. Yea, in faith, I will go from thee;
For when Strength goeth before
I follow after evermore.
EVERYMAN. Yet, I pray thee, for the love of the Trinity,
Look in my grave once piteously.
DISCRETION. Nay, so nigh will I not come.
Farewell, every one!
[*Exit* DISCRETION.]
EVERYMAN. O all thing faileth, save God alone,
Beauty, Strength, and Discretion;
For when Death bloweth his blast
They all run from me full fast.
FIVE WITS. Everyman, my leave now of thee I take;
I will follow the other, for here I thee forsake.
EVERYMAN. Alas! then may I wail and weep,
For I took you for my best friend.
FIVE WITS. I will no longer thee keep;
Now farewell, and there an end.
[*Exit* FIVE WITS.]
EVERYMAN. O Jesu, help! all hath forsaken me!
GOOD DEEDS. Nay, Everyman; I will bide with thee,
I will not forsake thee indeed;
Thou shalt find me a good friend at need.
EVERYMAN. Gramercy, Good Deeds! now may I true friends see;
They have forsaken me, every one;
I loved them better than my Good Deeds alone.
Knowledge, will ye forsake me also?
KNOWLEDGE. Yea, Everyman, when ye to death shall go;
But not yet, for no manner of danger.
EVERYMAN. Gramercy, Knowledge, with all my heart.
KNOWLEDGE. Nay, yet I will not from hence depart
Till I see where ye shall be come.
EVERYMAN. Methink, alas, that I must be gone
To make my reckoning and my debts pay,
For I see my time is nigh spent away.
Take example, all ye that this do hear or see,
How they that I loved best do forsake me,
Except my Good Deeds that bideth truly.
GOOD DEEDS. All earthly things is but vanity.
Beauty, Strength, and Discretion do man forsake,
Foolish friends and kinsmen, that fair spake,
All fleeth save Good Deeds, and that am I.
EVERYMAN. Have mercy on me, God most mighty,
And stand by me, thou mother and maid, Holy Mary!
GOOD DEEDS. Fear not, I will speak for thee.
EVERYMAN. Here I cry God mercy!

[14] Burst.

GOOD DEEDS. Short our end, and minish our pain.
Let us go and never come again.

EVERYMAN. Into thy hands, Lord, my soul I commend;
Receive it, Lord, that it be not lost.
As thou me boughtest, so me defend,
And save me from the fiend's boast,
That I may appear with that blessed host
That shall be saved at the day of doom.
In manus tuas — of might's most
For ever — *commendo spiritum meum.*[15]

[EVERYMAN *and* GOOD DEEDS *descend into the grave.*]

KNOWLEDGE. Now hath he suffered that we all shall endure;
The Good Deeds shall make all sure.
Now hath he made ending.
Methinketh that I hear angels sing
And make great joy and melody
Where Everyman's soul received shall be.

ANGEL [*Within*]. Come, excellent elect spouse to Jesu'!
Here above thou shalt go
Because of thy singular virtue.
Now thy soul is taken thy body fro,
Thy reckoning is crystal-clear.
Now shalt thou in to the heavenly sphere,
Unto the which all ye shall come
That liveth well before the day of doom.

[*Exit* KNOWLEDGE.]

[*Enter* DOCTOR *as Epilogue.*]

DOCTOR. This moral men may have in mind;
Ye hearers, take it of worth, old and young,
And forsake pride, for he deceiveth you in the end;
And remember Beauty, Five Wits, Strength, and Discretion,
They all at the last do Everyman forsake,
Save his Good Deeds there doth he take.
But beware, and they be small,
Before God he hath no help at all.
None excuse may be there for Everyman.
Alas, how shall he do then?
For, after death, amends may no man make,
For then mercy and pity do him forsake.
If his reckoning be not clear when he do come,
God will say — "*ite, maledicti, in ignem æternum.*"[16]
And he that hath his account whole and sound,
High in heaven he shall be crowned.
Unto which place God brings us all thither,
That we may live body and soul together.
Thereto help the Trinity!
Amen, say ye, for saint charity.

THUS ENDETH THIS MORAL PLAY OF EVERYMAN.

[15] In manus . . . meum: "Into thy hands . . . I commit my spirit."

[16] "Go, wicked ones, into the eternal fire."

¶ A MYRROVR FOR Magiſtrates.

Wherein maye be ſeen by example of other, with howe greuous plages vices are puniſhed: and howe frayle and unſtable worldly proſperity is founde, even of thoſe whom Fortune ſeemeth moſt highly to fauour.

Fœlix quem faciunt aliena pericula cautum.

Anno. 1563.

¶ Imprinted at London in Fleteſtrete nere to Saynct Dunſtans Churche by Thomas Marſhe.

INTRODUCTORY NOTE

The De Casibus Tradition: The Induction from *The Mirror for Magistrates*

The first edition of *The Mirror for Magistrates* (1559) offered nineteen verse tales of tragic misfortune written by several authors. These tragedies or rather tragic complaints are "spoken" by the ghosts of the unfortunates, who are historical figures drawn from the English Chronicles beginning with the reign of Richard II. The editor and guiding spirit of the *Mirror*, William Baldwin, also known for his *Treatise of Moral Philosophy* (1549), reveals in the preface to the first edition that an earlier edition was suppressed during printing in 1555. The second edition of 1563 added eight more tragedies and, more important, Thomas Sackville's "Induction," the only part of the *Mirror* with genuine literary merit. Whatever part Sackville may have played in the original conception of the *Mirror*, his "Induction" is evidently intended to preface his tragedy of Henry, Duke of Buckingham, not the *Mirror* as a whole. Augmented once again in 1578 and 1587, the *Mirror* was reprinted many times in the sixteenth century. The standard edition of the *Mirror* was prepared by Lily B. Campbell (Cambridge U. Press, 1938).

R. O.

THE INDUCTION FROM THE MIRROR FOR MAGISTRATES

BY

THOMAS SACKVILLE

The wrathful winter, 'proaching on apace,
With blustring blasts had all ybared the treen,
And old Saturnus, with his frosty face,
With chilling cold had pierced the tender green;
The mantles rent, wherein enwrapped been
The gladsome groves that now lay overthrown,
The tapets[1] torn, and every bloom down blown.

The soil, that erst so seemly was to seen,
Was all despoiled of her beauty's hue;
And soote[2] fresh flowers (wherewith the summer's queen
Had clad the earth) now Boreas' blasts down blew;
And small fowls flocking, in their song did rue
The winter's wrath, wherewith each thing defaced
In woeful wise bewailed the summer past.

Hawthorn had lost his motley livery,
The naked twigs were shivering all for cold,
And dropping down the tears abundantly;
Each thing (methought) with weeping eye me told
The cruel season, bidding me withhold
Myself within, for I was gotten out
Into the fields, whereas I walked about.

When lo, the night with misty mantles spread,
Gan dark the day and dim the azure skies;
And Venus in her message Hermes sped
To bloody Mars, to will him not to rise,
Which she herself approached in speedy wise;
And Virgo, hiding her disdainful breast,
With Thetis now had laid her down to rest.

Whiles Scorpio, dreading Sagittarius' dart,
Whose bow prest bent in fight, the string had slipped,
Down slid into the ocean flood apart;
The Bear, that in the Irish seas had dipped
His grisly feet, with speed from thence he whipped:
For Thetis, hasting from the Virgin's bed,
Pursued the Bear, that ere she came was fled.

And Phaethon now, near reaching to his race
With glistering beams, gold streaming where they bent,
Was prest[3] to enter in his resting place.
Erythius, that in the cart first went,
Had even now attained his journey's stent;
And, fast declining, hid away his head,
While Titan couched him in his purple bed.

And pale Cynthia, with her borrowed light,
Beginning to supply her brother's place,
Was past the noonstead six degrees in sight,
When sparkling stars amid the heaven's face
With twinkling light shone on the earth apace,
That, while they brought about the nightës chair,[4]
The dark had dimmed the day ere I was ware.

And sorrowing I to see the summer flowers,
The lively green, the lusty leas forlorn,
The sturdy trees so shattered with the showers,
The fields so fade that flourished so beforn,
It taught me well all earthly things be born
To die the death, for naught long time may last;
The summer's beauty yields to winter's blast.

Then looking upward to the heaven's leams,[5]
With nightës stars thick powdred everywhere,
Which erst so glistened with the golden streams
That cheerful Phoebus spread down from his sphere,
Beholding dark oppressing day so near:

[1] Tapestries of foliage. [2] Sweet.

[3] Ready. [4] The chariot of night.
[5] Rays of light.

The sudden sight reduced to my mind
The sundry changes that in earth we find.

That musing on this worldly wealth in thought,
Which comes and goes more faster than we see
The flickering flame that with the fire is wrought,
My busy mind presented unto me
Such fall of peers as in this realm had be,
That oft I wished some would their woes descrive,
To warn the rest whom fortune left alive.

And straight forth stalking with redoubled pace,
For that I saw the night drew on so fast,
In black all clad there fell before my face
A piteous wight, whom woe had all forwaste;
Forth from her eyne the crystal tears outbrast,[6]
And sighing sore, her hands she wrung and fold,
Tare all her hair, that ruth was to behold.

Her body small, forwithered and forspent,
As is the stalk that summer's drought oppresst;
Her welked [7] face with woeful tears besprent,
Her color pale, and (as it seemed her best)
In woe and plaint reposed was her rest;
And as the stone that drops of water wears,
So dented were her cheeks with fall of tears.

Her eyes swollen with flowing streams afloat,
Wherewith, her looks thrown up full piteously,
Her forceless hands together oft she smote,
With doleful shrieks that echoed in the sky;
Whose plaint such sighs did straight accompany,
That, in my doom, was never man did see
A wight but half so woebegone as she.

I stood aghast beholding all her plight,
'Tween dread and dolor, so distrained in heart,
That while my hairs upstarted with the sight,
The tears out streamed for sorrow of her smart;
But when I saw no end that could apart
The deadly deule [8] which she so sore did make,
With doleful voice then thus to her I spake:

Unwrap thy woes, whatever wight thou be,
And stint betime to spill thyself with plaint;
Tell what thou art, and whence, for well I see
Thou canst not dure, with sorrow thus attaint.
And with that word of sorrow, all forfaint
She looked up, and prostrate as she lay,
With piteous sound, lo, thus she gan to say:

Alas, I, wretch whom thus thou seest distrained
With wasting woes that never shall aslake,
Sorrow I am, in endless torments pained
Among the Furies in the infernal lake
Where Pluto, god of Hell, so grisly black,
Doth hold his throne, and Lethe's deadly taste
Doth reave [9] remembrance of each thing forepast.

Whence come I am, the dreary destiny
And luckless lot for to bemoan of those
Whom Fortune, in this maze of misery,
Of wretched chance, most woeful mirrors chose;
That when thou seest how lightly they did lose
Their pomp, their power, and that they thought most sure,
Thou mayst soon deem no earthly joy may dure.

Whose rueful voice no sooner had out brayed
Those woeful words wherewith she sorrowed so,
But Out, alas! she shright and never stayed,
Fell down, and all to-dashed herself for woe;
The cold pale dread my limbs gan overgo,
And I so sorrowed at her sorrows eft [10]
That, what with grief and fear, my wits were reft.

I stretched myself and straight my heart revives,
That dread and dolor erst did so appall;
Like him that with the fervent fever strives,
When sickness seeks his castle health to scale,
With gathered spirits so forced I fear to avale; [11]
And rearing her with anguish all fordone,
My spirits returned and then I thus begun:

O Sorrow, alas, sith Sorrow is thy name,
And that to thee this drear doth well pertain,
In vain it were to seek to cease the same;

[6] Burst forth. [7] Withered.
[8] Sorrow.

[9] Steal away. [10] In turn.
[11] Yield.

But as a man himself with sorrow slain,
So I, alas, do comfort thee in pain,
That here in sorrow art forsunk so deep
That at thy sight I can but sigh and weep.

I had no sooner spoken of a sike,[12]
But that the storm so rumbled in her breast
As Aeolus could never roar the like;
And showers down rained from her eyne so fast
That all bedrent the place, till at the last
Well eased they the dolor of her mind,
As rage of rain doth swage the stormy wind.

For forth she paced in her fearful tale;
Come, come (quod she) and see what I shall show;
Come hear the plaining and the bitter bale
Of worthy men by Fortune overthrow;
Come thou and see them rueing all in row:
They were but shades that erst in mind thou rolled;
Come, come with me, thine eyes shall them behold.

What could these words but make me more aghast,
To hear her tell whereon I mused whilere?
So was I mazed therewith, till at the last,
Musing upon her words, and what they were,
All suddenly well-lessoned was my fear;
For to my mind returned how she telled
Both what she was and where her wone[13] she held.

Whereby I knew that she a goddess was,
And therewithal resorted to my mind
My thought, that late presented me the glass
Of brittle state, of cares that here we find,
Of thousand woes to silly men assigned;
And how she now bid me come and behold,
To see with eye that erst in thought I rolled.

Flat down I fell, and with all reverence
Adored her, perceiving now that she,
A goddess sent by godly providence,
In earthy shape thus showed herself to me,
To wail and rue this world's uncertainty;
And while I honored thus her godhead's might,
With plaining voice these words to me she shright:

I shall guide thee first to the grisly lake
And thence unto the blissful place of rest;
Where thou shalt see and hear the plaint they make
That whilom here bare swing[14] among the best;
This shalt thou see, but great is the unrest
That thou must bide before thou canst attain
Unto the dreadful place where these remain.

And with these words, as I upraised stood,
And gan to follow her that straight forth paced,
Ere I was ware, into a desert wood
We now were come; where, hand in hand embraced,
She led the way and through the thick so traced
As, but I had been guided by her might,
It was no way for any mortal wight.

But lo, while thus amid the desert dark
We passed on with steps and pace unmeet,
A rumbling roar, confused with howl and bark
Of dogs, shook all the ground under our feet,
And struck the din within our ears so deep
As, half distraught, unto the ground I fell,
Besought return, and not to visit hell.

But she, forthwith, uplifting me apace,
Removed my dread, and with a steadfast mind
Bade me come on; for here was now the place,
The place where we our travail end should find;
Wherewith I arose, and to the place assigned
Astoined[15] I stalk, when straight we approached near
The dreadful place that you will dread to hear.

An hideous hole all vast, withouten shape,
Of endless depth, o'erwhelmed with ragged stone,
With ugly mouth and grisly jaws doth gape,
And to our sight confounds itself in one;
Here entered we, and yeding[16] forth, anon
An horrible loathly lake we might discern,
As black as pitch, that cleped is Avern.

A deadly gulf where naught but rubbish grows,
With foul black swelth[17] in thickened lumps that lies,
Which up in the air such stinking vapors throws

[12] Sigh.
[13] Dwelling.
[14] Command.
[15] Stunned.
[16] Going.
[17] Foul water.

That over there may fly no fowl but dies,
Chocked with the pestilent savors that arise;
Hither we come, whence forth we still did pace,
In dreadful fear amid the dreadful place.

And first, within the porch and jaws of hell,
Sat deep Remorse of Conscience, all besprent
With tears, and to herself oft would she tell
Her wretchedness, and cursing never stent
To sob and sigh; but ever thus lament
With thoughtful care as she that, all in vain,
Would wear and waste continually in pain.

Her eyes unsteadfast, rolling here and there,
Whirled on each place, as place that vengeance brought,
So was her mind continually in fear,
Tossed and tormented with the tedious thought
Of those detested crimes which she had wrought;
With dreadful cheer and looks thrown to the sky,
Wishing for death, and yet she could not die.

Next saw we Dread, all trembling how he shook,
With foot uncertain, proffered here and there,
Benumbed of speech, and with a ghastly look,
Searched every place, all pale and dead for fear,
His cap borne up with staring of his hair,
'Stoined and amazed at his own shade for dread,
And fearing greater dangers than was need.

And next, within the entry of this lake,
Sat fell Revenge, gnashing her teeth for ire,
Devising means how she may vengeance take,
Never in rest till she have her desire;
But frets within so far forth with the fire
Of wreaking [18] flames, that now determines she
To die by death, or venged by death to be.

When fell Revenge, with bloody foul pretense
Had showed herself as next in order set,
With trembling limbs we softly parted thence,
Till in our eyes another sight we met,
When from my heart a sight forthwith I fet,
Rueing, alas, upon the woeful plight
Of Misery, that next appeared in sight.

His face was lean and somedeal pined away,
And eke his hands consumed to the bone,
But what his body was I cannot say,
For on his carcass raiment had he none,
Save clouts and patches, pieced one by one;
With staff in hand and scrip on shoulders cast,
His chief defense against the winter's blast.

His food, for most, was wild fruits of the tree,
Unless sometime some crumbs fell to his share,
Which in his wallet long, God wot, kept he,
As on the which full daint'ly would he fare;
His drink, the running stream; his cup, the bare
Of his palm closed; his bed, the hard cold ground;
To this poor life was Misery ybound.

Whose wretched state when we had well beheld,
With tender ruth on him and on his feres,[19]
In thoughtful cares forth then our pace we held;
And by and by another shape appears,
Of greedy Care, still brushing up the breres,[20]
His knuckles knobbed, his flesh deep dented in,
With tawed [21] hands and hardy ytanned skin.

The morrow gray no sooner had begun
To spread his light, even peeping in our eyes,
When he is up and to his work yrun;
But let the night's black misty mantles rise,
And with foul dark never so much disguise
The fair bright day, yet ceaseth he no while,
But hath his candles to prolong his toil.

By him lay heavy Sleep, the cousin of Death,
Flat on the ground and still as any stone,
A very corpse, save yielding forth a breath;
Small keep took he whom Fortune frowned on
Or whom she lifted up into the throne
Of high renown; but as a living death,
So dead alive, of life he drew the breath.

The body's rest, the quiet of the heart,
The travail's ease, the still night's fere was he,
And of our life in earth the better part;
Reaver of sight, and yet in whom we see
Things oft that tide, and oft that never be;
Without respect, esteeming equally
King Croesus' pomp, and Irus' poverty.

And next in order sad Old Age we found,
His beard all hoar, his eyes hollow and blind,

[18] Avenging.

[19] Companions. [20] Briars.

[21] Tanned (as leather is).

With drooping cheer still poring on the ground,
As on the place where nature him assigned
To rest, when that the sisters had untwined
His vital thread and ended with their knife
The fleeting course of fast declining life.

There heard we him with broken and hollow plaint
Rue with himself his end approaching fast,
And all for naught his wretched mind torment
With sweet remembrance of his pleasures past,
And fresh delights of lusty youth forewaste;
Recounting which, how would he sob and shriek,
And to be young again of Jove beseek!

But, and the cruel fates so fixed be
That time forepast cannot return again,
This one request of Jove yet prayed he,
That in such withered plight and wretched pain
As eld, accompanied with his loathsome train,
Had brought on him, all were it woe and grief,
He might a while yet linger forth his life,

And not so soon descend into the pit
Where Death, when he the mortal corpse hath slain,
With retchless[22] hand in grave doth cover it,
Thereafter never to enjoy again
The gladsome light, but in the ground ylain,
In depth of darkness waste and wear to naught,
As he had never into the world been brought.

But who had seen him sobbing, how he stood
Unto himself and how he would bemoan
His youth forepast, as though it wrought him good
To talk of youth, all were his youth foregone,
He would have mused and marveled much, whereon
This wretched Age should life desire so fain,
And knows full well life doth but length his pain.

Crookbacked he was, tooth-shaken, and blear-eyed,
Went on three feet, and sometime crept on four,
With old lame bones that rattled by his side,
His scalp all pilled[23] and he with eld forlore;
His withered fist still knocking at Death's door,
Fumbling and driveling as he draws his breath;
For brief, the shape and messenger of Death.

And fast by him pale Malady was placed,
Sore sick in bed, her color all foregone,
Bereft of stomach, savor, and of taste,
Ne could she brook no meat, but broths alone;
Her breath corrupt, her keepers every one
Abhorring her, her sickness past recure,
Detesting physic and all physic's cure.

But oh, the doleful sight that then we see!
We turned our look and on the other side
A grisly shape of Famine mought we see,
With greedy looks and gaping mouth that cried
And roared for meat, as she should there have died;
Her body thin and bare as any bone,
Whereto was left naught but the case alone.

And that, alas, was gnawn on everywhere,
All full of holes that I ne mought refrain
From tears to see how she her arms could tear,
And with her teeth gnash on the bones in vain,
When all for naught, she fain would so sustain
Her starven corpse, that rather seemed a shade
Than any substance of a creature made.

Great was her force, whom stone wall could not stay,
Her tearing nails snatching at all she saw;
With gaping jaws that by no means ymay
Be satisfied from hunger of her maw,
But eats herself as she that hath no law;
Gnawing, alas, her carcass all in vain,
Where you may count each sinew, bone, and vein.

On her while we thus firmly fixed our eyes,
That bled for ruth of such a dreary sight,
Lo, suddenly she shright in so huge wise
As made hell gates to shiver with the might;
Wherewith a dart we saw, how it did light
Right on her breast, and therewithal, pale Death
Enthrilling it, to reave her of her breath.

And by and by a dumb dead corpse we saw,
Heavy and cold, the shape of Death aright,
That daunts all earthly creatures to his law;

[22] Careless.
[23] Bald.

Against whose force in vain it is to fight;
Ne peers, ne princes, nor no mortal wight,
No towns, ne realms, cities, ne strongest tower,
But all, perforce, must yield unto his power.

His dart, anon, out of the corpse he took,
And in his hand (a dreadful sight to see)
With great triumph eftsoons the same he shook,
That most of all my fears affrayed me;
His body dight with naught but bones, perdy,
The naked shape of man there saw I plain,
All save the flesh, the sinew, and the vein.

Lastly, stood War, in glittering arms yclad,
With visage grim, stern looks, and blackly hued;
In his right hand a naked sword he had,
That to the hilts was all with blood imbrued;
And in his left, that kings and kingdoms rued,
Famine and fire he held, and therewithal
He razed towns and threw down towers and all.

Cities he sacked and realms that whilom flowered
In honor, glory, and rule above the best,
He overwhelmed and all their fame devoured,
Consumed, destroyed, wasted, and never ceased
Till he their wealth, their name, and all oppressed;
His face forhewed with wounds, and by his side
There hung his targe, with gashes deep and wide.

In midst of which, depainted there, we found
Deadly Debate, all full of snaky hair,
That with a bloody fillet was ybound,
Out-breathing naught but discord everywhere,
And round about were portrayed, here and there,
The hugy hosts, Darius and his power,
His kings, princes, his peers, and all his flower.

Whom great Macedo vanquished there in sight
With deep slaughter, despoiling all his pride,
Pierced through his realms and daunted all his might;
Duke Hannibal beheld I there beside,
In Canna's field victor how he did ride,
And woeful Romans that in vain withstood,
And consul Paulus covered all in blood.

Yet saw I more: the fight at Thrasimene,
And Treby field, and eke when Hannibal
And worthy Scipio last in arms were seen
Before Carthago gate, to try for all
The world's empire, to whom it should befall;
There saw I Pompey and Caesar clad in arms,
Their hosts allied and all their civil harms.

With conquerors' hands forbathed in their own blood,
And Caesar weeping over Pompey's head;
Yet saw I Sulla and Marius where they stood,
Their great cruelty and the deep bloodshed
Of friends; Cyrus I saw and his host dead,
And how the queen with great despite hath flung
His head in blood of them she overcome.

Xerxes, the Persian king, yet saw I there
With his huge host that drank the rivers dry,
Dismounted hills, and made the vales uprear,
His host and all yet saw I slain, perdy;
Thebes I saw, all razed how it did lie
In heaps of stones, and Tyrus put to spoil,
With walls and towers flat evened with the soil.

But Troy, alas, methought above them all
It made mine eyes in very tears consume,
When I beheld the woeful werd [24] befall,
That by the wrathful will of gods was come;
And Jove's unmoved sentence and foredoom
On Priam king, and on his town so bent,
I could not lin, [25] but I must there lament.

And that the more, sith destiny was so stern
As, force perforce, there might no force avail,
But she must fall, and by her fall we learn
That cities, towers, wealth, world, and all shall quail;
No manhood, might, nor nothing mought prevail;
All were there prest, full many a prince and peer,
And many a knight that sold his death full dear.

Not worthy Hector, worthiest of them all,
Her hope, her joy, his force is now for naught;
O Troy, Troy, there is no boot but bale,
The hugy horse within thy walls is brought;
Thy turrets fall, thy knights, that whilom fought
In arms amid the field, are slain in bed,
Thy gods defiled and all thy honor dead.

The flames upspring and cruelly they creep
From wall to roof till all to cinders waste;

[24] A variant of *weird*: fated event. [25] Cease.

Some fire the houses where the wretches sleep,
Some rush in here, some run in there as fast;
In everywhere or sword or fire they taste;
The walls are torn, the towers whirled to the ground;
There is no mischief but may there be found.

Cassandra yet there saw I how they haled
From Pallas' house, with spercled [26] tress undone,
Her wrists fast bound and with Greeks' rout empaled;
And Priam eke, in vain how did he run
To arms, whom Pyrrhus with despite hath done
To cruel death, and bathed him in the baign
Of his son's blood, before the altar slain.

But how can I descrive the doleful sight
That in the shield so livelike fair did shine?
Sith in this world I think was never wight
Could have set forth the half, not half so fine;
I can no more but tell how there is seen
Fair Ilium fall in burning red gledes down,
And from the soil great Troy, Neptunus' town.

Herefrom when scarce I could mine eyes withdraw,
That filled with tears as doth the springing well,
We passed on so far forth till we saw
Rude Acheron, a loathsome lake to tell,
That boils and bubs up swelth as black as hell;
Where grisly Charon, at their fixed tide,
Still ferries ghosts unto the farther side.

The aged god no sooner Sorrow spied,
But hasting straight unto the bank apace,
With hollow call unto the rout he cried
To swerve apart and give the goddess place;
Straight it was done, when to the shore we pace,
Where, hand in hand as we then linked fast,
Within the boat we are together placed.

And forth we launch full fraughted to the brink,
When with the unwonted weight, the rusty keel
Began to crack as if the same should sink;
We hoise up mast and sail, that in a while
We fetched the shore, where scarcely we had while
For to arrive, but that we heard anon
A three-sound bark confounded all in one.

We had not long forth passed but that we saw
Black Cerberus, the hideous hound of hell,
With bristles reared and with a three-mouthed jaw
Fordinning the air with his horrible yell,
Out of the deep dark cave where he did dwell;
The goddess straight he knew, and by and by,
He peased [27] and couched while that we passed by.

Thence come we to the horror and the hell,
The large great kingdoms and the dreadful reign
Of Pluto in his throne where he did dwell,
The wide waste places and the hugy plain.
The wailings, shrieks, and sundry sorts of pain,
The sighs, the sobs, the deep and deadly groan,
Earth, air, and all, resounding plaint and moan.

Here puled the babes, and here the maids unwed
With folded hands their sorry chance bewailed,
Here wept the guiltless slain, and lovers dead,
That slew themselves when nothing else availed;
A thousand sorts of sorrows here, that wailed
With sighs and tears, sobs, shrieks, and all yfere, [28]
That oh, alas, it was a hell to hear.

We stayed us straight, and with a rueful fear,
Beheld this heavy sight, while from mine eyes
The vapored tears down stilled here and there,
And Sorrow eke, in far more woeful wise,
Took on with plaint, upheaving to the skies
Her wretched hands, that with her cry the rout
Gan all in heaps to swarm us round about.

Lo here (quoth Sorrow) princes of renown,
That whilom sat on top of Fortune's wheel,
Now laid full low, like wretches whirled down,
Even with one frown, that stayed but with a smile;
And now behold the thing that thou, erewhile,
Saw only in thought, and what thou now shalt hear,
Recount the same to kesar, king, and peer.

Then first came Henry, Duke of Buckingham,
His cloak of black all pilled and quite forworn,

[26] Disheveled.

[27] Grew still.

[28] Together.

Wringing his hands, and Fortune oft doth blame,
Which of a duke hath made him now her scorn;
With ghastly looks, as one in manner lorn,
Oft spread his arms, stretched hands he joins as fast
With rueful cheer and vapored eyes upcast.

His cloak he rent, his manly breast he beat,
His hair all torn, about the place it lay;
My heart so molt to see his grief so great,
As feelingly methought it dropped away;
His eyes they whirled about withouten stay,
With stormy sighs the place did so complain,
As if his heart at each had burst in twain.

Thrice he began to tell his doleful tale,
And thrice the sighs did swallow up his voice,
At each of which he shrieked so withal,
As though the heavens rived with the noise;
Till at the last, recovering his voice,
Supping the tears that all his breast berained,
On cruel fortune, weeping, thus he plained.

A DISCOVRSE VPON THE MEANES OF VVEL GOVERNING AND MAINTAINING IN GOOD PEACE, A KINGDOME, OR OTHER PRINCIPALITIE.

Divided into three parts, namely, The Counsell, the Religion, and the Policie, vvhich a Prince ought to hold and follow.

Against *Nicholas Machiavell* the Florentine.

Translated into English by Simon Patericke.

LONDON,

Printed by Adam Islip.

1602.

INTRODUCTORY NOTE

The Myth of the Machiavel: Innocent Gentillet's *Contre-Machiavel*

Innocent Gentillet's famous attack on Machiavelli was published in France in 1576 and reprinted four times by 1579. An English translation by Simon Patericke under the title of *A Discourse upon the meanes of wel Governing . . . a kingdome. . . Against Nicolas Machiavell, the Florentine* was published in 1602 and reprinted in 1609. The excerpts are taken from the 1602 edition.

R. O.

Moralist with high ideals —

The Prince - rulers <u>pretend</u> to be good...

better not to have a heart..

Elizabethans thought it was a "devil"

Italian - Italy dump all corruption...

CONTRE-MACHIAVEL

BY

INNOCENT GENTILLET

OF RELIGION

1. *MAXIME.*

A Prince above all things ought to wish and desire to be esteemed devout, though he be not so indeed.

THE WORLD (saith *Machiavell*) looketh but to the exterior, and to that which is in appearance; and iudgeth of al actions not by the causes, but by the issue and end: So that it sufficeth, if that the Prince seeme outwardly religious and devout, although he be not so at all. For let it be so, that some, which most narrowly frequent his companie, doe discover that feined devotion, yet he or they dare not oppugne the multitude, who beleeve, the Prince to be truly devout.

THIS MAXIME is a precept, whereby this Atheist *Machiavell* teacheth the Prince to be a true contemner of God and of Religion, and onely to make a shew and a faire countenance outwardly before the world, to be esteemed religious and devout, although he be not. For divine punishment, for such hypocrisie and dissimulation, *Machiavell* feares not, because he beleeves not there is a God; but thinkes that the course of the Sunne, of the Moone, of the Starres, the distinction of the Spring time, Summer, Autumne, and Winter, the pollitické government of men, the production that the earth makes of fruits, plants, living creatures, that all this comes by encounter and adventure: following the doctrine of *Epicurus*, (the doctor of Atheists, and master of Ignorance) who esteemes, that all things are done and come to passe by Fortune, and the meeting and encountring of atomes. But if *Machiavell* beleeved, that those things came by the disposition and establishment of a soveraigne cause (as common sence hath constrained *Plato*, *Aristotle*, *Theophrastus*, and all the other Phylosophers which have had any knowledge, to confesse it) he would beleeve there is one God, who ruleth & governeth the world, and all things within it. And if he beleeve there is one God, hee would also beleeve, that men ought to honour him as the soveraigne governour; and that hee will not be mocked of his creatures: And therefore will not he give such precepts, to make a shew to be devout, and not to be. For what is it to mocke God, if that be not? But they that learne such lessons of Atheisme, and which put out their eyes, that they may not see so cleare a light, and which take pleasure to be ignorant of that which (as *Cicero* saith) even nature it selfe teacheth the most barbarous nations, That there is a God which governeth all things; let them (I say) know, that if they will not know God well, God will well know them, and will make them well feele, that such as spit against heaven, shall spit against themselves; when they shall feele how heavie his hand weigheth, then shall they know, that there is a God, a revenger of them which reverence him not, but this knowledge shall be to their confusion and ruine. Many Atheists have been seene, which of a brutish boldness have made a mock of God: but it was never seene, that they felt not the punishment and vengeance of their audaciousnesse and impietie, as hereafter we will shew by examples. Yet wee have cause greatly to deplore the miserie and calamitie of the time wherein we are, which is so infected with Atheists, and contemners of God and of all Religion, that even they, which have no religion, are best esteemed, and are called in the court language, people of service: because being fraughted with all impietie and Atheisme, and having well studied their *Machiavell*, which they know upon their fingers, they make no scruple nor conscience at anything. Commaund them to slay and massacre, they slay and massacre; commaund them to rob and spoile good Catholickes, and Cleargie men, they rob and spoile all. They hold benefices with souldiers garments and short clokes, yet exercise no Religion, nor cares, but for the gaine therof. Commaund them to enterprise the betraying or impoysoning of this or that person, they make no scruple at it: yea, they themselves excogitate and devise all wickednesse and impieties, as the invention of so many new imposts upon the poore people, which they destroy and cause to die with hunger, without having any commiseration or compassion upon them, no more than upon brute beasts. . . . They alwayes have in their mouths their goodly Maximes of their *Machiavell,* to empeach and hinder a good peace. A prince (say they) must cause himselfe to bee feared, rather than loved: & this must be held as a resolved point. But if a peace be accorded to these rebels, such as they desire, then would it seeme that the king were afraid of his subjects, whereas he should make himselfe to be feared. True it is, that if such a peace could be made with them, as it might againe procure another S. *Bartholmewes* journey, nothing were so good & pleasant as that. For that is another resolved point and Maxime, That a prince ought not to hold any faith or promise, but so farre, as concernes his profit: and that hee ought to know how to counterfeit the foxe, to catch and entrap other beasts, and as soone as he hath them in his nets, to play the lion in slaying & devouring them. We have set downe unto us that goodly example of *Cæsar Borgia,* who in our country could so well counterfeit the said two beasts. Behold here the language and dealings of our Machiavelistes, which at this day men call people of Service: for that there is no wickednesse in the world so strange and detestable, but they wil enterprise, invent, and put it in execution, if they can. From whence comes it, that they be thus enclined to all wickednesse? It is because they are Atheists, contemners of God, neither beleeving there is a God which seeth what they doe, nor that ought to punish them. It is that goodly doctrine of *Machiavell,* which amongst other things complaines so much, that men cannot be altogether wicked (as we shall touch in his place.) These good disciples (seeing that their master found this imperfection amongst men, that they could not shew themselves altogether and in all things wicked) doe seeke by all meanes to attaine a degree of perfect wickednesse. And indeed they have so well studied and profited in their masters schoole, and can so well practise his Maximes, that none can deny, but they are come unto the highest degree of wickednesse. What need men then to be abashed, if they see in the world, and especially in this poore kindome of France, such famine, pestilence, civile warres, the father to band against his sonne, brother against his brother, they of the same Religion one against another, with all hatred, envie, disloyaltie, treasons, perfidies conspirations, empoysonments, & other great sinnes to raigne? Is there any marvaile if the people goe to wracke, the Cleargie be impoverished, the Nobilitie almost extinct? For it is the first judgement and vengeance of God, which he exerciseth against us: because some are filled with all impietie and Atheisme, which they have learned of *Machiavell:* and others which should resist such impieties, least they should take root, doe suffer them to encrease & augment. So that indeed all men are culpable of Atheisme, impietie, of the despight of God and Religion, which at this day raigneth. Therefore most righteously dooth God punish us all. For Atheisme and impietie is so detestable and abhominable before God, that it never remaineth unpunished. . . .

OF POLICIE

8. MAXIME.

A prince neede not care to bee accounted cruell, if so bee that hee can make himselfe bee obeyed thereby.

CÆSAR BORGIA (saith *Messier Nicholas*) was reputed cruell, yet by his crueltie hee brought into order, and into his obedience the whole countrie of Romania: Wherefore the prince neede take no great care, to see himselfe in reputation to be cruell, so that thereby he maintaine his people in a faithfull union and obedience. For the cruell and rigorous executions of a prince, doe but privately hurt certaine particulars, which ought not to be feared; and the too great lenitie of a pitifull prince, is the cause of infinit evils, which grow up and engender in their kingdomes, as murderes, thefts, and other like: Insomuch as a man may well say, that a pitifull prince, is cause of more evills than a cruell prince. The example of the emperour *Severus* may serve vs for proofe heereof, for hee was very cruell, and by his crueltie overcame *Albinus* & *Niger*, & the most part of their friends, & so wrought himselfe a peaceable empire, which hee long time held, beeing well obeyed, and reverenced of all the world.

I HAVE heeretofore shewed, how *Cæsar Borgia*, by his crueltie obtained for enemies, almost all the potentates of Italie, and thereby so well assured his estate, that incontinent as his father was dead, he was invironed with enemies, destitute of friends, despoiled of the lands he had usurped, and constrained to hide himselfe to save his life. This tragicall issue accordeth not very well, with that which *Machiavell* heere maintaineth, saying That the crueltie of *Borgia*, was the cause that hee got the peaceable domination of Romania: For to say truth, it was not his crueltie (which easilie might have beene resisted, *Borgia* of himselfe beeing without power) but it was the favour and feare of the pope his father, who commanded the French powers, and made himselfe feared of all christian princes. For at that time men feared more the popes simple buls, than at this day they feare either the keies of S. *Peter*, or the sword of S. *Paul* (which hee said hee had) or all his fulminations, excommunications, agravations, reagravations, interdicts, anathematizations, or all the forces and meanes hee can make. And who would make account of all those at this day? seeing even the Romanes themselves make but a mocke of them. But in the time of *Alexander Borgia*, yea in the time of Pope *Iulius* the eleaventh his successor, all that the Pope would and ordained, was held of christian princes for an ordinance as from the mouth of God, yea, even when the Pope ordained things manifestly wicked: as when *Iulius* delivered as a prey, the whole kingdome of France, and the lands of the kings allies. For the king of England, of Arragon, and the emperour *Maximilian*, beleeved all, that it was a sufficient cause to set upon the king and his allies, and that it was even as an expresse commandement of God. The world then, and even princes, being then overtaken with that beastly superstition and follie, wee neede not bee abashed, that *Cæsar Borgia*, had the meanes to possesse Romania, under the shadow and favour of the Pope his father, & that with the aide of the king of France: and it was plainly seene, that that good hap to subjugate Romania, proceeded from favour, and not from crueltie (as *Machiavell* saith) because as soone as that favour ceased, all his case was overthrowne, and it was straight seene, that his utter ruine arived, as is said. I doe then maintaine cleane contrary from the Maxime of *Machiavell*, and say, That crueltie is a vice which ordinarily bringeth to princes the ruine of them, & their estates, and that clemencie and gentlenes is the true meanes, to maintaine and establish a prince firme and assured in his estate.

For proofe heereof reasons are cleare and manifest: for wee call crueltie, all executions which are committed upon men, their lands and goods, without any forme of justice, or against all right and equitie: heereupon it followeth, that as violence is directly contrarie to right and equitie, so also is crueltie, and that crueltie is no other thing but manifest violence. But according to the Maximes, even of philosophers, *No violent thing can endure*; So it followeth, that an estate founded upon cruelty, cannot long endure. Moreover crueltie is alwaies hated of every one; for although it bee not practised upon all particulars, but upon some onely; yet they upon whom it is not exercised, cease not to feare, when they see it executed upon their parents, friends, allies and neighbours: But the feare of paine and punishment, engendreth hatred; for one can never love that, whereof hee feares to receive evill, especiallie when there is a feare of life, losse of goods and honours, which are the things wee hold most precious: and of that which wee hate, wee by the same meanes desire the losse and entier ruine, and search out, procure and advance it with all our power. But it is impossible when all a people shooteth at one same marke, that a tyrant or cruell prince (for all is one) can long endure, or that hee can doe so much, as there shall not arive unto him, some disastre or evill fortune: And if sometimes it please God to suffer him to live long, it is to cause him to take the higher leap, that in the end hee may have the sorer fall: As wee see it well painted in poets tragœdies, where many tyrants are seene (which enduring long time, have done no other thing during the space of their life, but knit cordes, fasten gallowes in some imminent places, whet swords and daggers, & temper poisons) for afterward to drinke the poison, to stab the dagger in their bosomes, or hang themselves on the gibet, in the sight of all the world; which laughing and mocking them, say, it is well employed: & we must not say, that such tragœdies are but poeticall fictions; for hystories are full of such tragicall ends of tyrants, which have delighted to shed their subjects bloud, and to handle them cruellie. . . .

OF POLICIE

12. MAXIME.

A prince ought to follow the nature of the Lyon, and of the Fox: not of the one without the other.

YOU MUST understand (saith this *Florentine*) that men fight in two manners: the one with lawes, when matters are handled by reason: the other with force: The first is proper to men, which have the use of reason: The second appertaineth to beasts, which have neither reason nor intelligence: But because the first is not sufficient to keepe men and to to maintaine them, in inioying of things belonging unto them, they must needes oftentimes have recourse to the second, which is force. Wherefore it is needefull, that a prince can well play the beast, and the man together: as our elders have taught, when they writ, that *Chiron* the Centaure, halfe a man and halfe a beast, was given as an instructor for the prince *Achilles*: For heereby hee gave to understand, that a prince ought to shew himselfe a man and a beast together. A prince then beeing constrained well to know how to counterfet the beast, hee ought amongst all beasts to chuse the complexion of the Fox, and of the Lyon together, and not of the one without the other: for the Fox is subtill, to keepe himselfe from snares, yet he is too weake to guard himselfe from wolves: and the Lyon is strong enough to guard himselfe from wolves, but hee is not subtill enough to keepe himselfe from nets: A man must then bee a Foxe to know all subtilties and deceits, and a Lyon to bee the stronger, and to make wolves afraid. The emperour *Didius Iulianus* knew well how to play the Fox, to come to the empire, in promising men of warre great sommes of mony, to obtaine the empire: For after he was chosen; hee played them a Foxes part, deceiving them, in giving them much lesse than hee promised: but not knowing withall how to play the Lyon, hee was incontinent overthrowne: For *Severus*, who was cunning to play both, came against him with great force; insomuch as hee was slaine by his owne souldiers of his guarde, which went to *Severus* side. And in the meane while *Severus* seeing that the captaine *Albinus*, was in Gaule, with a puissant armie; and captaine *Niger* in Levant likewise with a great army, hee played the Fox, to allure them by faire words: that they would not hinder him to obtaine the empire: for hee feared them, because they had great forces in their hands, and that they were more noble, and of more ancient houses than hee: Hee made them great promises, especiallie hee promised *Albinus* to associate him in the empire, and to give him the name and authoritie of *Çæsar*, which was the like title, as at this day is king of the Romanes: And as for *Niger*, hee held his children in his hands as hostages, under coulour of honour and favour, so that hee the lesse feared him. As soone as hee had thus by playing the Fox and deceit, stayed *Albinus* and *Niger*, hee ended his enterprise, to make himselfe knowne a peaceable emperour: But after this, taking unto him the nature of the Lyon, he turned his forces against *Albinus* & *Niger*, and overcame them both, one after another: So that by knowing well how to play these two beasts, the Lyon and the Fox, hee made himselfe a peaceable emperour without competitor. Contrary, the emperour *Maximin*, after he was elected emperour by the souldiers of his hoast, could not play one part of the Fox, but only of the Lyon, which was the cause that he endured not, and that many were elected, to hinder his quiet possession of the empire, insomuch as in the end, hee was overthrowne and slaine of his owne souldiers.

MACHIAVELL HATH not yet handled a discourse more worthie of his sufficiency than this: For hee teacheth by this Maxime the manner to be a beast, and especially how a prince should in all his behaviours use himselfe like a beast: Thinke you I pray you, that to teach, how being a man, you may imitate a beast, is a small matter? I know well that our *Machiavelists*, will say, that heerein is hid a secret of philosophie, & that *Machiavell* meaneth that a prince should be as subtill as a Fox, & violent like a Lyon; not that he must go with foure feet, or that he must dwell in the deserts of Arabia, or in holes in woods, or commit other such like actions, as the Fox & Lion doe. Well I am content to agree unto them this morall sense; and that their master meant here to declare some singular & memorable doctrine: Let us now come to examine it: He saith then, when a prince cannot fight like a man, that is by reason; he ought to fight like a beast, that is, to use force and subtiltie. To this I answere, that a prince in his quarrell hath either reason or right on his side, or els hee hath them not: If hee hath them not, he ought not to fight against any man: for each war ought to have his foundation upon reason, as other where wee have shewed: If the prince hath reason on his side, and he with whom hee hath to doe, refuseth to come to reason, then the prince may justly constraine him by force of armes: and this is not called to fight like a beast, nor like a Lion, but it is to fight as a man using reason, who employeth his owne corporall force, and the force of his horses, of his armies and walls, and of all other things offensive and defensive, to serve for instruments and meanes to execute that which reason commandeth and ordaineth: so that force employed to his right use, is no other thing but a servant of reason, which obeyeth her in all her commandements: and therefore therein there is nothing of a beast, and they which thus employ their forces, doe nothing that holds of a beast. As for guile and subtiltie, I say likewise, that in warre a man may lawfully use subtilties against his enemies, if so be his faith and the rights of warre bee not violated, and this is not called foxlike subtiltie, or unlawful deceiving, but it ought to be called militarie prudence: And therefore in warre to use subtiltie, fraud, and militarie sharpenesse of wit (for all those names may be well used) is not to counterfeit the beast, nor to play the Fox. But I know well, *Machiavell* is of another mind, namely, That a prince is not bound unto right, faith, or religious promise, to hinder him that he may not use now force, and now subtiltie, according as the one or the other may best serve him, to come to the end hee pretendeth: For of faith and promise, or of right and reason, men may not speake in *Machiavels* schoole, unlesse it be to mocke at them, which esteeme such, most holy bands of humane societie: but concerning faith and promises, we shall have another Maxime, wherein we shall rip up this matter to the bottome: but here only I will shew that these foxlike subtilties and deceits, where of *Machiavell* meanes in his speech, doe not ever succeed well to them who use them, but most commonly they fall into their owne nets. . . .

But should we call this beastlinesse, or mallice, which *Machiavell* saith of *Chiron*? or hath he read, that *Chiron* was both a man and a beast? Who hath told him, that he was delivered to the prince *Achilles*, to teach him that goodly knowledge to be both a man and a beast? *Xenophon* saith, that *Chiron* was *Iupiters* brother (so great a man he makes him) full of great knowledge, and of all vertue, generositie, pietie, and justice: nay. he saith further, that *Æsculapius*, *Nestor*, *Amphiaraus*, *Peleus*, *Telamon*, *Theseus*, *Ulisses*, *Castor*, *Pollux*, *Æneas*, *Achilles*, and almost all great persons, which the Grecians place amongst their gods, of him learned these vertues, whereby they have obtained immortall praise, and the reputation to be gods: Hee saith also, that *Chiron* was not in the time of *Achilles*, but long time before: but because the prince *Achilles* was instructed and nourished in his discipline, vertue, and manner of life, men say he was *Achilles* his instructor. True it is, that the Poets have called him a Centaure, because he tooke great pleasure in riding of horses, and in hunting, which are exercises well beseeming a prince: But although he loved horses, and the exercise of knighthood, yet was he never esteemed to hold any thing of a beast, but rather of the divinitie, as being endowed with all excellent vertues, which bring men nigh God, and take them fardest from beasts. And therefore the beastly mallice of *Machiavell* is seene, in perverslie abusing the example of that valiant and generous prince *Achilles*, to persuade a prince not to sticke to governe himselfe after the imitation of beasts; seeing that *Achilles* was instructed, as is said, by *Chiron* the Centaure, a man and a beast, which learned him how to live both like a man and a beast: for this is false and devised; for *Chiron* rather held of divinitie, than of a beast, neither was *Achilles* instructed, but in all heroicall vertues: And we never read, that hee ever used any Foxlike subtiltie or unlawfull policie, or any other thing unwoorthie of a magnanimous prince, well nourished and instructed in all high and royall vertues.

But since *Machiavell* travaileth so much to persuade princes to learne how to play the Lion and the Fox, wherefore doth he not persuade them also to carry those two beasts in their armes? We see many which beare

Lyons (because it is in some things a generous and a noble beast) but there are sildome seene in armes any Foxes pourtraied; because every noble and generous man which loveth vertue, disdaineth and hateth all deceit, falshood, and Foxlike dissembling, as things very unfit for gentlemen. The Machiavelists, which esteeme it so fit, that a prince should know how to play the Lion and the Fox together, the more to authorize this Maxime, should carie Foxes in their armes: But they would not be knowne to be that they are, to the end they might the better deceive the world, and lest men crie after them, The Fox, The Fox.

OF POLICIE

13. MAXIME.

Crueltie which tendeth to a good end is not to be reprehended.

Romulus (saith *Machiavell*) at the beginning of his kingdome, slew *Remus* his brother; and afterward consented to the death of *Tatius Sabinus*, king of the Sabines, whom he associated in his roialtie, that he might unite together in one same citie, the two people, the Romanes and Sabines. It would seeme to many men of grosse conceit, that *Romulus* proceeded evill, to begin his kingdome with the murder of his owne brother, and that it was an act of evill example: But as for me (saith *M. Nicholas*) I am of a far other opinion: For it is a generall Maxime, That the state of the Commonwealth cannot be well laid and compounded of new lawes, if the Lawmakers and Iudges be many, but there ought to be no more than one onely person and spirit, to doe, rule, and ordaine all: And therefore the prince which desireth to come to that point, is not worthy of any reprehension, if he commit any extraordinarie exploit to come thereunto: For that violence which destroyeth all, is greatly to be reprehended, but so is not that which tendeth to make things in better state: Therefore is *Romulus* worthie of praise, that he himselfe slew his brother, & caused to sley *Tatius* his companion, that hee alone might establish a good policie at Rome, as after he did, erecting there a Senate, by which hee was counselled in all his affaires both of peace and warre, and they made also good rules & ordinances. A like praise is due to *Agis*, king of Sparta, who sought to conforme the corrupted state of the Lacedæmonians, and to establish in use, the auncient ordinances of *Licurgus*, but knowing that the *Ephori* might hinder and contradict him in his deseignes, he caused them all to be slaine, whereby hee got great renowne, yea, as much or rather greater than *Licurgus* himselfe, the first author of such lawes: True it is, that *Agis* could not make an end of his good entents and purposes, because of the unluckie deseignes of the Macedonians, who making warre upon him, vanquished him to the hinderance of his gallant enterprises.

There was never murder nor crueltie, which is not coloured with some pretext or shew of good: some cover themselves with justice, affirming all that they doe, to be founded upon a good reason and equitie, and that justice would have done no lesse, than that which they have executed; and that their execution is the shortest way of justice, which would otherwise have beene too long: so that in place of murderers, cut-throates & massacrers, they are not ashamed to call themselves abbreviators of justice: And why should they bee ashamed; seeing that justice at this day, is so practised, as they make her serve but as a palliation or coverture, for all assassiments, murders, and vengeances? Every mans eye seeth, that in many places justice serveth to no other turne, but to lend her name to such as will seeme to doe well, when they doe evill against their owne consciences, therein following the doctrine of *Machiavell*: Murderers therefore & massacrers, may well from henceforth cover themselves, with the name of abreviators of justice, without reprehension, seeing officers of justice take also that trade upon them, and cause as unjust and wicked executions to bee done as they. Both of these truely (according to this Maxime of *Machiavell*) doe pretend for their mischievous wickednesse, a laudable end, and doe say, it is to minister and exercise justice, when they doe the aforesaid executions: Others cover their murders with another end; namely, the publike good, saying that their murders and massacres, are done to shun a greater evill, which would have come by him or them that they have slaine or murdered. There are some which make a covering of peace and tranquilitie, and so will say, That the murders which they did or caused to bee done, were executed to establish peace, and to make troubles to cease. Breefely, after *Machiavells* doctrine, there cannot bee found so cruell a tyrant and murderer, but hee should be justified, praised and remunerated, because all murders, massacres, and assasinates, are alwaies found done to a good end, and the most cruell hangman and executioners, will never want a colour for their most detestable and sanguinarie actions. Notwithstanding what pallations & shewes so ever that take, the worke alwaies shewes who was the workeman; and in the end their colours will deceive them, like the deceitfull painting of harlots: so that their maske or visard taken from them, murder will alwayes bee found murder, and theft, theft, and they wicked men, as they are, although most subtillie they play the Foxes, according to their masters doctrine, yet in the end, they wil be alwaies known for Foxes: And though they sometimes deceive, before they bee knowne, they are therefore after, double punished, in regard of the profit they get by deceiving, when none will beleeve or trust them in any manner, no not even then, when they have an intention and will, not to deceive at all: For alwaies men presume of them, as men ought to presume of deceivers and wicked men, which are without faith and promise, for men hold them for such, and they can bee held for no other, in regard of their actions and behaviours, of their lives past. This then is the first evill proceeding from *Machiavells* doctrine, which is that they themselves which practice it, bring evill to themselves, and are discryed, hated and evill beloved of all men.

The other inconvenience, which followeth this Maxime, is that, if the prince permit men to commit murders, under colour of a good intent and end, hee shall breake the order of justice, which hee ought to observe, in the punishment of offenders, and so shall turne all upside downe, and bring his estate and countrey into confusion and perill: for when justice goeth evill, all goes evill, & when well, all goes well, as in another place shall bee shewed more at full. Murders and massacres also never remaine long unpunished; for God incontinent sendes them their reward, as came to *Romulus* (*Machiavells* owne example) who was an unjust murtherer, and in the end was murdered himselfe. And in our time wee see examples enough, and I beleeve wee shall see more, in such as the hand of God hath not yet touched: But amongst those evills and inconveniences, which ordinarily lay hold of these murderers, and follow them, even to their graves, with furies, feares, and torments, which vexe their consciences, I could heere alledge, for a confirmation of this Maxime, that which S. *Paul* faith, That we must not doe evill, that good may come thereof: But I have alreadie said in another place, that I will not imploy the sacred armour of the holy scripture, to fight against this profane and wicked Atheist, but I will still give him this advantage, to contend with his owne armes; namely, with profane authors, which were not Christians, and which heerein alone resemble him; for in other things hee holds nothing of them, and especially in the matter whereof wee speake, they have beene most farre from his detestable doctrine.

When *Tarquin* the proude king of Rome, saw that hee had so behaved himselfe, as he had utterly lost the amitie of his subjects, then resolved to cause himselfe to be obeyed by feare; and to bring it to passe, hee tooke to himselfe, the knowledge of capitall causes against great men, which before appertained to the Senate, to make himselfe the better feared and obeyed, and so hee put to death, such as he thought good, under certaine pretextes and colours, thinking thereby the better to assure his estate; But how did hee assure it? Thus, hee so practised this doctrine of *Machiavell*, that hee became extreamely hated of all men, in such sort, as his subjects not being able to beare his tyrannie, did drive him out of his kingdome, where hee miserably died.

And so much there wanteth, that the ancient Romanes delighted in massacring and slaying, that they hated even the too rigorous punishments of offenders, as the punishment of *Metius Suffetius Albanois*, who was with foure horses drawne to death, for a strange and damnable treason by him entended: For although he merited to bee so handled, yet the Romanes had the crueltie of the punishment in so great disdaine and detestation, that every body turned away their eyes (saith *Titus Livius*) seeing so villanous a spectacle: And it was the first and last time that ever they used that rigorous punishment. Likewise it greatly displeased the Romanes, that some (thinking to doe well) caused to bee slaine a Tribune of the people, a very seditious man called *Genutius*, who ceased not to trouble the commonwealth, by divisions, whereby hee stirred the common people to uproares: If *Genutius* had had his lawfull tryall, it is likely hee would have beene condemned: but therein there was this mischiefe, that none durst lay hold upon him, for the reverence of his estate, during that yeere, but hee must needes have beene suffered either to doe what hee would, or els to resist his dessignes by other meanes, then by accusation, and not at all to condemne him, before hee were out of his office: This seemed a goodly colour to dispatch him, to shun seditions and troubles, which this Tribune raised, yet the execution which was made without course of law, was found nought, and of an evill example and consequence, and was the cause of great mischiefes and broyles which followed after.

And as for that which *Machiavell* writeth, that *Romulus* caused to slay *Tatius* his companion in the kingdome, the better to rule and governe the towne of Rome, this is false: for histories doe witnesse, that after hee had caused this execution to be made, hee became cruell and proud, towards the Senators, exercising tyrannie in many things, insomuch as the Senators themselves slew him, even in the senat house, and cut him in little pieces, whereof every man tooke one piece in his bosome: so that the bodie of *Romulus* was not found: for they hired one to say that hee did see the bodie flie into heaven, and the said Senators helping this bruite and report, placed him in the letanie of their Gods, and persuaded the people, that hee ascended into the heavens both in body and soule. But they gave *Romulus* his reward, for the murdering of his brother *Remus*, and his companion *Tatius*, and they murdered him, as hee had done them. For briefely it is a generall rule, that murderers are alwaies murdered, which rule hath seldome any exceptions.

But whereas *Machiavell* saith, That well to rule and governe a common wealth, there would bee but one person to medle therein, there hath beene alwaies the contrarie practised. When the Romanes thought it good, by good lawes and ordinances to governe the estate of their common weale, they considered, that the number of two Consuls (which were their soveraigne magistrates) were too few, and therefore they abrogated and tooke them cleane away, and elected ten men in their places, unto which they gave the same authoritie, which the Consuls before had, and especially gave them power and expresse charge, to make lawes and ordinances, for the pollicie, government and justice of the common weale. They made the lawes of the twelve tables, which endured long after them, yea at this day some of these are in good use and observance. Naturall reason also sheweth us, that a law and rule made and examined by many braines, must needes bee better, than when it is made by one alone: but because I have touched this point more at large in another place, I will wade no further therein.

As touching that which *Machiavell* saith, of *Agis*, *Plutarch* in his life, speaketh otherwise thereof; for hee saith, that hee was the most meeke and quiet man, in the world, who sought to reforme the estate of Sparta, by all good and honest meanes, and to bring into force and use, the ancient lawes of *Licurgus:* and because the *Ephori* opposed themselves against his desseignes and purposes, hee practised that *Lysander* and *Agesilaus*, should bee advanced to the estate of *Ephori*, as they were: But *Agesilaus*, overtaken with auarice, refused to sticke to the effecting of this good purpose of king *Agis*, so that he could not anyway bring to passe that good reformation which hee intended. Heere is all which *Plutarch* saith, he speakes no word that *Agis* should cause the *Ephori* to bee slaine, but contrary that the *Ephori* brought *Agis* to his death, neither speakes hee of any enterprise of the Macedonians: And I know not where *Machiavell* hath fished for that hee heere writeth, unles hee take it out of his owne braine, and then oweth hee nothing to any man, seeing it is his owne: But howsoever it bee, hee can learne it of no author, which shall not bee alwaies convinced of a lie, by that learned *Plutarch*, who speaketh as I have set it downe.

OF POLICIE

18. MAXIME.

A prince ought not to feare to bee periured, to deceive, and dissemble: for the deceiver alwaies findes some which are fit to bee deceived.

THE PRINCE (*saith master Nicholas*) which will become great, and make great conquests, it is necessarie that hee learne well the occupation and art of deceiving, as *John Galeace* did, who by that art tooke the dutchie of Millan, from Messire Bernard his uncle: The Romanes also under that name of allies and confederates, so deceived the Latine people and many others, that they reduced them into a servitude and subiection, yet they never espied it, untill the end. True it is, in this art of trompery & deceit, men must needes use great fainednesse, dissimulations, and periuries; and the prince which shall bee heereunto (as it were) made by nature and art, shall alwaies obtaine prosperous successe in his affaires: For men are commonly so simple, and doe so soone bend to present necessities, that the deceiver alwaies finds some, which will suffer themselves to be deceived: Heereupon we may alledge infinit examples of peace, truce, and promises which have beene broken by princes, yet have had good event: And heereof wee may alledge one example of fresh memorie, of Pope *Alexander* the sixt, who never did other thing, but made an art of abusing men, neither ever applied his minde to other studie, neither ever was there found man, that would confirme his promises with more horrible othes, nor that lesse kept and observed them: Yet his tromperies and periuries succeeded all well unto him, for hee knew well enough therein, how all sorts of men must be handled.

In this Maxime is an amplification of that which hath beene before set downe by *Machiavell*, when hee said, That a prince ought to know how to play the Fox; for now explicating, what it is to play the Fox, hee saith, it is to know how to deceive, to dissemble, and to bee perjured; and that a prince ought to bee adorned with these goodly vertues of trompery, dissimulation, and perjurie: But as for trompery, which men call subtiltie, wee have of it above sufficientlie spoken: And as for perfidie and perjurie, wee shall afterward speake in another Maxime, and therefore heereupon wee will make no long discourse, because wee will not often repeate one same thing: And with all that there is no man in the world, of so small a judgement, who doth not well see that this Maxime containeth a detestable doctrine, altogether unworthie not onely of a prince, but of every man, of what condition so ever hee bee: And I doe not beleeve that the Bohemians, who goe from countrey to countrey, telling good fortunes, juglers, or rather runnagate roagues, which make an occupation of deceits and abusing of the world, will not condemne this Maxime, as wicked and abhominable, if they bee made judges.

And as for that which *Machiavell* saith, That the deceiver will alwayes find some that will suffer themselves to bee deceived, I confesse there will bee ever found some idiot fooles and sots, that he may deceive, yea that sometimes he may deceive sharp witted and wise men: yet notwithstanding, it is as certaine, that there is not so great a deceiver, but he is sometimes deceived: For as soone as a deceiver is discovered to be one, every man takes heed to negotiate and traffique with him, or if they bee forced to have to do with him, for feare to be deceived, they will do their best to deceive him: And herein the most part of the world make no conscience, but thinke it not onely lawfull, but praiseworthie to deceive a deceiver: in-somuch, as he which hath once a name to be a cousener and deceiver, all men will dispence with themselves to deceive him if they can: and by that meanes the deceiver having cause to take heed of many sundry persons, it is impossible but he should be often deceived, and be often catched in his owne nets. Therefore *Machiavell* his reason, That the deceiver shall alwayes find them which will be deceived, doth not so well conclude, as it seemeth: For if the deceiver find alwaies some to deceive, he shall also find some which will deceive him: and it may be sometimes, for one that he deceiveth, hee may find sixe which will deceive him: because none can bee so perfect in the art of trompery (which art *Machiavell* so much recommendeth to a prince) but also hee shall alwaies finde others, which know more than himselfe in some points, and many together doe know more than one alone, in all points of that art, one in one point, and another in another: So that in the end hee himselfe shall see alwaies (according to the common proverbe) the deceiver shall bee deceived.

As it happened even to Pope *Alexander* the sixt, whose example *Machiavell* heere alledgeth; for the end of all his tromperies and perjuries, was to make his bastard *Cæsar Borgia*, lord & king of all Italie, and after, of all christendome if he could: But the issue of his desseignes and purposes was a tragicall act, as wee have before discoursed in another place. Moreover, the cause why that many times this Pope deceived christian princes, and even the king of France *Lewis* the twelfth, was: For that in that time men so greatlie feared the Popes bulls and interdictions, and that they beleeved him to bee a true lieutenant of God, on earth, so that they durst not discredit any thing hee did, but rather beleeved all his wordes as oracles: but at this day children would mocke at his actions, and few men will bee baited with his allurements.

But for whereas *Machiavell* saith, That the ancient Romanes under the deceit of those names, Allies and confederats, brought into their subjection and servitude the Latin people their neighbours, is a plaine and pure lie: For they subjugated all men by warre, at divers times as wee reade in hystories. True it is, that after once they vanquished and brought them under, they then made treaties of peace and confederations, which were not greatly to the advantage of such as were overcome, as in reason they might: For if by the right of nations, such as are vanquished by warres, may be bondslaves of the vanquishers: by a stronger reason may the vanquishers reserve to themselves some preheminence, over the vanquished: But the preheminences which commonly the Romanes reserved to themselves, in all their treaties, were that the allies and confederats, should not make warre upon any without their consent, and that they should contribute unto their souldiers in their warres: Moreover they left to all people, their franchises, liberties, goods, religion, magistrates, and all other things, without altering any thing, and without imposing upon them tributes of mony or such like. This cannot bee called a servitude, as *Machiavell* calls it; or if it bee a servitude, there are no people in christendome, whether they be subjects of princes, or common wealthes, which are not in a double, and quadruple servitude.

And whereas *Machiavell* saith, That a prince ought to know the art of trompery, deceit, some will aske (to take heede of it) which are the precepts of the art: Wherunto I answere for *Machiavell*, that no man can give precepts, practicale or singular which may bee applied to every busines, to avoide deceit and fraude: But the generall precepts of art (which the philosophers call Axiomes in philosophie) are these; Bouldly to forsweare themselves; Subtilly to dissemble, to insinuate into mens minds and to prove them; To breake faith and promise, and such like as heeretofore wee have handled, and shall doe heereafter: But heere we must note one thing, which is, That one well experienced in the art of trompery, will not alwaies practise that principle, To breake faith, for if he ordinarilie doe it, hee shall offend against another principle, which commands, To dissemble subtilly: For by, every where and ever breaking of faith, hee shall discover himselfe to bee a manifest deceiver, whereas hee ought to dissemble, and to make an outward countenance not to bee so, but rather to bee a good and an honest man: And therefore to observe all the principles, of that art together, without breaking one in observing another, hee shall in small matters keepe his faith, to breake it in great things, and in matters of consequence. Heereof *Fabius Maximus* admonisheth *Scipio* to take heede: Thou desirest *Scipio* (saith hee) to make warre upon the Carthaginians in Affricke, under an hope thou hast to have the favour of king *Siphax*, and of the Numidians, which have promised thee aide and succours: But take good advice how thou trustest in the barbarous nations, which commonly make no account to breake their faith & to deceive: True it is, in small matters they will keepe their faith with thee, well to assure thee in their promise and loyaltie, that they may afterward breake it, to their great profit and advantage, as soone as they see they have meanes and occasion in their hands, altogether to ruinate thee. This was the admonition, which that wise *Fabius*, gave to *Scipio*, then a yong captaine. What then should a man doe, to guard himselfe from such deceitfull faith of deceivers, which appeeres and shewes it selfe in little things, and is defective in great matters? A man must doe that which *Scipio* answered to *Fabius*: I know well (lord *Fabius* saith hee) how a man must leane upon the evill assured faith of *Syphax*, and the Numidians. I thinke so much to leane, and rest my selfe upon them, as may serve my turne, so that yet alwaies I hold my selfe upon my guardes, to warrant my selfe from all perfidie and treacherie.

Moreover there is yet another remedie against such deceivers and dissemblers, which promise much and in their hearts have no other intention, then in no thing to keepe their promises: that is to shun and flie from them, as from hell, and from more than capitall enemies, as *Homer* teacheth us:

Hee that one thing in heart, another in mouth dothe beare:
Fly him an enemie thine, and as hell-fire him feare.

OF POLICIE

19. MAXIME.

A prince ought to know how to winde and to turne mens mindes, that they may deceive and circumvent them.

In our time there have princes beene seene (saith our *Florentine*) which having knowledge how to cavalier the spirits of men, that is, which had the cunning subtillie to handle and proove mens mindes, have surmounted and gone beyond such men as stoode upon their simple loyaltie: And this is done, when a prince marketh the vertue or vice of him, whom hee meanes to undermine and deceive, by giving him a bait fittest to deceive and intrap him. As did *Appius Claudius*, one of the ten soveraigne potentates, that were created at Rome: For he meaning to lay hold for ever, of the soveraigne domination of the Romanes, enterprised to draw to his league and devotion, all the principall men hee could gaine: and knowing that *Quintus Fabius* (who before had alwaies beene so good a man as could possible bee) had a spirit, enclined to ambition and honour, hee gained him and drew him to the net, by promises of great estates and honours, insomuch as hee brought him to become as wicked as himselfe, knowing also many yong Romane gentlemen (which otherwise were well borne and well instructed) to bee desirous of wealth and riches to fulfill ther lusts, & giving them great gifts, & promising them much more, if they alwaies followed him at the taile, wheresoever hee went, as his guard and vassailes of his tyrannie: Even so a prince, who will thus handle and tosse mens mindes, shall easilie with deceit catch whom hee will, and alwaies obtaine the upper hand on them.

Ah poore Frenchmen (too simple) you see the nets and snares which so often catcheth you, you speake freely, you brag and vaunt, you discover your hearts, and will, unto the Machiavelists, which can cavalier your spirits, and discover the bottome of your hearts, and after bring you into their nets at their pleasure: But they are not such, they are slow and prolonging, secret, close, and they suffer not a word to fall from their mouths, without premeditation in what sence you may take them, and so doe make them serve to the end they meane; which is ordinarily contrarie to that which you thinke: They can also say, These Frenchmen are light and unconstant, they cannot keepe their secrets, they abound in words, are undiscreet, they speake many together, they have no retentive in their mouths, but discover their thoughts to every man: And in truth we must needs confesse, that France hath no neighbor nation, whose spirits are so easie to cavalier, as the spirits & minds of Frenchmen: And certainly, this Maxime is one of the greatest secrets of the Machiavelists Cabale, wherewith they aid themselves most, to execute that in France which they doe: And if Frenchmen could breake their practise, it should be easie to overthrow all their deseignes and purposes, whereby by little and little they ruinate all them that they feare & are suspected of them, to draw them afterward into a slavish and Turkish servitude, and to place amongst them Italian colonies.

But this Maxime is practised many wayes, as well by marking the vices as the vertues of men: For if he see a mans mind addicted to ambition, he needs but an office with a promise of a greater, and then may they doe all they will: So that having thus cavaliered and captivated his mind, hee brings him into his net, to make him serve his turne in all manner of wickednesse, that he will command him to do: For as *Salust* saith: Ambition, because it hath some resemblance of vertue, is often cause of great evils, yea, the ruine of great cities and commonweales: And indeed we see both by old and moderne examples, that this detestable ambition hath often drawn men to bandie and arme themselves, to the ruine & destruction of their owne countrey, most wickedly forgetting the dutie they owe to the conservation thereof, by divine, naturall, and humane right, to enjoy only the smoke of honor, which often bringeth the ruine of their goods, losse of their lives, and destruction of their soules. Such may we cal all them that make warre upon their owne nation, to deprive them, of the enjoying their goods, lives, conscience, and religion, & all other things which are theirs, and which they cannot take from them but by injustice and iniquitie: But behold they are blinded with ambition, and are their slaves which have brought them into their snares, which could so well cavalier their spirits, and even by that vice, which they have noted in them. In like manner, if these Machiavelists do mark the mind of a man to be given to lubricitie and *Venus* delights, then will they prepare for him, delicate and bravely adorned courtizans, which will soone take him in his owne lust as it were with the glew or fish-hooke of his owne vice. If they discover him to be covetous, they will bestow some gift upon him, as some benefice or other thing, and will promise him an hundred times as much: but withall, behold the man cavaliered and entrapped. Likewise, if they note a man vertuous, that hee is loyall and constant in his word, they will seeke to draw out of him some word and promise, and thereupon lay an ambush for him: If they see him of a mind enclined to the commonwealth, they will get him some charge, that thereby he may be some way entrapped: Breefely, in thus cavaliering mens minds, and by discovering their vertues, vices, courages, affections & passions, they frame craftie engines fit to make men fal into their devotion, or els altogether to take them out of the way, or to make them serve their deseigns and purposes. Lastly, the meanes to to shun their frauds and subtilties, are not difficult to wise men: for such cavaliering marchants are sufficiently knowne at this day: And therefore to cause them to fall into their owne snares and ambushes, men must antecavalier them, that is, men must worke against them.

OF POLICIE

23. MAXIME.

A prince ought to have a turning and winding wit, with art and practise made fit, to be cruell and unfaithfull, that he may shew himselfe such an one when there is need.

IT IS good (saith our Florentine) that a prince should appear to be loyall, piteous, liberall, yea, and effectually to bee so, whensoever hee seeth it is profitable unto him: But yet a princes spirits must be so flexible, so ductible and easie to bee led, so handsomely and naturally fitted, and with custome used, as he can do the contrarie at all times at a need: For most commonly necessitie requires, that a prince should shew himselfe disloyall, cruell, fierce, and niggardly.

THE PHILOSOPHERS call habitude that promptnesse & aptnesse which men acquire by frequent exercise of the actions of every art. As a Taylor by customable exercise of cutting and shaping, obtaines an habit and dexteritie, to know well how to make garments. An Archer in a crosbow or gunne, by the often exercise of shooting, obtaineth that habitude, to draw well, and to shoot nigh the white: and so it is in all other actions and sciences, every man may get an habitude by frequent exercise. *Machiavels* mind then is, That it is not sufficient for a prince sometimes to be cruell, perfidious, fierce, covetous, and illiberall; but by frequent exercise of crueltie, perfidie, and covetousnesse, he must obtaine an habitude, promptly, dexteriously, and handsomely at his pleasure to practice these goodly vertues at a need. For if by frequent exercise hee could not obtaine this habit, it might so fall out, that in his necessitie he should be found to [lacke] in the practise of them in that sort which should be requisite and necessarie: even as an Archer or Gunner cannot know how handsomely to handle his Bow and Gunne to come nigh the marke, who not past once or twice before hath handled them: Because (as *Aristotle* saith) one sole action makes not an habitude, no more than one alone Swallow brings a certaine assurance of the Springs comming; But I pray you, is not this a triumphant doctrine for a prince to be taught? nay, rather to teach some devill of hell: for since the nature of divels cannot tend but to evill, a man may say, that it should be very covenable that they had (as I beleeve they have) *Machiavell* to teach them the precepts of the art of wickednesse: As this Maxime must needs be one of them, whereby hee wills, that these vicious qualities of crueltie, perfidie, and niggardlinesse should be in a prince, not as in an habit and perfection: But I will not stand to confute here this Maxime: for before, we have sufficiently spoken of crueltie and perfidie, and at large demonstrated, how unworthy they are for a prince: And as for Covetousnesse, we shall have occasion to speak of it in another Maxime: yet I would desire all persons which have in them any pietie and love of vertue, to learne to detest so abhominable a doctrine, as this which *Machiavell* here teacheth: for there was never Arabian, Scythian, or Turke, which ever taught a more strange & barbarous doctrine, as to persuade men to make habitudes of vices? Let us also learne to discerne spirits before we beleeve them. If *Machiavell* had been knowne to be such a man as I hope he shall bee deciphered by this discourse, it is likely he should not have done so much harme as hee hath done. And finally, let us thanke our good God, which hath not permitted, that our spirits should be infected with such a corruption, as to approove or follow such abhorrent doctrine from pietie and reason, and such monstrous & savage opinions: For as *Thucidides* calleth them, servants and slaves of absurd opinions, such as follow evill counsell sooner than good, as the Athenians often did: So do I beleeve them to be double, yea, centuple slaves and miserable, which suffer their spirits to bee persuaded and deluded with the doctrine and impietie of *Machiavell.*

OF POLICIE

27. MAXIME.

A prince which will make a straight profession of a good man, cannot long endure in this world, in the companie of so many other that are so bad.

MANY (saith *Machiavell*) have written bookes, to instruct a prince, and to bring him to a perfection in all vertues, as *Xenophon* did in the institution of *Cyrus*: There are also many philosophers and others, which by their writings have formed Ideaes and figures of monarchies and common weales, whereof there were never seene the like in the world, because there is a great difference betwixt the manner, that the world liveth in, and that it ought to live: He then that will amuse and stick upon the formes of philosophers, monarchs, and commonweales, by dispising that which is done, and praising that which ought to bee done, hee shall sooner learne his owne ruine, than his conservation: Leaving then behinde, all that can bee imagined of a princes perfection, and staying ourselves upon that which is true, and subiect to bee practised: By experience I say (saith *Master Nicholas*) that the prince which will maintaine himselfe, ought to learne how hee may sometimes not bee good, and so ought to practise it, according to the exigence of his affaires: For if alwaies he will hould a straight profession of a good man, hee cannot long endure in the companie of so many others, which are of no valew.

THIS MAXIME meriteth no other confutation, than that which resulteth from the points before handled, for wee have at large demonstrated, that the truth is cleane contrary, to that which *Machiaveell* saith heere, and that princes which have beene good men, have alwaies raigned long and peceably, and have beene firme and assured in their estates: and the wicked contrary, have not raigned long, but have violently beene deposed from their estates: And as for ideaes and formes of perfect monarchs, and common weales, whereof some philosophers have written, they handled not that subject, saying there were any such, but to propose a patterne of imitation for monarchs, and government of commonweales: For when a man will propose a patterne to imitate, he must forme it the most perfect, and make it the best hee can; and after, every man, which giveth himselfe to imitate it, must come as nigh it as he can, some more nigh, others lesse: But a prince which proposeth to himselfe Machiavells patternes, such as *Cæsar Borgia, Oliver de Ferme, Agathocles,* how can hee doe any good thing, or approch to any good, seeing the patternes hould nothing thereof: Patternes then which men propose to imitate, must bee the best set downe that they can bee, that if in our imitation wee hap to erre, from a perfect image of Vertue, yet we may [follow] & in some sort expresse it in our manners: But what meanes *Machiavell,* when hee saith, That men must leave behinde, that which authors have written, of a princes perfection, to draw us unto that, which is now a daies practised: What is this? but in a word to tell us wee must leave the good precepts of vertue, to abide and stay our selves upon vices, and a tyrannie: For they which have written of a princes perfection, have set downe nothing which may not well bee practised, and if a prince cannot fully doe and practice all the precepts which are written, hee may at the least practice part of them, one more, another lesse: But wee must not say, that if a prince cannot bee perfect, that therefore hee must altogether forsake, and cast off all vertue and goodnesse, and take up a tyrannie and vice: For as *Horace* saith:

Hee that in highest place cannot abide,
Let not the meanest place him bee denied.

So that it seemes, *Machiavell* knowes not what hee would say, when hee houlds, That wee must not stay upon that which authors have written of a princes perfection, but upon that which is practised, and in use: For if hee meane, that vice alone is in use, hee then giveth wicked counsell and advice, and if hee will confesse that good and vertue is in use and practise, then will it follow, that wee must not reject that, which is written of a princes perfection, although a man cannot come to the perfectnesse thereof, for alwaies it is good and praiseable, to come as nigh thereunto as wee can.

And touching that which *Machiavell* saith, That a prince who is a good man, can not long endure amongst so many others, that valew nothing: I see well that hee meanes, heereby to persuade a prince to apply himselfe to the wicked, and to doe as they doe, and to bee wicked with them which valew nothing: But if *Machiavell* had well considered, That goodnesse and vertue, are alwaies in price and estimation, yea even with men of no valew, which are constrained to praise that, which they hate: And if hee were resolved (as it is certaine) that subjects doe commonly apply themselves willinglie to imitate their prince, (*Dion* witnesseth that in the time of the emperour *Antonine* the philosopher, many studied philosophie to be like him) hee would never have given this precept to a prince, to accommodate himselfe to the vices which are in facion and use: but contrary, hee would have taught him to follow goodnesse and vertue, to draw his subjects thereunto, and to receive honour and good reputation in the world: But in truth wee neede not mervaile, if *Machiavell* hould opinions so farre discrepant from the way of vertue, for that is not the path, whereby hee pretends to guide and conduct a prince; but his way is that which leadeth to all wickednesse and impietie, as wee have in many places demonstrated.

The ancient Romanes one day, found certaine verses of their prophetesse *Sibilla*, where it was said, That the Romanes should alwaies chase out of Italie, every strange enemie, if the mother of the gods were brought to Rome: The Romanes (which were very superstitious in a vaine religion) sent straight embassadors to Delphos, towards the oracle of *Apollo*, to know where they might finde the mother of the gods: The oracle sent them to king *Attalus* of of Pergamus: *Attalus* led them into Phrigia, and shewed them an old Image of stone, which in those quarters, they had alwaies called the mother of the gods: The said embassadors, caused that image straight to bee embarked, and brought to Rome, whereof the Senate being advertised, it fell in deliberation amongst them, who hee should bee, that at the gates should goe to receive the mother of the gods: and it was concluded, that that must be the best & most vertuous man in the citie: When then it came in question, who was the best in all the towne; every man (saith *Titus Livius*) desired the lot might fall upon him, and theere was not any, but he loved better to be elected the best man of the citie, than to bee chosen either Consul or Dictator, or into any other great estate: The election fell upon *Scipio Nasica* (coosin germane of the Affrican) who was a young man, but a very good man, and the sonne of a good father; who went to receive that old goddesse of stone, mother of the Gods: But I doe demand of you, if those good Romanes, had beene instructed in the doctrine of *Machiavell*, and had learned of this Maxime, That it is not good to make a straight profession of a good man; would they so much have wished, that this election had fallen upon them and preferred this title of a good man, before so high dignities of a Consull or Dictator? certainely no: but they which hould contrary to the doctrine of *Machiavell*, make more estimation of goodnesse and vertue, than of the greatest riches and dignities.

And indeed, there is nothing more certaine, but that it is the goodliest and most honourable title, that a man can possibly have, To bee a good man: And let it not displease great lords, which are imbarked in the highest title of honours of Constables, Marshals, Admirals, Chancelors, Presidents, Knights of the order, Governours, and Lieutenants of the king, and other like great States: for all those titles, without the title of a good man, valew nothing, and indeed are but smokes to stifle them which have them: But I confesse, that if they have the title of a good man, with these titles, then are they worthie of double honour, and to bee beloved and respected of all the world.

OF POLICIE

34. MAXIME.

A Prince ought to commit to another those affaires which are subiect to hatred and envie, and reserve to himselfe such as depend upon his grace and favour.

A PRINCE which will exercise some cruell and rigorous act (saith *M. Nicholas*) he ought to give the commission thereof unto some other; to the end, he may not acquire evill will and enmitie by it. And yet if he feare, that such a delegation cannot bee wholly exempted from blame (to have consented to the execution which was made by his Commissarie) he may cause the Commissarie to be slaine, to shew that he consented not to his crueltie, as did *Cæsar Borgia,* and *Messire Remiro Dorco.*

THIS MAXIME is a dependancie of that goodly doctrine, which *Machiavell* learned of *Cæsar Borgia* (which although it was very cruell) yet meaning to appeare soft and gentle, following therein the Maxime which enjoyneth dissimulation, committeth the execution of his crueltie to *Messire Remiro Dorco,* as at large before wee have discoursed that hystorie. And because we have fully shewed, that all dissimulation and feignednesse is unworthie of a prince, we will stay no longer upon this Maxime: Well will I confesse, that many things there be which seeme to be rigorous in execution (although they be most equall and just) which it is good a prince doe commit to others, to give judgement and execution by justice, as the case meriteth: For as the emperour *Marcus Antonine* said, It seemeth to the world, that that which the prince doth, hee doth it by his absolute authoritie and power, rather than of his civile and reasonable power. Therefore to shun that blame and suspition, it is good that the prince delegate and set over such matters to Iudges, which are good men, not suspected nor passionate, not doing as the emperour *Valentinian* did, who would never heare nor receive accusations against Iudges and Magistrates, which hee had established, but constrained the recusators or refusers, to end their cause before those Iudges only: Whereby he was much blamed, and his honor impeached and disgraced: For truly, the cheefe point which is required to cause good justice to be administred, is, That Iudges be not suspected nor passionat: because the passions of the soule and heart doe obfuscate and trouble the judgement of the understanding, and cause them to step aside and stray out of the way. It is also a thing of very evill example, when a prince with an appetite of revenge, or to please the passions of revengefull great men, dooth elect Iudges and Commissaries that bee passionate, and which have their consciences at the command of such as employ them: As was done in the time of king *Lewis Hutin,* in the judgement of *Messire Enguerrant de Marigni* great master of Fraunce; and in the time of king *Charles* the sixt, in the judgement of the criminall processe of *Messire Iean de Marests,* the kings Advocate in the parliament of Paris: And a man may put to them the judgements given in our time against *Amie du Bourg,* the kings Counsellor in the said parliament, and against captaine *Briquemand,* and *M. Arnand de Cavagnes,* master of the Requests of the kings houshold, and against the countie *de Montgomerie,* and many others: For the executions to death, which followed, manifested well, That the Iudges were passionate men, their consciences being at the command of strangers, which governed them.

THE TRIVMPHS OF GODS REVENEGE, AGAINST THE crying, and execrable Sinne of Murther:

OR

His Miraculous discoueries and seuere *punishments thereof:*

In thirty seuerall Tragicall Histories (digested in sixe *Bookes) acted in diuers Countries beyond the Seas, and neuer* till now published, or imprinted in any Language.

*Histories, which containe great variety of memo-*rable accidents, Amorous, Morall and Diuine, very *necessary to restraine, and deterre vs from this bloody* Sinne, which, in these our dayes, makes so ample, *and so lamentable a progression.*

Written by IOHN REYNOLDS.

THE FIRST BOOKE.

PSAL. 9.6.
The Lord is knowne in executing Iudgement, and the wicked in the worke of his owne hand.

PRO. 14.27.
The feare of the Lord is a wel-spring of life, to auoyde the snares of death.

LONDON,
Printed by FELIX KYNGSTON, for WILLIAM LEE, and are to be sold at his shop in *Fleete-streete*, at the signe of the golden Buck, neere *Serieants Inne.* 1621.

INTRODUCTORY NOTE

The Source of *The Changeling*:

John Reynolds' "tragicall historie" of Alsemero and Beatrice-Joanna

The plot of *The Changeling* was based on the fourth "historie" of Book I of Reynolds' *The Triumphs of Gods Revenge Against . . . Murther*, which was published in 1621. Amplified to six books and thirty tales by 1624, Reynolds' volume went through six editions and at least eight printings by 1679. The text reprinted here in its entirety is from the 1621 edition.

R.O.

THE TRIVMPHS OF GODS REVENGE AGAINST THE CRYING

and execrable sinne of *Murther*

BY

JOHN REYNOLDS

HISTORIE IV.

SITH in the day of Iudgement we shal answere at Gods great Tribunall for euery lewde thought our hearts conceiue, and idle words our tongues vtter, how then shall wee dare appeare, (much lesse thinke to scape) when wee defile our bodies with the pollution of adulterie, and taint our soules with the innocent blood of our Christian brethren? when, I say, with beastly lust and adultery, wee vnsanctifie our sanctified bodies, who are the receptacles and temples of the holy Ghost, and with high and presumptuous hands, stabbe at the Maiestie of God, by murthering of man, who is his Image. This is not the Ladder to scale heaven, but the shortest way to ride poast to hell: for how can wee giue ourselues to God, when in the heat of lust and fume of reuenge, we sell our hearts to the deuill? But did we euer loue God for his Mercy, or feare him for his Iustice, we would then not onely hate these sinnes in our selues, but detest them in others: for these are crying and capitall offences, seene in heauen, and by the sword of his Magistrates brought forth and punished here on earth. A lamentable and mournefull example whereof, I here produce to your viewe, but not to your imitation: may we all read it to the reformation of our liues, to the comfort of our soules, and to the eternall glorie of the most Sacred & Indiuidual Trinity.

IN *Valentia* (an ancient and famous Cittie of *Spaine*) there dwelt one *Don Pedro de Alsemero*, a noble young Cauallier, whose father, *Don Iuan de Alsemero*) beeing slayne by the Hollanders in the Sea-fight at *Gibralter*, he resolued to addict himselfe to Nauall & sea actions, thereby to make himselfe capeable to reuenge his fathers death: a braue resolution, worthy the affection of a sonne, and the generositie of a Gentleman!

To which end he makes two viages to the West-Indies, from whence he returnes flourishing and rich, which so spred the sayles of his Ambition, and hoysted his fame from top to top gallant, that his courage growing with his yeeres, he thought no attempt dangerous enough, if honourable, nor no honour enough glorious, except atchieued and purchased by danger. In the actions of *Alarache* and *Mamora*, hee shewed many noble proofes and testimonies of his valour and prowesse, the which he confirmed and made good by the receit of eleuen seueral wounds, which as markes and Trophees of Honour, made him famous in *Castile*.

Boyling thus in the heate of his youthfull blood, and contemplating often on the death of his father, he resolues to goe to *Validolyd*, and to imploy some Grando either to the King or to the Duke of *Lerma*, his great Fauorite, to procure him a Captains place and a Companie vnder the Arch-duke *Albertus*, who at that time made bloody warres against the Netherlanders, thereby to draw them to obedience: but as he beganne this sute, a generall truce of both sides layd aside Armes, which (by the mediation of *England* and *France*) was shortly followed by a peace, as a mother by the daughter: which was concluded at the *Hage* by his Excellency of *Nassaw* and *Marquis Spinola*, being chiefe Commissioners of either partie. *Alsemero* seeing his hopes frustrated, that the keyes of peace had now shut vp the temple of warre, and that muskets, pikes and corslets that were wont to grace the fields, were now rusting by the walles, hee is irresolute what course to take, resembling those fishes who delight to liue in cataracts and troubled waters, but die in those that are still and quiet: for he spurnes at the pleasures of the Court, and refuseth to haunt and frequent the companies of Ladies: and so not affecting, but rather disdaining the pompe, brauerie and vanitie of Courtiers, he withdrawes himselfe from *Validolyd*, to *Valentia*, with a noble and generous intent to seeke warres abroad, sith hee could finde none at home, where being ariued, although he were often inuited into the companies of the most Noble and Honourable Ladyes both of the Citty and Country: yet his thoughts ranne still on the warres, in which Heroike and illustrious Profession, hee conceiued his chiefest delight and felicity: and so taking order for his lands and affaires, hee resolues to see *Malta* that inexpugnable Rampier of *Mars*, the glorie of Christendome, and the terrour of Turkie, to see if he could gaine any place of command and honour either in that Iland, or in their Gallies; or if not, he would from thence into *Transiluania*, *Hungarie*, and *Germanie*, to inrich his iudgement and experience, by remarking the strength of their castles and Citties, their order and discipline in warre, the Potencie of their Princes, the nature of their Lawes and customes, and all other matters worthie the obseruation both of a Traueller and a Souldiour: and so building many castles in the ayre, he comes to *Alicant*, hoping to finde passage there for *Naples*, and from thence to ship himselfe vpon the *Neopolitan* Gallies for *Malta*.

There is nothing so vaine as our thoughts, nor so vncertain as our hopes: for commonly they deceiue vs, or rather wee our selues in relying on them, not that God is anyway vniust: (for to thinke so, were impiety:) but that our hopes take false obiects, and haue no true foundation, and to imagine the contrary, were folly: the which *Alsemero* findes true: for heere the winde doth oppose him, his thoughts fight and vanquish themselues, yea and the prouidence of God doth crosse him in his intended purposes, and giues way to that hee least intendeth.

For comming one morning to our Ladies Church at *Masse*, and being on his knees in his deuotion, hee espies a young Gentlewoman likewise on hers next to him, who being young, tender and faire, he thorow her thinne vaile discouered all the perfections of a delicate and sweet beautie, she espies him feasting on the daynties of her pure and fresh cheekes; and tilting with the inuisible lances of his eyes, to hers, he is instantly rauished and vanquished with the pleasing obiect of this Angelicall countenance, and now he can no more resist either the power or passion of loue.

This Gentlewoman (whose name as yet wee know not) is young and fayre, and cannot refraine from blushing, and admiring to see him admire and blush at her. *Alsemero* dies in conceit with impatiency, that hee cannot enioy the happinesse and meanes to speake with her, but hee sees it in vaine to attempt it, because shee is ingaged in the company of many Ladies, and he of many Caualiers: but Masse being ended, hee enquires of a good fellow Priest who walked by, what shee was, and whether she frequented that Church, and at what houre. The Priest informes him, that shee is *Don Diego de Vermandero's* daughter: hee being Captaine of the Castle of that City, that her name was *Dona Beatrice-Ioana*, and that shee is euery morning in that Church and Place, and neere about the same houre.

Alsemero hath the sweetnesse of her beautie so deepely ingrauen in his thoughts, and imprinted in his heart, that hee vowes *Beatrice-Ioana* is his Mistresse, and hee her seruant: yea, heere his war-like resolutions haue end, and strike sayle. And now hee leaues *Bellona* to adore *Venus*, and forsakes *Mars*, to follow *Cupid*: yea, so feruent is his flame, and so violent his Passion, as hee can neither giue nor take truce of his thoughts, till hee bee againe made happie with her sight, and blessed with her presence.

The next morne (as Louers loue not much rest) *Alsemero* is stirring very timely, and hoping to finde his Mistresse: no other Church will please him but our Ladies, nor place, but where he first and last saw her: but she is more zealous then himselfe; for shee is first in the Church, and on her knees to her deuotion, whom *Alsemero* gladly espying, he kneeles next to her: and hauing hardly the patience to let passe one poore quarter of an houre, he (resoluing as yet to conceale his name) like a fond Louer (whose greatest glory is in complements and courting his Mistresse), he boords her thus:

Faire Lady, it seemes, that these two mornings my deuotions haue beene more powerfull and acceptable then heretofore, sith I haue had the felicity to be placed next so faire and so sweet a Nimph as your selfe, whose excellent beautie hath so sodainely captiuated mine eyes, and so secretly rauished my heart, that he which heretofore reiected, cannot now resist the power of loue; and therefore hauing ended my deuotions, I beseech you excuse me, if I beginne to pray you to take pittie of mee: sith my flame is so feruent, and my affection so passionate, as either I must liue yours, or not die mine owne.

Beatrice-Ioana could not refraine from blushing vnder her vaile, to see an vnknowne Cauallier boord her in these termes in the Church: and as she gaue attentiue eare to his speech, so shee could not for a while refraine from glancing her eye vpon the sprucenesse of his person, and the sumptuousnesse of his apparell: but at last, accusing her owne silence, because shee would giue him no cause to condemne it, she with a modest grace, and a gracefull modestie, returnes him this answere:

Sir, as your deuotions can neither bee pleasing to God, nor profitable to your soule, if in this place you accompt it a felicity to inioy the sight of so meane a Gentlewoman as my selfe, so I cannot repute it to affection but flattery, that this poore beauty of mine (which you vniustly paint foorth in rich prayses) should haue power either to captiuate the eyes, or which is more, to rauish the heart of so Noble a Cauallier as your selfe. Such victòries are reserued for those Ladies, who are as much your equall, as I your inferiour: and therefore directing your zeale to them, if they finde your affection such as you professe to mee, no doubt but regarding your many vertues and merits, they will in honour grant you that fauour which I in modestie am constrained to deny you.

Alsemero (though a nouice in the art of Loue) was not so ignorant and cowardly to bee put off with her first repulse and refusall, but rather seeing that the perfections of her minde corresponded with those of her beautie, hee resolues now to make triall of his wit and tongue, as heeretofore hee had done of his courage and sword: and so ioynes with her thus:

It is a prettie Ambition in you, sweet Lady, to disparage your beautie, that thereby it may seeme the fayrer; as the Sunne, who appeares brighter by reason of the nights obscuritie; and all things are best, and more perfectly discerned by their contraries: but I cannot commend, and therefore not excuse your policy, or rather your dis-respect, to slight and poast me ouer from your selfe, whom I loue, to chose Ladies I neither know nor desire, which in effect is to giue mee a cloude for *Iuno*. No, no, it is onely to you, and to no other that I present and dedicate my seruice: and therefore it will be an ingratitude as vnworthy my receiuing, as your giuing, that I should bee the object of your discourtisie: sith you are that of my affection.

To these speeches of *Alsemero*, *Beatrice-Ioana* returnes this reply:

It is not for poore Gentlewomen of my ranke and complexion, either to be ambitious, or politike, except it bee to keepe themselues from the snares of such Caualliers as yourselfe, who (for the most part) vnder colour of affection, ayme to erect the trophees of your desires vpon the tombs of our dishonours; only I so much hate ingratitude, as you being to me a stranger, charitie and common courtesie commands me to thanke you for the proffer of your seruice; the which I can no other way either deserue or requite, except in my deuotions & prayers to God, for your glory and prosperitie on earth.

As she had ended this her speech, the Priest ends his Masse; when *Alsemero* arising, aduanced to lift her up from kneeling, and so with his Hat in his hand, (sequestring her from the crowd of people, who nowe began to depart the Church) he speakes to her to this effect:

Fayre Lady, as I know you to bee the Lady *Beatrice-Ioana*, (daughter to the noble knight *Don Diego de Vermanderos*, Captaine of the Castle of this Cittie: so I being a stranger to you, I admire that you offer so voluntary an iniurie to your iudgement and my intents, as to peruert my affection and speeches to a contrarie sence: but my innocencie hath this consolation, that my heart is pledge for my tongue, and my deeds shall make my words reall. In the mean time sith you will giue me no place in your heart, I beseech you lend me one in your Coach, & bee at least so courteous as to honour me, in accepting my company to conduct you home to your fathers Castle.

Beatrice-Ioana, calling to minde the freenesse of her speeches, and the sharpnesse of his answere, not blushing for ioy, but now looking pale for sorrow, repents her selfe of her errour, the which shee salues vp the best she could in this reply:

Noble Sir, when I am acquainted aswell with your heart as with your speeches, I shall then not onely repent, but recant mine errour, in iudging your selfe by others; in the meane time, if I haue any way wronged your merits and vertues; to giue you some part of satisfaction, if you please to grace mee with your company to the Castle, (although it bee not the custome of *Alicant*) I doe most kindly and thankfully accept thereof: when *Alsemero* giuing her many thanks, and kissing his hand, he takes her by the arme, & so conducts her from the Church to her Coach.

It is both a griefe and a scandall to any true Christians heart, that the Church ordained for thankes-giving and Prayer vnto God, should be made a Stewes, or at least, a place for men to meet and court Ladies: but in all parts of the Christian World, where the Romane religion reigneth, this sinfull custome is frequently practised, especially in *Italy* and *Spaine*, where, for the most part, men loue their Courtizans better then their God: and it were a happines for *France*, if her Popish Churches were freed of this abomination, and her people of this impiety. But againe to our Historie.

We will purposely omit the conference which *Alsemero* and *Beatrice-Ioana* had in the Coach, and allow them by this time arriued to the Castle: where first her selfe, then the Captaine her father, thanke him for his honour and courtesie: in requitall whereof, hee shewed him the rarities and strength of his Castle, and after some speeches and complements betweene them, he was so happie as to kisse *Beatrice-Ioana*, but had not the felicitie to entertain her: and so he departs, his Lacky attending him with his Gennet to the counterscarfe. So home he rides to his lodging, where, whiles the winde holds contrary, wee will a little leaue him to his thoughts, and they to resolue in what sort he might contriue his sute for the obtaining of his newe and fayre Mistris *Beatrice-Ioana*, and likewise her selfe, to muse vpon the speeches and extraordinarie courtesie, which this vnknowne Cauallier afforded her, and beginne to speake of *Don Alonso Piracquo*, a rich Cauallier of the Cittie, who vnknowne to *Alsemero*, was his riuall and competitor, in likewise seeking and courting *Beatrice-Ioana*, for his Mistris and wife.

This *Piracquo* being rich both in lands and money, and descended of one of the chiefest and Noblest families of *Alicant*, by profession a Courtier, and indeed (to giue him his dew) a Cauallier indued with many braue qualities and perfections, was so highly beloued, respected and esteemed in that Cittie, as the very fayrest and noblest young Ladies were, with much respect & affection, proffered him in marriage by their parents: but there was none either so precious or pleasing to his eye, as was our *Beatrice-Ioana*, whome he obserued for beauty to excell others, and for maiestie and grace to surpasse her selfe, and indeede hee could not refraine from louing her, nor be perswaded or drawne to affect any other: so as he settled his resolution either to haue her to his wife, or not to be the husband of any. Yea, he is so earnest in his sute, as scarce any one day passeth, but he is at the Castle.

Vermandero thinkes himselfe much honoured of him, in seeking his daughter, yea, he receiues him louingly, and entertaines him courteously; as knowing it greatly for her preferment, & advancement: and so giues *Piracquo* many testimonies of his fauour, and many hopes that he shall preuaile and obtaine his Mistris. But *Beatrice Ioana* stands not so affected to him, rather shee receiues him coldly; and when he beginnes his sute to her, shee turnes the deafe eare, and neuer answereth him, but in generall tearmes: only not peremptorily to disobey her parents, she seemes to be pleased with his company, and yet secretly in her heart wisheth him farther from her.

But *Piracquo* flattering him selfe in his hope, and as much doating on *Beatrice-Ioana's* beautie, as hee relies on her fathers constant affection to him, hee is so farre from giuing ouer his sute to her, as hee continueth it with more earnestnesse and importunitie, and vowes that he will forsake his life ere his Mistris: but sometimes wee speake true, when wee thinke wee iest: yet he findes her one and the same: for although shee were not yet acquainted with *Alsemero*, yet shee made it the thirteenth article of her Creede, that the supreme power had ordained her another husband, and not *Piracquo:* yea at that very instant, the remembrance of *Alsemero* quite defaced that of *Piracquo*, so that shee wholly refusd her heart to the last, of purpose to reserue and giue it to the first: as the sequell will shew.

Now by this time *Vermandero* had notice, & was secretly informed of *Alsemero's* affection to his daughter, and withall, that she liked him farre better then *Piracquo*: which newes was indeed very distastefull and displeasing to him, because he perfectly knew that *Piracquo's* meanes farre exceed that of *Alsemero.* Whereupon considering that hee had giuen his consent, and in a manner ingaged his promise to *Piracquo:* he, to preuent the hopes, and to frustrate the attempts of *Alsemero,* leaues his Castle to the command of *Don Hugo de Valmarino* his sonne, and taking his daughter *Beatrice-Ioana* with him, hee in his Coach very sodainely and secretly goes to *Briamata:* a fayre house of his, tenne leagues from *Alicant:* where he meanes to soiourn, vntill he had concluded and solemnized the match betwixt them: But he shall neuer be so happy, as to see it effected.

At the newes of *Beatrice-Ioana's* departure, *Alsemero* is extremely perplexed & sorrowfull, knowing not whether it proceed from her selfe, her father, or both; yea, this his griefe is augmented, when hee thinkes on the suddennesse thereof, which he feares may bee performed for his respect and consideration: the small acquaintance and familiarity he hath had with her, makes that hee cannot condemne her of vnkindnesse: yet sith he was not thought worthy to haue notice of her departure, hee againe hath no reason to hope, much lesse to assure himselfe of her affection towards him: hee knowes not how to resolue these doubts, nor what to thinke or doe in a matter of this nature and importance: for thus hee reasoneth with himselfe; if hee ride to *Briamata,* he may perchance offend the father; if hee stay at *Alicant,* displease the daughter; and although hee bee rather willing to runne the hazzard of his enuy, then of her affection, yet hee holds it safer to bee authorised by her pleasure, and to steere his course by the compasse of her commands: Hee therefore bethinkes himselfe of a meanes to auoyde these extremes, and so findes out a Channell to passe free betwixt that *Sylla* and this *Carybdis;* which is, to visit her by letters: he sees more reason to embrace, then to reiect this inuention, and so prouiding himselfe of a confident messenger, his heart commands his pen to signifie her these few lines:

AS long as you were in Alicant, *I deemed it a heauen vpon earth, and being bound for* Malta, *a thousand times blessed that contrary winde which kept mee from embarking and sayling from you: yea, so sweetly doe I suffer, and so dearely honour your beautie, as I entered into a resolution with my selfe, to end my voyage e're I beganne it, and to beginne another, which I feare will end mee. If you demand, or desire to know what this second voyage is, know, faire Mistris, that my thoughts are so honourable, and my affection so religious, that it is the seeking of your fauour, and the obtayning of your selfe to my wife, whereon not onely my fortunes, but my life depends. But how shall I hope for this honour, or flatter my selfe with the obtayning of so great a felicitie, when I see you have not onely left mee, but which is worse, as I vnderstand, the City for my sake? Fayre* Beatrice-Ioana, *if your crueltie will make mee thus miserable, I haue no other consolation left mee to sweeten the bitternesse of my griefe and misfortune, but a confident hope, that death will as speedily depriue mee of my dayes, as you have of my ioyes.*

ALSEMERO.

I know not whether it more grieued *Beatrice-Ioana* to leaue *Alicant,* without taking her leaue of *Alsemero,* then shee doth now reioyce to receiue this his Letter: for as that plunged her thoughts in the hell of discontent, so this rayseth them to the heauen of ioy: and as then shee had cause to doubt of his affection, so now shee hath not onely reason to flatter, but to assure her selfe thereof: and therefore, though shee will not seeme at first to grant him his desire, yet shee is resolued to returne him an answere, that may giue as well life to his hopes, as prayse to her modestie. Her Letter is thus:

AS I haue many reasons to be incredulous, and not one to induce mee to beleeue, that so poore a beautie of mine, should haue power to stoppe so braue a Cauallier (as your selfe) from ending so honourable a voyage as your first, or to perswade you to one so simple as your second: so I cannot but admire, that you in your Letter seeke mee for your wife, when in your heart, I presume, you least desire it; and whereas you alleadge, your life and fortunes depend on my fauour: I thinke you write it purposely, either to make triall of your owne wit, or of my indiscretion, by endeuoring to see whether I will beleeue that which exceedes all beliefe; now as it is true, that I haue left Alicant *so it is as true, that I left it not any way to afflict you, but rather to obey my father: for this I pray beleeue, that although I cannot bee kinde; yet I will neuer bee cruell to you: Liue therefore your owne friend, and I will neuer die your enemy.*

BEATRICE-IOANA.

This Letter of *Beatrice-Ioana*, giues *Alsemero* much despayre and little hope: yet though he haue reason to condemne her vnkindnesse, hee cannot but approue her modestie and discretion, which doth as much comfort, as that afflict him: so his thoughts are irresolute, and withall so variable, as hee knowes not whether hee should aduance his hand, or withdraw his penne againe to write to his Mistresse. But at last, knowing that the excellency of her Beautie, and the dignity of her Vertues deserue a second Letter: hee hoping it may obtaine and effect that which his first could not, calls for paper, and thereon traceth these few lines:

YOU haue as much reason to assure your selfe of my affection, as I to doubt of yours: and if words and Letters, Teares and Vowes, are not capable to make you beleeue the sincerity of my zeale, and the honour of my affection: what resteth, but that I wish you could diue as deepely into my heart, as my heart hath into your beautie, to the end you might be both witnesse and Iudge, if vnder heauen I desire any thing so much on earth, as to be crowned with the felicitie to see Beatrice-Ioana *my wife, and* Alsemero *her husband? But why should I striue to perswade that, which you resolue not to beleeue, or flatter my selfe with any hope, sith I see I must bee so vnfortunate to despaire? I will therefore henceforth cease to write, but neuer to love: & sith it is impossible for me to liue, I will prepare my selfe to dye, that the World may know, I haue lost a most faire Mistris in you, and you a most faithfull and constant seruant in me.*

ALSEMERO.

Beatrice-Ioana seeing *Alsemero's* constant affection, holds it now rather discretion, then immodesty to accept both his seruice and selfe, yea, her heart so delights in the agreeableness of his person, and triumphs in the contemplation of his vertues, that shee either wisheth her selfe in *Alicant* with him, or hee in *Briamata* with her: but considering her affection to *Alsemero* by her fathers hatred, and her hatred to *Piracquo*, by his affection; she thinks it high time to informe *Alsemero* with what impatiencie they both endeuour to obtaine her fauour and consent: hoping that his discretion will interpose and finde meanes to stop the progresse of these their importunities, and to withdraw her fathers inclination from *Piracquo*, to bestowe it on himselfe: but all this while she thinkes her silence is an iniurie to *Alsemero*: and therefore no longer to be vncourteous to him, who is so kinde to her, shee verie secretly conueyes him this Letter:

AS it is not for earth to resist heauen, nor for our wills to contradict Gods prouidence, so I cannot deny, but now acknowledge, that if euer I affected any man, it is your selfe: For your Letters, protestations, and vowes, but chiefly your merits; and the hope, or rather the assurance of your fidelitie, hath wonne my heart from my selfe to giue it you; but there are some important considerations and reasons, that enforce mee to craue your secresie herein, and to request you as soone as conueniently you may, to come priuately hither to mee: for I shall neuer giue content to my thoughts, nor satisfaction to my minde, till I am made ioyfull with your sight, and happie with your presence: in the meane time manage this affection of mine, with care and discretion, and whiles you resolue to make Alicant *your* Malta, *I will expect and attend your comming with much longing and impatiencie to Briamata.*

BEATRICE-IOANA.

It is for no others but for Louers to iudge how welcome this Letter was to *Alsemero*, who a thousand times kissed it, and as often blest the hand that wrote it, he had, as we haue formerly vnderstood, beene twice in the Indies: But nowe in his conceit, hee hath found a farre richer treasure in *Spaine*: I meane his *Beatrice-Ioana*, whom he esteemes the ioy of his life, and the life of his ioy: But shee will not prooue so: he is so inamored of her beautie, and so desirous to haue the felicitie of her presence: as the winde comming good, the ship sets sayle for *Malta* and hee (to giue a colour for his stay) feignes himselfe sicke, fetcheth backe his Trunkes, and remayneth in *Alicant*: and so burning with desire, to see his sweetely deare and dearely sweete Mistris, he dispatcheth away his confident messenger to *Briamata* in the morning, to aduertise her, that he will not fayle to bee with her that night at eleuen of the clocke.

Beatrice-Ioana is rauished with the ioy of this newes, and so prouides for his comming. *Alsemero* takes the benefit of the night, and shee giues him the aduantage of a posterne dore, which answeres to a Garden, where *Diaphanta* her waiting Gentlewoman attends his arriuall. He comes: she conducts him secretly thorow a priuate gallery, into *Beatrice-Ioana's* chamber; where (richly apparelled) shee verie courteously and respectiuely receiues him. At the beginning of their meeting they want no kisses: which they second with complements, and many louing conferences, wherein she relates him *Piracquo's* importunate sute to her, and her fathers earnestnesse, yea, in a manner, his constraint, to see the match concluded betwixt them: he being for that purpose there, in her fathers house, againe, after shee hath alleadged and shewne him the intirenesse of her affection to himselfe, with whome shee is resolued to liue and dye, shee lets fall some darke and ambiguous speeches, tending to this effect, that before *Piracquo* be in another World, there is no hope for *Alsemero* to inioy her for his wife in this. Lo here the first plot and designe of a lamentable and execrable murther: which we shall shortly see acted and committed.

There needes but halfe a word to a sharpe and quicke vnderstanding. *Alsemero* knowes it is the violence of her affection to him, that leades her to this dis-respect, and hatred to *Piracquo,* and because her content is his: yea, rather it is for his sake, that shee will forsake *Piracquo,* to liue and dye with him; Passion and affection blinding his Iudgement, and beautie triumphing and giuing a lawe to his conscience: he freely proffereth himselfe to his Mistris, vowing, that he will shortly send him a challenge, and fight with him, yea, had he a thousand liues, as he hath but one, he is ready, if shee please, to expose and sacrifice them all at her command and seruice. *Beatrice-Ioana* thankes him kindly for his affection & zeale, the which she sayth shee holds redoubled by the freenesse of his proffer: but being loth that he should hazard his owne life, in seeking that of another, shee coniures him by all the loue he beares her, neither directly nor indirectly to intermeddle with *Piracquo*: but that he repose and build vpon her affection and constancie: not doubting, but shee will so preuaile with her father, that he shall shortly change his opinion, and no more perswade her to affect *Piracquo,* whome shee resolutely affirmes, neither life nor death shall enforce her to marry. And to conclude, although shee affirme, his presence is dearer to her than her life; yet the better and sooner to compasse their desires, shee praies him to leaue *Alicant,* and for a while to returne to *Valentia,* not doubting but time may worke that, which perchance haste, or importunitie may neuer. Thus passing ouer their kisses, and the rest of their amorous conference, he assured of her loue, and shee of his affection, hee returnes for *Alicant,* packes vp his baggage which hee sends before, and within lesse then foure dayes, takes his iourney for *Valentia*: where wee will leaue him a while, to relate other accidents and occurrences: which (like riuers into the Ocean) fall within the compasse of this History.

This meeting, and part of *Alsemero's* and *Beatrice-Ioana's* conference at her fathers house of *Briamata,* was not so secretly carried and concealed, but some curious or trecherous person neere him, or her, ouer-heare and reueale it: which makes her father *Vermandero* fume and bite the lippe; but hee conceales it from *Piracquo*: and they still continue their intelligence and familiarity: *Vermandero* telling him plainely, that a little more time shall worke and finish his desire; and that sith his request cannot preuayle with his daughter, his commands shall: But he shall misse of his ayme.

There is not so great distance from *Briamata* to *Alicant,* but some of the Noblest of the city are aduertised hereof: and one among the rest, in great zeale and affection to *Piracquo,* secretly acquaints *Don Tomaso Piracquo* his younger brother therewith, being then in the citie of *Alicant*: who hearing of this newes, whereof he imagined his Brother was ignorant, loth that hee should any longer perseuere in his present errour, and to preuent his future disgrace, hee, like a faithfull and honest brother, takes occasion from *Alicant* to write him this ensuing Letter to *Briamata*:

BEING more ielous of your prosperity, then of mine owne; & knowing, it many times falls out, that louers lose the cleerenes & solidity of their iudgement, in gazing and contemplating on the Roses and Lillies of their Mistresses beauties: I desirous to preuent your disgrace, thought my selfe bound to signifie you, that I heere vnderstand by the report of those, whose speeches beare their perswasion with them, that your sute to Beatrice-Ioana *is in vayne, and shee unworthy of your affection, because she hath already contracted her selfe to* Alsemero *your riuall: I am as sorry to bee the Herald of this newes, as glad and confident, that as shee hath matched your inferiour, so you are reserued for her better: Wherefore, Sir, recall your thoughts, tempt not impossibilities, but consider that the shortest errours are best; and though you loue her well, yet thinke that at your pleasure you may finde variety of beauties, whereunto hers deserues not the honour to doe homage. I could giue no truce to my thoughts, till I had aduertised you hereof, and I hope either the name of a brother, or your owne generositie will easily procure pardon for my presumption.*

THOMASO PIRACQVO.

Piracquo, notwithstanding this his brothers Letter of counsell and advice, is so farre from retyring in his sute, as he rather aduanceth with more violence and zeale: and as many mens iudgements are dazled and obscured a little before their danger and misfortune, when indeed they haue most need to haue them sound and cleere: so he is not capable to bee disswaded from re-searching his Mistresse, but rather resembleth those Saylors, who are resolute to indure a storme, in hope of faire weather: but hee had found more security, and lesse danger, if hee had embraced and followed the counsell that his Brother gaue him. For *Beatrice-Ioana* seeing shee could not obtaine her desire in marrying *Alsemero,* e're *Piracquo* were remoued, doth now confirme that which formerly she had resolued on, to make him away, in what manner or at what rate soeuer. And now, after shee had ruminated, and runne ouer many bloody designes: the diuell, who neuer flies from those that follow him, proffers her an inuention as execrable as damnable. There is a Gallant young Gentleman, of the Garison of the Castle, who followes her father, that to her knowledge doth deepely honour, and dearely affect her: yea, she knowes, that at her request he will not sticke to murther *Piracquo*: his name is *Signiour Antonio de Flores*: shee is resolute in her rage, and approues him to be a fit instrument to execute her will.

Now, as soone as *Vermandero* vnderstands of *Alsemero's* departure to *Valentia,* he with his daughter and *Piracquo* returnes from *Briamata* to *Alicant*: where, within three dayes of their arriuall, *Beatrice-Ioana,* boyling still in her reuenge to *Piracquo,* which neither the ayre of the Country, nor City, could quench or wipe off, shee sends for *de Flores,* and with many flattering smiles, and sugered speeches, acquaints him with her purpose and desire, making him many promises of kindenesse and courtesies; if hee will performe it.

De Flores hauing a long time loued *Beatrice-Ioana,* is exceeding glad of this newes, yea, feeding his hopes with the ayre of her promises, hee is so caught and intangled in the snares of her beautie, that hee freely promiseth to dispatch *Piracquo*; and so they first consult, and then agree vpon the manner how, which foorthwith wee shall see performed, to which end, *de Flores* insinuates himselfe fairely into *Piracquo's* company and familiarity, as hee comes to the Castle; where watching his hellish opportunitie, he one day hearing *Piracquo* commend the thicknesse and strength of the Walles, told him that the strength of that Castle consisted not in the Walles, but in the *Casemates* that were stored with good ordnance to scoure the ditches. *Piracquo* very courteously prayes *de Flores* to be a meanes that he may goe downe and see the *Casemates. De Flores* like a bloody Fawkner, seeing *Piracquo* already come to his lure, tells him it is now dinner time, and the bell vpon ringing: but if hee please, hee himselfe will after dinner accompany him, and shew him all the strength and rarities of the Castle. Hee thankes *de Flores* for this courtesie, and accepts heereof, with promise to goe. So hee hies in to dinner, and *de Flores* pretending some businesse, walkes in the Court.

Whiles *Piracquo* is at dinner with *Vermandero*; *de Flores* is prouiding him a bloody banquet in the East *Casemate,* where, of purpose hee goes, and hides a naked Sword and Ponyard behinde the doore. Now dinner being ended, *Piracquo* findes out *de Flores,* and summons him of his promise: who tells him hee is ready to waite on him: so away they goe from the Walles, to the Rauellins, Sconces and Bulwarkes, and from thence by a Posterne to the ditches: and so in againe to the *Casemates,* whereof they haue already viewed three, and are now going to the last, which is the Theater, whereon wee shall presently see acted a mournfull and bloody Tragedy. At the descent hereof *de Flores* puts off his Rapier, and leaues it behinde him, trecherously informing *Piracquo,* that the descent is narrow and craggie. See heere the policy and villany of this diuellish and trecherous miscreant.

Piracquo not doubting, nor dreaming of any Treason, followes his example, and so casts off his Rapier: *De Flores* leades the way, and hee followes him: but, alas poore Gentleman, hee shall neuer returne with his life: they enter the Vault of the *Casamate*: *de Flores* opens the doore, and throwes it backe, thereby to hide his Sword and Ponyard: Hee stoopes and lookes thorow a Port-hole, and tells him, that that Peece doth thorowly scowre the ditch. *Piracquo* stoopes likewise downe to view it, when (O griefe to thinke thereon!) *de Flores* steppes for his weapons, and with his Ponyard stabbes him thorow the backe, and swiftly redoubling blow vpon blow, kills him dead at his feete, and without going farther, buries him there, right vnder the ruines of an old wall, whereof that *Casamate* was built. Loe heere the first part of this mourneful and bloody Tragedy.

De Flores (like a gracelesse villaine), hauing dispatched this sorrowfull businesse, speedily acquaints *Beatrice-Ioana* heerewith, who (miserable wretch) doth heereat infinitly reioyce, and thankes him with many kisses; and the better to conceale this their vilde and bloody murther, as also to cast a mist before peoples conceits and iudgements, shee bids him (by some secret meanes) to cause reports to be spred: first, that *Piracquo* was seene gone foorth the Castle gate; then, that in the City hee was seene take boate, and went (as it was thought) to take the ayre of the sea. But this wit of theirs shall proue folly: for though men as yet see not this murther, yet God in his due time will both detect and punish it.

By this time *Piracquo* is found wanting, both in the City and Castle; so these aforesayd reports runne for current, all tongues prattle hereof: *Vermandero* knowes not what to say, nor *Piracquo's* brother and friends what to doe herein: they euery houre and minute expect newes of him, but their hopes bring them no comfort, and amongst the rest, our diuellish *Beatrice-Ioana* seemes exceedingly to grieue and mourne heereat. *Don Tomaso Piracquo* with the rest of his friends, search euery corner of the City, and send scouts, both by land and Sea, to haue newes of him. *Vermandero* the Captaine of the Castle doth the like, and vowes that next his owne sonne, hee loued *Piracquo* before any man of the world: yea, not onely his friends, but generally all those who knew him, exceedingly weepe and bewayle the absence, and losse of this Cauallier; for they thinke sure he is drowned in the Sea.

Now in the middest of this sorrow, and of these teares, *Beatrice-Ioana* doth secretly aduertise her louer *Alsemero* heereof, but in such palliating tearmes, that thereby shee may delude and carry away his iudgement, from imagining, that shee had the least shadow, or finger heerein; and withall prayes him to make no long stay in *Valentia*, but to come away to her to *Alicant*. *Alsemero* wonders at this newes, and to please his faire Mistresse, beleeues part thereof, but will neuer beleeue all; but hee is so inflamed with her beautie, as her remembrance wipes away that of *Piracquo*: when letting passe a little time, hee makes his preparations for *Alicant*: but first hee sends the chiefest of his Parents to *Vermandero*, to demaund his Daughter *Beatrice-Ioana* in marriage for him, and then comes himselfe in person, and in discreete and honourable manner courts her Parents priuately, and makes shew to seeke her publikely.

In fine, after many conferences, meetings and complements, as *Alsemero* hath heretofore wonne the affection of *Beatrice-Ioana*; so now at last, hee obtaines likewise the fauour and consent of *Vermandero* her father. And heere our two Louers, to their exceeding great content, and infinite ioy, are vnited, and by the bond of marriage of two persons made one; their Nuptialls being solemnized in the Castle of *Alicant*, with much Pompe, State, and Brauery.

Hauing heeretofore heard the conference that past betwixt *Alsemero* and *Beatrice-Ioana* in the Church; hauing likewise seene the amorous Letters that past betwixt them, from *Alicant* to *Briamata*, and from *Briamata* to *Alicant*; and now considering the pompe and glory of their Nuptialls; who would imagine that any auerse accident could alter the sweetnesse and tranquillity of their affections, or that the Sunne-shine of their ioyes should so soone bee eclipsed, and ouertaken with a storme? But God is as iust as secret in his decrees.

For this married couple had scarce liued three moneths in the pleasures of wedlocke, (which if vertuously obserued, is the sweetest earthly ioy,) but *Alsemero*, like a fond husband, becomes ielous of his wife; so as hee curbes and restraynes her of her libertie, and would hardly permit her to see, yea, farre lesse to conferre or conuerse with any man: but this is not the way to teach a woman chastity: for if fayre words, good example, and sweete admonitions cannot preuaile, threatnings and imprisoning in a Chamber will neuer, yea, the experience thereof is dayly seene, both in *England, France* and *Germany*, where generally the women vse (but not abuse) their libertie and freedome, granted them by their husbands, with much ciuility, affection, and respect.

Beatrice-Ioana bites the lippe at this her husbands discourtesie: she vowes, shee is as much deceiued in his loue, as hee in his ielousie: and that shee is as vnworthie of his suspition, as hee of her affection: he watcheth her euery where, and sets spies ouer her in euery corner: yea, his ielousie is become so violent, as he deemes her vnchaste with many, yet knowes not with whome: but this tree of ielousie neuer brings foorth good fruit. Shee complaines hereof to her father, and prayes him to be a meanes to appease and calme this tempest, which threatens the shipwracke, not only of her content, but (it may be) of her life. *Vermandero* beares himself discreetly herein; but he may as soone place another Sunne in the Firmament, as roote out this fearefull frensie out of *Alsemero's* head: for this his paternall admonition is so farre from drawing him to hearken to reason, as it produceth contrary effects: for now *Alsemero*, to preuent his shame, and secure his feare, sodainly prouides a Coach, and so carries home his wife from *Alicant*, to *Valentia*. This sudden departure grieues *Vermandero*, and galles *Beatrice-Ioana* to the heart, who now lookes no longer on her husband with affection, but with disdayne and enuy. Many dayes are not past, but her father resolues to send to *Valentia*, to knowe how matters stand betwixt his daughter and her husband: hee makes choyce of *de Flores* to ride thither, and sends Letters to them both.

De Flores is extremely ioyfull of this occasion, to see his old Mistris *Beatrice-Ioana*, whom he loues dearer then his life: he comes to *Valentia*, and finding *Alsemero* abroade, and shee at home, deliuers her her fathers Letter, and salutes and kisseth her, with many amorous embracings and dalliances, (which modestie holds vnworthy of relation:) shee acquaints him with her husbands ingratitude: he rather reioyceth, then greeues hereat, and now reuiues his old sute, and redoubleth his newe Kisses: shee considering what he hath done for her seruice, and ioyning therewith her husbands ielousie, not onely ingageth her selfe to him for the time present, but for the future, and bids him visit her often. But they both shall pay deare for this familiarity and pleasure.

Alsemero comes home, receiues his fathers Letter, sets a pleasing face on his discontented heart, and bids him welcome: and so the next day writes backe to his father *Alsemero*, and dispatcheth *de Flores*, who for that time takes his leaue of them both, and returnes for *Alicant*.

Hee is no sooner departed, but *Alsemero* is by one of his spies, a wayting Gentlewoman of his wiues, whom hee had corrupted with money, aduertized, that there past many amorous kisses, and dalliances betweene her Mistris and *de Flores*: yea, shee reueales all that either shee sawe or heard; for shee past not to be false to her Lady, so shee were true to her Lord and Master. And indeede this waiting Gentlewoman was that *Diaphanta*, of whom we haue formerly made mention, for conducting of *Alsemero* to her Ladyes chamber at *Briamata*. *Alsemero* is all fire at this newes: he consults not with iudgement, but with passion, and so, rather like a deuill, then a man, flyes to his wiues chamber, wherein furiously rushing, hee with his sword drawne in his hand, to her great terrour and amazement deliuers her these words:

Minion (quoth he) vpon thy life, tell mee what familiaritie there hath nowe past betwixt *de Flores*, and thy selfe: whereat shee, fetching many sighs, and sheading many teares, answeres him, that by her part of heauen, her thoughts, speeches and actions haue no way exceeded the bonds of honour, and chastitie towards him; and that *de Flores* neuer attempted any courtesie, but such as a brother may shew to his own natural sister. Then quoth he, whence proceeds this your familiarity? Whereat shee growes pale, and withall silent. Which her husband espying, Dispatch, quoth he, and tell mee the truth, or else this sword of mine shall instantly finde a passage to thy heart. When loe, the prouidence of God so ordained it, that shee is reduced to this exigent and extremity, as she must bee a witnesse against her selfe, and in seeking to conceale her whoredome, must discouer her murther; the which she doth in these words:

Know, *Alsemero*, that sith thou wilt enforce mee to shew thee the true cause of my chaste familiarity with *de Flores*, that I am much bound to him, & thy selfe more, for he it was, that at my request, dispatched *Piracquo*, without the which (as thou well knowest) I could neuer haue enioyed thee for my husband, nor thou me for thy wife. And so shee reueales him the whole circumstance of that cruell murther, as wee haue formerly vnderstood: the which shee coniures, and prayes him to conceale, sith no lesse then *de Flores* and her owne life depended thereon, and that shee will dye a thousand deaths, before consent to defile his bed, or to violate her oath and promise giuen him in marriage.

Alsemero both wondering and grieuing at this lamentable newes, sayes little, but thinks the more: and although he had reason, and apparance to beleeue, that shee who commits murther, will not sticke to commit adultery, yet vpon his wiues solemne oaths and protestations, he forgets what is past; onely hee strictly chargeth her, no more to see, or admit *de Flores* into her company; or if the contrary, he vowes hee will so sharply bee reuenged of her, as he will make her an example to all posteritie.

But *Beatrice-Ioana*, notwithstanding her husbands speeches, continueth her intelligence with *de Flores*, yea, her husband no sooner rides abroade, but hee is at *Valentia* with her: and they are become so impudent, as what they before did secretly, they nowe in a manner doe publikely or at least, with chamber doores open. *Diaphanta* knowing this to be a great scandall, as well to her masters honour, as house, againe informes him thereof, who vowes to take a most sharpe reuenge of this their infamie and indignitie, as indeede he doth: for hee bethinkes himselfe (thereby to effect it) of an inuention as worthy of his ielousie, as of their first crime of murther, and of their second, of adultery: hee inioyneth *Diaphanta* to lay waite for the verie houre that *de Flores* arriues from *Alicant* to *Valentia*: which shee doth; when instantly pretending to his wife a iourney in the Countrey, he very secretly and silently hauing his Rapier and Ponyard, and a case of Pistols ready charged in his pocket. He (seeming to take horse) husheth himselfe vp priuately in his Studie, which was next adioyning, and within his bedchamber.

Beatrice-Ioana thinking her husband two or three leagues off, sends away for *de Flores*, who comes instantly to her: they fall to their kisses and embracings: shee reioycing extremely for his arriuall, and he for her husband *Alsemero's* departure; she relates him the cruelty and indignitie her husband hath shewed & offered her: the which *de Flores* vnderstands with much contempt and choller, as also with many threates. *Alsemero* heares all, but doth neither speake, cough, sneeze, nor spit. So from words, they fall to their beastly pleasures; when *Alsemero* no longer able to containe himselfe, much less to bee accessary to this his shame, and their villanie, throwes off the dore, and violently rusheth foorth; when finding them on his bed, in the middest off their adultery, he first dischargeth his Pistols on them, and then with his Sword and Ponyard runnes them thorow, and stabs them with so many deepe and wide wounds, that they haue not so much power, or time to speake a word, but there lye weltring and wallowing in their blood, whiles their soules flye to another world, to relate what horrible and beastly crimes their bodies haue committed in this. Thus by the prouidence of God, in the second Tragedie of our Historie we see our two murtherers murthered, and *Piracquo's* innocent blood reuenged in the guiltinesse of theirs.

Alsemero hauing finished this bloody businesse, leaues his Pistols on the Table, as also his Sword and Ponyard all bloody as they were: and without couering or remouing the breathlesse bodies of these two wretched miscreants, he shuts his Chamber doore, and is so farre from flying from the fact, as he takes his Coach, and goes directly to the Criminall Iudge himselfe, and reueales what hee had done, (but conceales the murther of *Piracquo*.) The Iudge is astonished, and amazed at the report of this mournefull and pittifull accident: hee takes *Alsemero* with him, returnes to his house, and findes those two dead bodies fresh smoaking and reeking in their blood: The newes hereof is spred in all the City. The whole people of *Valentia* flocke thither, to be eye-witnesses of these two murthered persons; where some behold them with pitty, others with ioy, but all with astonishment and admiration, and no lesse doe those of *Alicant*, where this newes is speedily posted; but all their griefes are nothing to those of *Don Diego de Vermandero's* (*Beatrice-Ioana's* father) who infinitly and extremely grieues, partly for the death, but especially for the crime of his daughter.

The Iudge presently commits *Alsemero* prisoner in another of his owne Chambers, and so examining *Diaphanta* vpon her oath, concerning the familiarity betwixt *de Flores* and *Beatrice-Ioana:* she affirmes constantly, that now and many times before, shee saw them commit adulterie: and that shee it was that first aduertised *Alsemero* her Master heereof. Whereupon, after a second examination of *Alsemero,* they, vpon mature deliberation, acquite him of this fact: so he is freed, and the dead bodies carried away and buried.

But although this earthly Iudge haue acquitted *Alsemero* of this fact, yet the Iudge of iudges, the Great God of Heauen, who seeth not onely our heart, but our thoughts, not onely our actions, but our intents, hath this and some thing else to lay to his charge: for hee (in his sacred Prouidence and Diuine Iustice) doth both remember and obserue, first, how ready and willing *Alsemero* was to ingage himselfe to *Beatrice-Ioana* to kill *Piracquo:* then, though hee consented not to his murther, yet how hee concealed it, and brought it not to publike arraignement and punishment: whereby the dead body of *Piracquo* might receiue a more honourable and Christian-like Sepulchre: and if these crimes of his bee not capable to deserue reuenge and chastisement; Lo, hee is entering into a new, wilfull and premeditated murther, and doth so dishonourably and trecherously performe it, as wee shall shortly see him lose his life vpon an infamous Scaffold, where hee shall finde no heart to pitty him, nor eye to bewaile him.

If wee would be so ignorant, wee cannot bee so malicious to forget that louing and courteous Letter, which *Don Tomaso Piracquo* wrote his brother *Alonso Piracquo* from *Alicant* to *Briamata,* to with-draw himselfe from his sute to *Beatrice-Ioana:* and although his affection and ielousie to preuent his brothers disgrace, was then the chiefe occasion of that his Letter: yet, sith hee was since disasterously and misfortunately bereaued of him, of that deare and sweet brother of his, whom he euer held and esteemed farre dearer then his life, his thoughts, like so many lines, concurre in this Centre, from whence hee cannot bee otherwise conceited or drawne, but that *Beatrice-Ioana* and *Alsemero* had a hand, and were at least accessaries, if not Authors of his losse: vpon the foundation of which beliefe, hee raiseth this resolution, that hee is not worthie to bee a Gentleman, nor of the degree and title of a brother, if hee craue not satisfaction for that irreparable losse which hee sustaineth in that of his brother: and the sooner is hee drawne thereunto, because hee beleeues that, as *Alsemero* was ordained of old to chastize *Beatrice-Ioana:* so hee was by the same power reserued to bee reuenged of *Alsemero.* Whereupon, although it be not the custome of *Spaine* to fight Duels (as desiring rather the death of their enemies, then of their friends) hee resolues to fight with him, and to that end vnderstanding *Alsemero* to bee then in *Alicant,* sends him this Challenge:

IT IS *with too much assurance, that I feare* Beatrice-Ioana's *vanity, and your rashnesse hath bereaued mee of a brother, whom I euer esteemed and prized farre dearer then my selfe: I were vnworthy to conuerse with the World, much lesse to beare the honour and degree of a Gentleman, if I should not seeke satisfaction for his death, with the hazard of mine owne life: for if a friend bee bound to performe the like courtesie and dutie to his friend, how much more a brother to his brother? Your Sword hath chasticed* Beatrice-Ioana's *errour, and I must see whether mine bee reserued to correct yours. As you are your selfe, meet mee at the foote of* Glisseran hill *to morrow at fiue in the morning without Seconds, and it shal be at your choyse, either to vse your Sword on horsebacke, or your Rapier on foote.*

THOMASO PIRACQVO.

Alsemero accepts this challenge, and promiseth that hee and his Rapier will not fayle to meet him: yet as hee one way wondereth at *Piracquo's* valor and resolution, so another way hee considereth the great losse hee hath receiued in that of his brother, and the iustnesse of his quarrell against him: who, although hee were not accessary to his murther; yet hee is, in concealing the cruelty thereof: and indeed this villany makes him lose his accustomed courage, & thinks of a most base cowardise and trecherous stratagem: but this dishonorable resolution and designe of his shal receiue an infamous recompence, and a reward, & punishment as bitter as iust.

They meet at the houre and place appointed: *Piracquo* is first in the field; & *Alsemero* stayes not long after, but hee hath two small Pistols charged in his pockets, which in killing his enemy shall ruine himselfe: they draw, and as they approach, *Alsemero* throws away his Rapier, & with his Hat in his hand, prayes *Piracquo* to heare him in his iust defence, & that hee is ready to ioyne with him to reuenge his Brothers murtherers. *Piracquo* being as courteous as couragious, and as honorable as valiant, likewise throws away his Rapier, & with his Hat in his hand comes to meet him: but it is a folly to vnarme our selues in our enemies presence; for it is better & fitter that hee stand at our courtesie, then we to his: when *Piracquo* fearing nothing lesse then treason, *Alsemero* drawes out his Pistols and dischargeth them, the first thorow his head, and the second thorow his brest; of which two wounds hee speaking onely thus, *O Villaine, O Traytor*! falls downe dead at his feete. Loe heere the third bloody part of our History.

It is a lamentable part for any one to commit murther: but for a Gentleman to destroy another in this base and cruell manner, this exceeds all basenesse and cruelty it selfe: yea, it makes him as vnworthy of his honour, as worthy of a halter.

The newes of this bloody fact, rattles in the Streets of *Alicant*, as thunder in the Firmament: *Piracquo's* Chirurgion being an eye-witnesse hereof, reports the death of his Master, and the trechery of *Alsemero*: all *Alicant* is amazed hereat, they extoll *Thomaso Piracquo's* valor, and his singular affection to his dead brother, and both detest and curse the trechery and memory of *Alsemero*. The Criminall Iudges are aduertised heereof, who speedily send poast after him: but hee is mounted on a swift Gennet; and like *Belerophon*, on his winged *Pegasus*, doth rather flie then gallop: but his haste is in vaine; for the Iustice of the Lord will both stoppe his horse, and arrest him. Hee is not recouered halfe way from *Alicant* towards *Valentia*, but his horse stumbles and breakes his fore-legge, and *Alsemero* his right arme: hee is amazed, perplexed, and inraged heereat, and knowes not what to doe, or whither to flie for safety: for hee sees no bush nor hedge to hide him, nor lane to saue him; and now he repents himselfe of his fact, but it is too late: his horse fayling him, hee trusteth to his legges, and so throwing off his cloake, runnes as speedily as hee may: but the foulenesse of his fact doth still so affright him, and terrifie his conscience, as hee is afrayd of his owne shaddow, lookes still backe, imagining that euery stone hee sees, is a Sergeant come to arrest him: yea, his thoughts, like so many Blood-hounds, pursue and follow him, sweating exceedingly, partly through his labour, but especially through the affliction & perturbation of his mind, yea, euery point of a minute hee hath expecteth and feares his apprehension.

Neither is his feare, or expectation vaine; for loe, hee at last perceiues foure come galloping after him, as fast as their horses can driue. So they finding first his poore horse, and now espying his miserable selfe, hee sees hee is enuironed of all sides, and thinkes the earth hath brought foorth *Cadmean* men to apprehend him; yet remembring himselfe a Gentleman, and withall a Souldiour, hee resolues rather to sell his life dearely in that place, then to bee made a spectacle vpon an infamous Scaffold: but this his courage and resolution shall neither preuaile, or rescue him.

Hee to this effect drawes his Rapier, the which, the foure Sergeants will him to yeeld, and render vp to the Kings Lawes and iustice: but hee is resolute to defend himselfe: they threaten him with their Pistols, but their sight doe as little amaze him, as their report and bullets. So they alight from their horses, and enuiron him with their swords, and hauing hurt two of them, and performed the part of a desperate Gladiator; the third, ioyning with him, they breake his Rapier within a foote of the hilt: whereat hee yeelds himselfe. *Alsemero* thus taken, is the same night brought backe to *Alicant*, in whose Gates and Streetes a wonderfull concourse of people assemble to see him passe, who as much pittie his person, as execrate and condemne his fact.

The Senate is assembled, and *Alsemero* brought to appeare, who considering the heynousnesse of his trecherous and bloody fact; which the deuill had caused him to commit, hee stayes for no witnesses, but accuseth himselfe of this murther, the which from poynt to poynt hee confesseth: and so they adiudge him to lose his head: but this is too honourable a death for a Gentleman, who hath so trecherously and basely dishonoured and blemished his Gentility. As hee is on the Scaffold, preparing himselfe to die, and seeing no farther hope of life, but the image of death before his eyes; knowing it no time now, either to dissemble with God, or to feare the Law; hee, to the amazement of all the World, tells the people, that although hee killed *Don Tomaso Piracquo*: yet, hee had no hand in the murther of his Brother *Don Alonso*, whom (he sayd) *de Flores*, at the instigation of his wicked and wretched wife, *Beatrice-Ioana*, had murthered and buried in the East *Casamate* of the Castle: and withall affirmed, that if hee were guiltie in any thing concerning that murther, it was onely in concealing it, which he had done till then, and whereof (hee sayd) he now most heartily repented himselfe, as being vnwilling any longer to charge his soule with it, sith hee was ready to leaue this World, and to goe to another, and so besought them all to pray vnto God to forgiue him; whose sacred Maiesty, he confessed, he had highly and infinitely offended; and wished them all to beware, and flie the temptations of the deuill, and to become better Christians by his example.

The Iudges aduertised hereof, cause his head to be strucken off, for murthering of *Don Tomaso Piracquo*: and his body to be throwne into Sea, for concealing that of *Don Alonso*: which was accordingly executed; and from the place of execution, they immediatly goe to the Castle, and so to the East *Casamate*, where causing the stones to be remoued, they finde the mournfull murthered body of *Don Alonso Piracquo*: which they giue to his kinsfolkes to receiue a more honourable buriall, according to his ranke and degree: and from thence they returne to the Churches, where the bodies of *de Flores* and *Beatrice-Ioana* were interred (after they were brought backe from *Valentia*) the which for their horrible murther, they at the common place of execution cause to be burned; and their ashes to be throwne into the ayre, as vnworthy to haue any resting place on earth, which they had so cruelly stayned and polluted with innocent blood.

Loe here the iust punishment of God against these deuillish and bloody murtherers! at the sight of whose executions, all that infinite number of people that were Spectators, vniuersally laude and prayse the Maiesty of God, for purging the earth of such vnnaturall and bloodie Monsters.

6 7 8 9 10